FREQUENTLY USED SYSTEM VARIABLES

SYSTEM VARIABLE	WHAT IT AFFECTS
Celtype	The default line type for new objects; has no effect on copied objects
Clayer	The current layer
Cmddia	If set to 1, enables command dialog boxes
Elevation	The default 3D elevation for new objects; has no effect on copied objects
Filedia	If set to 1, enables file dialog boxes where applicable
Insbase	The insertion point for the current drawing
Ltscale	Line type scaling; usually set to the scale factor of the drawing
Lunits	The unit style
Luprec	The unit precision
Menuctl	If set to 1, causes the screen menu to display options for keyboard commands
Pickadd	If set to 1, causes objects selection to be additive; Shift-pick removes items
Pickauto	If set to 1, selection windows are automatically issued when no objects are picked
Pickbox	The size of the pickbox
Pickfirst	If set to 1, enables preselection of objects for editing
Polysides	The default number of sides for polygons
Savetime	The time interval in minutes for automatic save; autosaved files have the .SV$ extension
Shadedge	The method for shading with the Shade command; range of 0 to 3
Snapang	The angle of the snap grid and cursor
Snapbase	The base point for the snap grid and hatch patterns
Sortent	The sorting method used for different operations like Osnap selection, regens, etc.
Surftab1	The number of facets in the M direction for 3D meshes created by some 3D commands
Surftab2	The number of facets in the N direction for 3D meshes created by some 3D commands
Thickness	The default thickness for new objects; has no effect on copied objects
Tilemode	Allows you to flip between Paperspace and Modelspace
Ucsfollow	If set to 1, causes AutoCAD to automatically display a plan view of the current UCS
Unitmode	If set to 1, displays feet and inches and surveyor's angles in AutoCAD input format instead of standard format
Visretain	If set to 1, causes AutoCAD to save layer visibility, color, and linetype settings for Xref files

For every kind of computer user, there is a SYBEX book.

All computer users learn in their own way. Some need straightforward and methodical explanations. Others are just too busy for this approach. But no matter what camp you fall into, SYBEX has a book that can help you get the most out of your computer and computer software while learning at your own pace.

Beginners generally want to start at the beginning. The **ABC's** series, with its step-by-step lessons in plain language, helps you build basic skills quickly. Or you might try our **Quick & Easy** series, the friendly, full-color guide.

The **Mastering** and **Understanding** series will tell you everything you need to know about a subject. They're perfect for intermediate and advanced computer users, yet they don't make the mistake of leaving beginners behind.

If you're a busy person and are already comfortable with computers, you can choose from two SYBEX series—**Up & Running** and **Running Start**. The **Up & Running** series gets you started in just 20 lessons. Or you can get two books in one, a step-by-step tutorial and an alphabetical reference, with our **Running Start** series.

Everyone who uses computer software can also use a computer software reference. SYBEX offers the gamut—from portable **Instant References** to comprehensive **Encyclopedias, Desktop References**, and **Bibles**.

SYBEX even offers special titles on subjects that don't neatly fit a category—like **Tips & Tricks**, the **Shareware Treasure Chests**, and a wide range of books for Macintosh computers and software.

SYBEX books are written by authors who are expert in their subjects. In fact, many make their living as professionals, consultants or teachers in the field of computer software. And their manuscripts are thoroughly reviewed by our technical and editorial staff for accuracy and ease-of-use.

So when you want answers about computers or any popular software package, just help yourself to SYBEX.

For a complete catalog of our publications, please write:

SYBEX Inc.
2021 Challenger Drive
Alameda, CA 94501
Tel: (510) 523-8233/(800) 277-2346 Telex: 336311
Fax: (510) 523-2373

SYBEX is committed to using natural resources wisely to preserve and improve our environment. As a leader in the computer book publishing industry, we are aware that over 40% of America's solid waste is paper. This is why we have been printing the text of books like this one on recycled paper since 1982.

This year our use of recycled paper will result in the saving of more than 15,300 trees. We will lower air pollution effluents by 54,000 pounds, save 6,300,000 gallons of water, and reduce landfill by 2,700 cubic yards.

In choosing a SYBEX book you are not only making a choice for the best in skills and information, you are also choosing to enhance the quality of life for all of us.

▼ ▼ ▼ ▼ ▼

Mastering AutoCAD
Release 12
for Windows

▼ ▼ ▼▼▼

MASTERING
AUTOCAD®
RELEASE 12
FOR WINDOWS™

George Omura

SYBEX ®

San Francisco

■

Paris

■

Düsseldorf

■

Soest

Acquisitions Editor: Dianne King
Associate Managing Editor: Joanne Cuthbertson
Editor: Savitha Varadan
Technical Editor: Kurt Hampe
Book Designer: Ingrid Owen
Production Artist: Helen Bruno
Screen Graphics: Aldo Bermudez, John Corrigan
Desktop Publishing Specialist: Thomas Goudie
Proofreader/ Production Assistant: Elisabeth Dahl
Indexer: Ted Laux
Cover Designer: Archer Design
Cover Photography: Courtesy of Autodesk
Screen reproductions produced with Collage Plus.

Collage Plus is a trademark of Inner Media Inc.

SYBEX is a registered trademark of SYBEX Inc.

TRADEMARKS: SYBEX has attempted throughout this book to distinguish proprietary trademarks from descriptive terms by following the capitalization style used by the manufacturer.

SYBEX is not affiliated with any manufacturer.

Every effort has been made to supply complete and accurate information. However, SYBEX assumes no responsibility for its use, nor for any infringement of the intellectual property rights of third parties which would result from such use.

Library of Congress Card Number: 92-82017
ISBN: 0-7821-1221-8

Manufactured in the United States of America
10 9 8 7 6 5 4 3 2 1

To all of my teachers

ACKNOWLEDGMENTS
▼ ▼ ▼ ▼ ▼

Mastering AutoCAD seems to have a life of its own. Over the years, it has evolved and grown with each new release of AutoCAD. This latest incarnation, *Mastering AutoCAD Release 12 for Windows,* is the result of many hours of preparation by the people at SYBEX. With gratitude, I'd like to thank Savitha Varadan, editor, for her excellent work in overseeing the progress of this Windows edition; and Kurt Hampe for the best technical review to date on Mastering AutoCAD.

Many thanks go to the SYBEX production staff for its efforts to get this book out on an accelerated schedule; Ingrid Owen, book designer; Helen Bruno, production artist; John Corrigan and Aldo Bermudez, screen graphics technicians; Thomas Goudie, desktop publishing specialist; and Elisabeth Dahl, proofreader. Thanks also to Ted Laux, indexer.

Christine Meredith, Robert Callori, Paul Richardson, Genevieve Katz, Allan Terry, and Fred Willsea provided helpful advice in earlier editions of the book.

At Autodesk, Matthew Gorton and Art Cooney of the Technical Support department offered courteous and timely assistance. Many thanks to Neele Johnston, manager of the Authors and Publishers Program, for providing us with the latest software, and a special thanks to Jim Quanci for putting up with my constant stream of phone calls.

And finally, a thanks to my family, Cynthia, Arthur, and Charles, for their encouragement.

CONTENTS AT A GLANCE

▼▼▼▼▼

Part Four

Modeling and Imaging in 3D

Part Five

Customization—Taking AutoCAD to the Limit

Appendices

TABLE OF CONTENTS
▼ ▼ ▼ ▼ ▼

Part Two

Discovering the AutoCAD Advantage

14 Getting and Exchanging Data from Drawings

Part Four
Modeling and Imaging in 3D

Part Five

Customization—Taking AutoCAD to the Limit

19   AutoCAD's Hidden Treasures

INTRODUCTION
▼ ▼ ▼ ▼ ▼

Welcome to *Mastering AutoCAD Release 12 for Windows*. As many readers have already discovered, *Mastering AutoCAD* offers a unique blend of tutorial and source book that offers everything you need to get started and stay ahead with AutoCAD.

HOW TO USE THIS BOOK

Rather than just showing you how each command works, *Mastering AutoCAD Release 12 for Windows* shows you AutoCAD in the context of a meaningful activity: you will learn how to use commands together to reach a goal. It also provides a foundation on which you can build your own methods for using AutoCAD and become an AutoCAD expert yourself. For this reason, I haven't covered every single command or every permutation of a command response. The AutoCAD help system (described in *Chapter 2*) and the AutoCAD Reference Manual are quite adequate for this purpose. You should think of this book as a way to get a detailed look at AutoCAD as it is used on a real project. As you follow the exercises, I encourage you to also explore AutoCAD on your own, applying the techniques you learn to your own work.

If you are not an experienced user, you may want to read *Mastering AutoCAD Release 12 for Windows* as a tutorial from front to back, since later chapters rely on the skills and information you learned in earlier ones. To help you navigate, the exercises are shown in numbered steps. *Mastering AutoCAD Release 12 for Windows* can also be used as a ready reference for your day-to-day problems and questions about commands. As suggested by many of you who have read earlier editions of this book, the exercises dealing with specific commands can quickly be located by means of the margin labels. Optional exercises at the end of each chapter will help you review what you have learned.

GETTING INFORMATION FAST

If you are already familiar with AutoCAD, you will appreciate the Fast Tracks at the beginning of each chapter. Fast Tracks are highly encapsulated instructions on the use of commands and functions found in the chapter. They include the page number in the chapter where you can find a more detailed description of the function or command. If you only need to refresh your memory on how to do something, check the Fast Tracks first.

I've also included marginal comments labeled as *Notes*, *Tips*, and *Warnings*. Notes supplement the main text; Tips are designed to make practice easier; and Warnings steer you away from pitfalls. Also, in each chapter you will find more extensive tips and discussions in the form of specially screened *side bars*. Together, they provide a wealth of information gathered over years of using AutoCAD on a variety of projects in different office environments. You may want to browse through the book, just reading the margin notes and side bars, to get an idea of how they might be useful to you.

In *Appendices D* and *E*, I provide tables of all the system variables and commands with comments on their use and options. You'll find an abbreviated summary of these tables in the front endpapers of the book so you don't have to do a lot of hunting around if you are just trying to remember a command or system variable name.

WHAT TO EXPECT

Mastering AutoCAD Release 12 for Windows is divided into five parts, each representing a milestone in your progress toward becoming an expert AutoCAD user. Here is a description of those parts and what they will show you.

Part One: The Basics

As with any major endeavor, you must begin by tackling small, manageable tasks. In this first part, you will get familiar with the way AutoCAD looks and feels. *Chapter 1, This Is AutoCAD*, shows you how to get around the AutoCAD screen. In *Chapter 2, Creating Your First Drawing*, you will learn how to start and exit the program and how to respond to

AutoCAD commands. *Chapter 3, Learning the Tools of the Trade*, tells you how to set up a work area, edit objects, and lay out a drawing. In *Chapter 4, Organizing Your Work*, you will explore some tools unique to CAD: symbols, blocks, and layers. As you are introduced to AutoCAD, you will also get a chance to make some drawings that you can use later in the book and perhaps even in future projects of your own.

Part Two: Discovering the AutoCAD Advantage

Once you have the basics down, you will begin to explore some of AutoCAD's more subtle qualities. *Chapter 5, Editing for Productivity*, tells you how to reuse drawing setup information and parts of an existing drawing. In *Chapter 6, Managing a Large Drawing*, you will learn how to assemble and edit a large drawing file. *Chapter 7, Printing and Plotting*, shows you how to get your drawing onto hard copy. *Chapter 8, Adding Text to Drawings*, tells you how to annotate your drawing and edit your notes. *Chapter 9, Using Dimensions*, gives you practice in using automatic dimensioning, another unique CAD capability. Along the way, I will be giving you tips on editing and problems you may encounter as you begin to use AutoCAD for more complex tasks.

Part Three: Getting the Most out of AutoCAD

At this point, you will be on the verge of becoming a real expert. *Part Three* is designed to help you polish your existing skills and give you a few new ones. *Chapter 10, Storing and Linking Data with Graphics*, tells you how to attach information to drawing objects. In *Chapter 11, Entering Pre-Existing Drawings*, you will learn three techniques for transferring paper drawings to AutoCAD. In *Chapter 12, Power Editing*, you will complete the tutorial, and in the process, will learn how to integrate what you've learned so far and gain some tips on working in groups and using multiple AutoCAD sessions. *Chapter 13, Drawing Curves and Solid Fills*, gives you an in-depth look at some special drawing objects such as spline and fitted curves. In *Chapter 14, Getting and Exchanging Data from Drawings*, you will practice getting information about a drawing, and will learn how AutoCAD can interact with other Windows applications, such as spreadsheets and desktop-publishing programs.

Part Four: Modeling and Imaging in 3D

While 2D drafting is AutoCAD's workhorse application, AutoCAD's 3D capabilities give you a chance to expand your ideas and look at them in a new light. *Chapter 15, Introducing 3D*, covers AutoCAD's basic features for creating three-dimensional drawings. *Chapter 16, Using Advanced 3D Features*, introduces you to some of the program's more powerful 3D capabilities. *Chapter 17, Rendering and Animating 3D Drawings*, shows how you can use the AutoCAD Renderer for this purpose. *Chapter 18, Mastering 3D Solids with the Advanced Modeling Extension*, is a guided tour of AutoCAD release 12's new Advanced Modeling Extension module.

Part Five: Customization— Taking AutoCAD to the Limit

In the last part of the book, you will learn how you can take full control of AutoCAD. *Chapter 19, AutoCAD's Hidden Treasures*, shows you some priceless but often overlooked tools that AutoCAD offers in the form of sample AutoLISP programs (AutoLISP is AutoCAD's built-in programming language). *Chapter 20, Exploring AutoLISP*, shows you how you can tap the power of this programming language to add new functions to AutoCAD. *Chapter 21, Integrating AutoCAD into Your Projects and Organization*, shows you how you can adapt AutoCAD to your own work style. Customizing menus, toolbar buttons, and line types are only three of the many topics. You'll also learn how to use other Windows programs to control AutoCAD.

The Appendices

Finally, this book has five appendices. *Appendix A, Hardware and Software Tips*, should give you a start on selecting hardware appropriate for AutoCAD. It also provides tips on improving AutoCAD's performance. *Appendix B, Installing and Setting Up AutoCAD*, contains an installation and configuration tutorial that you should follow before starting *Chapter 1* if AutoCAD is not already installed on your system.

If you're a beginner at Windows, you may want to browse through *Appendix C, A Windows Primer*, in conjunction with the earlier chapters. *Appendix D, System and Dimension Variables*, will illuminate the references to the system variables scattered throughout the book. *Appendix D* also discusses the many dimension settings and system features AutoCAD has to offer. Finally, *Appendix E, Standard AutoCAD Commands*, provides a listing of all the AutoCAD commands, with a brief description of their function and options.

THE MINIMUM
SYSTEM REQUIREMENTS

This book assumes you have an IBM-compatible 80386 computer that will run Windows 3.1 and support a mouse. Your computer should have at least one disk drive capable of reading a 5¼" 1.2 Mb disks or a 3½" 1.44 Mb disk, and a hard disk with 45 Mb or more free space (about 37 Mb for the AutoCAD program and another 8 Mb available for drawing files and work space for AutoCAD). AutoCAD release 12 for Windows runs best on systems with at least 8 Mb or more of RAM.

Your computer should also have a high-resolution monitor and a color display card. The current standard is the Video Graphics Array or VGA display, though most computers sold offer an enhanced version of the VGA called Super VGA. This is quite adequate for most AutoCAD work. The computer should also have at least one serial port. If you have only one, you should consider having another one installed, or at least getting a switch box. I also assume you are using a mouse and have the use of a dot-matrix printer or a plotter. If you are using a system with an 80386, you should also have a math coprocessor installed. AutoCAD release 12 for Windows does not run on older 80286-based computers.

If you want a more detailed explanation of hardware options with AutoCAD, look at *Appendix A*. You will find a general description of the available hardware options and their significance to AutoCAD.

DOING THINGS IN STYLE

Much care has been taken to see that the stylistic conventions in this book—the use of upper- or lowercase letters, italic or boldface type, and so on—will be the ones most likely to help you learn AutoCAD. On the whole, their effect should be subliminal. You may find it useful, however, to be conscious of the following rules that we have followed:

1. Pull-down selections are shown by a series of menu options separated by the ➤ symbol.

2. The terms *Side menu* and *Root menu* refer to the menu at the right of the screen.

3. Keyboard entries are shown in boldface (e.g. enter **Rotate** ↵).

4. Command line prompts are also shown in boldface.

MAKING AUTOCAD EASY

To help you gain even more productivity, you can purchase a disk containing software extensions to AutoCAD. These extensions make AutoCAD easier to use by simplifying many of AutoCAD's more common functions. You can get the basic bonus disk that contains general editing tools, or you can purchase the AEC disk for architecture, engineering, and construction applications. A third disk offers help to users who are combining AutoCAD with desktop publishing. These AutoCAD extensions are not available anywhere but on these disks. To find out more about these extensions, or to place an order, look at the order form at the end of this book.

NEW FEATURES OF RELEASE 12 FOR WINDOWS

AutoCAD release 12 for Windows offers a new level of speed, accuracy, and ease of use. Autodesk has improved its display speed and other operations, so learning and using AutoCAD is easier than ever. Other new features include:

- A fully Windows-compliant interface, which makes it easier to use.
- The ability to have multiple AutoCAD sessions running at the same time.
- The ability to link AutoCAD to other programs.
- Full Clipboard support for easy transport of drawings to other programs.
- Faster file-loading and regeneration times.
- Improved control of 3D display.
- Improved plotting controls that let you store several plotter configurations.
- An improved hatch command that allows you to select areas by boundaries, similar to a "fill" function.
- An improved zoom command that lets you instantaneously enlarge a view by a factor of up to 2.8 million.
- An improved online help system with graphics that lets you find information about commands quickly.
- A built-in renderer (AutoShade) that allows you to control surface reflectance and light sources.
- Support for PostScript Type 1 fonts.

THE MANUALS

You receive several manuals with AutoCAD. They are:

- The hard-bound AutoCAD Reference Manual
- The Interface, Installation, and Performance Guide
- The Advanced Modeling Extension Reference Manual
- The Render Reference Manual
- The Extras Manual

▼ NOTE

You may find the AutoCAD manuals pretty intimidating, especially if you feel uncomfortable with user manuals in the first place. But it's worth taking some time to browse through them and get to know their content, just in case you run into problems later.

- The Customization Manual
- A Tutorial
- The AutoCAD Development System Programmer's Reference Manual
- The AutoLISP Programmer's Reference Manual
- The AutoCAD SQL Extension Manual
- The AutoCAD IGES Interface Specifications
- The AutoCAD Resource Guide
- The Using AutoCAD for Windows Guide

You'll probably want to read the installation guide first, then browse through the reference manual to get a feel for the kind of information available there. The AutoCAD Resource Guide offers a listing of third-party developers for those of you looking for that special add-on to AutoCAD. Unless you already know AutoCAD inside and out, you probably won't want to look at the two programmer's references. The SQL Extension Manual is also geared toward programmers, though it does include a brief tutorial. You might want to browse through the remaining six manuals to see if there is anything of interest to you.

THE DISKS

AutoCAD comes with fifteen high-density program disks; twelve are for the main program and three are for the Advanced Modeling Extension. Before you do anything else, make copies of your disks and put the originals in a safe place. To do this, follow the instructions outlined in *Appendix B, Installing and Setting Up AutoCAD*.

THE DIGITIZER TEMPLATE

▼ NOTE

I won't specifically discuss the use of the digitizer for selecting commands, since the process is straightforward. If you are using a digitizer, you can use its puck like a mouse for all of the exercises in this book.

If you intend to use a digitizer tablet in place of a mouse, Autodesk also provides you with a digitizer template. Commands can be selected directly from the template by pointing at the command on the template and pressing the pick button. Each command is shown clearly by name and a simple icon. Commands are grouped on the template by the type of operation the command performs. Before you can use the digitizer template, you must configure the digitizer. See *Appendix A, Hardware and Software Tips,* for a more detailed description of digitizing tablets and *Appendix B* for instructions on configuring the digitizer.

I hope *Mastering AutoCAD Release 12 for Windows* will be of benefit to you and that, once you have completed the tutorials, you will continue to use the book as a reference. If you have comments, criticisms, or ideas about how the book can be improved, write to me at the address below. And thanks for choosing Mastering AutoCAD.

George Omura
Omura Illustration
P.O. Box 6357
Albany, CA 94706-0357

▼ ▼ ▼ ▼ ▼

PART ONE

THE
■
BASICS

As with any major endeavor, you must begin by tackling small, manageable tasks. In this first part, you will become familiar with the way AutoCAD looks and feels. You will also practice some of the basic commands that you will use most often in your work with AutoCAD. As you are introduced to AutoCAD, you will also get a chance to do some drawings that you can use later in this book and perhaps even in future drawings you create on your own. Finally, you will learn how to organize your work using blocks and layers.

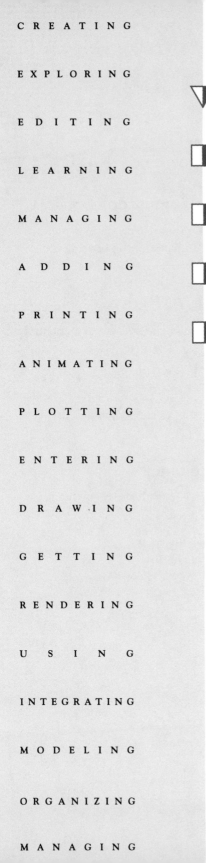

1

THIS IS
AUTOCAD

FAST TRACK

8 ▶ The AutoCAD drawing editor has six main components

These are the drawing area, the command prompt area, the side menu, the status line/toolbar, the pull-down menu bar, and the floating toolbox.

10 ▶ To tell AutoCAD what you want to do

Select commands from either the side menu or the pull-down menu or enter instructions with the keyboard.

10 ▶ To give instructions to AutoCAD

Use the command prompt area at the bottom of the screen and dialog boxes that appear in the drawing area.

10 ▶ To select locations in the drawing area

Position the crosshair cursor at the location you want and press the pick button.

17 ▶ To select a menu option

Highlight the option name and press the pick button. This is called *clicking* on a menu option.

21 ▶ To open a file from the file dialog box

Highlight the file name, then press the pick button twice in rapid succession. This is called *double-clicking*.

27 ▶ To exit a file

Choose File ➤ Exit AutoCAD.

28 ▶ To close one file and open another

Choose File ➤ Open.

Over the last decade, AutoCAD has emerged as the number-one CAD and drafting software package. When you learn to use AutoCAD, you not only have command over the most powerful PC-based CAD program, you also become a member of the largest community of CAD users in the world. This large user base offers a number of benefits:

▼ NOTE

Two independent publications, **Cadalyst** and **Cadence,** are devoted to AutoCAD users.

- A common file format across a variety of systems, from IBM to Silicon Graphics.

- A broad base of third-party software additions to enhance AutoCAD's functionality.

- The widest variety of hardware options for printing, plotting, and viewing CAD files.

- Support offered in the form of computer bulletin boards, user groups, and AutoCAD-specific publications.

- Easy access to training through Autodesk's official training centers.

WHAT MAKES RELEASE 12 FOR WINDOWS SPECIAL?

▼ TIP

If you are new to Windows, or if you want to better understand the dialog boxes, consult Appendix C. There you will find a Windows Primer, plus a section on the components of dialog boxes.

AutoCAD release 12 for Windows offers a new level of speed, accuracy, and ease of use. Its double-precision, floating-point database has always provided drawing accuracy to 16 decimal places. With this kind of accuracy, you can create a computer model of the earth and include details down to sub-micron levels. It also means that no matter how often you edit a drawing in AutoCAD, its dimensions will remain true. AutoCAD release 12 has improved its display speed and other operations, so learning and using AutoCAD is easier than ever. Other new features include:

- A fully Windows-compliant interface, which makes it easier to use.

- The ability to have multiple AutoCAD sessions running at the same time.

- The ability to link AutoCAD to other programs.

- Full Clipboard support for easy transport of drawings to other programs.

- Faster file-loading and regeneration times.

- Improved control of 3D display.

- Improved plotting control that lets you store several plotter configurations.

- An improved Hatch command that allows you to select areas by boundaries, similar to a "fill" function.

- An improved Zoom command that lets you instantaneously enlarge a view by a factor of up to 2.8 million.

- An improved online help system with graphics that lets you find information about commands quickly.

- A built-in renderer (AutoShade) that allows you to control surface reflectance and light sources.

- Support for PostScript Type 1 fonts.

A FIRST LOOK AT AUTOCAD

Now let's take a tour of AutoCAD. In this section, you will get a chance to familiarize yourself with the AutoCAD screen and how you communicate with AutoCAD. You will look at many of AutoCAD's basic operations like opening and closing files, getting a close-up look at part of a drawing, and making changes to a drawing.

Along the way, you will also get a feel for how to work with this book. Don't worry about understanding or remembering everything that you see in this chapter. You will get plenty of opportunities to probe the finer details of the program as you work through the later tutorials. If you are already familiar with earlier versions of AutoCAD, you may want to read through this chapter anyway to become familiar with new features. To help you remember the material, you will find a brief exercise at the end of each chapter. For now, just enjoy your first excursion into AutoCAD.

Starting AutoCAD

▼ TIP

If you are new to computers and you need a little help with Windows, consult Appendix C.

▼ TIP

You may notice a compass icon appear in the lower-left corner of the desktop. This icon is the Aerial View feature associated with AutoCAD's accelerated display driver option, the default display option when you configure AutoCAD. When you double click on this icon, a window appears that shows you an overall view of your drawing. You can use this window to pan and zoom over your drawing. The window can also be opened by clicking on the compass icon in the toolbar. See **Chapter 6** for more on the pan and zoom feature of AutoCAD.

▼ NOTE

A *layer* is like an overlay that allows you to separate different types of information. AutoCAD allows an unlimited number of layers. On new drawings the default layer is 0. There is a detailed discussion of layers in **Chapter 4**.

1. Start up Windows in enhanced mode.

2. If it isn't open already, open the AutoCAD program group by double-clicking on it.

3. Double-click on the AutoCAD program icon.

You will see a message telling you that AutoCAD is loading. Then AutoCAD's drawing editor appears with an opening message to tell you which version of AutoCAD you are using, who the program is registered to, and the AutoCAD dealer's name and phone number should you need help.

THE DRAWING EDITOR

The screen is divided into five parts, as shown in Figure 1.1. To the right you see the *side menu area* (the "side menu" is what Autodesk calls the "screen menu") ; at the bottom is the *prompt area*; and along the top is the *status line/tool bar* and the *menu bar*. The rest of the screen is occupied by the *drawing area*. In addition, you will see the *floating toolbox* to the right of the screen.

The drawing area occupies most of the screen and is your workspace. Everything you draw appears in this area. As you move your mouse around, you will see a cross appear to move within the drawing area. This is your drawing cursor. It lets you point to locations in the drawing area. Now let's look at each screen component in detail.

At the top of the drawing area (depicted in Figure 1.2), the status line/toolbar gives you information at a glance about the drawing. For example, the layer you are presently working on is displayed in the upper-left corner. The coordinate readout toward the center of the toolbar tells you the location of your cursor. To the far left, a box shows the current color. The rest of the toolbar offers buttons that perform special functions. Most of the buttons are customizable. You'll learn more about the toolbar buttons later in Part 1.

Right now, let's see how the coordinate readout works.

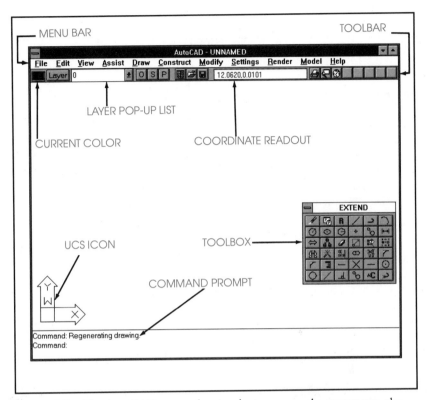

Figure 1.1: The AutoCAD screen, showing the menu area, the prompt area, the status line, the drawing area, the UCS icon, and the drawing cursor

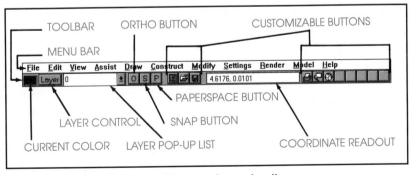

Figure 1.2: The components of the status line and toolbar

Picking points

1. Move the cursor to the middle of the screen, then press the pick button on your pointing device (usually the left button on a mouse or the top button on a digitizer puck) and let it go. The coordinate readout shows the coordinates of the cursor as you move it. As you move the cursor, a rectangle follows. This is a selection window. You'll learn more about this window later.

2. Move the cursor a bit in any direction, then press and let go of the pick button again while watching the coordinate readout. Notice that the rectangle disappears.

3. Try picking several more points in the drawing area.

You will notice that tiny crosses appear where you picked points. These are called blips. They are markers that show where you've selected points. They do not become a permanent part of your drawing, nor do they print onto hard copy output.

In the lower-left corner of the drawing area, you see a thick L-shape arrow. This is the *user coordinate system* (UCS) icon, which tells you your orientation in the drawing. This icon becomes helpful as you start to work with complex 2D drawings and 3D models. The X and Y inside the icon indicate the X and Y axes of your drawing. The W tells you that you are in what is called the *world coordinate system*. We will discuss this icon in detail in *Chapter 16*. For now, you can use it as a reference to tell you the direction of the X axis and the Y axis.

To the extreme right of the screen is the side menu. It offers a comprehensive selection of commands, as you will see later in the book.

At the bottom of the screen is the prompt area. This area displays AutoCAD's responses to your input. Right now, it shows the word *Command* at the very bottom. This tells you that AutoCAD is waiting for your instructions. *It is important to pay special attention to messages displayed in the prompt area, because this is how AutoCAD communicates with you.*

Finally, at the right of the screen, just below the side menu, you see the floating toolbox. The toolbox is a set of bitmap icon buttons that initiate a command or other function. It's called a floating toolbox because you can move it—to any location on the Windows desktop. Just click and drag its title bar.

Communicating with AutoCAD

AutoCAD is the perfect servant: It does everything you tell it to, and no more. You communicate with AutoCAD using *commands*. A command is a single-word instruction you give to AutoCAD telling it to do something, like draw a line (LINE) or erase an object (ERASE). Whenever you invoke a command, by either typing it in or selecting it from a menu, AutoCAD responds by presenting messages to you in the command-prompt area or by displaying a *dialog box*.

The messages in the command-prompt area often tell you what to do next or offer a list of options. A single command will often present several messages, which you answer to complete the command.

A dialog box is like a form you fill out on the computer screen. It lets you adjust settings or make selections from a set of options pertaining to a command. You'll get a chance to work with commands and dialog boxes later in this chapter.

THE SIDE MENU

You can think of the side menu to the right of the screen as a book listing all the commands available in AutoCAD. It contains many "pages" of menus. These pages are broken down into different categories like DISPLAY, DRAW, and EDIT. When you first open AutoCAD, the side

▼ NOTE

The side menu (or screen menu as it is often called) is turned off by default. If you are an experienced AutoCAD user who prefers to use the side menu, or if you feel that this menu can be useful to you, you can turn it on using the Edit ➤ Preferences ... option. This option opens the Preferences dialog box. See **Appendix B** to find out how to use the Preferences dialog box.

menu shows the first page, called the *Root menu*. You can think of this Root menu as the index or table of contents to the other pages of the side menu.

As you look at the menu, you will notice that three of the items listed—DIM, UCS, and SAVE—are followed by colons. (You may have to move the toolbox to see the commands on the side menu.) A colon tells you that the word preceding it is an AutoCAD command and selecting this option will start that command. Two of the items, LAYER and PLOT, are followed by a row of periods (...). These items are commands that display dialog boxes. All other items on the Root menu are the names of other menus (submenus) containing the commands related to that particular activity. For example, if you pick Edit, another menu will appear that contains the commands for editing objects.

Selecting options from the side menu

▼ TIP

If you experience difficulty picking menu options, the problem is most likely a sticky button on your pointing device. As you work through the exercises in this book, pay special attention to the way your pointing device's buttons work and make note of its idiosyncrasies.

1. Move your cursor to the far right. You will see a bar appear in the side menu.

2. Move the bar with your mouse until it is on the word *EDIT*.

3. Press the pick button then let it go. The Edit submenu appears. Figure 1.3 shows the Edit menu.

You see a new menu with several items followed by colons. Each of these items invokes a command. Near the bottom of the menu you will see *next* (you may have to click and drag the floating toolbox out of the way to see the bottom of the menu).

Moving through the menu system

1. Move your mouse forward and backward. Different options are highlighted.

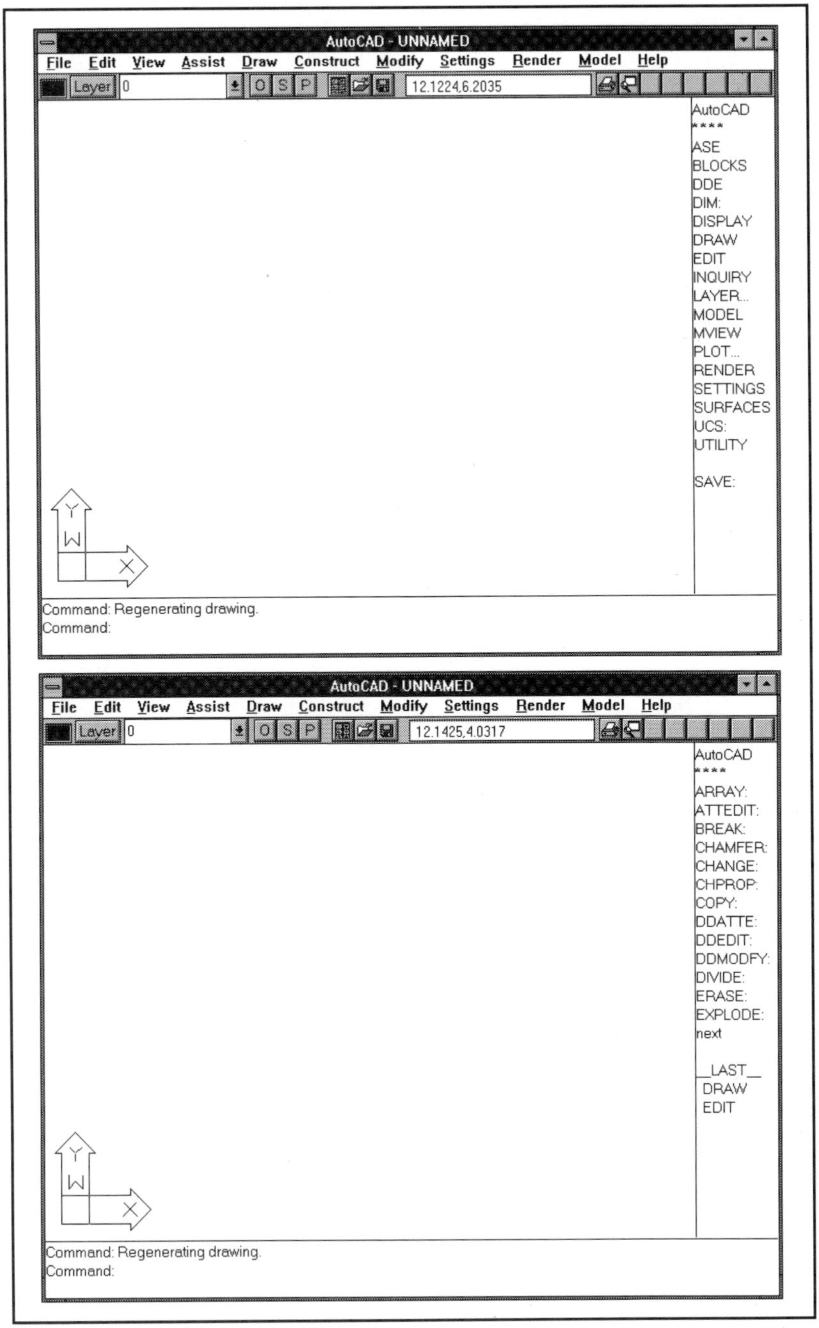

Figure 1.3: The Root and Edit menus

> **▼ NOTE**
>
> The operation you just performed—highlighting an item then pressing the pick button—is referred to as ***clicking on*** an item. From now on, I will use the expression "***click on***" to describe the process of placing the cursor on top of an item and pressing the pick button.

2. Click on **next** toward the bottom of the menu. Notice that another set of editing commands appears. This is a continuation of the Edit menu.
3. To get back to the original Edit menu, click on **previous** (see Figure 1.4).

Not all menus have a **next** option, but when you see **next**, you will know that the menu continues as a submenu. Also note that menu options are in alphabetical order.

You will also see **LAST**, **DRAW**, and **EDIT** at the bottom of the menu. These items allow you to go directly to the last menu or to the **Edit** or **Draw** menu from wherever you may be in the menu system. At the top, the item **AutoCAD** can be selected to bring you back to the Root menu. Just below AutoCAD is a row of asterisks. If you click on

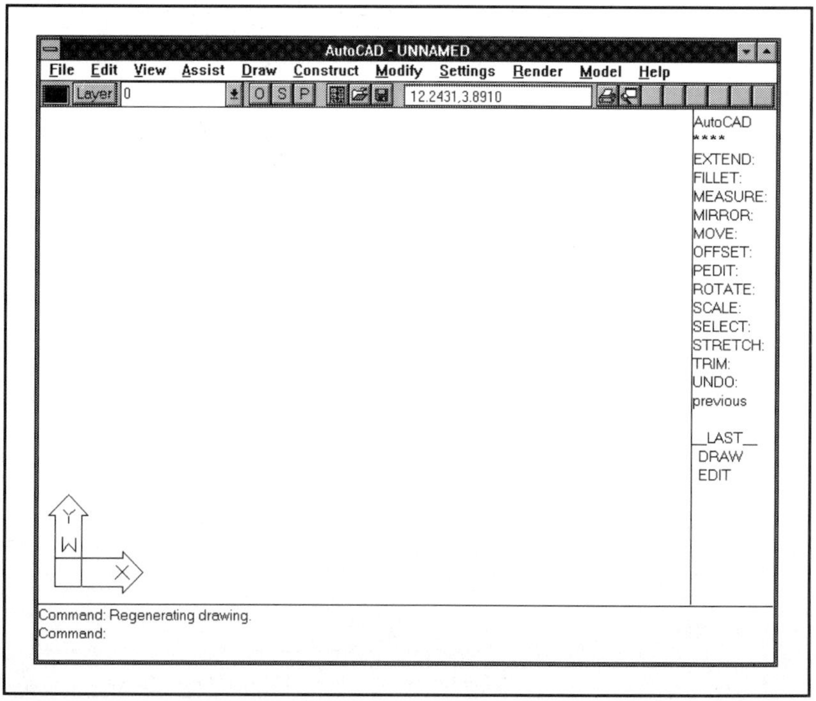

Figure 1.4: The Edit submenu with the previous option highlighted

▼ NOTE

It will help to remember that many of AutoCAD's commands offer several options that appear in both the side menu and in the prompt area. Options can be selected by clicking on them from the menu or by entering the option name from the keyboard.

this item, the **Osnap** (object snap) overrides will appear. The Osnap overrides menu is shown in Figure 1.5. These are *command modifiers* that allow you to pick specific locations in a drawing such as the midpoint of a line or the intersection of two lines. You will see how these work later.

The AutoCAD item, the row of asterisks, and the LAST, DRAW, and EDIT commands appear on nearly every menu. No matter where you are, you can get to the most commonly used menus.

The "pages" of the side menu are set up like a tree (see Figure 1.6). The Root menu is the trunk that branches to other menu "pages" specific to particular types of activities. From the branches, like leaves, spring the various commands related to the activity you have chosen.

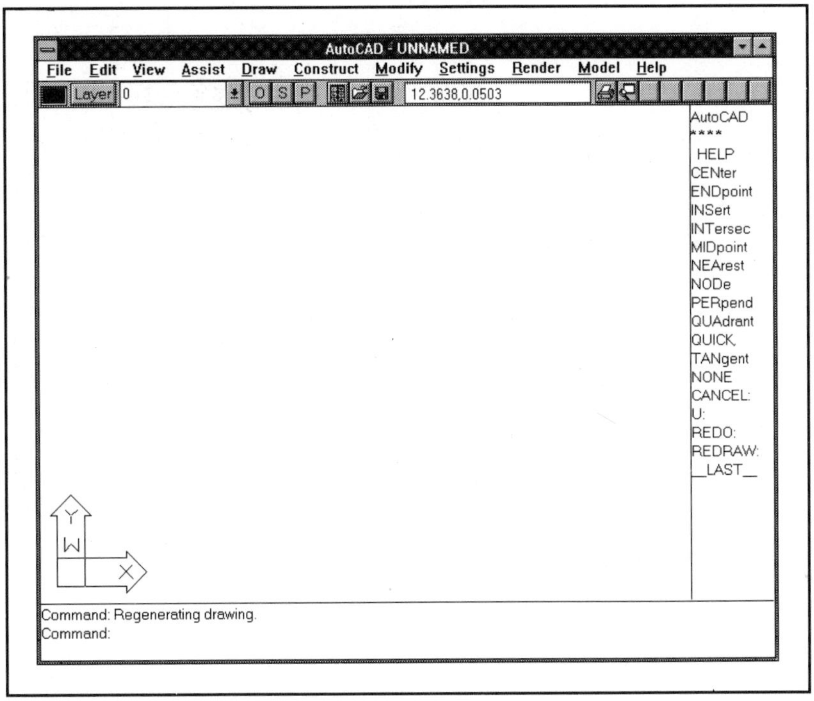

Figure 1.5:   The Osnap overrides menu

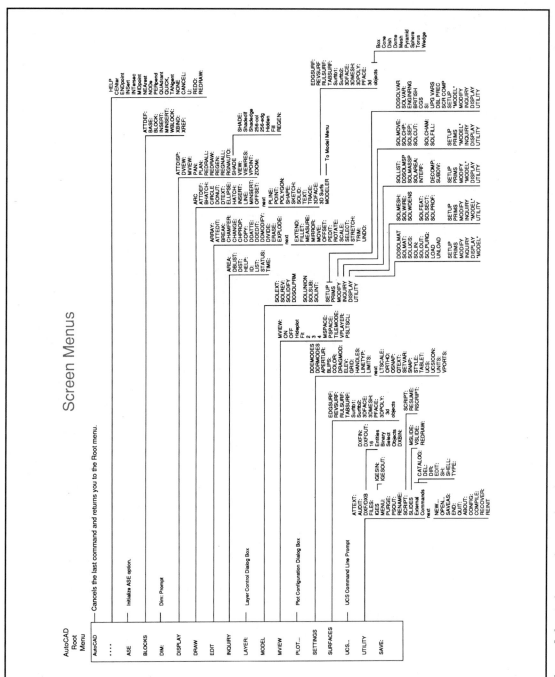

Figure 1.6: A diagram showing the side menu structure

THE PULL-DOWN MENUS

The side menu offers a way to access nearly all of AutoCAD's commands, but for many of the commands, you have to go through several layers of menus. The pull-down menus offer a quicker way to access the most commonly used commands that AutoCAD has to offer. Next, you will get a firsthand look at pull-down menus.

Navigating the pull-down menus

1. Place your arrow cursor on the Modify option and click on it. A menu drops down below the Modify option.

2. Some of the menu items have triangular pointers to their right. Click on the second icon from the top. Another set of options appears to the right. This second set of items is called a *cascading menu*. Many of AutoCAD's commands offer multiple options. These cascading menus give you easy access to those options.

3. To leave the pull-down menu, move the arrow pointer into the drawing area and press the pick button. Alternately, you can press the **Esc** (Escape) key. You must press Esc for each level of menu you have open.

CHANGING BITMAP ICONS TO PLAIN TEXT

If you prefer, you can set up three of the menus—Draw, Construct, and Modify—to use icons to represent commands.

Settings ➤ Menu Bitmaps

1. Click on Settings from the menu bar. Notice the option at the very bottom of the menu, Menu Bitmaps. This tells you that the icons (the menu bitmaps) are turned on.

2. Click on Menu Bitmaps. This has the effect of turning on the icons.

3. Click on Modify from the menu bar. Notice that the menu displays icons.

4. Go back to the Settings menu and click on Menu Bitmaps again. This sets the menu back to text.

From now on, to help simplify the description of command selection, I'll assume you have the menu bitmaps turned off. To show a menu-command combination, we will use the names of the menu and command in the form Menu ➤ Command. For cascading menus, we will use Menu ➤ Command ➤ Command (and so on to identify each successive command under the menu). If you need to correlate the bitmap icons with the plain-text equivalent, refer to Figure 1.7, which shows all of the pull-down menus at one time along with their bitmap icon menus. In addition, when a command has a menu-bitmap equivalent, we'll show the equivalent bitmap icon in the margin to help you locate a command in an icon menu or in the floating toolbox.

USING THE FLOATING TOOLBOX

The floating toolbox offers several of the more common AutoCAD functions in a set of icon buttons. To start a command, you simply click on a button. Just as with the toolbar at the top of the drawing area, the buttons on the floating toolbox are customizable. For now, you'll be using the options on the toolbox as they are set up by default.

Move the arrow pointer over the buttons of the toolbox and notice that the toolbox title bar displays the name of each button's function. The buttons are grouped loosely by their functions. The icons in the top set perform the same functions as the object snaps described earlier. The rest of the buttons are clustered in a way similar to the Draw, Construct, and Modify pull-down menus. In fact, many of the icons are the same as those found in the pull-down menus.

As you work through the exercises in this book, you will see icons in the margins. These icons will help you locate the buttons related to the commands being discussed in the accompanying text. In *Chapter 21*, I'll discuss how you can customize the toolbox.

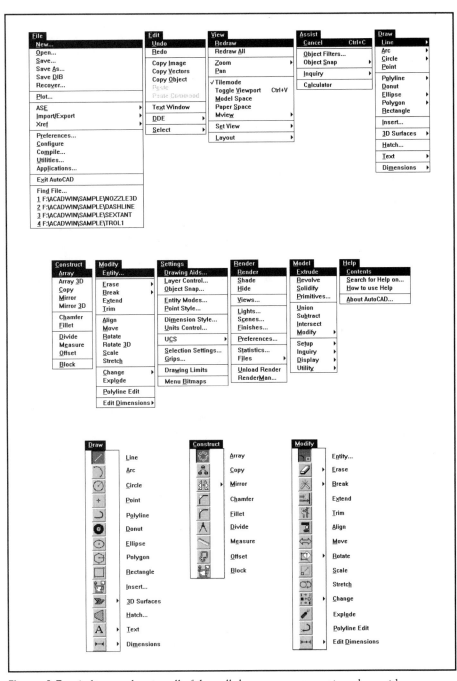

Figure 1.7: A diagram showing all of the pull-down menus at one time along with a comparison of the text and icon menus

Menus vs. the Keyboard

Throughout this book, you will be told to select commands and command options from the side menu or pull-down menus. Both kinds of menus offer new users an easy-to-remember method for accessing commands. You can also enter commands and command options through the keyboard. In fact, as you become more familiar with AutoCAD, you may prefer the keyboard over the menus. Keyboard entry of commands can speed up drawing input since it eliminates paging through the many layers of menus. Also, knowing the basic AutoCAD commands will allow you to work on any AutoCAD system no matter what kind of custom menus and program overlays the system may have. As you work through the tutorial, look for margin notes that show you alternate keyboard shortcuts to the operations being discussed in the tutorial.

If you decide that you prefer using the keyboard as a means of starting commands, you may want to make a habit of typing Ctrl-C twice, or clicking on the ^C button on the floating toolbox before entering a command. This will ensure that you are entering your commands at a fresh command prompt instead of in the middle of another command.

WORKING WITH AUTOCAD

Now that you've seen the drawing editor, let's try using a few of AutoCAD's commands. First, you'll open a sample file, then you'll make a few simple modifications to it. In the process, you'll get familiar with some common methods of operation AutoCAD uses.

OPENING AN EXISTING FILE

To start with, you will open an existing file. In this exercise, you will get a chance to see and use a typical file dialog box.

Opening a file

▼ NOTE

Pressing the pick button twice in rapid succession is called *double-clicking*. Double-clicking on a name in a list is a quick way of selecting that item. If you prefer, you can double-click on the file name to open that file, instead of highlighting the name and clicking on the OPEN button.

1. In the menu bar, choose File ➤ Open. A file dialog box appears, as shown in Figure 1.8. This is a typical Windows file dialog box.

2. In the directory list to the right, click on the directory named **SAMPLE** to highlight it, then press the pick button twice in rapid succession. You may need to scroll down the list to find the Sample directory. The file list to the left changes to show the contents of the Sample directory.

3. Move the arrow to the name **Nozzle3d** in the left-hand list and click on it. Notice that the name now appears in the file name input box near the bottom of the dialog box.

4. Click on the box labeled OK near the bottom left of the dialog box. AutoCAD proceeds to open the **Nozzle3d** file as shown in Figure 1.9.

▼ TIP

You will notice two check boxes in the File dialog box labeled Select Initial View and Read Only Mode. When Select Initial View is checked, you can open a drawing to a named view (see *Chapter 6* for more on named views). When Read Only Mode is checked, you are prevented from making changes to the drawing you open. Read Only Mode also lets you open files on non-writable media such as CD- ROMs.

Figure 1.8: The File dialog box and its components

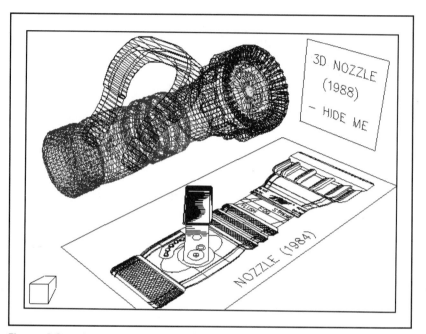

Figure 1.9: The Nozzle drawing

The Nozzle file opens to display the entire drawing. When you open a file, it is displayed in the same way you last saved it. Also notice that the AutoCAD window's title bar displays the name of the drawing. This offers easy identification of your drawing.

GETTING A CLOSER LOOK

Now suppose you want to get a closer look at a part of the nozzle. To do that, you use the *Zoom* command. To indicate the area you wish to enlarge, you will use what is called a *window*.

View ➤ Zoom ➤ Window

1. At the command prompt, enter **PLAN** ↵ or Click on View ➤ Set View ➤ Plan View ➤ Current UCS. Your view changes to display a 2D view.

2. Choose View ➤ Zoom ➤ Window.

3. The prompt area displays the words **First corner:**. Move the crosshair cursor to the lower-left corner of the square shown in Figure 1.10, then press the pick button. Now as you move the cursor you see a rectangle appear. One corner of the rectangle is fixed on the point you just picked while the other corner follows the cursor.

4. The prompt area now displays **First corner: Other corner:.** Position the other corner of the window so it encloses the handle of the nozzle as shown in Figure 1.10, then press the pick button. The handle enlarges to fill the screen.

In this exercise, you used the Window option of the Zoom command to define the area to enlarge for your close-up view. You saw how AutoCAD prompts you to indicate first one corner of the window, then the other. You will use the Window option frequently, not just to define views, but also to select objects for editing.

View ➤ Zoom ➤ Previous

Getting a close-up view of your drawing is crucial to allow you to work accurately with a drawing, but you'll often want to return to a previous view to get the overall picture. To do so, choose View ➤ Zoom ➤ Previous. The previous view—one showing the entire nozzle—returns to the screen.

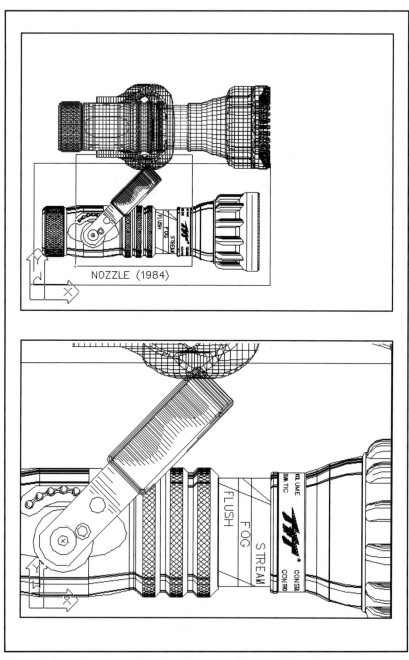

Figure 1.10: Placing the Zoom Window around the nozzle handle

▼ NOTE

By default, AutoCAD auto-matically saves your work at 120-minute intervals under the name AUTO.SV$. You can change the name of the save file or control the time be-tween saves by using system variables. See **Chapter 3** for more.

SAVING A FILE AS YOU WORK

It is a good idea to periodically save your file while you work. You can either save it under its original name or save it under a different name, thereby creating a new file.

First try the Save command. This quickly saves the drawing in its cur-rent state without exiting the program.

Choose File ➤ Save. You will notice some disk activity while AutoCAD saves the file to the hard disk. As an alternate to picking File ➤ Save, you can type **Qsave** at the command prompt, then press Return.

Now try the File ➤ Save As command. This command brings up a dialog box that allows you to save the current file under a new name.

File ➤ Save As

▼ NOTE

As an alternative, you can issue the File ➤ Save As com-mand by entering **Save** or **Save as** from the keyboard.

1. Choose File ➤ Save As. A dialog box similar to the File dialog box (shown in Figure 1.8) appears. Note that the cur-rent file name, *Nozzle3d*, appears highlighted in the File name input box at the bottom of the dialog box.

2. Type **Myfirst** from the keyboard. As you type, the name Nozzle disappears from the input box and the name you are typing takes its place. You don't need to enter the .DWG file name extension. AutoCAD will add it to the file name auto-matically when it saves the file.

3. Click on the OK button. The dialog box disappears and you will notice some disk activity.

You now have a copy of the nozzle file under the name *Myfile*.DWG. Also, you will notice that the name of the file displayed in the AutoCAD window's title bar has changed to Myfile. From now on, when you use the File ➤ Save option, your drawing will be saved under its new name. Saving files under a different name can be useful when you are creating alternatives or when you just want to save one of several ideas you are trying out.

MAKING CHANGES

You will be making frequent changes to your drawings. In fact, one of the chief advantages of CAD is the ease with which you can make changes. The following exercise shows you a typical sequence of operations involved in making a change to a drawing.

Modify ➤ Erase ➤ Select

1. Choose Modify ➤ Erase ➤ Select.

2. You will see the prompt **Select object:** at the bottom of the command prompt area. Also notice that the cursor has turned into a small square. This square is called the *pickbox*.

3. Place the pickbox on the diagonal pattern of the nozzle handle and click on it (see Figure 1.11). The 2D image of the nozzle becomes highlighted. The Select object prompt appears again.

4. Place the pickbox on the rectangular border that outlines the handle and click on it. The rectangle also highlights.

5. Now press **Return**. The nozzle and the rectangle disappear. You have just erased a part of the drawing.

In this exercise, you first issued the Erase command, then selected two objects by clicking on them using a pickbox. The *select object* prompt and the pickbox always appear together, telling you that you must select items on the screen. Once you've finished selecting objects, you press ↵ to move on to the next step. This sequence of steps is common to many of the commands you will work with in AutoCAD.

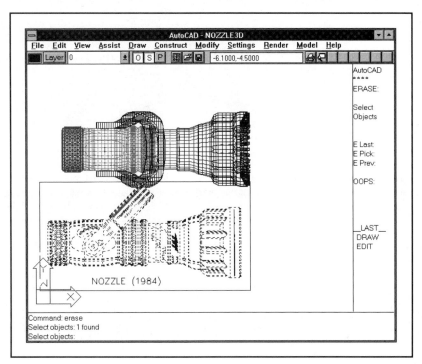

Figure 1.11:   Erasing a portion of the Nozzle handle

CLOSING AUTOCAD

When you are done with your work, you can open another drawing, temporarily leave AutoCAD, or close AutoCAD entirely. To close a file and exit AutoCAD, you use the *Exit AutoCAD* option on the File menu.

File ➤ Exit AutoCAD

1. Choose File ➤ Exit AutoCAD. A dialog box appears showing three buttons, labeled *Save Changes*, *Discard Changes*, and *Cancel Command* (see Figure 1.12).

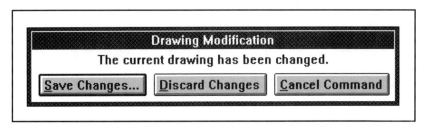

Figure 1.12:   The dialog box displayed when exiting a file

2. Click on *Discard Changes*. AutoCAD exits the nozzle drawing and closes without saving your changes.

When you attempt to exit a drawing that has been changed, you will get the dialog box in Figure 1.12. This dialog box is a safety feature that lets you save your changes before you exit AutoCAD. In this exercise, you discarded the changes you made, so the nozzle drawing reverted back to its condition before you erased the handle.

If you only want to exit AutoCAD temporarily, you can minimize it so it appears as an icon in the lower-left corner of the Windows desktop. You do this by clicking on the button showing the downward-pointing arrow in the upper-right corner of the AutoCAD window. Alternately, you can use the Alt-Tab key combination to switch to another program.

IF YOU WANT TO EXPERIMENT ...

Try opening and closing some of the sample drawing files.

1. Start AutoCAD by double-clicking on the AutoCAD pro-gram icon in the AutoCAD program group.

2. Click on File ➤ Open.

3. Use the dialog box to open the Myfile file again. Notice that the drawing appears on the screen with the handle enlarged. This is the view you had on the screen when you used the Save command in an earlier exercise.

4. Erase the handle as you did in the earlier exercise.

5. Click on File ➤ Open again. This time, open the Dhouse file. Notice that you get the *Save Changes* dialog box you got when you used the *Exit AutoCAD* option earlier. The Open menu option acts just like *Exit AutoCAD*, but instead of exiting AutoCAD altogether, it closes the current file and then opens a different one.

6. Click on the *Discard Changes* button. The 3D Dhouse drawing opens.

7. Click on File ➤ Exit AutoCAD. Notice that you exit AutoCAD without getting the Save Changes dialog box. This is because you didn't make any changes to the Dhouse file.

SUMMARY

In this chapter, we've covered some of the background on AutoCAD so you could get a feeling for what it has to offer. You also looked at the AutoCAD drawing editor and got a glimpse of the inner workings of AutoCAD. In the next chapter, you will get a chance to get more comfortable with AutoCAD's operations and start to do some drawing.

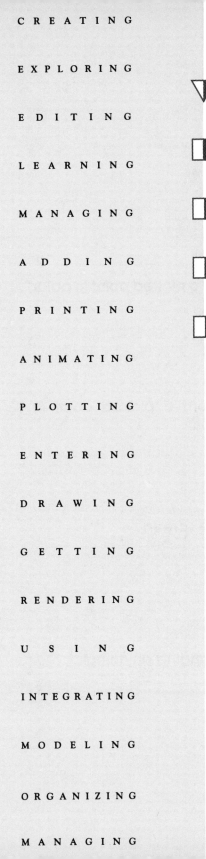

2
▼ ▼ ▼ ▼ ▼

**CREATING
YOUR FIRST
DRAWING**

FAST TRACK

35 ▶ **To draw a series of line segments**

Choose Draw ➤ Line ➤ Segments and click on the drawing area where you want to place lines.

37 ▶ **To specify exact distances from a picked point in polar coordinates**

Type @, the distance, <, and the angle. There should be no spaces between characters. For example, to specify a distance of 4 at an angle of 30 degrees, type **@4<30** ↵.

39 ▶ **To specify exact distances from a picked point in horizontal and vertical distances**

Type @, the horizontal distance, a comma, and the vertical distance. For example, to specify a location that is 4 units to the right and 6 units up, type **@4,6** ↵.

41 ▶ **To get rid of blips that clutter the screen**

Choose View ➤ Redraw.

43 ▶ **To cancel a command**

Hold down the **Ctrl** key and press **C**.

43 ▶ **To exit a dialog box without changing anything**

Press the **Esc** key.

46 ▶ To select objects to be edited

Click on them individually or pick two points defining a window.

56 ▶ To select the exact endpoint of an object at the From point: or to point: prompts

Hold down the **Shift** key and press the right mouse button. A pop-up menu appears. Click on *Endpoint* from the menu, then click on the endpoint you want to select.

56 ▶ To set up AutoCAD to allow preselection of objects

Enter '**Pickfirst** ↵; then at the next prompt, enter **1** ↵.

62 ▶ To set up AutoCAD to allow the use of Grips

Enter '**Grips** ↵, then at the next prompt, enter **1** ↵.

68 ▶ To get general information on AutoCAD

Click on Help ➤ Contents.

73 ▶ To move from the Text display to the Graphics display

Press the **F2** key or click on the minimize button.

In this chapter we'll look at some of AutoCAD's basic functions and practice using the drawing editor by building a simple drawing to use in later exercises. We'll cover giving input, interpreting prompts, and getting help when you need it. We'll also cover using coordinate systems to give AutoCAD exact measurements for objects, selecting objects you've drawn, and specifying base points for moving or copying.

If you're not a beginning AutoCAD user, you might want to complete the drawing quickly and move on to the more complex material in *Chapter 3*.

INTERPRETING PROMPTS

In *Chapter 1*, you looked at a sample drawing that came with AutoCAD. This time you will begin to draw on your own by creating a door that will be used in later exercises. First, though, you must learn how to tell AutoCAD what you want. Start a new file by choosing File ➤ New.

File ➤ New

1. Start AutoCAD the same way you did in the first chapter by going to your AutoCAD Program group and double-clicking on the AutoCAD icon.

2. Choose File ➤ New.

3. When the Create new drawing dialog box appears, type **Door**. As you type, the name appears in the file name input box.

4. Be sure the No Prototype check box is checked, then click on the **OK** button or press **Return**. The AutoCAD opening message will appear briefly and a new file will be opened.

▼ **NOTE**

The Create new file dialog box shows a checked box labeled **No Prototype** near the top. When this box is checked, AutoCAD creates a new file using the standard AutoCAD default settings. This is an important feature, because this book assumes you are using the standard default settings. (For more on the use of prototype files, see *Chapter 5*.)

When you see the command prompt

Command:

at the very bottom of the screen, you can enter any legal AutoCAD command either with the keyboard or from the side or pull-down menu. As you enter a command, other messages appear in the prompt area, asking you for additional information. The side menu will also change to show options available for the command. In this way the prompt guides you through a command, instructing you on what to do next, or offering options. The following exercise demonstrates this.

Draw➤ 🖊 Line ➤ Segments

1. Pick Draw ➤ Line ➤ Segments. AutoCAD responds with the prompt

   From point:

   asking you to select a point to begin your line. The side menu also changes to show you options available under the Line command. The cursor, too, has changed its appearance; it no longer has a square in the crosshairs.

2. Move your mouse around. You will see the cursor follow your movements within the drawing area.

3. Using the pick button, select a point on the screen near the center. As you select the point, AutoCAD adds

   To point:

   to the prompt.

Now as you move the mouse around, you will notice a line with one end fixed on the point you just selected and the other end following the cursor as you move the mouse (see panel 1 of Figure 2.1). This is called *rubber banding*. You will also see a tiny cross marking the first endpoint of the line. This cross is called a *blip*, and it appears every time you select a point during a command. Now continue with the line command.

1. Now move the cursor to a point to the right of the first point you selected and press the pick button again. The first rubber-banding line is now fixed between the two points you selected and a second rubber-banding line appears (see panel 2 of Figure 2.1).

2. If the line you drew isn't the exact length you want, you can back up during the Line command and change it. Pick undo

▼ NOTE

Alternately, you can pick Draw ➤ Line from the side menu or enter **Line** ↵ with the keyboard.

▼ NOTE

Though they show up on the screen, **blips** are not part of the drawing; they are a visual aid to you while you draw. AutoCAD provides a setting that lets you turn off blips. We will discuss this command in *Chapter 13*.

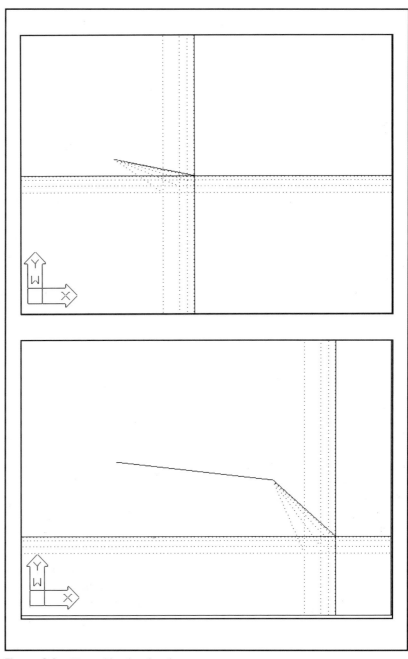

Figure 2.1: Two rubber-banding lines

from the Line side menu or type **U** from the keyboard and press **Return**. The line you drew previously will rubber-band as if you hadn't selected the second point to fix its length.

You've just drawn, then undrawn, a line at an arbitrary length. The line command is still active. You can tell you are in the middle of a command by looking at the bottom of the command prompt. If you don't see the word *Command*, you know a command is still active.

SPECIFYING DISTANCES WITH COORDINATES

Next, you will continue with the line command to draw a *plan view* (an overhead view) of a door to no particular scale. Later you will resize the drawing to use in future exercises. The door is to be 3.0 units long and 0.15 units thick. To specify these exact distances in AutoCAD, you can use either *relative polar* or *Cartesian* coordinates.

SPECIFYING A POLAR COORDINATE

To enter the exact distance of three units to the right of the last point you selected, do the following.

> Enter **@3<0** ↵. A line appears starting from the first point you picked and ending three units to the right of it (see Figure 2.2). You have just entered a relative polar coordinate.

▼ NOTE

If you are used to another CAD system that uses a different method for describing directions, you can use AutoCAD to set a vertical direction or downward direction to be 0°. (See *Chapter 3* for details.)

The at sign (**@**) tells AutoCAD that the distance you specify is from the last point you selected. The **3** is the distance. The less-than symbol (**<**) tells AutoCAD that you are giving it the angle at which the line is to be drawn. The last part is the value for the angle, which in this case is **0**. This is how to use *polar coordinates* to tell AutoCAD distances and direction.

Angles are given based on the system shown in Figure 2.3, where 0° is a horizontal direction from left to right, 90° is straight up, 180° is

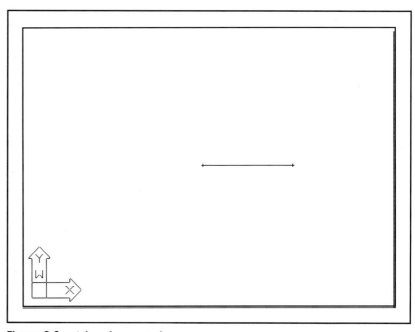

Figure 2.2: A line three units long

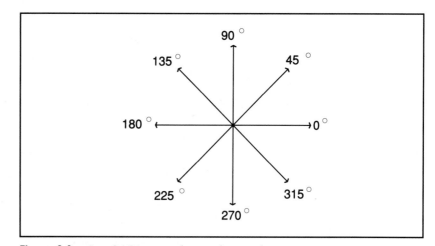

Figure 2.3: AutoCAD's system for specifying angles

horizontal from right to left, and so on. You can specify degrees, minutes, and seconds of arc if you want to be that exact. We'll discuss angle formats in more detail in *Chapter 3*.

SPECIFYING RELATIVE CARTESIAN COORDINATES

▼ NOTE

Once again the at sign tells AutoCAD that the distance you specify is from the last point picked. But in this example, you give the distance in *x* and *y* values. The *x* distance, 0, is given first, followed by a comma, and then by the *y* distance, 0.15.

For the next line segment let's try another method of specifying exact distances.

1. Enter **@0,.15** ↵. A short line appears above the endpoint of the last line. This is how to specify distances in relative Cartesian coordinates.

2. Enter **@-3,0**. The result is a drawing that looks like Figure 2.4.

The last distance you entered was also in *x,y* values. But you used a negative value to specify the *x* distance. Positive values in the Cartesian

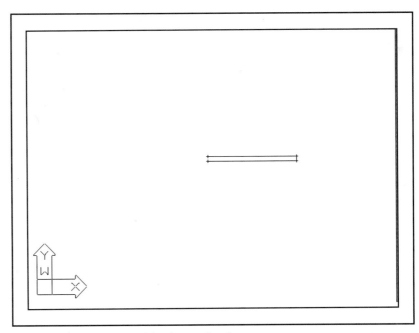

Figure 2.4:   Three sides of the door in the plan

coordinate system are from left to right and from bottom to top (see Figure 2.5). If you want to draw a line from right to left, you must give it a negative value.

1. Now pick *Close* from the side menu or type **C** ⏎. You can close any sequence of lines by picking *Close* from the menu during the Line command. A line connecting the first and last points of a sequence of lines will be drawn, and the Line command will terminate (see Figure 2.6).

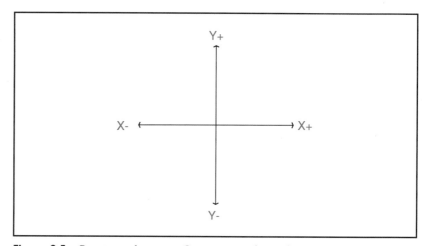

Figure 2.5:   Positive and negative Cartesian coordinate directions

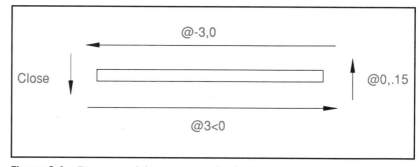

Figure 2.6:   Distance and direction input for the door

CLEANING UP THE SCREEN

By now the screen looks a bit messy with all the blips. To clean up a screen image, use the Redraw command.

View ➤ Redraw

1. Choose View ➤ Redraw and the screen will quickly redraw the objects, clearing them of the blips.

Another command, Regen, does the same thing but also updates the drawing database—which means it takes a lot longer to restore the drawing. In general you will want to avoid Regen. You will see how to use it in *Chapter 7*. (Regen can be found on the AutoCAD ➤ Display menu).

RESPONDING TO PROMPTS

In this section you will become familiar with some of the ways AutoCAD prompts you for input. Understanding the format of the prompts will help you learn the program more easily.

CHOOSING COMMAND OPTIONS

Virtually every command in AutoCAD has more than one option. Command options are presented to you in the prompt in a consistent format. The Arc command illustrates this point quite well.

Usually, in a drawing of a floor plan, an arc is drawn to indicate the direction of a door swing. Figure 2.7 shows some of the other standard symbols used in architectural style drawings. Next you'll draw the arc for the door you started in the previous exercise.

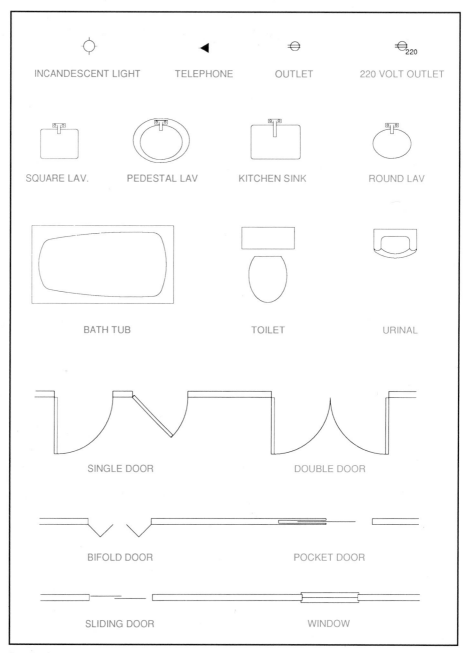

Figure 2.7: Samples of standard symbols used in architectural drawings

Getting Out of Trouble

Beginners and experts alike are bound to make a few mistakes. Before you get too far into the tutorial, I'd like to introduce you to some powerful yet easy-to-use tools to help you recover from accidents.

Backspace [←] If you make a typing error, you can use the **Backspace** key to back up to your error, then retype your command or response. This key is located in the upper right corner of the keyboard area.

Cancel [Ctrl-C] If you start a command and then decide not to use that command after all, you can hold down the **Control** key and simultaneously press **C**. This cancels the current command and returns you to the command prompt. You can also choose Assist ➤ Cancel. Alternately, you can pick a command from the pull-down menu to simultaneously cancel an active command and start a new one. Cancel also deselects objects that have been preselected using the noun/verb method.

Escape [Esc] If you want to quickly exit a dialog box without making changes, you can press the **Escape** key in the upper-left corner of your keyboard.

U If you accidentally change something in the drawing and want to reverse that change, you can enter **U** ↵ at the command prompt. Each time you enter **U**, AutoCAD will undo one operation at a time, in reverse order. This means that the last command performed will be undone first, then the next to last, etc. The prompt will display the name of the command being undone, and the drawing will revert to its condition prior to that command. You can undo everything back to the beginning of an editing session if you need to. U is a command unto itself. Though it acts in a similar way to the Line ➤ Undo option and the selection options (see Figure 2.20), it isn't really the same thing. A variation of the **U** command is the UNDO command, which we will discuss later.

Redo If you accidentally Undo one too many commands, you can redo the last undone command by entering **redo**. Unfortunately, Redo only restores one command.

Arc ↵

1. Initiate the command by typing **arc** ↵. The prompt **Center/<Start point>:** appears. This prompt tells you that you have two options. The *default* option always appears between angle brackets (<, >), and all options are separated by a slash (/). If you choose to take the default, you can simply input a point by picking a location on the screen with the mouse or entering a coordinate.

2. Type **C** ↵ to select the *Center* option. The prompt **Center:** appears. Notice that you only had to type in the **C** and not the whole word *Center*.

3. Now pick a point representing the center of the arc near the upper-left corner of the door (see panel 1 of Figure 2.8). The prompt **Start point:** appears.

4. Now type **@3<0**. The prompt **Angle/Length of chord/<End point>:** appears.

5. Move the mouse and you will see an arc originating from a point three units to the right of the center point you selected and rotating about that center, as in panel 2 of Figure 2.8. As the prompt indicates, you have three options. You can enter an angle, length of chord, or endpoint of the arc. The default, indicated by **<End point>** in the prompt, is to pick the arc's endpoint. To select this option, you need only pick a point on the screen indicating where you want the endpoint.

6. Pick a point directly vertical from the center of the arc. The arc is now fixed in place, as in panel 3 of Figure 2.8.

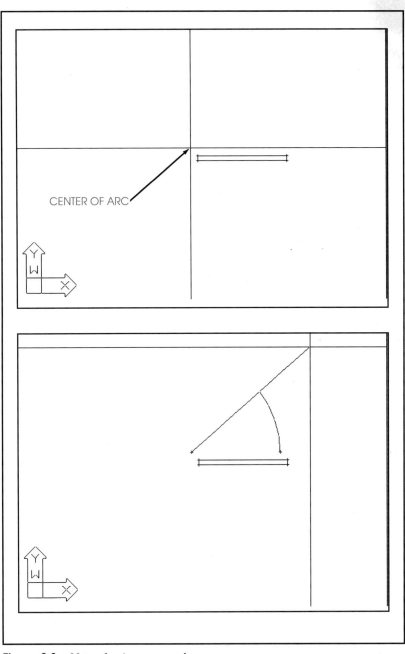

Figure 2.8: Using the Arc command

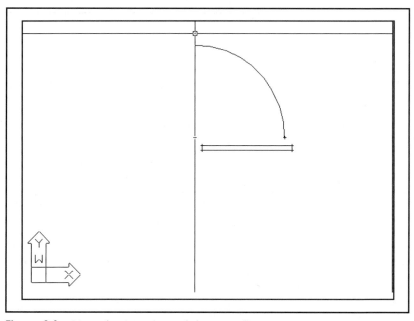

Figure 2.8:   Using the Arc command (continued)

As you can see, AutoCAD has a distinct structure in the way its commands work. You first issue a command, which in turn offers options in the form of a prompt. Depending on the option you pick, you will get another set of options or you will be prompted to take some action like picking a point, selecting objects, or entering a value.

As shown in Figure 2.9, the sequence is something like a tree. As you work through the exercise, you will become intimately familiar with this routine. Once you understand the working of the command prompts and the dialog boxes, you can almost teach yourself the rest of the program!

SELECTING OBJECTS

AutoCAD provides many options for selecting objects. With the introduction of release 12, many additional options have been added to the selection process. For this reason, I have split this section into two main

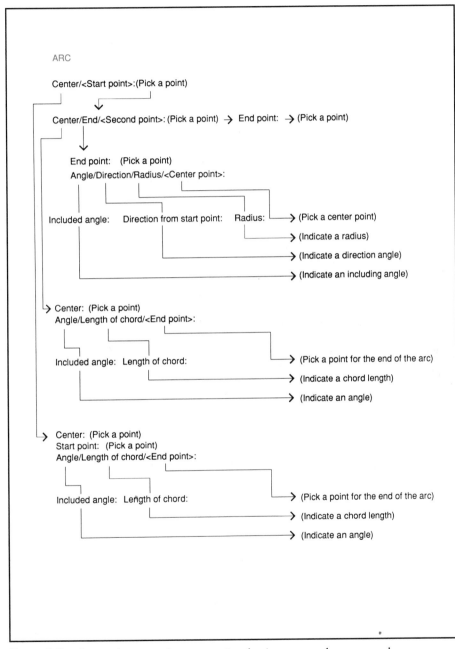

Figure 2.9: A typical command structure using the Arc command as an example

parts. The first part deals with object selection using the standard AutoCAD method; the second part deals specifically with object selection options using what is called the *noun-verb* method. This second method is popular with most graphics programs, and graphical interfaces such as those found in Microsoft Windows and the Apple Macintosh. I suggest you read both parts. You can then decide which method you prefer.

Selecting Objects: Noun/Verb

Many AutoCAD commands prompt you to **Select objects**. Whenever you see this prompt, you have several options while making your selection. Often, as you select objects on the screen, you may change your mind about a selection or accidentally pick an object you do not want. In this section, you will try out most of the available selection options and learn what to do when you make the wrong selection.

Modify ➤ ⇔ Move

1. Choose Modify ➤ Move.

2. At the prompt, **Select objects**, click on the two horizontal lines that compose the door. As you saw in the last chapter, whenever AutoCAD wants you to select objects, the cursor turns into a small square called a pickbox. This tells you that you are in *object-selection mode*. As you pick an object, the object *highlights* (see Figure 2.10).

3. After making your selections you may decide to unselect some items.

4. From the Side menu, click on Select Objects ➤ Undo or enter **U** ↵ with the keyboard. Notice that a line is no longer highlighted. The Undo option unselects objects, one at a time, in reverse order of selection.

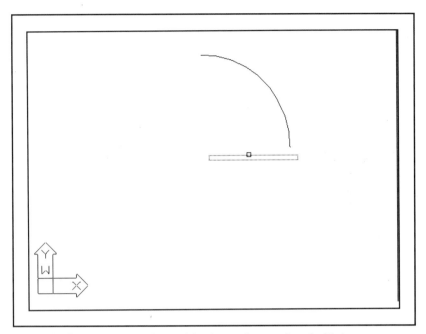

Figure 2.10: Selecting the lines of the door and seeing them highlight

5. There is also another way to unselect objects: from the side menu, click on Select Objects ➤ Remove or enter **R** ↵ with the keyboard. Now you can unselect objects by clicking on them.

6. Pick the other line you selected, and it will unhighlight to show that it is no longer among the selected objects.

7. By now you have probably unselected nearly everything. If you decide to reselect an object, pick Select Objects ➤ Add from the side menu or enter **A** ↵.

8. Another option for selecting objects is to *window* them. Pick Select Objects ➤ Window from the side menu or enter **W** ↵.

9. Now pick a point below and to the left of the rectangle representing the door. As you move your cursor across the screen, a box, or window, appears to stretch across the drawing area.

10. When the window completely encloses the door, but not the arc, press the pick button and all of the door will highlight. The Window option selects only objects that are completely enclosed by the window, as shown in Figure 2.11.

11. When you have selected the entire door but not the arc, press **Return**, and a new prompt, **Base point or displacement:**, will appear.

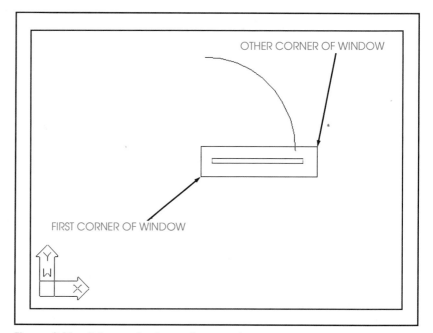

Figure 2.11: Selecting the door within a window

It is important to remember that you must press **Return** as soon as you have finished selecting the objects you want to edit. You must tell AutoCAD when you have finished selecting objects.

Now you have seen how the selection process works in AutoCAD. You are still in the middle of the Move command, so let's continue with a look at inputting base points and displacement distances.

Other Selection Options

There are several other selection options you haven't tried yet. The following describes these other options. You'll get a chance to use some of these other options later in the book. The keyboard equivalents of these options are shown in brackets next to their names.

All [all] selects all the objects in a drawing except those in frozen or locked layers (see *Chapter 4* for more on layers).

Auto [au] automatically produces a window or crossing window when a point is picked and no object is found. A window is produced when the two window corners are picked from left to right. A crossing window is produced when the two corners are picked from right to left. Once this option is selected, it remains active for the duration of the current command.

Crossing [c] is similar to a Window but will select anything that *crosses through* the window you define.

CPolygon [cp] acts exactly like WPolygon (see below), but, like the crossing option, will select anything that crosses through a polygon boundary.

Fence [f] selects objects that are crossed over by a temporary line called a fence. The operation is like crossing-out the objects you want to select.

Last [l] selects the last object you input.

Multiple [m] lets you select several objects first, before AutoCAD highlights them. In a very large file, picking objects individually can cause AutoCAD to pause after each pick while it locates and highlights each object. The Multiple option can speed things up by letting you first pick all the objects quickly and then highlighting them by pressing ↵.

Previous [p] selects the last object or set of objects that was edited or changed.

Single [si] forces the current command to select only a single object. If you use this option, you can pick a single object; then the current command will act on that object as if you had pressed ↵ immediately after selecting the object.

> **WPolygon [wp]** lets you select objects by enclosing them in an irregularly shaped polygon boundary. When you use this option, you see the prompt **First polygon point**. You then pick points to define the polygon boundary. As you pick points, the prompt
>
> **Undo/<Endpoint of line>** appears. You can select as many points as you need to define the boundary. You can Undo boundary line segments as you go by pressing the U key. Once you are done defining a boundary, you press ↵. The bounded objects are highlighted and the **Select object** prompt returns allowing you to use more selection options.

INDICATING POINTS

The last prompt asked you for a base point, which is a difficult concept to grasp. When you move or copy objects, AutoCAD must be told specifically *from* where and *to* where the move occurs. The base point is the exact location from which you determine the distance and direction of the move. Once the base point is determined, you can tell AutoCAD where to move the object in relation to that point.

Osnap: INTersec ENDpoint

▼ TIP

If you don't want to use the side menu to select the object snaps, you can get an Osnap pop-up menu by holding down the **Shift** key and pressing the right mouse button (or the number 2 button on most digitizer pucks). A menu will "pop-up" near the location of the cursor. You can then select an Osnap option from the menu. The pop-up menu disappears allowing you to select points.

1. To select a base point, pick the row of asterisks near the top of the side menu. Then pick INTersec from the Osnap menu that appears. Notice that a square appears on the cursor.

2. Now pick the lower-right corner of the door. When you see the square in the cursor you don't have to point exactly at the intersection. Just get the intersection within the square, and AutoCAD will find the exact point where the two lines meet (see Figure 2.12).

3. The prompt **Second point of displacement:** appears.

4. Pick the asterisks again and pick ENDpoint from the Osnap menu.

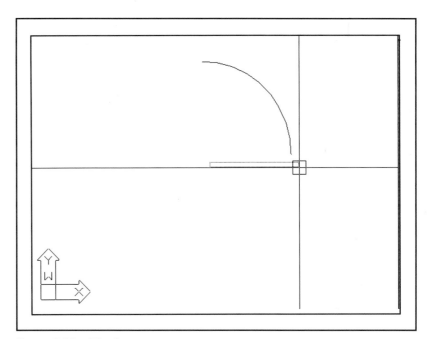

Figure 2.12: The Osnap cursor

5. Now pick the lower-right end of the arc you drew earlier. Remember, you need to place only the end of the arc within the square. The door moves so that the intersection of the door you picked connects exactly with the endpoint of the arc (see Figure 2.13).

As you can see, the Osnap overrides allow you to select specific points on an object. You used Endpoint and Intersect in this exercise, but other options are available. We will look at some of those later.

If you want to specify an exact distance and direction by typing in a value, you can select any point on the screen as a base point. Or you can just type an (@) at sign at the base point prompt; then enter the second point's location in relative coordinates. Remember that the at sign means the last point selected. Try moving the entire door an exact distance of 1 unit in a 45° angle.

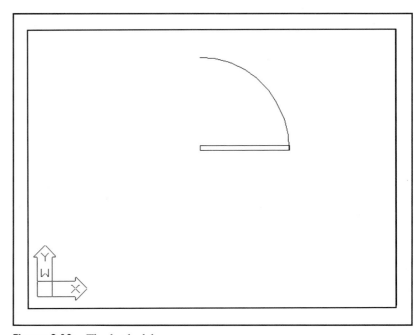

Figure 2.13: The finished door

Edit ➤ ⬌ Move

1. Pick Modify ➤ Move, then pick a point below and to the left of the door to start a selection window.

2. Now drag the window above and to the right of the door until the window completely encloses the door, then press the pick button. The entire door including the arc will highlight, as shown in Figure 2.14.

3. Now press **Return** to tell AutoCAD you have finished your selection.

4. At the prompt **Base point or displacement** pick a point on the screen between the door and the left of the screen (see Figure 2.14).

5. Move the cursor around slowly and notice that the door moves as if the base point you selected were attached to the door. The door moves with the cursor at a fixed distance from it. This visually shows you how the base point relates to the objects you select.

6. Now type **@1<45** ↵. The door will move to a new location on the screen at a distance of one unit from its previous location and at an angle of 45°.

This shows that the base point does not have to be on the object you are manipulating, provided you enter specific distances with the keyboard. The base point can be virtually anywhere on your drawing.

PRESELECTING OBJECTS: NOUN/VERB

Nearly all graphics programs today have tacitly acknowledged, the *noun/verb* method for selecting objects. This method requires you to

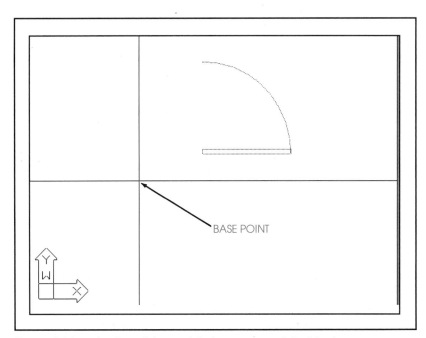

Figure 2.14: The ghosted door and the base point just left of the door

select objects *before* you issue a command to edit them. The next set of exercises shows you how you can use the noun/verb method in AutoCAD. First, you must make some changes to AutoCAD's settings.

Turning on Noun/Verb Selection

You can turn on the noun/verb selection option by entering 'Pickfirst ↵. At the prompt **New value for PICK-FIRST <0>:**, enter a *1* ↵ (entering a 0 turns the pick-first function off). Pickfirst is a system variable that is stored in the AutoCAD configuration file. See **Appendix D** for more on system variables.

This dialog box lets you control the degree to which AutoCAD conforms to standard graphical user interface (GUI) methods of operation (see the *Other Selection Settings* side bar). It also lets you adjust the size of the object selection pickbox.

In previous exercises, you were able to de-select objects by using the Undo or Remove selection options. You can also de-select objects by holding down the **Shift** key and simultaneously picking an object or picking points for a window.

1. Choose Settings ➤ Selection Settings. A dialog box appears (see Figure 2.15).

2. Toward the top of the dialog box, you will see a check box labeled Noun/Verb Selection. Click on this check box if it doesn't already have an X through it.

3. Click on the **OK** button at the bottom of the dialog box.

If it wasn't there before, you should now see a small square at the intersection of the cross-hair cursor. This square is actually a pickbox superimposed on the cursor. It tells you that you can select objects, even while the

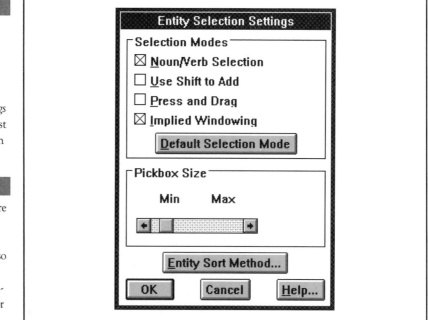

Figure 2.15:   The Selection Settings dialog box

command prompt appears at the bottom of the screen and no command is currently active. As you have seen earlier, the square will momentarily disappear when you are in a command that asks you to select points.

Now try moving objects by first selecting them and then using the Move command.

Move: Noun/Verb

1. First, click on the arc. The arc highlights. You also see squares appear at its endpoints and midpoint. These squares are called *grips*. You'll get a chance to work with them a bit later.

2. Choose Modify ➤ Move. The prompt **Base point or displacement:** appears.

3. Pick any point on the screen. The prompt **Second point of displacement:** appears.

4. Enter **@1<0**. The arc will move to a new location one unit to the right.

In this exercise, you picked the arc before issuing the Move command. Then, when you issued Move, you didn't see the Select objects prompt. Instead, AutoCAD assumed you wanted to move the arc you had preselected and went directly to the Base point prompt.

Next you will move the rest of the door in the same direction by using the Autoselect feature of the noun/verb setting.

Selecting with a window

1. Pick a point just above and to the left of the rectangle representing the door. Be sure not to pick the door itself. Now a window appears to drag across the screen as you move the cursor. If you move the cursor to the left of the last point selected, the window appears dotted (see panel 1 of Figure 2.16). If you move the cursor to the right of that point, it appears solid (see panel 2 of Figure 2.16).

▼ NOTE

These two different windows, the dotted and the solid, represent a crossing window and a standard window. If you use a crossing window, anything that crosses through the window will be selected. If you use a standard window, anything that is completely contained within the window will be selected. As long as the noun/verb setting is on, these two types of windows start automatically if no object is picked.

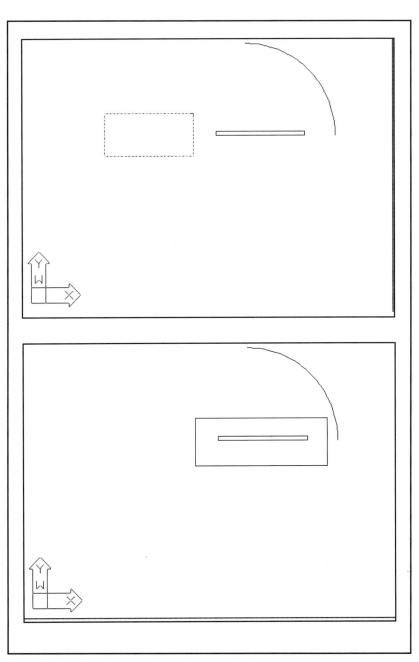

Figure 2.16: The dotted window and the solid window

2. Now pick a point below and to the right of the door, so that the door is completely enclosed by the window (see panel 2 of Figure 2.16). The door highlights (again, you may see small squares appear at the line's endpoints and midpoints).

3. Start the Move command again. Just as in the last exercise, the **Base** prompt appears.

4. Pick any point on the screen, then enter **@1<0**. The door will join with the arc.

Next you will pre-select objects with a crossing window.

Selecting with a crossing window

1. Pick a point below and to the right of the door. As you move the cursor to the left, the window appears dotted.

2. Select the next point so that the window encloses the door and part of the arc (see Figure 2.17). The entire door, including the arc, highlights.

3. Start the Move command.

4. Pick any point on the screen; then enter **@1<180**. The door will move back to its original location.

This noun/verb option is offered for those users who are accustomed to this method of working. Other options are also available to further enhance AutoCAD operation for those used to standard GUI operations (see *Other Selection Settings* side bar).

Now use the File ➤ Save command to save the door file. You won't want to save the changes you make in the next section, so saving now will store the current condition of the file on your hard disk for safe keeping.

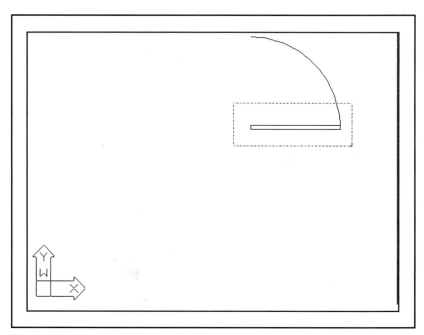

Figure 2.17: The door enclosed by a crossing window

File ➤ Save

1. Choose File ➤ Save.

2. If you wish to take a break and return later, Click on File ➤ Exit AutoCAD.

RESTRICTIONS ON NOUN/VERB SELECTION

If you prefer to use the noun/verb setting, you should know that its use is limited to a subset of AutoCAD commands. These commands are:

array	mirror	wblock	block
ddchprop	dview	move	explode
change	erase	rotate	chprop
hatch	scale	copy	list
stretch			

Other Selection Settings

You got to practice preselecting objects by turning on the noun/verb setting. This is just one of several AutoCAD settings that make AutoCAD work more like other programs that use a graphical user interface (GUI). Here is a description of some of the other options in the Selection Settings dialog box and how they work. If you are used to working with other GUIs, you may want to turn some of these settings on. I've included in parentheses the name of the system variable that controls each feature.

Use Shift to Add (pickadd)
With this option checked, you can use the standard GUI method of holding down the **Shift** key to pick multiple objects. If the **Shift** key is not held down, only the single object picked or group of objects windowed will be selected. Previously selected objects are deselected, unless the **Shift** key is held down during selection. To turn this feature on using system variables, set Pickadd to 0.

Click and Drag (pickdrag)
With this option checked, you use the standard GUI method for placing windows. To use this method, you first click and hold down the pick button on the first corner of the window, then while holding down the pick button, you drag the other corner of the window into position. When the other corner is in place, you let go of the pick button to finish the window. This setting applies to both verb/noun and noun/verb operations. Set Pickadd to 1 for this option.

Implied Window (pickauto)
When this option is checked, a window or crossing window will automatically start if no object is picked at the **Select objects:** prompt. This setting has no effect on the noun/verb setting (i.e., preselection of objects). Set Pickadd to 1 for this option.

For other modifying or construction oriented commands the Noun/Verb selection method is inappropriate because they require you to select more than one set of objects.

EDITING WITH GRIPS

Earlier, when you preselected the door, you may have seen squares appear at the endpoints and midpoints of the lines and arcs. These squares are called *grips*. Grips can be used to make direct changes to the shape of objects, or to quickly move and copy them.

So far, you have seen how operations in AutoCAD have a discrete beginning and ending. For example, to draw an arc, you first issue the arc command, then go through a series of operations that involve answering prompts and picking points. When you are done, you have an arc and AutoCAD is ready for the next command.

The grips feature, on the other hand, plays by a different set of rules. With grips, there are no discrete beginnings and endings of commands. Instead, grips offers a small yet powerful set of editing functions that don't conform to the lockstep command-prompt-input routine you have seen so far. For this reason, as you work through the following exercises, it will be helpful to think of the grips feature as a subset to the standard method of operation within AutoCAD.

To practice using the grips feature, you'll make some temporary modifications to the door drawing.

TURNING ON THE GRIPS FEATURE

Before you actually begin to use grips, let's make sure the grips feature is turned on.

▼ **TIP**

You can turn the Grips feature on and off by entering **'Grips** ↵. At the prompt **New value for GRIPS <0>:** enter a **1** to turn grips on, or **0** to turn grips off. Grips is a system variable that is stored in the AutoCAD configuration file. For more on system variables, see *Appendix D*.

1. Choose Settings ➤ Grips. The Grips dialog box appears (see Figure 2.18).

2. Near the top of the dialog box, you will see a pair of checkboxes. The box labeled Enabled Grips should have an X through it. If it doesn't, click on the box. An X will appear.

▼ NOTE

The Grips dialog box allows
you to set the grip color and
size and to determine whether
grips appear on objects that
compose a block. (See *Chapter
4* for more on blocks.) These
options can also be set using
system variables described in
Appendix D.

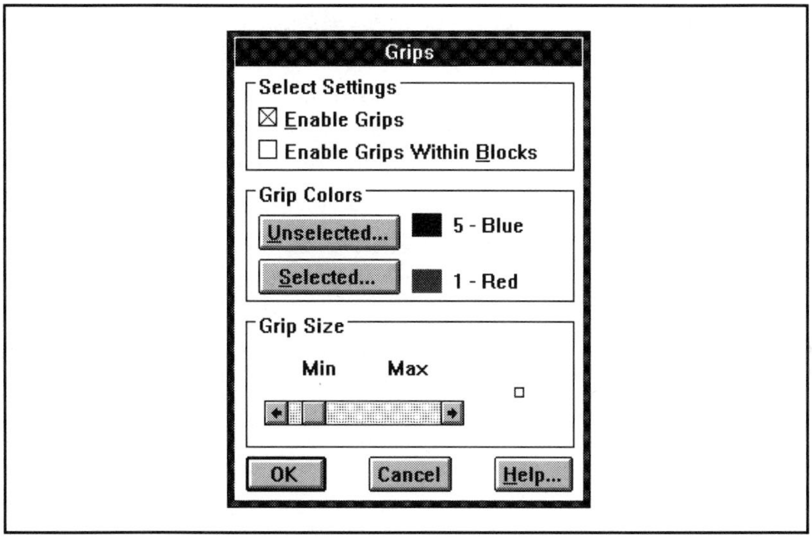

Figure 2.18:   The Grips dialog box

3. Click on the **OK** button at the bottom of the dialog box. You are now ready to proceed with the following exercises.

STRETCHING LINES USING GRIPS

In this exercise, you'll stretch one corner of the door by grabbing the grip points of two lines.

Stretch

▼ NOTE

When you select a grip by
clicking on it, it turns a solid
color. It is then called a
hot grip.

1. Click on a point below and to the left of the door. This starts a window.

2. Click above and to the right of the rectangular part of the door to preselect it.

3. Place the cursor on the lower-left corner of the rectangle but don't press the pick button yet. Notice that cursor jumps to the grip point.

4. Move the cursor to another grip point. Notice again how the cursor jumps to it. When the cursor is placed on a grip, the cursor moves to the exact center of the grip point. This means, for example, that if the cursor is placed on an endpoint grip, it is on the exact endpoint of the object.

5. Move the cursor to the upper-left corner of the rectangle and click on it. The grip becomes solid, and the prompt displays the following message:

```
**STRETCH**
<Stretch to point>/Base point/Copy/Undo/eXit:
```

This prompt tells you that the stretch mode is active. Note the options shown in the prompt. As you move the cursor, the corner follows and the lines of the rectangle stretch (see Figure 2.19)

6. Move the cursor upward toward the top end of the arc and pick that point. The rectangle deforms with the corner placed at your pick point (see Figure 2.19).

▼ NOTE

When you click on the corner grip point, AutoCAD selects the overlapping grips of two lines. When you stretch the corner away from its original location, the endpoints of both lines follow.

Here you saw that a command called ****stretch**** is issued simply by clicking on a grip point. As you will see, a handful of other commands are also available.

Several options to stretch are also presented at the prompt. Let's try some of those options next.

****Stretch****: Base Point/Copy

1. Click on the grip point that you moved before.

2. Enter **B** ↵. The prompt changes to **Base point:**.

3. Click on a point to the right of the hot grip. Now as you move the cursor, the hot grip moves relative to the cursor.

4. Type **C** ↵ to select the Copy option, then enter **@1<-90**. Instead of moving the hot grip and changing the lines, a copy of the two lines is made with their endpoints at a location 1 unit below the first set of endpoints.

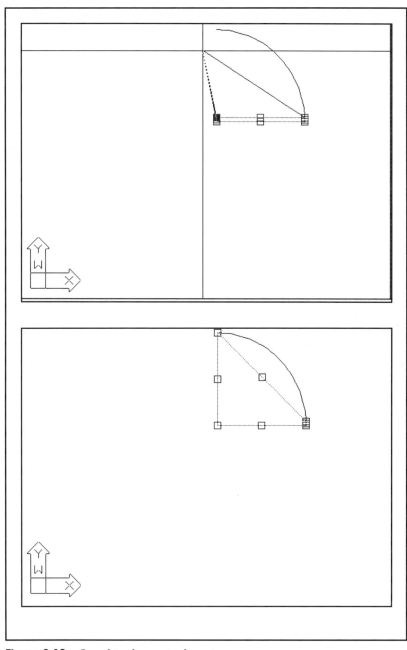

Figure 2.19:   Stretching lines using hot grips

5. Pick another point just below the last. More copies are made.

6. Press ↵ or enter **X** ↵ to exit the Stretch command.

In this exercise, you were shown that you can select a base point other than the hot grip. You also saw how you can specify relative coordinates to move or copy a hot grip.

MOVING AND ROTATING WITH GRIPS

As you've just seen, the grips feature offers an alternative method of editing your drawings. You've already seen how you can stretch endpoints. But there is much more you can do with grips. The next exercise will show some other options. You will start by undoing the modifications you made in the last exercise.

U

▼ TIP

Pressing ↵ at the command prompt causes AutoCAD to repeat the last command entered, in this case, **U**.

1. At the command prompt, enter **U** ↵. The copies of the stretched lines disappear.

2. Press ↵ again. The deformed door snaps back to its original form.

3. Choose View ➤ Redraw to clean up the display.

Now you're ready to make a rotated copy of the door.

Rotate: Copy

1. Preselect the entire door by first clicking on a blank area below and to the right of the door.

2. Move the cursor to a location above and to the left of the rectangular portion of the door and click on it. Since you went from right to left, you created a crossing window. You may recall that this selects anything enclosed and crossing through the window.

3. Click on the lower-left grip of the rectangle to turn it into a hot grip. Now as you move your cursor, the corner stretches.

4. Press ↵, or the right button on your mouse. The prompt changes to:

   ```
   **MOVE**
   <Move to point>/Base point/Copy/Undo/eXit:
   ```

   Now as you move the cursor, the entire door moves with it.

5. Position the door near the center of the screen and click there. You just moved the door to the center of the screen. Notice that the command prompt returns, yet the door remains highlighted telling you that it is still selected for the next operation.

6. Click on the lower-left grip again, then press ↵ or the right mouse button twice. This time, the command prompt changes to show

   ```
   **ROTATE**
   <Rotation angle➤/Base point/copy/Undo/Refer-
   ence/eXit:
   ```

   As you move the cursor, the door rotates about the grip point.

7. Position the cursor so that the door rotates 180° (see Figure 2.20). Then, while holding down the **Shift** key, press the pick button. A copy of the door appears in the new rotated position, leaving the original door in place.

8. Press ↵ to exit the rotate mode.

   In this exercise, you saw how new hot grip commands appear as you press ↵. Two more commands, **Scale** and **Mirror** are also available by continuing to press ↵ while a hot grip is selected. The commands then repeat if you continue to press ↵. The **Shift** key acts as a shortcut to the copy option.

▼ NOTE

You've seen how the Move command is duplicated in a modified way as a hot grip command. Other hot grip commands, **Stretch**, **Rotate**, **Scale**, and **Mirror**, also have similar counterpart in the standard set of AutoCAD commands. You'll see how those work later in this book.

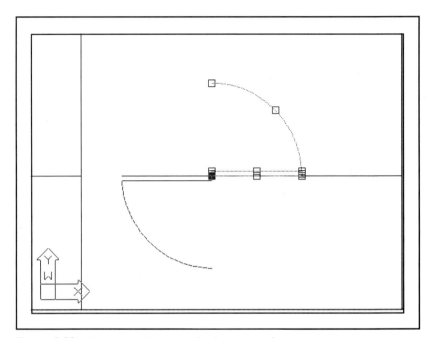

Figure 2.20:   Rotating and copying the door using a hot grip

▼ NOTE

You can also press the F1 function key to open the AutoCAD help window. If you are in the middle of a command, you can enter '**help** to get information about your current activity.

GETTING HELP

Eventually you will be somewhere without documentation and you will have a question about an AutoCAD feature. AutoCAD provides an on-line help facility that will give you information on nearly any topic related to AutoCAD.

Help

1. Click on Help ➤ Contents from the pull-down menu. A help window appears (see Figure 2.21). This window shows the contents of the Help system at a glance. Notice that several items appear in color and are underlined. When you click on these items, you will get further information.

Quick Summary
of the Grip Feature

The hot grip exercises in this chapter cover only a few options. You'll get a chance to use other hot grip commands in later chapters. Meanwhile, here is a summary of features offered by the grip function.

- Clicking on endpoint grips cause those endpoints to stretch.

- Clicking on midpoint grips cause the entire object or set of objects to move.

- If two objects meet end to end and you click on their overlapping grips, both grips are selected simultaneously.

- You can select multiple grips by holding down the **Shift** key and clicking on the desired grips.

- When a hot grip is selected, the Stretch, Move, Rotate, Scale, and Mirror commands are available to you.

- You can cycle through the Stretch, Move, Rotate, Scale, and Mirror commands by pressing ↵ while a hot grip is selected.

- All the hot grip commands allow you to make copies of the selected objects.

2. Scan down the screen until you see the topic labeled Commands & System Variables, then click on the word **AutoCAD**. A list of AutoCAD commands appears.

3. Notice that at the top of the list, you see an abbreviated alphabet. Below, you see a list of commands that begin with the characters A through C. You can click on the characters at the top to show more commands. For now, click on the word **Copy**. A detailed description of the copy command appears.

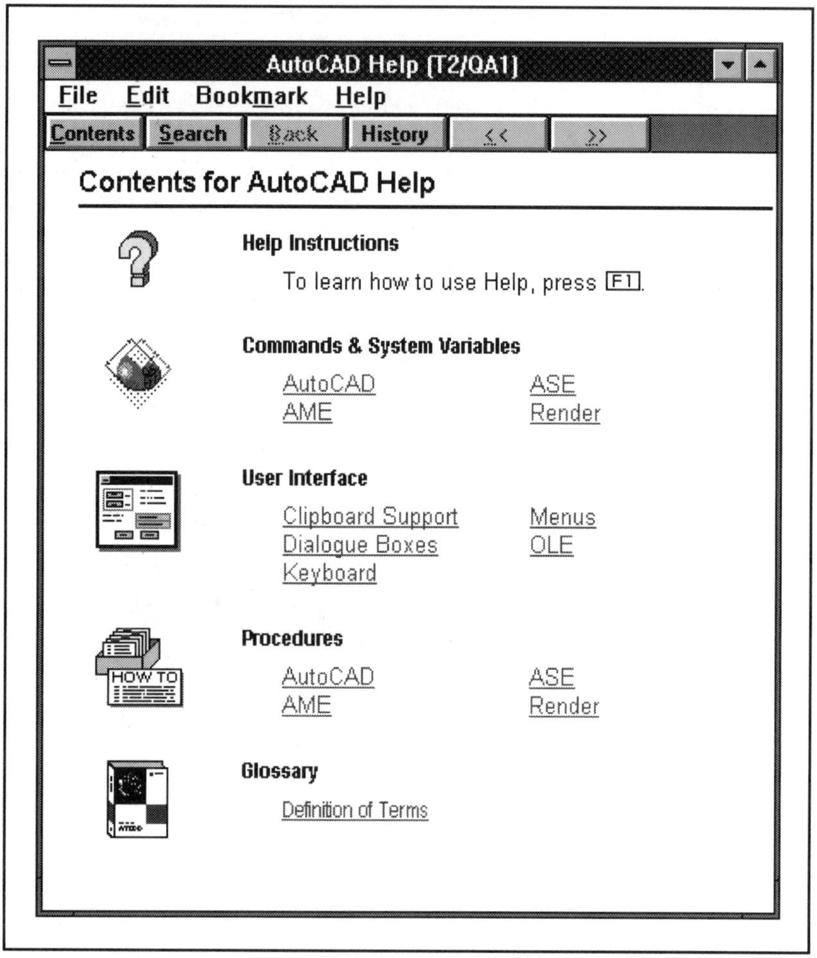

Figure 2.21:   The Help window

4. Click on the **Search** button at the top of the window. The Search dialog box appears showing a list of topics in alphabetical order (see Figure 2.22). You can enter a word to search or you can select a topic from the list box.

5. Type the word Change. Notice that the list box immediately goes to the word CHANGE in the list.

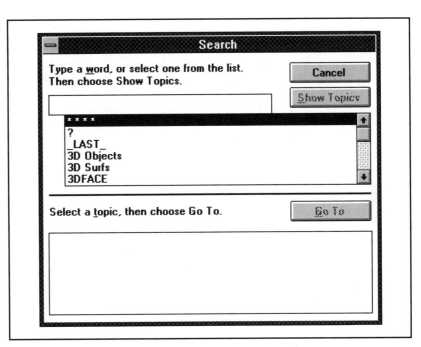

Figure 2.22:   The Search dialog box

6. Press ↵. The word CHANGE appears in the Go To list box at the bottom of the dialog box.

7. Click on the **Go To** button. You are shown a description of the Change command.

You can go directly to the Search dialog box by clicking on Help ➤ Search for Help on .... If you need more detailed information on using the Help system, click on Help ➤ How to use Help.

AutoCAD also provides what is called *context-sensitive help* to give you information related to the command you are currently using. To see how this works, try the following.

1. Start the Move command.

2. Enter 'Help ↵. The Help window appears, but this time, it shows a description of the selection options (see Figure 2.23).

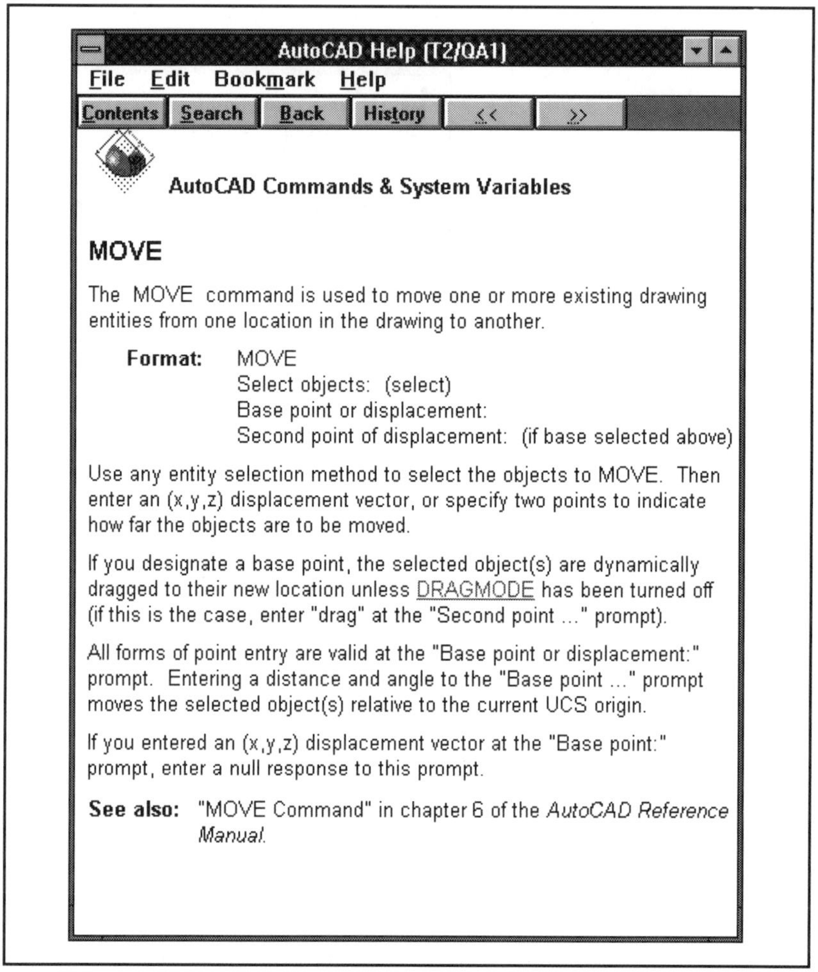

Figure 2.23:   A Help screen describing the Move command

Since AutoCAD was in the middle of asking you to select objects, the Help screen shows you a description of the options available under the Select object prompt.

3. Click on the **OK** button or press the **Esc** key.

4. Choose Assist ➤ Cancel or type **Ctrl-C** to exit the Move command.

SHOWING MORE
OF THE PROMPT TEXT

Some commands will display more information in the command prompt area than will fit there. This frequently happens when you are trying to get information about your drawing. The following exercise shows how you can get an enlarged view of the command prompt.

1. Choose Assist ➤ Inquiry ➤ List.

2. At the **Select objects** prompt, click on one of the arcs, then press ↵. Information regarding the arc is displayed in the prompt area, but it is more information than can be shown in three lines.

3. Press the F2 function key or click on Edit ➤ Text Window. The screen changes to display the AutoCAD prompt in a full-screen list. Toward the bottom is the list of the arc's properties (you'll get a detailed look at this information later in this book).

4. To go back to the drawing editor screen, click on the minimize key in the upper-right corner of the text window or press F2 again.

5. Repeat steps 3 and 4 a few times and see what happens. The F2 function key offers a quick way to switch between the two screens.

6. Now you are done with the door drawing, so choose File ➤ Exit AutoCAD.

7. At the dialog box, click on the Discard Changes button. You've already saved this file in the condition you want so you don't want to save it again at this time.

IF YOU WANT TO EXPERIMENT...

Try drawing the latch shown in Figure 2.24.

1. Start AutoCAD and open a new file called **Latch**.

2. When you get to the drawing editor, use the Line command to draw the straight portions of the latch. Start a line as indicated in the figure then enter relative coordinates from the keyboard. For example, for the first line segment, enter **@4<180** to draw a line segment 4 units long from right to left.

3. After drawing the lines, choose Draw ➤ Arc to draw the curved part. Do this by first clicking on Arc, then click on Start, End, Direction from the cascading menu.

4. Use the Endpoint Osnap override and pick the endpoint indicated in the figure to start your arc.

5. Using the Endpoint Osnap overrides again, click on the endpoint above where you started your line. A rubber-banding line and a temporary arc appear.

6. Position your cursor so the ghosted arc looks like the one in the figure then press your pick button. The arc is drawn in.

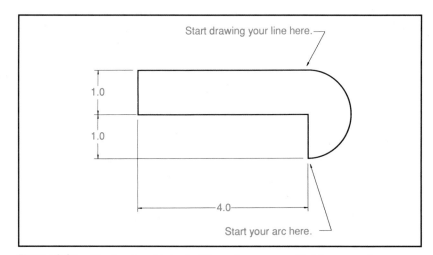

Figure 2.24: Try drawing this latch. Dimensions are provided for your reference.

SUMMARY

You now have the basic knowledge to start doing some serious drawing. You should be able to open a new file, input distances, and select commands from a menu with some confidence. In this chapter, we covered the following main points:

- AutoCAD commands always display *prompts* at the prompt line. This is how AutoCAD communicates with you.

- Most command prompts offer several options that are separated by a forward slash (/).

- Options can be selected either from the *side menu* or by entering the capitalized letter shown in the prompt.

- *Rubber-banding lines* are shown to aid you in determining the location of lines and displacements during the Move command.

- You can specify exact distances by entering coordinates from the keyboard. The *at sign* (@) indicates relative distances while the *less-than sign* (<) is used to indicate angles in the polar coordinates system.

- When you see the **Select object** prompt, you have several ways to select objects. You can select them individually, with a *window*, or with a *crossing window*.

- Objects can be deselected with the Remove or Undo options or with a Shift-selections.

- If you prefer, you can preselect objects for editing by turning on the *noun/verb* setting in the Selection Settings dialog box.

- You can pick exact geometric coordinates such as endpoints on lines by using the *object snap* (Osnap) *overrides*.

- You can clear the screen by using the Redraw command.

- Help is available through the Help command.

In *Chapter 3* you will start a project that shows you some of AutoCAD's basic drawing commands.

CREATING

EXPLORING

EDITING

LEARNING

MANAGING

ADDING

PRINTING

ANIMATING

PLOTTING

ENTERING

DRAWING

GETTING

RENDERING

USING

INTEGRATING

MODELING

ORGANIZING

MANAGING

3

▼ ▼ ▼ ▼ ▼

LEARNING
THE TOOLS
OF THE TRADE

FAST TRACK

81 ▶ To enable the use of feet and inch measurement

Click on Settings ➤ Units Control…. Click on the button labeled **Architectural** in the Units Control dialog box.

85 ▶ To define a work area

Determine the area you need, based on the scale of your drawing and final sheet size, then use the Limits command to define the area in AutoCAD.

89 ▶ To set the grid spacing

Click on Settings ➤ Drawing Aids, then enter the grid spacing in the **X spacing** input box under the Grid group. Turn the grid on and off by pressing the **F7** function key.

90 ▶ To force the cursor to snap to regularly spaced intervals

Click on Settings ➤ Drawing Aids, then enter the snap spacing in the **X spacing** input box under the Snap group. Turn snap on and off by clicking on the button labeled S in the toolbar.

92 ▶ To display the coordinates of the cursor dynamically as it moves

Click on the coordinate Readout box in the toolbar.

98   To copy an object

Pick Construct ➤ Copy, then select the object or objects you want to copy. Pick a base point for the copy, then either pick another point or enter a relative coordinate.

99   To trim an object

Pick Modify ➤ Trim, then select the objects you want to trim to. Next, select the objects you want to trim.

103   To make a parallel copy of an object

Pick Construct ➤ Offset, then enter the distance you want the copy to be. Next, select an object you want a parallel copy of and indicate the direction of the copy.

112   To join two objects with an arc

Pick Construct ➤ Fillet, then enter **R** ↵. Enter the radius of the joining arc. Start Fillet again and pick the two objects you want to join.

So far we have covered the most basic information you need to understand the workings of AutoCAD. Now you will put your knowledge to work by drawing a studio apartment building. This architectural tutorial illustrates how to use AutoCAD commands and will give you a solid understanding of the basic AutoCAD package. With that understanding, you can use AutoCAD to its fullest potential, regardless of the kinds of drawings you intend to create or the enhancement products you may use in the future. In this chapter you will start drawing an apartment's bathroom fixtures. In the process, you will learn how to use AutoCAD's basic tools.

SETTING UP A WORK AREA

Before beginning most drawings, you will want to set up your work area. To do this you must determine the *measurement system*, the *drawing sheet size*, and the *scale* you want to use. The default work area is 9"×12" at full scale, given a decimal measurement system where 1 unit equals 1 inch. If these are appropriate settings for your drawing, then you don't have to do any setting up. It is more likely that you will be doing drawings of various sizes and scales. For example, you may want to do a drawing in a measurement system where you can specify feet, inches, and fractions of inches at 1"=1′ scale and print it on an $8\frac{1}{2} \times 11$" sheet of paper. Once you have set up a drawing, you can use the setup for future drawings; I will explain how later in the book. In this section, you will learn how to set up a drawing the way you want.

▼ NOTE

You could have started drawing in the drawing editor immediately after you started up AutoCAD and then saved the file later under the name *Bath*, but I ask you to do this in case you are using a system that has an altered default setup for new files. I'll discuss default setups in *Chapter 5*.

SPECIFYING UNITS

Start by creating a new file called **Bath**.

1. Start up AutoCAD, then pick File ➤ New.

2. In the Create new file dialog box, enter the name **Bath**.

3. Make sure the check box labeled No Prototype is checked, then click on the **OK** button. The new file will open.

The first thing you will want to tell AutoCAD is the unit style you intend to use. So far, you've been using the default style, which is decimal inches. In this style, whole units represent inches and decimal units are decimal inches. If you want to be able to enter distances in feet, then you must change the unit style to one that accepts feet as input. This is done through the Units Control dialog box.

▼ TIP

The settings in the Units Control dialog box can also be controlled using several system variables. To set the unit style, you can enter 'lunits ⏎. At the **New value for Lunits <2> prompt**, enter **4** for architectural. See *Appendix D* for other settings.

1. Choose Settings ➤ Units Control…. The Units Control dialog box appears as seen in Figure 3.1, panel 1.

2. Look closely at the group of buttons to the left. They offer several unit styles. Click on the button labeled Architectural. Now before you close the dialog box, let's look at a few of the other options available.

3. Click on the down-pointing arrow to the right of the Precision pop-up list at the bottom of the Units group. Notice the set of options available. You can set the smallest unit AutoCAD will display in this drawing. For now, leave this setting at its default value of one-sixteenth of an inch.

4. Press the **Esc** key to close the pop-up list.

5. Click on the button labeled Direction. Another dialog box appears (see Figure 3.1, panel 2). This dialog box lets you set the angle for 0° and the direction for positive degrees.

6. You won't want to change these settings for now, so click on the **Cancel** button.

7. Click on the **OK** button in the main Units Control dialog box to return to the drawing.

You picked Architectural for this tutorial, but your own work may require a different unit style. You saw several unit styles to choose from in the Units Control dialog box. Table 3.1 shows examples of how the distance 15.5 is entered in each of these styles.

In the previous exercise, you needed to change only one setting. Let's take a moment to look at the other settings in more detail. You may want to refer to Figure 3.1 as you read.

▼ NOTE

This dialog box has two main groups of buttons labeled *Units* to the left and *Angles* to the right. Within both groups, toward the bottom, are pop-up lists labeled *Precision*. These lists let you control the degree of precision AutoCAD uses for distances and angles. The radio buttons in the Units group lets you select the unit type. In this exercise, you select Architectural. The radio buttons in the Angles group let you select the Angle type.

▼ NOTE

The Direction dialog box lets you set the direction for 0°. It also lets you determine the positive and negative direction for angles.

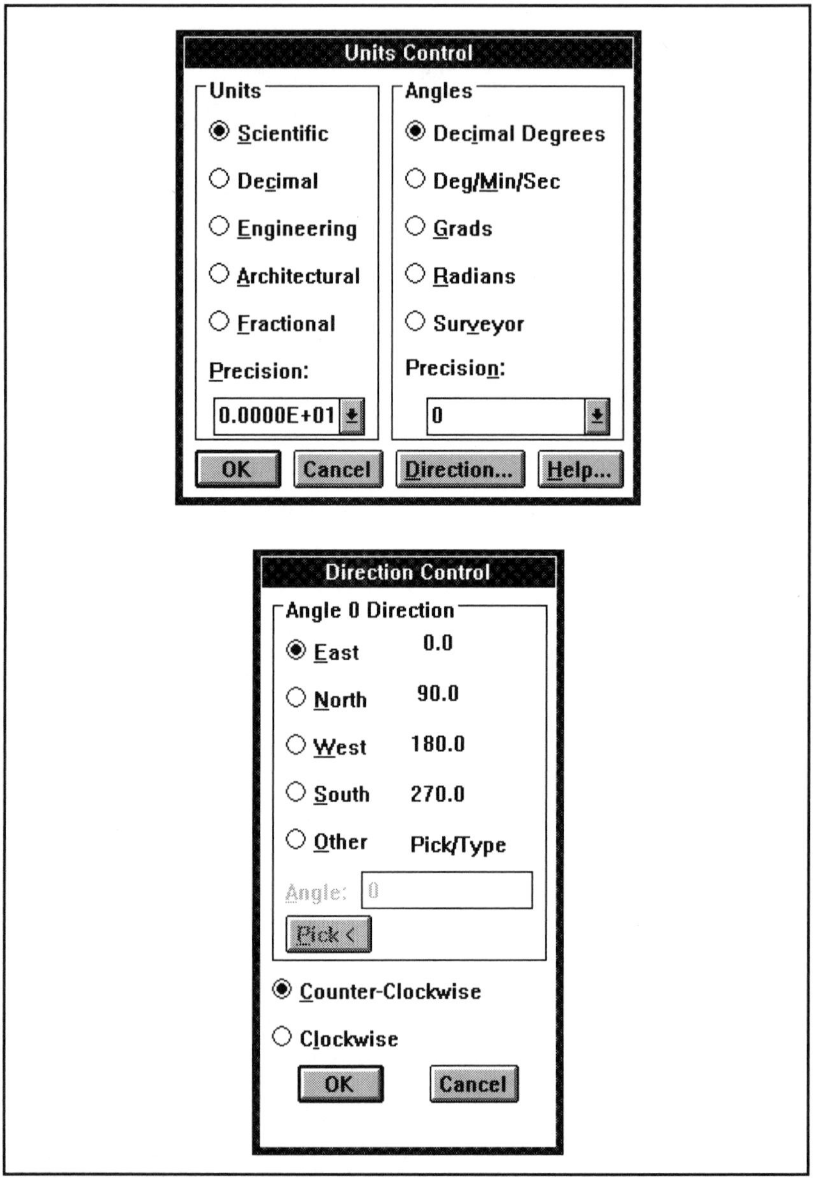

Figure 3.1: The Units Control dialog box and the Direction dialog box

Table 3.1: Measurement Systems Available in AutoCAD

MEASUREMENT SYSTEM	AUTOCAD'S DISPLAY OF MEASUREMENT
Scientific	1.55E+01 (inches)
Decimal	15.5000 (inches)
Engineering	1'-3.5" (input as 1'3.5")
Architectural	1'-3 1/2" (input as 1'3-1/2")
Metric	15.5000 (converted to metric at plot)
Fractional	15 1/2" (input as 15-1/2")

FINE-TUNING THE MEASUREMENT SYSTEM

Most of the time, you will be concerned only with the Units and Angles setting groups of the Unit Control Dialog box. But as you saw from the exercise, you can control many other settings related to the input and display of units.

The *Precision* pop-up list in the Units group lets you specify the smallest unit value AutoCAD is to display in the status line and in the prompts. If you choose a measurement system that uses fractions, this list also shows fractional units. This setting can also be controlled with Luprec system variables.

The *Angles* group lets you set the style for displaying angles. You have a choice of five angle styles: decimal degrees, degrees/minutes/seconds, Grads, Radians, and surveyor's units. The Precision pop-up list under Angles lets you determine the degree of accuracy you want AutoCAD to display for angles. These settings can also be controlled with the Aunits and Auprec system variables.

The *Direction* dialog box lets you set the direction of the base angle, 0°. The default base angle is a direction from left to right. You will use this as your base angle throughout this book. However, there may be times when you will want to designate another direction as the 0° base angle. You can also tell AutoCAD which direction is positive (either clockwise or counterclockwise). The default is counterclockwise, and this is the direction I'll be using throughout this book. These settings can also be controlled with the Angbase and Angdir system variables.

Things to Watch Out For

When you are using Architectural units, there are two points you should be aware of:

- Hyphens are used only to distinguish fractions from whole inches.

- You cannot use spaces while giving a dimension. For example, you can specify eight feet, four and one-half inches as **8′4-1/2"** or **8′4.5**, but *not* as **8′-4 1/2"**.

These idiosyncrasies are a source of confusion to many architects and engineers new to AutoCAD, since the program often *displays* architectural dimensions in the standard architectural format but does not allow you to *enter* dimensions that way.

Finally, here are some tips on inputting distances and angles in unusual situations.

- While inputting distances in inches and feet, you can leave off the inch (") sign.

- You can enter fractional distances and angles in any format you like, regardless of the current unit system. For example, you can enter a distance as **@1/2<1.5708r** even if your current unit system is set for decimal units and decimal degrees (*1.5708r* is the radian equivalent of 90°).

- If you have your angle units set to degrees, grads, or radians, you do not need to specify *g*, *r*, or *d* after the angle. You do have to specify *g*, *r*, or *d*, however, if you want to use these units when they are not the current default angle system.

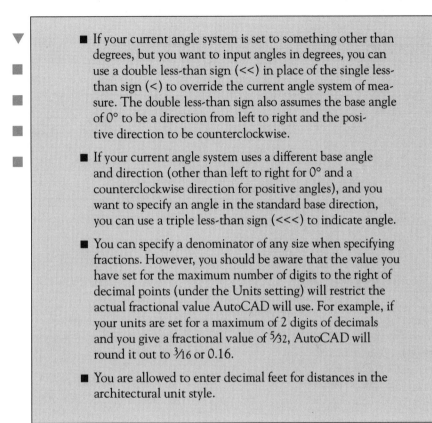

■ If your current angle system is set to something other than degrees, but you want to input angles in degrees, you can use a double less-than sign (<<) in place of the single less-than sign (<) to override the current angle system of measure. The double less-than sign also assumes the base angle of 0° to be a direction from left to right and the positive direction to be counterclockwise.

■ If your current angle system uses a different base angle and direction (other than left to right for 0° and a counterclockwise direction for positive angles), and you want to specify an angle in the standard base direction, you can use a triple less-than sign (<<<) to indicate angle.

■ You can specify a denominator of any size when specifying fractions. However, you should be aware that the value you have set for the maximum number of digits to the right of decimal points (under the Units setting) will restrict the actual fractional value AutoCAD will use. For example, if your units are set for a maximum of 2 digits of decimals and you give a fractional value of ⁵⁄32, AutoCAD will round it out to ³⁄16 or 0.16.

■ You are allowed to enter decimal feet for distances in the architectural unit style.

SETTING UP THE DRAWING LIMITS

One of the big advantages in using AutoCAD is that you can draw at full scale; you aren't limited to the edges of a piece of paper the way you are in manual drawing. But you still have to consider what will happen when you want a printout of your drawing. If you're not careful, you can create a drawing that won't fit on the paper size you want at the scale you want. You must limit your drawing area to one that can be scaled down to fit on a standard sheet size during printout.

In order to set up the drawing work area, you need to know how standard sheet sizes translate into full-scale drawing sizes. Table 3.2 lists widths and heights of drawing areas in inches according to scales and final printout sizes. The scales are listed at the far left while the output sheet sizes are listed across the top. To find the area needed in AutoCAD for your bath drawing, for instance, look across from the scale 1"=1'-0" to the column that reads $8\frac{1}{2} \times 11$ at the top. You find the value 102×132. This means that the drawing area needs to fit within an area 102" by 132" (8.5 feet by 11 feet) in AutoCAD in order to fit a printout of a 1"=1'-0" scale drawing on an $8\frac{1}{2} \times 11$" sheet of paper.

You will want the area to be oriented horizontally so that the 11 feet will be in the X axis and the 8.5 feet will be in the Y axis. Now that you know the area you need, you can use the Limits command to set up the area.

Settings ➤ Drawing Limits
View ➤ Zoom All

▼ **NOTE**

It's a good idea to let the origin of the drawing be the lower-left corner because it gives you a point of reference when using absolute coordinates. Also, you will want to set reasonable limits for your drawings. If the limits cover too great an area, AutoCAD will take longer to redraw.

1. Choose Settings ➤ Drawing Limits or enter **Limits** ↵ at the command prompt.

2. At the **ON/OFF/<Lower left corner> <0'-0",0'-0">:** prompt, you can specify the lower-left corner of your drawing work area. Press ↵ to accept the default.

3. At the **Upper right corner <1'0",0'9">:** prompt, you can specify the upper-right corner of your work area. The default is shown in brackets. Enter **132,102**. Or if you prefer, you can enter **11',8'6**.

4. Next, choose View ➤ Zoom All. Though it appears that nothing has changed, your drawing area is now set to a size that will allow you to draw your bathroom at full scale.

5. Pick a point in the upper-right corner of the drawing area and watch the coordinate readout. You will see that now the upper-right corner is near the coordinates 11',8'6. The coordinate readout also displays distances in feet and inches.

Table 3.2: Work Area in Drawing Units (Inches) by Scale and Plotted Sheet Size

SCALE	8½"×11"	11"×17"	17"×22"	18"×24"	22"×34"	24"×36"	30"×42"	36"×48"
3"=1'	34×44	44×68	68×88	72×96	88×136	96×144	120×168	144×192
1½"=1'	68×88	88×136	136×176	144×192	176×272	192×288	240×336	288×384
1"=1'	102×132	132×204	204×264	216×288	264×408	288×432	360×504	432×576
¾"=1'	136×176	176×272	272×352	288×384	352×544	384×576	480×672	576×768
½"=1'	204×264	264×408	408×528	432×576	528×816	576×864	720×1008	864×1152
¼"=1'	408×528	528×816	816×1056	864×1152	1056×1632	1152×1728	1440×2016	1728×2304
⅛"=1'	816×1056	1056×1632	1632×2112	1728×2304	2112×3264	2304×3456	2880×4032	3456×4608
¹⁄₁₆"=1'	1632×2112	2112×3264	3264×4224	3456×4608	4224×6528	4608×6912	5760×8064	6912×9216
¹⁄₃₂"=1'	3264×4224	4224×6528	6528×8448	6912×9216	8448×13056	9216×13824	11520×16128	13824×18432
1"=10'	1020×1320	1320×2040	2040×2640	2160×2880	2640×4080	2880×4320	3600×5040	4320×5760
1"=20'	2040×2640	2640×4080	4080×5280	4320×5760	5280×8160	5760×8640	7200×10080	8640×11520
1"=30'	3060×3960	3960×6120	6120×7920	6480×8640	7920×12240	8640×12960	10800×15120	12960×17280
1"=40'	4080×5280	5280×8160	8160×10560	8640×11520	10560×16320	11520×17280	14400×20160	17280×23040
1"=50'	5100×6600	6600×10200	10200×13200	10800×14400	13200×20400	14400×21600	18000×25200	21600×28800
1"=60'	6120×7920	7920×12240	12240×15840	12960×17280	15840×24480	17280×25920	21600×30240	25920×34560

▼ TIP

If you get the message ****Out-side limits**, you have selected a point outside the area defined by the limits of your drawing and the limits checking feature is on. (Some third-party programs may use the limits checking feature of the Limits command.) If you must select a point outside the limits, issue the Limits command then enter **off**. You can then select points outside the limits.

In the last step, the coordinate readout showed you that your drawing area is larger than before, but there are no visual clues to tell you where you are or what distances you are dealing with. To help you get your bearings, you can use the Grid mode, which you will learn about in the next set of exercises. But first, let's take a closer look at scale factors and how they work.

UNDERSTANDING SCALE FACTORS

All the drawing sizes in Table 3.2 were derived by using scale factors. Table 3.3 shows scale factors as they relate to standard drawing scales. These scale factors are the values by which you multiply the desired final printout size to get the equivalent full-scale size. For example, if you have a sheet size of 11×17", and you want to know the equivalent full-scale size for a ¼"-scale drawing, you multiply the sheet measurements by 48. In this way, 11" becomes 528" (48×11) and 17" becomes 816" (48×17). Your work area must be 528" by 816" if you intend to have a final output of 11" by 17" at ¼" = 1'. You can divide these inch measurements by 12" to get 44'×68'.

You will be using scale factors to specify text height and dimension settings, so getting to understand them now will pay off later.

Table 3.3: Scale Conversion Factors

Scale Factors for Engineering Drawing Scales								
1"= n	10'	20'	30'	40'	50'	60'	100'	200'
Scale factor	120	240	360	480	600	720	1200	2400
Scale Factors for Architectural Drawing Scales								
n=1'-0"	¹⁄₁₆"	⅛"	¼"	½"	¾"	1"	1¹⁄₂"	3"
Scale factor	192	96	48	24	16	12	8	4

USING THE AUTOCAD MODES AS DRAFTING TOOLS

After you have set up your work area, you can begin the plan of a typical bathroom in your studio. We will use this example to show you some of AutoCAD's tools. These tools might be compared to a background grid, scale, T square, and triangle.

USING THE GRID MODE AS A BACKGROUND GRID

Using the *grid mode* is like having a grid under your drawing to help you with layout. In AutoCAD, the grid mode also lets you see the limits of your drawing and helps you visually determine the distances you are working with in any given view. In this section, you will learn how to control the grid's appearance. The **F7** function key toggles the grid mode on and off.

▼ TIP

The scale factor for fractional inch scales is derived by multiplying the denominator of the scale by 12, then dividing by the numerator. For example, the scale factor for $\frac{1}{4}$" = 1'-0" is (4×12)/1 or 48/1. For whole-foot scales like 1" = 10', multiply the feet side of the equation by 12. Metric scales require simple decimal conversions.

Grid: On/Off

▼ TIP

You can use the Gridunit system variable to set the grid spacing. Enter '**Gridunit** ↵, then at the **New value for GRIDUNIT <0'0",0'0">:** prompt, enter **10,10**. Note that the grid unit value must be entered as an x,y coordinate.

1. Press **F7** or hold down the **Ctrl** key and press **G**. An array of dots appears. These dots are the *grid points*. They will not print or plot with your drawing. If the grid seems a bit too dense, you can alter the grid spacing by using the Grid command.

2. Choose Settings ➤ Drawing Aids. A dialog box displaying all the mode settings appears (see Figure 3.2). You see four button groups labeled *Modes, Snap, Grid,* and *Isometric Snap/Grid.* You'll get a chance to work with these groups later. For now you want to concentrate on the Grid group.

3. Notice the input box labeled X *Spacing* contains a value of 0'0". Above that, the On check box contains an X telling you that the grids are turned on.

4. Double-click on the X Spacing input box. The 0'0" highlights. You can now type in a new value for this setting.

▼ TIP

If you see an entry in an input box, you can double-click on it to highlight the whole entry. You can then replace the entry by simply typing in a new one. If you just want to change a part of the entry, you can click on the input box, then move the vertical bar cursor to the exact character you want to change using the cursor keys. You can use the backspace key to delete characters.

5. Enter **10** ↵ for 10". Notice that the Y Spacing input box automatically changes to 0'10". AutoCAD assumes you want the X and Y grid spacing to be the same unless you specifically ask for a different Y setting.

6. Click on the **OK** button. The grids now appear at a 10" spacing in your drawing area.

With the grid at a 10-unit spacing, the grid doesn't clutter the screen. Since the grid will appear only within the drawing limits, you are better able to see your work area. Next, you'll see how the snap mode works.

USING THE SNAP MODE

The *snap mode* has no equivalent in hand drafting. This mode forces the cursor to step a specific distance. It is useful if you want to maintain accuracy while entering distances with the cursor. The button labeled S in the toolbar toggles the snap mode on and off.

1. Click on the button labeled S in the toolbar or hold down the **Ctrl** key and press **B**, then move the cursor slowly around

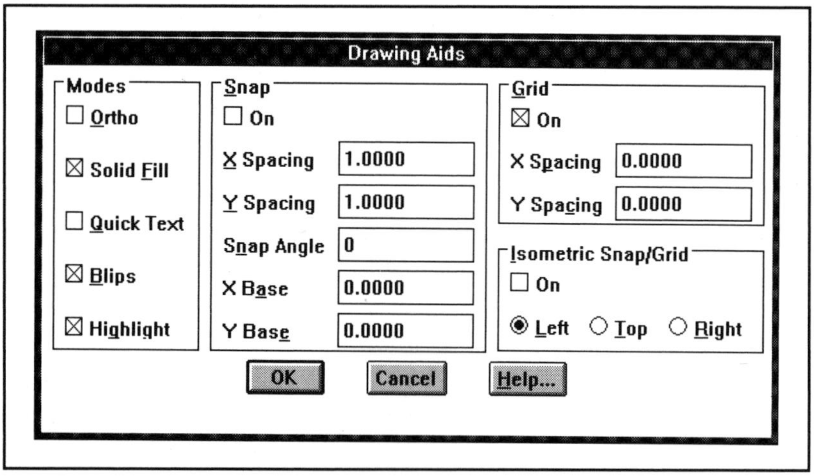

Figure 3.2: The Drawing Aids dialog box with the X Spacing input box highlighted

▼ TIP

You can use the Snapunit system variable to set the snap spacing. Enter ′**Snapunit** ↵, then at the **New value for SNAPUNIT <0′0",0′0">:** prompt, enter **4,4**. Note that the snapunit value must be entered as an x,y coordinate.

the drawing area. Notice how the cursor seems to step rather than move in a smooth motion. Also note that the S button in the toolbar appears to be depressed. This tells you that the snap mode is on.

2. Click on Settings ➤ Drawing Aids. The Drawing Aids dialog box appears again.

3. In the Snap group of the dialog box, double-click on the X Spacing input box, then enter **4** ↵. Just as with the Grid setting, AutoCAD assumes you want the X and Y snap spacing to be the same unless you specifically ask for a different Y setting.

4. Click on **OK**.

5. Now move the cursor around. Notice how it steps at a greater distance than before; 4" to be exact.

You might have noticed other options in the Snap group of the Drawing Aids dialog box. These other options allow you to set the snap origin point, rotate the cursor to an angle other than its current 0–90° (Snap angle), and set the horizontal snap spacing to a value different from the vertical spacing (Y Spacing). You can also adjust other settings like the grid/snap orientation that allow isometric-style drawings (Style option). We will look at these features in *Chapters 6* and *15*.

USING GRID AND SNAP TOGETHER

You can set the grid spacing to be the same as the snap setting, allowing you to see every snap point. The next set of exercises shows you how grid and snap work together.

1. Open the Drawing Aids dialog box again.

2. Double-click on the X Spacing input box in the Grid group.

3. Enter **0** ↵.

4. Click on the **OK** button.

Now the grid spacing has changed to reflect the 4" snap spacing. As you move the cursor, it snaps to the grid points.

1. Open the Drawing Aids dialog box again.

2. Double-click on the X Spacing input box in the Snap group.

3. Enter **1** ↵.

4. Click on the **OK** button.

The grid automatically changes to conform to the new snap setting. This shows you that when the grid spacing is set to 0, the grid then aligns with the snap points. At this density, the grid is overwhelming.

1. Open the Drawing Aids dialog box again.

2. Double-click on the X Spacing input box in the Grid group.

3. Enter **10** ↵.

4. Click on the **OK** button.

The grid spacing is now at 10 again, a more reasonable spacing for the current drawing scale.

USING THE COORDINATE READOUT AS YOUR SCALE

▼ NOTE

You can turn the dynamic coordinate readout on and off by clicking on it or by pressing the F6 function key.

Now you will draw the first item in the bathroom, the toilet. The toilet will be composed of a rectangle representing the tank and a truncated ellipse representing the seat. You will use the coordinate readout to help you find exact distances.

The coordinate readout dynamically displays its position in absolute Cartesian coordinates. This allows you to find a position on your drawing by locating it in reference to the drawing origin, 0,0, which is in the lower-left corner of the sheet. Throughout these exercises, coordinates will be provided to enable you to select points using the dynamic coordinate readout.

Draw ➤ [/] Line ➤ Segments

1. Choose Draw ➤ Line ➤ Segments.

2. Use your coordinate readout to start your line at the coordinate 5'-7", 6'-3". As you move the cursor you will see the coordinate readout change to polar coordinates. AutoCAD switches to polar coordinates to allow you to see your current location in reference to the last point selected. This is helpful when you are using a command that requires distance and direction input.

3. Move the cursor until the coordinate readout lists **1'-10"< 0**, then pick this point. As you move the cursor around, the rubber-banding line follows it at any angle. You can also force the line to be orthogonal.

4. Click on the button labeled O in the toolbar or hold down the **Ctrl** key and press **O** to toggle on the *ortho mode*, and move the cursor around. Now the rubber-banding line will only move vertically or horizontally. Notice that the O button appears to be depressed. This tells you that the ortho mode is on.

5. Move the cursor down until the coordinate readout lists **0'-9"< 270**, then click on this point.

6. Continue drawing the other two sides of the rectangle by using the coordinate readout. You should have a drawing that looks like Figure 3.3.

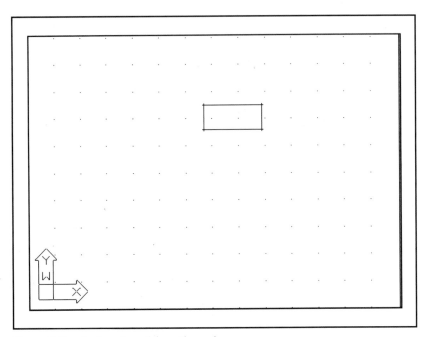

Figure 3.3: A plan view of the toilet tank

By using the snap mode in conjunction with the coordinate readout, you can measure distances as you draw lines. This is similar to the way you would draw using a scale. Be aware that the smallest distance the coordinate readout will register is dependant on the area you have displayed in your drawing area. For example, if you are displaying an area the size of a football field, the smallest distance you can indicate with your cursor may be 6". On the other hand, if you your view shows an area of only a one square inch, you can indicate distances as small as $1/1000$" using your cursor. The view on the screen does not affect the accuracy of distances entered through the keyboard.

The drawing modes can be indispensable tools when used properly. The Drawing Aids dialog box helps you visualize the modes in an organized manner and simplifies their management.

EXPLORING
THE DRAWING PROCESS

In this section, you will look at some of the more common commands and use them to complete this simple drawing. As you draw, watch the prompts and notice how your responses affect them. Also note how you use existing drawing elements as reference points.

While drawing with AutoCAD, you create gross geometric forms to determine the basic shapes of objects, then modify the shapes to fill in detail. This is where the differences between drawing with AutoCAD and manual drafting become more apparent.

AutoCAD provides eight basic drawing object types: lines, arcs, circles, traces, polylines, points, 3dfaces, and solids. All drawings are built on these objects. In addition, there are five different 3dmeshes. These meshes are three-dimensional surfaces composed of 3dfaces. You are familiar with lines and arcs, and these, along with circles, are the most commonly used objects. As you progress through the book, we will introduce you to the other objects and how they are used.

LOCATING AN OBJECT
IN REFERENCE TO OTHERS

To define the toilet seat, you will use an ellipse. AutoCAD's ellipse is actually a type of object called a *polyline,* which we will discuss in detail in *Chapter 13.*

Draw ➤ 〔⬭〕 Ellipse

1. Choose Draw ➤ Ellipse ➤ Axis, Eccentricity.

2. At the **<Axis endpoint 1>/Center:** prompt, pick the midpoint of the bottom horizontal line of the rectangle. Do this by bringing up the Osnap overrides and selecting MIDpoint, then pick the bottom line.

3. At the prompt **Axis endpoint 2:** move the cursor down until the coordinate readout lists **1'-10"< 270.**

4. Pick this as the second axis endpoint.

5. At the **<Other axis distance>/Rotation**: prompt, move the cursor horizontally from the center of the ellipse until the coordinate readout lists **0′-8″< 180**.

6. Pick this as the axis distance defining the width of the ellipse. Your drawing should look like Figure 3.4.

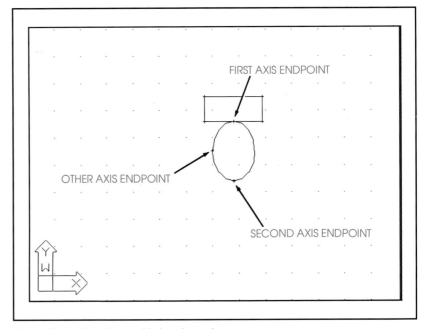

Figure 3.4: The ellipse added to the tank

GETTING A CLOSER LOOK

During the drawing process, you will want to enlarge areas of a drawing to more easily edit the objects you have drawn. In *Chapter 1*, you already saw how the Zoom command is used for this purpose.

View ➤ Zoom ➤ Window

1. Choose View ➤ Zoom ➤ Window.

2. At the **First corner:** prompt, pick a point below and to the left of your drawing at coordinate 5′-0″, 3′-6″.

3. At the **Other corner:** prompt, pick a point above and to the right of the drawing at coordinate 8′-3″, 6′-8″ so that the toilet is completely enclosed by the view window. The toilet enlarges to fill more of the screen (see Figure 3.5).

MODIFYING AN OBJECT

Now let's see how editing commands are used to construct an object. To define the back edge of the seat, let's copy the line defining the front of the toilet tank 3″ toward the center of the ellipse.

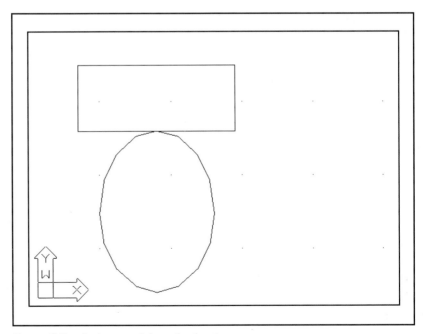

Figure 3.5:   A close-up of the toilet drawing

Construct ➤ 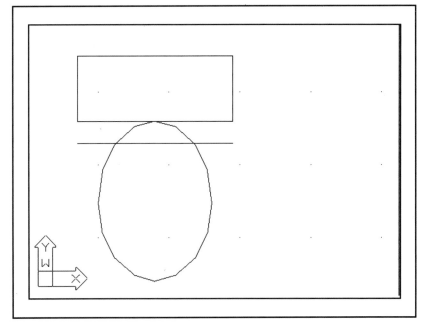 Copy

1. Choose Construct ➤ Copy.

2. At the **Select object:** prompt, pick the horizontal line that touches the top of the ellipse. The line highlights.

3. Press ↵ to confirm your selection.

4. At the **<Base point or displacement>/Multiple:** prompt, pick a base point near the line, then move the cursor down until the coordinate readout lists **0'-3"< 270**.

5. Pick this point. Your drawing should look like Figure 3.6.

You will have noticed that the Copy command acts exactly like the Move command you used in *Chapter 2*, except that Copy does not alter the position of the objects you select.

▼ **TIP**

You can also use the Grip feature to copy the line. See *Chapter 2* for more on Grips.

▼ **TIP**

Snap may be a hindrance at this point in your editing session because it may keep you from picking the points you want. The snap mode forces the cursor to move to points at a given interval, so you will have difficulty selecting a point that doesn't fall exactly on one of those intervals.

Figure 3.6:   The line copied down

Now you must delete the part of the ellipse that is not needed. You will use the Trim command to trim off parts of the ellipse.

Modify ➤ 🖾 Trim

1. First, turn the snap mode off by pressing the **F9** function key.

2. Choose Modify ➤ Trim. You will see the prompt

   Select cutting edge(s)...
   Select objects:

3. Click on the line you just created, the one that crosses through the ellipse, then press ↵ to finish your selection.

4. At the **<Select object to trim>/Undo:** prompt, pick the top-most portion of the ellipse above the line. The ellipse trims back to the line Press ↵ to exit the Trim command.

In step 2, the Trim command shows two lines of text in the prompt. The first line, **Select cutting edges...**, tells you that you must first select objects defining the edge to which you wish to trim. In step 4, you are again prompted to select objects, but this time, you are asked to select the **objects to trim**. Trim is one of a handful of AutoCAD commands that asks you to select two sets of objects. The first set defines a boundary and the second is the set of objects you want to edit. They are not mutually exclusive. You can, for example, select the cutting edge objects as objects to trim. The next exercise shows how this works.

First you will undo the Trim you just did, then you will use the Trim command again in a slightly different way to finish off the toilet.

Modify ➤ 🖾 Trim

1. Click on Edit ➤ Undo or enter **U** ↵ at the command prompt. The top of the ellipse returns.

2. Click on Modify ➤ Trim.

3. At the **Select cutting edge(s)... Select objects** prompt, click on the line crossing the ellipse and the ellipse (see Figure 3.7).

4. Press ⏎ to finish your selection and move to the next step.

5. At the **<Select object to trim>/Undo:** prompt, click on the top portion of the ellipse, as you did in the previous exercise. The ellipse trims back. (If some of the ellipse remains above the line, click on the remaining piece as well.)

6. Click on a point near the left end of the trim line, past the ellipse. The line trims back to the ellipse.

7. Click on the other end of the line. The right side of the line trims back to meet the ellipse.

8. Press ⏎ to exit the Trim command.

9. Erase any remnants of the ellipse.

Here you saw how the ellipse and the line are both used as trim objects, as well as object to be trimmed.

You've just seen one way to construct the toilet. But there are many ways to construct objects. For example, you could have just trimmed the top of the ellipse, as you did in the first Trim exercise, then used the Grips feature to move the endpoints of the line to meet the endpoints of the ellipse. As you become familiar with AutoCAD, you will start to develop your own style of working using the tools best suited to your way of working.

PLANNING AND LAYING OUT A DRAWING

For the next object, the bathtub, you will use some new commands to lay out parts of the drawing. This will help you get a feel for the kind of planning you must do to use AutoCAD effectively. You'll also get to use some keyboard shortcuts built into AutoCAD. First, though, you will want to go back to the previous view of your drawing to get more room to work.

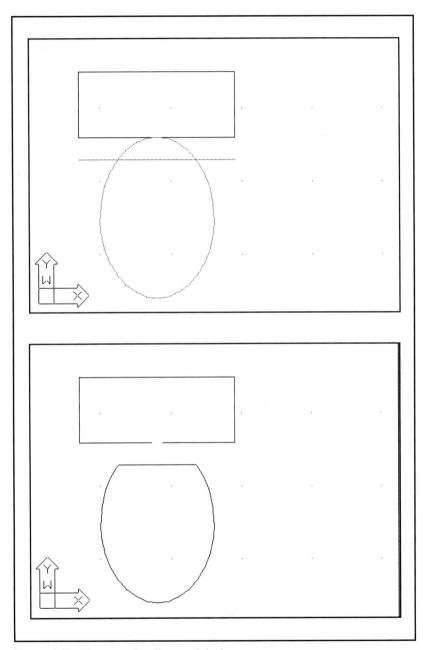

Figure 3.7: Trimming the ellipse and the line

View ➤ Zoom ➤ Previous

Choose View ➤ Zoom ➤ Previous. Your view will return to the one you had before the last Zoom command. Your drawing should look like Figure 3.8.

Begin the bathtub by using the Line command to draw a rectangle 2'-8"×5'-0" on the left side of the drawing area. This time, you'll use the keyboard shortcut to issue the line command.

L ↵ (Line Keyboard Shortcut)

1. Turn Snap on.
2. Enter **L** ↵, then, at the **From point** prompt, pick the coordinate location 0'-9", 0'-10".

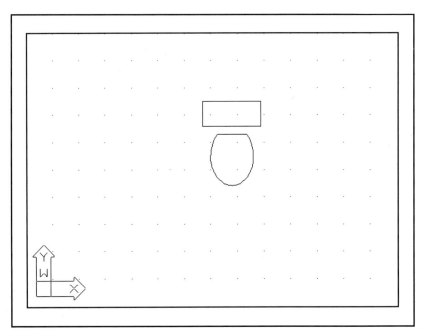

Figure 3.8:   The finished toilet

3. Enter **@2'8"<0** ↵ for the first side of the tub.

4. Enter **@5'<90** ↵ for the next side.

5. Enter **@2'8"<180** ↵ for the next side.

6. Enter **C** ↵ to close the rectangle.

This will be the outline of the tub. Note that as you enter feet and inches through the keyboard, you must avoid hyphens or spaces. Thus 2 feet 8 inches is typed as 2'8".

MAKING A PRELIMINARY SKETCH

The following exercise will show you how planning ahead can make your use of AutoCAD more efficient. When drawing a complex object, you will often have to do some layout before you do the actual drawing. This is similar to drawing an accurate pencil sketch using construction lines that you later trace over to produce a finished drawing. The advantage of doing this in AutoCAD is that your drawing doesn't lose any accuracy between the sketch and the final product. Also, AutoCAD allows you to use the geometry of your sketch to aid you in drawing. While planning your drawing, think about what it is you want to draw, then think what drawing elements will help you create that object.

▼ NOTE

The Offset command differs from the Copy command in that it allows only one object to be copied at a time, but it can remember the distance you specify.

You will use the Offset command to establish reference lines to help you draw the inside of the tub. This is where the Osnap overrides are quite useful.

SETTING UP A LAYOUT

The Offset command allows you to make parallel copies of a set of objects, such as the lines forming the outside of your tub.

Construct ➤ 🔲 Offset

1. Choose Construct ➤ Offset or enter **Offset** ↵ at the command prompt.

2. At the **Offset distance or Through <Through>:** prompt, enter **3** ↵. This enters the distance of 3" as the offset distance.

3. At the **Select object to offset:** prompt, click on the bottom line of the rectangle you just drew.

4. At the **Side to offset?** prompt, pick a point inside the rectangle. A copy of the line appears. You don't have to be exact about where you pick the side to offset. AutoCAD only wants to know which side of the line you want to make the offset copy.

5. The prompt **Select an object to offset:** appears again. Click on another side to offset then click on a point inside the rectangle again.

6. Continue to offset the other two sides, then offset these four new lines inside the rectangle toward the center. You will have a drawing that looks like Figure 3.9.

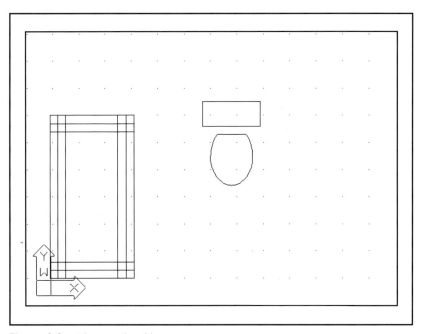

Figure 3.9:   The completed layout

7. Exit the Offset command by pressing ↵ when you are done.

You should be aware that the Offset command does not work with all types of objects. Lines, arcs, circles, and 2D polylines can be offset. All other objects cannot.

▼ TIP

Remember that you can bring up the Osnap pop-up menu by holding down the **Shift** key and pressing the right mouse button. Otherwise, you can select the Osnap overrides from the asterisk side menu or from the toolbox.

USING THE LAYOUT

Now you will begin to draw the inside of the tub, starting with the narrow end. You will use your offset lines as references to construct the arcs that make up the tub.

Draw ➤ ▢ Arc ➤ 3-Point

1. Choose Draw ➤ Arc ➤ 3-point (see Figure 3.10 for an explanation of *3-point* and the other options on the Arc menu).

2. Using the Intersection Osnap override, click on the intersection of the two lines located at coordinate 2'-11", 5'-4".

3. Using the Midpoint osnap override, pick the midpoint of the second horizontal line near the top.

4. Finally, pick the intersection of the two lines at coordinate 1'-3", 5'-4". Panel 1 of Figure 3.11 shows the sequence we've just described. An arc appears.

Next you will draw an arc for the left side of the tub.

Draw ➤ ▢ Arc ➤ Start, End, Dir

1. Pick Draw ➤ Arc ➤ Start, End, Direction, then enter @ ↵. This selects the last point you picked as the start of the next arc.

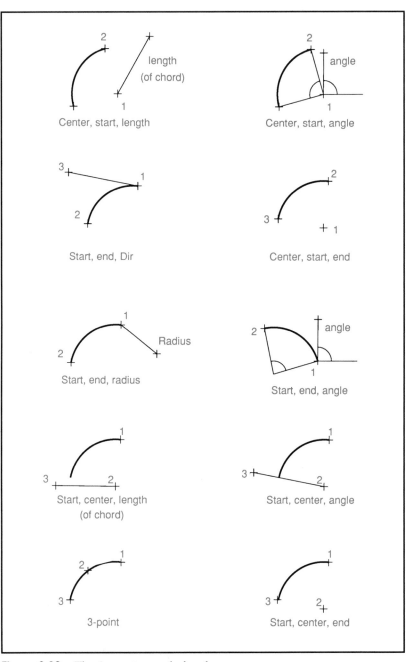

Figure 3.10:　The Arc options and what they mean

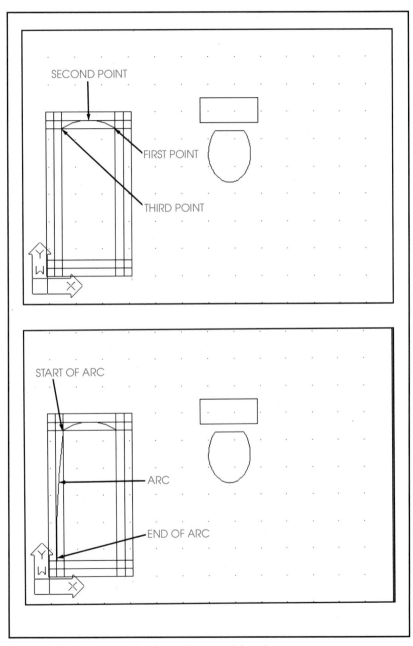

Figure 3.11: The top, left side, and bottom of the tub

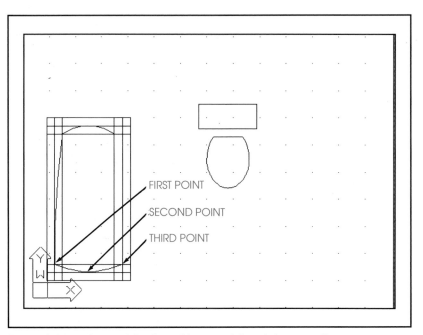

Figure 3.11: The top, left side, and bottom of the tub (continued)

2. At the **End point** prompt, use the Intersection osnap override to pick the intersection of the two lines at coordinate 1′-0″, 1′-4″ in the lower-left corner of the tub. See panel 2 of Figure 3.11 for the location of this point.

3. You will see the arc drag as you move the cursor along with a rubber-banding line from the starting point of the arc. Move the cursor to the left of the dragging arc until it touches the middle line on the left side of the tub. Then pick that point (see panel 2 of Figure 3.11).

Now you will draw the bottom of the tub.

1. Pick Draw ➤ Arc ➤ 3-point, and, using the Osnap overrides, pick the endpoint of the bottom of the arc just drawn.

2. Using the Osnap overrides, pick the midpoint of the middle horizontal line at the bottom of the tub.

▼ TIP

In step 3, the rubber-banding line indicates the direction of the arc. Be sure the ortho mode is off, as this will force the rubber-banding line and the arc in a direction you don't want. Check the status line to see if the O button is depressed. If it is, click on it or press the **F8** function key to turn ortho off.

3. Finally, pick the intersection of the two lines at coordinate 3'-2", 2'-4" (see panel 3 of Figure 3.11).

Now you will create the right side of the tub by mirroring the left side.

Construct ➤ Mirror

1. Choose Construct ➤ Mirror.

2. At the **Select objects** prompt, pick the long arc on the left side of the tub. The arc highlights.

3. Press ↵ to indicate that you've finished your selection.

4. At the **First point of mirror line:** prompt, pick the midpoint of the top horizontal line.

5. At the **Second point:** prompt, turn on the ortho mode and pick a point directly below the last point selected.

6. At the **Delete old objects?<N>** prompt, press ↵ to accept the default, no. A mirror image of the arc you picked appears on the right side of the tub. Your drawing should look like Figure 3.12.

> **▼ TIP**
>
> If you are preparing to erase objects that are in close proximity to other objects, you may want to use the preselection capabilities of AutoCAD. This feature allows you to carefully select objects you want to erase before you commit to actually using the Erase command.

For the next step, you will erase the layout lines you created using the Offset command. But this time, try preselecting the lines before issuing the Erase command.

E ↵ (Erase Keyboard Shortcut)

1. Be sure you have the noun/verb selection setting turned on. See *Chapter 3* on how to do this.

2. Click on each layout line individually. If you have problems selecting just the lines, try using a *Window* to select single lines. Remember that a window selects only objects that are completely within the window.

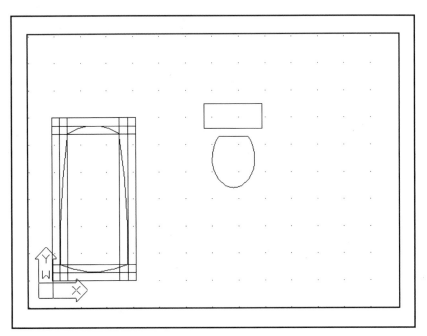

Figure 3.12:   The inside of the tub completed

3. Once all the layout lines are highlighted, enter **E** ↵. This is a keyboard shortcut to entering the Erase command.

You will notice that parts of the arcs you drew are missing. Don't be alarmed; they are still there. When an object that overlaps another object is changed or moved in any way, the overlapped object seems to disappear. This frequently occurs while you are using Change, Fillet, Move, Mirror, and Erase.

R ↵ (Redraw Keyboard Shortcut)

Enter **R** ↵. The screen redraws. After you've done that your drawing should look like Figure 3.13.

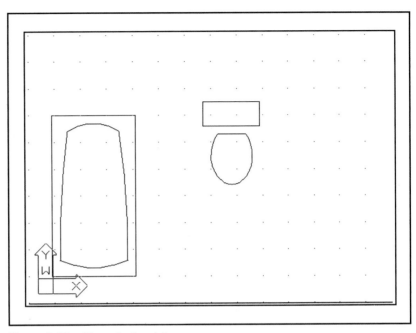

Figure 3.13: The redisplayed drawing

Many display options offer what are called *display list drivers* to help speed up AutoCAD's display. These drivers often use their own unique commands for refreshing the display. If you find that Redraw does not restore the screen properly, check to see if your system uses a display list driver. If it does, check further to see if it has some special means of refreshing the screen.

PUTTING ON THE FINISHING TOUCHES

The inside of the tub still has some sharp corners. To round out these corners, you can use the Fillet command. Fillet allows you to join lines and arcs end to end, and it can add a radius where they join so there is a smooth transition from arc to arc or line to line. Fillet can join two lines that do not intersect, or it can trim two crossing lines back to their point of intersection. This is one of the more frequently used commands because of its versatility.

Construct ➤ ⌐ Fillet

1. Choose Construct ➤ Fillet or enter **Fillet** ↵ at the command prompt.

2. At the **Polyline/Radius/<Select first object>:** prompt, pick **Radius** from the side menu or enter **R** ↵.

3. At the **Enter fillet radius <0′-0">:** prompt, enter **4** ↵. This tells AutoCAD that you want a 4" radius for your fillet.

4. Press ↵ to invoke the Fillet command again; this time, pick two adjacent arcs. The fillet arc joins the two larger arcs.

5. Press ↵ again and fillet another corner.

6. Repeat step 5 until all four corners are filleted. Your drawing should look like Figure 3.14.

7. Now save the bath file and exit AutoCAD.

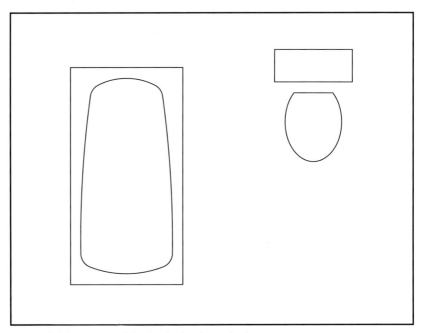

Figure 3.14: A plot of the finished toilet and tub

Using AutoCAD's Automatic Save Feature

As you work with AutoCAD, you may notice that AutoCAD periodically saves your work for you. The file is saved not as its current file name but as a file called *Auto.SV$*. The time interval between automatic saves is 120 minutes. You can change this interval by doing the following:

1. Enter **Savetime** ↵ at the command prompt.

2. At the **New value for SAVETIME < 120 >:** prompt, enter the time interval in minutes you want the automatic save to occur.

To disable the automatic save feature entirely, enter 0 at the prompt in step 2.

IF YOU WANT TO EXPERIMENT...

As you draw, you will notice that you are alternately creating objects, then copying and editing them. This is where the difference between hand drafting and CAD really begins to show.

Try drawing the part shown in Figure 3.15. The figure shows you step by step what to do. Note how you are applying the concepts of layout and editing to this drawing.

SUMMARY

As you learned to use each tool in this chapter, you probably noticed that many of them used the object-selection prompt introduced in *Chapter 2*. Change, Copy, Mirror, and Erase all allow you to select multiple objects, though in these examples you only had to choose one object. You also used the Osnap overrides to select exact points on the objects you were editing.

In *Chapter 4*, you will learn how to organize your drawing for faster editing and drawing control.

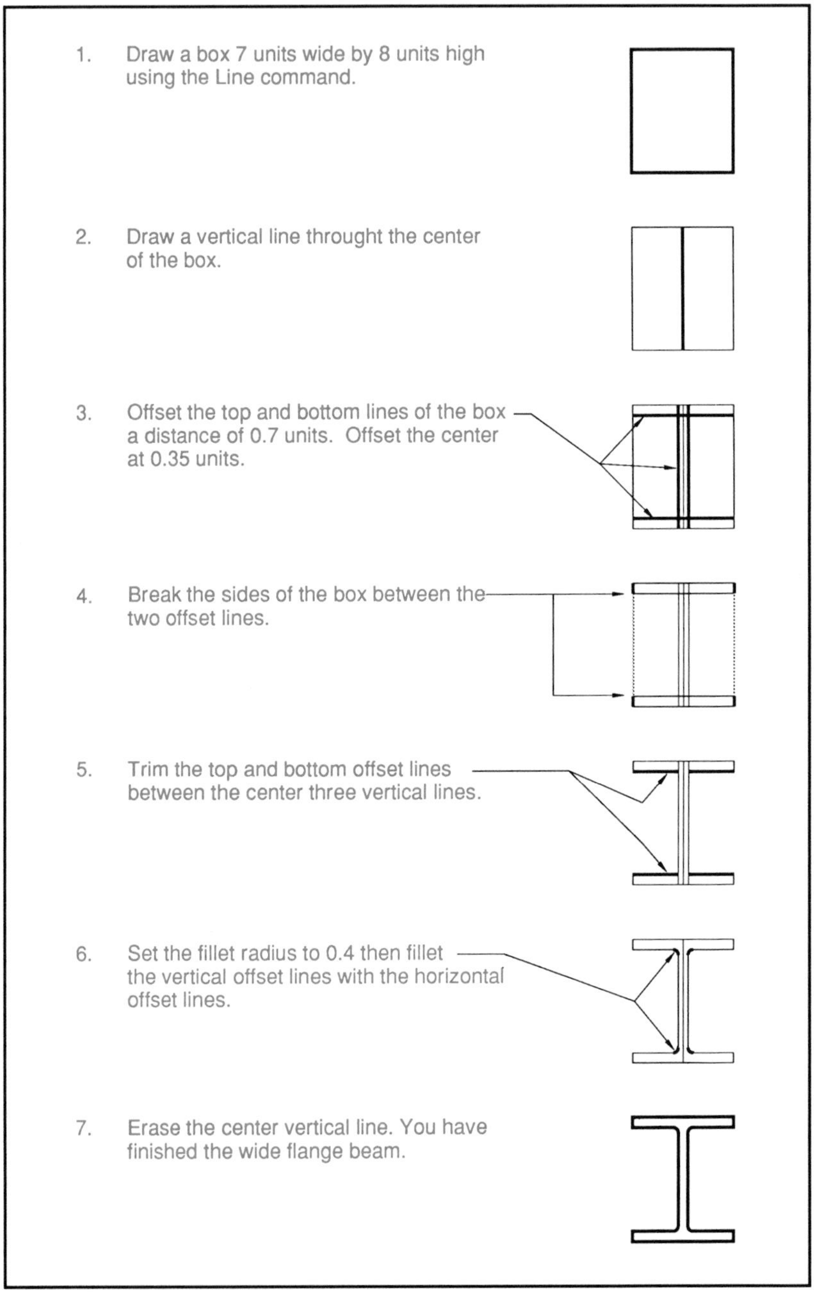

1. Draw a box 7 units wide by 8 units high using the Line command.

2. Draw a vertical line throught the center of the box.

3. Offset the top and bottom lines of the box a distance of 0.7 units. Offset the center at 0.35 units.

4. Break the sides of the box between the two offset lines.

5. Trim the top and bottom offset lines between the center three vertical lines.

6. Set the fillet radius to 0.4 then fillet the vertical offset lines with the horizontal offset lines.

7. Erase the center vertical line. You have finished the wide flange beam.

Figure 3.15: Drawing a section view of a wide flange beam

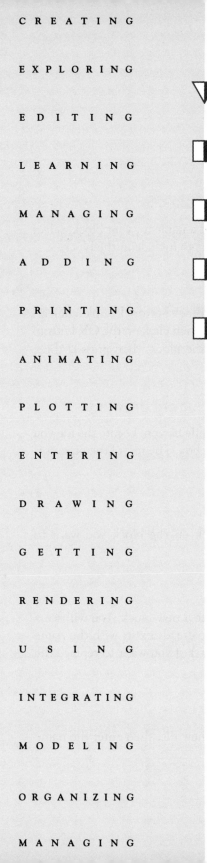

ORGANIZING YOUR WORK

FAST TRACK

118 ▶ **To turn a set of objects into a block**

Click on CONSTRUCT ➤ Block, enter a name for your block, select an insertion point, then select the objects to include in the block.

120 ▶ **To insert a block into a drawing**

Click on Draw ➤ Insert…. Click on the Block button. Double-click on the name of the block you want to insert, then click on the **OK** button. Click on the location where you want the block, then press ↵ three times.

122 ▶ **To insert a drawing file into the current drawing**

Click on Draw ➤ Insert…. Click on the **File** button. Locate the file you want to insert using the Insert File dialog box. The rest of the process is the same as for inserting blocks.

127 ▶ **To unblock a block**

Click on Modify ➤ Explode, then click on the block you want to unblock.

128 ▶ **To redefine a block**

Use the same procedure you use to create a new block. You will see a warning message telling you that a block already exists with the name you are entered for the new block. Enter **Y** if you want to replace the existing block with the new one.

130 ▶ **To turn a block into a file on disk**

Enter Wblock ↵, , enter a name for the new file, then enter the name of the block you want to turn into a file.

135 ▶ To create a new layer

Click on the button labeled Layer in the toolbar. Type in the new layer name at the Layer Control Dialog box. Click on the **New** button, then click on **OK**.

136 ▶ To change the color of a layer

With the Layer Control dialog box open, highlight the name of the layer you want to change, then click on the Set Color button. Double-click on the desired color from the Set Color dialog box, then click on **OK** to exit the dialog box.

138 ▶ To change the layer assignment of an object

Click on Modify ➤ Change ➤ Properties. Select the objects you want to change, press ↵, then at the Change properties dialog box, click on the button labeled Layer. Double-click on the layer name you want for the selected objects, then click on **OK** to exit the dialog box.

142 ▶ To make a layer the current default

Click on Settings ➤ Layer Control. Click on the layer you want to make current in the list of layers, then click on the **Current** button near the bottom of the list. Click on **OK** to exit the dialog box.

144 ▶ To turn a layer off

Click on Settings ➤ Layer Control. Click on the layer or layers you want to turn off from the list of layers, then click on the **Off** button to the right of the list. Click on **OK** to exit the dialog box.

148 ▶ To change the line type assignment of a layer

First load the line type you want using the Linetype command. Click on Settings ➤ Layer Control. Highlight the name of the layer you want to change, then click on the **Set Ltype** button. Double-click on the desired line type from the Set Ltype dialog box, then click on **OK** to exit the dialog box.

You may think it took an inordinate amount of time to draw the tub and toilet. As you continue to use AutoCAD, however, you will learn to draw objects faster. You will also need to draw fewer of them because you can save drawings as *symbols* to be used like rubber stamps, duplicating them instantaneously wherever they are needed. Re-using such symbols can save you a lot of time when composing drawings.

To make effective use of AutoCAD, you should begin a *symbol library* of drawings you use frequently. A mechanical designer might have a library of symbols for fasteners, cams, valves, or any number of parts for his or her application. An electrical engineer might have a symbol library of capacitors, resistors, switches, and the like, while a circuit designer may have another set of frequently used symbols.

In *Chapter 3* you drew two objects, a bathtub and a toilet, that architects often use. In this chapter, you will learn how to create symbols from those drawings. You will also learn about layers and how you can use them to organize information.

CREATING A SYMBOL

To save a drawing as a symbol, you use the **BLOCK** command. If you use a word processor, you are probably familiar with the idea of a block. In word processing, a block is used to group words or sentences to be copied elsewhere within the same file, other files, or saved separately on disk for future use. AutoCAD uses blocks in a similar fashion. Within a file, you can turn parts of your drawing into blocks that can be saved and recalled at any time. You can also use entire existing files as blocks.

Construct ➤ 🖾 Block

▼ **TIP**

You can also enter **Block** ↵ at the command prompt to start the block command.

1. Start AutoCAD and open the existing Bath file. The drawing appears just as you left it in the last session.

2. Click on CONSTRUCT ➤ Block.

3. The prompt **BLOCK Block name (or ?):** appears asking you to supply a name for the block you are about to define. Type **Toilet** ↵.

▼ NOTE

The insertion base point of a block is similar to the base point you used as a handle on an object in *Chapter 2*.

▼ NOTE

You can press ↵ to start the BLOCK command again.

4. The prompt **Insertion base point:** asks you to select a base point for the block. Use the Osnap overrides and pick the midpoint of the back of the toilet.

5. You will now see the familiar object-selection prompt. Window the entire toilet. The toilet will highlight.

6. Press ↵ to confirm your selection, and the toilet will disappear. It is now a block with the name *Toilet*.

7. Go through the same process for the tub, but this time use the upper-left corner of the tub as the insertion base point and give the block the name *Tub*.

RECALLING BLOCKED OR ERASED OBJECTS

When you turn an object into a block, it is stored within the drawing file, ready to be recalled at any time. The block remains part of the drawing file even when you end the editing session. When you open the file again, it will be available for your use. A block acts like a single object even though it is really made up of several objects. It can only be modified by unblocking it using the EXPLODE command. You can then edit it and turn it back into a block. We will look at the block-editing process later in this chapter.

If for some reason you want to restore the object you just turned into a block, you can use the OOPS command.

OOPS

▼ NOTE

The OOPS command can also be used in any situation where you want to restore an object you erased by accident.

1. Pick OOPS from the Side BLOCK menu or enter **OOPS** ↵. The tub reappears in its former condition, not as a block.

2. Since you don't need this restored tub, enter **U** ↵ to undo the OOPS command. Be careful you don't press ↵ more than once.

OOPS can be useful when you want to create several blocks that are only slightly different. For example, suppose you want several versions of the tub. You can save the tub as a block, then use OOPS to restore it, then modify it to a different shape, then save this new tub as a different block.

INSERTING A SYMBOL

Although the tub and toilet blocks disappeared, they can be recalled at any time, as many times as you want. In the following exercise you'll first draw the interior walls of the bathroom, then you'll insert the tub and toilet.

Draw ➤ 🔲 Insert... ➤ Block

▼ TIP

If you are in a hurry, enter **Insert** ↵ at the command prompt, then enter **Tub** ↵, then go to step 6.

1. Draw a rectangle 5′×7½′. Orient the rectangle so the long sides go from left to right and the lower-left corner is at coordinate 1′-10″, 1′-10″. Your drawing will look like Figure 4.1.

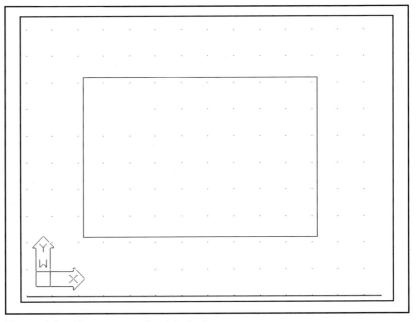

Figure 4.1: The interior walls of the bathroom

2. Choose Draw ➤ Insert... ➤. The Insert dialog box appears (see Figure 4.2).

3. Click on the button labeled Block at the top of the dialog box. Another dialog box appears showing a list of available blocks in the current drawing.

4. Double-click on the name *Tub*. You return to the Insert dialog box and the name *Tub* appears in the input box next to the **Block** button.

5. Click on the **OK** button. Next, AutoCAD will prompt you for more information.

6. At the **Insertion point:** prompt, move the cursor across the screen slowly. Notice that the tub now appears and follows the cursor. The upper-left corner you picked for the tub's base point is now on the cursor intersection.

7. Pick the upper-left intersection of the room as your insertion point.

▼ NOTE

The Insert dialog box lets you insert a block or an external file into your current drawing. It also lets you manually enter the insertion point and scale factor for blocks and external files.

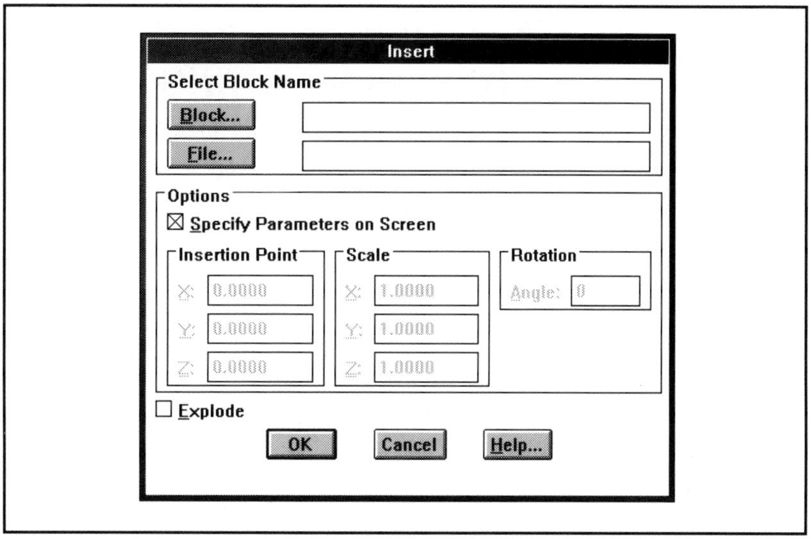

Figure 4.2:   The Insert dialog box and block list

▼ NOTE

The X scale factor and Y scale factor prompts let you stretch the block in one direction or another. You can even specify a negative value to mirror the block. The defaults on these prompts are always 1, which inserts the block or file at the same size as they were created.

8. At the **X scale factor <1> / Corner / XYZ:** prompt, press ↵ to accept the default, 1.

9. At the **Y scale factor (default=X):** prompt, press ↵ to accept (default=X).

10. At the **Rotation angle <0>:** prompt, press ↵ to accept the default of 0. You should have a drawing that looks like panel 1 of Figure 4.3.

11. Repeat steps 2 through 10, but this time, in place of steps 3 and 4, click on the Block input box and enter *toilet*. Place the toilet along the top of the rectangle representing the room and just to the right of the tub, at coordinate 5′-8″, 6′-10″, as shown in panel 2 of Figure 4.3.

In steps 8 and 9, you might have noticed that as you moved the cursor, the tub distorted. This shows you how the X and Y scale factors can affect the item being inserted. Also in step 10, you can see the tub rotate as you move the cursor. You can pick a point to fix the block in place, or you can enter a rotation value. The default 0 angle inserts the block or file at the orientation it was created.

USING AN EXISTING DRAWING AS A SYMBOL

Now you need a door into the bathroom. Since you already drew a door and saved it as a file, you can bring the door into this drawing file and use it as a block.

Draw ➤  Insert... ➤ File

1. Click on Draw ➤ Insert....

2. Click on the **File** button just below the **Block** button. The familiar File dialog box appears.

3. Double-click on the Door file name in the File list.

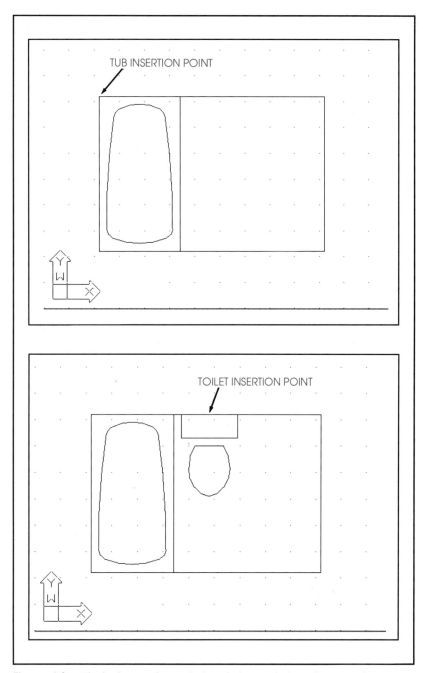

Figure 4.3: The bathroom, first with the tub then with the toilet inserted

4. As you move the cursor around, you will notice the door appear above and to the right of the cursor intersection as in Figure 4.4.

5. The door looks too small for this bathroom. This is because you drew it 3 units long, which translates to 3". Pick a point near coordinate 7'-2",2'-4", so that the door is placed in the lower-right corner of the room.

6. At the **x scale factor** prompt, enter **12** ↵ .

7. Press **Return** twice to accept the default y = x and the rotation angle of 0°.

The command prompt appears, but nothing seems to happen to the drawing. The reason is that when you enlarged the door, you also enlarged the distance between the base point and the object. This brings up another issue to be aware of when considering drawings as symbols.

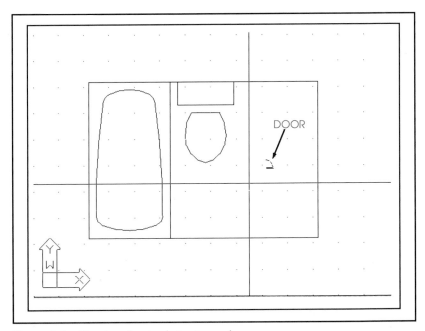

Figure 4.4: The door drawing being inserted

All drawings have base points. The default base point is the absolute coordinate 0,0, otherwise known as the *origin*, which is located in the lower-left corner of any new drawing. When you drew the door in *Chapter 2*, you didn't specify the base point. So, when you try to bring the door into this drawing, AutoCAD uses the origin of the door drawing as its base point (see Figure 4.5).

Since the door appears outside the bathroom, you must first use the Zoom ➤ All option to show more of the drawing, then use the MOVE command to move the door to the right side wall of the bathroom.

Click on View ➤ Zoom ➤ All. The view of the room will shrink away and the door will be revealed. Notice that it is now the proper size for your drawing (see Figure 4.6).

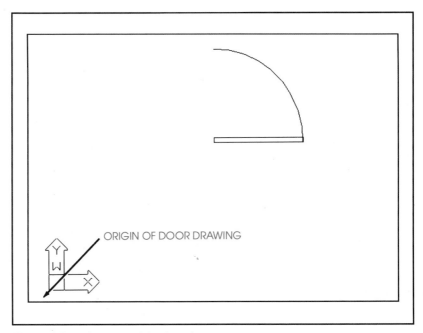

Figure 4.5: The origin of the door drawing

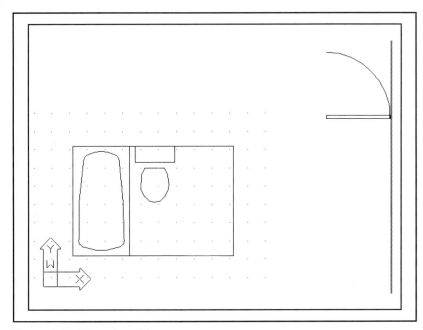

Figure 4.6:   The enlarged door

Modify ➤ ⬌ Move

1. Click Modify ➤ Move.

2. To find the door you just inserted, at the **Select objects** prompt, click on a point anywhere on the door, then press ↵.

3. At the **Base point** prompt, pick the lower-left corner of the door.

4. At the **Second point** prompt, use the Nearest Osnap modifier and position the door so your drawing looks like Figure 4.7.

Because the door is an object you will use often, it should be a common size so you don't have to specify an odd value every time you insert

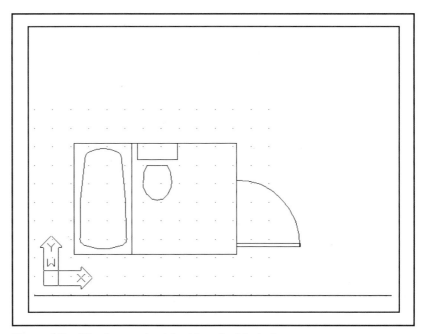

Figure 4.7:   The door on the right side wall of the bathroom

it. It would also be helpful if the door's insertion base point were in a more convenient location.

Next, you will modify the Door block to better suit your needs.

UNBLOCKING A BLOCK

You can modify a block by breaking it down into its components, editing them, and then turning them back into a block. To break a block into its components you use the EXPLODE command.

Modify ➤ Explode

1. Click on Modify ➤ Explode or enter **Explode** ↵ at the command prompt.

2. Click on the door.

3. Press ↵ to confirm your selection.

▼ TIP

You can simultaneously insert and explode a block by clicking on the Explode check box in the lower-left corner of the Insert Dialog box (see Figure 4.2).

You can now edit the individual objects that make up the door if you so desire. In this case, you only want to change the door's insertion point because you already made it a more convenient size.

Now turn the door back into a block, this time using the door's lower-left corner for its insertion base point.

Construct ➤ 🖾 Block (Redefining)

1. Issue the BLOCK command as you did earlier in this chapter.

2. At the **Block name** prompt, enter **Door** for the name of the block, the following prompt appears:

   > Block DOOR already exists.
   > Redefine it? <N>

   AutoCAD provides this prompt so you won't inadvertently change a block you want to leave alone.

3. Enter **Y** ↵ for yes.

▼ NOTE

To mirror an object using the Grips feature, first be sure Grips are turned on. Once you've selected the objects to mirror, click on a grip then press the right mouse button until you see the ****MIR-ROR**** message in the prompt.

4. At the **Insertion base point:** prompt, pick the lower-left corner of the door, then proceed with the rest of the command.

5. Now insert the door again, using the Block option of the dialog box, but this time use the Nearest Osnap override and pick a point on the right side wall of the bathroom near coordinate 9'-4", 2'-1".

6. After you complete this, use the Grips feature to mirror the door using the wall as the mirror axis so that the door is inside the room. Your drawing will look like Figure 4.8.

If you redefine a block that has been inserted in a drawing, each occurrence of that block will change to reflect the new block definition. You can use this block redefinition feature to make rapid changes to a design.

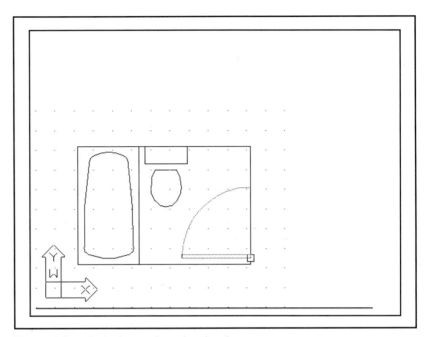

Figure 4.8:   The bathroom floor plan thus far

SAVING A BLOCK AS A DRAWING FILE

You've seen that, with very little effort, you can create a symbol that can be placed anywhere in a file. Suppose you want to use this symbol in other files. When you create a block using the BLOCK command, the block exists within the current file only. For an existing drawing that has been brought in and modified, like the door, the drawing file on disk associated with that door is not automatically updated. You must update the door file to reflect the changes you made to the door block. You do this using the WBLOCK (short for Write Block) command. Let's see how WBLOCK works. In the next exercise, you'll also get to try some new options on the File dialog box.

To turn the tub and toilet blocks into individual files on disk, do the following:

AutoCAD ➤ Blocks ➤ Wblock (Create New File)

▼ **TIP**

You can enter **Wblock** ↵ from the command prompt to quickly get to step 2.

1. Click on AutoCAD ➤ BLOCKS from the side root menu, then click on WBLOCK. The Create Drawing File dialog box appears. By now you should know how this dialog box works.

2. Click on the button labeled **Type it**. The dialog box disappears, then you get the prompt **File Name:**.

3. Enter **Tub** ↵.

▼ **NOTE**

AutoCAD gives you the option to save the file of a block under either the same name as the original block or a different one. Usually you will want to use the same name, which you can do by entering an equals sign (=) after the block name prompt or picking the equals sign from the WBLOCK menu.

4. At the **Block name** prompt, enter the name of the block you wish to save on disk as the tub file—in this case also **Tub**. The tub block is now saved as a file.

5. Repeat steps 1 through 4 for the toilet block. Give the file the same name as the block.

You could have just entered the name **tub** when the dialog box appeared in step 1. You would have then gotten the Block name prompt, just as in step 4. Here you had an opportunity to explore the File dialog box.

REPLACING EXISTING FILES WITH BLOCKS

Let's try using the WBLOCK command again, this time to save the door block you modified.

AutoCAD ➤ Blocks ➤ Wblock (Replace Existing File)

1. Issue the WBLOCK command again.

2. At the File Creation dialog box, enter the file name **Door**. A warning message appears (see Figure 4.9).

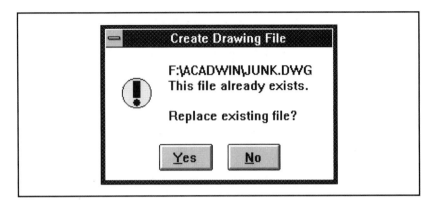

Figure 4.9:   The File warning message

3. In this case, you want to update the door you drew in *Chapter 2*, so click on **Yes**. Then enter Door at the block name prompt. The new door will replace the old one.

OTHER USES FOR BLOCKS

So far, you have used BLOCK to create symbols and WBLOCK to save those symbols to disk. As you can see, symbols can be created and saved any time while you are drawing. The tub and toilet symbols are now drawing files you can see when you check the contents of your current directory. However, creating symbols is not the only use for the IN-SERT, BLOCK, and WBLOCK commands. You can use them in any situation that requires grouping objects. WBLOCK also allows you to save to disk a part of a drawing. These other uses of BLOCK and WBLOCK are explained throughout *Chapters 5–8* and in *Chapter 12*.

BLOCK and WBLOCK are both extremely versatile and, if used judiciously, can boost your productivity and make your work easier. If you are not careful, however, you can also get carried away and create more blocks than you can keep track of. Planning your drawings helps you determine which elements work best as blocks and where other methods of organization are more suitable.

▼ NOTE

Third-party developers that produce software for making shapes often advertise in Cadalyst Magazine. Their address is: Cadalyst, Aster Publishing, P.O. Box 10460, Eugene, OR 97440-2460. Telephone: (503) 343-1200.

▼

■

■

■

■

An Alternative to Blocks

Another way to create symbols is by creating *shapes*. Shapes are special objects made up of lines, arcs, and circles. They can regenerate faster than blocks and they take up less file space. Unfortunately shapes are considerably more difficult to create and less flexible to use than blocks. You create shapes by using a coding system developed by Autodesk. The codes define the sizes and orientations of lines, arcs, and circles. You first sketch your shape, then convert it into the code, then copy that code into a DOS text file. We won't get into detail on this subject, so if you want to know more about shapes look in the AutoCAD Customization Manual, or refer to the SYBEX book *Advanced AutoCAD Release 12* by Robert Thomas, which gives an excellent description of shapes.

One way to get around the difficulty of creating shapes is to purchase one of the third-party software products available for this purpose. These are add-on programs capable of converting AutoCAD drawings into shape libraries. They usually require that you draw your shape within a predefined area in a special drawing file supplied with the software. If you intend to do drawings that will be composed mostly of very simple symbols, you may want to look into this alternative. Since AutoCAD fonts are created the same way shapes are, these programs also allow you to create your own fonts

Another way of using symbols is to use AutoCAD's cross-reference capabilities. Cross-referenced, or Xref, files are those inserted into a drawing in a way similar to blocks. The difference between Xref files and blocks is that Xref files do not actually become part of the drawing's database. Instead, they are loaded along with the current file at start-up time. It is as if AutoCAD opens several drawings at once: the main file you specify when you start AutoCAD, and any Xref files associated with the main file.

By keeping Xref files independent from the current file, you make sure that any changes made to the Xref file will automatically appear in the current file. You don't have to update the Xref file manually the way you do blocks. For example, if XREF were used to insert the tub, and you later made changes to the tub drawing, the next time you opened the bath file, you would see the new version of the tub in place of the old.

Xref files are especially useful in work-group environments where several people are working on the same project. One person might be updating several files that have been inserted into a variety of other files. Before XREF was available, everyone in the workgroup would have had to be notified of the changes and update all the affected blocks in all the drawings that contained them. With XREF, the updating is automatic. There are many other features unique to Xref files. I will discuss XREF in more detail in *Chapters 6* and *12*.

ORGANIZING INFORMATION WITH LAYERS

Another tool for organization is the layer. A layer is like an overlay on which you keep various types of information (see Figure 4.10). In a floor plan of a building, for example, you want to keep the walls, ceiling, plumbing fixtures, wiring, and furniture separate, so you can display or plot them separately or combine them in different ways. You also want to keep notes and reference symbols on their own layers, as well as dimensions. As your drawing becomes more complex, these different layers can be turned on and off to allow easier display and modification.

For example, one of your consultants may need a plot of just the dimensions and walls without all the other information, while another consultant may need only a furniture layout. Using manual drafting,

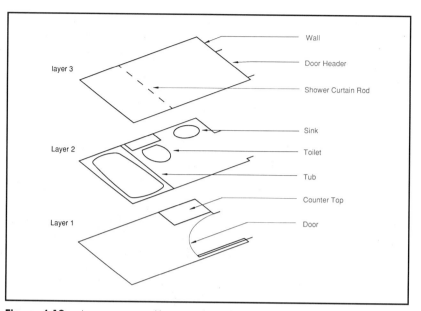

Figure 4.10: A comparison of layers and overlays

you would have to redraw your plan for each consultant. Using AutoCAD, you can turn off the layers you don't need and plot a drawing containing only the required information. A carefully planned layering scheme helps you produce a document that combines the different types of information needed in each case.

Using layers also enables you to modify your drawings more easily. For example, suppose you have an architectural drawing with separate layers for the walls, the ceiling plan, and the floor plan. If any change occurs in the wall locations, you can turn on the ceiling plan layer to see where the new wall locations affect the ceiling and make the proper adjustments.

AutoCAD allows an unlimited number of layers, and you can name each layer anything you want.

CREATING AND ASSIGNING LAYERS

To continue with your bathroom, you will create some new layers.

Settings ➤ Layer Control

▼ NOTE

Layer colors are designated by numbers, with the exception of the first seven colors, so when you select a color above 7, a number appears in the color input box toward the bottom of the dialog box.

1. Click on the Layer button in the toolbar or on Settings ➤ Layer Control. The Layer Control Dialog box appears (see Figure 4.11).

2. Type **Wall**. As you type, the name appears in the input box at the bottom of the dialog box.

3. When you are done typing, click on the button labeled **New** just above the input box. The new layer appears in the layer list that occupies the upper half of the dialog box.

4. Click on the Wall layer shown in the list. The item highlights. Notice that some of the buttons to the right changed from gray to black. This tells you that they are available for use.

▼ NOTE

The Layer Control Dialog box shows you at a glance the status of your layers. Right now, you only have two layers, but as your work expands, so will the number of layers. You will then find this dialog box indespensable.

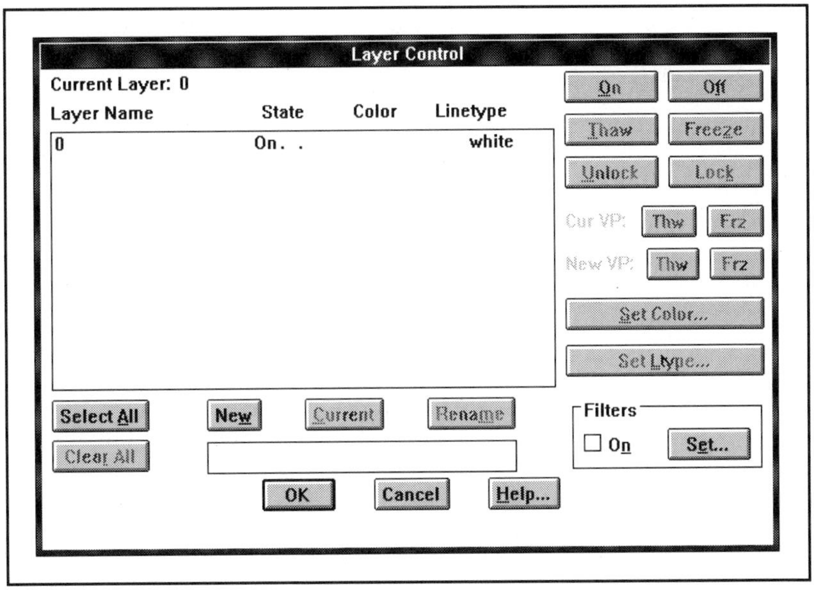

Figure 4.11: The Layer Control dialog box

5. Click on the button labled **Set Color**. Another dialog box appears showing you the selection of colors available.

6. Click on the green square in the top row of colors labeled Standard Colors.

7. Click on the **OK** button.

8. Click on the **OK** button in the main Layer Control dialog box.

The Layer Control dialog box offers a way to view and edit layer information in an easy-to-understand form. Layer colors can be easily selected from a palette that appears on the screen. But layers can also be controlled through the command prompt.

Controlling Layers through the Layer Command

Layer (Command Prompt)

1. First press **Ctrl-C**.

2. At the command prompt, enter **Layer** ↵. The following prompt appears:

   ?/Make/Set/New/ON/OFF/Color/Ltype/Freeze/Thaw
   /Lock/Unlock:

3. Click on New from the side menu or enter **N** ↵ to select the New option.

4. At the **New layer name(s)** prompt, enter **Wall2** ↵. The **?/Make/Set/New** prompt appears again.

5. Enter C ↵.

6. At the Color prompt, enter **yellow** ↵. Alternately, you can enter **2** ↵, the numeric equivalent to the color yellow in AutoCAD.

7. At the **Layer Names for color 2 (yellow) <0>:** prompt, enter **Wall2** ↵. The **?/Make/Set/New** prompt appears again.

8. Press ↵ to exit the Layer command.

The two methods of controlling layers you just tried each have their advantages. The dialog box offers more information about your layers at a glance. On the other hand, the Layer command offers a quick way to control and create layers if you're in a hurry. Also, if you intend to write custom macros, you will want to know how to use the Layer command as opposed to the dialog box, since dialog boxes cannot be controlled through scripts.

Understanding Colors

As you saw in each exercise, AutoCAD assigns a number to each color, and you can use this number to select it. Number assignments vary among the numerous display options available with AutoCAD, so 2 may not always correspond to the color yellow. AutoCAD provides a quick way to find the number that corresponds to a color.

Layer ↵ Color ➤ Chroma

▼ NOTE

The topmost row of colors shows the first nine. The first column to the left shows the next ten colors, with even-numbered colors in the upper half and odd-numbered colors in the lower half. As you move from left to right, the color numbers increase by ten.

1. Enter **Layer** ↵, then select Color ➤ Chroma from the side menu. The screen changes to show all the colors available in AutoCAD.

2. The Chroma image is an AutoCAD *slide* file. We will discuss slides in *Chapter 15*. To restore your previous view, you can click on LAST ➤ Restore from the side menu or enter **'redraw** ↵, then enter **Ctrl-C** twice to exit the layer command.

Assigning Layers to Objects

When you create an object, that object is assigned to the current layer. Up until now, only one layer existed, layer 0. All the objects you've drawn so far are assigned to layer 0. Now that you've created some new layers, you can use the CHANGE command to re-assign objects to them.

Modify ➤ Change ➤ Properties

1. Click on Modify ➤ Change ➤ Properties.
2. At the **Select objects** prompt, click on the four lines representing the bathroom walls. If you have problems singling out the wall to the left, use a window to select the wall line.
3. Press ↵ to confirm your selection. The Change Properties dialog box appears (see Figure 4.12).
4. Click on the button labeled **Layer**. Another dialog box appears, listing all the existing layers. Notice that the layers you just created appear in the list.
5. Double-click on the Wall layer listed in the box. You return to the Change Properties dialog box.
6. Click on the **OK** button. The dialog box closes.

▼ NOTE

This dialog box allows you to change the layer assignment, color, line type, and thickness of an object. You'll learn about line types and object thickness in later chapters.

The bathroom walls are now on the new layer, Wall. You will see the walls change to green. Layers are more easily distinguished from each other when colors are used to set them apart.

Next, you will practice the commands you learned in this section by creating some new layers and changing the layer assignments of the rest of the objects in your bathroom.

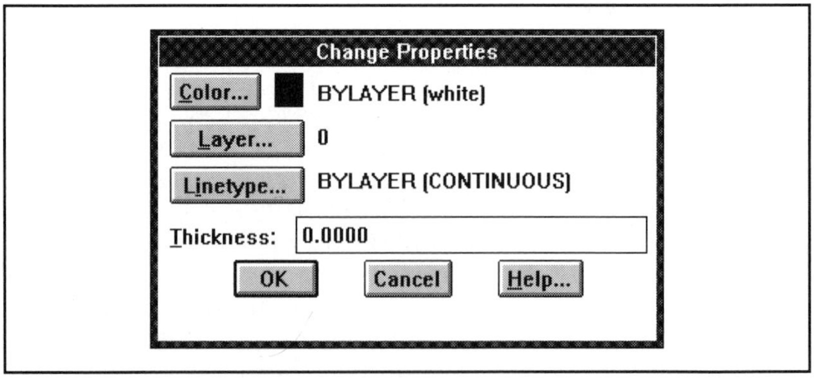

Figure 4.12: The Change Properties dialog box

Settings ➤ Layer Control
Modify ➤ ⊞ Change ➤ Properties

1. Create a new layer called **Fixture** and give this new layer the color blue.

2. Use the Change Properties dialog box to change the tub and toilet to the Fixture layer.

3. Now create a new layer for the door. Call the layer **Door** and make it red.

4. Change the door to that layer.

5. Create three more layers for the ceiling, door jambs, and floor, and assign magenta to Ceiling, green to Jamb, and cyan to Floor.

WORKING ON LAYERS

So far you have created layers, then assigned objects to those layers. However, the current layer is still 0, and every new object you draw will be on layer 0. Here's how to change the current layer.

Toolbar: *Layer Name*

1. Click on the layer name that appears next to the Layer button on the toolbar. A popup list appears showing you all the layers available in the drawing.

2. Click on the Jamb layer name. The popup list closes and the name Jamb appears next to the Layer button. This tells you that Jamb is now the current layer. Also notice that the current color shown in the box to the far left is green, the color of the Jamb layer.

3. Zoom into the door and draw a line 5" long toward the right from the lower-right corner of the door.

Controlling Colors and Line Types of Blocked Objects

Layer 0 has special importance to blocks. When objects assigned to layer 0 are used as parts of a block, those objects will take on the characteristics of the layer the block is inserted on. On the other hand, if those objects are on a layer other than 0, they will maintain their original layer assignment no matter what layer the block is inserted on or changed to. For example, suppose you drew the tub on the Door layer, instead of on layer 0. Then suppose you turn the tub into a block and insert it on the Fixture layer. The objects the tub is composed of will maintain their assignment to the Door layer although the Tub block is assigned to the Fixture layer.

It might help to think of the block function as a clear plastic bag that holds together the objects that make up the tub. The objects inside the bag maintain their assignment to the Door layer even while the bag itself is assigned to the Fixture layer.

AutoCAD also allows you to have more than one color or line type on a layer. You can use the color or **Linetype** button on the Change Properties dialog box to alter the color or line type of an object on layer 0, for example. That object then maintains its color and line type assignment no matter what layer it is assigned to. Likewise, objects specifically assigned a color or line type will not be affected by their inclusion into blocks.

▼ NOTE

You can also use the Layer command to set the current layer to Jamb. To do this, you enter **Layer** at the command prompt, then at the *?/Make...* prompt, enter **S** for set. At the **New current layer** prompt, enter *Jamb* ↵, then press ↵ again to exit the Layer command.

4. Draw a similar line from the top-right end of the arc. Your drawing should look like Figure 4.13.

The two lines you just drew in steps 3 and 4 to represent the door jambs are green. Remember that you assigned the color green to the Jamb layer. Since you know the Jamb layer is green, seeing objects appear green as you draw gives you immediate feedback about what layer you are on.

Now you will use the part of the wall between the jambs as a line representing the door header (the part of the wall above the door). To do

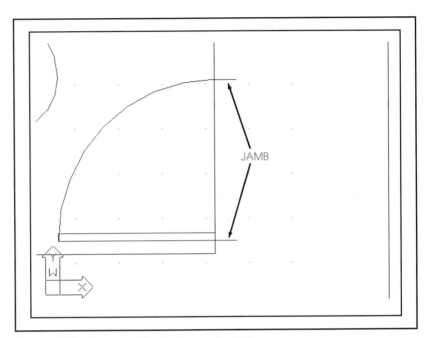

JAMB

Figure 4.13:   Door at wall with door jamb added

this, you will have to cut the line into three line segments, then change the layer assignment of the segment between the jambs to a new layer.

Modify ➤ ⬚ Break ➤ Select Objects, Two Points

1. Click on Modify ➤ Break ➤ Select object, two points.

2. At the **Select object** prompt, click on the wall between the two jambs.

3. At the **Enter first point** prompt, use the Endpoint osnap override to pick the endpoint of the door's arc that is touching the wall.

4. At the **Enter second point** prompt, click on the at sign on the Break menu. This breaks the wall line into two lines at the intersection of the wall, the jamb, and the arc.

5. Repeat steps 1 through 4, this time using the jamb near the door hinge location to locate the break point.

6. Now change the line between the two jambs to the Ceiling layer. When you complete the change, the line will turn to magenta, telling you it is now on the Ceiling layer.

7. Click on View ➤ Zoom ➤ Previous to return to the previous view.

The Break command allows you to cut an object at a single point. You can also use Break to create a gap in an object.

Settings ➤ Layer Control ➤ New, Set Color

1. Using the Layer Control dialog box, create a layer called *Casework*.

2. When the Casework layer name appears in the layer list, highlight it then click on the check box labeled Current.

3. Using the Set Color dialog box, set its color to blue. When you exit the LAYER command, the status line indicates that the current layer is Casework.

Now you'll finish the bathroom by adding a sink. Notice that as you draw, the objects appear in the color blue, the color of the Casework layer you just created.

View ➤ Zoom
Draw ➤ 🔲 Line ➤ Segments
🔘 Ellipse ➤ Axis, Eccentricity
Modify ➤ 🔳 Change ➤ Properties

1. Click on View ➤ Zoom ➤ All.

2. Draw a rectangle 28"×18" representing a sink countertop. Orient the countertop so that it fits into the upper-right

corner of the room as in Figure 4.14. Use coordinate 7'-0",
5'-4" for the lower-left corner of the counter.

3. Draw an ellipse 17"×14" in the center of the countertop.

4. Change the ellipse to the Fixture layer. Your drawing will
   look like Figure 4.14.

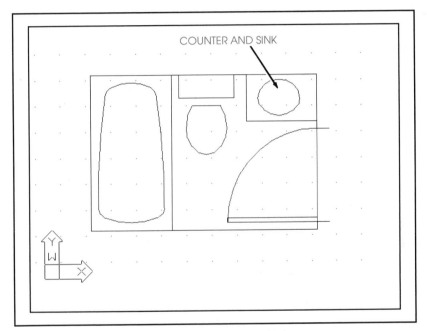

Figure 4.14: Bathroom with sink and countertop added

CONTROLLING LAYER VISIBILITY

We mentioned earlier that at times you want to be selective about what
layers you are working with on a drawing. In this bathroom, a door
header is shown that normally appears only in the ceiling plan. To turn
off a layer so that it becomes invisible, use the **Off** button in the Layer
Control dialog box.

Settings ➤ Layer Control: Off

1. Open the Layer Control dialog box.

2. Click on the Ceiling layer in the layer list.

3. Click on the **Off** button to the right of the list.

4. Click on the **OK** button to exit the dialog box. When you return to the drawing, the header disappears (see Figure 4.15).

The header didn't go anywhere. It is just invisible since you turned off the layer it was assigned to.

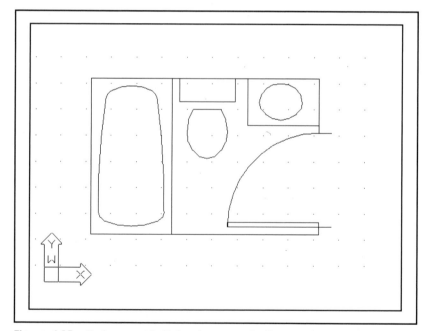

Figure 4.15: Bathroom with Ceiling layer turned off

FINDING THE LAYERS YOU WANT

With only a handful of layers, its fairly easy to find the layer you want to turn off. But when the number of layers exceeds 20 or 30, it becomes more difficult to find the layer you are looking for. The Layer Control dialog box offers the Filters option that helps you search through your layer names to find specific ones.

To use filters, you click on the Set button of the Filters group in the lower-right area of the Layer Control dialog box. Another dialog box appears (see Figure 4.16). From this dialog box, you can specify the layers you want to show in the layer list by indicating the layer's characteristics.

Now suppose you have several layers whose names begin with C-, like *C-lights, C-header,* and *C-pattern,* and you want to display only those layers in the Layer Control dialog box. You can enter **C-*** in the Layer Names input box, then click on the **OK** button. Once this is done, only

▼ TIP

The asterisk in **C-*** is called a *wildcard* character. Wildcards can be used to help locate names in DOS and AutoCAD. See *Appendix C* for more on wildcard characters.

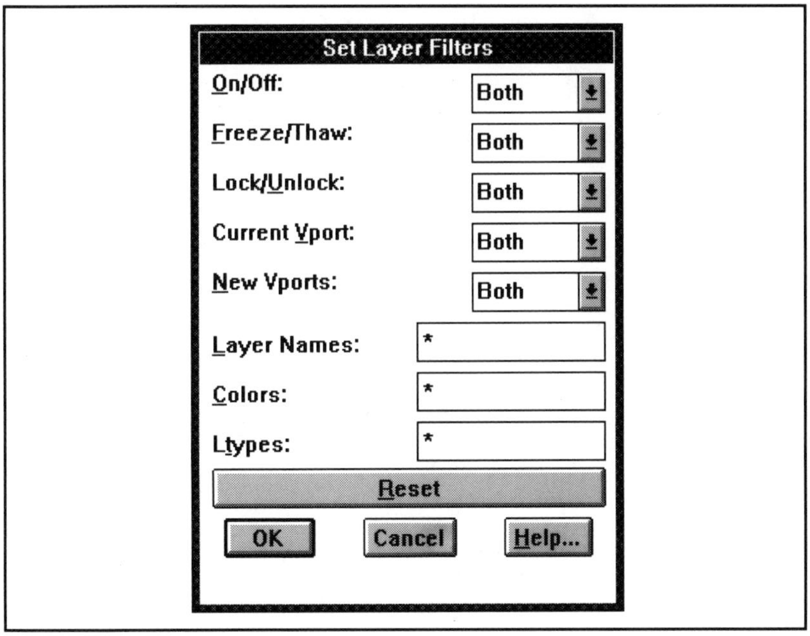

Figure 4.16:   The Filters dialog box

the layers whose names begin with C- will appear in the list of layers. You can then easily turn all these layers off, change their color assignment, or change other settings quickly, without involving other layers you don't want to touch.

The other two input boxes, Colors and Ltypes, let you control what layers appear in the list by virtue of their color or line-type assignments. The five pop-up lists at the top of the dialog box let you display layers in the layer list by virtue of the status: On/Off, Freeze/Thawed, Locked/Unlocked, etc.

As the number of layers grow, you will find this tool indispensable. Also keep in mind the wildcard feature as you name layers: you can use it to group layers and later quickly select those groups to turn on and off.

Now try changing the layer settings again. You can turn off all the layers except Wall and Ceiling and be left with a simple rectangle. In the exercise, you'll get a chance to experiment with the On/Off options of the Layer Control dialog box.

▼ NOTE

If you want to delete all the objects on a layer, you can set the current layer to the one you want to edit, then freeze or lock all the others. Then, from the Root menu, click on Edit ➤ Erase ➤ Select objects ➤ All. See also the discussion of DELLAYER in *Chapter 19.*

Settings ➤ Layer Control: Off

1. Click on Settings ➤ Layer Control.

2. Turn on the Ceiling layer by first clicking on it in the list and then clicking the **On** button.

3. Click on the **Select All** button in the bottom-left corner of the dialog box. The entire list highlights.

4. Click on the Wall and Ceiling layers. They become un-highlighted.

5. Click on the **Off** button in the upper-right corner of the dialog box. Notice that the list changes to show that the layers have been turned off.

6. Click on the **OK** button. A message appears, warning you that the current layer will be turned off. Click **OK**. The drawing appears with only the Wall and Ceiling layers displayed (see Figure 4.17).

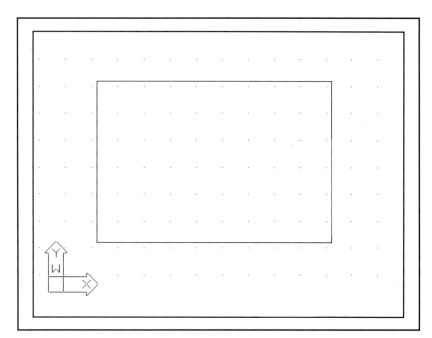

Figure 4.17:   Bathroom with all layers except Wall and Ceiling turned off

7. Open the Layer Control dialog box again, click on the **Select All** button, then click on the **On** button to turn on all the layers at once.

8. Click on the **OK** button to return to the drawing.

ASSIGNING LINE TYPES TO LAYERS

You will often want to use different line types to show hidden lines, center lines, or other noncontinuous lines. You can set a layer to have not only a color assignment but also a line-type assignment. To see how line types work, add a dash-dot line in the bathroom plan to indicate a shower-curtain rod.

The first step in adding a new line type is to load the line type you want. This is done through the Linetype command.

▼

■

■

■

■

Other Layer Options

You may have noticed the *Freeze* and *Thaw* options in the Layer control dialog box. These options are similar to ON and OFF. However, Freeze not only makes layers invisible, it also tells AutoCAD to ignore the contents of those layers when you use the All selection option. Freezing layers can also save time when you issue a command that regenerates a complex drawing. This is because AutoCAD ignores objects on frozen layers during a regen. You will get first-hand experience with Freeze and Thaw in *Chapter 6*.

Another pair of options, *Lock* and *Unlock*, offer a similar function to Freeze and Thaw. If you lock a layer, you will be able to view and snap to objects on that layer, but you won't be able to edit those objects. This feature is useful when you are working on a crowded drawing and you don't want to accidentally edit portions of the drawing. You can lock all the layers except those you intend to edit, then proceed to work without fear of making accidental changes.

Settings ➤ Linetyp ➤ ?, Load

▼ NOTE

AutoCAD stores line type descriptions in an external file named ACAD.LIN. You can edit this file in a word procesor to create new line types or to modify existing ones. You will see how this is done in *Chapter 21*.

1. From the Root menu, click on AutoCAD ➤ SETTINGS ➤ LINETYP ➤ ?. You can also enter LINETYPE ⏎ ? ⏎. The Select Linetype File dialog box appears. Note that the name *ACAD* is highlighted.

2. Click on **OK** to select the default ACAD line-type file. Change the screen to text mode and you will see a listing of the different line types available (see Figure 4.18).

3. Notice the message at the bottom of the screen telling you to press **Return** for more. Press ⏎ to view the rest of the list.

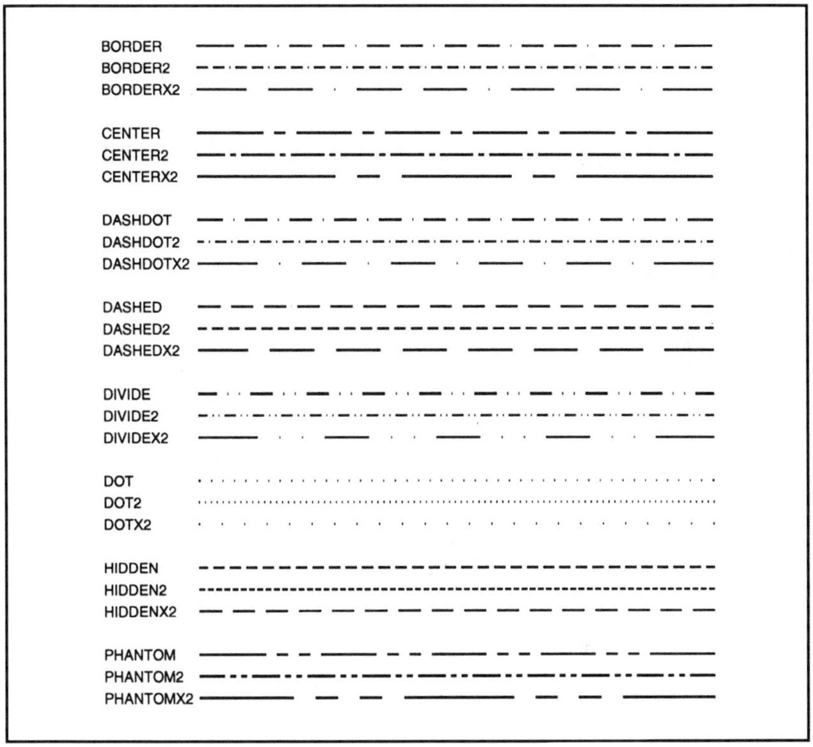

Figure 4.18: The line type listing shown under the Linetype command

▼ NOTE

Be sure the Filedia system variable is set to 1 if you do not see the files dialog box.

4. At the **?/Create/Load/Set:** prompt, click on Load from the side menu or enter **L** ↵.
5. At the **Linetype(s) to load:** prompt, enter **Dashdot** ↵.
6. Again, you will see the Select Linetype File dialog box. Click on **OK**.
7. The message **Linetype DASHDOT loaded** appears in the prompt. Press ↵ to exit the Linetype command.

You used two options in this exercise: the question mark and the Load option. The question mark option appears in many commands. It offers a way to get a list of items to choose from. In the case of the linetype command, you saw a list of available line types. The Load option performed the actual loading of the desired line type. Once a line type is loaded, you are able to assign it to a layer.

Settings ➤ Layer Control ➤ Set Ltype

▼ TIP

If you are in a hurry, you can simultaneously load a line type and assign it to a layer by using the Layer command. Enter **Layer** ↵ at the command prompt, then enter **L** ↵, **dashdot** ↵, **pole** ↵, then enter ↵ to exit the Layer command.

1. Click on Settings ➤ Layer Control.
2. Enter **Pole** in the input box, then click on **New**. Click on the Pole layer from the layer list.
3. Click on the **Set Ltype** button. You will see a listing of the available line types (see Figure 4.19).
4. Double-click on the sample view of the Dashdot line type.

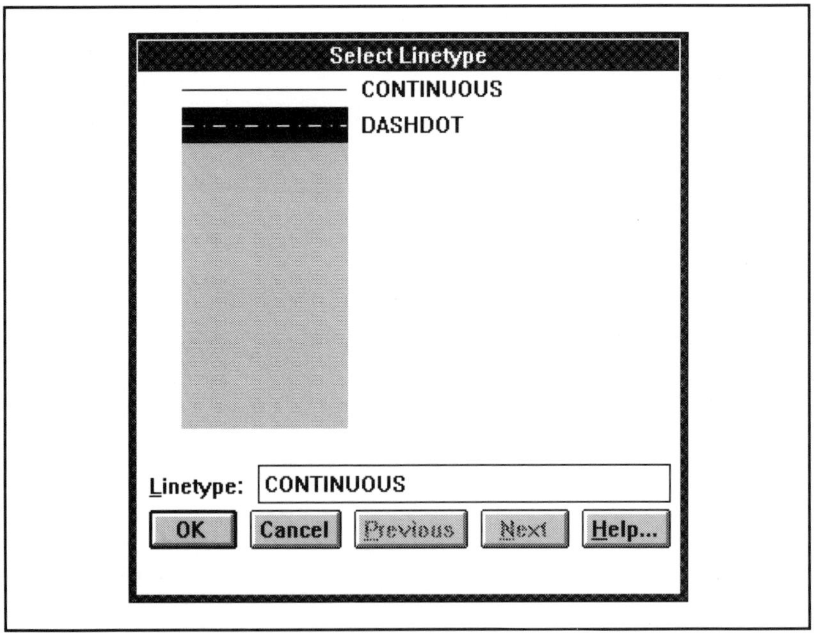

Figure 4.19: The Select Linetype dialog box

5. Make sure the Pole layer is the current default layer by clicking on the **Current** button.

6. Click on the **OK** button to exit the dialog box.

7. Draw a line across the opening of the tub area from coordinate 4'-4", 1'-10" to coordinate 4'-4", 6'-10".

Although this line should have been a dash-dot line, it appears to be solid. If you zoom into a small part of the line, you will see that the line is indeed a dash-dot line.

Since you are working at a scale of 1"=1', you must adjust the scale of your line types accordingly. You do this by using the LTSCALE command.

Settings ➤ Next ➤ Ltscale

1. From the Root menu, click on SETTINGS ➤ next ➤ LTSCALE or enter **Ltscale** ↵.

2. At the **LTSCALE New scale factor <1.0000>** prompt, enter **12** ↵. This is the scale conversion factor for a 1"=1' scale (see *Table 3.3*). The drawing regenerates, and the rod is shown as the line type you want. Your drawing will look like Figure 4.20.

▼ TIP

If you change the line type of a layer or object but the object remains a continuous line, then check the LTSCALE setting. It should be set to your drawing scale factor. If this doesn't work, set VIEWRES (see *Chapter 6*) to a higher value.

AutoCAD comes with 24 line types and also allows you to create your own very easily. Remember that if you assign a line type to a layer, everything you draw on that layer will be of that line type. This includes arcs, polylines, circles, and traces. As we mentioned earlier, you can also assign different colors and line types to individual object, instead of relying on their layer assignment to define color and line type. However, this can create confusion as your drawing becomes more complex. You should assign colors and line types directly to objects until you have some experience with AutoCAD and a good grasp of your drawing's organization.

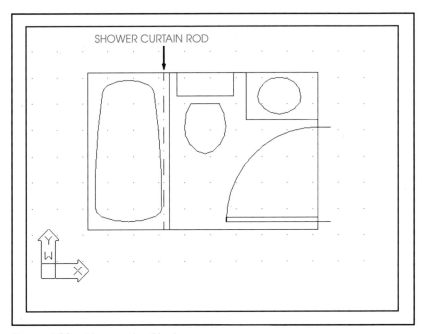

Figure 4.20: The completed bathroom

If the objects you draw appear in a different line type from that of the layer they are on, check the default line type using the Linetype command or use the Set option under the Linetype command to set the default linetype to Bylayer. You can also use the Entity Creations Modes dialog box to set the default linetype.

Before you continue, you must set up an insertion point for the current drawing to facilitate its insertion into other drawings in the future.

AutoCAD ➤ Blocks ➤ Base

1. From the side menu, click on AutoCAD ➤ BLOCKS ➤ *BASE*.

2. At the **Base point <0′-0″,0′-0″>:** prompt, pick the upper-left corner of the bathroom. The bathroom drawing is now complete. Save the drawing before you continue.

▼
■
■
■
■

Understanding
Colors and Line Types

If you prefer, you can set up AutoCAD to assign specific colors and line types to objects, instead of having objects take on the color and line type settings of the layers they are assigned to. Normally, objects are given a default color and line type called *Bylayer*. Bylayer means that an object takes on the color or line type of the layer it is on. You could use the COLOR command to set the current default color to red, for example, instead of Bylayer. Then everything you drew would be red regardless of the current layer color.

Another possible color assignment is Byblock, which you also set with the COLOR command. Byblock makes everything you draw white until you turn your drawing into a block, then insert the block on a layer with an assigned color. The objects then take on the color of that layer. This is similar to the way objects drawn on layer 0 act.

KEEPING TRACK
OF BLOCKS AND LAYERS

The Insert and Layer Control dialog boxes let you view the blocks and layers available in your drawing by listing them in a window. The Layer Control dialog box also includes information on the status of layers. However, you may forget what layer an object resides on. The List command on the Inquiry menu enables you to get information about individual objects as well as blocks.

Assist ➤ Inquiry... ➤ List

1. Click on Assist ➤ Inquiry... ➤ List from the pull-down menu.

2. Click on the tub at the object-selection prompt, then press ↵. The text screen will appear, and you will see not only the

▼ **NOTE**

The Space category you see listed as a property of the tub block refers to whether the object resides in modelspace or paperspace. You'll learn more about these spaces in *Chapter 6*.

layer that the tub is on but its space, insertion point, name, color, line type, rotation angle, and scale.

Eventually, you will want a permanent record of block and layer listings. This is expecially true if you work on drawing files that are being used by others. Here's a way to get a permanent record of the layers and blocks within a drawing.

1. Click on Files ➤ Preferences .... The Preferences dialog box appears (see Figure 4.21).

2. Locate the Log File Open check box in the upper-right corner of the dialog box and click on it. An X should appear in the check box.

3. Click on OK, then at the command prompt enter **LAYER** ↵, then **?** ↵. A listing of all the layers will appear in the prompt area. You can press the F2 function key to view the list.

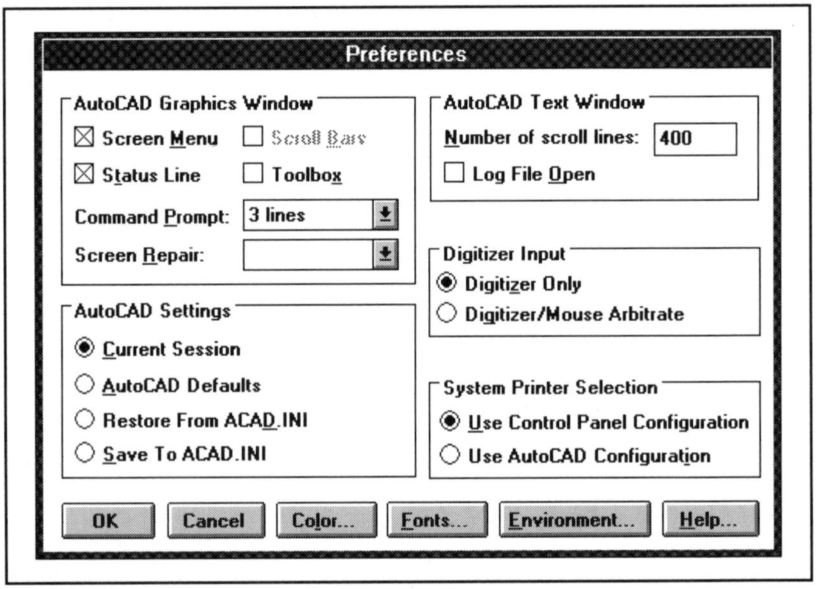

Figure 4.21:   The Preferences dialog box

4. Click on Files ➤ Preferences … to view the Preferences dialog box again, then click on the Log File Open check box to remove the X.

5. Click on OK, then use the Windows Notepad program to open the AutoCAD log file ACAD.LOG located in the \ACADWIN\SUPPORT directory. You will see that the layer listing is recorded there.

Through the Log File Open option, you can record virtually anything that appears in the command prompt. You can even record an entire AutoCAD session. You can then get hard copy of the log file by printing the file from an application like the Notepad or any other word processor. The log file can also be helpful in constructing script files to automate tasks.

If you want to place the log file in a directory other than the default Support subdirectory, click on the Environment button at the bottom of the Preferences dialog box. Another dialog box opens, revealing the environment settings for AutoCAD. You can then set the path and file name for the log file in this dialog box. See Appendix B for more on environment settings.

LOCATING FILES ON YOUR HARD DISK

As your library of symbols and files grows, you may begin to lose track of them. Fortunately, AutoCAD offers a utility that lets you quickly locate a file anywhere in your computer. The Find File utility searches your hard disk for specific files. You can have it search one drive or several, or you can limit the search to one directory. You can limit the search to specific file names or you can use DOS wildcard characters to search for files with similar names. The following exercise steps you through a sample of Find File's use.

1. Click on File ➤ Find File …. The Find File dialog box appears (see Figure 4.22). Toward the top right of the dialog

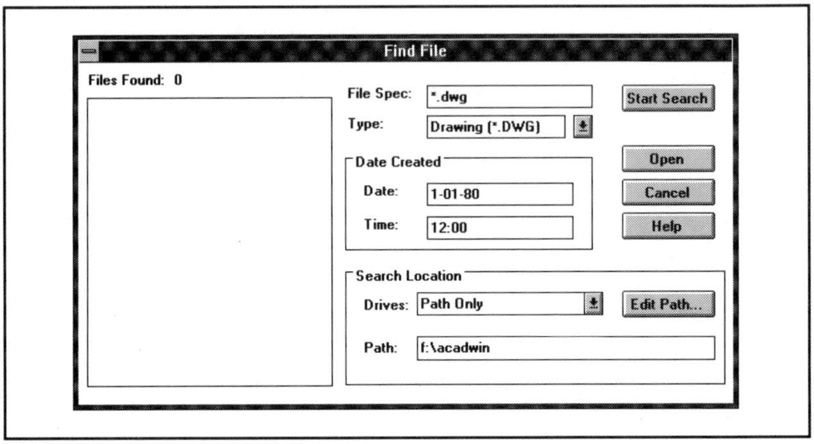

Figure 4.22:   The Find File dialog box

▼ TIP

Find File can also be accessed from any AutoCAD File Dialog box. With the File dialog box open, click on the Find File button.

box is an input box labeled File Spec. This is where you enter the name of the file you wish to search for. The default is .DWG, which will cause Find File to search for all AutoCAD drawing files. Several other input boxes let you set a variety of other search criteria.

2. Click on the Start Search button. In a second, a listing of files that meet the criteria listed in the input boxes appears in the list box to the left. You can click on a file name in the list, then click on the Open button to open the file in the drawing editor.

3. For now, click on Cancel to exit the the Find File dialog box.

In the previous exercise you performed a search using the default settings. These settings caused AutoCAD to search for files with the .DWG extension created after 12.00, January 1, 1980, in the \acadwin directory. The following describes the other options available in the Find File dialog box.

File Spec lets you give specific file name search criteria using DOS wildcard characters.

Type lets you select from a set of standard file types to search.

Date lets you specify a cutoff date.

Time lets you specify a cutoff time.

Drives lets you specify the drives to search.

Path lets you specify a path to search.

Start Search begins the search process.

Open opens the file highlighted in the file list, after a search is performed.

Cancel exits the Find File dialog box.

Help provides information on the use of Find File.

Edit Path ... opens a dialog box that displays a directory tree from which you can select a search path.

INSERTING SYMBOLS WITH DRAG AND DROP

If you prefer to manage your symbols library using the Windows File Manager, or if you prefer to use another third-party file manager to locate and manage your symbols, you'll appreciate AutoCAD's support for *Drag and Drop*. With this feature, you can click and drag a file from the File Manager into the AutoCAD window. AutoCAD will automatically start the Insert command to insert the file. Drag and Drop also works with a variety of other AutoCAD support files. Table 4.1 shows a list of files with which you can use Drag and Drop and the functions associated with them.

▼ TIP

Use the object snap modes you learned about in *Chapter 2* to select the insertion points.

IF YOU WANT TO EXPERIMENT...

If your application is not architecture, you may want to experiment with creating some other types of symbols. You might also start thinking about a layering system that suits your particular needs. Open a new file

Table 4.1: This table shows the file types you can use with the Drag and Drop feature. It also indicates the command issued when you use Drag and Drop with the file.

EXTENSION	COMMAND	FUNCTION
.DXF	Dxfin	Import DXF files
.IGS	Igesin	Import IGES files
.DWG	Insert, Plot	Import or Plot Drawing Files
.TXT	Dtext	Import Texts via Dtext
.LIN	Linetype	Load line types
.MNU, .MNX	Menu	Load menus
.PS	Psin	Import PostScript files
.PSB, .SHP, .SHX	Style	Load Fonts or Shapes
.SCR	Script	Run Script
.LSP	(Load..)	Load AutoLISP routine
.EXE, .EXP	(Xload..)	Load ADS application

called **Mytemp**. In it, create layers named 1 through 8 and assign each layer the color that corresponds to its number. For example, give layer 1 the color 1 (red), layer 2 the color 2 (yellow) and so on. Draw each part shown in Figure 4.23, then turn each part into a file on disk using the WBLOCK command. When WBLOCK prompts you for a file name, use the name indicated for each part in the figure. For the insertion point, also use the points indicated in the figure.

When you are done creating the parts, exit the file using the END command then open a new file. Use View ➤ Layout ➤MVsetup and set up the drawing as an engineering drawing with a scale of $\frac{1}{4}$" = 1" on an 11"×17" sheet. Create the drawing in Figure 4.24 using the INSERT command to place your newly created parts.

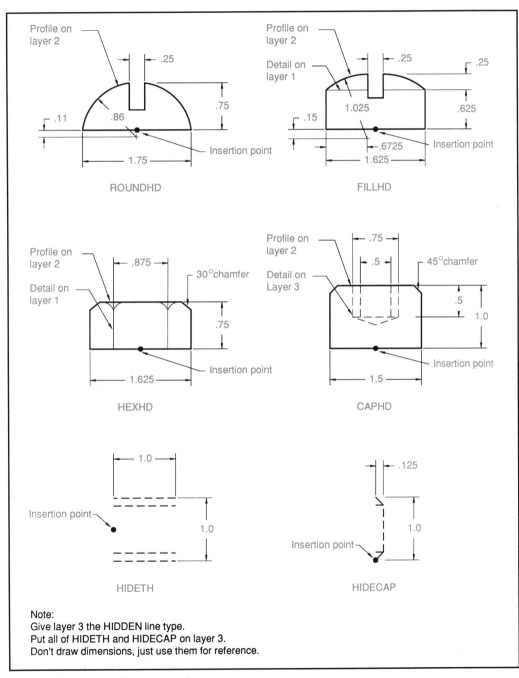

Figure 4.23: A typical set of symbols

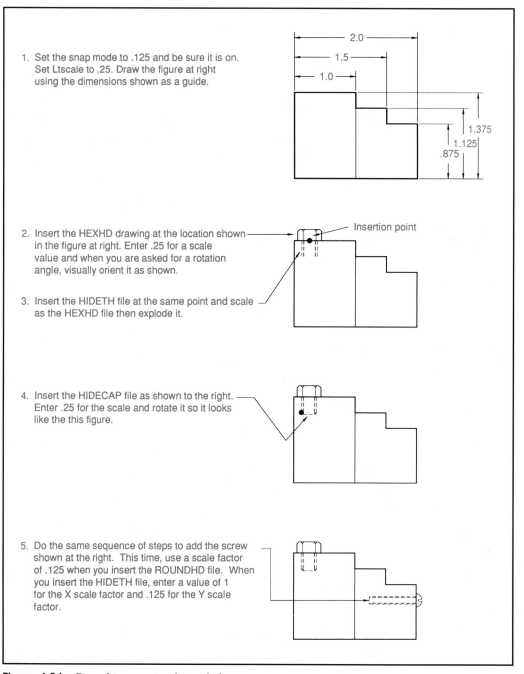

1. Set the snap mode to .125 and be sure it is on. Set Ltscale to .25. Draw the figure at right using the dimensions shown as a guide.

2. Insert the HEXHD drawing at the location shown in the figure at right. Enter .25 for a scale value and when you are asked for a rotation angle, visually orient it as shown.

3. Insert the HIDETH file at the same point and scale as the HEXHD file then explode it.

4. Insert the HIDECAP file as shown to the right. Enter .25 for the scale and rotate it so it looks like the this figure.

5. Do the same sequence of steps to add the screw shown at the right. This time, use a scale factor of .125 when you insert the ROUNDHD file. When you insert the HIDETH file, enter a value of 1 for the X scale factor and .125 for the Y scale factor.

Figure 4.24: Draw this part using the symbols you create.

SUMMARY

Blocks and layers can help you organize your drawing task in ways not possible in manual drawing. In this chapter, you learned some of the ways to use these features effectively.

This concludes *Part I* of *Mastering AutoCAD*. You now have the basic knowledge to create accurate drawings. In *Part II*, you will continue to draw your apartment building and in the process will learn how to use AutoCAD to create larger, more complex drawings. You will also learn how to annotate drawings and how to print or plot them.

PART TWO

DISCOVERING
■
THE
■
AUTOCAD
■
ADVANTAGE

Now that you have the basics down, you can begin to explore some of AutoCAD's more subtle qualities. First, you will look at issues regarding productivity and how to deal with a large drawing file. You will learn how to annotate your drawings and will take your first steps in producing hard copy. Along the way, I will also be giving you tips on drawing with greater precision, on editing, and on solving problems you may encounter as you become more involved with AutoCAD.

5

▼ ▼ ▼ ▼ ▼

EDITING FOR
PRODUCTIVITY

FAST TRACK

169 ► **To use an existing file as a prototype for a new file**

Click on File ➤ New. Make sure the No Prototype check box is un-checked, then enter the name of the prototype file in the prototype file name input box at the top of the dialog box. Click on **OK**.

171 ► **To create a circular pattern of copies**

Click on Construct ➤ Array, select the objects you want to copy, select the polar option, enter the total number of items you want, enter the degrees to fill, then tell AutoCAD whether you want the copies rotated as they are copied or not.

172 ► **To create row and column copies**

Click on Construct ➤ Array, select the objects you want to copy, select the rectangular option, enter the number of horizontal rows and vertical columns you want, then enter the row and column spacing.

180 ► **To create randomly spaced copies**

Click on Construct ➤ Copy, select the objects, enter **M** ↵ then click on the locations where you want the copies. You can also use the move mode of the Grips feature to make multiple random copies.

181 ► **To re-use layers from another drawing**

Insert the drawing containing the layers and other settings you want.

184 ► **To construct walls from existing single lines**

Use the offset command to place parallel copies of lines at wall thick-ness, then use the Fillet command to join lines end to end for corners.

187 ▶ To extend lines to points in space

Draw a construction line pointing in a direction that intersects another line at the desired point in space, then use the FILLET command to join the construction line with the line you want to extend.

190 ▶ To draw an opening in a wall

Draw a line between and perpendicular to the two sides of the wall, preferably at a corner location. Offset the line the distance from the corner to the beginning of the opening. Offset the new line to the width of the opening. Erase the original line. Use the break or trim command to break the wall lines between the two copies of the line.

201 ▶ To locate a cord distance along an arc

Draw a circle with its center at the beginning of the cord location on an arc. Make the circle's radius equal to the cord length. Draw a line from the intersection of the circle and arc to the center of the circle. The line represents the desired cord.

202 ▶ To locate an exact distance along an arc

Set the Pdmode system variable to 3. Click on Construct ➤ Measure then click on the arc near the endpoint you wish to measure from. Enter the distance you want to measure. Xs appear along the arc at the distance specified.

204 ▶ To export a block as a drawing file for use in other drawings

Click on BLOCKS ➤ WBLOCK, enter a name for the new file, then enter the name of the block.

There are at least five commands devoted to duplicating objects, ten if you include the options available under the grips feature. Why so many? If you're an experienced drafter, you know that technical drawing is often tedious, repetitive work. So AutoCAD offers a variety of ways to re-use existing geometry, thereby automating much of the tedious work usually associated with manual drafting.

In this chapter, while you finish drawing the studio apartment unit, you will explore some of the ways to exploit existing files and objects while constructing your drawing. For example, you will use existing files as prototypes for new files, eliminating the need to set up layers, scales, and sheet sizes for similar drawings. With AutoCAD you can also duplicate objects in multiple arrays. You have already seen how to use the Osnap overrides on objects to locate points to draw complex forms. We will look at other ways of using lines to aid your drawing.

And, because you will begin to use ZOOM more, you will review this command as you go along. I'll also introduce you to the PAN command, another tool to help you get around in your drawing.

You're already familiar with many of the commands you will use to draw the apartment unit, so I won't take you through every step of the drawing process. Instead, I will sometimes ask you to copy the drawing from a figure, using the notes and dimensions as guides and putting objects on the indicated layers. If you have trouble remembering a command you've already learned, review the appropriate section of the book.

USING AN EXISTING DRAWING AS A PROTOTYPE

AutoCAD allows you to use an existing drawing as the starting point or *prototype* for a new drawing. A prototype is a file that contains necessary settings or objects for making a drawing. For example, you may want to create a drawing with the same scale and sheet size as an existing drawing. You may even want to use some of the objects, layers, and blocks in it. By using the existing drawing to begin your new one, you can save a lot of time.

CHANGING THE STANDARD AUTOCAD PROTOTYPE DRAWING

▼ **TIP**

If you find most of the default settings unsatisfactory for your application, you can open ACAD.DWG and reset them however you want. Then, leave the No Prototype check box unchecked whenever you create a new file.

You may recall that in the exercises where you created new files, I asked that you make sure the No Prototype check box in the Create New File dialog box had an X in it. This ensures that you are working with the standard AutoCAD settings. (If the No Prototype option is not checked, AutoCAD uses the ACAD.DWG file that comes with AutoCAD, which contains the default settings for modes, text, limits, etc.) AutoCAD copies the ACAD.DWG file, then gives the copy the name you enter for your drawing. When you save your file or exit AutoCAD, the ACAD.DWG file is left untouched.

If you are working on a system with a nonstandard ACAD.DWG template file, and you want to create a file based on the standard AutoCAD file, you can do so by ensuring the No Prototype option is checked.

But you may have several sets of default settings you would like to use. In this case, you can create several empty drawing files, each with its own default settings. One may have layers already set up, while another may have predefined blocks ready to use. Then when you want to use one of these files as a prototype, proceed as if you were opening a new file, then at the Create New File dialog box, make sure the No Prototype option is not checked, then enter the name of the prototype in the input box just above the check box. The following exercise guides you through creating and using a prototype drawing for your studio's kitchenette.

Because the kitchenette will use the same layers, settings, scale, and sheet size as the bathroom drawing, you can use the Bath file as a prototype.

File ➤ New (Use Prototype)

1. First start AutoCAD in the usual way.

2. Click on File ➤ New.

3. If the check box labeled No Prototype is checked, click on it to turn it off.

4. Click on the prototype file input box at the top of the dialog box and type **bath**.

5. Click on the File name input box at the bottom of the dialog box and type **kitchen**.

6. When you are done typing, click on **OK**. The bathroom drawing appears on the screen.

The bathroom drawing now appears in the drawing editor. This does not mean that you have opened the Bath file, however. Because the Kitchen file used the Bath file as a prototype, it contains everything in the Bath file, including objects. You don't need these objects, so erase them. Your new kitchenette file still contains the layers and settings used in the Bath file, and is set up for a 1"=1' drawing on an 8½×11" drawing area.

COPYING AN OBJECT MULTIPLE TIMES

▼ NOTE

An array can be in either a circular pattern called a *polar array* or a matrix of columns and rows called a *rectangular array*.

Now let's explore the tools that let you quickly duplicate objects. First you will draw the gas range top. In the process you will learn how to use the ARRAY command to create *arrays*, or multiple copies of an object, and to control the number and orientation of the copies.

MAKING CIRCULAR COPIES

To start the range top, you will have to first set the layer you want to draw on, then draw a circle representing the edge of one burner.

Draw ➤ Circle ➤ Center, Radius

▼ TIP

You can also enter **C** ↵ at the command prompt to start the Circle command. The Center, Radius options are the defaults for Circle.

1. Set the current layer to Fixture and toggle the snap mode on.

2. Click on Draw ➤ Circle ➤ Center, Radius.

3. At the **3P/2P/TTR/<Center point>:** prompt, pick a point at coordinate 4',4'.

4. At the **Diameter/<Radius>:** prompt, enter **3** ↵. The circle appears.

Now you're ready to use the Array command to draw the burner grill. You will first draw one line representing part of the grill, then use Array to create the copies.

Construct ➤ 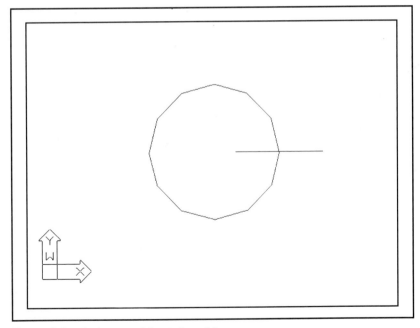 Array (Polar)

1. Draw a line 4" long starting from the coordinate 4'-1", 4'-0" and ending to the right of that point.

2. Zoom into the circle and line to get a better view. Your drawing should look like Figure 5.1.

Figure 5.1:   A close-up of the circle and line

3. Click on Construct ➤ Array.

4. At the **Select objects** prompt, enter **L** ↵ or pick Select Objects ➤ Last from the side menu to select the last object drawn. The line you just drew will highlight.

5. Press ↵ to confirm your selection.

6. At the **Rectangular or Polar array (R/P) <R>** prompt, click on Polar from the side menu or enter **P** ↵.

7. At the **Center point of array** prompt, pick the center of the circle using the Center osnap override. Be sure you click on the circle's circumference.

8. At the **Number of items** prompt, enter **8** ↵. This tells AutoCAD you want seven copies plus the original.

9. At the **Angle to fill (+=ccw,-=cw) <360>:** prompt, press ↵ to accept the default. The default value of 360 tells AutoCAD to copy the objects so that they are spaced evenly over a 360° arc. (If you had instead entered 180°, the lines would be evenly spaced over a 180° arc, filling only half the circle.)

10. At the **Rotate objects as they are copied? <Y>** prompt, press ↵ again to accept the default. The line copies around the center of the circle, rotating as it copies. Your drawing will look like Figure 5.2.

MAKING ROW AND COLUMN COPIES

Now you will draw the other three burners of the gas range by creating a rectangular array from the burner you just drew. You will first zoom back a bit to get a view of a larger area. Then you will proceed with the Array command.

▼ NOTE

If you want to copy in a clockwise (CW) direction, you must enter a minus sign (−) before the number of degrees.

▼ NOTE

In step 10, you can have the line maintain its horizontal orientation as it is copied around by entering **N** ↵. Since you want it to rotate about the array center, accept the default, Y.

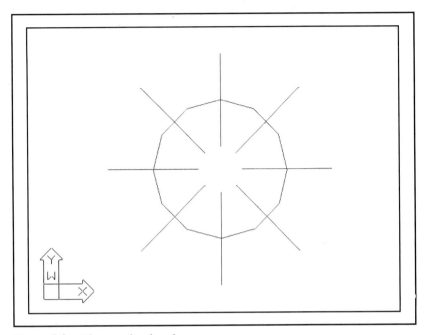

Figure 5.2:   The completed gas burner

Display ➤ Zoom (Out)

1. From the side menu, click on AutoCAD ➤ DISPLAY ➤ ZOOM or enter **Z** ↵ at the command prompt.

2. Enter **.5x** ↵. Your drawing will look like Figure 5.3.

Entering **.5x↵**, tells AutoCAD you want a view that reduces the width of the current view to fill half the display width area, allowing you to see more of the work area. If you specify a value greater than 1–5, for example, you will magnify your current view. If you leave off the x, your new view will be in relation to the drawing limits rather than the current view.

Now you will finish the range top. Here you will get a chance to use the Rectangular Array option to create three additional burners.

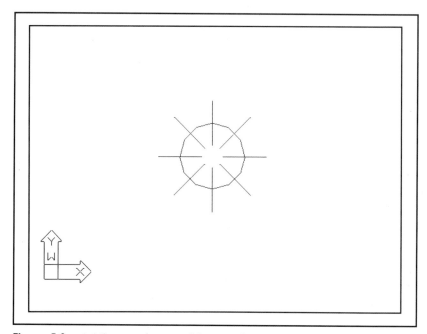

Figure 5.3: A 0.5x magnification of the preceding view

Construct ➤  Array (Rectangular)

1. Click on Construct ➤ Array or enter **ARRAY** ↵ at the command prompt.

2. At the **Select objects** prompt, use the Window selection option to window the entire burner, then press ↵ to confirm your selection.

3. At the **Rectangular or Polar array (R/P) <P>** prompt, click on the *Rectang* option from the Array menu or enter **R** ↵. As I mentioned earlier, a rectangular array is a matrix of columns and rows.

4. At the **Number of rows (----) <1>** prompt, enter **2**↵. This tells AutoCAD the number of copies you want vertically.

5. At the **Number of columns (| | | |) <1>** prompt, enter
   2 ↵ again. This tells AutoCAD the number of copies you
   want horizontally.

6. At the **Unit cell or distance between rows (----)** prompt,
   enter **14** ↵. This tells AutoCAD that the vertical distance
   between the rows of burners is 14".

7. At the **Distance between columns (| | | |)** prompt, enter
   16 ↵ to tell AutoCAD the horizontal distance between the
   columns of burners, 16". Your screen will look like Figure 5.4.

AutoCAD usually draws a rectangular array from bottom to top, and
left to right. You can reverse the direction of the array by giving negative values for the distance between columns and rows.

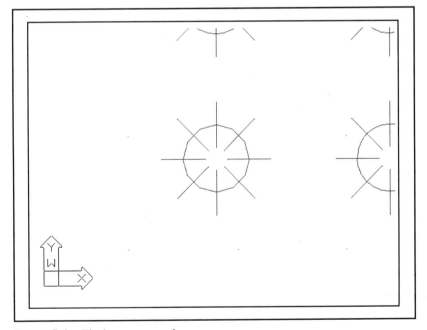

Figure 5.4: The burners arrayed

You can also use the cursor to graphically indicate an *array cell* (see Figure 5.5). An array cell is a rectangle defining the distance between rows and columns. You may want to use this option when an object is available to use as a reference from which to determine column and row distances. For example, you may have drawn a crosshatch pattern like a calendar within which you want to array an object. You could use the intersections of the hatch lines as references to define the array cell, which would be one square in the hatch pattern.

You'll notice that most of your burners do not appear on the display shown in Figure 5.4. You can use the PAN command to move the view over so you can see all the burners. PAN is similar to ZOOM in that it changes your view of the drawing. However, PAN does not alter the magnification of the view the way ZOOM does. Instead it maintains the current magnification while moving your view across the drawing, just as you would pan a camera across a landscape.

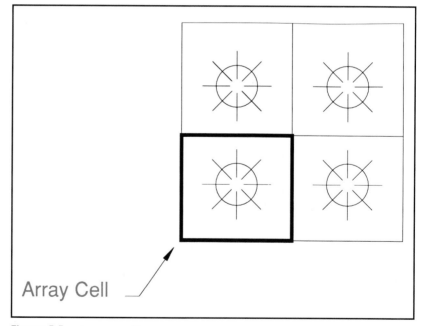

Figure 5.5: An array cell

View ➤ Pan

▼ TIP

You can also enter **P** ↵ at the command prompt to start the Pan command.

1. Click on View ➤ Pan.

2. At the **'PAN Displacement:** prompt, pick a point near co-ordinate 3′-7″, 3′-7″.

3. At the **Second point:** prompt, turn the ortho mode off if it is still on, then move the cursor to the lower-left corner of the screen, as shown in Figure 5.6. The rubber-banding line you see indicates the pan displacement. Pick this point. Your drawing will be panned to the view shown in Figure 5.7.

The burners are still not entirely visible, because the current zoom magnification is too great for you to see the entire range.

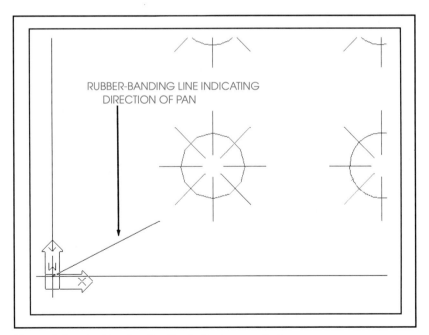

Figure 5.6: A rubber-banding line indicating pan displacement

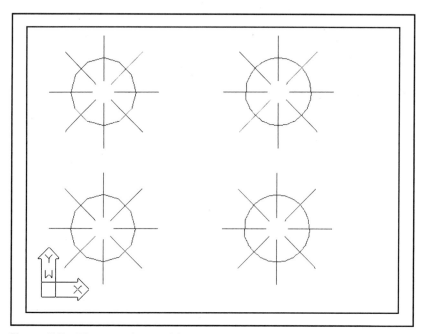

Figure 5.7: The panned view of the gas range

Z ↵ (Zoom Shortcut Key)

1. Enter **Z** ↵.

2. At the **All/Center/Dynamic**... prompt, enter **1** ↵. This has the effect of zooming back out to include an area equivalent to the limits of your drawing.

3. Now complete the kitchenette as indicated in Figure 5.8.

You will be using this drawing as a symbol, inserting it into the overall plan of the studio unit. To facilitate accurate placement of the kitchenette, you will want to change the location of the base point of this drawing to the upper-left corner of the kitchenette. This will then be the "handle" of the drawing.

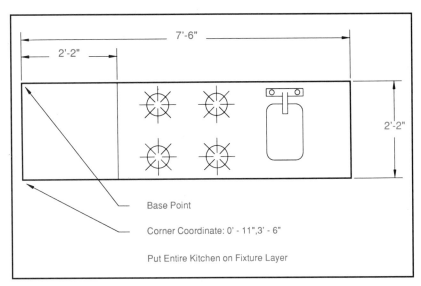

Figure 5.8: Drawing the kitchenette

AutoCAD ➤ Blocks ➤ Base

1. Click on AutoCAD ➤ BLOCKS ➤ BASE or enter **base** ⏎.

2. At the **Base point <1'-10",6'-10",0'-0">** prompt, pick the upper-left corner of the kitchenette as indicated in Figure 5.8. The kitchenette drawing is complete.

3. Click on File ➤ Save.

▼
■
■
■
■

Making Random Multiple Copies

The Array command is useful when you want to make multiple copies in a regular pattern. But what if you need to make copies in a random pattern? You have two alternatives for making copies in a random pattern. The Copy command offers an option for making multiple copies. The Grips feature also lets you make multiple copies under its move mode.

To use the COPY command to make random multiple copies, follow these steps:

1. Click on Construct ➤ Copy.

2. At the **object-selection** prompt, select the objects you want to copy, then press ⏎ to confirm your selections.

3. At the **<Base point or displacement>/Multiple:** prompt, enter **M** ⏎ to select the Multiple option.

4. At the **base point** prompt, select a base point as usual.

5. At the **second point** prompt, select a point for the copy. The copy command prompts you again for a second point, allowing you to make yet another copy of your object.

6. Continue to select points for more copies.

7. Press ⏎ to exit the Copy command when you are done.

To use the Grips feature to make multiple random copies, follow these steps:

1. Preselect the objects you want to copy.

2. Click on a grip point as your Base point. The ****STRETCH**** prompt appears telling you that you are in the stretch mode.

3. Press the right button on your mouse once to change to the move mode. You'll see ****MOVE**** in the prompt.

4. Move the cursor to the location for your copy and, while holding down the **Shift** key, click on the new location. Alternately, you can enter **C** ⏎ to issue the Copy option before you click on the new location.

5. You can then click on other locations for more copies without holding down the **Shift** key.

The Grips feature offers an added level of functionality since you can also rotate, mirror, and stretch copies by pressing the right mouse button.

DEVELOPING YOUR DRAWING

▼ NOTE

As you go through the exercise, observe how the drawings evolve from simple forms to complex, assembled forms.

I mentioned briefly in *Chapter 3* that when using AutoCAD, you first create the most basic forms of your drawing, then refine them. In this section you will create two drawings, the studio apartment unit and the lobby, that demonstrate this process in more detail.

First you will construct a typical studio apartment unit using the drawings you have created thus far. In the process, you will explore the use of lines as reference objects.

You will also further explore how to use existing files as blocks. In *Chapter 4*, you inserted a file into another file. There is no limit to the size or number of files you can insert. As you may have already guessed, you can also *nest* files and blocks—that is, have blocks or files inserted within other blocks or files. Nesting can help reduce your drawing time by allowing you to build one block out of smaller blocks. For example, the door drawing you created can be inserted into the bathroom plan. The bathroom plan can in turn be inserted into the studio unit plan, which also contains doors. Finally the unit plan can be inserted into the overall floor plan for the studio apartment building.

IMPORTING SETTINGS

In this exercise, you will use the Bath file as a prototype for the studio unit plan. However, you must make a few changes to it first. Once the changes are made, you will import the bathroom and thereby import the layers and blocks contained in the bathroom file.

1. First, open the Bath file.

2. Use the BASE command and select the upper-left corner of the bathroom as the new base point for this drawing, so you can position the Bath file more accurately.

3. Save the Bath file.

4. Open a new file called **Unit**. This time, make sure the No Prototype check box is checked.

5. Use Settings ➤ Units Control to set the unit style to Architectural.

6. Use Settings ➤ Limits to set up a ¼"=1'-0" scale, drawing on an 8½×11" sheet. This means your limits should include an area 528" wide by 408" high. If you need help, turn to the instructions for setting up a drawing at the start of *Chapter 3*.

7. Turn the snap mode on and set the grid spacing to 12".

8. Begin the unit by drawing two rectangles, one 14' wide by 24' long, the other 14' wide by 4' long. Place them as shown in Figure 5.9.

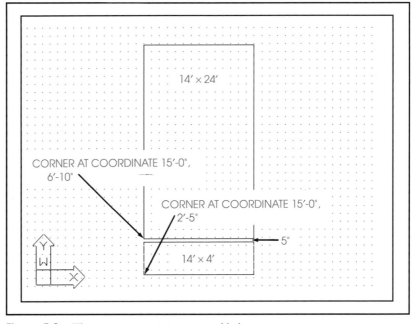

Figure 5.9: The apartment unit interior and balcony

9. Insert the bathroom drawing using the upper-left corner of the unit's interior as the insertion point (see Figure 5.10). You can use the Endpoint Osnap override to accurately place the bathroom. Use a scale factor of 1.0 and a rotation angle of 0°.

10. Use Modify ➤ Change ➤ Properties to change all the lines you drew to the Wall layer.

▼ WARNING

If two drawings contain the same layers and blocks, and one of these drawings is imported into the other, the layer settings and block definitions of the current file will take priority over those of the imported file. This is a point to remember in cases where the layer settings and block definitions are different in the two files.

By inserting the bathroom, you imported the layers and blocks contained in the Bath file. You were then able to move previously drawn objects to the imported layers. You could set up several drawings containing different layering schemes, then insert them into new drawings as a quick way of setting up layers. This method is similar to using an existing drawing as a prototype, but it allows you to start work on a drawing without having to decide which template to use right away.

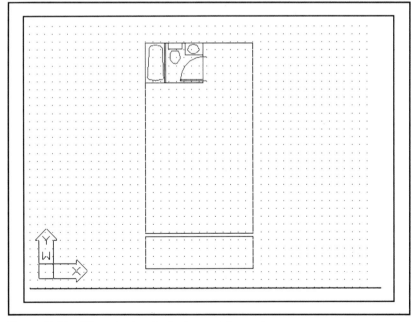

Figure 5.10: The unit after the bathroom is inserted

▼
■
■
■
■

Importing Settings from Cross-Referenced Files

As explained in *Chapter 4*, you can use the XREF command to use another file as a background or cross-referenced file. Cross-referenced files are similar to blocks except that they do not actually become part of the current drawing's database. Settings from the cross-referenced file do not automatically become part of the referencing drawing either. If you want to import layers, line types, text styles, etc., from a cross-referenced file, you must use the XBIND command. XBIND allows you to attach Dimstyle settings, layers, line types, or text styles from a cross-referenced file to the current file.

You can also use XBIND to turn a cross-referenced file into an ordinary block, thereby importing all the new settings contained in that file. See *Chapter 12* for a more detailed description of how to use the XREF and XBIND commands.

USING AND EDITING LINES

The majority of your work involves drawing lines, so it is important to know how to manipulate them to your best advantage. In this section, you will look at some of the more common ways to use and edit these primary drawing objects. The following exercises are intended to show you the process of drawing rather than just how individual commands work.

Roughing In the Line Work

The bathroom you inserted in the last section has only one side of its interior walls drawn (walls are usually shown by double lines). Next you will draw the other side.

1. Zoom into the bathroom so that the entire bathroom and part of the area around it are displayed on the screen, as in Figure 5.11.

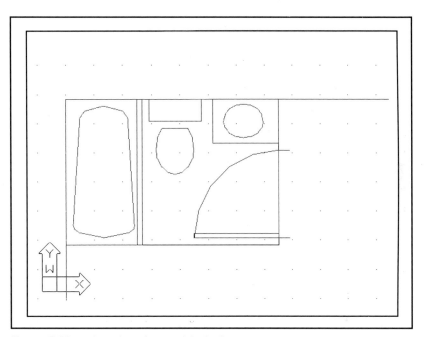

Figure 5.11:   The enlarged view of the bathroom

You may notice that the arcs are not smooth. Don't be alarmed; this is how AutoCAD displays arcs and circles in enlarged views. The arcs will be smooth when they are plotted, or, if you want to see them as they actually are, you can regenerate the drawing clicking on DISPLAY ➤ REGEN from the Root menu. We will look more closely at regeneration in *Chapter* 6.

2. Use Settings ➤ Layer Control to make Wall your current layer.

3. Draw a line from the lower-right corner of the bathroom down a distance of 5". This is only a reference line establishing the thickness of the wall; it will be erased.

4. Continue the line horizontally to the left to slightly cross the left wall of the apartment unit, as in panel 1 of Figure 5.12.

5. Erase the first short line you drew from the corner of the bathroom.

6. Draw another line from the endpoint of the top door jamb near coordinate 22′-11", 29′-2" upward to meet the top wall of the unit. Use the ortho mode and the Perpendicular

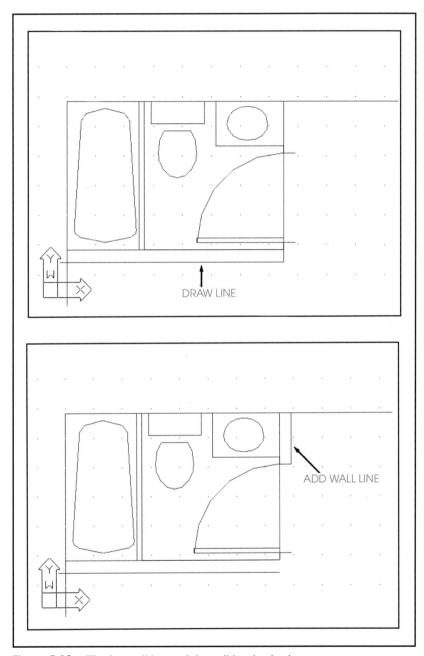

Figure 5.12:   The first wall line and the wall line by the door

▼ TIP

The Perpendicular Osnap override can also be used to draw a line perpendicular to a non-orthogonal line—one at a 45° angle, for instance.

Osnap override to pick the top wall of the unit. This will cause the line to end precisely on the wall line in perpendicular position, as in panel 2 of Figure 5.12.

7. Draw a line connecting the two door jambs. Then change that line to the Ceiling layer.

8. Draw a line 6" downward from the endpoint of the jamb nearest the corner at coordinate 22'-11", 26'-0", as in panel 1 of Figure 5.13.

Cleaning Up the Line Work

You've drawn some of the wall lines, approximating their endpoint locations. Next you will use the Fillet command to join lines exactly end to end.

Construct ➤ ⌐ Fillet

▼ NOTE

CHAMFER is a command that operates in a similar way to Fillet. Unlike FILLET, however, it allows you to join two lines with an intermediate beveled line as opposed to an arc. CHAMFER can be set to join two lines at a corner in exactly the same manner as FILLET.

1. Click on Construct ➤ Fillet.

2. Make sure the fillet radius is zero by using the radius 0 option on the Fillet menu.

3. Fillet the two lines by picking the vertical line at coordinate 22'-11", 25'-7" and the horizontal line at coordinate 22'-0", 25'-5". Your drawing will look like panel 2 of Figure 5.13.

4. Fillet the bottom wall of the bathroom with the left wall of the unit.

5. Fillet the top wall of the unit with the right side wall of the bathroom. Be sure you click on the side of the line you want to retain after fillet has done its work.

6. Use the REDRAW command to refresh the drawing. Your drawing should now look like Figure 5.14.

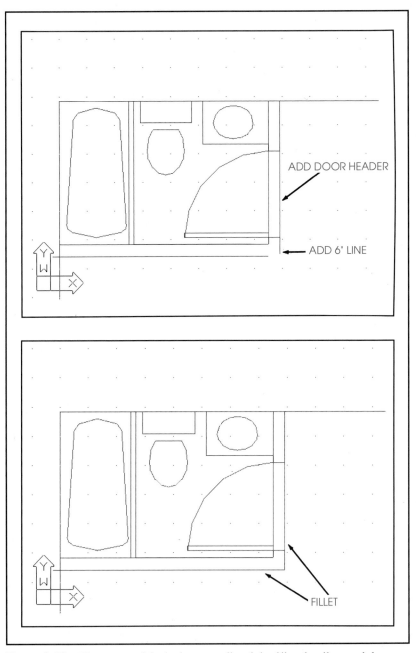

Figure 5.13: The corner of the bathroom wall and the filleted wall around the bathroom

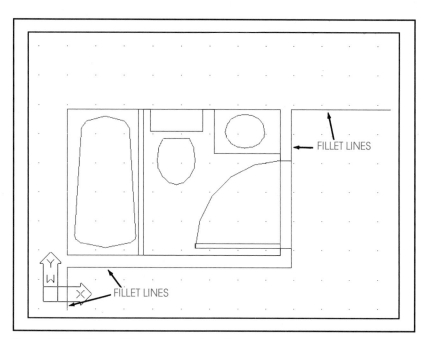

Figure 5.14:   The wall intersections cleaned up

Fillet will join two nonparallel lines exactly end to end. But where you select the lines will affect how the lines are joined. As you select objects for Fillet, the side of the lines you click on is the side that remains when the lines are joined. Figure 5.15 illustrates how Fillet works.

Now let's finish this end of the unit plan.

Draw ➤ 🔲 Insert

Modify ➤ ✳ Break

Construct ➤ 🔲 Offset

1. Use Draw ➤ Insert to place the kitchen drawing at the wall intersection at coordinate 15'-0", 25'-5".

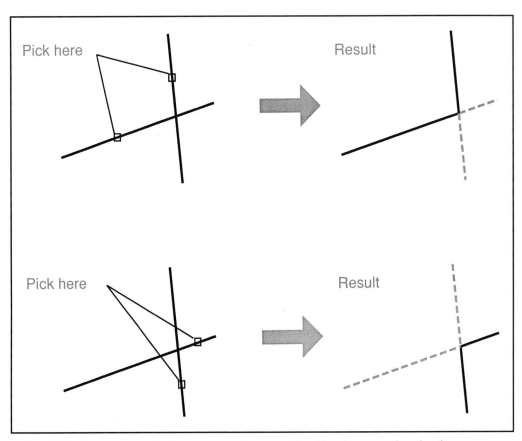

Figure 5.15:   You can control what part of an object gets filleted by where you select the object.

▼ TIP

You can also insert the kitchen roughly where you want it, then move it into position.

2. Press ↵ three times to accept the default x and y scale factors of 1.0 and a rotation angle of 0°.

3. Pan your view so that the upper-right corner of the bathroom is in the center of the drawing area. Your view will look like panel 1 of Figure 5.16.

4. Insert a door on the unit wall at coordinate 23′-4″, 30′- 10″. Then press ↵ twice to accept the default scale factors.

5. At the **Rotation angle** prompt, enter **270** ↵ or use the cursor (make sure the ortho mode is on) to orient the door so that it is swinging into the unit.

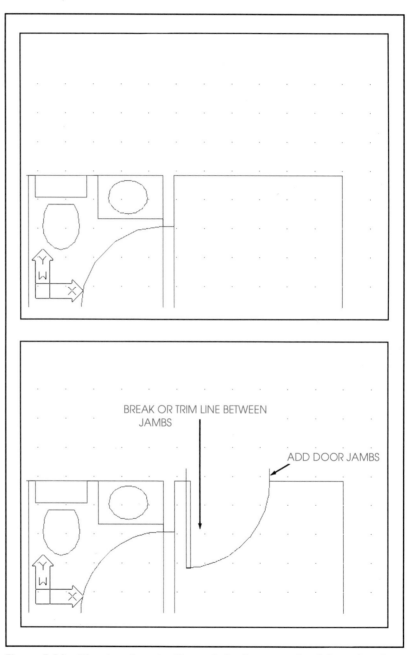

Figure 5.16:   The view after using Pan, with the door inserted and the jamb and header added

▼ NOTE

If you need some help with the BREAK command, see *Modifying an Object* in *Chapter 3*.

6. Make sure the door is on the Door layer.

7. Add 5" door jambs and break the header over the door (see panel 2 of Figure 5.16). Be sure the door jambs are on the Jamb layer.

8. Draw the door header on the Ceiling layer.

9. Use the Offset command to copy the top wall lines of the unit and the door header up 5" so they connect with the top end of the door jamb, as shown in Figure 5.17. Don't forget to include the short wall line from the door to the bathroom wall. Be sure this line is on Wall layer.

10. Save your file.

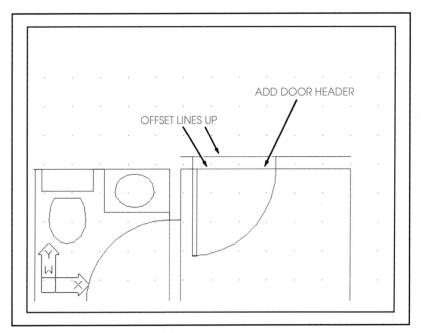

Figure 5.17: The other side of the wall

DRAWING PARALLEL LINES

AutoCAD provides an option to draw double lines that can be used to represent walls. The following exercise explains how it works. You may want to try it out later on your own.

⬛ Dline

▼ NOTE

The double line option is really an AutoLISP application. See *Chapter 21* for more on AutoLISP.

1. Click on Draw ➤ Line ➤ Double Lines. You'll get the message

   Initializing... DLINE loaded.
   Dline, Version 1.11, (c) 1990-1992 by Autodesk, Inc.
   Break/Caps/Dragline/Offset/Snap/Undo/Width/<start point>:

2. Pick on a point to start the double line.

3. Enter **W** ↵ to enter the distance between the double lines, or pick a second point to draw the first segment of the double line, or select an option (see list below).

4. Continue to select points or enter options. By clicking on another line, the double line will automatically join that line and you will exit Dline.

The following describes the options available with the Dline program.

Break	Controls whether the start or endpoint of the double line breaks another line on which the start or endpoint is placed. With this and Snap turned on, this option lets you join double lines in a clean intersection. This is on by default. See **Snap** below.
CAps	Controls whether a cap is placed at the end of a double line.

Dragline	Controls how far off center the double lines are drawn. The default is to make the double lines equidistant from the points you pick. You can adjust the distance to be greater from one side of the pick points or the other, or you can set the pick points to be the location of one side of the double line.
Offset	Lets you specify the start point of the double line relative to another location such as a corner or other wall endpoint.
Snap	Controls whether the start or endpoint of the double line is snapped to an object. With this turned on, Dline will automatically adjust the double line endpoints to align with the object being snapped to. If Break is also turned on, the object being snapped to will be broken between the double lines to form a uniform joint between the double line and the line being snapped to. The Size sub-option of Snap allows you to set the size of the snap area in pixels. Snap is on by default.
Undo	Removes double line segments in reverse order of their creation.
Width	Lets you set the width of the double line.
Arc	Switches from double lines to double arcs. When this option is active, you will also see the Line option appear in the prompt allowing you to return to drawing double lines.
CLose	Closes a sequence of double lines much like the line commands close option.

Using Lines as Tools

Now you need to extend the upper wall line 5" beyond the right-side interior wall of the unit. To accomplish this, you will draw some lines you'll use for layout only.

1. Draw a reference line at a 45° angle from the upper-right corner of the unit at coordinate 29'-0", 30'-10" (see panel 1 of Figure 5.18). The length of this line is not important.

2. Fillet this diagonal line with the wall line you wish to extend, then erase the diagonal line when you are done. Your drawing should look like panel 2 of Figure 5.18.

3. Click on View ➤ Zoom ➤ Previous to view the left side of the unit.

4. Draw another reference line at 135°, then use Fillet to join this line with the wall line (see Figure 5.19).

5. Erase the last reference line you drew.

6. Click on View ➤ Zoom ➤ All to view the entire drawing. Your drawing will look like Figure 5.20.

In this exercise, you used a reference line to help you accurately locate two other lines used for the exterior walls of the Studio unit. This shows you that you can freely use objects to help you construct your drawing.

Now you will finish the balcony by adding a sliding glass door and rail. Again you will be using lines for construction as well as parts of the drawing. First, you will add the door jamb by drawing a short line, then you'll move and copy it into position to locate the door.

▼ TIP

Alternately, you can use the Offset command to make copies of the line in step 3, then erase the original line.

1. Zoom into the balcony area.

2. Draw a line connecting the lower-right corner of the unit's interior to the upper-right corner of the balcony from co-ordinate 29'-0", 6'-5" to 29'- 0", 6'-10".

3. Move that line to the left 3'-6", then copy the line 7'-0" to the left.

4. Change these lines to the Jamb layer.

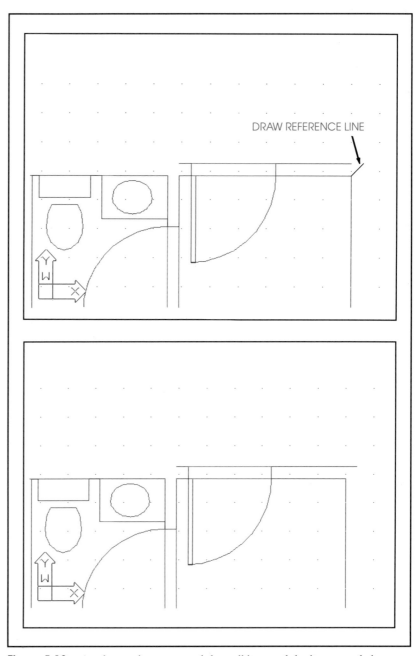

Figure 5.18: A reference line to extend the wall line, and the line extended

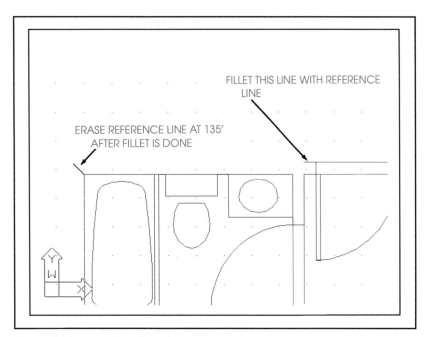

Figure 5.19:   The left-side wall line extended

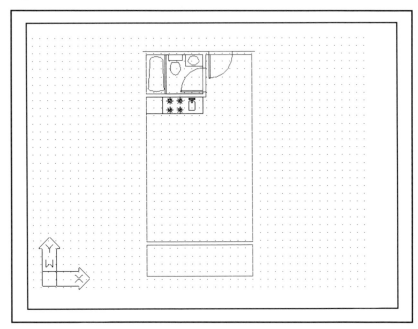

Figure 5.20:   The unit plan thus far

▼ TIP

Break the lines by clicking on Modify ➤ Break ➤ Select objects, 2 points, then pick the line you wish to break. Next, use the osnap overrides to pick the endpoints of the door jambs.

5. Break the wall lines between the two jambs using option in the Break ➤ First menu. Do this for both wall lines. Your drawing will look like Figure 5.21.

6. Add lines on the Ceiling layer to represent the door header.

7. Now draw lines between the two jambs (on the door layer) to indicate a sliding glass door (see Figure 5.22).

The wall facing the balcony is complete. To finish off the unit, you need to show a hand rail and the corners of the balcony wall.

1. Offset the bottom line of the balcony 3" toward the top of the drawing.

2. Create a new layer called **F-rail** and assign this line to it.

3. Add a 5" horizontal line to the lower corners of the balcony as shown in Figure 5.22.

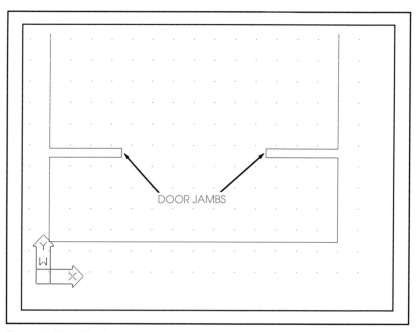

Figure 5.21:   The door opening

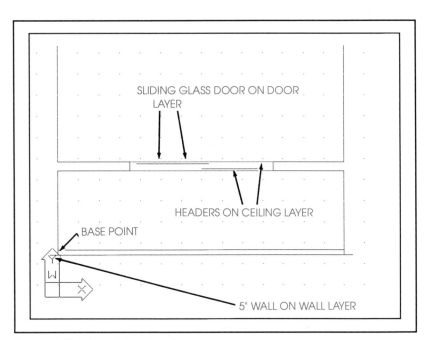

Figure 5.22: The sliding glass door

4. Now use AutoCAD BLOCKS ➤ BASE from the side menu to set the base point at the lower-left corner of the balcony at the coordinates 15', 2'-5".

5. Change the lines indicating walls to the Wall layer and the sliding glass door to the Door layer (see Figure 5.22).

6. Zoom back to the previous view. Your drawing should look like Figure 5.23.

7. Click on File ➤ Save to save the drawing.

Your studio apartment unit plan is now complete. The exercises you've just completed shows you a typical set of operations you'll perform while building your drawings. In fact, nearly 80% of what you will do in AutoCAD is represented here.

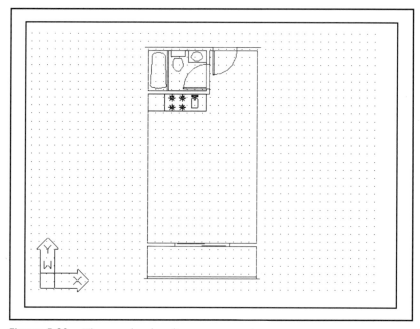

Figure 5.23:   The completed studio apartment unit

Now, to review the drawing process, and to create a drawing you'll use later, draw the apartment house's lobby. As you follow the steps, refer to Figure 5.24.

1. Create a new file called **Lobby** using the Unit file as a prototype.

2. Erase the entire unit.

3. Draw the three main rectangles representing the outlines of the stair shaft, the elevator shaft, and the lobby first.

4. To draw the stairs, offset the left wall of the stair shaft to the right a distance of 4′. This will create the first line representing the steps.

5. Array this line in one row of ten columns using an 11" column spacing.

6. Draw the center line dividing the two flights of stairs.

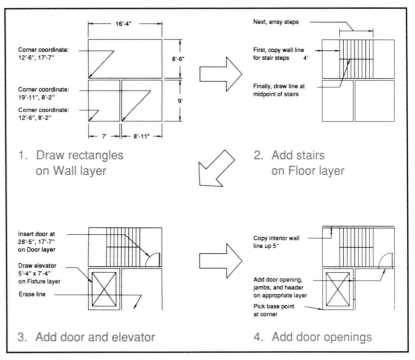

Figure 5.24: Drawing the lobby plan

7. Draw the elevator and insert the door.

8. Draw in the door jambs, and edit the door openings to add the door headers. Your plan should resemble the one in Figure 5.24, panel 4.

9. Once you are finished, save the Lobby file.

FINDING DISTANCES ALONG ARCS

You've seen how you can use lines to help locate objects and geometry in your drawing. But if you need to find distances along a curved object like an arc, lines don't always help. Here are two ways of finding exact distances on arcs. Try these exercises when you're not working through the main tutorial.

At times you need to find the location of a point on an arc that lies at a known distance from another point on the arc. The distance could be described as a cord of the arc, but how do you find the exact cord location?

To find a cord along an arc, do the following:

1. Click on Draw ➤ Circle ➤ Center, Radius, then use the osnap overrides to click on the endpoint of the arc.

2. At the **end of diameter/<radius>** prompt, enter the length of the cord. The point where the circle intersects the arc is the endpoint of the cord distance from the endpoint of the arc (see Figure 5.25).

You can then use the intersect osnap override to select the circle and arc intersection.

To find an exact distance along an arc (non-linear), do the following:

1. Click on Settings ➤ Point Style.

2. At the Point Style dialog box, click on the icon that looks like an X in the top row. Also be sure the Set Size Relative to Screen radio button is selected. Then click on OK.

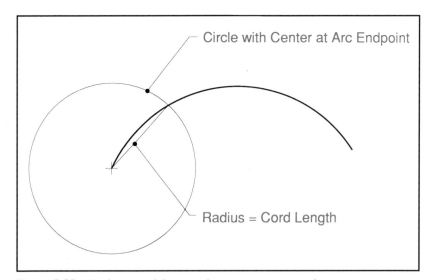

Figure 5.25:   Finding a cord distance along an arc using a circle

▼ TIP

The Block option of the Measure command allows you to specify a block to be inserted at the specified segment length, in place of the **X**s. You are given the option to align the block with the arc as it is inserted. This is similar to the Rotate objects as they are copied option in the Polar Array.

3. Click on Construct ➤ Measure.

4. At the **Select object to measure** prompt, click on the arc near the end from which you wish to find the distance.

5. At the **<Segment length>/Block** prompt, enter the distance you are interested in. A series of Xs appears on the arc, marking off the specified distance along the arc. You can select the exact location of the Xs using the Node osnap override (see Figure 5.26).

The Measure command also works on bézier curves. You'll get a chance to get a more detailed look at the Measure command in *Chapter 13*.

As you work with AutoCAD, you'll find that constructing temporary geometry such as the circle and points in these two examples will help you solve problems in new ways. Don't hesitate to experiment! Remember, you've always got the Save and U commands to help you recover from mistakes.

CREATING A NEW DRAWING USING PARTS FROM ANOTHER DRAWING

You can create a separate stair drawing using the stair you've already drawn for the lobby. Later, you will use the new stair drawing for a fire

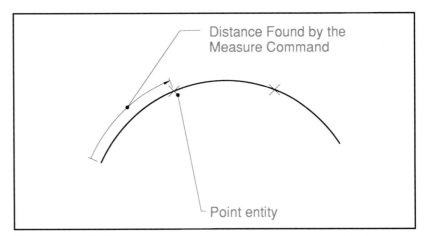

Figure 5.26: Finding an exact distance along an arc using points and the Measure command

escape. To accomplish this, you will use the WBLOCK command you used in *Chapter 4*. Although you haven't turned the stair into a block, you can still use WBLOCK to turn parts of a drawing into a file.

Wblock (Objects)
Oops

1. Click on AutoCAD ➤ BLOCKS ➤ WBLOCK from the root menu.

2. When the Create Drawing File dialog box appears, enter **stair**, then pick **OK**. Alternately, you can pick the Type it box and then enter **stair** at the File name prompt.

3. At the **Block name** prompt, press ↵. By doing this, you are telling AutoCAD that you want to create a file from part of the drawing, rather than a block.

4. At the **Insertion base point:** prompt, pick the lower-right corner of the stair shaft at coordinate 28'-10", 17'-7". This tells AutoCAD the base point for the new drawing.

5. At the **Select objects** prompt, use a window to pick the stair shaft as shown in Figure 5.27.

6. When the stair shaft, including the door, is highlighted, press ↵ to confirm your selection. The stair disappears.

7. Since you want the stair to remain in the lobby drawing, use the OOPS command to bring it back.

GETTING RID OF BLOCKS, LAYERS, LINE TYPES, SHAPES, AND STYLES

A template may contain blocks and layers you don't need in your new file. For example, the lobby you just completed contains the bathroom block because you used the Unit file as a template. Even though you erased this block, it remains in the drawing file's database. It is considered unused because it doesn't appear as part of the drawing. Such

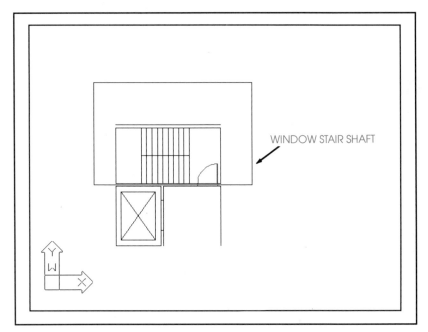

Figure 5.27: A window enclosing the stair shaft

extra blocks can slow you down by increasing the amount of time needed to open the file. They can also unnecessarily increase the size of your file. There are two commands for getting rid of unused elements: PURGE and WBLOCK.

SELECTIVELY REMOVING UNUSED ELEMENTS

The PURGE command is used to remove unused individual blocks, layers, line types, shapes, and text styles from a drawing file. You cannot issue a PURGE command once you do something to change the drawing database. This includes adding, deleting, or changing an object or its location in a drawing. Display commands like Zoom or Pan will not affect the drawing database.

AutoCAD ➤ Utility ➤ Purge

As you can see from the PURGE command prompt, you can purge other unused drawing elements like line types and layers. You should be aware that PURGE will not delete certain primary drawing elements, namely, Layer 0, the continuous line type, and the standard text style.

1. Click on File ➤ Open and open the Lobby file. Remember, you saved this file to disk so now you are simultaneously closing the file, then re-opening the saved version.

2. Click on AutoCAD ➤ UTILITY ➤ PURGE from the Root menu.

3. At the **Purge unused Blocks/Dimstyles/LAyers/LTypes /SHapes/Styles/All:** prompt, click on Blocks from the side menu or enter **B** ↵.

4. At the **Purge block BATH? <N>** prompt, enter **Y** ↵.

5. The **purge block** prompt repeats for each unused block in the file. Continue to enter **Y** ↵ to all the prompts until the PURGE command is completed.

6. Use File ➤ Save to save the file to disk.

The Lobby file is now purged of most, but not all, of the unused blocks. In the next section, you will learn how to delete all the unused elements at once.

REMOVING ALL UNUSED ELEMENTS

Files inserted by using the XREF command do not have to be purged since they never actually become part of the drawing's database.

The PURGE command has its limitations. We already mentioned that PURGE can only be used if you haven't changed the drawing database. PURGE also does not remove nested blocks on its first pass. For example, although you purged the Bath block from the Lobby file, it still contains the Tub and Toilet blocks that were nested in the Bath block. And last, using PURGE is a time-consuming way to delete large numbers of elements.

The WBLOCK command enables you to remove *all* unused elements, including blocks, nested blocks, layers, line types, shapes, and styles, at any time in the editing session. You cannot select specific elements or types of elements to remove. Because a block you want to keep may be unused, you may want to keep a copy of the unpurged file.

AutoCAD ➤ Blocks ➤ Wblock

1. If you've exited the Lobby file, open it again.

2. Click on AutoCAD ➤ BLOCKS ➤ WBLOCK.

3. At the Create Drawing File dialog box or the File name prompt, enter **Lobby1**. This tells AutoCAD to create a new file called Lobby1, which will be the Lobby file with the unused elements removed.

4. At the **Block name** prompt, enter * ↵. This tells AutoCAD that you want to create a new file containing all the drawing elements of the current file, including settings. AutoCAD now saves the current file to the disk, less all the unused blocks, layers, etc.

5. Now open the Lobby1 file and click on Draw ➤ Insert….

6. Click on the **Block** button to get a view of blocks contained in this file. Note that the list shows only the Door block. All the unused blocks have been purged.

Wblock indiscriminately strips a file of all unused elements, so you will want to use this method of purging files with care. Still, WBLOCK offers a quick way of clearing out the deadwood in a file.

IF YOU WANT TO EXPERIMENT...

Try using the techniques you learned in this chapter to create new files. Use the files you created in *Chapter 4* as prototypes to create the symbols shown in Figure 5.28.

SUMMARY

You have seen how you can use existing drawings to help you create new ones in many different ways. By understanding these capabilities, you can save yourself a good deal of time.

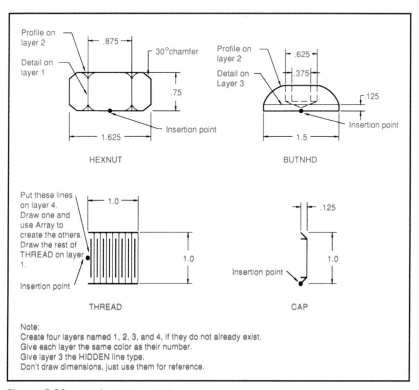

Figure 5.28: Mechanical symbols

As your drawings become more complex, you will have to use different strategies to edit them. In *Chapter* 6, you will assemble the components you have created into a larger file. You will then look at ways to edit and view a file more easily once it becomes very large.

6

▼ ▼ ▼ ▼ ▼

MANAGING
A LARGE
DRAWING

FAST TRACK

216 ▶ To get a quick overall view of your drawing

Click on View ➤ Zoom ➤ Dynamic. You'll get an overall view of your drawing from which you can select a view.

218 ▶ To prevent annoying accidental regens

Click on DISPLAY ➤ RGNAUTO ➤ OFF from the Root menu.

221 ▶ To recall a view

Click on View ➤ Set View ➤ Named View…. Double-click on the name of the view you want to restore.

222 ▶ To quickly save a view that you will want to refer to later

Set up the view you want to save. Type **View** ↵, **S** ↵, then enter a name for the view. No spaces or odd characters are allowed for the name.

225 ▶ To set up a drawing to allow the hiding of sets of objects

Group objects into blocks, then assign the blocks to their own unique layers. Freeze and thaw the block layers to hide their contents or make their contents visible again.

227 ▶ To get to part of a drawing not currently visible while in the middle of another command

Use View ➤ Zoom ➤ Dynamic, View ➤ Pan, or View ➤ Set View options.

230 ▶ To add a hatch pattern to an area

Click on Draw ➤ Hatch, then click on Hatch Options. Click on **Stored Hatch Pattern** to select a pattern from the standard set. Then pick the pattern button and select a pattern. Click on **OK**, then click on Pick Points. Click on a point inside the area to be hatched, near any object that borders the area to be hatched. Click on **Preview Hatch** to preview the pattern, then click on **OK** to accept the location.

235 ▶ To position a hatch pattern accurately

Use the Snapbase system variable to set the origin of the hatch pattern.

239 ▶ To generate a polyline outline of the hatch boundary

Once you've defined a boundary, click on the **Advanced Options** button in the Boundary Hatch dialog box. Click on the **Retain Boundaries** button, then proceed to hatch the selected area.

243 ▶ To globally update blocks

Type **Insert** ↵, then at the **Block name** prompt, enter the block name followed by an equals sign, then the name of the new block or file name. Do not include spaces between the names and the equals sign.

246 ▶ To add a cross-reference file

Click on File ➤ Xref ➤ Attach; then at the dialog box, double-click on the name of the file you wish to add as a cross reference. Answer the rest of the prompts according to your needs.

Now that you have created drawings of a typical apartment unit and the apartment house's lobby and stairs, you can assemble them to complete the first floor of the apartment house. In this chapter, you will learn how to take full advantage of AutoCAD's features to enhance your drawing skills and reduce the time it takes for you to create accurate drawings.

As your drawing becomes larger, you will find yourself using the ZOOM and PAN commands more often. And as the drawing becomes more dense, regenerations will take longer. I'll show you how to take control of regenerations through the careful use of display options.

Larger drawings also require different editing methods. You will learn how to assemble drawings in ways that will save you time and effort as your design progresses. Along the way, you'll learn how you can enhance the appearance of your drawings by adding hatch patterns.

ASSEMBLING THE PARTS

Start by creating a new file for the first floor and inserting and copying the unit file.

▼ NOTE

If you have problems with using your mouse to pick the exact point we specify, enter the values through the keyboard. Or you can move the cursor close to the specified point by using your cursor, then switch to the cursor keys with the snap mode on and close in on the point.

1. Open a new file, called **Plan**, to contain the drawing of the apartment house's first floor. This is the layer on which you will place the Unit Plan.

2. Set the unit style to architectural, then set up the drawing for a ⅛"=1'-0" scale on an 18"×24" drawing area.

3. Create a layer called **Plan1** and make it the current layer.

4. Turn the snap mode on and set the grid to 5'.

5. Insert the unit drawing at coordinate 31'-5", 43'-8". Accept the default values at all the prompts, since you want to insert this drawing just as you drew it.

6. Zoom into the apartment unit plan.

7. Draw a line from the upper-right corner of the unit's interior at coordinate 45'-5", 72'-1" to the right 2.5".

8. Use the endpoint of that line to mirror the unit plan to the right. By mirroring the unit plan at the endpoint of the 2.5"

line, you will get a wall thickness of 5" between studio units. Keep the original unit plan in place. Your drawing should look like Figure 6.1.

9. Now erase the short line you used as a mirror reference and draw another line vertically from the same corner a distance of 24".

10. Use the endpoint of that line to mirror the two unit plans on a horizontal axis.

11. Click on View ➤ Zoom ➤ Extents to get a view of the four plans. Your drawing will look like Figure 6.2.

12. Erase the reference line and copy the four units horizontally a distance of 28'-10", the width of two units.

13. Insert the lobby at coordinate 89'-1", 76'-1".

14. Copy all the unit plans to the right 74'-5", the width of four units plus the width of the lobby.

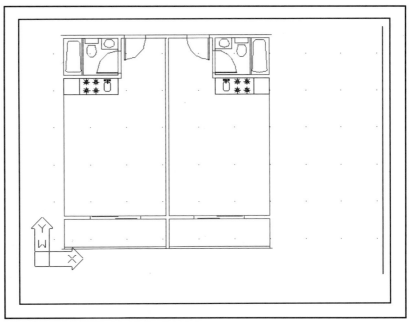

Figure 6.1: The unit plan mirrored

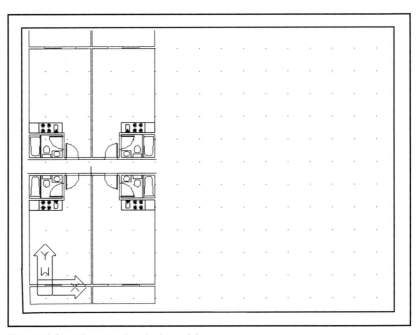

Figure 6.2: The unit plan duplicated four times

15. Click on View ➤ Zoom ➤ All to view the entire drawing. From here on, I will refer to the View ➤ Zoom ➤ All option as the Zoom All command. Your display will look like Figure 6.3.

16. Now use the File ➤ Save option to save this file to disk.

CONTROLLING REGENERATION

You may have noticed that the drawing takes considerably longer to regenerate than it did before. This is because AutoCAD must recalculate more information during commands that regenerate the drawing. In this section, you will discover how to minimize the number of regenerations during an editing session, thus making it easier to create a large and complex drawing. You can control regeneration in three ways: by using the virtual screen to speed up zooming and panning; by saving views to return to without zooming; and by freezing layers that do not need to be viewed or edited.

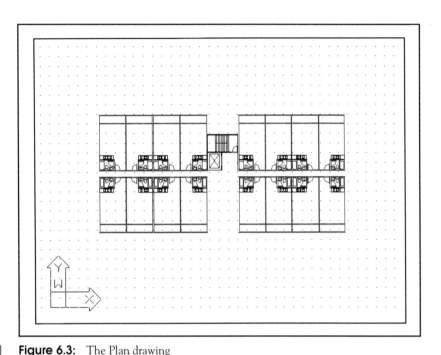

Figure 6.3: The Plan drawing

▼ TIP

If you configure AutoCAD to use AutoCAD's accelerated display driver option, you can use an Aerial View window to get around in your drawing. The Aerial View window is a separate window with scroll bars that shows you the overall view of your drawing, similar to the Dynamic option of the Zoom command. This window allows you to pan and zoom over your drawing while maintaining an overall view. To access this Aerial View window, double click on the compass icon in the toolbar or on the desktop. See *Appendix B* for more on configuring AutoCAD.

USING THE VIRTUAL SCREEN

AutoCAD uses two types of numbers for storing and displaying drawings: floating-point numbers and integers. The drawing database is stored in a floating-point format while the display is modeled using integers. When AutoCAD does a regeneration, it converts the floating-point drawing database into an integer format that is in turn used to generate the display you see on the screen. This integer display format is called the *virtual display*. The virtual display is a computer model of the actual display you see on the screen. AutoCAD can recalculate these integers and therefore the virtual display much faster than the floating-point coordinates when you do zooms and pans. As long as you select view windows within the virtual display area, your zooming speed will be as fast as a redraw.

Redrawing is used to refresh the screen drawing area by clearing blips and restoring any lines that appear to get lost during editing. This can take as little as one-tenth the time of a regeneration. A typical architectural drawing can take a minute or more to regenerate if you are using an Intel 386 or similar computer. At that rate, you can find yourself spending more time waiting for a drawing to regenerate than you spend on actual editing. With this in mind, you can appreciate the speed of redrawing while moving around in your drawing.

The virtual display is on by default. You can turn it off or on by using the VIEWRES command on the DISPLAY menu. This command also controls the smoothness of line types, arcs, and circles when they appear in an enlarged view. With the virtual screen active, line types sometimes appear as continuous even when they are supposed to be dotted or dashed. Also, you may have noticed in previous chapters how arcs appeared to be segmented lines on the screen, though they are always plotted as smooth curves. You can adjust the VIEWRES value to control the number of segments an arc appears to have: the lower the value, the fewer the segments and the faster the redraw and regeneration. However, a low VIEWRES value will cause noncontinuous line types to appear as continuous.

Another way to improve redraw speed is to keep your drawing limits to a minimum area. If the limits are set to an unnecessarily large area, AutoCAD can slow down noticeably. Also, make sure the drawing origin falls within the drawing limits.

The size of the virtual display is roughly determined as three times the most recent regenerated view of the drawing. For example, if a Zoom ➤ All command causes the entire drawing to regenerate, the virtual screen is roughly three times the area defined by the drawing's limits. You can set the virtual screen area to equal three times the limits of the drawing by issuing Zoom ➤ All. The virtual screen is then forced to include an area roughly three times the drawing limits. To help you visualize the virtual screen, do the following.

1. Click on View ➤ Zoom ➤ Dynamic or enter **Z** ↵ **D** ↵ at the command prompt. You will get a display that looks like Figure 6.4.

2. Press the pick button on your mouse. As you move the mouse from left to right, the left side of the view box remains stationary, while the box changes in size. As you move the mouse up and down, the view box also moves up and down. This allows you to determine the window size of your zoom.

You see several boxes surrounding the drawing. The solid white box represents the drawing limits. The dotted box represents the current display area. The corner marks show the virtual screen area. The box that moves with your cursor input is your *view box,* which determines the next view you will select.

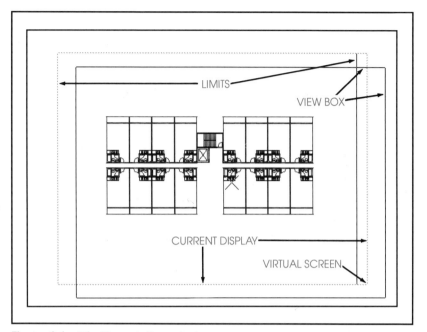

Figure 6.4: The Dynamic Zoom display

The view box maintains its proportion of width to height as you resize it. AutoCAD forces the box to maintain the same proportions as the drawing area, ensuring that the window you pick will be displayed and you don't accidentally cause a regen.

3. Adjust the size of the box to about a quarter of the display area, then press the pick button again. The view box is now smaller and it moves freely as it did before. Now you can pick a view framed by the view box.

4. When you finally decide on a view, press **Return** or the right mouse button to select it. The new view will be displayed.

If your drawing is dense and you are in a hurry, you can approximate a view position with the view box and then, once the view is on the screen, pan to the exact position.

Using Dynamic Zoom is another way to move from one part of the drawing to another without having to do a Zoom All or Zoom Vmax to see the entire drawing. The Dynamic Zoom window does not display the entire drawing very quickly unless the view box is held still. An alternative is to stop the view box movement by lifting your mouse off the desktop until the entire drawing finishes redrawing, then select your view.

SAVING VIEWS

A few walls in the Plan drawing are not complete. You have to zoom into the areas that need work to add the lines, but these areas are spread out over the drawing. You could use the Dynamic option on the ZOOM menu or the Zoom Dynamic (or Dynamic) option on the Display pull-down menu to view each area. Another way to edit widely separated areas is to first save views of the areas you want to work on, then jump from view to view. This technique is especially helpful when you know you will often want to return to a specific area of your drawing.

View ➤ Set View ➤ Name View (New)

1. Click on View ➤ Zoom ➤ All to get an overall view of the plan.

2. Click on View ➤ Set View ➤ Named View. The View Control dialog box appears (see Figure 6.5).

▼

■

■

■

■

Preventing Accidental Regens

Another way to control regeneration is by turning off the REGENAUTO (RGNAUTO) command on the Display menu. If you then use PAN, ZOOM, or another command that can trigger a regen, AutoCAD tells you it is about to regenerate the drawing and asks if you are sure you want to proceed. Some commands that normally regenerate a drawing won't give you a regeneration prompt. When you globally edit attributes, redefine blocks, thaw layers, change the LTSCALE setting, or, in some cases, change a text's style, you must use the REGEN command to display the effects of these commands. If you don't care whether you see the changes, then you won't have to regenerate the drawing. The drawing database is still updated when you save or end the file.

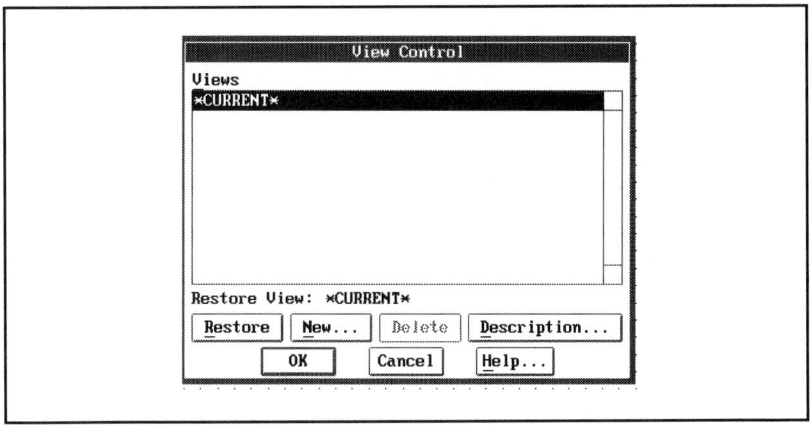

Figure 6.5: The View Control dialog box

▼ NOTE

From this dialog box, you can call up an existing view (Restore), Create a new view (New) or get detailed information about a view (Description...).

3. Click on the **New** button. The Define New View dialog box appears.

4. Click on the button labeled **Define Window**. Notice that the grayed options become solid.

5. Click on **Window<**. The dialog boxes momentarily disappear.

6. At the **First corner** prompt, click on the coordinate 26′-3", 40′-1".

7. At the **Other corner** prompt, click on the coordinate 91′-2", 82′-8". The dialog boxes reappear.

8. Type **1** for the name of the view you just defined.

9. Click on the **Save View** button. The Define New View dialog box closes and you see *first* listed in the View Control list.

10. Repeat steps 3 through 8 to define 5 more views. Using Figure 6.6 as a guide for where to define your windows.

11. Click **OK** when you are done.

You've saved several views. Now let's see how you recall these saved views.

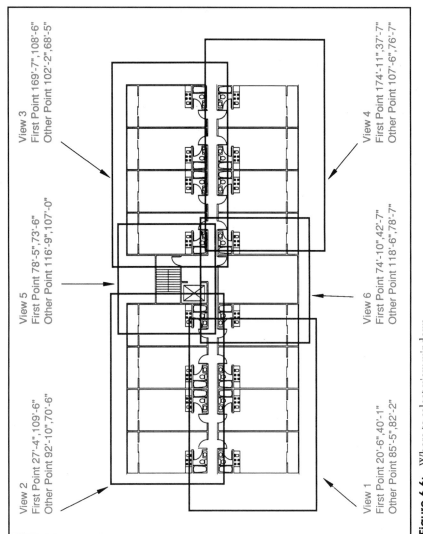

View 3
First Point 169'-7",108'-6"
Other Point 102'-2",68'-5"

View 4
First Point 174'-11",37'-7"
Other Point 107'-6",76'-7"

View 5
First Point 78'-5",73'-6"
Other Point 116'-9",107'-0"

View 6
First Point 74'-10",42'-7"
Other Point 118'-6",78'-7"

View 2
First Point 27'-4",109'-6"
Other Point 92'-10",70'-6"

View 1
First Point 20'-6",40'-1"
Other Point 85'-5",82'-2"

Figure 6.6: Where to select view windows

View ➤ Set View ➤ Named View... ➤ Restore

1. With the View Control dialog box open, click on *first* from the list of views.

2. Click on the **Restore** button then click on **OK**. Your screen displays the first view you selected.

3. Set your current layer to Wall and proceed to add the stairs and exterior walls of the building as shown in Figure 6.7.

4. Use the View Control dialog box again to restore the view named 2. Then add the wall indicated in Figure 6.8.

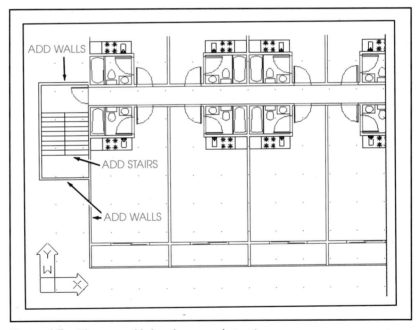

Figure 6.7: The stairs added to the restored view 1

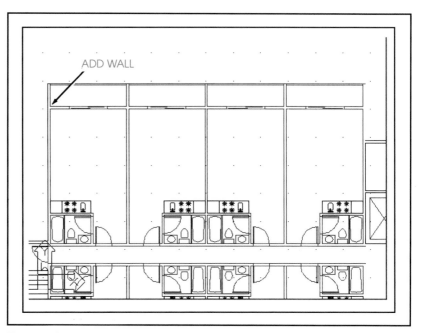

Figure 6.8:   A wall added to the restored view 2

5. Continue to the other views and add the rest of the exterior walls as you have done in these examples. Use Figure 6.9 as a guide to completing the views.

You can also use the keyboard to invoke the View command and avoid all the dialog boxes.

View ↵

1. Click on View ➤ Zoom ➤ All.
2. Enter **View** ↵ at the command prompt.
3. At the **?/Delete/Restore/Save/Window** prompt, enter **S**↵.
4. At the **View name to save** prompt, enter **overall** ↵.
5. Now save the Plan file to disk.

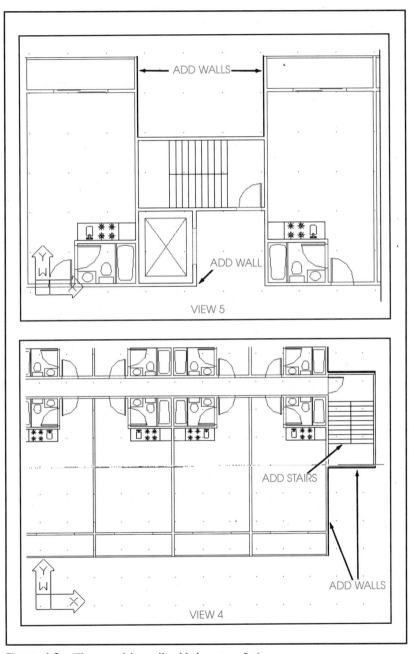

Figure 6.9: The rest of the walls added to views 3–6

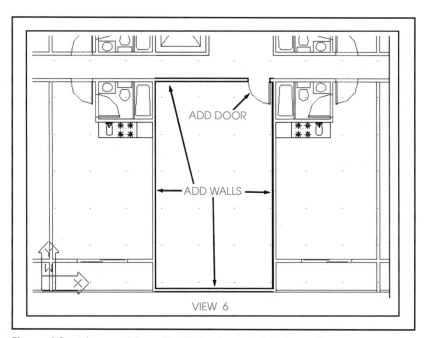

Figure 6.9: The rest of the walls added to views 3–6 (continued)

As you can see, this is a quick way to save a view. I asked you to save this view as *overall* so you can easily recall the overall view at any time. The View ➤ Zoom ➤ Vmax option gives you an overall view, but it may zoom out too far for some purposes.

FREEZING LAYERS TO CONTROL REGENERATION TIME

I mentioned earlier that you may wish to turn certain layers off to plot a drawing containing only selected layers. I also mentioned that the LAYER command's Freeze option acts like its OFF option, except that Freeze causes AutoCAD to ignore frozen layers when regenerating a drawing. By freezing layers that are not needed for reference or editing, you can speed up drawing regenerations.

But Freeze also affects blocks in a way that Off does not, as demonstrated by the following exercise.

Settings ➤ Layer Control ➤ Freeze

1. Turn on all the layers, then turn off the Plan1 layer. Nothing happens because none of the objects were drawn on that layer.

2. Use the Freeze option to freeze the Plan1 layer. Every block you inserted disappears.

Even though none of the objects within those blocks were drawn on layer Plan1, when Plan1 is frozen, so are the blocks assigned to that layer. To help you understand what Freeze does to blocks, I'll use the clear plastic bag analogy again. You may remember that I likened a block function to a plastic bag that holds objects together. You can further think of the bag as an object that is not affected by the Layer commands Off option. In the last exercise, the items inside the bag are assigned to layers independent of the bag's (block's) layer assignment. When you turn off the layer assigned to the bag, nothing happens because the bag is unaffected by the Off option and none of the objects within the bag are on the layer you turned off. However, you can freeze the layer assigned to the bag, causing the bag and its contents to disappear. Figure 6.10 helps you visualize this idea.

Cross-referenced files inserted using the Xref command also act like blocks when it comes to the Freeze option. For example, you can Xref several drawings on different layers. When you want to view a particular drawing, you can freeze all the layers except the one containing that Xref drawing.

You can also put parts of a drawing you may want to plot separately on different layers. For example, three floors in your apartment house plan may contain the same information with some variation from floor to floor. In this case, you can have one layer contain blocks of the objects common to all the floors. Another layer contains the blocks and

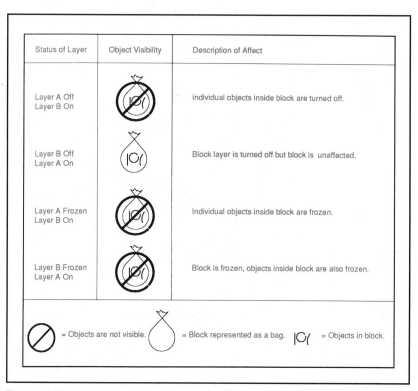

Status of Layer	Object Visibility	Description of Affect
Layer A Off Layer B On		individual objects inside block are turned off.
Layer B Off Layer A On		Block layer is turned off but block is unaffected.
Layer A Frozen Layer B On		Individual objects inside block are frozen.
Layer B Frozen Layer A On		Block is frozen, objects inside block are also frozen.

= Objects are not visible.   = Block represented as a bag.   = Objects in block.

Figure 6.10: A graphic showing the relationship of the Freeze Layer option to blocks

objects specific to the first floor, and yet other layers contain information specific to the second and third floors. When you want to view or plot one floor, you can freeze the layers associated with the others. You will practice this technique in *Chapter 12*.

Using layers and blocks this way requires careful planning and record keeping. It also makes your files quite large, slowing down overall regeneration time and making it difficult to transfer files from your hard disk to floppy disks. If used successfully, however, it can save a great amount of time with drawings that use repetitive objects or that require similar information that can be overlaid.

Now thaw all the layers you froze, turn off the Ceiling layer, and use File ➤ Exit AutoCAD to exit the Plan file. Discard any changes.

Zooming and Panning During Other Commands

At times you may want to do something that requires you to pan beyond the current view while in the middle of another command. For example, suppose you have the view named *first* on the screen and you want to draw a line from the lower-left corner of the building to the upper-right corner. You can start the LINE command, pick the starting point of the line, then click on View ➤ Pan and pan your view so that the upper-right corner of the building appears on the screen. Once the view appears, the LINE command automatically continues and you can pick the other corner. Likewise, you can use the View ➤ Zoom ➤ Dynamic option to zoom or pan over your drawing while in the middle of another command.

This only works within the virtual screen area, however, and you cannot use the All or Extents Zoom options. But you can use the Vmax Zoom option or the View command to get an overall view of the virtual screen area while in another command.

Commands that can be used in the middle of other commands are called *transparent commands*. A handful of standard AutoCAD commands as well as all the system variables are accessible as transparent commands.

▼ NOTE

In modelspace, you can use the VPORTS command to split your screen into several viewports that can be neither plotted nor shaped and controlled individually the way Paperspace viewports can. The VPORTS command only works in Modelspace (see *Chapter 16* for details).

UNDERSTANDING MODELSPACE AND PAPERSPACE

You have the capability to set up multiple views of your drawing called *viewports*. Viewports are accessed by using two modes of display: *Paperspace* and *Modelspace*. To get a clear understanding of these two modes, imagine that your drawing is actually a full-size replica or model of the object you are drawing. Your computer screen constitutes your window into a "room" where this model is being constructed, and the keyboard and mouse are your means of access to this room. You can control your window's position in relation to the object through the use of the PAN and ZOOM commands. You can also construct or modify the model by using drawing and editing commands. This is your *Modelspace*.

So far, you have been working on your drawings by looking through a single "window." Now suppose you suddenly had the ability to step back and add different view windows looking into your Modelspace. The effect would be as if you had several video cameras in your Modelspace "room," each connected to a different monitor: you could view all your windows at once on your computer screen, or enlarge a single window to fill the entire screen. Further, you could control the shape of your windows and easily switch from one window to another. This is what *Paperspace* is like.

Paperspace allows you to set up several views into your drawing's Modelspace. Each view acts like an individual virtual screen. One window can have an overall view of your drawing while another can be a close-up view. Layer visibility can also be controlled individually for each window, allowing you to display different versions of the same area of your drawing if you so choose. You can move, copy, stretch, and even overlap viewports just as you would any object.

If you draw something in Paperspace, it doesn't become part of your Modelspace but it can be plotted. This is significant because, as you will see in *Chapter 12*, Paperspace lets you plot several different views of the same drawing on one sheet of paper. You can even include drawing borders and notes that appear only in Paperspace. In this function, you might think of Paperspace as a kind of page layout area where you can "paste up" different views of your drawing. Figure 6.11 shows the plan drawing set up in Paperspace mode to display several different views.

I will discuss using Paperspace in more detail in *Chapter 12*. For now, let's continue with our look at managing large drawings.

ADDING TEXTURE
TO YOUR DRAWINGS

To help communicate your ideas to others, you will want to add graphic elements that represent types of materials, special regions, or textures. AutoCAD provides hatch patterns that enable you to quickly place a

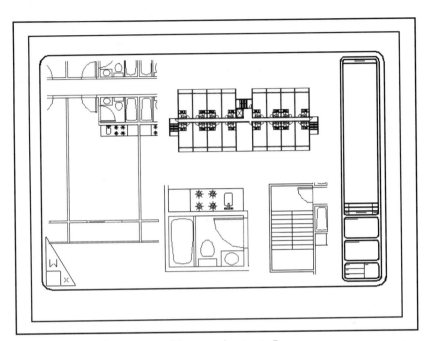

Figure 6.11: Different views of the same drawing in Paperspace

texture over an area of your drawing. In this section, you will add a hatch pattern to the floor of the studio apartment unit. In so doing, you will see how you can quickly enhance the appearance of one drawing. Then later, you'll learn how you can quickly update all the units in the overall floor plan to reflect the changes in the unit.

The first step is to provide a layer for the hatch pattern.

Setting up for the hatch

1. Open the Unit file and zoom into the bathroom and kitchenette area.

2. Create a new layer called **Flr-pat**. Then turn off the Door layer.

3. Make Flr-pat the current layer.

Draw ➤ Hatch...

1. Click on Draw ➤ Hatch. The Boundary Hatch dialog box appears (see Figure 6.12).

2. Click on the **Hatch Options** button. The Hatch Options dialog box appears (see Figure 6.13).

3. Click on the **User-Defined Pattern (U)** button in the Pattern type button group. The Spacing input boxes turn from gray to solid allowing you to enter values. The **User-Defined Pattern** button lets you define a simple cross hatch pattern by specifying the hatch line spacing and whether it is a single hatch or double hatch pattern.

4. Click on the Spacing input box and enter **6**. This tells AutoCAD you want the hatch line spacing to be 6".

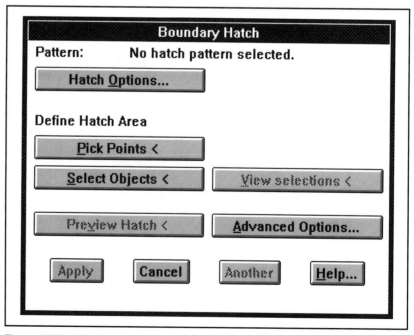

Figure 6.12: The Boundary Hatch dialog box

The Hatch Options dialog box lets you select a hatch pattern from a set of predefined patterns (Stored Hatch Pattern, Pattern), select a pattern that already exists in your drawing (Copy Existing Hatch), or define your own pattern based on a simple cross hatch (User-Defined Pattern). You can also control how the hatch pattern is affected by boundaries using the Hatching Style button group.

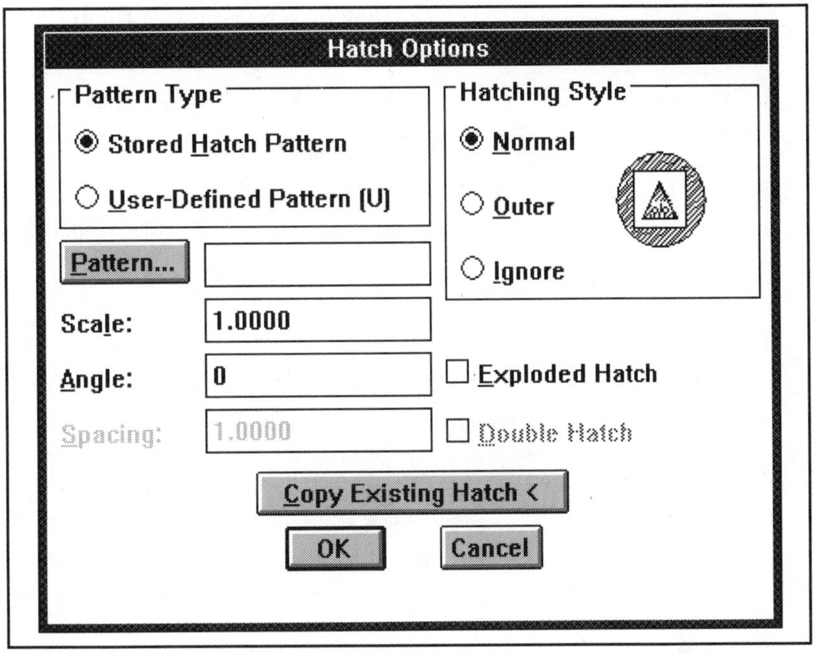

Hatch Options

Pattern Type
- ◉ Stored Hatch Pattern
- ○ User-Defined Pattern (U)

[Pattern...] [   ]

Scale: 1.0000

Angle: 0

Spacing: 1.0000

Hatching Style
- ◉ Normal
- ○ Outer
- ○ Ignore

☐ Exploded Hatch

☐ Double Hatch

[Copy Existing Hatch <]

[OK] [Cancel]

Figure 6.13: The Hatch Options dialog box

5. Click on the Double Hatch check box to the right of the Spacing input box. This tells AutoCAD you want the hatch pattern to run both vertically and horizontally.

6. Click on **OK**.

7. Click on **Pick Points**. The dialog box momentarily disappears, allowing you to pick a point inside the area you want hatched.

8. Click on a point anywhere inside the bathroom floor area away from the toilet. Notice that a highlighted outline appears in the bathroom. This shows you the boundary AutoCAD has selected to enclose the hatch pattern. It outlines everything including the door swing arc. However, it misses the toilet seat.

9. Click on a point inside the toilet seat. The toilet seat is highlighted.

10. Press ⏎. The Boundary Hatch dialog box appears again.

11. Click on **Preview Hatch**. The hatch pattern appears everywhere on the floor.

12. Press ⏎ to return to the hatch dialog box then click on **Apply** to place the hatch pattern in the drawing.

13. Turn the Door layer back on.

Hatch lets you first define the boundary within which you want to place a hatch pattern. You do this by simply clicking on a location inside the boundary area, as in step 8. AutoCAD finds the actual boundary for you. You might have noticed that, in the case of the toilet seat, you also select any area within the main boundary that you want to exclude from hatching. You might think of the toilet seat as a nested boundary area to be excluded from hatching. You can control how AutoCAD treats these nested boundaries using the Hatching Styles button group (see Figure 6.14) in the Hatch Options dialog box.

Here are the Hatch Style buttons and their uses:

    Normal causes the hatch pattern to alternate between nested boundaries. This is the default setting.

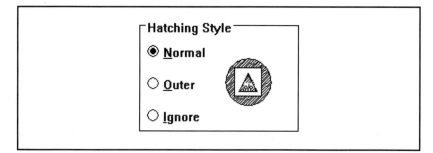

Figure 6.14:   The Hatching Style button group

Outer causes the hatch pattern to hatch an area defined by the outermost boundary and any boundaries nested with the outermost boundary. Any boundaries nested within the nested boundaries will be ignored.

Ignore causes the hatch pattern to hatch the entire area within the outermost boundary, ignoring any nested boundaries.

The graphic to the right of the buttons shows an example of how the selected option affects the hatching of nested boundaries.

Boundary Hatch lets you select sets of boundaries. Each set is hatched independently. For example, in the hatch exercise, you selected the main area to be hatched, then you selected the toilet seat. That was one boundary set. You then selected the **Another** button telling AutoCAD that you were done defining one boundary set and wanted to find another boundary to be hatched separately. You then proceeded to select the area inside the door swing. If you were to select the hatch lines for editing, you would see that the door swing hatch is separate from the Main bathroom floor area. The next section, *Things to Watch out for While Using Boundary Hatch*, describes why you were asked to select the hatch areas the way you did.

THINGS TO WATCH OUT FOR WHILE USING BOUNDARY HATCH

Here are a few tips on using the Boundary Hatch feature:

- Watch out for boundary areas that are part of a very large block. AutoCAD will examine the entire block when defining boundaries. This can take time if the block is quite large. In cases like this, you can use the Ncopy.lsp utility described in *Chapter 20* to copy a portion of a block into the hatch area.

- The Boundary Hatch feature is view dependent; that is, it locates boundaries based on what is in visible in the current

> ▼ NOTE
>
> Hatch patterns are actually blocks and they act like single objects. You can explode a hatch pattern to edit its individual lines. You can also select the Explode Hatch option in the Hatch Options dialog box to automatically explode the hatch after it is placed in the drawing. An exploded hatch pattern, however, will increase the size of your file.

view. To improve Bhatch speed, zoom into the area to be hatched.

■ If the area to be hatched is to cover a very large area, yet require fine detail, you should first outline the hatch area using a polyline (see *Chapter 13* for more on Polylines), then use the Select Objects option to select the polyline boundary manually, instead of depending on Boundary Hatch to find the boundary for you.

■ Consider turning off layers that might interfere with AutoCAD's ability to find a boundary. For example, in the previous exercise, you could have turned off the door layer, then used the Pick Points option to locate the boundary of the hatch pattern.

■ Boundary Hatch works on nested blocks so long as the nested block entities are parallel to the current UCS and are uniformly scaled in the X and Y axis.

Finally, if you need to hatch an area bounded by a distorted block, you can use the standard Hatch command to do it. The following steps describe how to use the Hatch command:

1. Using a Polyline, trace over any boundaries not defined by a block (see *Chapter 13* for more on Polylines).

2. Type **Hatch** ↵ at the command prompt.

3. At the **Pattern (? or name/U,style) <U>:** prompt, enter the name of the pattern you want or **U** to set up a user defined pattern. The U option prompts you for an angle, space between lines, and whether you want double hatching or not. If you enter a hatch pattern name, you are prompted for a scale and angle.

4. At the **Select objects**: prompt, pick the blocks and other objects bounding the hatch area.

POSITIONING HATCH PATTERNS ACCURATELY

In the last exercise, the hatch pattern is placed in the bathroom without regard for the location of the lines that make up the pattern. Most likely, you will want to control where the lines of the pattern are placed.

Hatch patterns use the same origin as the snap origin. By default, this origin is the same as the drawing origin, 0,0. You can change the snap origin and thus the hatch pattern origin by using the *Snapbase* system variable. The following exercise will step you through the process of placing a hatch pattern accurately, using the example of adding floor tile to the kitchenette.

1. Pan your view so that you can see the area below the kitchenette as shown in Figure 6.15.

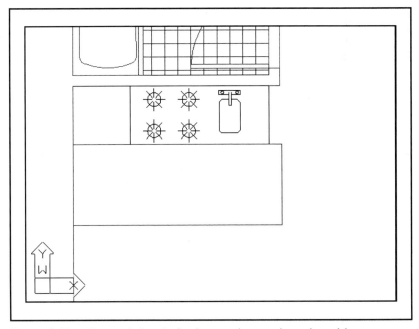

Figure 6.15:   The area below the kitchenette showing the outline of the area

2. Draw the 3′-0″×8′-0″ outline of the floor tile area as shown in Figure 6.15.

3. Type **Snapbase** ↵.

4. At the **New value for SNAPBASE <0′-0″,0′-0″>:,** use the endpoint osnap override and click on the lower-left corner of the area you just defined (see Figure 6.15).

5. Click on Draw ➤ Hatch.

6. At the Boundary Hatch dialog box, click on **Hatch Option**.

7. At the Hatch Option dialog box, click on the button labeled **Stored Hatch Pattern** in the Pattern Type button group, then click on **Pattern**. An icon menu appears showing some sample patterns.

8. Click on the **Next** button at the bottom of the menu, then click on the pattern labeled *AR-PARQ1*.

9. Click on **OK**, then click on **Pick Points**.

10. Click on the interior of the area to be tiled, then press ↵.

11. Click on **Apply**. A Parquet tile pattern appears in the defined area.

12. Now save the Unit file.

Notice that each tile is shown whole; none of the tiles is cut off as in the bathroom example. This is because you used the Snapbase system variable first to set the origin for the hatch pattern. You could now move the snapbase setting back to the 0,0 setting and not affect the hatch pattern.

You got a chance to use a predefined hatch pattern from an Icon menu. Figure 6.16 shows you all the patterns available. You could also create your own custom patterns. *Chapter 21* describes how this is done.

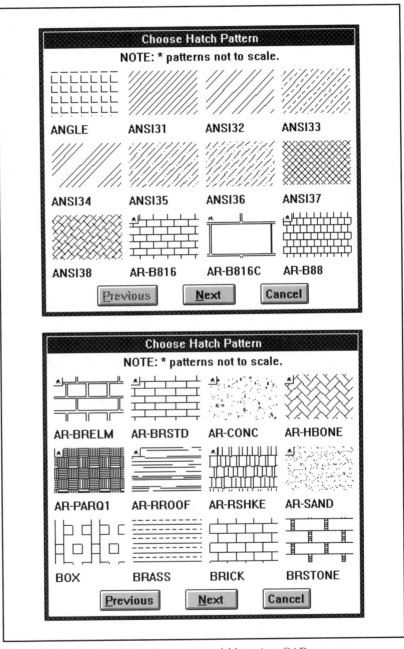

Figure 6.16:   Predefined hatch patterns available in AutoCAD

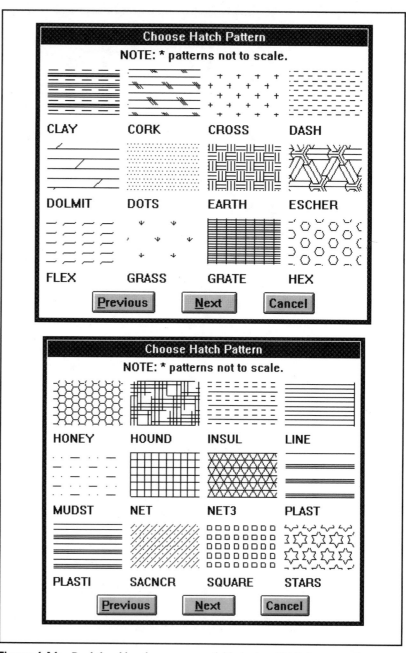

Figure 6.16: Predefined hatch patterns available in AutoCAD (continued)

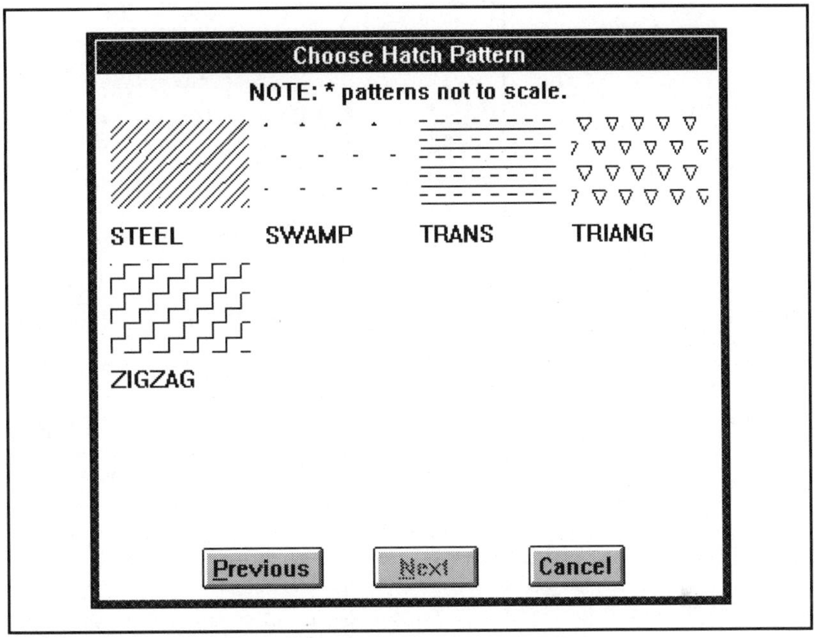

Figure 6.16:   Predefined hatch patterns available in AutoCAD (continued)

UNDERSTANDING THE ADVANCED HATCH OPTIONS

At times, the standard settings for the Boundary Hatch dialog box will not produce the desired hatch boundary. AutoCAD provides the Advanced Options dialog box to help you control how AutoCAD locates hatch boundaries (see Figure 6.17).

The following describes the function of the options in this dialog box:

Make New Boundary Set	Lets you select the objects from which AutoCAD is to determine the hatch boundary. The screen clears and lets you select objects. This option discards previous boundary sets.

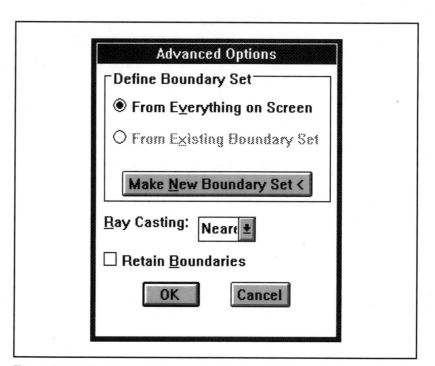

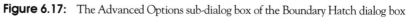

Figure 6.17: The Advanced Options sub-dialog box of the Boundary Hatch dialog box

From Existing Working Set	If you have already used Boundary Hatch to generate a hatch boundary, this option is on by default. It simply indicates that a boundary set already exists and will be used unless the Make New Boundary Set or From Everything on Screen button is selected.
From Everything on Screen	If you haven't already used Boundary Hatch to generate a hatch boundary, this option is on by default. If it isn't already on, clicking on this button creates a new boundary set based on everything visible on the screen. This can take some time if the current view is dense with objects.

Retain Boundaries
The Boundary Hatch command works by creating temporary polyline outlines of the hatch area. These polyline boundaries are automatically removed after the hatch pattern is inserted. If you want to retain the polyline in the drawing, make sure this box is checked. Retaining the boundary can be useful in situations where you know you will be hatching the area more than once, or if you are hatching a fairly complex area. It is also useful if you want to know the area in square inches or feet of a hatched area. This option is only available if a boundary is already defined.

Ray Casting
This is a pop-up list that lets you control how AutoCAD searches for a boundary. The options are Nearest, −X, +X, −Y, and +Y. Nearest is the default. With Nearest selected, AutoCAD searches for a boundary by starting with the object nearest to the point you pick when you use the Pick Points button in the main Boundary Hatch dialog box. The − X options causes AutoCAD to search in negative X direction for the first object in the boundary. The +X options causes AutoCAD to search in a positive X direction. Likewise for the -Y and +Y settings.

SPACE PLANNING AND HATCH PATTERNS

If you are working on a plan where you are constantly moving equipment and furniture, you may be a little hesitant to place a hatch pattern on the floor, because you will have to rehatch the area every time you move a piece of equipment. This situation frequently arises in space planning projects where you are not only designing the layout of equipment and furniture, but also designing the floor covering. You have two options in this situation.

Outlining Your Area and Blocks

The first option is to outline the floor area with a polyline; then, make sure your equipment is also outlined with polylines. Make sure the outlining polylines are on their own layer. Turn off all layers except the layer for the floor pattern and the outlining polylines. Finally, use the hatch command to hatch the floor, making sure the polylines outlining your equipment are included in the boundary set. Whenever you move equipment or furniture, erase the old hatch pattern and repeat the hatch command.

Using 3D Features to Trick AutoCAD

The second option requires the use of some 3D features of AutoCAD. First, draw the equipment at an elevation above the floor level (you can set up AutoCAD to draw objects with a Z coordinate other than 0). Use the 3Dface command to generate a 3D surface that matches the outline of the equipment. Make sure the 3Dfaces are drawn at an elevation that places them between the floor and the equipment. Turn each individual piece of equipment, complete with 3Dface, into individual blocks that you can easily move around. Once this is done, hatch the entire floor, making sure the hatch pattern is at an elevation below the 3Dface elevation (see Figure 6.18).

As you work with the drawing, the floor pattern will show through the equipment. Don't worry. When it is time to plot your drawing, use the Hide option. This causes anything behind the 3Dface to be hidden in the plotter output. This means any hatch pattern underneath your equipment will not appear. You can also use the Hide command (discussed in *Chapter 15*) from time to time, to see what your design will look like without having to wait for hard copy. This method is analogous to using paper cut-outs over a plan.

Using AutoCAD 3D features this way can save you time and give your more flexibility in your work. And while the Hide command takes a minute or two to do its work, it is still faster than rehatching an area each time you move a piece of equipment. For more on the 3D functions mentioned here, see *Part Four* of this book.

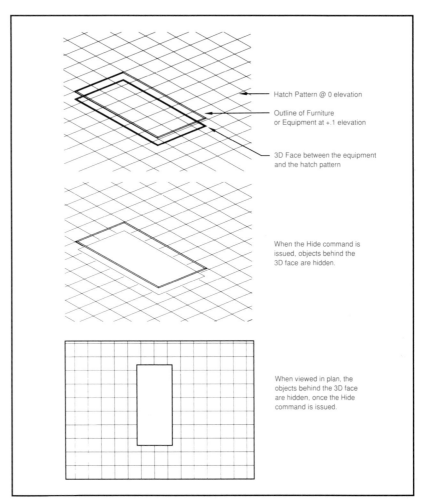

Hatch Pattern @ 0 elevation

Outline of Furniture
or Equipment at +.1 elevation

3D Face between the equipment
and the hatch pattern

When the Hide command is
issued, objects behind the
3D face are hidden.

When viewed in plan, the
objects behind the 3D face
are hidden, once the Hide
command is issued.

Figure 6.18:   Using 3D functions for space planning

UPDATING BLOCKS

As you progress through a design project, you make countless revisions. If you are using traditional drafting methods, revising a drawing like the studio apartment floor plan takes a good deal of time. If the bathroom layout is changed, for example, you have to erase every occurrence of the bathroom and redraw it sixteen times. If you are using AutoCAD, however, revising this drawing can be a very quick operation. The studio unit you just modified can be updated throughout the overall plan drawing by replacing the current Unit block with the updated Unit file. AutoCAD automatically updates all occurrences of the Unit block. In the following exercise, we show you how this is accomplished.

1. Start by opening the Plan file.

2. When the drawing editor appears, press **Ctrl-C** to cancel the initial regeneration.

3. Click on Draw ➤ Insert....

4. Click on the **File** button; then from the Select Drawing File dialog box, double-click on the Unit file name.

5. Click on **OK**. A warning message tells you that a block already exist with the same name as the file. You have the option to cancel the operation or redefine the block in the current drawing.

6. Click on **Redefine**. Your prompt will display a series of messages telling you that AutoCAD is ignoring duplicate blocks. Then, unless you have REGENAUTO turned off, the drawing will regenerate.

7. At the **Insertion point** prompt, press **Ctrl-C**. You do this since you really don't want to insert a Unit plan into your drawing, you are just using the Insert feature to update an existing block.

8. If REGENAUTO is turned off, click on AutoCAD ➤ DISPLAY ➤ REGENALL from the Root menu.

9. Now zoom into one of the units. You will see that the floor tile appears in the unit as you drew it in the Unit file (see Figure 6.19).

▼ WARNING

This method does not update exploded blocks. If you plan to use this method to update parts of a drawing, do not explode the blocks you plan to update. See *Chapter 4* under *Unblocking a Block*.

▼ TIP

You don't have to wait for the drawing to regenerate to edit it, and canceling this regeneration can save some time when you update blocks.

▼ NOTE

If REGENAUTO is turned off, you must use the REGEN command to force a regeneration of the drawing before the updated Unit block will appear on the display, even though the drawing database has been updated.

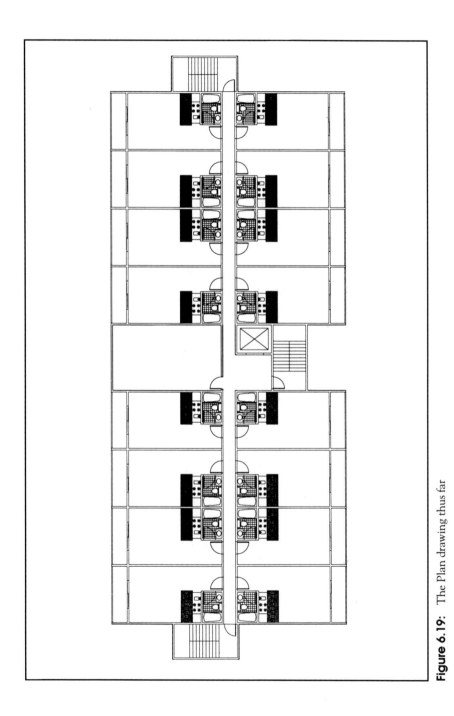

Figure 6.19: The Plan drawing thus far

Nested blocks must be updated independent of the parent block. For example, if you had modified the Toilet block while editing the Unit file, then updated the Unit drawing in the Plan file, the old Toilet block would not have been updated. This is because even though the toilet is part of the Unit file, it is still a unique, independent block in the Plan file and AutoCAD will not modify it unless specifically instructed to do so. In this situation, you must edit the original Toilet file, then update it in both the Plan and Unit file.

Also, block references and layer settings of the current file take priority over those of the imported file. For example, if a file to be imported has layers of the same name as the current file but those layers have different color and line type assignments, then the layer color and line type assignments of the current file will determine the layer color and line types of the imported file. This does not mean, however, that the actual imported file on disk is affected; only the inserted drawing is affected.

CROSS-REFERENCING DRAWINGS

I've mentioned that you can use cross-referenced drawing files in a way similar to blocks. You can use the Xref option on the File menu to access this feature. The difference between files inserted with File ➤ Xref and those inserted with Draw ➤ Insert is that cross-referenced files do not actually become part of the drawing's database. Instead, they are "loaded" along with the current file at start-up time. It is as if AutoCAD were opening several drawings at once, the currently active file you specify when you start AutoCAD, and any file inserted with XREF.

If you keep cross-referenced files independent from the current file, any changes you make to the cross-reference will automatically appear in the current file. You don't have to manually update the cross-referenced file the way you do blocks. For example, if XREF were used to insert the Unit file into the Plan file, and you later made changes to the Unit file, the next time you opened the Plan file you would see the new version of the Unit file in place of the old.

Substituting Blocks

In the example under the section *Updating Blocks*, you updated a block in your Plan file using the File option in the Insert dialog box. In that exercise, both the block name and the file name were the same. You can also replace a block with another block or file of a different name. To do this, you issue the Insert command from the keyboard as follows.

1. Type **Insert** ↵.

2. At the **Block name (or ?) <>:** prompt, enter **unit=***alternate* ↵ where *alternate* is the name of the replacing block or file name. You will get the message *Block unit redefined*, and if Regenauto is turned off, your drawing will regenerate.

3. At the **Insertion point:** prompt, press **Ctrl-C**.

You can use this method of replacing blocks if you would like to see how changing one element of your project can change your design.

You could, for example, draw three different apartment unit plans, each with a different name. You could then generate and plot three different apartment house designs in a fraction of the time it would take you to do it by hand.

You can also use block substitution to reduce a drawing's complexity and speed up regenerations. To do this, you temporarily replace large, complex blocks with schematic versions of those blocks. For example, you could replace the Unit block in the Plan drawing with another drawing that contains just a single line representation of the walls and bathroom fixtures. You would still have the wall lines for reference when inserting other symbols or adding mechanical or electrical information, but the drawing would regenerate much faster. When it came time to do the final plot, you would reinsert the original Unit block showing every detail.

Another advantage to cross-referenced files is that since they do not actually become part of a drawing's database, drawing size is kept to a minimum. This translates to more efficient use of your hard disk space. The next exercise shows how you can use Xref in place of Insert to construct the studio apartment building.

File ➤ Xref ➤ Attach

1. In the Windows File Manager, make a copy of the Unit file and call the copy **Unitxref.DWG**.

2. Open a new file called **Planxref** and set up the drawing for a ⅛"=1′-0" scale on an 11"×17" drawing area.

3. Click on File ➤ Xref ➤ Attach.

4. At the Select File to Attach dialog box, click on the *unitxref* file name. You see the message **Unitxref loaded** in the prompt.

5. At the **Insertion point:** prompt, insert the drawing at co-ordinate 31′-5",43′-8". The rest of the Xref command acts just like the INSERT command.

6. Press ↵ at all the prompts to accept the defaults.

7. Once the Unitxref file appears, make several copies of it in the same way you made copies of the Unit plan in the first part of this chapter.

8. Save the Planxref file then open Unitxref.

9. Erase the hatch pattern for the floors then save the file.

10. Open Planxref again and notice what happens to the Unitxref file you inserted using XREF.

Here you saw how a cross-referenced file doesn't have to be updated the way blocks do. Also, you don't have the problem of having to update nested blocks, since AutoCAD updates nested cross-references as well. There are a few other differences between cross-referenced files and inserted files.

- Any new layers, text styles, or line types brought in with cross-referenced files do not become part of the current file. You must use the XBIND command to import these items.

- If you make changes to the layers of a cross-referenced file, those changes will not be retained when the file is saved unless you set the Visretain system variable to 1. Visretain will then instruct AutoCAD to remember any layer color or visibility settings from one editing session to the next.

- Layers on the cross-referenced file are prefixed with the file's name to segregate those layers from the ones in the current drawing. A vertical bar separates the file name prefix and the layer name, as in *Unitxref | wall.*

- Cross-referenced files cannot be exploded. If you want to make a cross-referenced file a permanent part of your current drawing, you must use the Bind option under the XREF command. This turns the Xref into a block that can be exploded.

- If a cross-referenced file is moved to a different location on your hard disk or if it is renamed, AutoCAD won't be able to find it when it opens other files that the cross-reference is attached to. If this happens, you must use the Path option under the XREF command to tell AutoCAD where to find the cross-referenced file.

XREF files are especially useful in work-group environments where several people are working on the same project. For example, one person might be updating several files that are inserted into a variety of other files. Using blocks, everyone in the work group would have to be notified of the changes and would have to update all the affected blocks in all the drawings that contained them. With XREF, however, the updating is automatic, so there can be no confusion about which files need to have their blocks updated.

There are many other features unique to XREF files. Let's briefly look at some of the other options under the XREF command.

Bind converts a cross-referenced file into a simple block. This is useful if you plan to send a file to someone on a diskette or if you want to explode a cross-referenced file. When using this option, you get the prompt **Xref(s) to bind**. Enter the name of the cross-referenced file or files you wish to convert to a block. Wildcard characters are accepted for multiple file names.

Detach deletes cross-referenced files from the drawing they are imported from; this is equivalent to purging a block. You can specify individual cross-references or indicate all cross-referenced files at once by using an asterisk or other wildcard characters.

Path lets you specify a different path for a cross-referenced file. This is used when a cross-referenced file has been moved from one directory to another and AutoCAD cannot find the cross-referenced file, or if the cross-referenced file's name has been changed.

Reload lets you update a cross-referenced file that has been modified since you opened your current file. This is useful when you are working in a network environment and you know that someone is concurrently editing a cross-referenced file that you need.

▼ TIP

The XREF log file can become quite large. If you find you are running out of disk storage space, you may want to delete any .XLG files you may accumulate as you work.

To aid in housekeeping, AutoCAD maintains a log file that keeps a record of all your XREF activity. The name of the file is the same as the drawing file it is associated with except that the .XLG extension is used. This file stores a record of cross-referenced files and their associated blocks. AutoCAD creates this file automatically if it does not already exist. If it does exist, AutoCAD will append further records of XREF activity.

IF YOU WANT TO EXPERIMENT...

If you'd like to see firsthand how block substitution works, try doing the exercise in Figure 6.20. It shows how quickly you can change the configuration of a drawing by careful use of block substitution. As you work through the exercise, keep in mind that some planning is required to use blocks in this way. If you know that you will have to try different configurations in a drawing, you can plan to set up files to accommodate them.

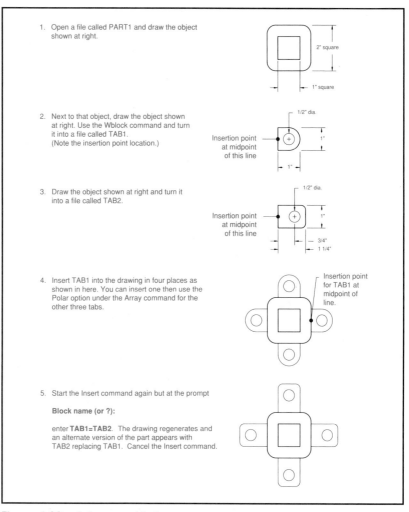

Figure 6.20:   Substituting blocks

You might also try doing the exercise using the XREF command in place of the INSERT command. Once you've attached the cross-reference, try detaching it by using the Xref ➤ Detach option. When you get the prompt **Xref(s) to Detach**, enter the name of the cross-referenced file.

By now, you may be anxious to see how your drawings look on paper. In the next chapter you will learn how to use AutoCAD's printing and plotting commands.

SUMMARY

AutoCAD has a variety of tools to enhance your ability to produce drawings quickly. You've seen how some of these tools work together. You've also seen how you can enhance your work visually through the use of hatch patterns. The tools you learned to use in this chapter will prove to be some of the most useful in your day-to-day work with AutoCAD.

7

▼ ▼ ▼ ▼ ▼

PRINTING
AND
PLOTTING

FAST TRACK

274 ▶ To adjust the location of a plot on the paper

From the Plot dialog box, click on the **Rotation and Origin**... button. At the next dialog box, enter an offset value in the X origin input box, then enter an offset value in the Y origin input box. Use negative values for offsets to the left or down.

275 ▶ To control line weights

From the Plot dialog box, click on **Pen Assignments**, then assign pens of different weight to the different drawing colors by highlighting a color item from the list and entering the new pen assignment in the input box to the right.

279 ▶ To view a plot before you commit it to paper

Click on the Full radio button in the Plot Preview button group, then click on the **Preview** button.

280 ▶ To save your plotter settings for easy retrieval

Click on the Device Default selection in the Plot dialog box, then click on the **Save Defaults to File**... button. At the file dialog box, enter the name you want to save the settings under.

282 ▶ To use AutoCAD as a plot station

Include the **-p** command switch in the Program Item Properties dialog box under the Windows Program Manager File ▶ Properties option.

288 ▶ To plot using a script file

Use the Script command while in AutoCAD.

▼ **NOTE**

For more information on choosing between printers and plotters, see *Appendix A*.

Getting hard copy output from AutoCAD is something of an art. It requires an intimate familiarity with both your output device and the settings available in AutoCAD. You will probably spend a good deal of time experimenting with AutoCAD's plotter settings and your printer or plotter to get your equipment set up just the way you want.

With the huge array of output options available, I can only provide a general discussion of plotting. It is up to you to work out the details and fine-tune the way you and AutoCAD work with your plotter. In this chapter, I'll describe the features available in AutoCAD and discuss some general rules and guidelines to follow while setting up your plots. I'll also discuss alternatives to using a plotter, such as plotter service bureaus and using common dot-matrix printers. There won't be much in the way of a tutorial, so look at the material in this chapter as more of a reference.

PLOTTING THE PLAN

To see first-hand how the Plot command works, try plotting the Plan file.

File ➤ Plot

1. First, be sure your printer or plotter is connected to your computer and is turned on.

2. Start AutoCAD and open the plan file.

3. Click on View ➤ Zoom ➤ All to display the entire drawing.

4. Click on File ➤ Plot. The Plot dialog box appears (see Figure 7.1).

5. Click on **OK**. The dialog box closes and you see the following message:

▼ **NOTE**

The width and height values shown here may vary from your system.

    Command: PLOT Effective plotting area: 10.50 wide by 7.59 high

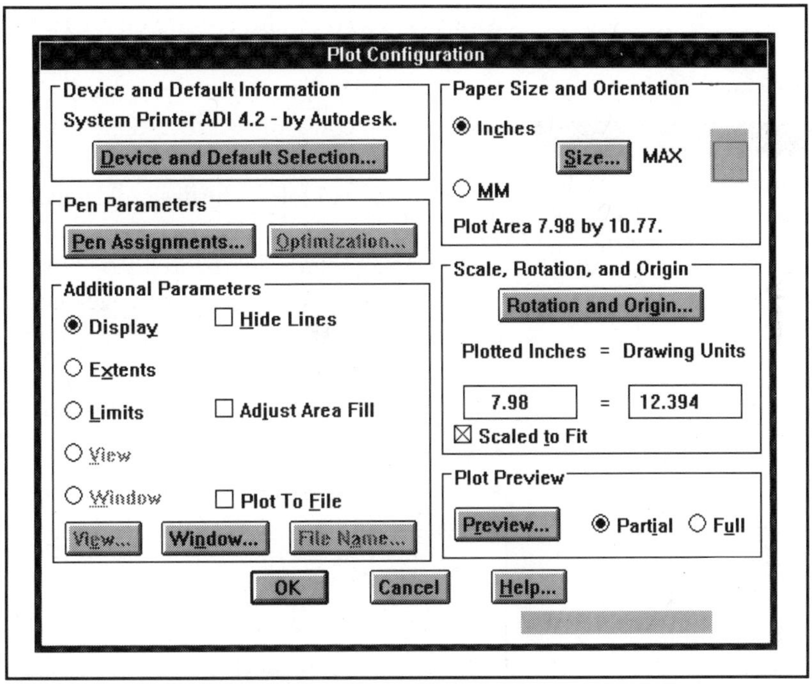

Figure 7.1:   The Plot dialog box

6. Your plotter or printer will print out the plan to no particular scale. When the plot is done you see the message

   Regeneration done 100%
   Plot complete.

   You may see other messages while AutoCAD is plotting.

You've just done your first printout. Now let's take a look at the wealth of settings available when you plot, starting with the selection of an output device.

SELECTING AN OUTPUT DEVICE

Frequently, users will have more than one device for output. You may have a laser printer for your word processed documents in addition to a plotter. You may also require PostScript file output for presentations. AutoCAD offers you the flexibility to use several types of devices quickly and easily.

When you configure AutoCAD, you have the option to specify more than one output device. Once you've configured several printers and plotters, you can select the desired device using the **Device and Default Selection** button. When you click on this button, you will see the Device and Default Selection dialog box (see Figure 7.2).

To select a device, highlight the device name from the list, then click on **OK**. The rest of the Plot Configuration options will reflect the requirements of the chosen device. For this reason, be sure you select the output device you want before you adjust the other plotter settings.

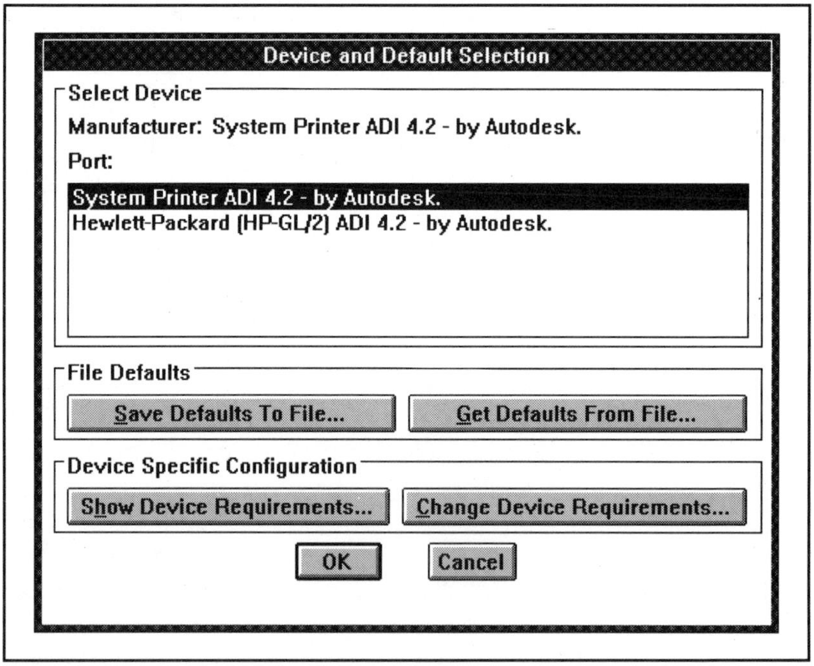

▼ NOTE

The current default device is shown just above the **Device and Default Selection** button.

Figure 7.2: The Device and Default Selection dialog box

▼

■

■

■

■

Using the Windows System Printer

Under Windows, you have even more output options since Windows itself offers you the option to output to a wide range of plotters and printers. If you configure AutoCAD to use the System Printer, AutoCAD will then use the Windows output device. You set the Windows output device through the Printers option of the Windows Control Panel application. Consult your Windows manual for more on the use of output devices and Windows.

UNDERSTANDING YOUR PLOTTER'S LIMITS

If you're familiar with a word processor or desktop publishing program, you know that you can set the margins of a page, thereby telling the program exactly how far from each edge of the paper you want the text to appear. With AutoCAD, you don't have that luxury. To accurately place a plot on your paper, you must know the plotter's *hard clip limits*. The hard clip limits are like built-in margins, beyond which the plotter will not plot. They vary from plotter to plotter (see Figure 7.3).

It is crucial that you know where these limits are on your printer or plotter in order to accurately place your drawings on the sheet. Take some time to study your plotter manual and find out exactly what these hard clip limits are. Then make a record of these limits somewhere in case you or someone else needs to format a sheet in a special way.

Hard clip limits for printers are often dependent on the software that drives them. You may need to consult your printer manual or use the trial-and-error method of plotting several samples and see how they come out.

Once you've established the limits of your plotter or printer, you can begin to lay out your drawings to fit within those limits (see the section *Setting the Output's Origin and Rotation* later in this chapter). You can then establish some standard drawing limits based on your plotter's limits.

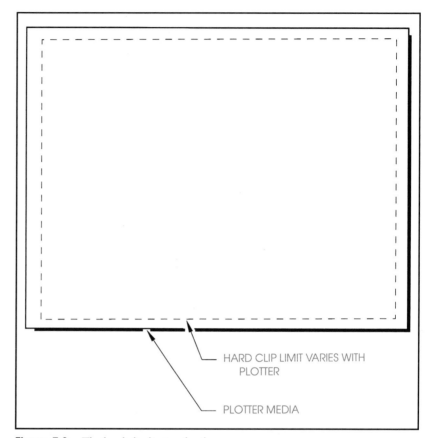

Figure 7.3: The hard clip limits of a plotter.

KNOWING YOUR PLOTTER'S ORIGINS

Another important consideration is the location of your plotter's origin. For example, the Hewlett Packard 7470 and 7475 use the lower-left corner of the plot area as the origin. When plotting a drawing that is too large to fit on a 7475 plotter, the image is pushed toward the top and to the right of the sheet (see Figure 7.4).

The origin determines a point of reference from which you can relate your drawing in the computer to the physical output. Once you understand this, you are better equipped to accurately place your electronic drawing on the physical media.

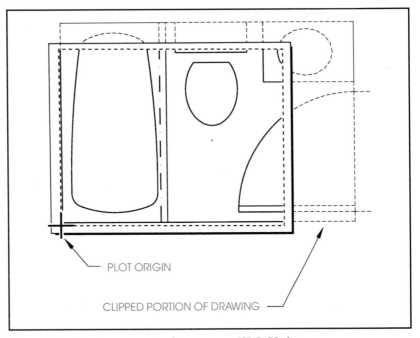

PLOT ORIGIN

CLIPPED PORTION OF DRAWING

Figure 7.4:   Plotting an oversized image on an HP 7475 plotter

These origin placements also apply to plotter-emulation software that allows you to plot to a raster printer using the HPGL or Houston Instrument Graphic Language formats.

SELECTING A PAPER SIZE AND ORIENTATION

▼ TIP

If you need to convert from inches to millimeters, the scale factor is 1" = 25.4 mm.

Next let's look at the Paper Size and Orientation button group. This is where you determine the size media and standard unit of measure you are using. The two radio buttons labeled Inches and MM let you determine the unit of measure you want to work with in the Plot Configuration dialog box. This is the unit of measure you will use when specifying sheet sizes and view location on the sheet. If you choose MM, sheet sizes are shown in millimeters and you must specify distances and scales in millimeters for other options.

Once you've chosen a unit of measure, you can click on the Size button to select a sheet size. The Paper Size and Orientation dialog box appears (see Figure 7.5).

The range of sheet sizes will vary, depending on what plotter you have selected in the Device and Default selection option (described later). To select a sheet size, you simply highlight it, then click on **OK**. Optionally, you can enter a non-standard sheet size in the input boxes to the right. As you can see, you can store up to five custom sheet sizes.

Toward the bottom right, you can use the Portrait and Landscape radio buttons to set the sheet orientation in the plotter (landscape is wide and portrait is tall).

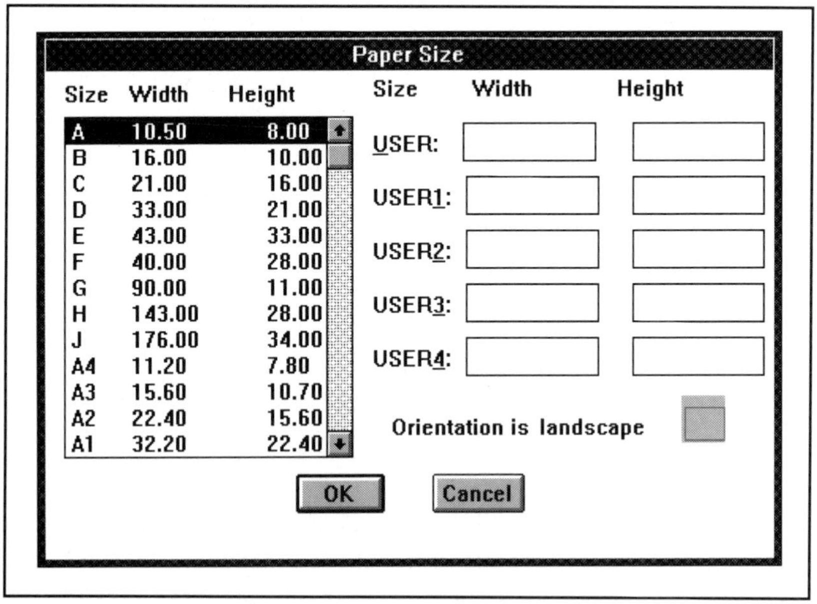

Figure 7.5: The Paper Size and Orientation dialog box

CONTROLLING THE APPEARANCE OF OUTPUT

On the left side of the Plot Configuration dialog box, you see the Additional Parameters button group. These buttons give you the most control over the appearance of your plot. From here, you can control what gets plotted and how.

CONTROLLING HIDDEN LINES, FILLS, AND REDIRECTING OUTPUT

Let's start by looking at the three check boxes down the right side of this group. Using these check boxes, you can tell AutoCAD to store the plot in a file on disk, instead of sending the plot data to a plotter or printer for immediate output. You can specify whether to plot a 3D drawing with hidden lines removed, or whether your plotter is to compensate for pen widths when drawing solid fills.

Hide Lines

The Hide Lines check box is generally only used for 3D images. When this is checked, AutoCAD will perform a hidden line removal on the drawing as it plots. This option will add a minute or two to your plotting time.

Adjust Area Fill

This option tells AutoCAD to compensate for pen width around the edges of a solid filled area in order to maintain dimensional accuracy of the plot. To understand this feature, you need to understand how most plotters draw solid areas.

Plotters draw solid fills by first outlining the fill area, then crosshatching the area with a series of lines, much as you would do by hand. For example, if a solid filled area is drawn at a width of 0.090", the plotter will outline the area using the edge of the outline as the center line for the pen, then proceed to fill the area with a cross-hatch motion. Unfortunately, by using the outline as the center line for the pen, the solid fill's actual width is 0.090" plus the width of the pen. If you check the Adjust Area Fill box, AutoCAD pulls in the outline of the solid area half the pen width. AutoCAD uses the pen width setting you enter under the Pen Assignments dialog box (described later in this chapter) to determine the amount of offset to use. Figure 7.6 illustrates what Adjust Area Fill does.

Plot to File

This option enables you to divert your printout to a file on disk and print it later. This can be useful if you are in an office that must share a plotter between several CAD stations. When the plotter is busy, plot to a file, then later download the plot file to your plotter when it is available.

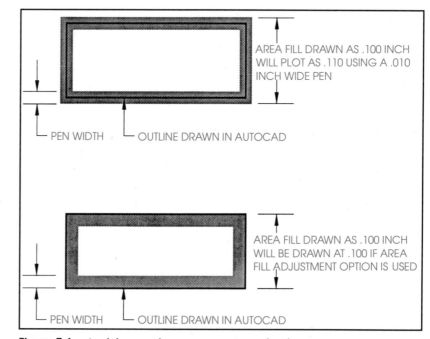

Figure 7.6: A solid area without compensation and with compensation

To use this option, do the following:

1. First click on the check box next to the Plot to file label.

2. Next click on the **File Name** button. The Create Plot File dialog box appears. This is the same dialog box used for most other file operations.

3. Enter the name for your plot file. Or if you prefer, you can accept the default plot file name, which is usually the same name as the current file. The .PLT file name extension is the default.

4. Click on **OK** to accept the file name.

If you don't use the Create Plot File dialog box to specify a plot file name, AutoCAD will create a plot file using the Drawing file name and the .PLT extension.

DETERMINING WHAT TO PRINT

The radio buttons to the left of the Additional Parameters button group let you specify which part of your drawing you wish to plot. You might notice some similarities between the Zoom command options and these settings.

Display

The default radio button option, Display, tells AutoCAD to plot what is currently displayed on the screen (see Figure 7.7). If you let AutoCAD fit the drawing onto the sheet, the plot will display exactly the same thing that you see on your screen.

Extents

The Extents option draws the entire drawing, eliminating any space that may border the drawing (see Figure 7.8). If you let AutoCAD fit the drawing onto the sheet using the Scale to Fit check box, the plot will display exactly the same thing that you would see on the screen had you clicked on View ➤ Zoom ➤ Extents.

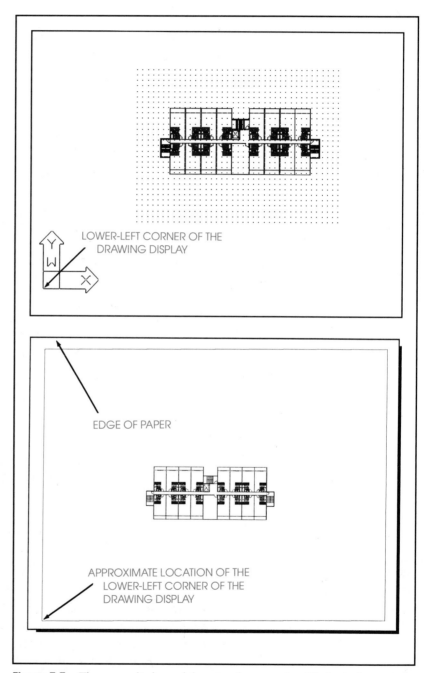

LOWER-LEFT CORNER OF THE
DRAWING DISPLAY

EDGE OF PAPER

APPROXIMATE LOCATION OF THE
LOWER-LEFT CORNER OF THE
DRAWING DISPLAY

Figure 7.7:   The screen display and the printed output when Display is chosen and no scale is used (the drawing is scaled to fit the sheet)

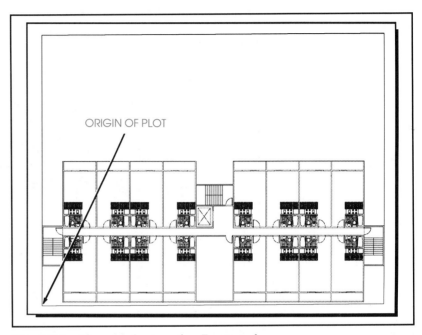

ORIGIN OF PLOT

Figure 7.8: The printed output when Extents is chosen

At times when using this plot option, you may find that you don't get exactly the same plot as your drawing extents. When a drawing changes in size, AutoCAD will often have to recalculate its size twice by performing two drawing regenerations to display the drawing extents. When plotting, AutoCAD doesn't do the second regeneration, so you end up with the wrong display. To avoid this problem, you may want to use the VIEW command to set up a view of the area you want to plot and use the Additional Parameters View option, described below. This will ensure that you will always get the plot you want regardless of your drawing extents.

Limits

The Limits printing option uses the limits of the drawing to determine what to print (see Figure 7.9). If you let AutoCAD fit the drawing onto the sheet using the Scale to Fit check box, the plot will display exactly the same thing that you would see on the screen had you clicked on View ➤ Zoom ➤ All.

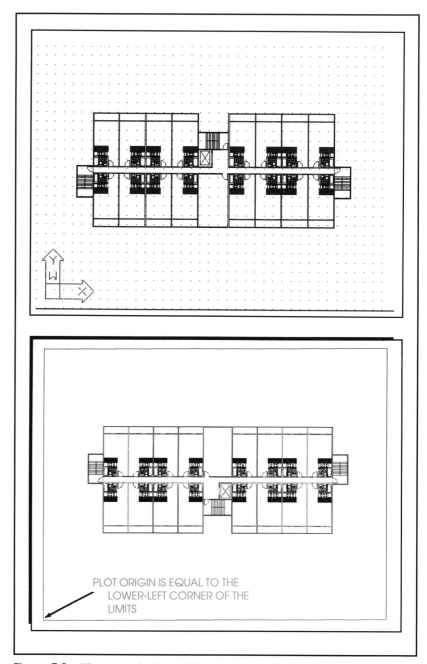

Figure 7.9: The screen display and the printed output when Limits is chosen

View

The View printing option uses a previously saved view to determine what to print (see Figure 7.10). To use this option, do the following.

1. First click on the button labeled **View**....

2. Double-click on the desired view name from the dialog box list that appears.

If you let AutoCAD fit the drawing onto the sheet using the Scale to Fit check box, the plot will display exactly the same thing that you would see on the screen if you recalled the view you are plotting.

Window

Finally, the Window option allows you to indicate the area you wish to plot with a window (see Figure 7.11). Nothing outside the window will print. To use this option, do the following.

1. Click on the button labeled **Window**....

2. Enter the coordinates of the window in the appropriate input boxes.

3. Alternately, you can click on the button labeled **Pick** to indicate a window in the drawing editor screen. The dialog box will temporarily close to allow you to select points.

4. Click on **OK**.

If you let AutoCAD fit the drawing onto the sheet using the Scale to Fit check box, the plot will display exactly the same thing that you enclose within the window.

CONTROLLING SCALE AND LOCATION

You will notice another button group to the right called Scale, Rotation, and Origin. This is where you tell AutoCAD the scale of your

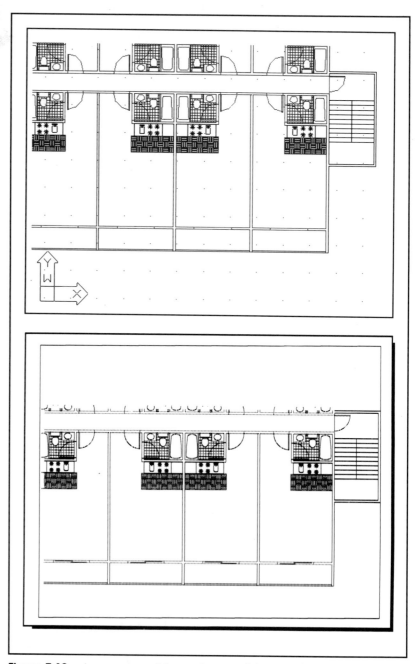

Figure 7.10: A comparison of the saved view and the printed output

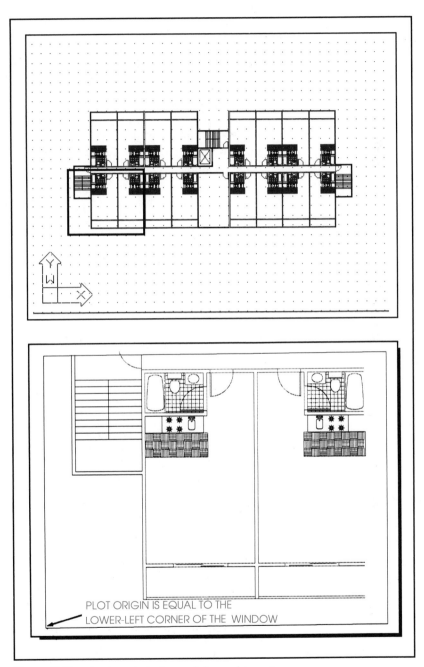

Figure 7.11:   A selected window and the resulting printout

drawing, as well as how the image is to be rotated on the sheet, and the location of the drawing origin on the paper.

You probably couldn't help noticing that in the previous section, I qualified the descriptions of the plotter output by saying that the Scale to Fit check box must be checked. When you start to apply a scale factor to your plot, the effects of the Additional Parameters radio buttons begin to change and problems can arise that are not obvious. This is usually where most new users have problems.

For example, the apartment plan drawing fits nicely on the paper when you use the Scale to Fit option. But if you tried to plot the drawing at a scale of 1"=1', you would probably get a blank piece of paper, because, at that scale, hardly any of the drawing would fit on your paper. AutoCAD would tell you that it was plotting and when it was done, it would tell you that the plot was finished. You wouldn't have a clue as to why your sheet was blank.

If an image is too large to fit on a sheet of paper because of improper scaling, the plot image will be clipped differently depending on whether the plotter uses the center of the image or the lower-left corner for its origin (see Figure 7.3). Keep this in mind as you specify scales in this area of the dialog box.

SPECIFYING DRAWING SCALE

▼ NOTE

See *Chapter 3* for a discussion on unit styles and scale factors.

To indicate scale, two input boxes are provided in the Scale, Rotation, and Origin button group: Plotted Inches and Drawing Units. For example, if your drawing is of a scale factor of 96, do the following.

1. Double-click on the Plotted Inches input box. Enter **1** ↵.

2. Double-click on the Drawing Units input box then enter **96**.

▼ NOTE

Metric users will see the Plotted MM label for the input box on the left.

For a drawing set up using the architectural unit style, you can enter a scale as a fraction of 1" = 1'. For example, for a ⅛" scale drawing you would do the following.

1. Double-click on the Plotted Inches input box, then enter **1/8"**.

2   Double-click on the Drawing Units input box, then enter **1′**.

You can specify a different scale from the one you chose while setting up your drawing, and AutoCAD will plot your drawing to that scale. You are not restricted in any way. Entering the correct scale is important, because if it is too large, AutoCAD will think your drawing is too large to fit on the sheet, though it will attempt to plot your drawing anyway.

The Scale to Fit check box, as I've already described, allows you to avoid giving a scale altogether and forces the drawing to fit on the sheet. This works fine if you are doing illustrations that are not to scale.

SETTING THE OUTPUT'S ORIGIN AND ROTATION

To adjust the position of your drawing on the media, you enter the location of the view origin in relation to the plotter origin in x and y coordinates (see Figure 7.12).

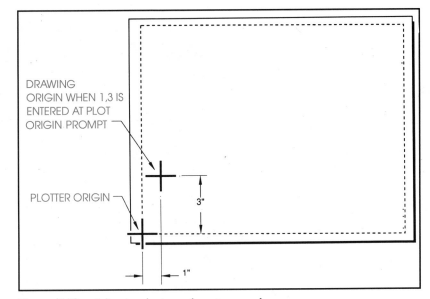

Figure 7.12:   Adjusting the image location on a sheet

▼ WARNING

If you encounter problems with rotating plots, try setting up a UCS that is rotated 90° from the world coordinate system. Then use PLAN to view your drawing in the new rotated orientation. Next, save the view using VIEW. Once you do this, you can use the View option under the Additional Parameters group to plot the rotated view. See *Chapter 16* for more on UCS.

For example, suppose you plot a drawing, then realize that it needs to be moved 1" to the right and 3" up on the sheet. You would re-plot the drawing by making the following changes in the Plot Configuration dialog box:

1. Click on the **Rotation and Origin**… button in the Scale, Rotation, and Origin button group. The Plot Rotation and Origin dialog box appears (see Figure 7.13).
2. Double-click on the X Origin input box, then type **1**.
3. Double-click on the Y Origin input box, then type **3**.
4. Click on **OK**.
5. Proceed with the rest of the plot configuration as before.

When the plot is done, the image will be shifted on the paper exactly 1" to the right and 3" up.

You might have noticed the four radio buttons labeled 0, 90, 180, and 270. These buttons allow you to rotate the plot on the sheet. The default is 0, but if you need to rotate the image to a different angle, click on the appropriate radio button, then click on **OK**.

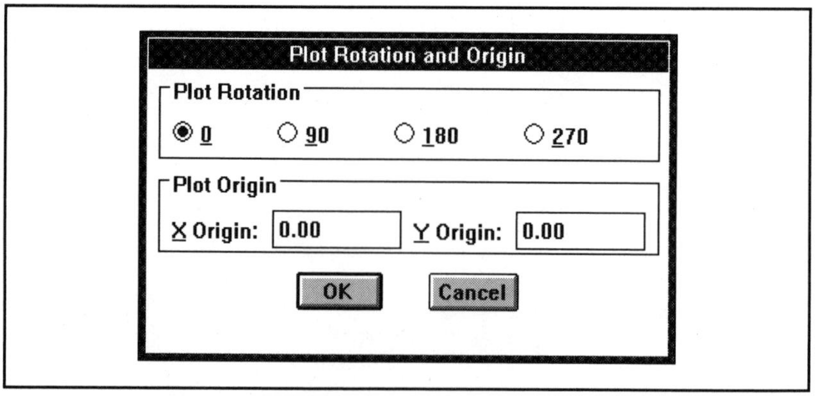

Figure 7.13: The Plot Rotation and Origin dialog box

ADJUSTING PEN PARAMETERS AND LINE WEIGHTS

▼ NOTE

You can also control line weights through the use of Polylines. See *Chapter 13* for details.

In most graphics programs, you control line weights by adjusting the actual width of lines in the drawing. In AutoCAD, you generally take a different approach to line weights. Instead of specifying a line weight in the drawing editor, you match plotter pen widths to colors in your drawing. For example, you might designate the color red to correspond to a fine line weight or the color blue to a very heavy line weight. To make these correlations between colors and line weights, you tell AutoCAD to plot with a particular pen for each different color in the drawing.

The **Pen Assignments...** button in the Plot Configuration dialog box is the entry point to setting the drawing colors to the pens on your plotter. When you click on this button, the Pen Assignment dialog box appears (see Figure 7.14).

▼ NOTE

This dialog box shows a listing for a Hewlett Packard 7580 plotter.

The predominant feature of this dialog box is the list that shows the pen assignments. The color numbers in the first column of the list correspond to the colors in your drawing. The other columns show you what pen number, line type, pen speed, and pen width are assigned to those colors.

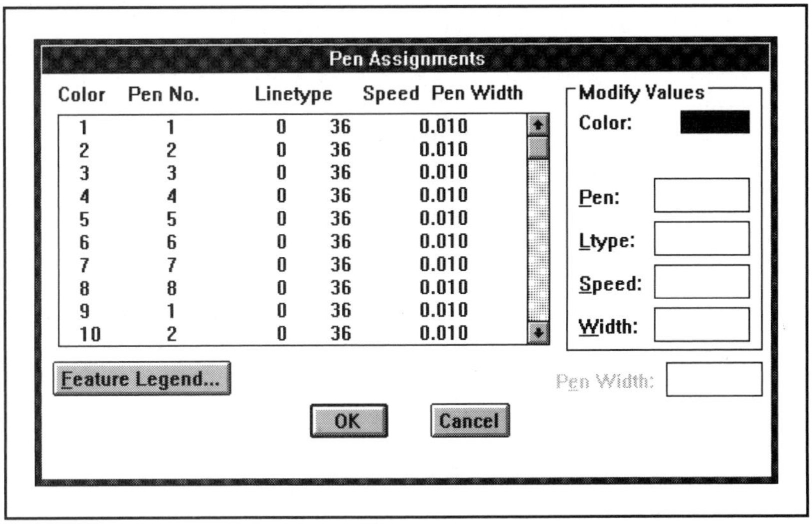

Figure 7.14: The Pen Assignments dialog box

To change these settings, you click on the item in the list you want to change. The input box to the right then fills with the same information as the selection you just highlighted. You can then change the values listed in the input box. You can highlight more than one color at a time with a shift-click to change the pen assignments of several colors at once.

PEN NO.

You assign different line weights to colors by entering a pen number in the pen input box. The default for the color red, for example, is pen 1. You can then place a pen with a fine tip in the slot designated for pen 1 in your plotter. Then everything that is red in your AutoCAD drawing will be plotted with the fine pen.

▼ NOTE

If your plotter can generate its own line types, you can also assign line types to colors. This feature is very seldom used because it is simpler to assign line types to layers directly in the drawing.

LTYPE

Some plotters offer line types independent of AutoCAD's line types. You can force a pen assignment to a hardware line type using the Ltype input box. If your plotter supports hardware line types, you can click on the button labeled **Feature Legend** to see what line types are available and what their designations are. Usually line types are given numeric designations, so a row of dots might be designated as line type 1, or a dash-dot might be 5.

SPEED

The pen speed setting lets you adjust the pen speed in inches per second. This is important because different pens have different speed requirements. Refillable technical pens that use India ink generally require the slowest settings, while roller pens are capable of very high speeds. Pen speeds will also be affected by the media you are using. Selecting pens and media for your plotter can be a trial-and-error proposition. If you would like to learn more about the details of plotter pens and media, read *Appendix A*.

WIDTH

AutoCAD uses this setting in conjunction with the Adjust Area Fill option under the Additional Parameters button group discussed earlier. When AutoCAD draws solid fills, it draws a series of lines close together much as you would do by hand (see Figure 7.15). To do this efficiently, AutoCAD must know the pen width. If this setting is too low, AutoCAD will take longer than necessary to draw a solid fill; if it is too high, solid fills will appear as cross hatches instead of solids.

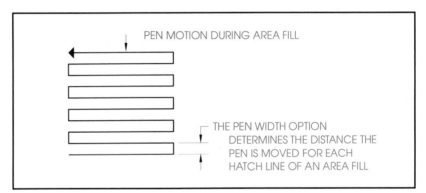

Figure 7.15:   How solid-fill areas are drawn by a plotter

OPTIMIZING PLOTTER SPEED

AutoCAD does a lot of preparation before sending your drawing to the plotter. One of the things it does is optimize the way it sends vectors to your plotter so your plotter doesn't waste time making frequent pen changes and moving from one end of the plot to another just to draw a single line.

The **Optimization…** button opens a dialog box that lets you control the level of pen optimization AutoCAD is to perform on your plots (see Figure 7.16).

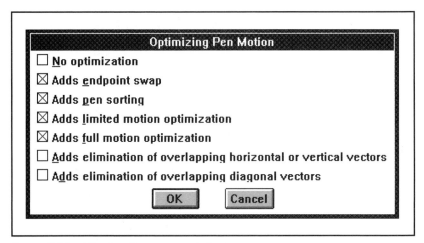

Figure 7.16: The Pen Optimization dialog box

Here are brief descriptions of each setting:

No optimization causes AutoCAD to plot the drawing just as it regenerates it on the screen.

Adds endpoint swap forces the plotter to draw (as best as it can) parallel lines in a back-and-forth motion so that the pen moves the minimum distance between the end of one line and the beginning of another.

Adds pen sorting sorts pens so that all of one color is plotted at once. This is fine if your plotter has a self-capping penholder, or if it is a single-pen plotter. You may not want this option if you have a multi-pen plotter that does not cap the pens.

Adds Limited motion optimization and **Adds Full motion optimization** further minimize pen travel over a plot.

Adds elimination of overlapping horizontal or vertical vectors, as it says, eliminates overlapping lines. With pen plotters, overlapping lines can cause the weight of the line to increase noticeably. This feature helps reduce line weight build-up when a drawing contains numerous line overlaps. This setting does not affect raster plotters or printers.

Adds elimination of overlapping diagonal vectors performs a similar function as the previous option on diagonal lines.

PREVIEWING A PLOT

If you are a seasoned AutoCAD user, you're probably all too familiar with the following scenario:

You're rushing to meet a deadline. You've got one hour to plot a drawing that you know takes 45 minutes to plot. You set up AutoCAD and start the plot, then run off to finish some paperwork. When you come back 45 minutes later, the plot image is half the size it is supposed to be.

You can avoid this situation with the *Plot Preview* feature. Once you've made all the settings you think you need, click on the Full radio button in the Plot Preview group, then click on **Preview**…. AutoCAD will show you what your drawing will look like according to the settings you've chosen. Preview also lists any warning messages that would appear during the actual plotting process.

While in the Full Preview, you can zoom in on an area and pan around, but be aware that each zoom and pan requires the preview function to "re-plot" the image.

The Full preview can take some time, though not as long as an actual plot. If you're just interested to see how the drawing fits on the sheet, you can click on the Partial radio button before clicking on **Preview**. This option shows the sheet edge, image orientation triangle, and the image boundary. The image itself is not shown. Instead it shows how the image is oriented on the sheet with a small triangle in the corner of the drawing. This triangle indicates the lower-left corner of the drawing.

▼ TIP

You can press the **Esc** key to speed up the preview. Once the preview plot is done, you are immediately returned to the Plotter Configuration dialog box. You can also press **Ctrl-C** to terminate the preview generation when you've seen enough.

▼

▼ Re-initializing Your Input/Output Ports

If you are using two output devices on the same port, like a printer and a plotter, you may want to know about the Reinit command. This command lets you re-initialize a port for use by AutoCAD after another program has used it. For example, you may have a printer and a plotter connected to the same port through a switch box. You may use the AutoCAD Shell command to temporarily exit AutoCAD to print out a document on your printer. When you return to AutoCAD to plot something, you will want to use Reinit to restore AutoCAD's connection to your plotter.

To use Reinit, enter **Reinit** at the command prompt. You will see a dialog box showing you check boxes labeled Digitizer, Plotter, Display, and PGP file. You can check them all if you like or just check the items you are concerned most with.

Reinit can also be accessed using the Re-init system variable.

SAVING YOUR SETTINGS

At times, drawings will require special plotter settings, or you may find that you frequently use one particular setting configuration. Instead of trying to remember the settings every time you plot, you can store settings as files that you can recall at any time. To use this feature do the following.

1. Set up the plotter settings exactly as you want them.

2. Click on the **Device and Default Selection** button. The Device and Default Selection dialog box appears.

3. Click on the button labeled **Save Defaults to File**…. The Save to File dialog box appears.

4. Enter a name for the settings. The default name is the current drawing name with the .PCP file name extension.

5. Click on **OK**. A file with the .PCP extension will be created.

To recall a setting, do the following.

1. Click on File ➤ Plot.

2. Click on the **Device and Default Selection** button. The Device and Default Selection dialog box appears.

3. Click on the button labeled **Get Defaults From File**…. The Obtain From File dialog box appears.

4. Click on the name of the desired plotter settings file.

5. Click on **OK**. The settings will be loaded. You can then proceed with your plot.

The ability to store plotter settings in .PCP files gives you greater control over your output quality. It allows you to reproduce similar plots more easily at a later date. You can store several different plotter configurations for one file, each for a different output device.

You can also open the .PCP file with a text editor. You can even create your own .PCP file by copying an existing one and editing it.

FREEPLOTTING WITH AUTOCAD

At times, you may want to use AutoCAD just to plot a set of drawings. For this purpose, AutoCAD provides the Freeplot feature. The Freeplot feature offers the following advantages:

■ No Network License requirements

■ Files are not loaded, so you don't get drawing regenerations

■ No temporary files are created

To use Freeplot, you start AutoCAD by entering **acad -p** at the DOS prompt. AutoCAD will open in the usual way; however, you are restricted to the following commands:

About	Help	Script
Compile	Plot	Status
Config	Quit	Textscr
Delay	Reinit	Time
Files	Resume	Vslide
Graphscr	Rscript	

AutoLISP and ADS applications are also not available; however, you can plot drawings, view slides, and run scripts.

PLOTTING FROM THE COMMAND LINE

Many readers may already be used to the command line method of plotting from AutoCAD and have devised methods for storing plotter settings. One common method is to use script files to plot from AutoCAD (see *Plotting from Scripts*, below). You can still use the older method of issuing the plot command from the command prompt and script files. You must first change the CMDDIA system variable to 0 to do this. The following describes the command prompt method for configuring the plotter.

First set the CMDDIA system variable to 0.

Enter **Plot** from the command prompt. You will get the following prompt.

What to plot—Display, Extents, Limits, View, or Window <D>:

Enter the desired option. The screen switches to text mode and you see the following list of settings:

```
Plot device is Hewlett-Packard (HPGL) ADI 4.2 by -
Autodesk
Description: HP 7585
Plot Optimization level = 4
Plot will NOT be written to a selected file
Sizes are in Inches and the style is landscape
Plot origin is at (0.00,0.00)
Plotting area is 10.50 wide by 8.00 high (A)
Plot is NOT rotated
Area fill will NOT be adjusted for pen width
Hidden lines will NOT be removed
Plot will be scaled to fit available area
Do you want to change anything?(No/Yes/File/Save) <N>
```

If you answer **Y** to the last prompt and you have a multiple pen plotter driver loaded, you get the prompt

```
Do you want to change plotters? <N>:
```

If you answer **Y**, you get a listing of the available plotters:

```
1.Hewlett-Packard (HPGL) ADI 4.2 - by Autodesk
Description HP 7585
2.PostScript device ADI 4.2 - by Autodesk
Description LaserWriter II
Enter selection <1>:
```

▼ NOTE

This list is just an example. The list you see on your computer will depend on how you have configured the AutoCAD plotter option.

If you answer **No** to the **Do you want to change plotters?** prompt and you have selected a multi-pen plotter, AutoCAD then asks if you want to configure your plotter pen assignments. If you answer **Y**, you will get a list showing the current settings for pen assignments, as shown in Figure 7.17.

```
How many seconds should we wait for the plotter
port to time-out (0 means wait forever), 0 to 500 <30>:

Pen widths are in Inches.
Entity       Pen  Line   Pen   Pen
Color        No.  Type  Speed  Width
1 (red)       1     0    36    0.010
2 (yellow)    2     0    36    0.010
3 (green)     3     0    36    0.010
4 (cyan)      4     0    36    0.010
5 (blue)      5     0    36    0.010
6 (magenta)   6     0    36    0.010
7 (white)     7     0    36    0.010
8             8     0    36    0.010

Entity       Pen  Line   Pen   Pen
Color        No.  Type  Speed  Width
9             1     0    36    0.010
10            2     0    36    0.010
11            3     0    36    0.010
12            4     0    36    0.010
13            5     0    36    0.010
14            6     0    36    0.010
15            7     0    36    0.010
16            8     0    36    0.010

Linetypes
0 = continuous line
1 = ...............
2 = ---  ---  ---  ---
3 = ----  ----  ----
4 = -----  .  -----  .  -----
5 = ----  .  ----  .  ----
6 = --- --- --- ---

Do you want to change any of the above parameters? <N>
```

Figure 7.17: The pen assignments for a Hewlett Packard 7585 plotter—other plotters will show different pen assignments.

You may also see messages pertaining to your specific plotter, such as paper tray selection and number of copies.

If you answer **Y** to this prompt, the prompt shown in Figure 7.18 appears.

Notice how this prompt duplicates the information on the first color listed in the previous prompt. To the right is a line prompting you to enter a pen number for the color. The default is 1. You can select a pen number corresponding to the color red or accept the default pen number, 1. The bottom line of the prompt changes to show the following:

    1 (red)   2   0   36   Line type <0>:

The prompt reflects the change in pen assignments you just made and asks you what line type you wish to use (unless your plotter does not offer built-in line types). Finally, you are prompted for pen width. Once you have selected an option, the prompt will change to:

    1 (red)   2   0   36   Pen speed <60>:

Now AutoCAD prompts you for pen speed (unless your plotter does not offer the pen speed option). Once you answer this prompt, the prompt advances to displays the settings for color number 2, yellow. You can now select pen number, pen speed, and line type for yellow the same way you did for red. You can then continue through all 15 colors.

At any time, you can enter one of the following options:

S	To review your settings.
C(*color number*)	To change the settings of another color. For example, enter **C4** ↵ to change the settings for color number 4.
X	To exit the pen assignments and move on to the next setting.

Once you've exited the pen assignments, you will get the series of prompts shown in Figure 7.19.

Once you've answered these prompts, you can start your plot.

```
Enter values, blank=Next value, Cn=Color n, S=Show current values, X=Exit

Entity          Pen     Line    Pen
Color           No.     Type    Speed
1 (red)         1       0       36      Pen number <1>:
```

Figure 7.18: This prompt lets you change pen parameters.

▼ NOTE

Sheet sizes shown here may vary from those you see on your computer.

```
Write the plot to a file? <N>
Size units (Inches or Millimeters) <Inches>:
Plot origin in Inches <0.00,0.00>:
Standard Values for plotting size

Size        Width            Height
A           10.50             8.00
B           16.00            10.00
MAX         16.00            10.00

Enter the Size or Width,Height (in Inches) <A>:
Rotate plot 0/90/180/270/ <0>:
Adjust area fill boundaries for pen width? <N>
Remove hidden lines? <N>
Specify scale by entering:
Plotted Inches=Drawing Units or Fit or ? <F>
```

Figure 7.19: You are prompted for information on print options.

Plotting in the Background

Plotting is often the most time-consuming function in AutoCAD. In the past, plotting often meant you couldn't do anything but wait for your plot to finish. AutoCAD for Windows lets you run multiple sessions of AutoCAD, so you can have one AutoCAD session plotting, while you continue to work on your drawings. The only requirement for multiple AutoCAD sessions is that you have an adequate amount of RAM to run more than one AutoCAD session.

To start a second or third AutoCAD session, you simply return to the Program Manager and start AutoCAD again as you normally do. You then use the second session as you would any other session of AutoCAD.

PLOTTING FROM SCRIPTS

A popular method for automating plotting is to use *script files*. Script files act like DOS batch files. They are ASCII text files that contain the exact keystrokes used to perform some task (see *Appendix C* for a description of ASCII files). To create a script file, you would use a text editor and create a file containing the exact keystrokes necessary to perform the plotter setup. Figure 7.20 shows a listing of a typical script file called Plotter.SCR for a Hewlett-Packard plotter. (Script files must always have the file extension .SCR.) Once the file is created, you use the SCRIPT command to run the script. See *Chapter 12* for more on Script files and their use.

You can also initialize script files for plotting at the same time you start AutoCAD. To do this, you enter the following at the DOS prompt:

acad -p *script*.scr

where *script* is the name of the script file.

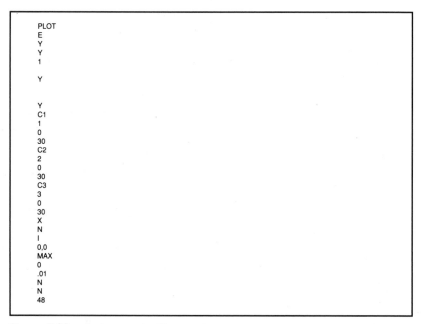

```
PLOT
E
Y
Y
1

Y


Y
C1
1
0
30
C2
2
0
30
C3
3
0
30
X
N
I
0,0
MAX
0
.01
N
N
48
```

Figure 7.20:   A plotter script file

SENDING YOUR DRAWINGS TO A SERVICE

Using a plotting service can be a good alternative to purchasing your own plotter. Or you might consider using a low-cost plotter for check plots, then sending the files to a service for your final plots. Many reprographic services such as blueprinters offer plotting in conjunction with their other services. Quite often these services include a high-speed modem that allows you to send files over phone lines, eliminating the need to courier or mail files to the service bureau.

These service bureaus will often use an *electrostatic plotter*. Because they are costly, you probably won't want to purchase one yourself. However, the electrostatic plotter is excellent for situations where high volume and fast turnaround are required. It produces high-quality plots, often better than a laser printer, and it is fast. A 30"×42" plot can take as little as 2 minutes. One limitation, however, is that these plotters require special media, so you can't use your pre-printed title blocks. Check with your prospective plotter service organization on media limitations.

Another device used by service bureaus is the *laser photo plotter*. This device uses a laser to plot a drawing on a piece of film. The film negative is later enlarged to the finished drawing size by means of standard reprographic techniques. This device yields the highest-quality output of any device, and it offers the flexibility of reproducing drawings at any size.

Finally, many service bureaus can produce full E size plots of PostScript files. With AutoCAD's full PostScript support, you can get presentation quality plots from any AutoCAD drawing. See *Chapter 14* for more on PostScript and AutoCAD.

IF YOU WANT TO EXPERIMENT...

At this point, when you aren't rushing to meet a deadline, you may want to experiment with some of the plotter and printer variables and see firsthand what each one does. Figure 7.21 shows an exercise you can do to try out printing from the command line.

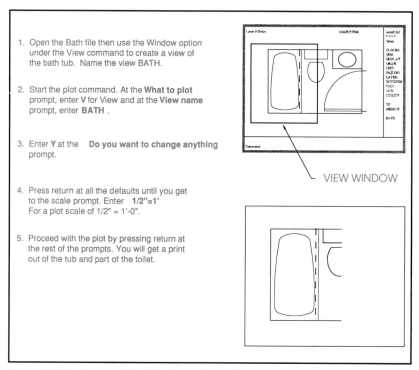

1. Open the Bath file then use the Window option under the View command to create a view of the bath tub. Name the view BATH.

2. Start the plot command. At the **What to plot** prompt, enter **V** for View and at the **View name** prompt, enter **BATH** .

3. Enter **Y** at the   **Do you want to change anything** prompt.

4. Press return at all the defaults until you get to the scale prompt. Enter   **1/2"=1'** For a plot scale of 1/2" = 1'-0".

5. Proceed with the plot by pressing return at the rest of the prompts. You will get a print out of the tub and part of the toilet.

VIEW WINDOW

Figure 7.21:   Printing the tub at $1/2''=1'-0''$ scale

SUMMARY

In this chapter, you learned the rudiments of printing and plotting. These are complex functions that take some practice to master. But in time, you will be able to judge exactly how your drawing will appear when it is printed or plotted.

AutoCAD offers many tools to help you get exactly the plot you want. The Paperspace mode I discussed in *Chapter 6* allows you to paste up different views of your drawing in a way similar to many desktop publishing programs. Also, you can apply some tricks to combine drawings of different scales in one plot. I will discuss both Paperspace and mixing scales in one drawing in more detail in *Chapter 12*; here, you should just try to get comfortable with the basic printing and plotting functions.

In *Chapter 8*, you will learn how to annotate your drawings with text.

8

▼ ▼ ▼ ▼ ▼

ADDING
TEXT TO
DRAWINGS

FAST TRACK

294 ▶ To enter text in a drawing

Click on Draw ➤ Text ➤ Dynamic, enter the desired height if you are prompted for it, enter a rotation angle, then start typing. A ↵ starts a new line. A ← lets you back up as far as you like.

294 ▶ To set the justification of text you are about to enter

Click on Draw ➤ Text ➤ Dynamic, then enter the desired justification style (e.g., **Center**, **Right**, **TL** (top left), **Middle**, etc.). Answer the rest of the prompts, then start typing.

298 ▶ To find the appropriate height of text for a drawing according to its scale

Multiply the desired final text height by the scale factor. For example, if you want ⅛" high letters in a drawing that is to be plotted at ¼" = 1′, multiply ⅛ times 48. (See *Chapter 3* for more on scale factors.)

300 ▶ To continue text where you left off

Start the Dtext command. The last line of text you entered should high-light. Press Return at all the prompts until you see the **Text** prompt. You should see a text cursor just below the last text line.

301 ▶ To include text in scripts and macros

Use the Text command instead of the Dtext command.

306 ▶ To create a new text style

Click on Draw ➤ Text ➤ Set Style. At the Dialog box, click on the style you want to use, then click on **OK**. Answer the prompts that follow.

310 ▶ To rename a text style

Ascertain the name of the style whose name you wish to change. Type **RENAME** ↵ at the command prompt. At the **RENAME** prompt, type **S** ↵. Enter the old style name, then enter the new style name.

311 ▶ To select a text style for use with the Dtext command

Ascertain the name of the style you want to use. Click on Draw ▶ Text ▶ Dynamic. Enter **S** ↵, then enter the name of the style you want to use.

314 ▶ To change the style of existing text

Click on Modify ▶ Entity..., then click on the text whose style you want to change. The Modify Text dialog box appears. Click on the arrow of the Style pop-up list, then click on the desired text style. Click on **OK**.

316 ▶ To change the justification of text already entered

Click on Modify ▶ Entity..., then click on the text you want to modify. The Modify Text dialog box appears. Click on the arrow of the Justification pop-up list, then click on the desired justification style. Click on **OK**.

320 ▶ To edit text

Type **Ddedit** ↵, then click on the text you wish to edit. A dialog box appears with the text. You can use the standard input box editing methods to edit your text. When you are done, click on **OK**. Click on the next line to edit or press ↵ when you are done.

One of the more tedious drafting tasks is applying notes to your drawing. Anyone who has had to draft a large drawing containing lots of notes knows the full effect of writer's cramp. AutoCAD not only makes this job go faster by allowing you to type your notes, it enables you to create more professional-looking notes by using a variety of fonts, type sizes, and type styles.

In this chapter you will add notes to your apartment house plan. In the process, you will explore some of AutoCAD's text creation and editing features. You will learn how to control the size, slant, type style, and orientation of text, and how to import text files.

LABELING A DRAWING

In this first section, you will add simple labels to your Unit drawing to identify the general design elements: the bathroom, kitchenette, and living room.

Draw ➤ A Text ➤ Dynamic (Continued)

1. Start AutoCAD and open the Unit file.

2. Turn off the Flr-pat layer. Otherwise, the floor pattern you added previously will obscure the text you will enter in this chapter.

3. Create a layer called **Notes**, then make Notes the current layer. Notes is the layer on which you will keep all your text information.

4. Click on Draw ➤ Text ➤ Dynamic or enter **Dtext** ↵ from the command prompt.

5. At the **DTEXT Justify/Style/<Start point>:** prompt, pick the starting point for the text you are about to enter, just below the kitchenette at coordinate 16'-2", 21'-8". By picking a point you are accepting <start point>, which is the default.

▼ **TIP**

It is a good idea to keep your notes on a separate layer so you can plot drawings containing only the graphic information or freeze the notes layer to save regeneration time.

▼ NOTE

You may wonder why you would want the text to be so high. Remember that you are drawing at full scale and anything you draw will be reduced in the plotted drawing. We will discuss text height in more detail later in this chapter.

▼ TIP

If you make a typing error, back up to the error with the ← key, then retype the rest of the word. If you need to, you can backspace over several lines.

6. At the **Height <0′-0 3/16">:** prompt, enter **6"** to indicate the text height.

7. At the **Rotation angle <0>:** prompt, press ⏎ to accept the default, 0°. You can specify any angle other than horizontal if you wish—for example, if you want your text to be aligned with a rotated object. You'll see a small square appear at the point you picked in step 5. This is your text cursor.

8. At the **Text:** prompt, enter the word **Kitchenette**. As you type, the word appears in the drawing.

9. Press ⏎ and the cursor moves down to start a new line.

10. This time you want to label the bathroom. Pick a point to the right of the door swing at coordinate 19′-11", 26′-5". The text cursor moves to that point.

11. Enter **Bath** ⏎. Figure 8.1 shows how your drawing should look. The text is in the default font, Txt (we'll discuss fonts later in this chapter).

12. Press ⏎ again to exit the Dynamic Text command.

Dynamic text or *Dtext*, as the command is called, lets you enter a column of text by pressing ⏎ at the end of each line. You can also click on a location for the next line as you did in step 10.

JUSTIFYING TEXT

▼ NOTE

The baseline of text is an imaginary line on which the lowercase letters of the text sit.

When you pick a point at the Dynamic text's **Justify/Style/<Start point>:** prompt, your text is automatically justified to the right of the selected point and the text uses that point as its baseline location. You can change the justification setting so that the text you enter will be justified either to the center or to the right. You can also specify whether the text baseline is on, above, or below the start-point prompt.

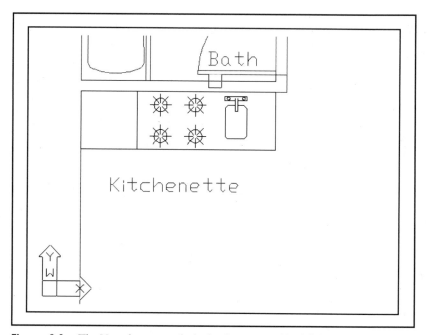

Figure 8.1: The Unit drawing with the kitchenette and bath labeled

▼ NOTE

If you are working through the tutorial, you don't have to do this exercise. It's here for reference only.

▼ TIP

To select one of the Top, Bottom, or Middle justification styles from the side menu, first click on Top-, Bottom-, or Middle-, then click on -Left, Center, or -Right.

To change the justification setting, follow these steps.

1. Click on Draw ➤ Text ➤ Dynamic or enter **Dtext** ↵, just as you would to start text.

2. At the **DTEXT Justify/Style/<Start point>:** prompt, enter **J** ↵ or click on Justify from the side menu.

3. At the **Align/Fit/Center/Middle/Right/TL/TC/TR/ML/MC/MR /BL/BC/BR:** prompt, select the justification style you want by entering the name of the style or by clicking on the name from the side menu.

4. Once you select one of these options, you are prompted for a point to locate your text. You can then start to enter your text.

When you start to enter text, it will first appear as though no change has been made to the justification style. The text will come in as it does using the default, left justification. Don't be alarmed. The text will move into position after you've exited the text command.

Here is a list describing each justification option, except Align and Fit.

Center causes the text to be centered on the start point with the baseline on the start point.

Middle causes the text to be centered on the start point with the baseline slightly below the start point.

Right causes the text to be justified to the right of the start point with the baseline on the start point.

TL, **TC**, and **TR** stand for *top left*, *top center*, and *top right*. These options will cause the text to appear entirely below the start point and justified left, center, or right, depending on which of the three options you choose.

ML, **MC**, and **MR** stand for *middle left*, *middle center*, and *middle right*. These options act in a similar way to TL, TC, and TR, except that the start point will determine a location midway between the baseline and the top of the lowercase letters of the text.

BL, **BC**, and **BR** stand for *bottom left*, *bottom center*, and *bottom right*. Again, these options are similar to TL, TC, and TR, but here the start point determines the bottom-most location of the letters of the text (the bottom of letters with descenders, like *p*, *q*, and *g*).

Figure 8.2 shows the relationship between the text start point and these options.

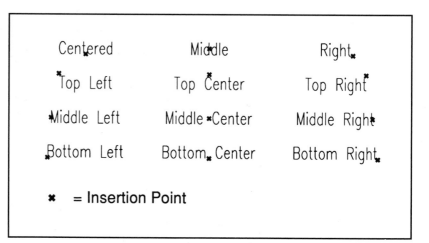

Figure 8.2:   Text inserted by using the various Justify options

The Fit and Align options allow you to specify a dimension within which the text must fit. For example, you may want the word *Refrigerator* to fit within the 26"-wide box representing the refrigerator. To do this, you could use either the Fit or the Align option. Fit stretches or compresses the letters to fit within the width and text height you specify. You use this option when the text must be a consistent height throughout the drawing and you don't care about distorting the font. Align automatically adjusts the text height to fit within the specified width without distorting the font. You use this option where it is important to maintain the font's shape and proportion. Figure 8.3 shows you how these options work.

UNDERSTANDING TEXT AND SCALE

Text scale conversion is a concept many people have difficulty grasping. As you discovered in previous chapters, AutoCAD allows you to draw at full scale, that is, to represent distances as values equivalent to the actual size of the object. When you later plot the drawing you tell AutoCAD what scale you wish to plot it to and the program reduces the

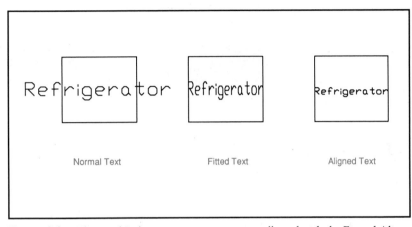

Figure 8.3: The word *Refrigerator* as it appears normally and with the Fit and Align options

drawing accordingly. This allows you the freedom to input measurements at full scale and not worry about converting them to various scales every time you enter a distance. Unfortunately, this feature also creates problems when you enter text and dimensions. Just as you had to convert the plotted sheet size to an enlarged size equivalent at full scale in the drawing editor, you must convert your text size to its equivalent at full scale.

To illustrate this point, imagine you are drawing the Unit plan at full size on a very large sheet of paper. When you are done with this drawing, it will be reduced to a scale that will allow it to fit on an 8½×11" sheet of paper. So you have to make your text quite large to keep it legible once it is reduced. This means that if you want text to appear ⅛" high when the drawing is plotted, you must convert it to a considerably larger size when you draw it. To do this, you multiply the desired height of the final plotted text by a scale conversion factor. If your drawing is at ⅛"=1′ scale, you multiply the desired text height, ⅛", by the scale conversion factor of 96 (found in *Table 3.3*) to get a height of 12". This is the height you must make your text to get ⅛"-high text in the final plot. Table 8.1 shows you some other examples of text height to scale.

Table 8.1:   8.1: ⅛" high Text Converted to Size for Various Drawing Scales

DRAWING SCALE	SCALE FACTOR	AUTOCAD DRAWING HEIGHT FOR ⅛" HIGH TEXT
1/16" = 1'-0"	192	24.0"
1/8" = 1'-0"	96	12.0"
1/4" = 1'-0"	48	6.0"
1/2" = 1'-0"	24	3.0"
3/4" = 1'-0"	16	2.0"
1" = 1'-0"	12	1.5"
1 1/2" = 1'-0"	8	1.0"
3" = 1'-0"	4	0.5"

ENTERING A COLUMN OF TEXT

You will often want to enter a note or description of an object that re-quires more than one line of text. You've already gotten a glimpse of how to do this. The next exercise will let you try it out.

CONTINUING TEXT FROM WHERE YOU LEFT OFF

One feature of the text function is that it lets you stop to do something else, then return to add text in a column below the last line you entered. This exercise shows you the process.

Draw ➤ A Text ➤ Dynamic (Continued)

▼ **NOTE**

Dynamic text can be issued from the command prompt by entering **Dtext** ↵.

1. Click on Draw ➤ Text ➤ Dynamic or enter **Dtext** ↵.

2. Click on a point at coordinate 24'-0", 26'-5" to locate the beginning of your text.

3. Enter **6** ↵ for the height and press ↵ at the angle prompt.

4. Enter **Entry** ↵.

5. Press ↵ again to exit the Dynamic text command.

At this point, you can move to another part of the drawing to make changes. The point is, you've exited the Dynamic text command. Next, you'll pick up where you left off.

1. Pan to the area where you just added the text.

2. Start Dynamic Text again. Notice that the word *Entry* highlights.

3. At the **Justify/Style/<Start point>:** prompt, press ↵. The **Text** prompt appears (skipping the prompts for height and insertion angle).

4. Enter the entry dimensions **6'-0" × 7'-0"** ↵. The cursor moves down a line.

5. Enter the words **to the kitchenette** ↵. You should have something that looks like Figure 8.4.

6. Press ↵ to exit the Dynamic text command.

UNDERSTANDING THE TEXT COMMAND

Another way of entering text is to use the TEXT command. While Dynamic text is easier to use than the TEXT command, it cannot be incorporated into menus, scripts and AutoLISP macros. The TEXT command is best suited in menus and macros. TEXT and Dtext work in nearly identical ways except for the following:

- TEXT does not show your text in the drawing as you type.

- TEXT requires you to press ↵ twice between lines in a column of text.

- TEXT does not let you position text "on the fly" the way Dtext does.

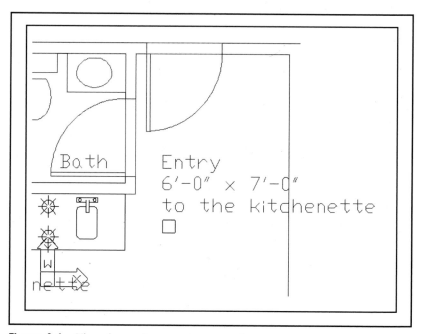

Figure 8.4: The column of text you just entered

To get a feel for how TEXT works, try the following:

Text ↵

1. Click on View ➤ Zoom ➤ All or enter Z ↵ A↵ .

2. Enter **text** ↵ or click on AutoCAD ➤ DRAW ➤ next ➤ TEXT:. Notice that the same starting point prompt appears as when you use Dynamic Text.

3. Pick a point on the balcony at coordinate 19′-8", 4′-4". Press ↵ twice to accept the default height and angle.

4. Type the word **Balcony**. As you type, the letters appear only in the prompt area. They do not appear in the drawing yet.

5. Press ↵. The word *Balcony* appears in the drawing and the command prompt appears (see Figure 8.5).

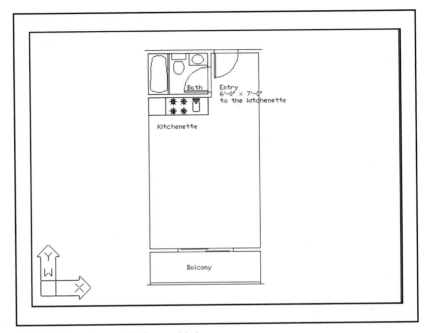

Figure 8.5: The word *Balcony* added

CHOOSING FONTS AND SPECIAL CHARACTERS

AutoCAD offers twenty fonts that can be displayed in a number of different ways. These include two foreign fonts, Greek and Cyrillic. Symbols for astronomy, mapping, math, meteorology, and music are also provided. You can compress or expand these fonts and symbols, or you can modify them to create different type styles. Figure 8.6 shows you the fonts available with AutoCAD.

I should mention that the more complex the font, the longer it takes AutoCAD to regenerate your drawing. Before you choose a font for a particular job, consider how much text the drawing will contain. Use the Txt font if you like its looks; it regenerates the fastest. Monotxt is a fixed-width font (like a typewriter font) that is useful for aligned

▼ NOTE

AutoCAD's fonts are contained in the files with the .SHX extension in your AutoCAD directory. You can get other popular fonts such as Helvetica or Times Roman from third-party software companies (for more information, consult *Chapter 19*).

This is Txt
This is Monotxt
This is Simplex (Old version of Roman Simplex)
This is Complex (Old version of Roman Complex)
This is Italic (Old version of Italic Complex)
This is Romans (Roman Simplex)
This is Romand (Roman double stroke)
This is Romanc (Roman Complex)
This is Romant (Roman triple stroke)
This is Scripts (Script Simplex)
This is Scriptc (Script Complex)
This is Italicc (Italic Complex)
This is Italict (Italic triple stroke)
Τηισ ισ Γρεεκσ (This is Greeks - Greek Simplex)
Τηισ ισ Γρεεκχ (This is Greekc - Greek Complex)
Узит ит Вшсиллив (This is Cyrillic - Alphabetical)
Тхис ис Чйрилтлч (This is Cyriltc - Transliteration)
This is Gothice (Gothic English)
This is Gothicg (Gothic German)
This is Gothici (Gothic Italian)

font \ key	A	B	C	D	E	F	G	H	I	J	K	L	M	N	O	P	Q	R	S	T	U	V	W	X	Y	Z	[	\	]	^	_	`
Symap																											[	\	]	^	_	`
Syastro																											[	\	]	^	_	`
Symath																											[	\	]	^	_	`
Symeteo																											[	\	]	^	_	`
Symusic																											[	\	]	^	_	`
Greeks	A	B	X	Δ	E	Φ	Γ	H	I		K	Λ	M	N	O	Θ	P	Σ	T	T	Υ	Ω	Ξ	Ψ	Z		[	\	]	^	_	`
Greekc	A	B	X	Δ	E	Φ	Γ	H	I		K	Λ	M	N	O	Θ	P	Σ	T	T	Υ	Ω	Ξ	Ψ	Z		[	\	]	^	_	`
Cyrillic	А	Б	В	Г	Д	Е	Ж	З	И	Й	К	Л	М	Н	О	П	Р	С	Т	У	Ф	Х	Ц	Ч	Ш	Щ	Ъ	Ы	Ь	Э	Ю	Я
Cyriltc	А	Б	Ч	Д	Е	Ф	Г	Х	И	Ш	К	Л	М	Н	О	П	Ц	Р	С	Т	У	В	Ш	Ж	Й	З	Ь	Ы	Ъ	Э	Ю	Я

font \ key	a	b	c	d	e	f	g	h	i	j	k	l	m	n	o	p	q	r	s	t	u	v	w	x	y	z	{	|	}	~	<	>
Symap																											{	|	}	~	<	>
Syastro																											{	|	}	~	<	>
Symath																											{	|	}	~	<	>
Symeteo																											{	|	}	~	<	>
Symusic																											{	|	}	~	<	>
Greeks	α	β	χ	δ	ε	φ	γ	η	ι		κ	λ	μ	ν	o	π	ϑ	ρ	σ	τ	υ	ϵ	ω	ξ	ψ	ζ	{	|	}	~	<	>
Greekc	α	β	χ	δ	ε	φ	γ	η	ι		κ	λ	μ	ν	o	π	ϑ	ρ	σ	τ	υ	ϵ	ω	ξ	ψ	ζ	{	|	}	~	<	>
Cyrillic	а	б	в	г	д	е	ж	з	и	й	к	л	м	н	о	п	р	с	т	у	ф	х	ц	ч	ш	щ	ъ	ы	ь	э	ю	я
Cyriltc	а	б	ч	д	е	ф	г	х	и	ш	к	л	м	н	о	п	ц	р	с	т	у	в	ш	ж	й	з	ь	ы	ъ	э	ю	я

Figure 8.6: The AutoCAD script and symbol fonts

columns of numbers or notes (see Figure 8.7). If you want something less boxy-looking, you can use the Romans font. Use the Romanc, Italicc, and other more complex fonts with discretion, as they will slow down the drawing regeneration considerably. Use the more complex fonts where you want a fancier type style, such as when drawing titles or labels in an exploded parts diagram (see Figure 8.8). You could use the Greeks font in conjunction with the Symath symbols for mathematical text.

CREATING A TYPE STYLE USING FONTS

Your drawings could look pretty boring using the same text style over and over. AutoCAD provides the ability to create any number of text

Room #	Door #	Thick	Rate	Matrl	Const
116	116	1 3/4'	20 MIN	WOOD	SOLID CORE
114	114	1 3/4'	20 MIN	WOOD	SOLID CORE
112	112	1 3/4'	20 MIN	WOOD	SOLID CORE
110	---	1 3/4'	45 MIN	METAL	MINERAL CORE
108	108	1 3/4'	20 MIN	WOOD	SOLID CORE
106	106	1 1/2'	NO RATE	WOOD	HOLLOW
102	102	1 1/2'	NO RATE	WOOD	HOLLOW
104	104	1 3/4'	20 MIN	WOOD	SOLID CORE
107	107	1 3/4'	45 MIN	METAL	MINERAL CORE
105	105	1 3/4'	20 MIN	WOOD	SOLID CORE
101	101	1 3/4'	20 MIN	WOOD	SOLID CORE

Room #	Door #	Thick	Rate	Matrl	Const
116	116	1 3/4'	20 MIN	WOOD	SOLID CORE
114	114	1 3/4'	20 MIN	WOOD	SOLID CORE
112	112	1 3/4'	20 MIN	WOOD	SOLID CORE
110	---	1 3/4'	45 MIN	METAL	MINERAL CORE
108	108	1 3/4'	20 MIN	WOOD	SOLID CORE
106	106	1 1/2'	NO RATE	WOOD	HOLLOW
102	102	1 1/2'	NO RATE	WOOD	HOLLOW
104	104	1 3/4'	20 MIN	WOOD	SOLID CORE
107	107	1 3/4'	45 MIN	METAL	MINERAL CORE
105	105	1 3/4'	20 MIN	WOOD	SOLID CORE
101	101	1 3/4'	20 MIN	WOOD	SOLID CORE

Figure 8.7: Columns in the Txt (top) and Monotxt (bottom) fonts

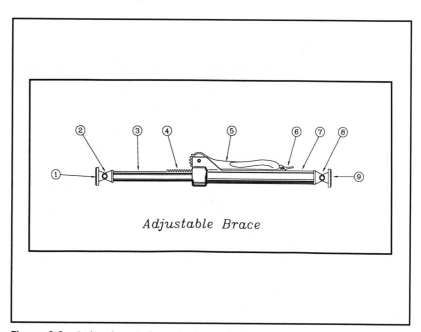

Figure 8.8: Italicc font used as title of parts diagram

styles based on a set of predefined fonts. You create a style using Draw
➤ Text ➤ Set Style.... You can then select from the fonts available
from AutoCAD, or you can use PostScript Fonts if you have them. This
next exercise will show you how to create a text style quickly from the
predefined set of AutoCAD fonts.

Draw ➤ A Text ➤ Set Style

1. Click on Draw ➤ Text ➤ Set Style. An icon menu appears.
   To the left is a list of fonts to choose from. To the right, each
   font is represented as an icon.

2. Click on **Next** to view the next group of fonts. Note that the
   button labeled **Previous** changes from gray to solid black.
   This button brings you back to the first group of icons (see
   Figure 8.9).

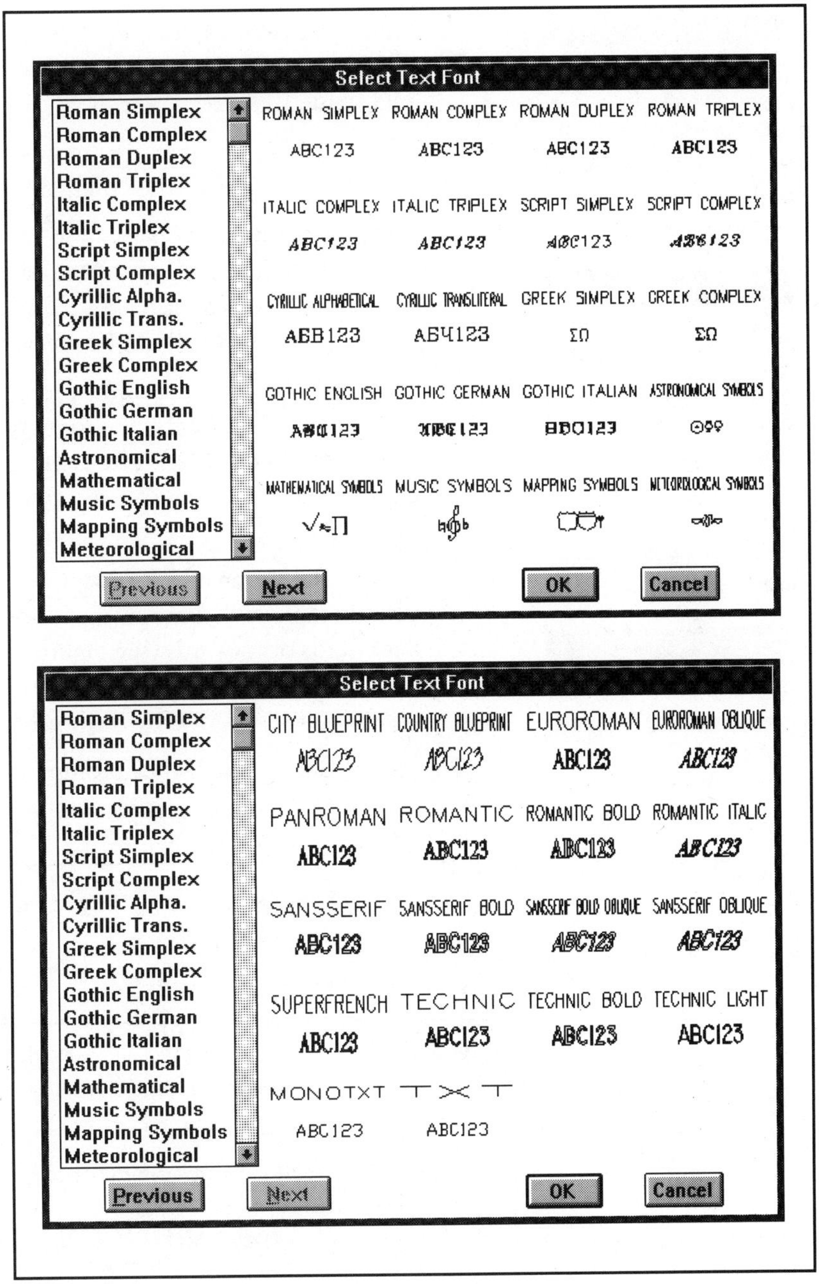

Figure 8.9:   The text font icon menus

3. Click on **Previous**, then click on the Roman Simplex icon. The Roman Simplex icon and the scroll list to the left are highlighted.

4. Click on **OK**. The icon menu disappears. The rest of the settings are set through the command prompt.

5. At the **Height <0'-0">** prompt, enter **6** ↵ for a fixed 6" text height. When you enter a value other than 0 at this prompt, it becomes the default height for this style. Then, when you use this style, you will not be prompted for a text height.

6. At the **Width factor <1.00>** prompt, Enter **.8** ↵. Here, you can compress or expand the font. You may find that you need a compressed font to fit into tight spaces. Or you may want to expand a font because of some graphic design consideration (see Figure 8.10).

7. At the **Obliquing angle <0>** prompt, press ↵ to accept the default angle of 0. This prompt allows you to slant the font backwards or forwards (see Figure 8.11). This allows you to give an italic look to any font but it doesn't slow down regeneration the way the Italic font does.

8. At the **Backwards? <N>** prompt, enter ↵.

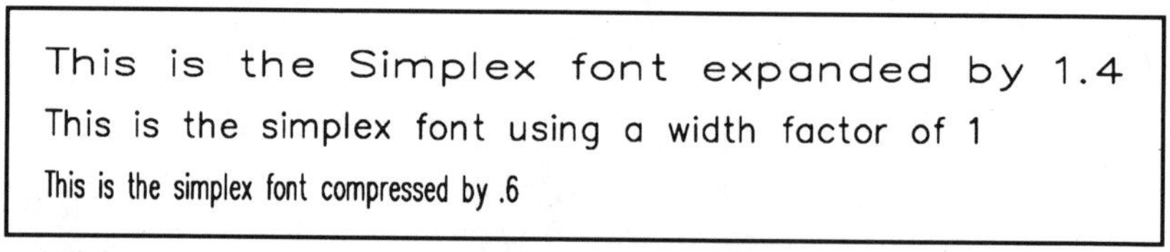

This is the Simplex font expanded by 1.4
This is the simplex font using a width factor of 1
This is the simplex font compressed by .6

Figure 8.10: Examples of compressed and expanded fonts

This is the simplex font using a 12−degree oblique angle

Figure 8.11: The Simplex font with a 12-degree oblique angle

If you need to use several different text heights in a drawing, you may want to keep the text height at 0. However, if you are using only two or three heights, you would be better off creating two or three different type styles with different heights.

9. At the **Upside-down? <N>** prompt, press ↵.

10. At the last prompt, **Vertical? <N>**, press ↵.

When you are done, you get the message, **ROMANS is now the current text style**, telling you that now when you enter text, it will be in the style you just created, Romans.

TURNING TEXT UPSIDE DOWN AND BACKWARDS

For several of the Style prompts, you just pressed ↵ to accept the N default. Chances are, you will never use these other style options. But here are descriptions for those rare instances that you do need to use them.

Backwards? <N> This prompt allows you to have the text appear backwards as if in a mirror (see Figure 8.12).

Upside-down? <N> This prompt allows you to set the style to appear upside down, rather than entering the text and rotating it (see Figure 8.13).

Vertical? <N> This prompt allows you to arrange lines of text vertically.

Figure 8.12: A text style using the Backwards option

Figure 8.13: A text style using the Upside-down option

RENAMING A TYPE STYLE

Romans is the default name AutoCAD gives to this style when you select Roman Simplex from the icon menu. AutoCAD uses the name of the Font to name the style. But suppose you want to use a different name for your newly created style. For example, you might want to create two styles of differing height using the same Romans font. Here's how you can change the style name.

AutoCAD ➤ Utility ➤ Rename

1. Click on AutoCAD ➤ UTILITY ➤ RENAME from the Root menu or enter **Rename** ↵ at the command prompt.

2. At the **RENAME Block/Dimstyle/LAyer/LType/Style /UCS/VIew/VPorts:** prompt, click on Style from the side menu or enter **S** ↵.

3. At the **Old text style name:** prompt, enter **Romans** ↵.

4. At the **New text style name:** prompt, enter the word **Note2** ↵. You have just renamed the text style you created using the icon menu.

Since you renamed the current style from *Romans* to *Note2*, Note2 is your current style. You'll get a chance to see how this style will look in your drawing, but first, let's look at another way of creating a text style.

FINE-TUNING A TYPE STYLE

The last text style you created drew from the predefined set of AutoCAD fonts. It also automatically assigned a name for the style, which you then changed using the RENAME command. Another way of creating text styles is to use the Style command. The Style command allows you to select from PostScript fonts, as well as the standard AutoCAD fonts, or any other third-party fonts you might obtain for AutoCAD. It also lets you enter a name for the text style instead of automatically providing one.

AutoCAD ➤ Settings ➤ next ➤ Style

1. Click on AutoCAD ➤ SETTINGS ➤ next ➤ STYLE from the Root menu or enter **Style** ↵ at the command prompt.

2. At the **Text style name (or ?) <STANDARD>** prompt, enter **Note** ↵ for your text style name. The Select Font File dialog box appears. This is a typical file dialog box.

3. Use the Files list to locate the PostScript font file *TE_____.PFB*, then double-click on it. The dialog box disappears.

4. Enter a Height of 6" and press ↵ at the rest of the prompts.

The rest of the command operates exactly as if you had used the Draw ➤ Text ➤ Set style option when you created the Note2 style.

▼ NOTE

PostScript fonts will appear as outline fonts no matter what type of font they are. Plotting PostScript fonts will also yield outline letters. You can, however, use the PSout function to export your drawings as fully PostScript-compatible files. You can then download the file to a PostScript device for accurate text reproduction (see *Chapter 14* for more on PSout).

USING A TYPE STYLE

Now let's see how to use the text styles you created. In the next exercise, you'll also get to see how the justification option works.

Draw ➤ A Text ➤ Dynamic (Centered)

1. Click on Draw ➤ Text ➤ Dynamic.

2. Click on Justify ➤ Center from the side menu or enter **C** ↵.

3. Pick a point near the center of the living room at coordinate 21'-11", 15'-2".

4. At the **rotation angle** prompt, press ↵ to accept the default 0 angle.

5. At the **Text** prompt, enter **Living room** ↵. As you type, AutoCAD does not yet center the text.

6. Press ↵ again to exit the Dtext command. Notice how the text centers on the point you selected.

You might have noticed that in step 4 the **rotation angle** prompt appeared, skipping over the Height prompt. Remember that when you use a style with a non-zero height, AutoCAD doesn't bother to ask you what height you want. In this example, the style has a preset height of 6, so you are not prompted for a height.

Compiling PostScript Fonts for Speed

Some PostScript fonts may slow AutoCAD down due to the added overhead of having to translate PostScript font descriptions into a format AutoCAD can understand. To improve AutoCAD performance, you can compile PostScript fonts into AutoCAD's native .SHX font format. Here's how it's done.

1. Click on File ➤ Compile. The Compile Shape or Font file dialog box appears.

2. Double-click on the PostScript font you want to convert into the AutoCAD format. AutoCAD will work for a moment, then give you the message:

   Compiling shape/font description file
   Compilation successful. Output file
   E:\ACAD\FONTS\TE_____.shx contains 59578 bytes.

3. When AutoCAD is done, you will have a file with the same name as the PostScript font file but with the .SHX file extension.

AutoCAD will use this compiled version of the font instead of the original PostScript .PFB file. It is important to note that license restrictions still apply to the AutoCAD compiled version of the PostScript font. Compiled PostScript fonts can also take up large amounts of disk space, so only compile the fonts you need. Finally, some fonts may not load into AutoCAD at all due to subtle differences in PostScript formatting.

▼ NOTE

When you use the STYLE command, your default style becomes the one you most recently edited or created.

In the last exercise, you entered text using the current default style. If you want to use a different style from the current one, you can use the Dtext style option.

Draw ➤ A Text ➤ Dynamic (Style)

1. Click on Draw ➤ Text ➤ Dynamic or enter **Dtext** ↵.

2. Click on Style from the side menu or enter **S** ↵.

3. At the **Style name (or ?) <Note>:** prompt, enter **Standard** ↵.

4. Type **C** ↵ or click on the Centered option from the side menu.

5. Pick the point at coordinate 21′-11″, 14′-4″. This time the height prompt appears, because you are now using a font whose height is set to 0. Notice how the default height is still at the last size you entered.

6. Press ↵ to accept the default height.

7. Press ↵ again to accept the default angle.

8. Enter **14′-0″ by 16′-5″** ↵.

9. Press ↵ again to exit dynamic text.

10. Zoom into this group of text.

▼ NOTE

You can enter a question mark at step 3 to get a list of available styles; enter the name of an available style to make it current; or press ↵ to accept Note, the current style.

▼ TIP

If you remember all the justification options, you can enter them directly at the **Justify/Style/<Start point>** prompt and skip the **Justify** prompt.

Now you can see the different styles you entered (see Figure 8.14). The words *Living room* use a smoother letter form than the dimensions *14′-0″ by 16′-5″*.

1. Start Dynamic Text again, and at the starting point prompt, press ↵.

2. Enter **231 square feet** ↵.

3. Press ↵ again to exit Dtext.

4. Now zoom to your previous view.

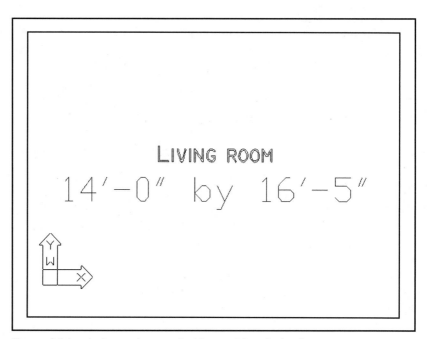

Figure 8.14:   A closeup showing the Note and Standard styles

Notice how the text you just entered is centered below the previously entered text (see Figure 8.15). AutoCAD remembers not only the location of the last text you entered, but the starting point you selected for it. If you had moved the last line of text, the new text would still appear below it.

MODIFYING EXISTING TEXT

AutoCAD offers a variety of ways to modify text. Nearly every property associated with text, from height to width, can be edited. Of course, you can also edit the contents of the text. In this section, you will learn the various ways that text can be controlled to do exactly what you want it to do.

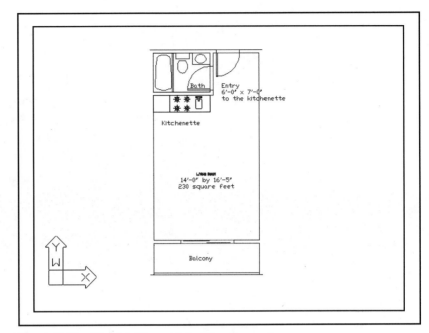

Figure 8.15: The third line added to the column of text

Table 8.1: Codes for Adding Special Characters to AutoCAD Text

CODE	DESCRIPTION
%%o	Toggles overscore on and off.
%%u	Toggles underscore on and off.
%%d	Places a degree sign (°) where the code occurs.
%%p	Places a plus-minus sign where the code occurs.
%%%	Forces a single percent sign. This is useful where a double percent sign must be entered or when a percent sign must be entered in conjunction with another code.
%%*nnn*	Allows the use of extended ASCII characters when these characters are used in a text-definition file. The *nnn* is the three-digit value representing the character.

▼

■

■

■

■

Adding Special Characters

AutoCAD offers the ability to add special characters to your text. For example, you can add the degrees symbol (°) to a number or underscore text. To accomplish this, you need to use a double percent (%%) sign in conjunction with a special code (see Table 8.2). For example, to underscore (i.e., underline) text, you enclose it with the underscore code. To get the following text:

This is <u>underscored</u> text.

you would enter **This is %%uunderscored%%u text.** Overscore operates in the same manner. You just place the other codes in the correct positions for the symbols they represent. For example, to enter

100.5°

you would type **100.5%%d.**

CHANGING THE PROPERTIES OF TEXT

Perhaps the simplest way to modify text is to use the Modify ➤ Entity... menu option. This option will give you access to virtually all of the properties that control the appearance of text. Let's see how it works.

Modify ➤ Entity...

1. Zoom into the entry area again.

2. Click on Modify ➤ Entity....

3. At the **Select object to modify** prompt, click on the bottom line of the currently displayed text. The Modify Text dialog box appears (see Figure 8.16). Take a moment to review the options.

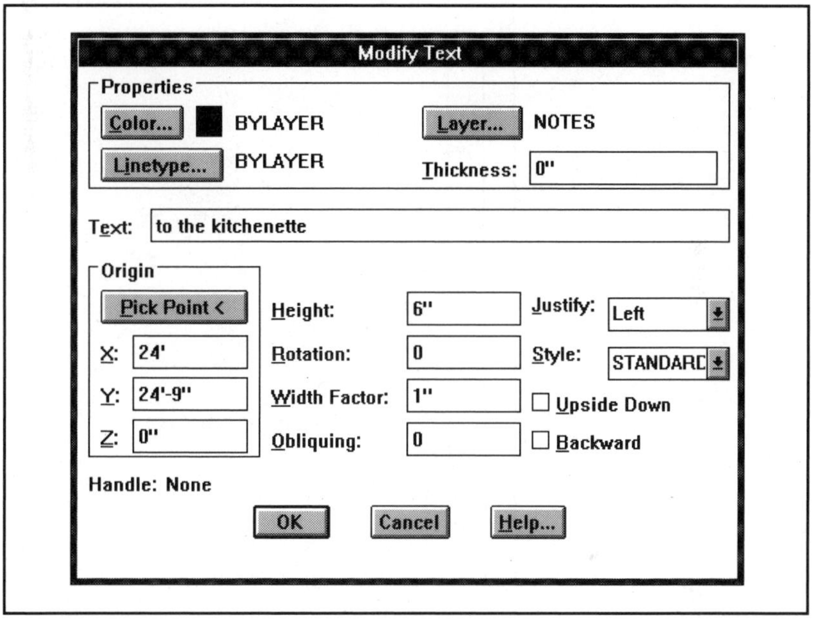

Figure 8.16:   The Modify Text dialog box

4. Click on the down-pointing arrow of the Style pop-up list in the lower-right corner of the dialog box. You will see all three text styles available in this file listed.

5. Click on **Note**. The pop-up list closes.

6. Click on **OK**. The dialog box closes and the text you selected changes to the new style (see Figure 8.17).

The Modify Text dialog box lets you change everything from the text's justification style to its contents. But as powerful as it is, this dialog box only handles one line of text at a time. Suppose you want to modify several lines at once.

CHANGING PROPERTIES OF MULTIPLE TEXT

Often you will need to change the properties of several pieces of text at once. To do this, you will have to enlist the aid of AutoLISP. AutoCAD comes with several helpful utilities that you'll explore as you proceed

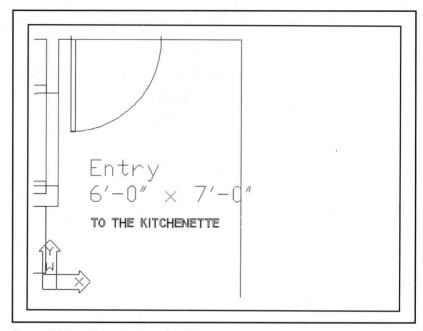

Figure 8.17: The style changed to Note

through this book. One such utility is Chtext, which helps you modify the properties of multiple text objects. First, you'll have to load it from your hard disk.

File ➤ Applications

▼ TIP

You can quickly load this AutoLISP utility by entering **(Load "Chtext")** ↵.

1. Click on File ➤ Applications.

2. At the Load AutoLISP and ADS files dialog box, click on **File**….

3. Go to the Support subdirectory.

4. Double-click on CHTEXT.LSP from the Files scroll list. You may have to use the scroll bar to find it. You will see CHTEXT.LSP added to the list in the main dialog box.

5. Click on CHTEXT.LSP to highlight it, then click on the button labeled LOAD.

6. You see the message **CHText loaded. Start command with CHT.**

You've just loaded an AutoLISP program. You'll have access to it for the rest of the time you are in the current file. Let's try it out.

Cht ↵

▼ WARNING

If you have problems starting this program, consult *Chapter 19* on how to load AutoLISP programs.

1. Enter **CHT** ↵.

2. At the **Select objects** prompt, select the bottom two lines of text.

3. At the **Height/Justification/Location/Rotation/Style/Text /Undo/Width:** prompt, enter **H** ↵ for Height.

4. At the **Individual/List/<New height for all text entities>:** prompt, enter **12**. The selected text changes in height to 12" and the **Height/Justification/Location** prompt returns.

5. Enter **U** to undo this edit.

6. Press ↵ to exit the Chtext program.

With Chtext, you modify a group of text at once. It may not be as elegant as the Modify Text dialog box, but it can save you a good deal of time when you must modify large blocks of text.

You probably noticed several other options in the Chtext prompt. The following briefly explains what each option offers:

Height changes the height of text. If you have selected more than one line of text, you can enter a new text height to change the height of all text at once, enter **I** to change the height of each line of text individually, or enter **L** to get a listing of the range of heights of the existing text you selected.

Justification lets you change the justification of text. You are prompted for a justification option. You can enter any of the justification options that are normally available. Once you enter a justification style, you are asked to select new insertion points for the selected text.

Location, **Rotation**, and **Style** let you change the position, angle, and text style of the selected text.

Text lets you edit the selected text either through a dialog box or directly from the keyboard. This option has the further sub-options of **Individual/Retype/Global**. Individual lets you edit the selected text in a dialog box (see the next section). Retype lets you re-enter each selected line. Global lets you replace a specific string of text in the selected group.

Undo will undo the last Chtext operation performed.

Width changes the width factor of the selected text.

There are two other utilities available on the bonus disk that came with this book. ET.LSP lets you quickly replace several lines of text with the same line that you enter. ETS.LSP lets you change a group of text objects into a sequence of numbers. Both of these utilities are useful when you are editing tables or schedules where sets of numbers change or where data is repeated in several places.

TEXT EDITING SIMPLIFIED

If you have to change the contents of several lines of text, you may find using the Modify Text dialog box a bit too clumsy. AutoCAD offers a quick way to edit several lines of text using the DDEDIT command.

Ddedit ↵

1. Enter **Ddedit** ↵ or click on AutoCAD ➤ EDIT ➤ DDEDIT from the side menu.

2. At the **<Select a TEXT or ATTDEF object>/Undo:** prompt, click on the second-to-last line of text displayed on the screen. A dialog box appears displaying that text (see Figure 8.18).

3. Click on the **X** between the two dimensions.

4. Press the ← key to delete the **X**, then enter **by**.

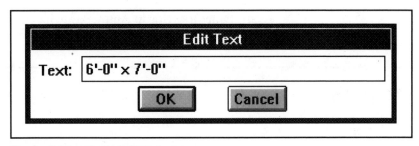

Figure 8.18:   The Ddedit dialog box

5. Click on **OK**. The text changes to reflect the changes you made in the dialog box.

6. At the **Select a TEXT**... prompt, click on the next line down. The dialog box appears again allowing you to make more changes.

7. Click on **OK**.

8. Now enter **U** to select the Undo option. The text you just edited changes back to its previous form, and again the *Select a TEXT*... prompt remains.

9. Press ↵ to exit DDEDIT.

10. Now save this file.

You can edit the text in the DDEDIT dialog box just as you would in any other input box. You can double-click on the input box, then proceed to enter an entirely new line of text. Or, as you have just seen, you can easily edit one or two letters within the current line of text.

Another way to edit multiple lines of text is to use the Text option under the Chtext utility described in the previous section. The Text option has a suboption called Individual, which automatically applies DDEDIT to the set of text lines you select for CHText.

KEEPING TEXT FROM MIRRORING

At times you may want to mirror a group of objects that contain some text. Normally, if you do this, the mirrored text appears backward. You can change a setting in AutoCAD to make the text read the regular way even if it is mirrored.

Mirrtext ↵

1. Enter **Mirrtext** ↵.
2. At the **New value for MIRRTEXT <1>:** prompt, enter **0** ↵.

Once you have done this, any mirrored text that is not in a block will read normally. The text position, however, will still be mirrored, as shown in Figure 8.19.

SPEEDING UP ZOOMS
AND REGENS WITH QTEXT

If you need to edit a drawing that contains lots of notes, but you are not going to edit the notes, you can use the QTEXT command to help speed up redraws and regenerations. QTEXT turns lines of text into rectangular boxes, saving AutoCAD from having to form every letter. This

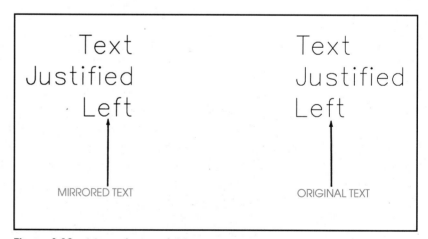

Figure 8.19:   Mirrored text with Mirrtext set to 0

allows you to see the note locations so you don't accidentally draw over them. To turn on QTEXT, do the following:

▼ NOTE

You can also control Qtext from the Drawing Aids dialog box. Click on Settings ➤ Drawing Aids, then check the box labeled Quick Text.

1. Enter **Qtext** ↵ at the command prompt or click on AutoCAD ➤ *Settings* ➤ next ➤ *Qtext* from the Root menu.

2. At the **ON/OFF <OFF>:** prompt, enter **ON** ↵.

3. Issue the REGEN command to display the results of QTEXT.

When QTEXT is off, text is generated normally, as shown in panel 1 of Figure 8.20. When QTEXT is on, a rectangle appears showing the approximate size and length of text, as shown in panel 2.

IMPORTING TEXT INTO AUTOCAD

If you have a good deal of text in a drawing, or a sheet of general notes for a set of drawings, you may want to create it in a word processor with advanced features for moving around, editing, and copying. You may also want a drawing to contain text already generated with a spreadsheet or database program.

You can import ASCII text into your drawings using Draw ➤ Text ➤ Import Text. Here's how to use it.

At ↵

1. Click on Draw ➤ Text ➤ Import Text.

2. At the File dialog box, locate the text file you wish to import.

3. At the **Start point or Center/Middle/Right/?:** prompt, pick the location for the first line of text. You can also specify justification at this prompt.

4. At the **Height: <6">:** prompt, enter a height or press ↵ to accept the default.

5. At the **Rotation angle <0>** prompt, enter an angle or press ↵ to accept the default.

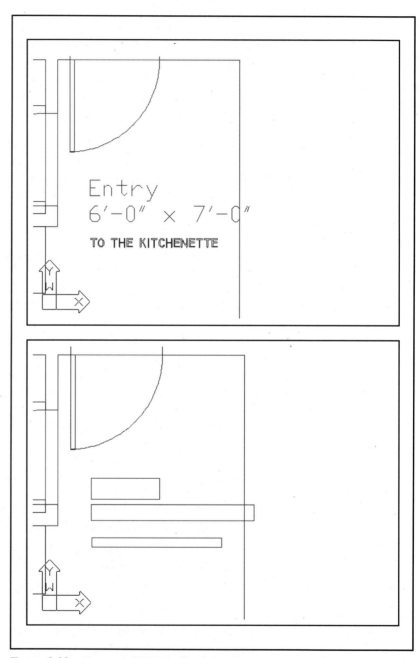

Figure 8.20: Text with QTEXT off and on

6. At the **Change text options? <N>:** you could press ↵ to accept the default, *No*, and your text would be imported. You can, however, change several other settings to enhance the imported text. If you enter **Y**, AutoCAD continues with the following set of prompts.

7. At the **Distance between lines/<Auto>:** prompt, you can specify the line spacing if you want it to be different from the default.

8. At the **First line to read/<1>:** prompt, you can tell AutoCAD to skip the beginning of the file if you so desire.

9. At the **Number of lines to read/<All>:** prompt, you can restrict how much of the file you want read into your drawing.

Using the Windows Clipboard to Import Text

You can also use the Windows Clipboard to cut and paste text from a Windows word processor into AutoCAD. Here's how it's done.

1. While in AutoCAD, click on Draw ➤ Text ➤ Dynamic, or enter **Dtext** at the command prompt.

2. Pick a point to locate the text, then enter the text height and rotation angle.

3. At the Text prompt, switch to your word processor and highlight the text you want to import to AutoCAD.

4. While still in the word processor, click on Edit ➤ Copy.

5. Return to AutoCAD, then click on Edit ➤ Paste Command. The text is entered into the drawing.

6. Press ↵ to exit the Dtext command.

10. At the **Underscore each line? <N>:** and **Overscore each line? <N>:** prompts, you can tell AutoCAD to add underscores or overscores.

11. At the **Change text case? Upper/Lower/<N>:** prompt, you can change the case of the incoming text.

12. At the **Set up columns? <N>:** prompt, you can specify the distance between columns and the number of lines per column. If you answer **N**, the text will be imported.

IF YOU WANT TO EXPERIMENT...

At this point you may want to try adding notes to drawings you have created in other *If You Want to Experiment...* sections. Try the exercise shown in Figure 8.21. You might also try importing a schedule in the Monotxt font to see how that works.

SUMMARY

In this chapter we have introduced you to AutoCAD's features for entering, editing, and importing text. You may end up using only a few of the available options, but it is useful to be aware of them all. You never know when you will have to enter a large text file into an AutoCAD drawing, or when you will have to replace every occurrence of the word *widget* with the word *doodad* in a drawing full of text.

Along with notes, dimensions help convey information about a design. In the next chapter, you will add dimensions to the studio unit plan. You will also discover how to add arrows for pointing to objects from notes.

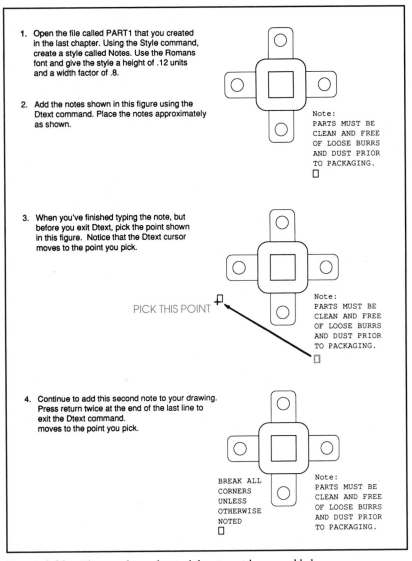

1. Open the file called PART1 that you created in the last chapter. Using the Style command, create a style called Notes. Use the Romans font and give the style a height of .12 units and a width factor of .8.

2. Add the notes shown in this figure using the Dtext command. Place the notes approximately as shown.

   Note:
   PARTS MUST BE
   CLEAN AND FREE
   OF LOOSE BURRS
   AND DUST PRIOR
   TO PACKAGING.

3. When you've finished typing the note, but before you exit Dtext, pick the point shown in this figure. Notice that the Dtext cursor moves to the point you pick.

   PICK THIS POINT

   Note:
   PARTS MUST BE
   CLEAN AND FREE
   OF LOOSE BURRS
   AND DUST PRIOR
   TO PACKAGING.

4. Continue to add this second note to your drawing. Press return twice at the end of the last line to exit the Dtext command.
   moves to the point you pick.

   BREAK ALL
   CORNERS
   UNLESS
   OTHERWISE
   NOTED

   Note:
   PARTS MUST BE
   CLEAN AND FREE
   OF LOOSE BURRS
   AND DUST PRIOR
   TO PACKAGING.

Figure 8.21: The sample mechanical drawing with notes added

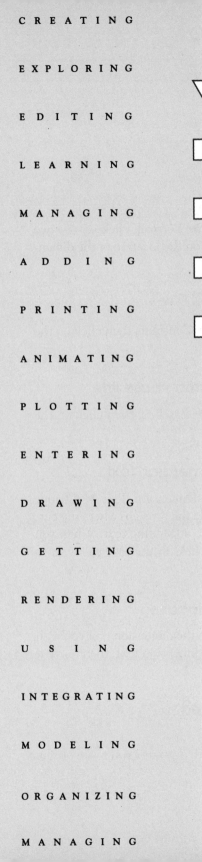

9

USING
DIMENSIONS

FAST TRACK

332 ▶ **To draw a vertical dimension**

Click on Draw ➤ Dimension ➤ Linear ➤ Vertical, click on the two points you want to dimension, then click on the location of the dimension line.

337 ▶ **To add to a string of dimensions**

Click on Draw ➤ Dimension ➤ Linear ➤ Continue, then click on the next point you want to dimension.

339 ▶ **To draw dimensions from a common base line**

Click on Draw ➤ Dimension ➤ Linear ➤ Baseline, then click on the next point you want to dimension.

341 ▶ **To append text to an existing dimension text**

Click on Modify ➤ Edit Dimensions ➤ Dimension Text ➤ Change Text, enter the appending text and include the <> signs where the current text is to be placed in relation to the appending text. When you are done typing the text, press ↵, then click on the text you wish to change. Press ↵ to finish your selection.

343 ▶ **To move dimension text to new location**

With the Grips feature turned on, click on the dimension text you wish to move. Click on the grip located at the dimension text, then move it into place.

343 ▶ **To ensure dimensions are updated when a drawing changes**

Include a dimension's definition point with any edits you make on the drawing.

351 ▶ To set up specific Osnap overrides to be the default when picking points

Click on Settings ➤ Object Snaps..., then check any object snap settings you want to be active at all times.

351 ▶ To set up several dimension styles

Click on Settings ➤ Dimension Style..., then enter a name in the input box. Press ↵ to make the name you entered into a style. Enter more names this way to create more styles. Once a style is defined, you can click on the labeled buttons to make adjustments to each style.

359 ▶ To dimension an arc

Click on Draw ➤ Dimension ➤ Angular, click on the arc to be dimensioned, pick the dimension line location, enter a new dimension value or press ↵ to accept the default, then pick the text location.

361 ▶ To add a note with a leader

Click on Draw ➤ Dimension ➤ Leader, pick the arrow side of the leader, pick points defining the leader lines, press ↵ when you are done placing the leader lines, then type the note.

364 ▶ To skew the extension lines of a linear dimension

Click on Modify ➤ Edit Dimensions ➤ Oblique Dimension, select the dimensions you want to skew, then enter the new angle for the extension lines. The angle you enter describes the angle of the extension line to the 0 angle.

Before you determine the dimensions of a project, your design is in flux and many questions may be unanswered. Once you begin dimensioning, you see if things fit or work together. Dimensioning can be crucial to how well a design works and how quickly it develops. Communicating even tentative dimensions to others can speed up design development.

With AutoCAD, you can easily add tentative or final dimensions to any drawing. AutoCAD gives you an accurate dimension without your having to take measurements. You simply pick the two points to be dimensioned and the dimension line location, and AutoCAD does the rest. AutoCAD's *associative dimensioning* capability automatically updates dimensions whenever the size or shape of the dimensioned object is changed. These *dimensioning features* can save you valuable time and reduce the number of dimensional errors in your drawings.

USING AND ADJUSTING THE DEFAULT DIMENSION SETTINGS

AutoCAD's dimensioning feature has a large number of settings. While they give you an enormous amount of flexibility in formatting your dimensions, they can be a bit intimidating to the new user. In this first section you will enter some dimensions to see what happens when you use the default settings. This will show you that you needn't know everything about dimensions to get some useful results.

PLACING HORIZONTAL AND VERTICAL DIMENSIONS

The most common type of dimension you'll be drawing is the *vertical* or *horizontal dimension*. In this first exercise, you will see how to draw these types of dimensions, and along the way, discover how to take control of a few dimension settings.

Draw ➤ ⊢⊣ Dimension ➤ Linear ➤ Vertical

▼ TIP

You can also enter **dim1** ↵
vert ↵ to start the vertical
dimension.

1. Open the Unit file and click on View ➤ Zoom ➤ All to get an overall view.

2. Click on Draw➤ Dimension➤ Linear➤ Vertical.

3. At the **First extension line origin or Return to select:** prompt, pick the upper-right corner of the entry at the co-ordinate 29′-0″, 30′-10″. This prompt is asking you for the first point of the distance to be dimensioned.

▼ NOTE

The *dimension line* is the line
indicating the direction of the
dimension and containing the
arrows or tick marks.

4. At the **Second extension line origin:** prompt, pick the lower-right corner of the living room at coordinate 29′-0″, 6′-10″.

5. At the **Dimension line location:** prompt, move your cursor from left to right. You see a temporary dimension appear. This allows you to visually select a dimension line location.

6. Enter @4′<0 to tell AutoCAD you want the dimension line four feet to the right of the last point you selected. You could pick a point using your cursor, but you may want to place the dimension line more accurately.

▼ NOTE

You have the option to enter a
different dimension text or to
append information to the
default. You'll learn how to append text to dimensions later
in this chapter.

7. At the **Dimension text <24′>:** prompt, press ↵ to accept the default, *24′*.

The dimension lines and extension lines appear, but there are no dimensions or arrows (see Figure 9.1). To see what happened, do the following.

1. Enter ′**zoom** ↵, then enter **C** ↵.

▼ NOTE

The value in brackets indicates the current view height.

2. At the **Center point:** prompt, pick a point midway between the two dimension extension lines, as shown in Figure 9.2.

3. At the **Magnification or Height (34′-0″):** prompt, enter 8 ↵ for an 8″ height. Your view will look like Figure 9.3.

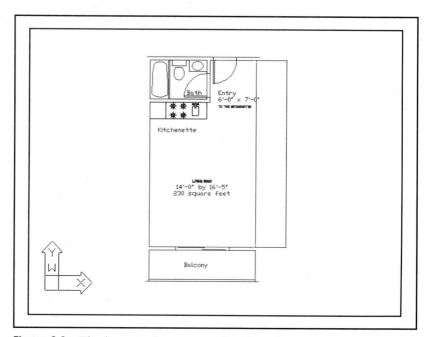

Figure 9.1: The dimension lines, apparently without dimensions or arrows

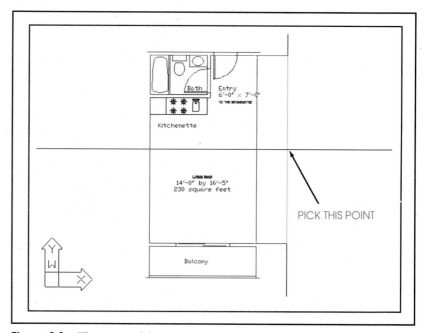

Figure 9.2: The center of the zoom view

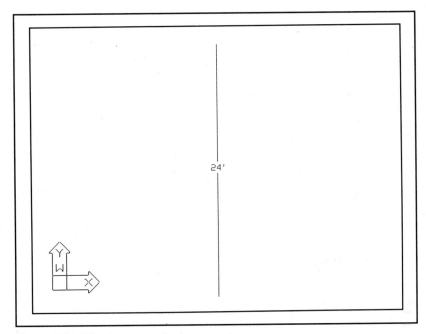

Figure 9.3:   The dimension after you zoom in

The dimension is there after all, but it is so small that it cannot be read in a normal view. The dimension arrows were also inserted, but because they are so small and so close to the extension lines, they don't appear.

SETTING A DIMENSION SCALE

A new user will often try adding dimensions to a drawing, only to find that many things seem not to work. Most of these problems come from not understanding that dimensions require a scale adjustment, just as sheet sizes and text do. Next you will set the dimension scale so the dimension appears at the right scale for this drawing.

'Dimscale ↵

1. Click on View ➤ Zoom ➤ Previous or enter **'Zoom** ↵ **P** ↵ to get back to the overall view of the unit plan.

▼ **TIP**

A simple way to figure out scale factors is to divide 12 by the decimal equivalent of the inch scale. For ¼" you divide 12 by 0.25 to get 48. For ⅛" you divide 12 by 0.125 to get 96. For 1½" you divide 12 by 1.5, and so on.

2. Enter **dimscale** ↵ at the command prompt. This is a dimension variable you can set from the command prompt.

3. At the **New value for DIMSCALE <1.0000>** prompt, enter **48** ↵. As you can see from the default value, the current setting is for a one-to-one scale. Your current scale, however, is ¼"=1'-0". You know from previous chapters that the scale conversion factor for ¼" scale is 48.

Next, you will update a dimension to conform to the new dimension-scale factor setting.

Modify ➤ ⊢⊣ Edit Dimensions ➤ Update Dimensions

▼ **NOTE**

You can also simply enter **DIM1** ↵ **UPDATE** ↵ at the Dim prompt.

1. Click on Modify ➤ Edit Dimensions ➤ Update Dimension.

2. At the **Select objects** prompt, click on the dimension line you just entered, then press ↵. The dimension will appear at the proper scale, as shown in Figure 9.4.

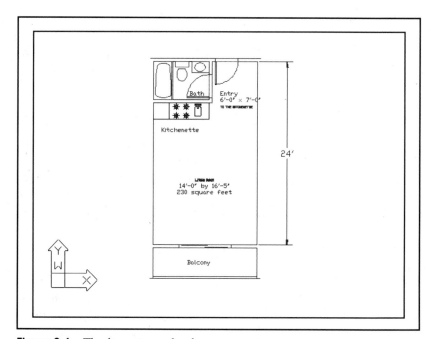

Figure 9.4: The dimension updated

CONTINUING A DIMENSION

You will often want to input a group of dimensions strung together in a line. For example, you may want to dimension the balcony and have it aligned with the dimension you just entered. To do this, you use the Continue option.

Draw ➤ ⊢⊣ Dimension ➤ Linear ➤ Continue

▼ TIP

You can also enter **dim1** ↵ **cont** ↵ to continue a dimension.

1. Click on Draw ➤ Dimension ➤ Linear ➤ Continue.

2. At the **Second extension line origin or RETURN to Select:** prompt, pick the right end of the rail on the balcony at coordinate 29'-0", 2'-8".

3. At the **Dimension text <4'-2">** prompt, press ↵ to accept the default. See Figure 9.5 for the results.

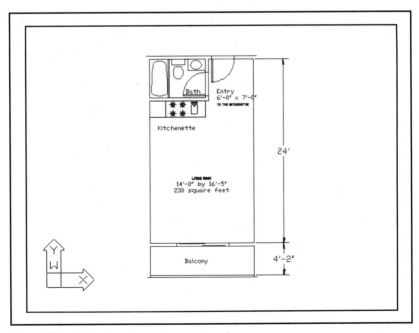

Figure 9.5:   The dimension string continued

The Continue option adds a dimension from where you left off. It uses the last drawn extension line as the first extension line for the continued dimension.

Dimensioning from the Keyboard

AutoCAD provides two commands for dimensioning that you can use from the keyboard. These commands are *Dim* and *Dim1*. The Dim command is like a self-contained program. Once you enter it, you get the **Dim:** prompt instead of the familiar command prompt. Also, you cannot use any other AutoCAD commands (with the exception of transparent commands); only the commands that relate to dimensioning are allowed (see below). To exit the Dim prompt, you enter **Exit** ↵ or press **Ctrl-C**.

The Dim1 command allows you to enter a single dimension, then automatically returns you to the standard command prompt to enter other AutoCAD commands. Most of the pull-down menu selection options use this command. This is useful for dimensioning parts of an object quickly, when you don't have to enter lots of dimensions. Dim1 uses the same settings as Dim.

The dimensioning commands are as follows:

Aligned	Hometext	Radius	Tedit
Angular	Horizontal	Redraw	Trotate
Baseline	Leader	Restore	Undo
Center	Newtext	Rotate	Update
Continue	Oblique	Save	Variables
Diameter	Ordinate	Status	Vertical
Exit	Override	Style	

All of these dimensioning commands can be issued using just the first three letters. For example, you can enter **Dim1**↵ **Ver** ↵ to draw a vertical dimension.

As you work through the tutorial, you will see these command names appear, usually as the last part of a menu selection sequence or as part of a dialog box. If you prefer to use the keyboard to issue dimensioning commands, use Dim1 when you are adding single dimensions and Dim where you are adding strings of dimensions or when you want to add several dimensions at once. By using Dim, you avoid having to re-enter the dimensioning feature for each additional dimension.

Both Dim and Dim1 are accessible from the Root menu by clicking on Dim.

DRAWING DIMENSIONS FROM A COMMON BASE EXTENSION LINE

At times you will want several dimensions to originate from the same extension line. To accommodate this, AutoCAD provides the *baseline* option. To see how this works, first you will start another dimension across the top of the plan. In doing this, you will get a chance to use the Horizontal option to draw a horizontal dimension.

Draw ➤ |↔| Dimension ➤ Linear ➤ Horizontal

▼ TIP

You can also enter **dim1 ↵ hor** ↵ to start the horizontal dimension.

1. Click on Draw ➤ Dimension ➤ Linear ➤ Horizontal.

2. At the **First extension line**... prompt, pick the upper-left corner of the bathroom near coordinate 15′-0″, 30′-10″.

3. At the **Second extension line**... prompt, pick the upper-right corner of the bathroom near coordinate 22′-6″, 30′-10″.

4. At the **Dimension line**... prompt, pick a point near coordinate 22′-5″, 33′-5″.

5. At the **Dimension text** prompt, press ↵ (see Figure 9.6).

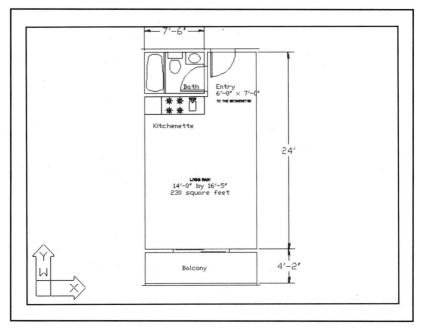

Figure 9.6: The bathroom with horizontal dimensions

Now you're set to draw another dimension from the same first extension line.

Draw ➤ Dimension ➤ Linear ➤ Baseline

Zoom is one of a handful of *transparent* commands. These are commands that can be used even while another command is active. To use the transparent feature of a command from the keyboard, you precede its name with an apostrophe.

1. Click on Draw ➤ Dimension ➤ Linear ➤ Baseline or enter **Dim1** ↵ **Base** ↵.

2. At the **Second extension line…** prompt, click on the upper-right corner of the entry.

3. At the **Dimension text** prompt, press ↵. Although you cannot see it, the overall width dimension appears above the 7'-6" dimension.

4. Click on View ➤ Zoom ➤ All to see the entire drawing, as shown in Figure 9.7.

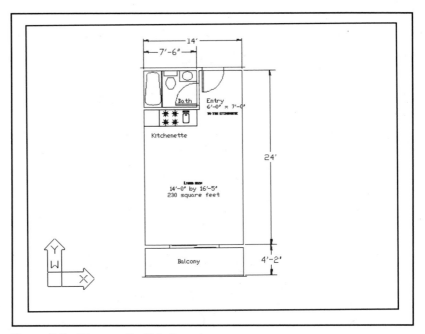

Figure 9.7: The overall width dimension

▼ TIP

You may want to continue a dimension string or add a dimension to a baseline dimension that is not the most recently added one. Use Modify ➤ Edit Dimensions ➤ Update Dimension on the dimension you want to refresh, then use the Linear ➤ Baseline or Linear ➤ Continue options to add the new dimension.

In this example, you see that the Baseline option is similar to the Continue option, except that it allows you to use the first extension line as the base for a second dimension.

APPENDING DATA TO DIMENSION TEXT

▼ TIP

You can append text to several dimensions at once by using Modify ➤ Edit Dimensions ➤ Dimension Text ➤ Change Text.

So far, you've been accepting the default dimension text. Whenever you see the **Dimension text…** prompt, you can append information to the default dimension value shown in brackets. By using the less-than (<) and greater-than (>) signs, you can add text either before or after the default dimension. Let's see how this works by changing a dimension text.

Modify ➤ |↔| Edit Dimensions ➤ Dimension Text ➤ Change Text

▼ TIP

You can also enter **Dim1** ↵ **Newtext** ↵ to start the Change Text option.

1. Click on Modify ➤ Edit Dimensions ➤ Dimension Text ➤ Change Text.

2. At the **Enter new dimension text:** prompt, type **<> to face of stud** ↵.

3. At the **Select objects** prompt, pick the last horizontal dimension you added to the drawing at the top of the screen. The **Select objects** prompt remains, allowing you to select more dimensions.

4. Press ↵ to finish your selection. The dimension changes to read *14′ to face of stud*.

5. Enter **U** ↵ to undo the appended text. You don't really need the new appended text for the tutorial.

6. Now save the Unit file.

Using the Change Text option, you were able to combine the dimension text *14′* with the text *to face of stud*. You can also have AutoCAD automatically add a *dimension suffix* to all dimensions, instead of just a chosen few, by using the Dimpost and Dimapost system variables or the Text Prefix and Text Suffix options in the Dimension Styles... Text format dialog box. See *Appendix D* for more on these options.

EDITING DIMENSIONS

AutoCAD provides the associative dimensioning capability to automatically update dimension text when a drawing is edited. Objects called *definition points* are used to determine how edited dimensions are updated.

LOCATING THE DEFINITION POINTS

The definition points are located at the same points you pick when you determine the dimension location, plus there is another definition point at the center of the dimension text. For example, the definition points for linear dimensions are located at the extension line origin and the intersection of the extension line and the dimension line. The definition points for a circle diameter are the points used to pick the circle and the opposite side of the circle. The definition points for a radius are the points used to pick the circle, plus the center of the circle.

Definition points are actually point objects. They are very difficult to see, since they are usually covered by the feature they define. You can, however, see them indirectly using grips. The definition points of a dimension are the same as the dimension's grip points. You can see them simply by clicking on a dimension. Try the following.

1. Make sure the Grips feature is turned on (see *Chapter 2* to refresh your memory on the Grips feature).

2. Click on the longer of the two vertical dimensions you drew earlier in this chapter. You will see the grips of the dimension (see Figure 9.8).

▼ TIP

Since the Defpoints layer has the unique feature of being visible even when turned off, you can use it as a layer for laying out your drawing. If Defpoints is turned off, you can still see objects assigned to it, but the objects won't plot.

The definition points, whose location you can see through their grips, are located on their own unique layer called Defpoints. Definition points are displayed regardless of whether the Defpoints layer is on or off. To give you an idea of how these definition points work, the following exercises will show you how to manipulate them directly.

MAKING MINOR ADJUSTMENTS TO DIMENSIONS

Once you've placed some dimensions, you may want to make some minor changes to the dimensions themselves. Perhaps the most common type of change is to move the dimension text to a new location.

This situation frequently arises when several dimensions occupy a very tight space. The following exercise shows how you can use the Grips feature to adjust parts of a dimension.

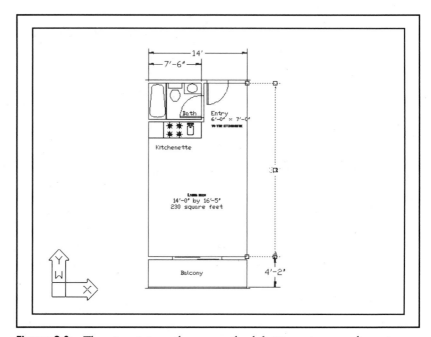

Figure 9.8: The grip points are the same as the definition points on a dimension

1. Click on the grip at the center of the dimension text, then move the cursor around. Notice that the dimension text now follows the cursor.

2. Click on a point to the left of the original dimension text location (see Figure 9.9). The dimension text moves to its new location. The dimension remains highlighted, telling you that it is still available for editing.

The Grips feature lets you effortlessly move parts of a dimension. Now let's try moving the location of the dimension line.

1. Click on the grip near the top of the dimension line.

2. Move the cursor around. Notice that the dimension line follows the cursor only in the horizontal direction, keeping its parallel orientation to the dimensioned floor plan.

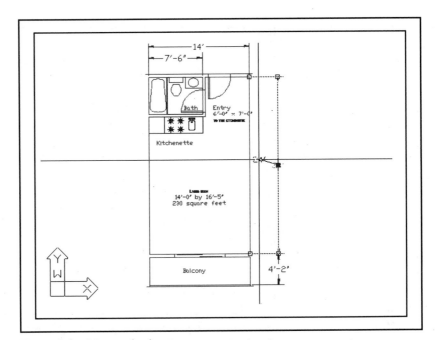

Figure 9.9: Moving the dimension text using its grip

3. Enter **@9<0** ↵. The dimension line and the dimension extensions move to the new location right of the text (see Figure 9.10).

The text and the dimension line act independently of each other when being edited with grips. Also in step 3, you saw that you can specify an exact distance for the new dimension line location by entering a relative polar coordinate. Cartesian coordinates work just as well. You can even use object snaps to relocate dimension lines. Try moving the dimension line back using the perpendicular Osnap override.

1. Click on the same dimension line grip you used last.

2. Shift-click the right mouse button to bring up the pop-up Osnap overrides menu.

3. Click on Nearest.

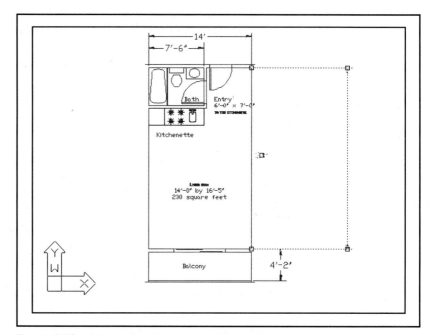

Figure 9.10: Moving the dimension line using its grip

4. Using the nearest Osnap override, click on the vertical dimension line just below the one you have selected. The selected dimension line moves to align with the other vertical dimension, back to its original location.

The Grips feature is especially well suited to editing dimensions. You can copy, rotate, mirror, and scale dimensions using grips. You aren't limited to selecting dimensions with the grips feature. Still, you may need to rotate the dimension text or you may prefer not to use the grips feature. Two other options are available that allow you to rotate or move dimension text without the use of grips. They are the Rotate Text and Move Text options on the Modify ➤ Edit Dimensions ➤ Dimension Text cascading menu. Their use is self-explanatory.

Understanding the Stretch Command

The tool you used for moving the wall and the dimension line extensions is the Stretch command. This is one of the most useful, yet least understood commands offered by AutoCAD. You should think of Stretch as a vertex mover: its sole purpose is to move the vertices (or endpoints) of objects.

Stretch actually requires you to do two things: select the objects you want to edit, then select the vertices you wish to move. The crossing window and the Cpolygon window are convenient ways of killing two birds with one stone: they select objects and vertices in one operation. But if you want to be more selective, you can click on objects and window vertices instead. For example, suppose in the last exercise you wanted to move the walls, but not the dimension line extensions. To do that, follow these steps.

1. Enter **stretch** ↵ at the command prompt. You enter Stretch through the keyboard because the Stretch option in the Modify pull-down menu automatically includes the Crossing selection option.

2. At the **Select objects** prompt, enter **w** ↵ or **WP** ↵.

3. Window the vertices you wish to move. Since the window selection options select objects completely enclosed within the window, most of the items you want to stretch will already be selected.

4. Click on the vertical walls to include them in the set of objects to be edited.

5. Press ↵ to finish your selection.

6. Indicate the base point and second point for the stretch.

You could also have used the Remove selection option and clicked on the dimensions to deselect them in the previous exercise. Then, when you entered the base and second points, the walls would have moved, but the dimensions would have stayed in place.

Stretch will stretch only the vertices included in the last window, crossing window, crossing polygon, or window polygon (see *Chapter 2* for more on these selection options). This means that if you had attempted to window another part of your drawing in the last exercise, nothing would have moved. Objects need to be highlighted (i.e., selected) and their endpoints must have been windowed before Stretch will do anything.

The Stretch command is especially well suited to editing dimensioned objects, and when you use it with the crossing polygon (cp) or window polygon (wp) selection options, you can have a lot of flexibility over what gets edited.

EDITING DIMENSIONED OBJECTS

You've just seen how you can edit a dimension directly using its grips. But the key feature of AutoCAD's dimensions is their ability to automatically adjust themselves to changes in the drawing. As long as you include the dimension's definition points when you select objects to edit, the dimensions themselves will automatically update to reflect the change in your drawing.

To see how this works, try moving the living room closer to the bathroom wall. You can move a group of lines and vertices using the STRETCH command and the Crossing option.

Modify ➤ ▭ Stretch

▼ **TIP**

You can also enter **stretch** ↵ **c** ↵ to start the stretch command or use the Grips feature.

1. You don't really want to save the changes you are about to make, so click on File ➤ Save before you do anything else.

▼ NOTE

You can also be more selective about the vertices you move by using a standard window instead of a crossing window to select the vertices, then picking the individual objects whose vertices you wish to move.

2. Click on Modify ➤ Stretch. You will see the following prompt:

    At the Select objects to stretch by window or
    polygon...
    Select objects: C
    First corner:

3. Pick a crossing window as indicated in Figure 9.11.

4. Once you have picked the window, press ↵ to confirm your selection.

5. At the **base point** prompt, pick any point on the screen.

6. At the **new point** prompt, enter **@2′<90** to move the wall 2′ in a 90° direction. The wall will move and the dimension text will change to reflect the new dimension, as shown in Figure 9.12.

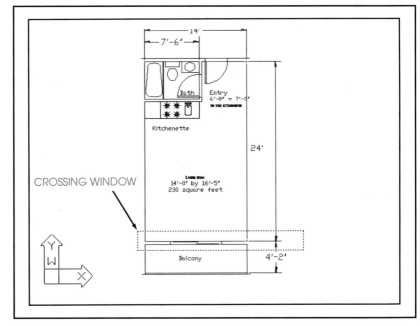

Figure 9.11:   The STRETCH crossing window

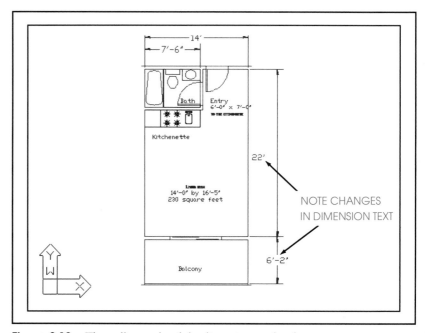

Figure 9.12: The wall moved and the dimensions updated

When you selected the crossing window corners, you included the definition points of both vertical dimensions. This allowed you to move the dimension extension lines along with the wall, thereby updating the dimensions automatically.

TURNING OFF ASSOCIATIVE DIMENSIONS

You can also use the standard Mirror, Rotate, and Stretch commands with dimensions. The polar arrays will also work, and Extend and Trim can be used with linear dimensions. So, when editing dimensioned objects, be sure you select the dimension associated with the object being edited. Using the Crossing or Cpolygon selection options when selecting objects will help you include the dimensions.

If you don't want to use the Associative dimensioning feature—for example, when you want to edit dimension lines individually—you can turn it off. To do this, follow these steps.

1. Enter **dimaso** ↵.

2. At the **New value for DIMASO <1>** prompt, enter 0 ↵.

Remember that if you explode a dimension or turn off Associative dimensioning, then the dimensions will no longer update automatically, nor will you be able to use any of the options on the Modify ➤ Edit Dimensions menu.

USING OSNAP WHILE DIMENSIONING

▼ WARNING

The drawback to setting a constant Osnap mode is that when your drawing gets crowded, you may end up picking the wrong point by accident.

You may find that when you pick intersections and endpoints frequently, as during dimensioning, it is a bit inconvenient to use the Osnap overrides menu. Fortunately, you can set a default active Osnap mode or combination of modes. To accomplish this, follow these steps.

1. Click on Settings ➤ Object Snaps…. The Running Object Snap dialog box appears (see Figure 9.13).

2. You can now select the desired default mode. You can even pick more than one mode, say Intersection, Endpoint, and Midpoint, so that whichever geometry you happen to be nearest will be the point selected.

▼ TIP

You can also enter **osnap** ↵, then enter the name of the Osnap modes you want to use. If you want to enter more than one mode, enter their names separated by commas, such as *endpoint,midpoint,intersect*.

3. Click on **OK** once you have made your selections.

The next time you are prompted to select a point, the selected Osnap modes will be automatically activated. You can still override the default settings using the Osnap pop-up menu (Shift-right mouse button) or the Osnap side menu (asterisks).

SETTING UP AND SAVING A DIMENSION STYLE

Because different professions use different styles of dimensioning, AutoCAD allows you to modify the way its dimensions appear. In your apartment unit plan, you used the default dimension settings, which are

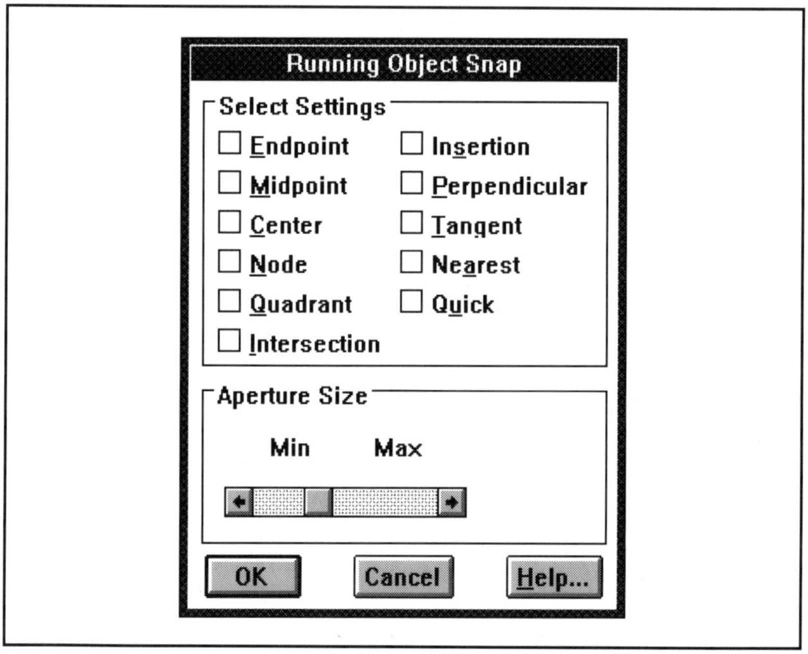

Figure 9.13: The Running Object Snap dialog box

more frequently used in engineering and mechanical drawings than in architectural ones. Other available options include tick marks, which are generally used in architectural drawings instead of arrows. You can align the dimension text along the dimension line rather than have them always appear horizontal, and you can place them above the dimension line rather than break them. You can even have the dimension automatically display a plus or minus value, which is useful if you are doing mechanical drawings of machined parts.

Other settings give you the ability to set the color of the individual parts of a dimension. For example, you can set the color of dimension text so that, at plot time, the text color is assigned to a thick pen that causes the dimension text to be thicker than other dimension lines. The following exercise gives you a glimpse of what you can do with these settings.

Start by saving the current settings as a dimension style called **Standard**.

Settings ➤ Dimension Style...

1. Click on Settings ➤ Dimension Style.... The Dimension Style dialog box appears (see Figure 9.14).

2. Type **standard** ↵. You see the message *New style STAN-DARD created from *UNNAMED* appear in the dialog box, and the name **UNNAMED* changes to *STANDARD* in the list box.

3. Double-click on the input box and type **architect** ↵. The name *ARCHITECT* appears in the list box.

You have just created two dimension styles. They are identical since they are copies of each other. Now you can change the settings for one of these styles.

▼ NOTE

This dialog box shows a list of dimension styles currently available in the list box to the left. The right side shows a button group for the dimension variable settings. These settings are categorized into several buttons that each open a dialog box. See *Appendix D* for a detailed explanation.

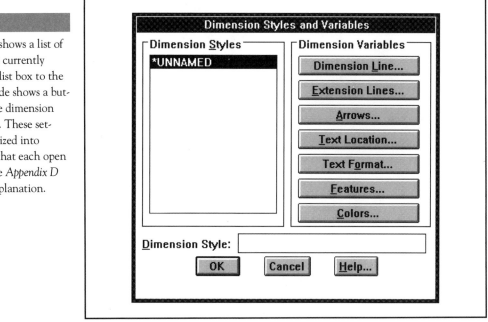

Figure 9.14:   The Dimension Style dialog box

1. Make sure the ARCHITECT style is highlighted in the list box.

2. Click on the button labeled Arrows…. The Arrows dialog box appears (see Figure 9.15).

3. Click on the radio button labeled Tick.

4. Click on **OK**.

5. Click on the **OK** button in the Dimension Style dialog box.

You now have two dimension styles. One uses tick marks for arrows while the other one uses arrows. Since you had highlighted the ARCHITECT dimension style, it is the current one. Update a dimension to see the effect of the new style.

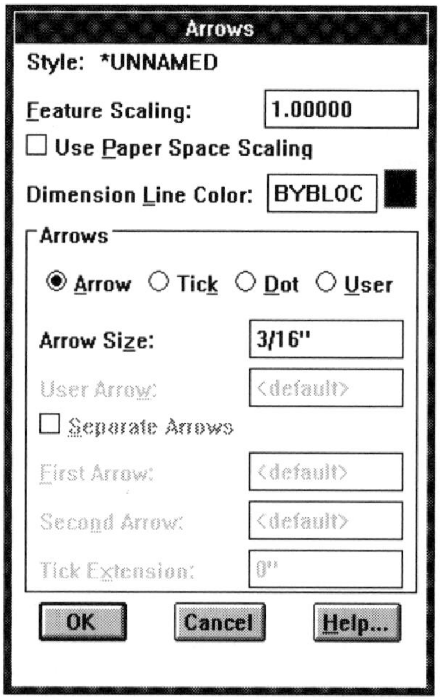

Figure 9.15: The Arrows dialog box

Modify ➤ ⊞ Edit Dimensions ➤ Update Dimensions

1. Click on Modify ➤ Edit Dimensions ➤ Update Dimension.
2. Click on the longer of the two vertical dimensions.
3. Press ↵. The arrows of the dimension change to tick marks.

▼ TIP

If you prefer to use the keyboard, you can enter **Dim1** ↵ **Save** ↵. You are prompted for a dimension style name. Once you enter a name, the current settings are stored under that name.

You can set up and store several different dimension styles that can be recalled at will. This feature is especially helpful if you mix styles—architectural tick marks and engineering arrows, for instance—in one drawing. There is a bewildering array of settings to choose from. Fortunately, the dialog box makes their use painless. For a detailed discussion all the dimension settings, see *Appendix D*.

DIMENSIONING NONORTHOGONAL OBJECTS

So far, you've seen how to use the linear dimensions. You can also dimension nonorthogonal objects, such as circles, arcs, triangles, and trapezoids. In this section you will practice dimensioning nonorthogonal objects by drawing an elevation of a window that might appear as part of the set of plans for your studio apartment building. You'll start by drawing the window itself.

Draw ➤ ⬡ Polygon ➤ Circumscribed

1. Open a new file called **Window** (don't bother to save your work).
2. Set the file up as an architectural drawing at a scale of 3"=1'-0" on an 8½ × 11" sheet.
3. Click on Draw ➤ Polygon ➤ Circumscribed.

4. At the **Number of sides**... prompt, enter **6** ↵ or enter **Polygon** ↵.

5. At the **Edge/<center of polygon>** prompt, pick the center of the polygon at coordinate 1′-10″, 1′-6″. If you started the command with the keyboard, enter **C** ↵ at the **Inscribe in circle/circumscribe**... prompt.

6. At the **Radius of circle:** prompt, you will see the hexagon drag along with the cursor. You could pick a point with your mouse to determine its size.

7. Enter **8** ↵ to get an exact size for the hexagon.

8. Draw a circle with a radius of 7″ using coordinate 1′-10″, 1′-6″ as its center. Your drawing will look like Figure 9.16.

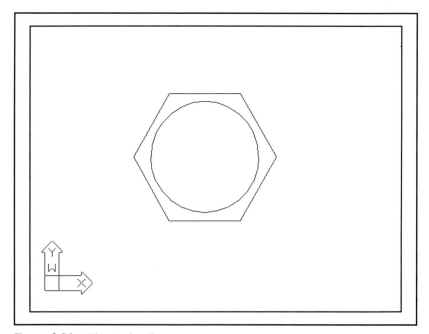

Figure 9.16: The window frame

DIMENSIONING NONORTHOGONAL LINEAR DISTANCES

Now you will dimension the window. The unusual shape of the window prevents you from using the horizontal or vertical dimensions you've used already. However, the Draw ➤ Dimension ➤ Linear ➤ Aligned option will allow you to dimension at an angle.

Draw ➤ ⊢⊣ Dimension ➤ Linear ➤ Aligned

▼ TIP

You can also enter **dim1** ↵ **ali** ↵ to start the aligned dimension.

1. Start by setting the dimension scale to 4. Enter **dimscale** ↵ **4** ↵.

2. Click on Draw ➤ Dimension ➤ Linear ➤ Aligned.

3. At the **First extension line origin or RETURN to select:** prompt, press ↵. You could have picked extension line origins as you did in earlier examples, but using the RETURN to select option will show you firsthand how it works.

4. At the **Select line, arc, or circle:** prompt, pick the upper-right face of the hexagon near coordinate 2′-5″, 1′-10″. As the prompt indicates, you can also pick an arc or circle for this type of dimension.

5. At the **Dimension line location:** prompt, pick a point near coordinate 2′-10″, 2′-2″.

6. At the **Dimension text <9 1/4">:** prompt, press ↵ to accept the default dimension. The dimension appears parallel to the line you picked, as in Figure 9.17.

Next you will dimension a face of the hexagon. But instead of its actual length, you will dimension a distance at a specified angle. In this example, you will dimension a face of the hexagon to show the distance from the center of the face.

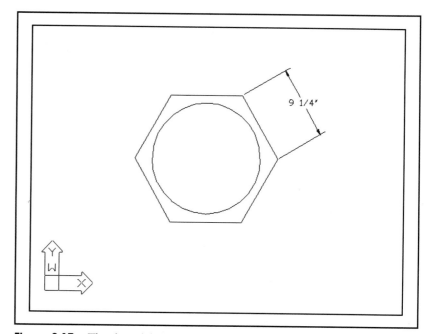

Figure 9.17: The aligned dimension of a nonorthogonal line

Draw ➤ ┣━┫ Dimension ➤ Linear ➤ Rotated

1. Click on Draw ➤ Dimension ➤ Linear ➤ Rotated or enter **Dim1 ↵ Rot ↵**.

2. At the **Dimension line angle <0>** prompt, enter 30 ↵.

3. At the **First extension line origin or RETURN to select:** prompt, press ↵.

4. At the **Select line, arc, or circle:** prompt, pick the lower-right face of the hexagon near coordinate 2'-6", 1'-4".

5. At the **Dimension line location:** prompt, pick a point near coordinate 2'-11", 0'-8".

6. At the **Dimension text <8">:** prompt, press ↵ and the dimension of the line at 30° appears. Your drawing will look like Figure 9.18.

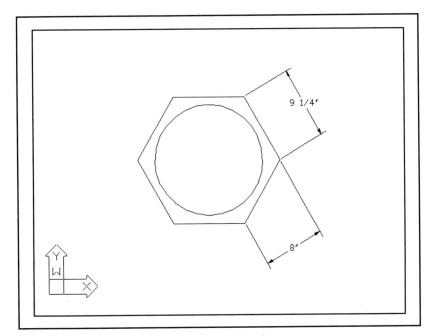

Figure 9.18:   A linear dimension using the rotated option

DIMENSIONING RADII, DIAMETERS, AND ARCS

To dimension circular objects, you use another set of options from the Draw ➤ Dimension menu.

Draw ➤ ⊢⊣ Dimension ➤ Angular

▼ **TIP**

You can also enter **dim1** ↵ **ang** ↵ to start the angular dimension.

1. Click on Draw ➤ Dimension ➤ Angular or enter **Dim1** ↵ **Ang** ↵. This option allows you to dimension the angle between two lines.

2. At the **Select arc, circle, line, or RETURN:** prompt, pick the upper-left face of the hexagon near coordinate 1'-3", 1'-10".

3. At the **Second line:** prompt, pick the top face at coordinate 1′-9″, 2′-2″.

4. At the **Enter dimension line arc location:** prompt, pick a point near coordinate 1′-8″, 1′-11″.

5. At the **Dimension text <120>:** prompt, press ↵ to accept the default dimension text.

6. At the **Enter text location:** prompt, pick a point near coordinate 1′-8″, 1′-9″. The angle between the two lines you picked appears with an arrow indicating the angle (see Figure 9.19).

Now try the Diameter option, which shows the diameter of a circle.

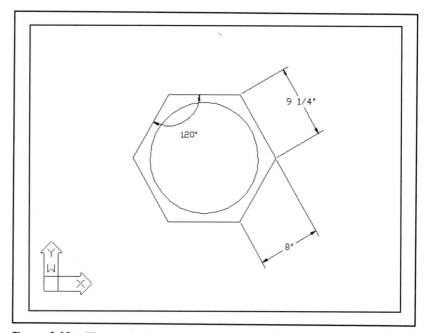

Figure 9.19:   The angular dimension added to the window frame

Draw ➤ 🖼 Dimension ➤ Radial ➤ Diameter

▼ TIP

You can also enter **dim1** ↵ **dia** ↵ to start the diameter dimension.

1. Click on Draw ➤ Dimension ➤ Radial ➤ Diameter.

2. At the **Select arc or circle:** prompt, pick the circle near coordinate 2'-5", 1'-6".

3. At the **Dimension text <1'-2">:** prompt, press ↵ to accept the default dimension text.

4. At the **Enter leader length for text:** prompt, you will see a temporary, highlighted dimension on the drawing. As you move your cursor, the temporary leader and dimension text move horizontally.

5. Adjust your cursor so that the dimension looks like Figure 9.20, then press the pick button.

The Draw ➤ Dimension ➤ Radial ➤ Radius option works the same way as Diameter, except that it gives you a radius dimension (see Figure 9.21). The Draw ➤ Dimension ➤ Radial ➤ Center Mark option just places a center mark in the shape of a cross at the center of the selected arc or circle.

You can control the format of diametric and radial dimensions using the Dimtix and Dimtofl dimension variables (see Figure 9.22). See *Appendix D* for further information.

ADDING A NOTE WITH AN ARROW

Finally, there is the Draw ➤ Dimension ➤ Leader option. This option allows you to add a note with an arrow pointing to the object the note describes.

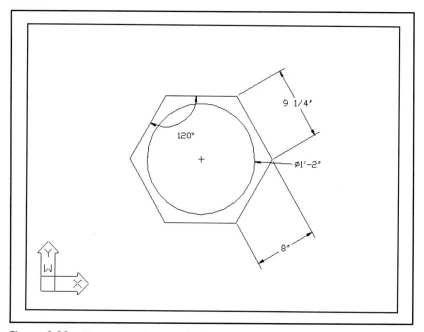

Figure 9.20: Dimensions showing the diameter of a circle

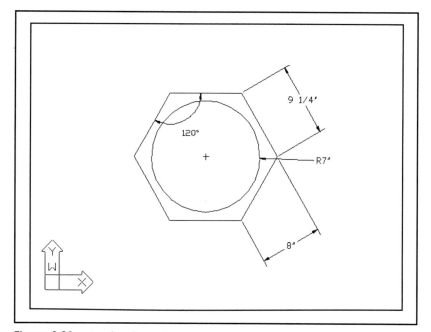

Figure 9.21: A radius dimension

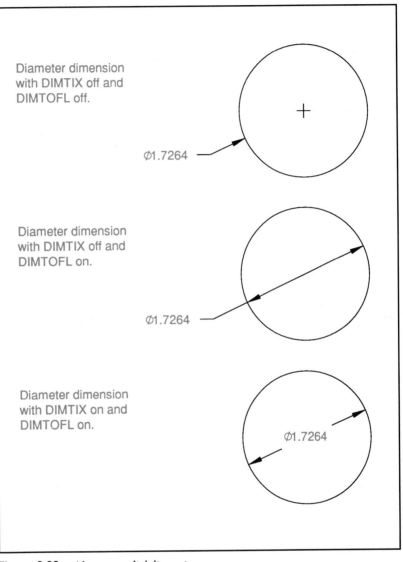

Figure 9.22:   Alternate radial dimensions

Draw ➤ ⊬⊣ Dimension ➤ Leader

▼ TIP

You can also enter **dim1** ↵
lead ↵ to start the leader.

1. Click on Draw ➤ Dimension ➤ Leader.

2. At the **Leader start:** prompt, pick a point near coordinate 1′-4″, 2′-0″.

3. At the **To point:** prompt, enter **@6<110** ↵. The leader appears.

4. At the **To point:** prompt, you can continue to pick points just as you would draw lines. Press ↵ instead. A short horizontal line appears at the end of the leader line.

5. At the **Dimension text <1′-2″>:** prompt, you might notice that the default value for this prompt is the last dimension you entered. If this is the first dimension you enter in a drawing session, it will be a blank. You can enter a different value or press ↵ to accept this default.

6. Enter **Window frame** ↵ as the label for this leader. Your drawing will look like Figure 9.23.

The problem with the *leader* option is that it does not allow you to enter more than one line of text. If you have a lot of text you would like to use with the leader, you will have to enter the text using Draw ➤ Text ➤ Dynamic, then use the leader option on the Dim menu to add the leader. When you do this, enter **spacebar** ↵ at the dimension text prompt.

SKEWING DIMENSION LINES

At times, you may find it necessary to force the extension lines to take on an angle other than 90° to the dimension line. This is a common requirement of isometric drawings, where most lines are at 30° or 60° angles instead of 90°. To facilitate nonorthogonal dimensions like these, AutoCAD offers the Oblique Dimension command.

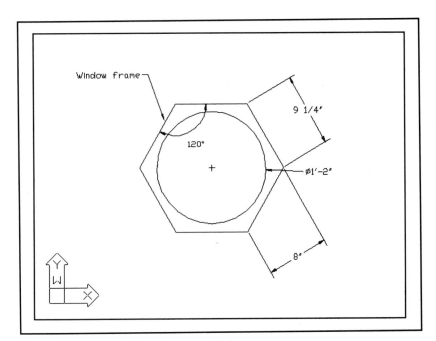

Figure 9.23: The leader with a note added

Modify ➤ ↦ Edit Dimensions ➤ Oblique Dimension

1. Click on Modify ➤ Edit Dimensions ➤ Oblique Dimension.

2. At the **Select objects:** prompt, pick the aligned dimension at the upper right of the drawing, then press ↵ to confirm your selection.

▼ TIP

You can also enter **dim1** ↵ **obl** ↵ to start the oblique dimension.

3. At the **Enter obliquing angle (RETURN for none):** prompt, enter **60** for 60°. The dimension will skew so that the extension lines are at 60° (see Figure 9.24).

4. Now exit AutoCAD. You are done with the tutorials in this chapter.

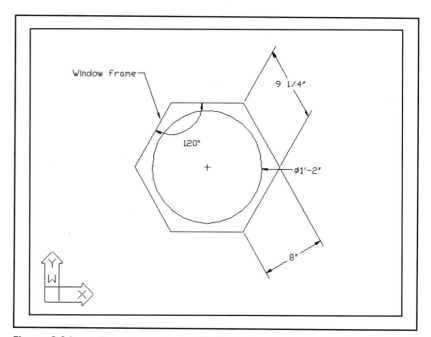

Figure 9.24: A dimension using the OBLIQUE dimension command

APPLYING ORDINATE DIMENSIONS

In mechanical drafting, *ordinate dimensions* are used to maintain accuracy of machined parts by establishing an origin on the part. All major dimensions are described as X or Y coordinates of that origin. The origin is usually an easily locatable feature of the part, such as a machined bore or two machined surfaces. Figure 9.25 shows a typical application of ordinate dimensions.

To use Ordinate dimensions, follow these steps.

▼ **TIP**

You can also enter **dim1** ↵ **ord** ↵ to start the Ordinate dimension.

1. Click on Settings ➤ UCS ➤ Origin.

2. At the **Origin point <0,0,0>:** prompt, click on the exact location of the origin of your part.

3. Toggle the Ortho mode on.

4. Click on Draw ➤ Dimension ➤ Ordinate ➤ Automatic.

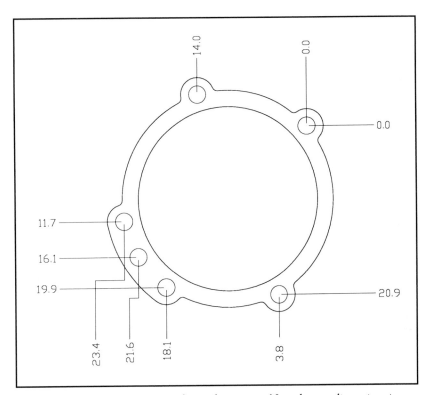

Figure 9.25: A drawing using ordinate dimensions. Note the two dimensions in the lower left whose leaders are jogged. Also note the origin location in the upper right.

5. At the **Select feature:** prompt, click on the item you want to dimension.

▼ NOTE

The direction of the leader will determine whether the dimension will be of the X datum or the Y datum.

6. At the **Leader endpoint (Xdatum/Ydatum):** prompt, indicate the length and direction of the leader. Do this by positioning the rubber-banding leader perpendicular to the coordinate direction you want to dimension, then clicking on that point.

7. At the **Dimension text:** prompt, press ↵ or enter a value.

In steps 1 and 2, you used the UCS feature to establish a second origin in the drawing. The Ordinate dimension then uses that origin to determine the ordinate dimensions. You will get a chance to work with the UCS feature in *Chapter 16*.

The other two options on the Draw ➤ Dimension ➤ Ordinate cascading menu, Xdatum and Ydatum, force the dimension to be of the X coordinate or Y coordinate no matter what direction the leader takes. The Automatic option shown in the sample steps will make the best guess at which direction you want dimensioned, based on the orientation of the leader.

If you turn Ortho mode off, the dimension leader will be drawn with a jog, in order to maintain orthogonal lines (see Figure 9.25).

IF YOU WANT TO EXPERIMENT...

At this point, you might want to experiment with the settings to identify the ones that are most useful for your work. Review *Appendix D* for details on how to do this. You can then set these settings up as defaults in a prototype file or the Acad.DWG file. Because you will still have to alter them from time to time, it's also a good idea to experiment with the settings you don't think you will need often.

▼ TIP

Try using Move Text and Rotate Text on the Modify ➤ Edit Dimensions ➤ Dimension Text cascading menu.

As an added exercise, try the steps shown in Figure 9.26. It will give you a chance to see how you can update dimensions on a drawing that has been scaled down.

SUMMARY

AutoCAD's dimensioning capabilities are extensive and take some practice. This chapter has given you the necessary background to use the dimensioning feature successfully.

You've now completed *Part Two, Discovering the AutoCAD Advantage*, and are at an intermediate level of using AutoCAD. You should feel

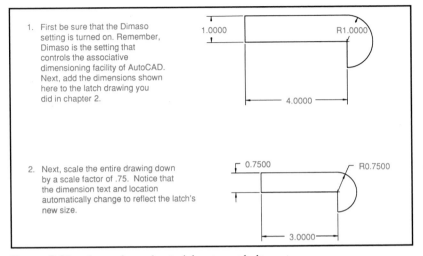

1. First be sure that the Dimaso setting is turned on. Remember, Dimaso is the setting that controls the associative dimensioning facility of AutoCAD. Next, add the dimensions shown here to the latch drawing you did in chapter 2.

1.0000   R1.0000

4.0000

2. Next, scale the entire drawing down by a scale factor of .75. Notice that the dimension text and location automatically change to reflect the latch's new size.

0.7500   R0.7500

3.0000

Figure 9.26:   A sample mechanical drawing with dimensions

confident that you can tackle just about any project. *Part Three: How to Get the Most from AutoCAD* will fill out your knowledge of two-dimensional drawing by showing you how to store and retrieve data, input existing paper drawings, and use some tools, both familiar and new, to edit drawings more efficiently.

PART THREE

GETTING THE
■
MOST OUT OF
■
AUTOCAD

At this point, you are on the verge of becoming a real expert. To make sure you reach expert status, Part Three provides you with the kind of instruction you need to begin to store data with your drawings, input pre-existing paper drawings, use curves and solids, and exchange data with database and spreadsheet programs. You will also look at ways to make complex editing tasks easier.

10

STORING
AND
LINKING DATA
WITH GRAPHICS

FAST TRACK

376 ▶ **To create a block with an attribute**

Click on Draw ➤ Text ➤ Attributes ➤ Define, fill in the Attribute Definition dialog box with the appropriate tag, prompt, and default value information, specify the text size and angle, and use the **Pick Point** button to pick a location for the attribute, then click on **OK**. Next, include the attribute definition you just created in a block.

381 ▶ **To change an attribute definition**

Click on Modify ➤ Entity…, then click on the attribute definition you wish to modify. Make the appropriate changes in the Modify Attribute Definition dialog box. Alternately, you can use the Ddedit command to modify only the tag, prompt, and default value of an attribute definition.

383 ▶ **To set up an attribute so it will be invisible**

Place a check in the Invisible check box of the Attribute Definition dialog box or the Modify Attribute Definition dialog box.

383 ▶ **To set up an attribute so it doesn't prompt you at insertion time**

Place a check in the Preset check box of the Attribute Definition dialog box or the Modify Attribute Definition dialog box.

388 ▶ **To set up AutoCAD to display a dialog box to enter attribute values**

Enter **Attdia** ↵ at the command prompt, then enter 1 ↵.

389 ▶ **To edit a single attribute value of a block**

Click on Draw ➤ Text ➤ Attributes ➤ Edit, then click on the attribute to edit. Make changes in the Edit Attribute dialog box that appears.

391 ▶ To change the appearance of a visible attribute

Enter **Attedit** ↵ at the command prompt. Press ↵ at all the prompts until you see the **Select Attribute** prompt. Select the attribute(s) you want to change, then press ↵. At the **Value/Position/Height/Angle/Style/Layer/Color /Next…** prompt, enter the option that best describes the characteristic you wish to change, then answer the prompts. Press ↵ to go to the next selected attribute.

393 ▶ To make the same change to several attribute values at once

Enter **Attedit** ↵, then, at the **Edit attributes one at a time** prompt, enter **N** ↵. Press ↵ at all the prompts until you see the **Select Attributes** prompt. Select the attributes you want to edit, then press ↵. Enter the text to change, then enter the replacement text.

396 ▶ To make invisible attributes visible

Enter **Attdisp** ↵ then enter **ON** ↵.

397 ▶ To specify what data to export from the attributes in a drawing

Using a text editor, create a file containing the name of the attribute tags you want to export, plus the code specifying whether the attribute is a character or number, and the number of characters and decimal places to set aside for the extracted value. Each tag and value should occupy one line of the file. Each line must be followed by a ↵.

401 ▶ To specify how to delimit fields in the export file

Click on Draw ➤ Text ➤ Attributes ➤ Extract, enter the name of the template file and extract file in the appropriate input boxes, then click on the CDF, SDF, or DXF radio button from the file format button group.

▼ NOTE

For some of the exercises in this chapter, you will need to know how to create and manipulate ASCII files, and you should be familiar with Windows. If you need more information on Windows, look at *Appendix C* of this book or your Windows manual. It is helpful, but not essential, for you to know how to use a database-management program as well.

▼ TIP

You can even set up a default value for the attribute, such as hollow core, or hc. That way you only have to enter a value when it deviates from the default.

▼ NOTE

A door type symbol is a graphic code used to indicate special characteristics of the associated door. The code refers to a note on another drawing or in a set of written specifications.

Attributes are unique to computer-aided design and drafting; nothing quite like them exists in traditional drafting. Because of this, they are often poorly understood. Attributes enable you to store information as text you can later extract to use in database managers, spreadsheet programs, and word processors. By doing this, you can keep track of virtually any object in a drawing.

But keeping track of objects is just one way of using attributes. You can also use them in place of the text objects where you must enter the same text, with minor modifications, in many places in your drawing. For example, if you are drawing a schedule that contains several columns of information, you can use attributes to help simplify your data entry. Attributes can also be used where you anticipate global editing of text. For example, suppose a note that refers to a part number occurs in several places. If you think you will want to change that part number in every note, you can make the part a block with an attribute. Later, when you know the new part number, you can use the global editing capability of the attribute feature to change the old part number for all occurrences in one step.

In this chapter you will use attributes for one of their more common functions: maintaining lists of parts. In this case, the parts are doors. We will also describe how to import these attributes into a database-management program. As you go through these exercises, think about the ways attributes can help you in your particular application.

CREATING ATTRIBUTES

Attributes depend on blocks. You might think of an attribute as a tag attached to a block. That tag contains information about that block. For example, you could have included an attribute definition with the door drawing you created in *Chapter 2*. Then, every time you subsequently inserted the door, you would have been prompted for a value associated with that door. The value can be a number, a height or width value, a name, or any type of text information you like. When you insert the block, you get the usual prompts, then a prompt for an attribute value. Once you enter a value, it is stored as part of the block within the drawing database. This value can be displayed as text attached to the door, or it can be made invisible. You can even specify what the prompts say as they ask you for the attribute value.

But suppose you don't have the attribute information when you design the door. You may not want to add an attribute to a block that will not have a specific value early in the design process. As an alternative, you can add the attribute to a symbol that is later placed by the door when you know enough about the design to specify what type of door goes where. The standard door type symbol suits this purpose nicely because it is an object that can be set up and used as a block independent of the actual door block.

In the following exercises, you will create a door type symbol with attributes for the different values normally assigned to doors, namely, size, thickness, fire rating, material, and construction.

ADDING ATTRIBUTES TO BLOCKS

In this exercise, you will create a door type symbol, which is commonly used to describe the size, thickness, and other characteristics of any given door in an architectural drawing. The symbol is usually a circle, hexagon, or diamond with a number in it. The number can be cross-referenced to a schedule that lists all the door types and their characteristics.

Draw ➤ **A** Text ➤ Attribute ➤ Define

▼ TIP

Since this is a new drawing, the circle is placed automatically on layer 0. Remember that objects in a block that are on layer 0 will take on the color and line type assignment of the layer on which the block is inserted.

▼ NOTE

The tag can be up to 31 characters long but it cannot contain spaces. If you plan to use the attribute data in a database program, check for other restrictions on field names.

1. To create the door type symbol with these attributes attached, open a new file and call it **S-door** (for symbol-door). Since the symbol will fit in the default limits of the drawing, I won't ask you to change the limits setting.

2. Draw a circle 0.25 units in diameter with its center at coordinate 7,5. Next, zoom into the circle.

3. Click on Draw ➤ Text ➤ Attributes ➤ Define. The Attribute definition dialog box appears (see Figure 10.1).

4. Click on the input box labeled Tag in the Attribute group. Enter **d-type**. This will be your shorthand for door type.

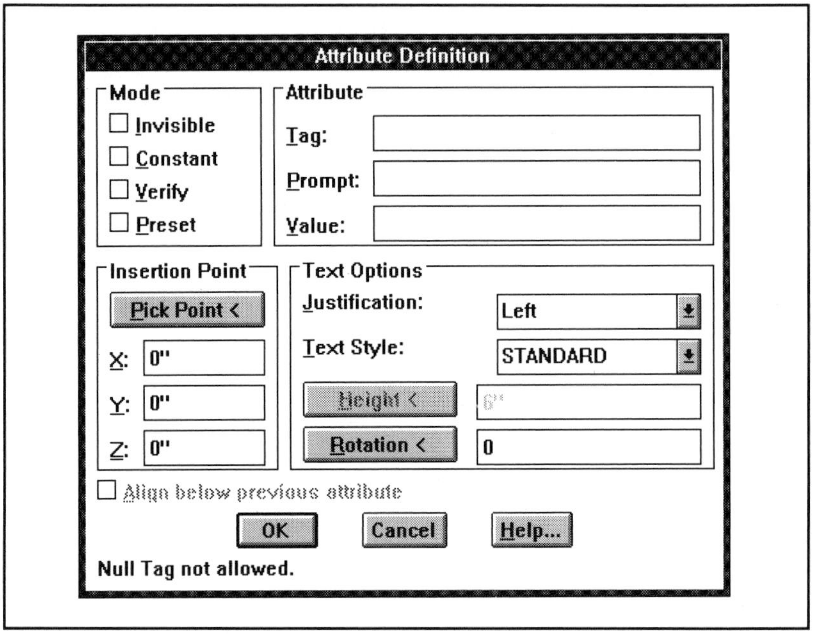

Figure 10.1: The Attribute Definition dialog box

▼ TIP

Use a prompt that gives explicit instructions so the user will know exactly what is expected. You can even include an example in the prompt in brackets, which is the way AutoCAD prompts often display defaults.

5. Click on the input box labeled Prompt just below the Tag input box, then enter **Door type**. Here you enter the text for the prompt that appears when you insert the block containing this attribute. Often the prompt is the same as the tag, but it can be anything you like. Unlike the tag, you are allowed to include spaces in the prompt.
6. Click on the input box labeled Value. This is where you enter a default value for the door type prompt. Enter a hyphen.
7. Click on the arrow on the Justification pop-up list, then highlight Middle. This will allow you to center the attribute on the circle's center. You might notice several other options in the Text Options group. Since attributes appear as text, you can apply the same settings to them as you would to ordinary text.

▼ TIP

If an attribute is to contain a number that will later be used for making sorts in a database, use a default such as 000 to indicate the number of digits required. The zeros may also serve to remind the user that values less than 100 must be preceded by a leading zero, as in 099.

8. Double click on the input box next to the button labeled Height <, then enter **0.125**. This will make the attribute text 0.125 inches high.

9. Check the box in the Modes group labeled Verify. This option instructs AutoCAD to verify any answers you give to the attribute prompts at insertion time (you'll see how Verify works later).

10. Click on the button labeled **Pick Point <** in the Insertion point group. The dialog box closes momentarily to let you pick a location for the attribute.

11. Using the Center Osnap override, click to pick the center of the circle. The dialog box re-appears.

12. Click on **OK**. You will see the attribute definition at the center of the circle (see Figure 10.2.)

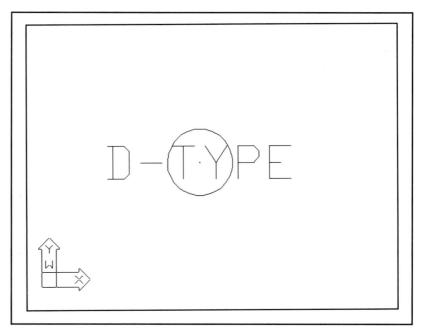

Figure 10.2: The attribute inserted in the circle and the second attribute added

You have just created your first attribute definition. The attribute definition displays its tag in all uppercase to help you identify it. When you later insert this file into another drawing, you will see that the tag turns into the value you assign to it when it is inserted. If you only want one attribute, you can stop here and save the file. The next section shows you how you can quickly add several more attributes to your drawing.

CHANGING ATTRIBUTE SPECIFICATIONS

Next, you will add a few more attribute definitions, but instead of using the Attribute Definition dialog box, you will make an arrayed copy of the first attribute, then edit the attribute definition copies. This method can save you time when you want to create several attribute definitions that have similar characteristics. By making copies and editing them, you'll also get a chance to see first-hand how to make changes to an attribute definition.

Construct ➤ 🔘 Array

1. Click on Construct ➤ Array or enter **Array** ↵.

2. At the **Select objects** prompt, click on the attribute definition you just created, then press ↵.

3. At the **Rectangular or Polar array** prompt, enter **R** ↵.

4. At the **Number of rows prompt**, enter **7** ↵.

5. At the **Number of columns** prompt, press ↵.

6. At the **Distance between rows** prompt, enter **−.18** ↵. This is about 1.5 times the height of the attribute definition. Be sure to include the minus sign. This will cause the array to be drawn downward.

Now you are ready to modify the copies of the attribute definitions.

Modify ➤ Entity...

▼ **TIP**

The Ddedit command also lets you edit the tag, prompt, and default value of an attribute definition. It doesn't let you change an attribute definition's mode, however.

1. Click on Modify ➤ Entity....

2. At the **Select object to modify:** prompt, click on the attribute definition just below the original. The Modify Attribute Definition dialog box appears (see Figure 10.3).

3. Click on the Invisible check box in the lower-right corner of the dialog box. This will cause this attribute to be invisible when the file is later inserted.

4. Double-click on the input box labeled Tag, then enter **d-size**.

5. Press **Tab** to move to the Prompt input box, then type **Door number**.

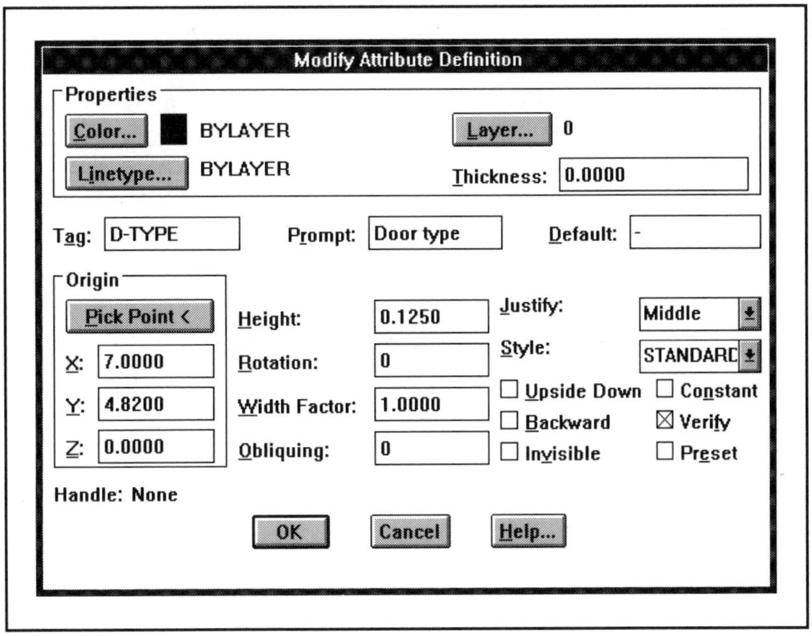

Figure 10.3: The Modify Attribute Definition dialog box

6. Click on **OK**. You will see the attribute definition change to reflect the new tag.

7. Continue to edit the rest of the attribute definitions using the attributes settings listed in Table 10.1. Also make sure all but the original attributes have the invisible option turned on.

8. After you have modified all the attributes, use the Base command to change the base point of this drawing to center of the circle.

9. Now you have finished creating your door type symbol with attributes. Save the S-door file and open the Plan file.

When you later insert a file or block containing attributes, the attribute prompts will appear in the order that their associated definitions were created. You can therefore control the order of the prompts at insertion time by editing the attribute definitions so their creation order corresponds to the desired prompt order.

I should mention that although you created a new file containing attribute definitions, you can also include such definitions in blocks you create using the BLOCK command or in files you create using the WBLOCK command. Just create the attribute definitions, then include them with the BLOCK or WBLOCK selections.

Table 10.1:   Attributes for the Door Type Symbol

TAG	PROMPT	DEFAULT
D-number	Door number	-
D-thick	Door thickness	-
D-rate	Fire rating	-
D-matrl	Door material	-
D-const	Door construction	-

▼ Understanding
■ Attribute Definition Modes

In the Attribute Definition dialog box, you saw several check boxes in the Mode group. I've briefly described what two of these modes do. You won't be asked to use any of the other modes in this tutorial, so the following set of descriptions is provided in case they might be useful for your work.

Invisible	Controls whether the attribute is shown as part of the drawing.
Constant	Creates an attribute that does not prompt you to enter a value. Instead the attribute simply has a constant, or fixed, value you give it during creation. *Constant* is used in situations where you know you will assign a fixed value to an object. Once they are set in a block, constant values cannot be changed using the standard set of attribute editing commands.
Verify	Causes AutoCAD to review the attribute values you enter at insertion time and asks you if it is correct.
Preset	Causes AutoCAD to automatically assign a default value to an attribute when its block is inserted. This saves time, since a preset attribute will not prompt you for a value. Unlike the Constant option, you can edit an attribute that has the Preset option turned on.

You can have all four modes on, all four off, or any combination of modes. With the exception of the Invisible mode, none of these modes can be altered once the attribute becomes part of a block. Later in this chapter we will discuss how to make an invisible attribute visible.

INSERTING BLOCKS CONTAINING ATTRIBUTES

In the last section, you created a door type symbol at the desired size for the actual plotted symbol. This means that whenever you insert that symbol, you have to specify an x and y scale factor appropriate to the scale of your drawing. This allows you to use the same symbol in any draw-ing, regardless of its scale. You could have several door type symbols, one for each scale you anticipate using, but this would be inefficient.

▼ NOTE

Refer to *Chapter 6* if you need to refresh your memory about views.

1. Use the VIEW command to restore view 1.

2. Be sure the Ceiling and Flr-Pat layers are off. Normally in a floor plan the door headers are not visible, and they will interfere with the placement of the door symbol.

3. Click on Draw ➤ Insert.

4. At the Insert dialog box, click on the File button.

5. Locate the S-door file in the file list and double-click on it.

6. Click on **OK**.

7. Insert the symbol at coordinate 41′-3″, 72′-4″.

8. At the **X scale factor** prompt, enter **96**.

9. Press ↵ at the **Y scale factor** prompt, and again at the **Rota-tion angle** prompt.

10. At the **Door type <->:** prompt, enter **A** ↵. Note that this prompt is the prompt you created. Note also that the default value is the hyphen you specified.

11. At the **Door number <->:** prompt, enter **116** ↵. Continue to enter the values for each prompt as shown in Table 10.2.

12. When you are done entering the values, the prompts repeat themselves to verify your entry (because you selected Verify from the modes group of the Attribute Definition dialog box). You can now either change an entry or just press ↵ to accept the original entry.

Table 10.2: Attribute Values for the Typical Studio Entry Door

PROMPT	VALUE
Door type	A
Door number	Same as room number
Door thickness	1 ¾"
Fire rating	20 min.
Door material	Wood
Door construction	Solid core

13. When you are done and the symbol appears, the only attribute you can see is the one you selected to be visible, the door type.

14. Add the rest of the door type symbols for the apartment entry doors by copying or arraying the door symbol you just inserted. You can use the previously saved views to help you get around the drawing quickly. Don't worry that the attribute values won't be appropriate for each unit. I'll show you how to edit the attributes in a later section.

As a review exercise, create another file for the room number symbol. This will be a rectangular box with the room number that you will place in each studio apartment.

1. Save the Plan file and open a new file to create the apartment number symbol shown in Figure 10.4.

2. Give its attribute the tag name **A-number**, the prompt Enter apartment number, a default value of 000, and a text height of 0.125 inches.

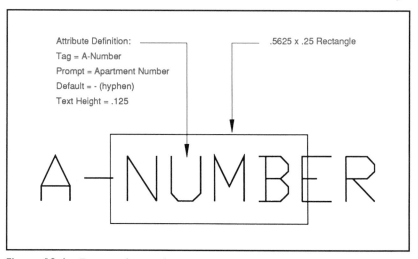

Figure 10.4: Drawing showing how to construct the apartment number symbol

3. Make the base point of this drawing the lower-left corner of the rectangle.

4. Use File ➤ Save As and save this file under the name **S-apart** for *Symbol-apartment*.

5. Open the Plan file again and insert the apartment number symbol into the lower-left unit at a scale of 96. Give this attribute the value of **116**.

6. Copy or array this room number symbol so that there is one symbol in each of the units, as shown in Figure 10.5. You'll learn how to modify the attributes to reflect their proper values in the following section, *Editing Attributes*. Figure 10.6 shows you what view 4 should look like once you have entered the door symbols and apartment numbers.

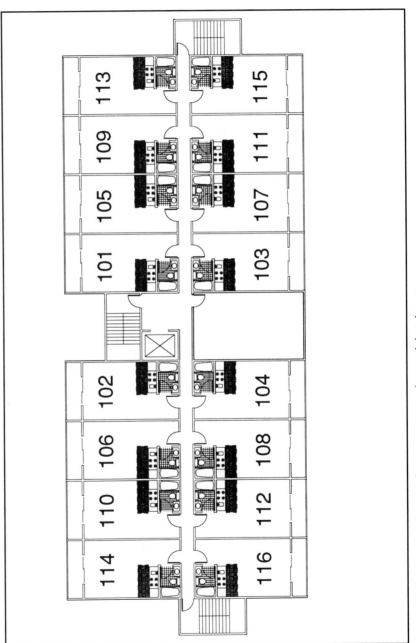

Figure 10.5:   Drawing showing the apartment numbers and their locations

USING A DIALOG BOX
TO ANSWER ATTRIBUTE PROMPTS

You can set up AutoCAD to display a dialog box for entering the attribute values at insertion time. This dialog box allows you to enter the values for each attribute using the input boxes next to the attribute name. Since it lets you change your mind about a value before confirming your entry, the dialog box allows greater flexibility in entering attributes. You can also see all the attributes associated with a block at once, making it easier to understand what information is required for the block.

To turn this feature on, do the following.

1. Enter **attdia** ↵ at the command prompt.

2. At the **New value for ATTDIA <0>:** prompt, enter 1 ↵.

Attributes set with the Preset mode on will also appear in the dialog box and are treated no differently from other nonconstant attributes.

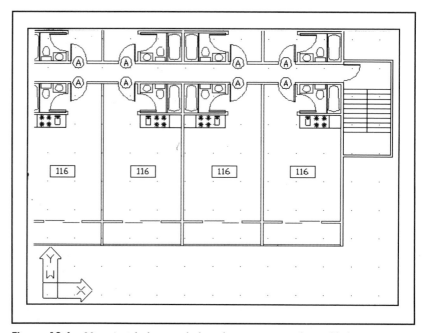

Figure 10.6: View 4 with door symbols and apartment numbers added

EDITING ATTRIBUTES

Because drawings are usually in flux even after actual construction or manufacturing begins, you will eventually have to edit previously entered attributes. In the example of the apartment building, many things can change before the final set of drawings is completed.

Attributes can be edited globally, meaning you can edit several occurrences of a particular attribute tag at once or individually. In this section you will make changes to the attributes you have entered so far, using both individual and global editing techniques, and you will practice editing invisible attributes.

EDITING ATTRIBUTES ONE AT A TIME

AutoCAD offers an easy way to edit attributes one at a time through a dialog box. The following exercise demonstrates this feature.

Draw ➤ A Text ➤ Attributes ➤ Edit

▼ TIP

You can also enter **Ddatte** ↲ at the command prompt to edit attributes one at at time.

1. Use the View ➤ Set View ➤ Named View option to restore view 1.

2. Click on Draw ➤ Text ➤ Attributes ➤ Edit.

3. At the **Select block** prompt, click on the apartment number attribute in the unit just to the right of the first unit in the lower-left corner. A dialog box appears showing you the value for the attribute in an input box. Highlight the attribute value in the input box and enter **112**, then click on **OK** to make the change (see Figure 10.7).

4. Do this for each room number, using Figure 10.4 to assign room numbers.

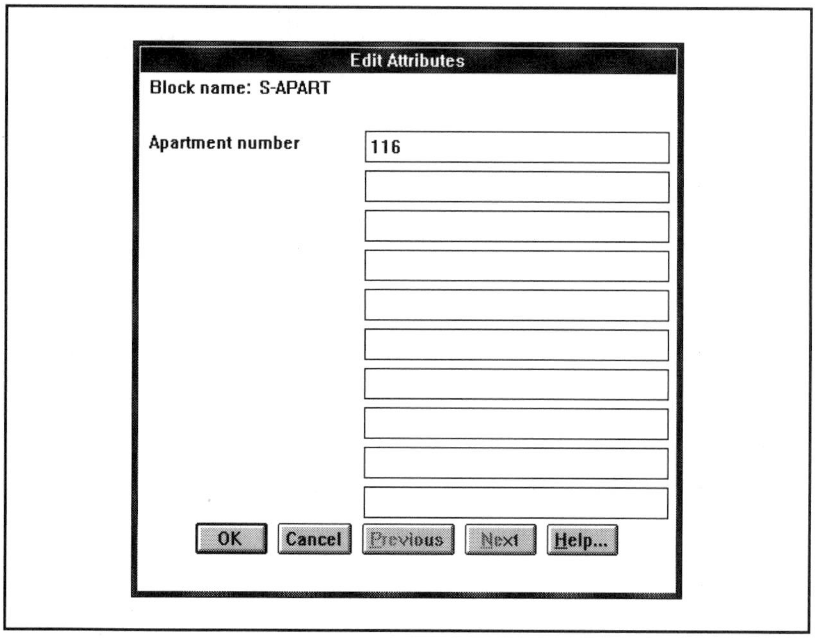

Figure 10.7: The Edit Attributes dialog box

EDITING SEVERAL ATTRIBUTES IN SUCCESSION

The Draw ➤ Text ➤ Attributes ➤ Edit option is useful for reviewing attributes as well as editing them, because both visible and invisible attributes are displayed in the dialog box. This option is the same as the Ddatte command. If you wish to review several attributes, you can use the multiple command modifier to force AutoCAD to repeat the Ddatte command.

Multiple ↵ Ddatte ↵

▼ NOTE

The multiple command modifier affects all other commands in the same way by automatically repeating them until you press **Ctrl-C**.

1. Enter **multiple ↵ ddatte ↵**.
2. Click on a Door Symbol block containing attributes. A dialog box appears as before (see Figure 10.8).

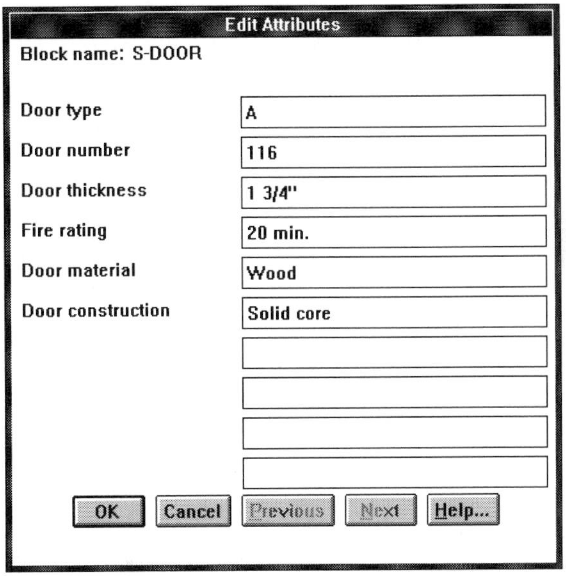

Figure 10.8: Apartment numbers for one floor of the studio apartment building

3. Change the door number to match the room number. Once you exit the dialog box, AutoCAD automatically restarts the DDATTE command. This enables you to pick the next block without re-entering ddatte ↵.

4. Change the rest of the Door Symbol attributes so the door numbers match the room numbers. To exit DDATTE, press **Ctrl-C** or click on Assist ➤ Cancel.

MAKING MINOR CHANGES TO AN ATTRIBUTE'S APPEARANCE

Eventually, you will want to make a change to an attribute that doesn't involve its value, like moving the attribute's location relative to the block it's associated with, or changing its color, its angle, or even its text style. To make these types of changes, you must use the Attedit command. Here's how to do it.

1. Enter **attedit** ↵ at the command prompt.

2. At the **Edit attributes one at a time? <Y>** prompt, press ↵ to accept the default Y.

3. At the **Block name specification <*>** prompt, press ↵. Optionally, you can enter a block name to narrow the selection to specific blocks.

4. At the **Attribute tag specification <*>** prompt, press ↵. Optionally, you can enter an attribute tag name to narrow your selection to specific tags.

5. At the **Attribute value specification <*>** prompt, press ↵. Optionally, you can narrow your selection to attributes containing specific values.

6. At the **Select Attributes** prompt, you can pick the set of blocks that contain the attributes you wish to edit. Once you press ↵ to confirm your selection, one of the selected attributes highlights, and an X appears at its base point (see Figure 10.9).

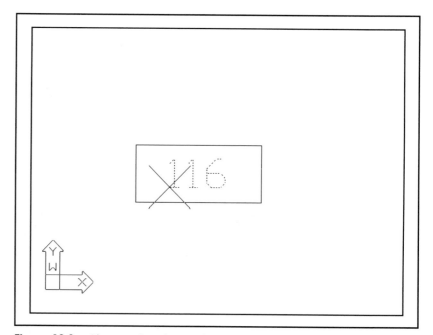

Figure 10.9: Close-up of attribute with X

7. At the **Value/Position/Height/Angle/Style/Layer/Color /Next <N>:** prompt, you can enter the option that best describes the attribute characteristic you wish to change. After making the change, the prompt returns allowing you to make another change to the attribute. If you press ↵ to accept the default, N, another attribute highlights with an X at its base.

8. The **Value/Position/Height**… prompt appears again, allowing you to make changes to the next attribute.

9. This process repeats until all the attributes have been edited or until you press **Ctrl-C**.

Attedit lets you change only one attribute at a time. If you need to make appearance changes to all the attributes of a block, you can enlist the aid of an AutoLISP utility provided with AutoCAD called ATTREDEF.LSP. You will get a chance to look at ATTREDEF.LSP in *Chapter 19*.

MAKING GLOBAL CHANGES TO ATTRIBUTES

There will be times when you'll want to change the value of several attributes in a file to be the same value. If you need to make global changes to attribute values, you can use the Attedit command.

Suppose you decide you want to change all the entry doors to a type designated as B, rather than A. Perhaps door type A was an input error, or type B happens to be better suited for an entry door.

1. Use the VIEW command to restore view 4.

2. Enter **Attedit** ↵ at the command prompt.

3. At the **Edit attributes one at a time? <Y>** prompt, enter **N** ↵ for *No*. You will see the message **Global edit of attribute values.** This tells you that you are in the global edit mode.

4. At the **Edit only attributes visible on screen? <Y>** prompt, press ↵. As you can see from this prompt, you have the option to edit all attributes including those out of the view area. You'll get to work with this option later.

5. At the **Block name specification <*>** prompt, press ↵. Optionally, you can enter a block name to narrow the selection to specific blocks.

6. At the **Attribute tag specification <*>** prompt, press ↵. Optionally, you can enter an attribute tag name to narrow your selection to specific tags.

7. At the **Attribute value specification <*>** prompt, press ↵. Optionally, you can narrow your selection to attributes containing specific values.

8. At the **Select Attributes** prompt, window the door type symbols for units 103 to 115.

9. At the **String to change** prompt, enter **A** ↵.

10. At the **New string** prompt, enter **B** ↵. The door type symbols all change to the new value.

In step 8, you are asked to select the attributes to be edited. AutoCAD limits the changes to those attributes you select. If you know you need to change every single attribute in your drawing, you can do so by answering the series of prompts in a slightly different way, as in the following exercise.

1. Try the same procedure again, but this time enter **N** at the **Edit only attributes visible on screen:** prompt (step 4 in the previous exercise). The message **Drawing must be regenerated afterwards.** appears. The display will flip to text mode.

2. Once again, you are prompted for the block name, the tag, and the value (steps 5, 6 and 7 in the previous exercise). Respond to these prompts as you did before. Once you have done that, you get the message **16 attributes selected**. This tells you the number of attributes that fit the specifications you just entered.

3. At the **String to change:** prompt, enter **A** ↵ to indicate you want to change the rest of the A attribute values.

4. At the **New string:** prompt, enter **B** ↵. A series of B's appear, indicating the number of strings that were replaced.

5. Now save your file.

You may have noticed that the **Select Attribute** prompt is skipped and you go directly to the **String to change** prompt. AutoCAD assumes that you want it to edit every attribute in the drawing, so it doesn't bother asking you to select specific attributes.

MAKING INVISIBLE ATTRIBUTES VISIBLE

You may eventually want to make invisible attributes visible to check their location or make other changes to them. The following describes how to make all attributes visible.

Using Spaces in Attribute Values

At times, you may want the default value to begin with a blank space. This enables you to more easily specify text strings when you edit the attribute. For example, you may have an attribute value that reads *3334333*. If you want to change the first 3 in this string of numbers, you have to specify *3334* when prompted for the string to change. If you start with a space, as in *_3334333*, you isolate the first 3 from the rest by specifying *_3* as the string to change (an underline here represents a space). You must enter a backslash character (\) before the space in the default value to tell AutoCAD to interpret the space literally, rather than as a press of the **spacebar** (which is equivalent to pressing ↵).

Attdisp ↵

▼ NOTE

You get a chance to see the results of the ON and Normal options. The OFF option will make all attributes invisible, regardless of the mode used when they were created.

1. Enter **Attdisp** ↵.

2. At the **Normal/ON/OFF <Normal>:** prompt, enter **ON** ↵. Your drawing will look like Figure 10.10. If Regenauto is turned off, you may have to issue the Regen command. At this point you could edit the invisible attributes individually, as in the first attribute-editing exercise. For now, set the attribute display back to normal.

3. Enter **Attdisp** ↵ again, then at the **Normal/ON/OFF** prompt, enter **N** ↵ for normal.

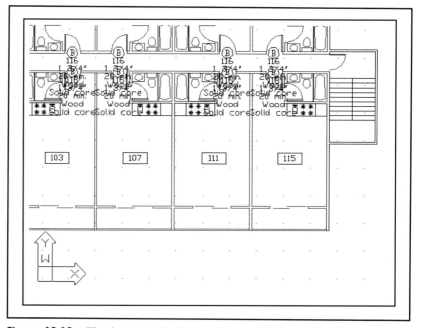

Figure 10.10: The drawing with all the attributes visible. Since the door type symbols are so close together, the attributes overlap.

REDEFINING BLOCKS CONTAINING ATTRIBUTES

Finally, you should be aware that attributes act differently from other objects when included in redefined blocks. Normally, blocks that have been redefined change their configuration to reflect the new block definition. But if a redefined block contains attributes, the attributes will maintain their old properties. This means that the old attribute position, style, etc., do not change even though you may have changed them in the new definition. Fortunately, AutoCAD supplies an AutoLISP program called Attredef.LSP that allows you to redefine blocks, including any of their attribute definitions. See *Chapter 19* for details on how to use this program.

EXTRACTING AND EXPORTING ATTRIBUTE INFORMATION

Once you have entered the attributes into your drawing, you can extract the information contained in them and use it in other programs. You may, for example, want to keep track of the door information in a database manager. This is especially true if you have a project that contains thousands of doors, such as a large hotel.

▼ NOTE

This template file shouldn't be confused with the drawing prototype file you use to set up various default settings.

The first step in extracting attribute information is to create a template file using a text editor like Windows Notepad. The template file used with attributes is a text file containing a list of the attributes you wish to extract and their characteristics. You can also extract information about the block an attribute is associated with. The block name and its *x* and *y* coordinates, layer, orientation, and scale are all available for extraction.

DETERMINING WHAT TO EXTRACT

In the template file, for every attribute you wish to extract, you must give its tag name, followed by a code that determines whether the attribute value is numeric or text, how many spaces to allow for the value, and, if it is a numeric value, how many decimal places to give the number. If you are familiar with database-management programs, you'll know these are typical variables you determine when you set up a database.

For example, to get a list of rooms containing the B door type, you create a DOS text file with the following contents.

```
D-ROOM N005000
D-TYPE C001000
```

The first item on the line is the tag of the attribute you want to list, D-ROOM or D-TYPE. This is followed by at least one space, then a code that describes the attribute. This code may look a little cryptic at first glance. The following list describes how the code is broken down from left to right:

- The first character of the code is always a C or an N to denote a character (C) or numeric (N) value.

- The next three digits are where you enter the number of spaces the value will take up. You can enter any number from 001 to 999, but you must enter zeros for null values. The D-ROOM example shows the value of 005 for five spaces. Note that 005 is used to indicate five spaces. The two leading zeros are needed because AutoCAD expects to see three digits in this part of the code.

- The last three digits are for the number of decimal places to allow if the value is numeric. For character values, these must always be zeros. Once again, AutoCAD expects to see three digits in this part of the code, so even if there are no decimal digits for the value, you must include 000.

Now you will use the Windows Notepad application to create a template file. If you like, you can use any Windows word processor that is capable of saving files in the ASCII format.

Notepad ↵

1. Switch over to the Program Manager, then locate and start up the Notepad application.

2. Enter the following text as it is shown. Enter one line carefully, then press ↵ when you are sure it is correct. Repeat the process for each line until you are done.

   ```
   D-NUMBER C005000 ↵
   D-THICK C007000 ↵
   D-RATE C010000 ↵
   D-MATRL C015000 ↵
   D-CONST C015000 ↵
   ```

3. Click on File ➤ Save, then enter **DOOR.TXT** for the file name.

4. Close the Notepad, then return to AutoCAD.

You've just completed the setup for attribute extraction. Now that you have a template file, you can extract the attribute data.

EXTRACTING BLOCK INFORMATION USING ATTRIBUTES

▼ WARNING

A template file containing these codes must also contain at least one attribute tag, because AutoCAD must know which attribute it is extracting before it can tell what block the attribute is associated with. The code information for blocks works the same as for attributes.

I mentioned that you can extract information regarding blocks, as well as attributes. To do this you must use the following format.

```
BL:LEVEL      N002000
BL:NAME       C031000
BL:X          N009004
BL:Y          N009004
BL:Z          N009004
BL:NUMBER     N009000
BL:HANDLE     C009000
BL:LAYER      C031000
```

```
BL:ORIENT    N009004
BL:XSCALE    N009004
BL:YSCALE    N009004
BL:ZSCALE    N009004
BL:XEXTRUDE  N009004
BL:YEXTRUDE  N009004
BL:ZEXTRUDE  N009004
```

I have included some typical values for the attribute codes in this example. The following describes what each line in the above example is used for.

BL:LEVEL returns the nesting level.

BL:NAME returns the block name.

BL:X returns the X coordinate of the insertion point.

BL:Y returns the Y coordinate of the insertion point.

BL:Z returns the Z coordinate of the insertion point.

BL:NUMBER returns the order number of the block.

BL:HANDLE returns the blocks handle. If no handle exists, a 0 is returned.

BL:LAYER returns the layer the block is inserted on.

BL:ORIENT returns the insertion angle.

BL:XSCALE returns the X scale.

BL:YSCALE returns the Y scale.

BL:ZSCALE returns the Z scale.

BL:XEXTRUDE returns the block's X extrusion direction.

BL:YEXTRUDE returns the block's Y extrusion direction.

BL:ZEXTRUDE returns the block's Z extrusion direction.

PERFORMING THE EXTRACTION

AutoCAD allows you to extract attribute information from your drawing as a list in one of three different formats. These are the *CDF*
(comma delimited format), *SDF* (space delimited format), and *DXF*
(data exchange format).

The CDF format can be read by many popular database-management
programs, as well as programs written in BASIC. This is the format you
will use in this exercise.

Draw ➤ [A] Text ➤ Attributes ➤ Extract
(CDF)

1. Click on Draw ➤ Text ➤ Attributes ➤ Extract. The Attribute Extraction dialog box appears (see Figure 10.11).

2. Click on the radio button labeled CDF.

3. Double click on the Template File input box and enter
DOOR.TXT.

4. Press the **Tab** key to move to the Output File input box, then
type **PLAN.TXT**.

5. Click on **OK**. The computer will pause for several seconds,
and when it is done, the message **16 records in extract file.**
appears.

▼ NOTE

You can select file names of
existing template and output
files by clicking on the
Template File or **Output File**
buttons. The file dialog box appears, allowing you to select
files from a list.

AutoCAD has created a file called Plan.TXT that contains the extracted list. Let's take a look at its contents.

1. Enter **Type** ↵ or click on UTILITY ➤ External Commands
➤ TYPE.

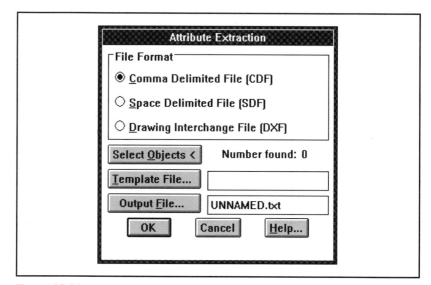

Figure 10.11: The Attribute Extraction dialog box

▼ NOTE

You may have noticed the **Select Objects** button in the Attribute Extraction dialog box. When you click on this button, the dialog box temporarily closes to let you single out attributes to extract by picking their associated blocks from the display.

2. At the **File to list:** prompt, enter **Plan.TXT** ↵. You will get the following list:

```
'116','1 3/4"','20 MIN','WOOD','SOLID CORE'
'114','1 3/4"','20 MIN','WOOD','SOLID CORE'
'112','1 3/4"','20 MIN','WOOD','SOLID CORE'
'110','1 3/4"','20 MIN','WOOD','SOLID CORE'
'108','1 3/4"','20 MIN','WOOD','SOLID CORE'
'106','1 3/4"','20 MIN','WOOD','SOLID CORE'
'102','1 3/4"','20 MIN','WOOD','SOLID CORE'
'104','1 3/4"','20 MIN','WOOD','SOLID CORE'
'107','1 3/4"','20 MIN','WOOD','SOLID CORE'
'105','1 3/4"','20 MIN','WOOD','SOLID CORE'
'101','1 3/4"','20 MIN','WOOD','SOLID CORE'
'103','1 3/4"','20 MIN','WOOD','SOLID CORE'
'111','1 3/4"','20 MIN','WOOD','SOLID CORE'
'109','1 3/4"','20 MIN','WOOD','SOLID CORE'
'113','1 3/4"','20 MIN','WOOD','SOLID CORE'
'115','1 3/4"','20 MIN','WOOD','SOLID CORE'
```

Notice that the individual values are enclosed in single quotes. These quotes delimit character values. If you had specified numeric values, the quotes would not have appeared. Also note that the fields are in the order they appear in the template file.

Since you picked the comma delimited format, AutoCAD placed commas between each extracted attribute value (or *field* in database terminology).

The commas are used by some database-management programs to indicate the separation of fields in ASCII files. This example shows everything in uppercase letters because that's the way they were entered when I inserted the attribute blocks in my own working sample. The extracted file maintains the case of whatever you enter for the attribute values.

USING OTHER DELIMITERS

Some database managers require the use of other symbols, such as double quotes and slashes, to indicate character values and field separation. AutoCAD allows you to use a different symbol in place of the single quote or comma. For example, if the database manager you use requires double-quote delimiters for text in the file to be imported, you can add the statement

    c:quote "

to the template file to replace the single quote with a double quote. A line from an extract file using *c:quote "* in the template file would look like this:

    "115","1 3/4" ","20 MIN","WOOD","SOLID CORE"

Notice that the single quote (') is replaced by a double quote ("). You can also add the statement

    c:delim /

to replace the comma delimiter with the slash symbol. A line from an extract file using both *c:quote "* and *c:delim /* in the template file would look like this:

    "115"/"1 3/4" "/"20 MIN"/"WOOD"/"SOLID CORE"

Here the comma is replaced by a forward slash. You can add either of these statements to the beginning or end of your template file.

Using the SDF Format

The SDF format, as well as the CDF format, can be read by most database-management programs. You can also use this format if you intend to enter information into a word-processed document. You can even import it into an AutoCAD drawing using the method described in *Chapter 8* to import text. Now try using the SDF option to extract the same list.

Draw ➤ A Text ➤ Attributes ➤ Extract
(SDF)

1. Click on Draw ➤ Text ➤ Attributes ➤ Extract again.

2. At the Attribute Extraction dialog box, use the same template file name, but for the attribute extract file name, use **Plan-SDF.TXT** to distinguish this file from the last one you created.

3. Click on the SDF radio button, then click on **OK**.

4. After AutoCAD has extracted the list, use the TYPE command to view the contents of the file. You will get a list similar to this one:

```
116 1 3/4" 20 MIN WOOD SOLID CORE
114 1 3/4" 20 MIN WOOD SOLID CORE
112 1 3/4" 20 MIN WOOD SOLID CORE
110 1 3/4" 20 MIN WOOD SOLID CORE
108 1 3/4" 20 MIN WOOD SOLID CORE
106 1 3/4" 20 MIN WOOD SOLID CORE
102 1 3/4" 20 MIN WOOD SOLID CORE
104 1 3/4" 20 MIN WOOD SOLID CORE
107 1 3/4" 20 MIN WOOD SOLID CORE
105 1 3/4" 20 MIN WOOD SOLID CORE
101 1 3/4" 20 MIN WOOD SOLID CORE
103 1 3/4" 20 MIN WOOD SOLID CORE
111 1 3/4" 20 MIN WOOD SOLID CORE
```

```
109 1 3/4" 20 MIN WOOD SOLID CORE
113 1 3/4" 20 MIN WOOD SOLID CORE
115 1 3/4" 20 MIN WOOD SOLID CORE
```

This format shows text without any special delimiting characters.

Using the DXF Format

The third file format is the DXF format. There are actually two DXF commands. The Draw ➤ Text ➤ Attributes ➤ Extract option extracts only the data from blocks containing attributes. The File ➤ Import/Export ➤ DXF Out option converts an entire drawing file into a special format for data exchange between AutoCAD and other programs (for example, other PC CAD programs). I will discuss the DXF format in more detail in *Chapter 14*.

USING EXTRACTED ATTRIBUTE DATA WITH OTHER PROGRAMS

Suppose you want to import the list you just created into dBASE IV by using the CDF option. First, you create a database file with the same field characteristics you entered for the template file (i.e., length of fields and character or number). Then enter:

```
Append from \
AutoCAD directory\plan.txt Delimited
```

where **AutoCAD directory** is the directory where the Plan.TXT file can be found. To use the file created by the SDF option, replace Delimited in the line above with **SDF** and use **plan-SDF.TXT** instead of *plan.txt*.

You can import any of these lists into any word-processing program that accepts ASCII files. They will appear as shown in our examples. You may want to use the SDF format for word processing because it leaves out the commas and quotes.

You can also use the SDF format for importing files into Lotus 1-2-3. However, you must change the SDF file extension from .TXT to .PRN. Once you have done this, you can use Lotus's File Import command to create a spreadsheet from this file. Use the Numbers option on the

Lotus Import submenu to ensure that the numeric values are entered as discrete spreadsheet cells. Any items containing text are grouped together in one cell. For example, the last three items in the Plan-SDF.TXT file are combined into one cell because each item contains text.

If you want to export data to Excel, you will have to use the .CDF format. There are no other special requirements for Excel, but importing into Excel is made somewhat easier if you give your export file an extension that begins with .*XL*, as in Plan.XLA.

As we mentioned earlier, the extracted file can be made to conform to other data formats. If you are using a database manager other than dBASE IV, find out what its format requirements are for imported files and use the quote and delim options described earlier to make adjustments.

LINKING TO EXTERNAL DATABASES

AutoCAD offers a way to link your drawing directly to an external database. Through the AutoCAD SQL Extension (ASE) you can read and manipulate data from external database files. You can also link parts of your drawing to an external database. There are numerous reasons for doing this. The most obvious is to keep inventory on parts of your drawing. If you are an interior designer do office planning, you can link inventory data from a database to your drawing. If you are a facilities manager, you can track the movement of people and facilities using AutoCAD linked to a database file.

The following tutorial is intended to give you an overview of the ASE capabilities, and by no means constitutes complete coverage of this feature. I specifically avoid the more complex programming issues of database management systems and I do not discuss the SQL language on which much of ASE is based. Still, you should be able to make good use of ASE with the information provided here. I do assume a small degree of familiarity with databases in these exercises.

OPENING A DATABASE FROM AUTOCAD

The ASE doesn't actually create database files. You must have created a database file before you use ASE. Before you begin to access database files, you must first set the DOS environment to tell AutoCAD where to look for them. In this exercise, you will use the sample tutorial DbaseIII files provided with AutoCAD. These files can be found in the \acad\tutorial\dbf directory. The directory containing your database files can then be viewed as the database with each .DBF file being a table.

1. Before you start AutoCAD, exit Windows, then enter **set asedb=c:\acad \tutorial\dbf** ↵ at the DOS prompt. This creates an alias for the directory path to your database files.

2. Go to the \acad\tutorial\dbf directory and enter **dir** ↵. You see the following list of files:

```
COMPUTER DBF 667  03-30-92  6:42p
EMPLOYEE  DBF 3612 07-04-92  11:12a
INVENTRY  DBF 3489107-04-92  11:11a
```

These are dBASEIII database files. The contents of the first database file you will work with are shown in Figure 10.12.

EMPLOYEE.DBF

EMP_ID	LAST_NAME	FIRST_NAME	DEPT	TITLE	ROOM	EXT
1000	Meredith	Dave	Sales	V.P.	101	8600
1001	Williams	Janice	Sales	Western Region Mgr.	102	8601
1003	Smith	Jill	Sales	Central Region Mgr.	104	8603
1004	Nelson	Kirk	Sales	Canadian Sales Mgr.	105	8604
1005	Clark	Karl	Sales	Educational Sales Mgr.	106	8605
1006	Wilson	Cindy	Accounting	Accountant	110	8455
1007	Ortega	Emilio	Accounting	Accountant	109	8607
1008	Benson	Adam	Accounting	Accountant	109	8608
1009	Rogers	Kevin	Accounting	Accountant	109	8609
1012	Simpson	Paul	Engineering	Mechanical Engineer	124	8612
1013	Debrine	Todd	Engineering	Design Engineer	125	8613
1014	Frazier	Heather	Engineering	Application Engineer	126	8614
1016	Taylor	Patrick	Engineering	Software Engineer	128	8616
1017	Chang	Yuan	Engineering	Software Engineer	129	8617
1018	Dempsy	Phil	Engineering	Application Engineer	112	8618
1019	Kahn	Jenny	Engineering	Programmer	113	8619
1020	Moore	George	Engineering	Programmer	114	8620
1021	Price	Mark	Engineering	Software Engineer	115	8621
1022	Quinn	Scott	Engineering	Software Engineer	116	8622
1023	Sanchez	Maria	Engineering	Mechanical Engineer	117	8623
1024	Ross	Ted	Engineering	Application Engineer	118	8624
1026	Fong	Albert	Engineering	Programmer	120	8626
0	Vacant					

Figure 10.12: The contents of Employee.DBF dBASEIII file that comes with AutoCAD

3. Start Windows and AutoCAD.

4. Click on File ➤ ASE ➤ Initialize or enter **ASEinit** ↵.

5. Click on File ➤ ASE ➤ Set ➤ DBMS or enter **Asesetdbms** ↵, then click on Dbase3 at the DBMS Drive dialog box (see Figure 10.13).

6. Click on File ➤ ASE ➤ Set ➤ DB… or enter **Asesetdb** ↵. The Set Current Database dialog box appears (see Figure 10.14).

7. Enter **asedb** ↵ in the input box then click on **OK**. Remember that this is the database alias you set up in step 1 pointing to the directory containing the .DBF files. The Set Database Please Enter dialog box appears (see Figure 10.15).

8. Press ↵ twice as the user name and password are not important to this tutorial.

9. Click on File ➤ ASE ➤ Set ➤ Table… or enter **Asesettable** ↵. The Set Current Table dialog box appears (see Figure 10.16).

10. Enter **Employee** ↵. The Select Key Columns dialog box appears (see Figure 10.17).

11. Click on the first item in the list, EMP_ID, and click the **ON** button. Click on **OK**. You are now connected to the Employee.DBF File.

FINDING A RECORD IN THE DATABASE

Now that you are connected to the database, suppose you want to find the record of a specific individual. You might know that individual is in the Accounting department.

1. Click on File ➤ ASE ➤ Set Row or enter **Asesetrow** ↵. You see the Set Row Options dialog box (see Figure 10.18).

2. Enter **dept='Accounting'** in the input box, then click on the **Search** button. The Set Current Row by Search Criteria dialog box appears (see Figure 10.19). Notice that the box tells you how many rows fill the criteria.

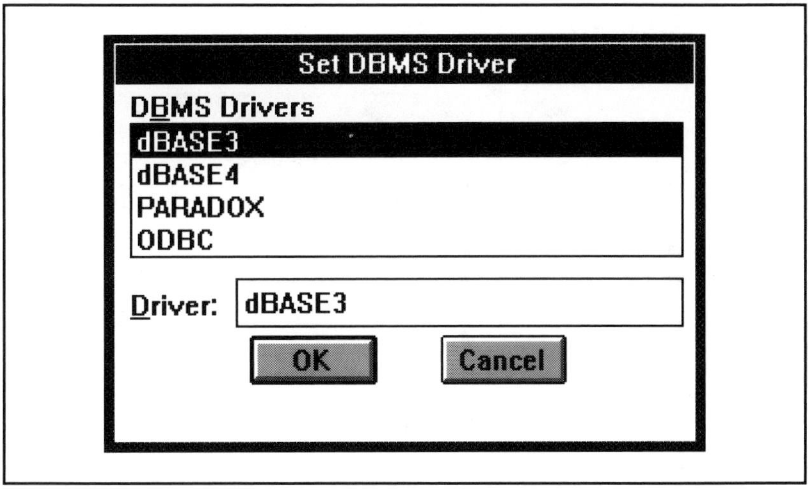

Figure 10.13: The DBMS Driver dialog box

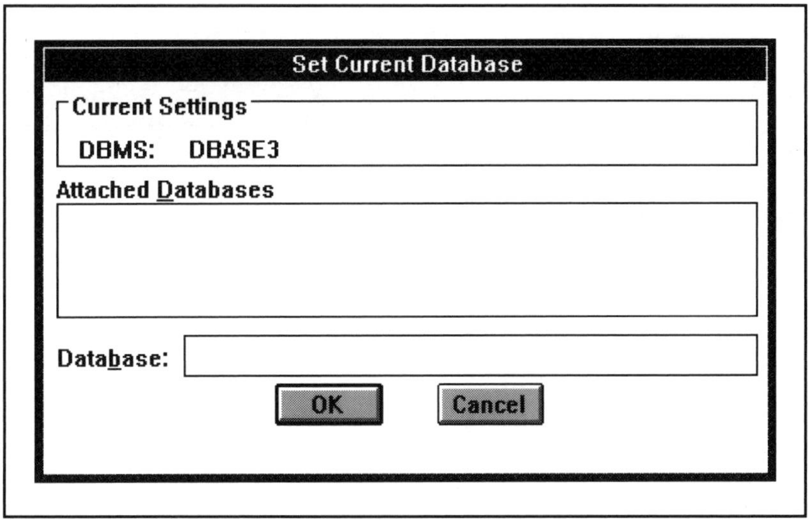

Figure 10.14: The Set Current Database dialog box

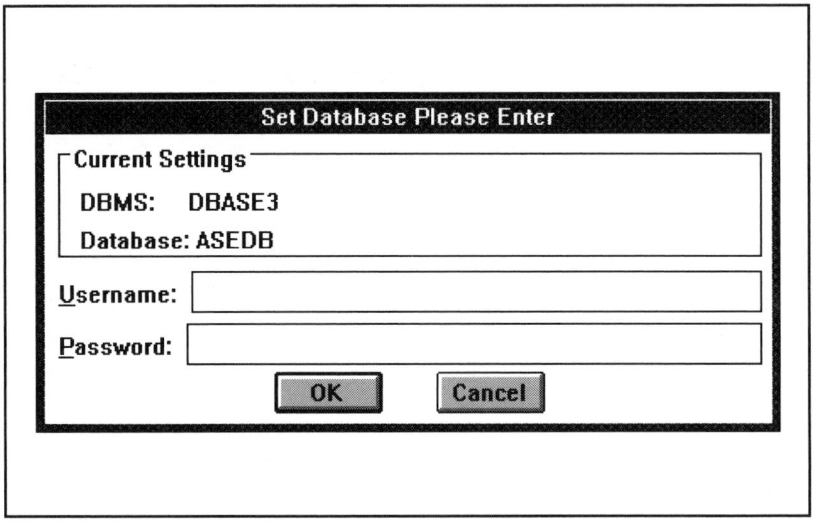

Figure 10.15:   The Set Database Please Enter dialog box

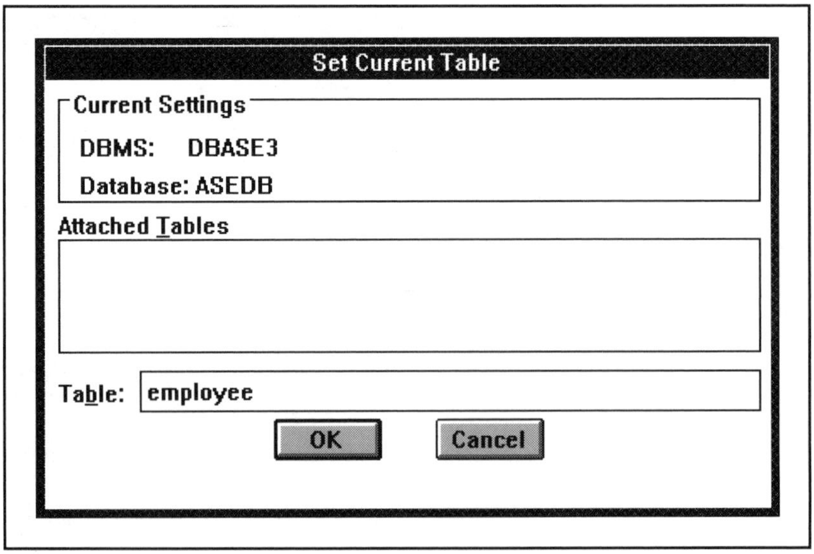

Figure 10.16:   The Set Current Table dialog box

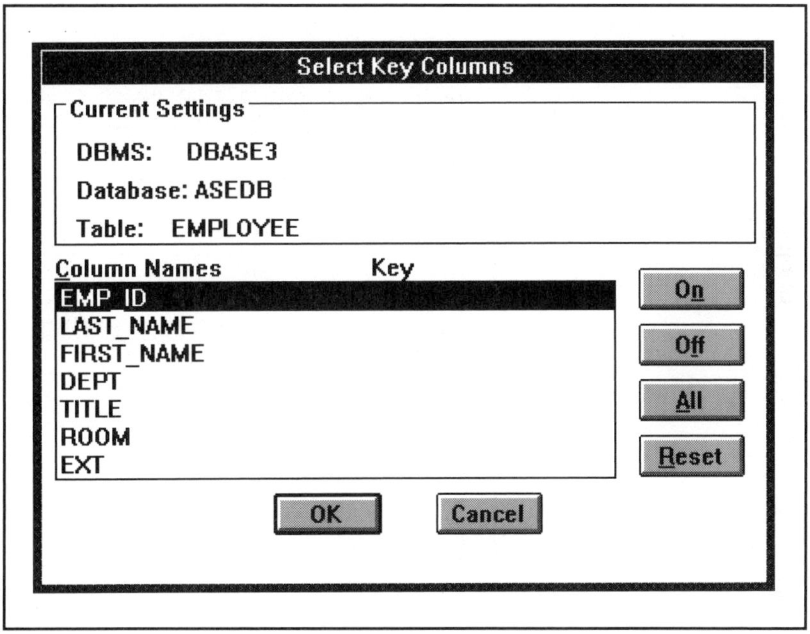

Figure 10.17: The Select Key Columns dialog box

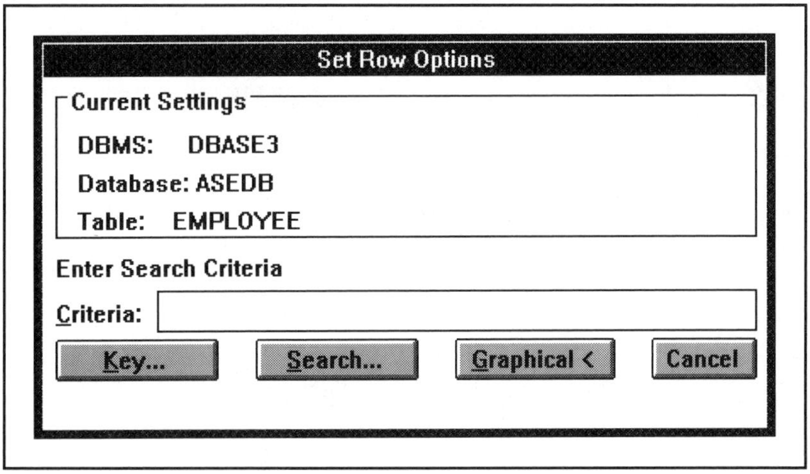

Figure 10.18: The Set Row Options dialog box

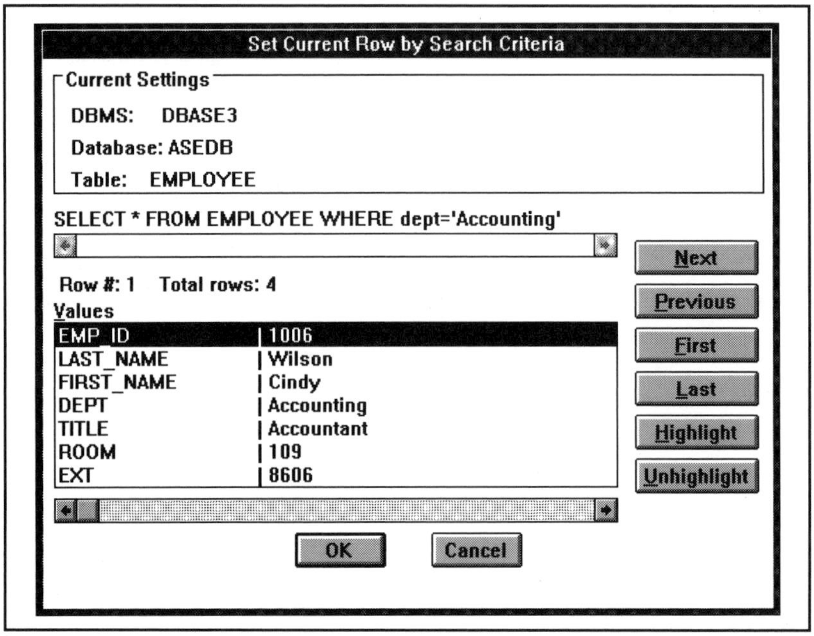

Figure 10.19: The Set Current Row by Search Criteria dialog box

3. Click on the **Next** button to view the next row that meets the search criteria.

4. Click on **Last** to view the last row, with Kevin Rogers's name.

5. Click on **OK** to close the dialog box.

The row with Kevin Rogers' name becomes the current one. This is important because the current row is the one that can be deleted or edited. If you want to perform either a deletion or edit, you must first set the desired record to be the current one, then use Asedelrow (ASE ➤ Row ➤ Delete) to delete it or Aseeditrow (ASE ➤ Row ➤ Edit) to edit it.

You can also click on **Search** without entering anything in the input box in step 2. This essentially tells ASE to select all the rows in the current database table. You would then be able to scan the entire table in the Set Current Row by Search Criteria dialog box.

If you enter a search criteria that finds only one row, that row automatically becomes the current one and you do not see the Set Current Row dialog box.

ADDING A ROW TO A DATABASE TABLE

Now suppose you have a new employee who will need to be set up in an office. The first thing you will want to do is add his or her name to the database. Here's how it's done.

1. Click on File ➤ ASE ➤ Row ➤ Add or enter **Aseaddrow** ↵. The Add Row dialog box appears (see Figure 10.20).

2. Enter the following data for each item in the dialog box. To add an item, highlight the item in the list, then add the information in the input at the bottom of the dialog box. Press ↵ at the end of entry.

   ```
   EMP_ID |      2000
   LAST_NAME |   Knopfler
   FIRST_NAME |  Mark
   DEPT |        R&R
   TITLE |       Composer
   ROOM |        -
   EXT |         8888
   ```

3. When you are done entering the list, click on **OK**. You've just added a row to the database and it is the current one.

FINDING AND SELECTING GRAPHICS THROUGH THE DATABASE

Accessing a database from AutoCAD in itself can be useful, but the real advantage of using AutoCAD with a database is being able to link data to graphics in your drawing. The following exercise will show you how you can locate parts of a drawing using a database search similar to the one you just performed. For the following exercises, you will use a tutorial drawing that comes with AutoCAD.

The first thing you must do is reset the DOS environment to assign a different database alias to the \acad\tutorial\dbf directory.

1. Exit AutoCAD and Windows, then at the DOS prompt, enter **set asetut=***d:*\acad\tutorial\dbf ↵, where *d:*\acad is the directory where you have installed AutoCAD.

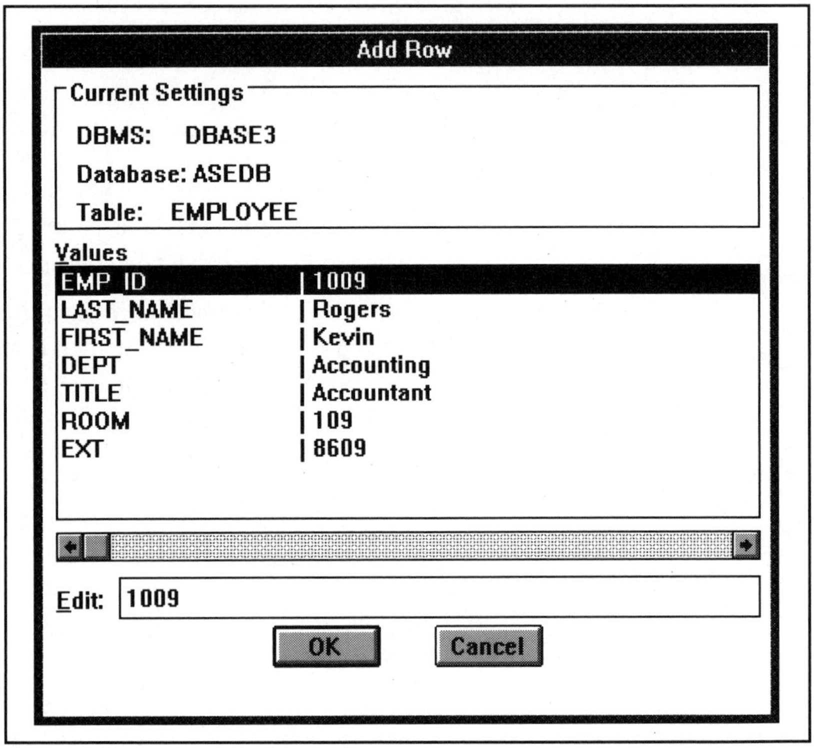

Figure 10.20:   The Add Row dialog box

2. Start up Windows and AutoCAD, then open the file called Asetut in the Tutorial subdirectory (in the AutoCAD directory). You will see the drawing shown in Figure 10.21.

3. Click on File ➤ ASE ➤ Initialize. You will see the messages **Current DBMS is DBASE3** and **Current database is ASETUT**. Since this drawing already has links to a database, these connections are defined in the drawing.

4. In the Set Database dialog box, click on **OK**.

5. Click on File ➤ ASE ➤ Set Table and at the Set Current Table dialog box, highlight Employee and click **OK**.

6. Click on File ➤ ASE ➤ Set Row or enter **Asesetrow** ↵.

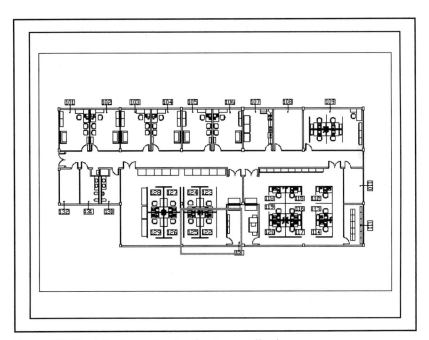

Figure 10.21:   The Asetut drawing showing an office layout

7. At the Set Row Options dialog box, click on the **Search…** button.

8. At the Set Current Row by Search Criteria dialog box, click on **Last**. Notice that the record you added appears at the end of the table.

9. Click on **Previous**. The row listing Vacant as the Employee's last name appears.

10. Click on **Highlight**. The dialog box temporarily closes and you see the prompt **Press < enter > or spacebar…:**. Notice that some of the room numbers are highlighted. The highlighted room numbers show you which rooms are linked to the row that has *Vacant* for the last-name field.

11. Press ↵, then click on **OK**.

The room numbers are linked to the Employee's database table. As you can see, several drawing objects can be linked to a single row in a database. In this exercise, you used that link to visually locate the rooms that were listed as Vacant in the database table. You could then decide where to place your new employee.

Another capability of the linked database is the ability to select objects for editing. You'll look at that a bit later. Now let's see how you can create a link to the database by linking your new employee to one of the vacant rooms.

DELETING AND CREATING A LINK

Now that you've spotted the vacant offices, it's time to link your new employee to one of them. But first, you should unlink the current Vacant link assigned to the room you select.

1. Zoom into the area shown in Figure 10.21.

2. Click on File ➤ ASE ➤ Link ➤ Delete or enter **Asedellink** ↵.

3. At the **All/DBMS/Database/Table/<row>:** prompt, press ↵ to accept the default, *row*.

4. At the **select object** prompt, click on room number 122, then press ↵. This is the room for your new employee.

5. At the Delete Linkages dialog box, click on **Yes**. All links to the room number are removed.

Now you are ready to add a link to room 122.

1. Enter **Asesetrow** ↵ and at the Set Row Options dialog box, enter **emp_id=2000**, then click on **OK**. This sets the current row to be the one for your new employee. Like other options, you must first set the desired row to be current before you can link it to an object.

2. Click on File ➤ ASE ➤ Make Link or enter **Asemakelink** ↵; then at the **select objects** prompt, click on room number 122.

3. To check the link, click on File ➤ ASE ➤ Quick View or enter **Aseqview** ↵, then click on room number 122. You will see the row data for your new employee appear in a dialog box.

4. Click on **OK** to exit the dialog box.

You can also make a link quickly by using File ➤ ASE ➤ Quick Link or by entering **Aseqlink**. This brings up the Set Row Options dialog box allowing you to select a row, then it immediately asks you to select an object to link to that row.

You could have added your link to room 122 without deleting the Vacant link. You would then have two links to the room number. This is perfectly legal and in some cases quite desirable.

ADDING LABELS WITH LINKS

You will often want to place data from your database in your drawing as text or labels. Suppose, for example, that you want to add a label to room 122 showing the name of the new employee and his extension. The following shows how this is done.

▼ WARNING

Each time you add a label, you are adding a new block to your drawing and increasing your file size.

1. First create a layer called **roomlbl** for your labels and make it the current layer.

2. Click on File ➤ ASE ➤ Quick Make DA or enter **aseqmakeda** ↵.

3. At the **select object** prompt, pick the room number 122.

4. At the **Justify/Style/<start point>** prompt, click on a point just below the chair in room 122 (see Figure 10.22.)

5. At the **Height** prompt, enter **6** ↵ and press ↵ at the rotation prompt. The Make Displayable Attribute dialog box appears (see Figure 10.23). Don't confuse the term *Displayable Attribute* with the attributes you created earlier using the AutoCAD attribute definitions. They are not the same.

6. Double click on FIRST_NAME from the column at the left, then double click on LAST_NAME. Notice that they appear in the list box to the right in the order you selected them.

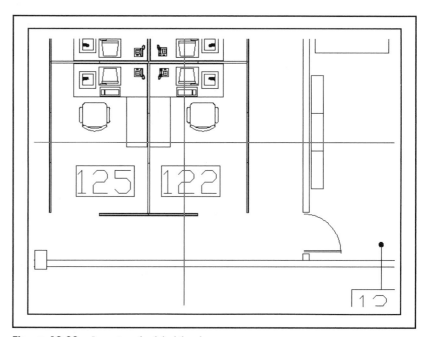

Figure 10.22:   Locating the label for the room occupant

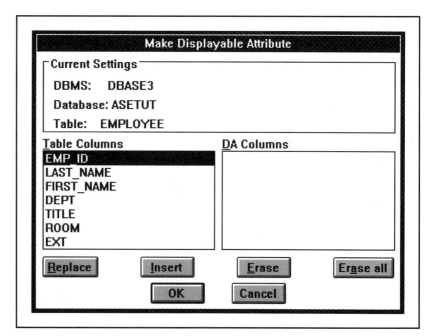

Figure 10.23:   The Make Displayable Attribute dialog box

7. Double click on Title then click on **OK**. The items you selected from the dialog box appear in the drawing.

8. Press ↵ to repeat the Aseqmakeda command, then click on the chair in room 125.

9. At the **Justify/Style/<start point>** prompt, pick a point just below the chair, then press ↵ twice to accept the default for height and angle.

10. At the dialog box, double click on DESCRIPT then click on **OK**. The label *adjustable chair* appears in the drawing.

The Aseqmakeda command actually does two things. It first changes the current row by asking you to select an object linked to a row. It uses that link to determine which row to make current. Then it runs the Asemakeda command to place the current row information in the drawing. If you were to issue the Aseviewrow command now, you would see that the current row is now the one for the chair you labeled in steps 9 and 10 of the last exercise.

As an alternate to using Aseqmakeda, you can use Asesetrow and Asemakeda to place a linked label in your drawing. This alternative is useful if you do not want to maintain the current row setting for the next operation.

UPDATING ROWS AND LABELS

Things are constantly changing and chances are your database will change frequently. In the following exercise, you will get to change a database row and update one of the labels you just placed in your drawing. You will start by quickly setting the current row by selecting an object.

1. Click on File ➤ ASE ➤ Set Row, then at the dialog box, click on **Graphical<**. The dialog box closes and the **select object** prompt appears.

2. Click on the number 122. The current row is now set to the one for your new employee.

3. Click on File ➤ ASE ➤ Row ➤ Edit or enter **Aseeditrow** ↵, then at the Edit Row dialog box, highlight TITLE.

4. Press ↵ to highlight the input box and enter **Great Composer** ↵, then click on **OK**.

You have just edited a row in the database. Next, you will update the label you placed earlier in room 122.

1. Click on File ➤ ASE ➤ Reload DA or enter **Asereloadda** ↵.

2. At the **select objects** prompt, click on the label in room 122, then press ↵. The drawing regenerates and the label updates to reflect the change in the database table.

CHANGING A LINK

Earlier, you had to change a link to a room number from Vacant to your new employee. In that exercise, you first deleted a link, then added a new one. This next exercise shows you how you can change a link from one database table row to another in one step.

Now suppose you want to change the label in room 125 to reflect the desk and not the chair in the room. Here's how this is done.

1. Click on File ➤ ASE ➤ Set Row or enter **Asesetrow** ↵, then at the dialog box, click on **Graphical**.

2. Click on the *adjustable chair* label in room 125. The row assigned to that label is now the current row.

3. Click on File ➤ ASE ➤ Link ➤ Edit or enter **Aseeditlink**.

4. At the **All/DBMS/dataBase/Table/<row>** prompt, press ↵.

5. At the **select object** prompt, click on the *adjustable chair* label. The Edit Link dialog box appears (see Figure 10.24).

6. Click on the **Proceed...** button. The Edit Link Options dialog box appears. Notice that it is similar to the Set Row Options dialog box.

7. Enter **room='125'** ↵ in the input box. The Set Current Row by Search Criteria dialog box appears. You can now scan through the list of items in the Inventory table that have a ROOM field value equal to '125'.

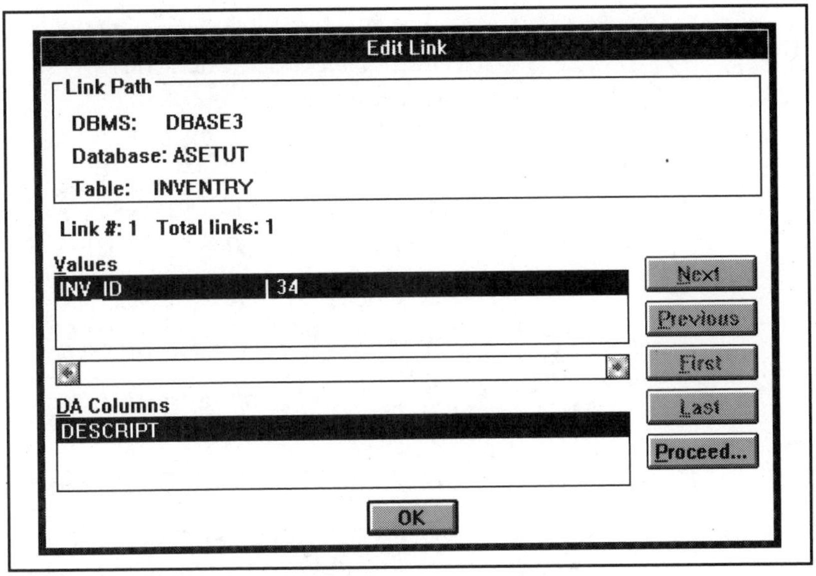

Figure 10.24:   The Edit Link dialog box

8. Click on the **next** button to view the next item, a two-piece desk, then click on **OK**; click on **OK** again at the dialog box. The label changes to reflect its new link.

If you look at the prompt in step 4, you will notice other options you didn't try. You can change a link all the way across to another database if you want.

SELECTING OBJECTS BASED ON THEIR DATABASE LINKS

I mentioned earlier that you can select objects based on their database links. This is a kind non-graphical method of selecting objects. Try the following exercise to see how it works.

First, you must set the current table for the criteria you want your selection to fall under. Then you can use the Aseselect command to do the actual selecting.

1. Zoom out to the extents of the drawing.

2. Click on File ➤ ASE ➤ Set ➤ Table or enter **Asesettable**; then at the dialog box, click on Employee then **OK**.

3. Click on File ➤ ASE ➤ Select or enter **Aseselect** ↵.

4. At the **Export/<Selection set>:** prompt, press ↵.

5. At the **Union/Subtract/<Intersection>:** prompt, press ↵ again.

6. At the **Graphical/<Textual>:** prompt, press ↵ again.

7. At the **Enter search criteria for DBASE3/ASETUT /EMPLOYEE**: prompt, enter **last_name='Vacant'** ↵.

8. At the **Select objects:** prompt, window the entire plan, then press ↵.

9. Enter **Erase** ↵, then enter **P** ↵ to select the previous selection set. Notice that some of the room numbers highlight.

10. Press ↵ again to complete the Erase command. All the room numbers that are linked to the Vacant database table row are erased.

11. Exit the file without saving it.

▼ WARNING

Erasing linked objects or deleting linked records in a database using a database manager can cause conflicts between the drawing the database file. To correct such conflicts, enter **Asepost** ↵ at the Command prompt, then choose the FIX option.

You could have windowed only half the area of the floor plan to isolate a particular region of the drawing for the selection. The following describes what happens with the various options in step 4.

Intersection selects only the items in the windowed area that fit the search criteria entered in step 6.

Subtract selects only items outside the windowed area that fit the search criteria entered in step 6.

Union selects all the items selected with the window, plus all the items that fit the search criteria entered in step 6.

WHERE TO GO FROM HERE

You've seen how you can access and link your drawing to a database. I hope that in this brief tutorial, you can find the information you will need to develop your own database needs. Chances are, you are already familiar with at least one database program, and as you may have noticed, ASE provides support for dBASE III, dBASE IV, and the DOS version of Paradox. But you don't have to have these specific programs to work with ASE. Many other database and spreadsheet programs can read and write to dBASE III files. You can use Excel to create database files for use with AutoCAD ASE. Borland's Object Vision works with dBASE and Paradox files.

If you understand SQL, you can take advantage of it to perform more sophisticated searches. You can also expand the functionality of the basic ASE package included with AutoCAD. These topics are, unfortunately, beyond the scope of this book. For more detailed information about the ASE and SQL, refer to the AutoCAD SQL Extension reference manual.

IF YOU WANT TO EXPERIMENT...

Attributes can be used to help automate data entry into drawings. To demonstrate this, try the following exercise.

Create a drawing file called **Record** with the attribute definitions shown in Figure 10.25. Note the size and placement of the attribute definitions as well as the new base point for the drawing. Save and exit the file, then create a new drawing called **Schedule** containing the schedule shown in Figure 10.26. Use the INSERT command and insert the Record file into the schedule at the point indicated. Note that you are prompted for each entry of the record. Enter any value you like for each prompt. When you are done, the information for one record is entered into the schedule.

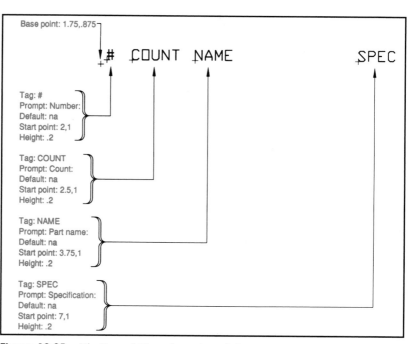

Base point: 1.75,.875

COUNT NAME SPEC

Tag: #
Prompt: Number:
Default: na
Start point: 2,1
Height: .2

Tag: COUNT
Prompt: Count:
Default: na
Start point: 2.5,1
Height: .2

Tag: NAME
Prompt: Part name:
Default: na
Start point: 3.75,1
Height: .2

Tag: SPEC
Prompt: Specification:
Default: na
Start point: 7,1
Height: .2

Figure 10.25: The Record file with attribute definitions

SUMMARY

AutoCAD's attribute feature offers flexibility and power to those who take the time to master its use. It may seem a bit cumbersome at first, but with some standardization of procedures and names for attributes and template files, you can simplify the process of extracting information.

At times you will want to enter hand-drafted drawings to be used as templates or backgrounds for other drawings. In the next chapter, you will look at alternate methods of input, such as tracing, that enable you to quickly enter existing drawings. You will also learn what to do with a drawing once it has been traced.

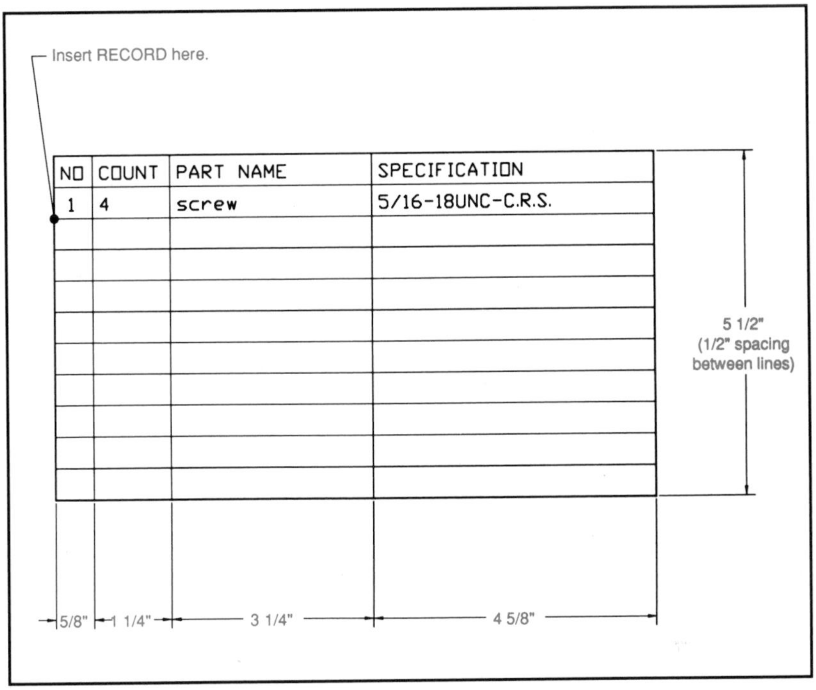

Figure 10.26: The Record file with attribute definitions

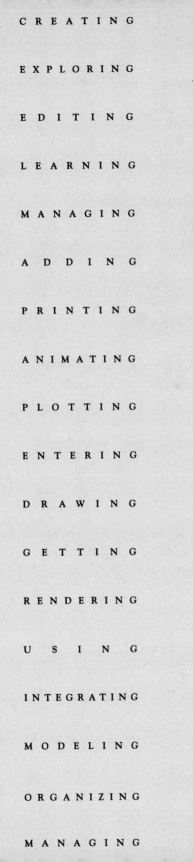

11

ENTERING
PRE-EXISTING
DRAWINGS

FAST TRACK

431 ▶ To set up a drawing to be traced on a digitizer

Secure the drawing on the digitizer. Enter **Tablet** ↵ **Cal** ↵, pick a known point on your drawing, then enter its coordinates. Pick another point on your drawing, then enter its coordinates. Continue until you have selected enough points to your satisfaction.

434 ▶ To trace a perspective view so it looks like an orthogonal one

Secure the drawing or photograph on the digitizer, then Enter **Tablet** ↵ **Cal** ↵. Calibrate the four corners of the facade. At the **Orthogonal/ Affine/Projective/<Repeat table>** prompt, enter **P** ↵.

435 ▶ To access the menus once you've calibrated your tablet

Press the **F10** function key to toggle the tablet mode on and off.

440 ▶ To relocate a set of endpoints

Turn on the Verb/ Noun and Grips features. Select all the objects whose endpoints you want to relocate. Turn ortho mode on then Shift-click on the rest of the grips you want to move. Click on one of the hot grips a second time, then stretch the grips to their new location.

440 ▶ To straighten sets of lines

Click on Modify ➤ Change ➤ Points. Select the lines you want to straighten, then click on a point indicating roughly their endpoint location.

447 ▶ To scale a drawing that contains curves without using a digitizer

Draw a grid in AutoCAD that conforms to the area of the drawing you intend to scale. Plot the grid, then overlay the grid onto the paper drawing. Locate key points on the grid then transfer those points back into the grid drawing in AutoCAD.

450 ▶ To import a raster image into AutoCAD

Click on File ➤ Applications, locate the Rasterin.EXP utility in the Support subdirectory, then load it. At the command prompt, enter **Gifin**, **Tiffin**, or **Pcxin** to import one of the three formats represented by these commands. Answer the prompt regarding insertion point, scale, and angle.

454 ▶ To import a PostScript image into AutoCAD

Click on File ➤ Import/Export ➤ PostScript In, or enter **Psin** ↵ at the command prompt. Answer the prompt regarding insertion point, scale, and angle.

At times you will want to turn a hand-drafted drawing into an AutoCAD drawing file. It may be because you are modifying a design you created before you started using AutoCAD, or because you are converting your entire library of drawings for future AutoCAD use. This chapter discusses three ways to enter a hand-drafted drawing: *tracing*, *scaling*, and *scanning*.

Each method of drawing input has its advantages and disadvantages. *Tracing* with a digitizing tablet is the easiest method, but a traced drawing usually requires some cleaning up and reorganization. If dimensional accuracy is not too important, tracing is the best method for entering existing drawings. It is especially useful for entering irregular curves, such as the contour lines of a topographical map.

Scaling a drawing is the most flexible method, since you don't need a tablet to do it and you usually have less cleaning up to do afterwards. It also affords the most accurate input of orthogonal lines, since you can read dimensions directly from the drawing and enter those same dimensions into AutoCAD. Its main drawback is that if the drawing does not contain complete dimensional information, you must constantly look at the hand-drafted drawing and measure distances with a scale. Also, irregular curves are difficult to scale accurately.

Scanning produces a file that requires the most cleaning up of all these input methods. In fact, you often spend more time cleaning up a scanned drawing than you would have spent tracing or scaling it. It is also difficult to scan text in a drawing (even though some scanners can read straight text files). Unfortunately, there is no easy way to transfer text from a hand-drafted drawing to an AutoCAD file. Scanning is best used for drawings that are difficult to trace or scale, such as complex topographical maps containing more contours than are practical to trace, or nontechnical line art.

If you don't have a digitizing tablet, you can use scaling to enter the utility room drawing used in the tracing exercise (you will insert it into your apartment house plan in *Chapter 12*).

▼ TIP

Be sure to read the tracing information anyway, because some of it will help you with your editing. For example, because traced lines are often not accurately placed, you will learn how to fix such lines in the course of cleaning up a traced drawing.

TRACING A DRAWING

The most common and direct method for entering a hand-drafted drawing is tracing. If it is a large drawing, and you have a small tablet, you may have to cut the drawing into pieces your tablet can manage, trace each piece, then assemble the completed pieces into the large drawing. The best solution is to have a large tablet to begin with, but many of us can't afford the five or ten thousand dollars these large-format tablets usually cost.

In the following exercises, we assume you have an 11"×11" or larger tablet. The sample drawings are small enough to fit completely on this size of tablet. You can use either a stylus or a puck to trace them, but the stylus offers the most natural feel since it is shaped like a pen. A puck has crosshairs that you have to center on the line you want to trace. This requires a bit more dexterity.

RECONFIGURING THE TABLET FOR TRACING

▼ TIP

You can save several different AutoCAD configurations that can be easily set at the DOS level by using batch files. See *Appendix B*.

When you first installed AutoCAD, you configured the tablet to use most of its active drawing area for AutoCAD's menu template. Since you will need the tablet's entire drawing area to trace this drawing, you now have to reconfigure the tablet to get rid of the menu. Otherwise you won't be able to pick points on the drawing outside the 4"×3" screen pointing area AutoCAD normally uses (see Figure 11.1).

Tablet ↵ Cfg ↵

1. Start AutoCAD and open a new file called **Utility**.

2. Set up the file as a $1/4$"=1' scale architectural drawing on an $8^1/_2 \times$ 11" sheet.

3. Enter **Tablet** ↵ or click on SETTINGS ➤ Next ➤ TABLET from the Root menu.

4. At the **TABLET Option (ON/OFF/CAL/CFG):** prompt, enter **CFG** ↵. This tells AutoCAD you want to configure your tablet. (We will discuss the other options later in this section.)

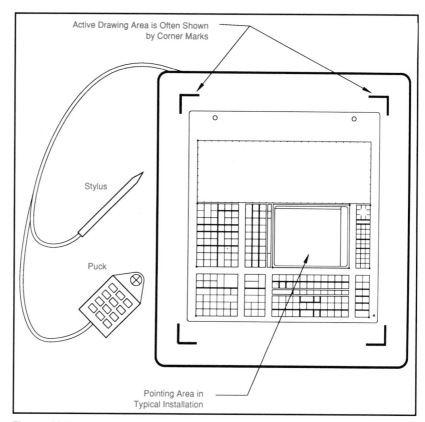

Figure 11.1: The template's active drawing area

5. At the **Enter number of tablet menus desired (0-4):** prompt, enter **0** ↵.

6. At the **Do you want to respecify the screen pointing area?** prompt, enter **Y** ↵.

7. At the **Digitize lower left corner of screen pointing area:** prompt, pick the lower-left corner of the tablet's active drawing area.

8. At the **Digitize upper right corner of screen pointing area:** prompt, pick the upper-right corner.

▼ NOTE

On some tablets, a light appears to show you the active area; other tablets use a permanent mark, such as a corner mark. AutoCAD won't do anything until you have picked a point, so you don't have to worry about picking a point outside this area.

Now as you move your stylus or puck you will notice that the relationship between your hand movement and your screen cursor is different. The cursor moves more slowly and it is active over more of the tablet surface.

CALIBRATING THE TABLET FOR YOUR DRAWING

Now photocopy Figure 11.2, which represents a hand-drafted drawing of a utility room for your apartment building. Place the photocopied drawing on your tablet so that it is aligned with the tablet and completely within the tablet's active drawing area (see Figure 11.3).

Before you can trace anything into your computer, you must *calibrate* your tablet. This means that you must give some points of reference so AutoCAD can tell how distances on the tablet relate to distances in the

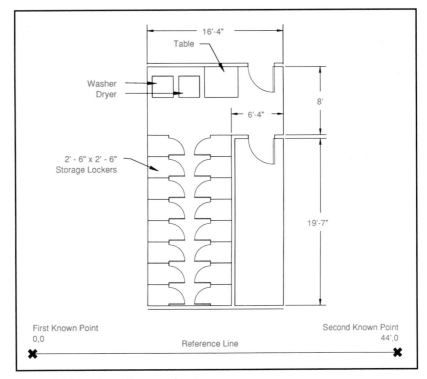

Figure 11.2: The utility room drawing

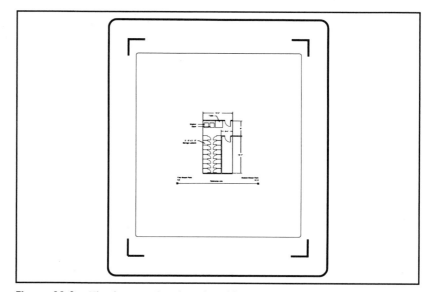

Figure 11.3: The drawing placed on the tablet

drawing editor. For example, you may want to trace a drawing that was drawn at a scale of ⅛"=1'- 0". You will have to show AutoCAD two specific points on this drawing, then where those two points should appear in the drawing editor. This is accomplished by using the TABLET command.

On Figure 11.2, we have already determined the coordinates for two points on a reference line.

Tablet ⏎ Cal ⏎

1. Enter **Tablet** ⏎ at the command prompt or click on TABLET from the side menu.

2. At the **TABLET Option (ON/OFF/CAL/CFG):** prompt, enter **CAL** ⏎.

3. The message **Calibrate tablet for use… Digitize first known point:** appears, asking you to pick the first point that you know the absolute coordinates for. Pick the X on the left end of the reference line.

4. At the **Enter coordinates for first point:** prompt, enter **0,0** ↵. This tells AutoCAD that the point you just picked is equivalent to the coordinate 0,0 in your drawing editor.

5. The **Digitize second known point:** prompt asks you to pick another point that you know the coordinates for. Pick the X on the right end of the reference line.

6. At the **Enter coordinates for second point:** prompt, enter **44′,0** ↵.

7. At the **Digitize third known point (or RETURN to end):** prompt, press ↵.

The tablet is now calibrated.

The word **Tablet** appears on the status line to tell you that you are in *tablet mode*. While in tablet mode, you can trace the drawing, but you cannot access the menus. If you want to pick a menu item, you must toggle the tablet mode off by using the **F10** function key. Or you can enter commands through the keyboard. If you have forgotten a keyboard command, enter **help** ↵ to get a list.

CALIBRATING MORE THAN TWO POINTS

▼ NOTE

The next section is not crucial to the tutorial and can be skipped for now. You may want to just skim through it and read it more carefully later on.

You may have noticed that you could have continued to calibrate a third point in the previous exercise. In fact, you can calibrate as many as 31 points. Why would anyone want to calibrate so many points? Often the drawing or photograph you are trying to trace will be distorted in one direction or another. For example, blue-line prints are usually stretched in one direction because of the way prints are rolled through a print machine.

You can compensate for distortions by specifying several known points during your calibration. For example, I could have included a vertical distance on the sample drawing to indicate a distance in the Y axis. You could have then picked that distance and calibrated its point. AutoCAD would then have a point of reference for the Y distance as well as the X distance. If you calibrate only two points, as you did in the exercise, AutoCAD will scale X and Y distances equally. Calibrating three points causes AutoCAD to scale X and Y distances separately, making adjustments for each axis based on their respective calibration points.

Now suppose you want to trace a perspective view of a building, but you want to "flatten" the perspective out so all the lines are parallel. You can calibrate the four corners of the buildings facade to stretch the narrow end of the perspective view out to be parallel with the wide end. This is a limited form of what cartographers call "rubber sheeting," where different areas of the tablet are stretched by different scale factors.

When you select more than two points for calibration, you will get a message similar to Figure 11.4.

Across the top, you see the labels *Orthogonal*, *Affine*, and *Projective*. These are the three major types of calibrations or *Transformation types* I discussed previously. *Orthogonal* scales the X and Y axis using the same values. *Affine* scales the X and Y axes separately and requires at least three points. *Projective* will stretch the tablet coordinates differently, depending on where you are on the tablet. It requires at least four calibration points.

Just below each of these labels you will see the message *Success*, *Exact*, and *Impossible*. This tells you whether any of these transformation types are available to you. Since this example shows what you see when you pick three points, you get *Impossible* for the projective transformation type.

The column to the left tells you what is shown in each of the other three columns. The screen also shows statistical data on the accuracy of AutoCAD transformation of points.

Finally, the prompt at the bottom of the screen lets you select which transformation type to use. If you calibrate four or more points, the Projective transformation type is added to the prompt. The Repeat Table option simply refreshed the table.

Take care when you calibrate points on your tablet. Here are a few points to watch out for when calibrating your tablet.

- Use only known calibration points.
- Try to locate calibration points that cover a large area of your image.
- Don't get carried away with points. Try to limit calibration points to only those necessary to get the job done.

```
3 calibration points

Transformation type:      Orthogonal    Affine    Projective

Outcome of fit:           Success       Exact     Impossible
RMS Error:                0.4143
Standard deviation:       0.0922
Largest residual:         0.5087
At point:                 2
Second-largest residual:  0.5087
At point:                 3

Select transformation type....
Orthogonal/Affine/<Repeat table>:
```

Figure 11.4: AutoCAD's assessment of the calibration

ENTERING LINES FROM A DRAWING

Now you are ready to trace the utility room.

Draw ➤ ▨ Line ➤ Segments

1. Click on Draw ➤ Line ➤ Segments.

2. Press **F10** to turn the tablet mode on and trace the outline of all the walls except the storage lockers.

3. Add the doors by inserting the Door file at the appropriate points, then mirroring them. The doors may not fit exactly. You'll get a chance to make adjustments later.

4. Trace the washer and copy it over to the position of the dryer. Since the washer and dryer are the same size, you can draw the washer then copy it for the dryer.

Your drawing should look something like panel 1 of Figure 11.5. It is a close facsimile of the original drawing, but not as exact as you might like. Zoom into one of the doors. Now you can see the inaccuracies of tracing. Some of the lines are crooked, and others don't meet at the right points. These inaccuracies are caused by the limited resolution of your tablet, coupled with the lack of steadiness in the human hand. The best digitizing tablets have an accuracy of 0.001 inch, which is actually not very good when you are dealing with tablet distances of ⅛" and smaller. In the following section you will clean up your drawing.

CLEANING UP A TRACED DRAWING

In Figure 11.5, panel 1, one of the door jambs is not in the right position (see the close-up in panel 2). You can move a group of objects and keep their vertices intact by using the Grips feature.

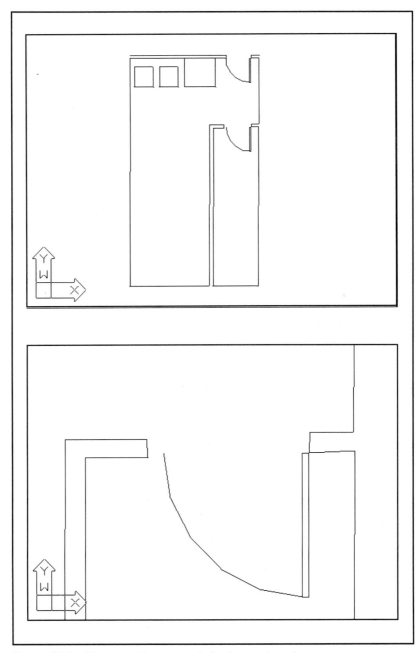

Figure 11.5: The traced drawing, with the door jamb in close-up

Verb/Noun, Grips **STRETCH**

1. With the Verb/ Noun and Grips features turned on, pick a crossing window enclosing the door jamb to be moved (see panel 1 of Figure 11.6).

2. Click on one of the grips at the end of the wall, then Shift-click on the other grip. You should have two hot grips at the door jamb.

3. Click on the lower of the two hot grips, then drag the corner away to see what happens (see panel 2 of Figure 11.6).

4. Use the Endpoint osnap override to pick the endpoint of the arc. The jamb repositions itself and all the lines follow (see Figure 11.7).

Another problem in this drawing is that some of the lines are not orthogonal. The Change command together with the ortho mode can be used to straighten them.

Modify ➤ 〔icon〕 Change ➤ Points

▼ NOTE

Modify➤ Change➤ Points does not work on polylines. Use grips to change polyline vertices.

1. Toggle the ortho mode on. Then press **Ctrl-C** to clear the grips selection.

2. Click on Modify ➤ Change ➤ Points.

3. At the object-selection prompt, pick the two lines representing the wall just left of the door.

4. Press ↵ to confirm your selection.

5. Then use the Perpend Osnap override and pick the wall to the left of the lines you just selected. The two lines will straighten out and their endpoints will align with the wall left of the two lines (see Figure 11.8).

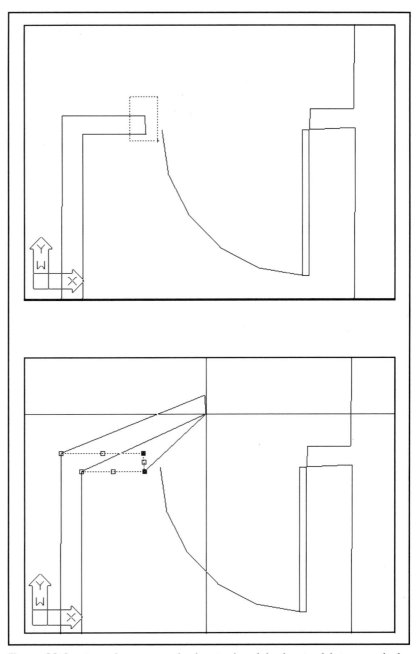

Figure 11.6: A window crossing the door jamb and the door jamb being stretched

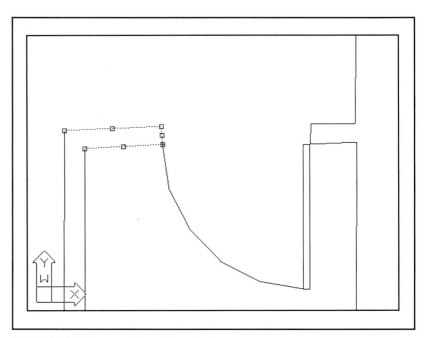

Figure 11.7: The repositioned door jamb

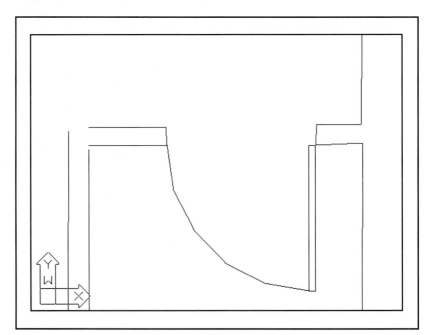

Figure 11.8: The lines, after Change is used

▼ TIP

You can also use the Snap Angle input box in the Settings ➤ Drawing Aids dialog box to rotate the cursor.

▼ WARNING

The Change command's Change Point option is similar to the Fillet command in that it changes the location of the endpoint closest to the new point location. This can cause erroneous results when you are trying to change groups of lines.

As you have just seen, you can use Modify ➤ Change ➤ Points not only to straighten lines, but to make them meet another line at a perpendicular angle. This only works with the ortho mode on, however. To extend several lines to be perpendicular to a nonorthogonal line, you have to rotate the cursor to that line's angle, using the Snapang system variable, then use the process just described to extend or shorten the others (see Figure 11.9). Be careful not to pick a point too close to the endpoints you want to move, or you may get unwanted results, as shown in Figure 11.10.

The overall interior dimension of the original utility room drawing is 16'-4" × 28'-0". Chances are the dimensions of the drawing you traced vary somewhat from these.

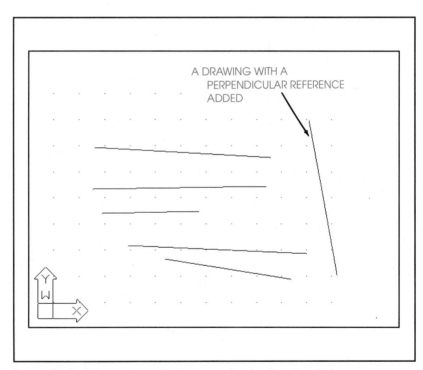

Figure 11.9: How to change lines at an angle other than 0 or 90 degrees

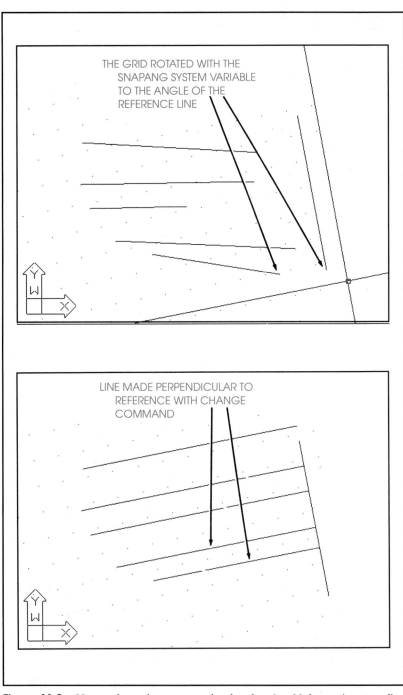

Figure 11.9: How to change lines at an angle other than 0 or 90 degrees (continued)

When changing several lines to be perpendicular to another line, you must be careful not to select too many. If the width of the group of lines is greater than the distance between the ends of the lines and the line they are to be perpendicular to, some of the lines will not change properly (see Figure 11.10). Once the lines have been straightened out, you can use the Fillet command to make the corners meet.

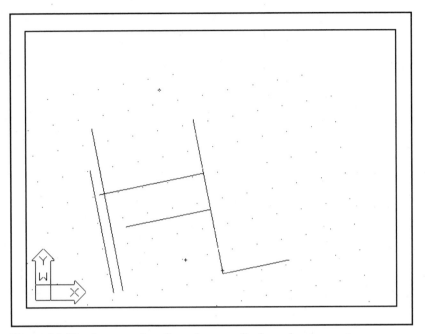

Figure 11.10:   Lines accidentally made perpendicular to the wrong point

Assist ➤ Inquiry ➤ Distance

1. Use Assist ➤ Inquiry ➤ Distance to find your drawing's dimensions.

2. Use Modify ➤ Stretch or the Grips feature to adjust the walls to their proper positions (see Figure 11.11).

3. Use **Base** ↵ to make the base point the upper-left corner of the utility room near coordinate 13′,30′.

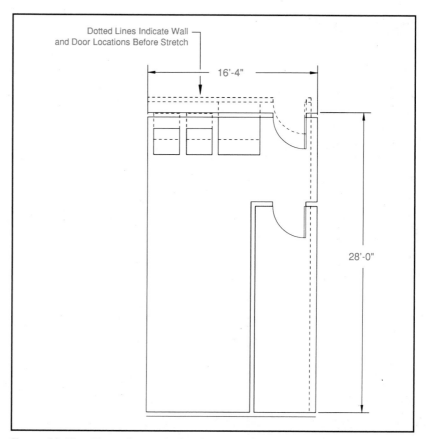

Figure 11.11:   The walls stretched to the proper dimensions

Since the utility room example had mostly orthogonal lines, you could have set the snap and ortho modes on while you traced. This would have kept the lines orthogonal and saved you the time of straightening them out. By leaving these modes off, however, you practiced some new editing options.

To add the storage lockers, draw them in using the dimensions provided on the traced drawing. This is actually a faster and more accurate method than tracing for entering objects repeatedly. If you tried to trace each locker, you would also have to clean up each one.

1. Draw one locker accurately.

2. Then use the MIRROR and ARRAY commands, to create the others.

Finally, you may want to add the dimensions and labels shown in Figure 11.2.

Settings ➤ Layer Control... ➤ New

1. Create a layer called **Notes** to add these dimensions and labels.

2. Set the Dimscale dimension setting to **48** before you start dimensioning.

3. Set the text height to **6"**.

4. When you are done, save the file and exit AutoCAD.

WORKING SMARTER WITH DIGITIZERS

▼ TIP

If you've only got a small 12×12 format digitizer, but you need to digitize large drawings, you might consider hiring a finish carpenter to cut a hole in your table to accommodate the digitizer. You could then recess you digitizer into your table so you can lay your drawings flat over the digitizer.

Although in the first exercise, I asked you to trace the entire drawing, you could have just traced the major lines with the Ortho mode on, then use the offset command to draw the wall thicknesses. Fillet and trim could then be used to "clean up" the drawing where lines cross or where they don't meet.

If you are a civil engineer, you would take a different approach. If you are laying out a road, you might first trace in the center lines, then use the offset command to place the curb and gutter. You could trace curved features using arcs, just to see what the radius of the curve is. Then you could redraw the arc accurately joining straight line segments. The digitizer can be a great tool if it is used with care and a touch of creativity.

SCALING A DRAWING

If a hand-drafted drawing is to scale, you can read the drawing's own dimensions or measure distances using an architect's or engineer's scale, then enter the drawing as you would a new drawing using these dimensions. Entering distances through the keyboard is slower than tracing, but you don't have to do as much cleaning up since you are entering the drawing accurately.

If a drawing contains lots of curves, you have to resort to a different scaling method, which is actually an old drafting technique for enlarging or reducing a drawing. First draw a grid in AutoCAD to the same proportions as your hand-drafted drawing. Plot this grid on translucent media and place it over the drawing. Then place points in the AutoCAD grid file relating to points on the grid overlay that intersect with the hand-drafted drawing (see Figure 11.12).

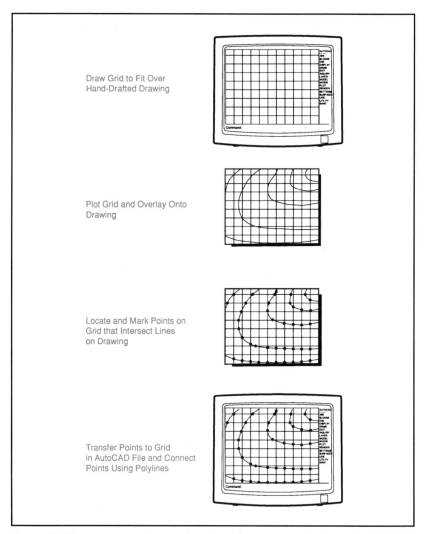

Figure 11.12: Using a grid to transfer a hand-drafted drawing

Once you have located these points in your AutoCAD file, you can connect them to form the drawing by using polylines. Because this method can be time-consuming and is not very accurate, it is best to purchase a tablet and trace drawings if you must enter a lot of drawings containing curves. You might also consider scanning or a scanning service for drawings that contain lots of curves.

If you don't have a tablet, enter the utility room drawing in Figure 11.2 using the dimensions provided (ignore the reference line).

SCANNING A DRAWING

No discussion of drawing input can be complete without mentioning the scanner. The scanner has become a subject of interest lately because of its ability to read text from a typewritten page (called *character recognition*), thereby saving the time and effort of typing the text into a word processor. It is also popular with desktop publishers because a scanner allows the user to import bitmap grayscale or color images into their documents. Imagine how easy it would be to convert an existing library of drawings into AutoCAD drawing files by simply running them through one of these devices.

Unfortunately, it is not that simple. Desktop scanners are generally limited to an $8^{1}/_{2} \times 14''$ sheet size. There are many low-cost hand-held scanners available that will scan a $4'' \times 14''$ area. Larger-format scanners are available but very expensive; they can cost ten thousand dollars or more. Once the drawing is scanned and saved as a file, it must be converted into a file AutoCAD can use. This conversion process is time-consuming and it requires special translation software. Finally, the drawing usually requires some cleaning up, which can be much more involved than cleaning up a traced drawing. The poorer the condition of the original drawing, the more cleanup you have to do. The net result is a very expensive alternative to tracing with a digitizer that may or may not save you time.

Whether a scanner can help you depends on your application. If you have drawings that would be very difficult to trace—large, complex topographical maps, for example—the scanner may well be worth a look. You don't necessarily have to buy one; there are scanning services, some of which offer excellent value. And if you can accept the quality

▼ TIP

There are three programs that will convert scanned images into formats that AutoCAD can read: *CADmate* from Microtek Labs, Inc., 16901 South Western Avenue, Gardena, CA 90247; *Scan Pro* from American Small Business Computers, 118 South Mill Street, Pryor, OK 74361; and *AI-Pro* from Palisades Research, 869 Via De La Paz, Pacific Palisades, CA 90272.

of a scanned drawing before it is cleaned up, you can save a lot of time. On the other hand, drawings composed mostly of orthogonal lines and notes may be more easily traced by hand with a large tablet or entered directly by using the drawings' dimensions.

HYBRID SCANNING SYSTEMS

A few software products use scanner technology in a different way. One such product, *CAD Overlay* from Image Systems Technology, allows you to view a scanned image as a background while in AutoCAD. A drawing is first scanned using any one of several popular scanners available. The file generated by the scanner is then translated into a form that the CAD Overlay software can read. This file is brought into AutoCAD as a background that you can trace over for your final drawing. The background image always remains in place in relation to your AutoCAD drawing, even when you perform a pan or zoom. The conversion from scanned image to background is considerably faster than from scanned image to an AutoCAD file, and you can build an intelligent drawing using the standard AutoCAD drawing entities. If you are an illustrator, this can be an easy way of digitizing hand-drawn images or other types of art. Since you usually have to do the work of converting a scanned drawing into an intelligent CAD drawing anyway, CAD Overlay can offer a more direct and faster conversion method for many types of drawings.

Image Systems Technology also offers *CAD ESP*, another unique product that allows you to merge hand-drafted drawings with CAD drawings. Instead of redrawing the entire scanned drawing in CAD, you only edit the portion of the scanned drawing that needs updating. You can then get a printout that combines the scanned drawing and the edited portion of the drawing done in AutoCAD.

▼ TIP

For more information on these products, you can contact Image Systems Technology, at 120 DeFreest Drive, Rensselaer Technology Park, Troy, NY 12180.

IMPORTING AND TRACING RASTER IMAGES

If you have a scanner and you would like to use it to import drawings to AutoCAD, you can use AutoCAD's Rasterin.EXP ADS application. Rasterin is actually a suite of commands that allow you to import .TIF,

.GIF, and .PCX files. Most scanners have facilities to store scanned images in at least one of these formats.

But before you get too excited, though, there are some definite drawbacks to Rasterin. The biggest problem with importing scanned bitmap files is that AutoCAD file you are importing to becomes enormous. A simple line drawing that is $8^{1}/_{2} \times 11$" scanned at 200 dpi can become a 2Mb AutoCAD file. Another problem is that some files simply won't import for one technical reason or another. TIFF files are particularly troublesome because there are so many versions of TIFF in the marketplace.

If the drawing you want to scan is not too complicated, and it is a fairly clean drawing that will scan well without a lot of background, then Rasterin can be helpful. The following gives step-by-step instructions on using Rasterin for tracing purposes. The example used is for a .PCX file. If you've got a .PCX file, you can try Rasterin using these steps. Or better yet, if you have a scanner (a hand scanner will do) scan Figure 11.2 and try importing it.

▼ TIP

You can load Rasterin from the command prompt by entering (**Xload "rasterin"**).

▼ NOTE

You don't need to set Riedge to 1 if you plan to import an image for viewing or as a background for 3D modeling.

1. Click on File ➤ Applications, then at the dialog box, click on **Files**....

2. Locate the Rasterin file in the Support subdirectory of the AutoCAD directory and double-click on it.

3. Highlight Rasterin.EXP in the list box then click on **Load**.

4. At the command prompt, enter **Riedge** ↵.

5. At the **Raster input edge detection <0>:** prompt, enter **1**. This tells AutoCAD to draw the image into AutoCAD using the bounding edges of filled areas.

6. At the command prompt, enter **Pcxin** ↵.

7. At the **PCX file name** prompt, enter the name of the .PCX file you wish to import. You needn't enter the file extension since Rasterin assumes .PCX. AutoCAD will seem to pause as it works to convert the .PCX file into an AutoCAD image.

8. At the **Insertion point** prompt, you'll notice a square at the cursor. This is a schematic representation of the imported image intended to help you place it. Pick a point for the lower-left corner of the image.

9. At the **Scale factor** prompt, you can enter a scale or use the cursor to indicate the size you want the image to be. You can scale it again more accurately later if you need to. Once you select a scale factor, the image will gradually appear on your screen.

Once the image is in, you can use it as a background to trace over, and then discard the image when you are done. As I mentioned earlier, the file size is greatly increased when importing raster images. TIF files create especially large files. You will have to try it out to see how large a file you can tolerate.

The method for importing .TIF and .GIF images is the same as for .PCX files, only you use the Tiffin and Gifin commands respectively. In addition, there are several settings that let you control how the image gets translated. One of these settings, Riedge, is useful for importing line drawings. The following describes these settings.

Riaspect lets you modify the aspect ratio of .TIF and .GIF files being imported. For example, if you are importing a 320×200 mode .GIF file from 3D Studio or Autodesk Animator, you may want to set Riaspect to 0.8333.

Ribackg controls the background color of the imported image. The default background color is 0, however, and if your background is not black, you will want to change Ribackg's setting. For example, if you have your background set to white (7), set Ribackg to 7.

Riedge controls the detection of boundary edges between colors in an image. Turn this feature on (1) when you want to import an image for tracing. Leave it at its default setting (0) for importing full images for viewing.

Rigamut controls the number of colors used when importing images. The default is 256 but you can set it to 16 or 8 to reduce the size of the imported image or to make the image conform to your display limitations.

Rigrey allows you to import an image in greys. The default setting is off (0). This can be used to reduce the size of the imported image as AutoCAD has a limited palette of greys.

Rithresh controls what gets translated into AutoCAD based on a brightness threshold. The default setting is off (0). Raster uses higher values to determine what level of brightness to accept for translation into the AutoCAD file. The higher the value, the brighter the import threshold.

You will have to experiment with these settings to determine which is best for your needs. There are a few points you should consider if you plan to use Rasterin for tracing drawings:

- Scan your drawing in using a greyscale scanner or convert your black-and-white scanned image to a greyscale one using your scanner software.

- Use a paint program or your scanner software to clean up unwanted grey or spotted areas in the file before importing into AutoCAD.

- If your scanner software or paint program has a de-speckle or de-spot routine, use it. It can help clean up your image and ultimately reduce AutoCAD file size and import time.

- Scan at a reasonable resolution. Remember that the human hand is usually not more accurate than a few thousandths of an inch, so scanning at 150 to 200 dpi may be more than adequate.

- If you plan to make heavy use of Rasterin, upgrade your computer to the fastest processor you can afford and don't spare the memory.

If you can get past some of the annoying features of Rasterin, you'll find a tool that can prove to be indispensable for some applications. I've already mentioned tracing scanned drawings. Another is to incorporate paper maps or plans into 3D AutoCAD drawings for presentations. I know of one architectural firm that produces some very impressive presentations with very little effort by combining 2D scanned images with 3D massing models for urban design studies. If you have the memory capacity, you can include raster images on 3D surfaces to simulate storefronts, people, or other surface features.

IMPORTING POSTSCRIPT IMAGES

In addition to the Rasterin utility, you can use the built-in Psin command to import PostScript files. Psin can be accessed by clicking on File ➤ Import/Export ➤ PostScript In. A dialog box lets you easily locate a file to be imported. Once you select a file, the rest of the program works just like the Rasterin commands. You are asked for an insertion point, scale, and rotation angle. Once you've answered all the prompts, the image appears in the drawing.

You can make adjustments to the quality of imported PostScript files by using the Psquality setting. This setting takes an integer value from −75–75. 75 is the default setting. The absolute value of this setting is taken as the ratio of pixels to drawing units. If, for example, Psquality is set to 50 or −50, then Psin will convert 50 pixels of the incoming Post-Script file into 1 drawing unit. You use negative values to indicate that you want outlines of filled areas rather than the full painted image. Using outlines can save drawing space and improve readability on monochrome systems or systems with limited color capability.

Finally, if Psquality is set to 0, only the bounding box of the imported image is displayed in the drawing. While you may only see a box, the image data is still incorporated into the drawing and will be maintained as the image is exported using Psout.

IF YOU WANT TO EXPERIMENT...

If you want to see how the Psin command works firsthand, you can try the following.

1. Use the Config command to add a PostScript plotter to your plotter configuration. You can click on File ➤ Configure to access it.

2. Open the Plan file then issue the Plot command.

3. Use the Device and Default Selection sub-dialog box of the Plot dialog box to select the PostScript plot configuration.

4. Use the **File Name** button to specify the name Plan.EPS for the plot file.

5. When the plot is complete, close the plan file and open a new file. It can be an unnamed file.

6. Enter **Psin** ↵ or click on File ➤ Import/Export ➤ PostScript In.

7. Locate the Plot file you just created and double-click on it. The file appears in your drawing.

This sequence of steps I just described can be a quick way to convert a 3D model into a 2D line drawing. You may want to make note of this as you work through the later chapters on 3D.

SUMMARY

This chapter has shown you the three basic methods of entering a hand-drafted drawing. The method you choose depends on your equipment and the complexity of the drawing to be entered. You may decide you need a digitizing tablet, or you may want to go to a scanning service. Perhaps your input requirements are not very demanding and you can get by with scaling. A careful evaluation of your particular needs will save you time in the long run.

By now, you have enough knowledge of AutoCAD to do some serious work with it. In the next chapter, you will see how all your knowledge can be integrated to efficiently perform real-world drawing tasks. You will also learn how you can create computer presentations by using the AutoCAD slide facility.

12

POWER
EDITING

FAST TRACK

463 ▶ To copy a set of lines using the Grips feature

Select the lines, Shift-click on the midpoint grips, click again on one of the hot grips, enter **C** ↵, and enter a relative coordinate for the location of the copies.

476 ▶ To rotate an object using Grips

Select the object or objects, click on a grip point close to the rotation point, press ↵ twice, then enter a rotation angle or indicate an angle using the cursor.

478 ▶ To scale an object using Grips

Select the object or objects, click on a grip point close to a scale center point, press ↵ three times, then enter a scale factor or indicate a new scale using the cursor.

481 ▶ To be able to select objects close together based on their order of creation

Click on Settings ➤ Selection Settings ➤ Entity Sort Method, then check the box labeled Object Selection. Click on **OK** to exit the dialog box.

487 ▶ To insert a cross reference drawing

Click on File ➤ Xref ➤ Attach. At the dialog box, locate the file you wish to cross reference and double-click on it. Answer the prompts for insertion point, scale, and angle.

493 ▶ To import a named element such as a layer or block from a cross reference

Enter **Xbind** ↵, then enter the type of named element you wish to import. Next, enter the name of the element, including the file name prefix.

495 ▶ To enter and exit Paperspace

Click on View ➤ Tilemode.

496 ▶ To create a Paperspace Viewport

While in Paperspace, click on View ➤ Mview, then select the type or number of desired viewports from the cascading menu.

502 ▶ To accurately scale a view in a Paperspace viewport

While in Paperspace, enter **MS** ↵, click on the viewport to be set, enter **Zoom** ↵, then enter the inverse of the desired scale factor of the view, followed by **XP**. For example, you would enter **1/48XP** for a ¼"=1' scale view.

505 ▶ To freeze a layer in a particular viewport

While in Paperspace, enter **MS** ↵, click on the viewport to be set, then click on Settings ➤ Layer Control. Click on the layer you wish to freeze, then click on the **FRZ** button across from the Cur PV: label in the right side of the dialog box.

Because you may not know what all the requirements are at the beginning of a project, you usually base the first draft of a design on the early requirements. As the project proceeds, you make adjustments for new requirements as they arise. As more people enter the project, more design restrictions come into play and the design is further modified. This process continues throughout the project, from first draft to end product.

In this chapter you will review much of what you've already learned. In the process, you will look at some ways that you can set up drawings to help manage continuous changes in a project. You will also learn what steps you can take to minimize duplication of work. AutoCAD can be a powerful timesaving tool if used properly. In this chapter, I hope to show you methods that will help you harness that power.

EDITING MORE EFFICIENTLY

The apartment building plan is currently incomplete. For example, the utility room you created needs to be added. In the real world, this plan would also undergo innumerable changes. Wall and door locations would change, and more notes and dimensions would be added. In the space of this tutorial, we can't develop these drawings to full completion. However, we can give you a sample of what is in store while using AutoCAD on such a project.

In this section, you will add a closet to the Unit plan (you will update the Plan file later in this chapter). In the editing you've already done, you've probably found you use certain commands frequently: Move, Offset, Fillet, Trim, Grips, and the Osnap overrides. Now you will learn some ways to shorten your editing time by using them more efficiently.

EDITING AN EXISTING DRAWING

First, let's look at how you can add a closet to the unit plan. You'll begin by copying existing objects to provide the basis for the closet.

Grips ➤ Copy
Offset

1. Open the Unit plan, make Wall the current layer, and freeze the Notes and Flr-pat layers to keep your drawing clear of objects you won't be editing.

2. If they are not already on, turn on the Noun/Verb and Grips modes.

3. Click on the right side wall, then click on its midpoint grip.

4. Enter **C** ↵ to start the Copy mode, then enter **@2'<180** (see Figure 12.1).

5. Press Ctrl-C twice to clear the grips selection, then zoom into the entry area.

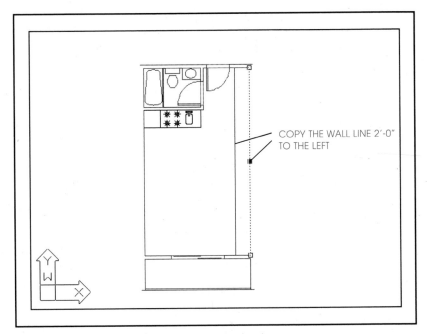

Figure 12.1: Where to copy the wall to start the closet

6. Issue the Offset command and at the **Offset distance or through** prompt, use the Nearest Osnap override and pick the outside wall of the bathroom near the door (see Figure 12.2).

7. At the **Second point:** prompt, use the Perpend Osnap override and pick the other side of that wall (see Figure 12.2 again).

8. Click on the copy of the wall line you just created, click on a point to the left of it, and then press ↵ to edit offset.

In steps 7 and 8, you determined the offset distance by selecting existing geometry. If you know you want to duplicate a distance, but don't know what that distance is, you can often use existing objects as references.

Next, you'll use the same idea to copy a few more lines for the other side of the closet.

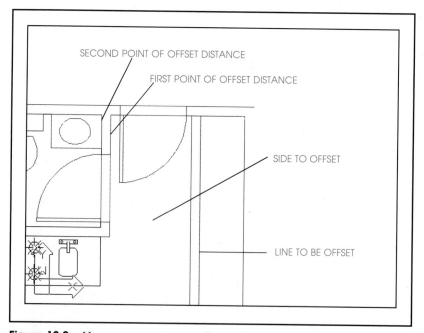

Figure 12.2: How to use an existing wall as a reference for copying

Grips ➤ Copy

1. ZOOM back so you can see the kitchenette in your screen view.

2. Click on the two lines that make up the wall at the top of your view to highlight them.

3. Shift-click on the midpoint grips of these lines (see Figure 12.3).

4. Click again on one of the midpoint grips, then enter **C** ↵. to select the Copy option.

5. Enter **B** ↵ to select a basepoint option.

6. Use the upper-right corner of the bathroom for the base point and the lower-right corner of the kitchenette as the second point. When you are done, press ↵.

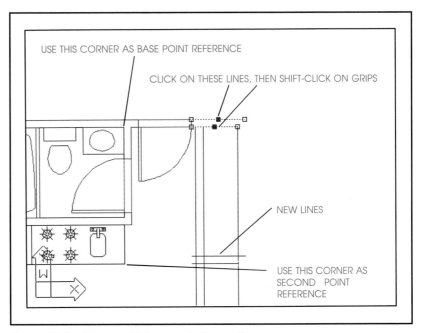

Figure 12.3:   How to add the second closet wall

Now you've got the general layout of the closet. Note that you haven't been too precise about the placement of lines. Where accuracy does count, you've used existing geometry to aid in specifying distances. The next step is to clean up the corners. First, you'll have to do a bit of prep work and break the wall lines near the wall intersections, as shown in Figure 12.4.

Modify ➤ ⚹ Break ➤ At Selected Point

1. Click on Modify ➤ Break ➤ At Selected Point.

2. Click on the vertical wall to the far right at a point near the location of the new wall (see Figure 12.4).

3. Click on Modify ➤ Break ➤ At Selected Point again, then click on the horizontal line just below the topmost line on the screen (see Figure 12.4).

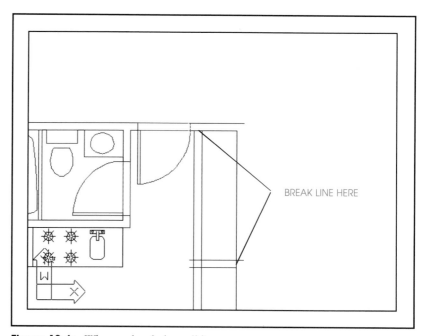

BREAK LINE HERE

Figure 12.4:   Where to break the wall lines

4. Now use Construct ➤ Fillet or the **Fillet** command from the keyboard to join the wall lines that don't meet (see Figure 12.5). You may have to zoom into the upper wall to select the lines to fillet.

In steps 2 and 3, you didn't have to be too exact about where to pick the break points because the Construct ➤ Fillet option takes care of joining the wall lines exactly. Now you are ready to add the finishing touches.

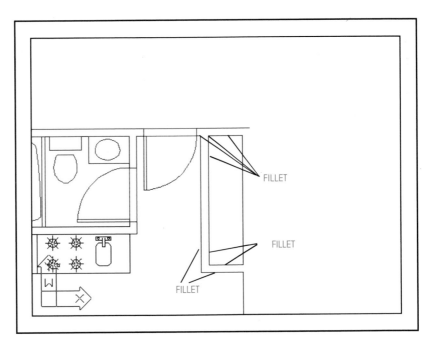

Figure 12.5: Where to fillet the corners

Modify ➤ 🗒 Trim

1. At the closet door location, draw a line from the midpoint of the interior closet wall to the exterior (see Figure 12.6).

2. Offset the new line 3′ in both directions. These new lines are the closet door jambs.

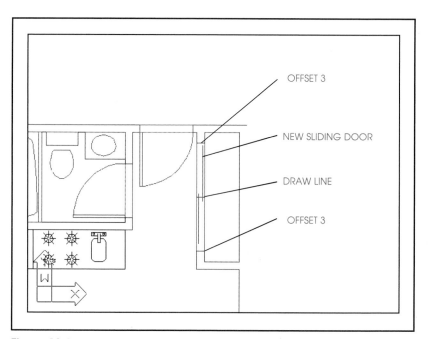

Figure 12.6:   Constructing the closet door jambs

3. Click on Modify ➤ Trim, click on the two jambs, then press ↵.

4. Click on the two vertical lines between the jambs.

5. Add door headers and the sliding doors as shown in Figure 12.7.

6. Now use File ➤ Save to save the file.

Sometimes it's easier to trim lines back, then draw them back in, as in steps 4 and 5. At first it may seem a bit backward, but trimming the lines then drawing in headers actually takes fewer steps and is a less tedious operation than some other routes. The end result is a door that is exactly centered on the closet space.

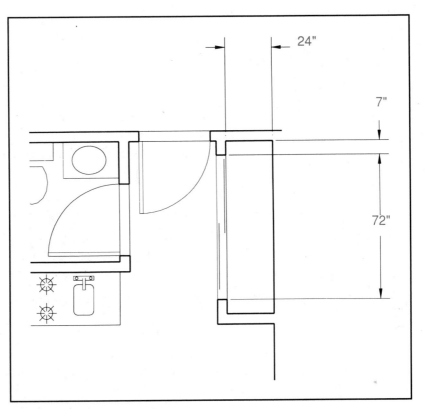

Figure 12.7: The finished closet

BUILDING ON PREVIOUSLY DRAWN OBJECTS

Suppose your client decides your design needs a few one-bedroom units. In this exercise, you will use the drawing of the studio unit as a basis for the drawing of a one-bedroom unit. To do so, you will double the studio's size, add a bedroom, move the kitchenette, rearrange and add closets, and move the entry doors. In the process of editing this new drawing, you will see how you can build on previously drawn objects.

Start by setting up the new file.

Modify ➤ Erase
Construct ➤ Copy
Construct ➤ Fillet

1. Open a new file called **Unit2** and use the Unit file as a prototype.

2. You will be moving the kitchenette later, so first turn on the Notes and Flrpat layers, then erase the floor pattern.

3. MOVE the dimension string at the right of the unit 14'-5" further to the right, and copy the unit the same distance to the right. Your drawing should look like Figure 12.8.

4. Now erase the bathroom, kitchenette, door, closet, and wall lines and notes, as shown in Figure 12.9.

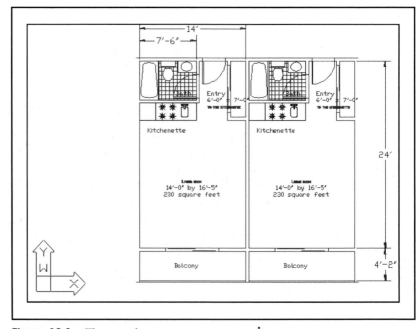

Figure 12.8: The copied unit

5. Copy the short interior wall of the closet to the right about 4′ to replace that side of the wall (see Figure 12.10).

6. Use Construct ➤ Fillet to join and extend walls where they have been broken, as shown in Figure 12.10.

7. Extend the topmost line so its endpoint is 5″ beyond the right interior wall line. You've already done this once before in *Chapter 5*.

8. MOVE the kitchenette to the opposite corner of the unit, as shown in Figure 12.11.

9. MOVE the remaining closet down 5′-5″, as shown in Figure 12.12. You can use the corners of the bathroom as reference points.

You could have been more selective about the objects you erased in step 4 and then added line segments where there were gaps in walls, but this is

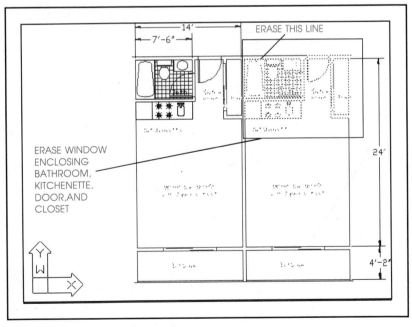

Figure 12.9: Objects to be erased

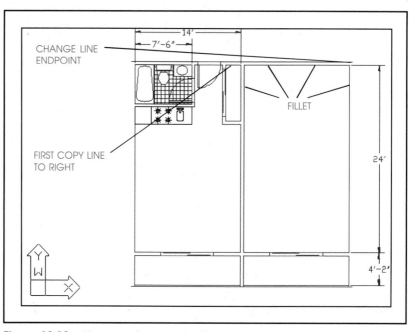

Figure 12.10: How to replace erased walls

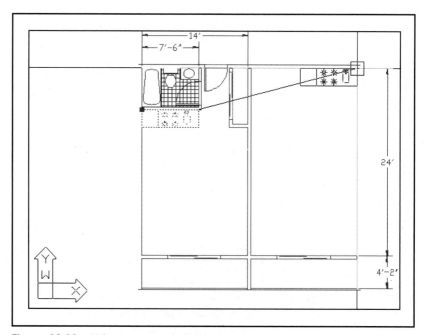

Figure 12.11: Where to move the kitchenette

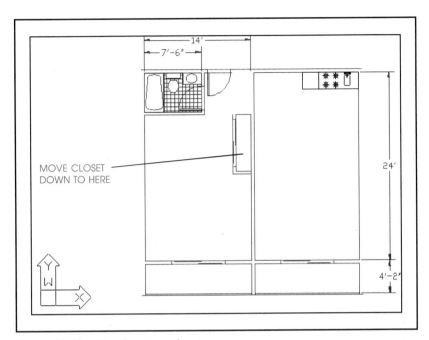

Figure 12.12:   The closet's new location

considered bad form. *When editing files, it is a good idea to keep lines continuous, rather than fragmented.* Adding line segments to a drawing increases the size of the drawing database and slows down editing operations.

Next, you'll work on finishing the new bedroom door and entry.

View ➤ Zoom
Construct ➤ 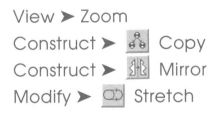 Copy
Construct ➤ Mirror
Modify ➤ Stretch

1. Zoom into the area that includes the closet and the two doors.

2. Copy the existing entry door downward, including header and jambs (see Figure 12.13).

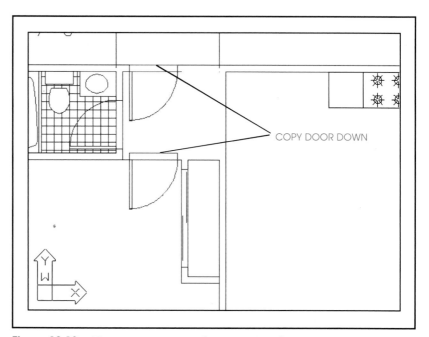

COPY DOOR DOWN

Figure 12.13:   How to use an existing door to create a door opening

3. Clean up the walls by adding new lines and filleting others, as shown in Figure 12.14.

4. Mirror the door you just copied so it swings in the opposite direction.

▼ TIP

Use the midpoint of the door header as the first axis endpoint.

5. Use Modify ➤ Stretch to move the entry door from its current location to near the kitchenette, as shown in Figure 12.15.

6. Once you've moved the entry door, mirror it as you mirrored the other door.

Once again, you are re-using parts of the drawing instead of creating new parts. Only in a few instances are you adding new objects.

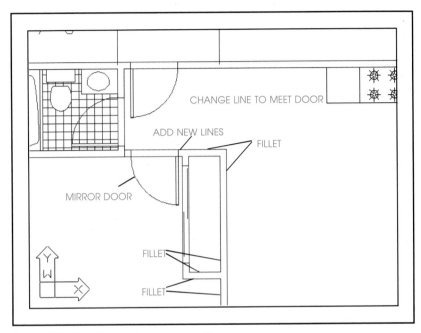

Figure 12.14:   How to clean up the walls

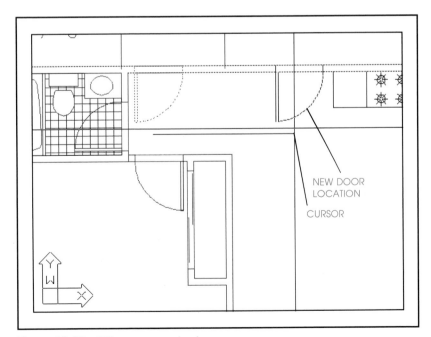

Figure 12.15:   Where to move the door

Modify ➤ 🔲 Extend

1. Now set the view of your drawing so it looks similar to Figure 12.16.

2. Click on Modify ➤ Extend or enter **Extend** ↵.

3. At the **Select boundary edge(s)… Select objects:** prompt, pick the wall at the bottom of the screen, as shown in Figure 12.16, and press ↵. Just as with Trim, Extend requires you to first select a set of objects to define the extend boundary, then select the objects you wish to extend.

4. At the **Select object to extend:** prompt, you will want to pick the two lines just below the closet door. To do this, first enter **F** ↵ to use the Fence selection option.

5. At the **First Fence point** prompt, pick a point just to the left of the lines you want to extend.

6. At the **Undo/<Endpoint of line>** prompt, pick a point to the right of the two lines, so the fence crosses over them (see Figure 12.6).

7. Press ↵. The two lines extend to the wall.

8. Use a combination of trim and fillet to clean up the places where the walls meet.

9. Add another closet door on the right side of the new closet space you just created. Your drawing should look like Figure 12.17.

▼ NOTE

You may have to pick the lines several times if they don't extend on the first try.

USING GRIPS

Now suppose you want to change the location and orientation of the kitchenette. Next, you will use the Grips feature to do just that.

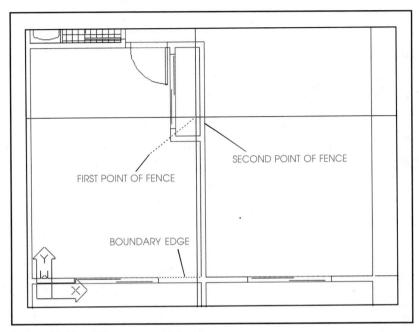

SECOND POINT OF FENCE

FIRST POINT OF FENCE

BOUNDARY EDGE

Figure 12.16: Where to extend the lines

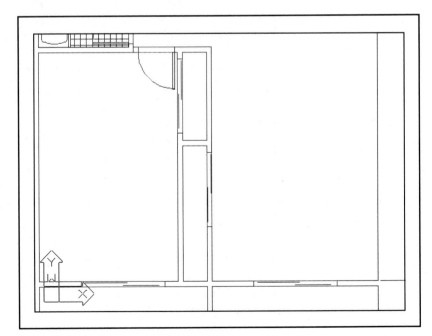

Figure 12.17: The second closet added

Grips ➤ Rotate

1. Set up a view similar to the one in Figure 12.18.

2. Click on the kitchenette.

3. Click on the grip in the upper-right corner.

4. Press the right mouse button or the ↵ key twice until you see the ***ROTATE*** message at the prompt.

5. Enter –90.

6. Click on the kitchenette's grip again, then, using the endpoint Osnap override, click on the upper-right corner of the room. Press **Ctrl-C** twice to clear the grips section. Your drawing should look like Figure 12.19.

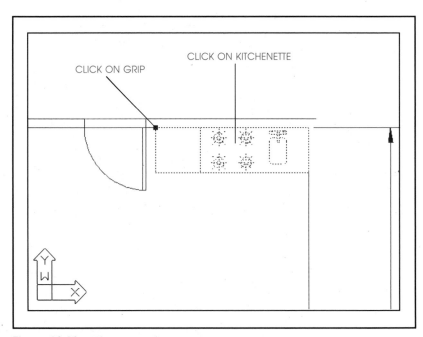

Figure 12.18: The rotation base point

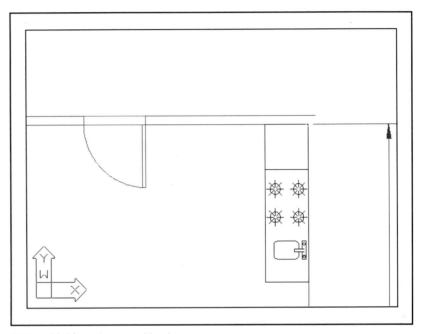

Figure 12.19: The revised kitchenette

▼ NOTE

The STRETCH command will ignore blocks so long as you do not include the block's insertion point in the stretch window.

Since the kitchenette is a block, its grip point is the same as its insertion point. This makes blocks great candidates for grip editing. Remember that the door is also a block. Try the following exercise involving a door and its surrounding wall.

Now suppose you want to widen the entrance door from 36 to 42".

Grips ➤ Stretch

1. Use a crossing window to select the left door jamb.

2. Shift-click on both of the door jamb's grips.

3. Click on one of the hot grips again.

4. Enter **@6<180**. The door should now look like Figure 12.20.

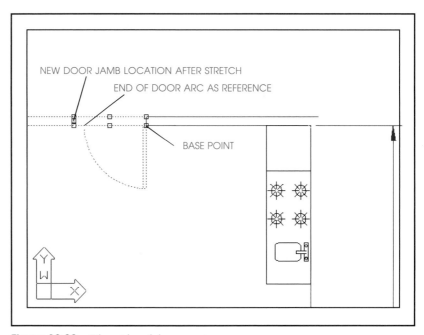

NEW DOOR JAMB LOCATION AFTER STRETCH

END OF DOOR ARC AS REFERENCE

BASE POINT

Figure 12.20: The widened door opening

You might notice that in step 4, you didn't have to specify a base point to stretch the grips. AutoCAD assumes the base to be the original location of the selected hot grip. Now you can enlarge the door using the SCALE command. In this exercise, you will use the current door width as a reference.

Grips ➤ Scale

1. Press **Ctrl-C** twice to clear your selection set.

2. Click on the door.

3. Click on the door's grip point.

4. Press the right mouse button (or ⏎) three times to get to the scale mode.

5. At the **<Scale factor>/Base point/Copy/Undo/Reference /eXit:** prompt, enter **R** ↵ to select the Reference option.

6. At the **Reference length <01′–1″>:** prompt, click on the door's grip point.

7. At the **Second point:** prompt, click on the endpoint of the door's arc at the wall line. As you move the cursor, the door changes in size relative to the distance between the grip and the end of the arc.

8. At the **<New length>/Base point/Copy/Undo/Reference /eXit:** prompt, click on the grip at the door jamb directly to the left of the arc endpoint. The door enlarges to fit the new door opening (see Figure 12.21).

9. Now save the file.

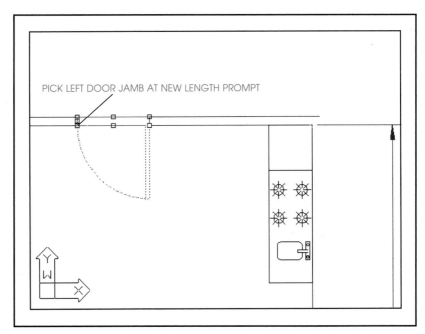

Figure 12.21: The enlarged door

You could have used the Modify ➤ Scale option to accomplish the same thing. This option acts in a very similar way to the Grips Scale option. The advantage to using grips is that you don't need to use the Osnap overrides to select exact grip locations, thereby reducing the number of steps you must take to accomplish a given task.

In the next section, you will update the Plan file to include the revised studio apartment and the one-bedroom unit you just created (see Figure 12.22). Changes like these will continue into the later stages of your design project. As you have seen, AutoCAD's ability to make changes easily and quickly can ease your work and help you test your design ideas more accurately.

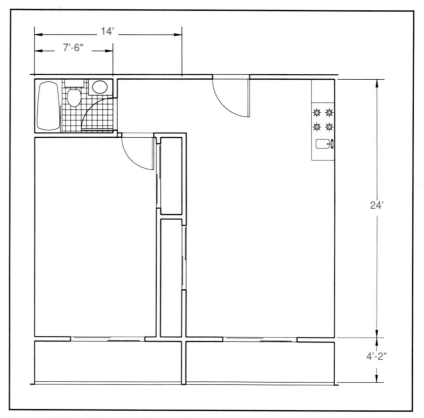

Figure 12.22: The finished one-bedroom unit

SETTING THE ENTITY SORT METHOD

If you've used earlier versions of AutoCAD, you may have noticed that if you try to select two objects close together, the most recently drawn object will be selected. This was because when you selected objects, AutoCAD would sort through the drawing database, starting with the most recently added entities. To improve performance, release 12 no longer sorts through the database the old way.

But you may have grown accustomed to the old sort method, especially when applied to the selection process. If you find you are clicking on one object only to find that AutoCAD selects another object nearby, you may want to try changing the Entity Sort Method settings. These settings lie buried in the Entity Selection Settings dialog box as a sub-dialog box called Entity Sort Method (see Figure 12.23). You can get to this dialog box by clicking on Settings ➤ Selection Settings..., then clicking on the Entity Sort Method button.

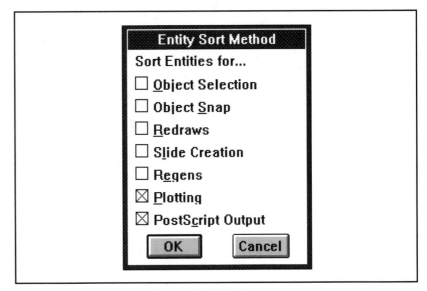

Figure 12.23: The Entity Sort Method dialog box

This dialog box lets you set the sort method for a variety of operations. If you check any of the operations listed, AutoCAD will use the prerelease 12 sort method for that operation. You will probably not want to change the sort method for object snaps or regens. But by checking the object selection, plotting, and PostScript output options, you can control a variety of things. For the object selection, you can control which of two overlapping lines are selected when you click on them. For Plotting and PostScript output, you can control the overlay of screened or hatched areas.

The settings can also be controlled through system variables. See *Appendix D* for details.

USING CROSS REFERENCES

We mentioned in *Chapter 6* that careful use of blocks, cross references, and layers can help you improve your productivity. In this section you will see firsthand how to use them to help reduce design errors and speed up delivery of an accurate set of drawings. You do this by controlling layers in conjunction with blocks and cross-referenced files to create a common drawing database for several drawings.

PREPARING EXISTING DRAWINGS FOR CROSS REFERENCING

You may recall that in *Chapter 6* we discussed using the Freeze option to control layers. You can think of layers as being different z coordinate locations in your drawing. For example, you can create a layer for each of the three floors of your apartment building, then insert the Unit blocks on the appropriate layers. You can create a fourth layer to contain the blocks common to all the floors, such as the lobby, stairs, utility room, and some of the units (see Figure 12.24). To display or plot a particular floor, you freeze all the layers except that floor and the layer containing the common information. The following exercise shows you how to do this.

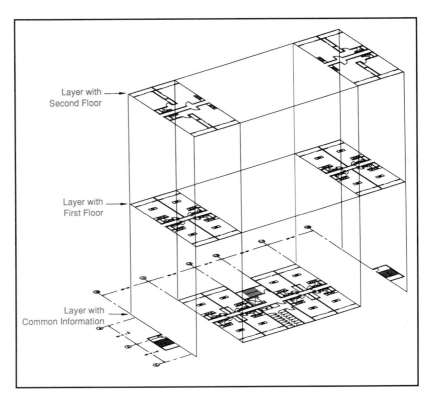

Figure 12.24: A 3D representation of how layers might be considered

---

Modify ➤ 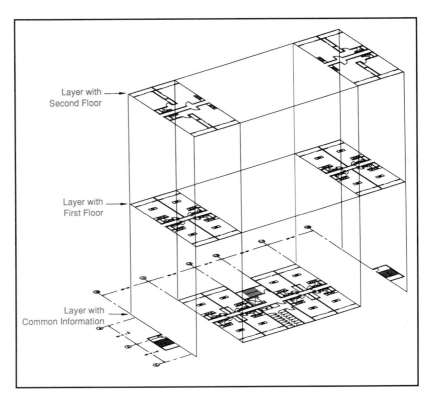 Entity...
Wblock ↵

Gridline and related dimensions are used in architectural drawings as a system to establish references from which accurate dimensions can be taken. They are usually based on key structural elements, such as columns and foundation wall locations.

1. Open the Plan file.

2. Create a layer called Gridline and add the grid and dimension information shown in Figure 12.25.

3. Use Modify ➤ Entity... to make the grid lines a *center* line type. This is a typical center line composed of a long line, then a short dash, then another long line. It is usually used to denote the center of an object—in this case, a wall. Be sure LTSCALE is set to 96.

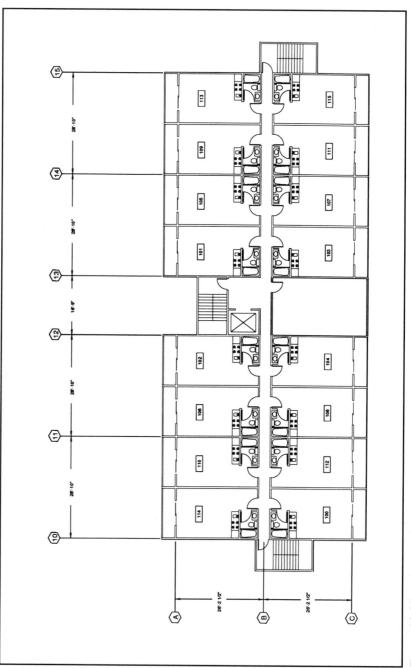

Figure 12.25: The overall plan with grid lines added

4. Use the WBLOCK command to write the grid lines and other grid information to a file called **Col-gr**. Use the drawing origin, 0,0, for the insertion base point.

5. Use the WBLOCK command again to write the eight units in the corners of your plan to a file called **Floor1** (see Figure 12.26). Be sure to include the door symbols for those units when you select objects for the wblock. Use 0,0 again for the wblock insertion base point.

6. Insert Unit2 into the corners where the other eight units had been. Use Figure 12.27 as a guide.

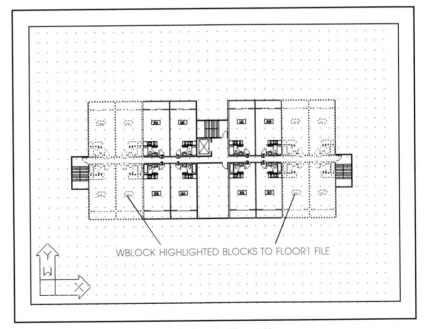

Figure 12.26:   Units to be wblocked to the Floor1 file

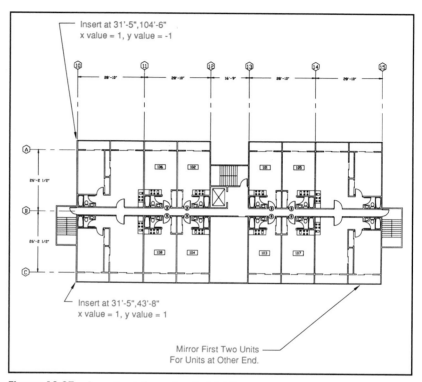

Figure 12.27: Insertion information for Unit2

7. Once you've accurately placed the corner units, use the WBLOCK command to write these corner units to a file called **Floor2**. Again, use the 0,0 coordinate as the insertion base point for the wblock.

8. Now use the WBLOCK command to turn the remaining set of unit plans into a file called **Common**. Remember that you can select everything in the drawing by entering **ALL** ↵ at the **Select objects** prompt.

You've just created four files: Col-gr, Floor1, Floor2, and Common. Each of these files contains unique information about the building. Next, you'll use the XREF command to recombine these files for the different floor plans in your building.

ASSEMBLING CROSS REFERENCES TO BUILD A DRAWING

Next, you will create composite files for each floor with cross references of only the files needed for the individual floors. You will use the Attach option of the XREF command to insert all the files you wblocked from the Plan file.

Ltscale ↵

File ➤ Xref ➤ Attach

1. Close the Plan file (don't save the changes) and open a new file called **Xref-1**.

2. Set this file up as an architectural drawing 18"×24" with a scale of ⅛ "=1'.

3. Set LTSCALE to 96.

4. Click on File ➤ Xref ➤ Attach. You see the Attach Xref dialog box. This is a typical file dialog box.

5. Double-click on the COMMON file name.

6. At the **Insertion point** prompt, enter **0,0** ↵.

7. Press ↵ at the X and Y scale factor prompts and the rotation angle prompt.

8. Repeat the XREF command and insert the Floor1 file and the Col-gr file. You now have the plan for the first floor.

9. Save this file, then create a new file called **Xref-2**. Repeat steps 2 through 8, but in place of the Floor1 file in step 8, use the XREF command and insert the Floor2 file. This new file represents the plan for the second floor.

10. Save this file.

▼ NOTE

Because the insertion points of all the files are the same, they will fit together perfectly when they are inserted into the new files.

Now when you need to make changes to Xref-1 or Xref-2, you can edit the individual cross-referenced files that make them up. Then the next time you open either Xref-1 or Xref-2, the updated cross-referenced files will automatically appear in their most recent forms.

Cross references need not be permanent. You can attach and detach cross references easily at any time. This means that if you need to get information from another file—to see how well an elevator core aligns, for example—you can temporarily cross reference the other file to quickly check alignments, then detach it when you are done.

You can think of these composite files as final plot files that are only used for plotting and reviewing. Editing can then be performed on the smaller, more manageable cross-referenced files. Figure 12.28 diagrams the relationship of these files. The combinations of cross references are limited only by your imagination, but AutoCAD does not allow a circular reference, a cross-referenced file that, in turn, cross references the current file.

There are several advantages to using composite cross-referenced files. Since the cross references don't become part of the drawing file's database, these composite files remain quite small. Also, because cross-referenced files are easily updated, work can be split up among several people in a work-group environment or on a network. One person could be editing the Common file while another worked on Floor1, and so on.

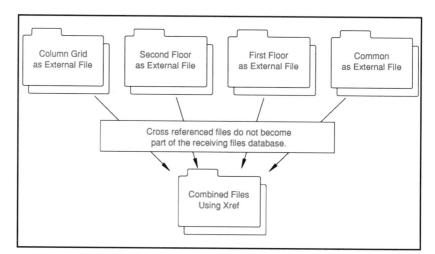

Figure 12.28: Diagram of cross-referenced file relationships

The next time the composite file is opened, it will automatically reflect any new changes that had been made in the cross-referenced files. Now let's see how this works.

USING MULTIPLE AUTOCAD SESSIONS TO EDIT CROSS REFERENCES

▼ TIP

You can change the default settings of each AutoCAD session by editing the Edit ➤ Preferences ... dialog box. You can also set up multiple configurations so each AutoCAD session has its own set of permanent default settings. See *Appendix B* for details.

You can see firsthand how cross references might work in a work-group environment by simultaneously editing one file and updating another file that is cross referenced to it.

1. Open the Xref-1 drawing again.

2. Without exiting AutoCAD, go to the Program Manager and start another AutoCAD session by double clicking on the AutoCAD program icon. You can get to the Program Manager by pressing the Alt-Tab key combination until you see the Program Manager icon appear in the center of the screen.

3. Open the Common file and press **Ctrl-C** to stop the drawing regeneration. Don't be alarmed if nothing appears on the screen. The drawing is still there.

4. Update the Unit plan you edited earlier in this chapter by selecting Draw ➤ Insert.

5. At the Insert dialog box, click on the **File** button and double-click on the UNIT file name.

6. Click on **OK**.

7. At the warning message, click on **Redefine**.

8. At the **Insertion point:** prompt, press **Ctrl-C**.

9. If you have Regenauto turned off, enter **Regen** ↵ to regenerate the drawing. You will see the new Unit plan in place of the old one (see Figure 12.29).

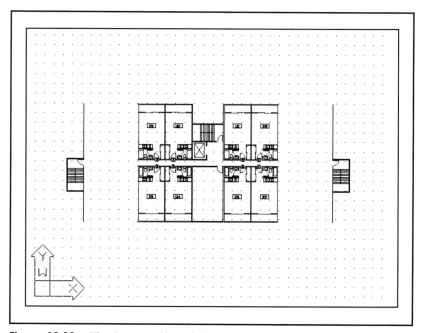

Figure 12.29: The Common file with the revised Unit plan

10. Use Draw ➤ Insert again to replace the empty room across the hall from the lobby with the utility room you created in *Chapter 11* (see Figure 12.30).

11. Save the Common file.

12. Return to the AutoCAD session containing the Xref-1 file then click on File ➤ Xref ➤ Reload.

13. At the **Xref(s) to reload** prompt, enter *↵. The revised floor plan will look like Figure 12.31.

In this exercise, you simulated having two people edit cross-referenced files by running two sessions of AutoCAD. You are able to make changes to a cross-referenced file, then quickly switch to a second file that is using the cross reference to update it. Of course, as this exercise demonstrates, you can take advantage of multiple sessions and cross references on your own.

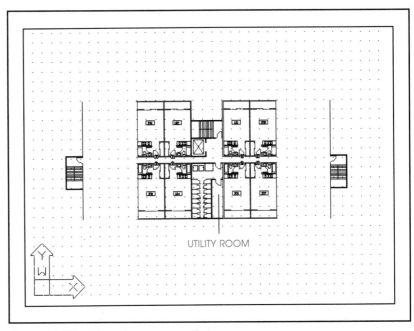

Figure 12.30:   The utility room installed

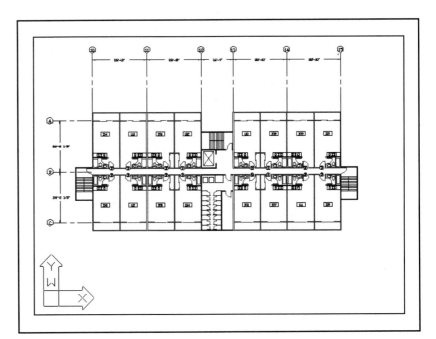

Figure 12.31:   The Xref-1 file with the units updated

Cutting and Pasting between AutoCAD Sessions

New users frequently ask how they can transport part of a drawing to another file. Before AutoCAD release 12 for Windows, you had to first use the Wblock command to export the part of the drawing from the source file as a new file. Then you had to close the source file and open the destination file. Once it was open, you used the Insert command to insert the Wblocked portion of the source drawing into the destination file.

With Windows, the process is much simpler. You can start two sessions of AutoCAD, then open both the source and destination files. Next, while in the source file, you click on Edit ➤ Copy Vectors to copy objects to the Windows Clipboard. When you see the familiar **Select object** prompt, you can proceed to select the objects you want to transfer. Once this is done, you can switch to the destination file and click on Edit ➤ Paste. AutoCAD inserts the object from the Clipboard. Pasting from the Clipboard into AutoCAD is just like using the Insert command. You are prompted for an insertion point, an X and Y scale factor, and a rotation angle. Pasted items use the origin of the source file as the insertion base point, so if the objects in the source file are far from the drawing origin, you may not see the pasted item right away. Also, pasted objects are inserted as a single block, even if the original object in the source file is not a block. You may want to use Modify ➤ Explode to reduce the pasted block to its component objects, then purge the file.

IMPORTING NAMED ELEMENTS FROM CROSS REFERENCES

▼ TIP
You can use the Visretain system variable to force AutoCAD to remember layer settings of cross-referenced files. See *Appendix D* for details.

In *Chapter 5*, I discussed how layers, blocks, line types, and text styles are imported at the same time that one file is inserted into another. Cross-referenced files, on the other hand, do not import such *named elements*. You can, however, review their names and use a special command to import those named elements you want to use in the current file.

AutoCAD renames named elements from cross references by giving them the prefix of the file name from which they come. For example, the Wall layer in the Floor1 file will be called *Floor1 | wall* in the Xref-1 file and the Toilet block will be called *Floor1 | toilet*. You cannot draw on the layer Floor | wall, nor can you insert Floor1 | toilet; but you can view cross-referenced layers in the Layer Control dialog box, and cross-referenced blocks can be viewed using the Insert dialog box.

Next you'll look at how AutoCAD identifies layers and blocks in cross-referenced files, and you'll get a chance to import a layer from a cross reference.

Settings ➤ Layer Control
Xbind ↵

1. While in the X-ref1 file, click on Settings ➤ Layer Control. Notice that the names of the layers from the cross-referenced files are all prefixed with the file name and the | (vertical bar).

2. Click on Cancel, then enter **Xbind** ↵ or click on AutoCAD ➤ BLOCKS ➤ XBIND from the root menu.

3. At the **Block/Dimstyle/LAyer/LType/Style:** prompt, enter **LA** ↵ for *LAyer*.

4. At the **Dependent Layer Name(s):** prompt, enter **FLOOR1 | WALL**. You then get the next message: **Scanning... 1 Layer(s) bound**. You have now imported the Wall layer from the Floor1 file. However, AutoCAD maintains the imported layer's uniqueness by giving it another name.

5. Click on Settings ➤ Layer Control again.

6. Scroll down the list of layer names until you get to the ones that start with the Floor1 prefix. Notice that *Floor1 | wall* no longer exists. In its place is a layer called *Floor1$0$wall*.

As you can see, when you use XBIND to import a named item such as the layer Floor1 | wall, the vertical bar sign (|) is replaced with two dollar signs surrounding a number, which is usually zero. If for some reason the imported layer name Floor1$0$wall already exists, then the zero in that name is changed to 1, as in *Floor1$1$wall*. Other named items are also renamed in the same way using the dollar sign-zero-dollar sign replacement for the vertical bar.

GETTING INTO PAPERSPACE

Your set of drawings for this studio apartment building would probably have a larger-scale, more detailed drawing of the typical unit plan. You already have the beginnings of this drawing in the form of the Unit file. As you have seen, the notes and dimensions you entered into the Unit file can be frozen in the Plan file so they don't interfere with the graphics of the drawing. The Unit file can be part of another drawing file that contains more detailed information on the typical unit plan at a larger scale. To this new drawing you can add other notes, symbols, and dimensions. Whenever the Unit file is altered, you update its occurrence in both the large-scale drawing of the typical unit and the Plan file (see Figure 12.32). By doing this, you can update the units quickly and assure good correspondence between all the drawings for your project.

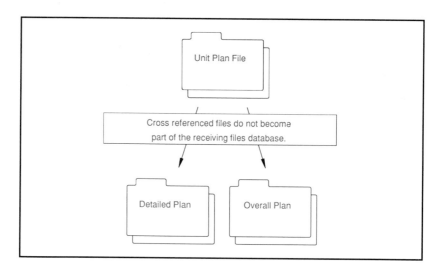

Figure 12.32: Relationship of drawing files

Now suppose that you want to combine drawings with different scales in the same drawing file—the overall plan of one floor, for example, plus an enlarged view of one typical unit. This can be accomplished by using the Paperspace mode I discussed in *Chapter* 6. First, let's see how to get into Paperspace.

The key to Paperspace is the Tilemode system variable. You might think of Tilemode as the gateway to Paperspace.

View ➤ Tilemode

1. If it isn't already open, open the Xref-1 file, making sure your display shows all of the drawing.

2. Click on View ➤ Tilemode or enter **Tilemode** ↵ **Off** ↵. Your screen goes blank and your UCS icon changes to a triangular shape.

You may have noticed that the Tilemode option had a check mark next to it. This tells you that Tilemode is on. Tilemode is a system variable that controls access to Paperspace. When Tilemode is set to 1, the default setting, you cannot enter Paperspace; when it is set to 0, you can freely move from Paperspace to Modelspace.

The new UCS icon tells you that you are in Paperspace. But where did your drawing go? Before you can view it, you must create the windows, or *viewports* as they are called, that let you see into Modelspace. But before you do that, let's explore Paperspace.

Settings ➤ Drawing Limits

1. Click on Settings ➤ Drawing Limits or enter **Limits** ↵, then note the default value for the lower-left corner of the Paperspace limits. It is 0'-0", 0'-0".

2. Press ↵ and note the current default value for the upper-right corner of the limits. It is 1'-0", 9", which is the standard default for a new drawing. This tells us that the new Paperspace area is 12" wide by 9" high—an area quite different from the one you set up originally in this drawing.

3. Click on Settings ➤ Drawing Limits again.

4. At the **ON/OFF:** prompt, press ↵.

5. At the **upper-right corner:** prompt, enter **42,30** to give yourself an area that is 42"×30".

6. Click on View ➤ Zoom ➤ All.

Now you've got your Paperspace set up. The next step is to create your viewports so you can begin to paste up your views.

View ➤ Mview ➤ 3 Viewports

▼ TIP

If you are using Paperspace to combine different 3D views of a 3D model, you can control which viewport plots with hidden lines removed using the View ➤ Mview ➤ Hideplot option. You can selectively turn Hideplot on or off for any viewport.

1. Click on View ➤ Mview ➤ 3 Viewports

2. At the **Horizontal/Vertical/Above/Below/Left/<Right>:** prompt, enter **A** ↵ for *Above*. This option creates one large viewport along the top half of the screen with two smaller viewports along the bottom.

3. At the **Fit/<first point>:** prompt, enter **F** ↵ for the *Fit* option. Three rectangles appear in the formation shown in Figure 12.33. Each of these is a viewport to your Modelspace.

Next you'll see how to get access to those viewports in order to display and edit your drawing.

View ➤ Modelspace

▼ TIP

If you prefer, you can click on the button labeled P in the toolbar to switch between Modelspace and Paperspace.

1. Click on View ➤ Modelspace. This gives you control over Modelspace.

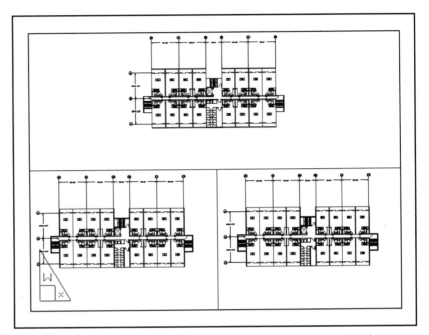

Figure 12.33:   The newly created viewports. Notice that the viewport at the top fills the whole width of the drawing area, while the bottom half of the screen is divided into two.

2. Click on the top viewport, then click on View ➤ Zoom ➤ Extents. The view enlarges to fill in the current active viewport.

3. Click on the lower-left viewport to make this viewport active.

4. Click on View ➤ Zoom ➤ Window and window the elevator area.

5. Click on the lower-right viewport and use View ➤ Zoom ➤ Window to enlarge your view of a typical unit.

When you use View ➤ Modelspace to move into Modelspace mode, the UCS icon changes: instead of one triangular-shaped icon you have three arrow-shaped ones, one for each viewport on the screen. Also, as you move your cursor, it appears as an arrow until you enter the currently active viewport. Then it turns into the usual cross-hair cursor. You can also tell which viewport is the active one by its double border. You can move from viewport to viewport even while you are in the middle of most commands. For example, you can issue the LINE command, then pick the start point in one viewport, then go to a different viewport to pick the next point, and so on. To make a different viewport active, you simply click on it. See Figure 12.34.

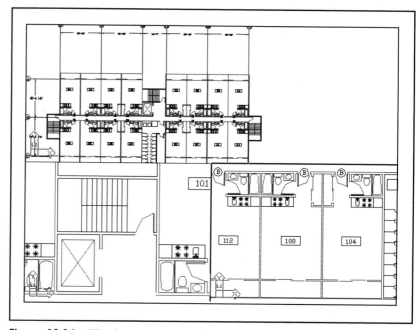

Figure 12.34: The three viewports with the plan in view

GETTING BACK TO MODELSPACE

Once you've created viewports, you can then re-enter Modelspace through the viewport using View ➤ Modelspace. But what if you want to quickly get back into the old full-screen Modelspace you were in before you entered Paperspace? The following exercise demonstrates how this is done.

View ➤ Tilemode

1. Click on View ➤ Tilemode or enter **Tilemode** ↵ **On** ↵. Your drawing returns to the original full-screen view of your drawing. Now everything is back to normal.

2. Click on View ➤ Tilemode. You are back in Paperspace.

Notice that all the viewports are still there when you return to Paperspace. Once you've set up Paperspace, it remains part of the drawing until you delete all the viewports.

You may prefer doing most of your drawing in Modelspace and use Paperspace for setting up views for plotting. Since viewports are retained, you won't lose anything when you go back to Modelspace to edit your drawing.

WORKING WITH PAPERSPACE VIEWPORTS

Paperspace is intended as a page-layout or composition tool. You can manipulate viewports' sizes, scale their view independently of each other, and even set layering and line type scale independently. Let's see how you can manipulate the shape and location of viewports.

Modify ➤ ▱ Stretch

Modify ➤ ▱ Erase ➤ Single

Modify ➤ ⟺ Move

▼ TIP

You can enter **PS** ↵ as a keyboard shortcut to return to Paperspace mode.

1. Click on View ➤ Paperspace to get back into the Paperspace mode, if you aren't already there.

2. Click on Modify ➤ Stretch and stretch the two viewport corners as shown in Figure 12.35. Notice how the view within each viewport changes.

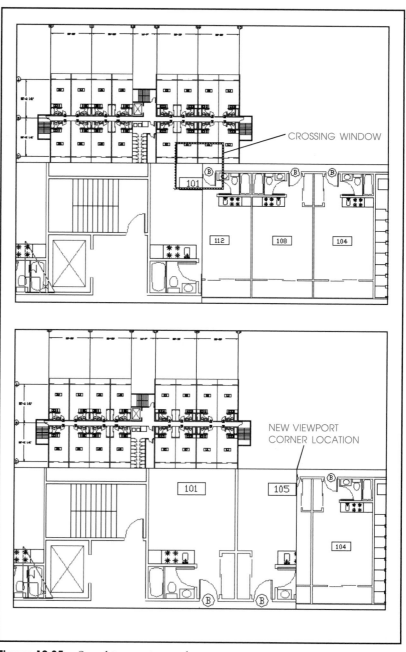

Figure 12.35: Stretching, erasing, and moving viewports

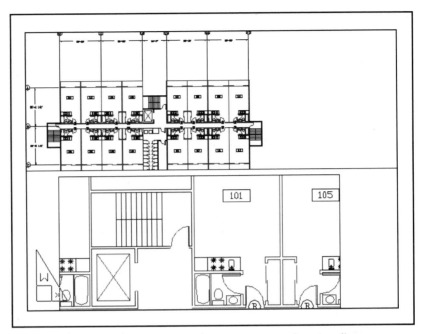

Figure 12.35: Stretching, erasing, and moving viewports (continued)

▼ TIP

You can also click on the viewport frames, then stretch their corners using their grips. A viewport remains rectangular even if you try to stretch only one corner of it.

3. Click on Modify ➤ Erase ➤ Single, then click on the frame of the lower-right viewport.

4. Use the MOVE command to move the lower-left viewport to a new position, as shown in Figure 12.35.

Viewports are actually objects, so they can be affected by all the editing commands just as any other object would be affected. Here, you moved, stretched, and erased viewports. Next, you'll see the effects that layers have on viewports.

1. Create a new layer called *Vport*.

2. Use Modify ➤ Entity… to change the viewport borders to the Vport layer.

3. Finally, turn off the Vport layer. The viewport borders will disappear.

A viewport's border can be assigned a layer, color, or line type. If you put the viewport's border on a layer that has been turned off, that border will become invisible, just like any other object on such a layer. Making the borders invisible is helpful when you want to compose a final sheet for plotting. Even when turned off, the active viewport will show a heavy border around it to simplify editing.

SCALING VIEWS IN PAPERSPACE

▼ **NOTE**

While in Paperspace, you cannot edit objects in Modelspace, and vice versa. You must use View ➤ Modelspace and View ➤ Paperspace to move from one mode to the other. Paperspace and Modelspace each have separate scales, just as they have separate objects.

Paperspace has its own unit of measure. You have already seen how you can set the limits of Paperspace independently of Modelspace. When you first enter Paperspace, regardless of the area your drawing takes up in Modelspace, you are given limits that are 12 units wide by 9 units high. This may seem incongruous at first, but if you keep in mind that Paperspace is like a paste-up area, this difference of scale becomes easier to accept. Just as you might paste up photographs and maps representing several square miles onto an 11"×17" board, so you can use Paperspace to paste up views of scale drawings representing city blocks or houses.

You must carefully consider scale factors when composing your Paperspace paste-up. Let's see how you can put together a sheet in Paperspace and still maintain accuracy of scale.

Zoom ↵ Xp

▼ **NOTE**

The *xp* suffix appended to the *1/96* tells AutoCAD that the current view should be scaled to ¹⁄₉₆th of the Paperspace scale. You get the 1/96 simply by taking the inverse of the drawing's scale factor, 96.

1. Click on View ➤ Modelspace or enter **MS** ↵ to return to Modelspace.

2. Click on the top view to make it active.

3. Pan the view so that the plan is centered in the viewport (see Figure 12.36).

4. Enter **Zoom** ↵.

5. At the **All/Center/Dynamic/Extents**… prompt, enter **1/96xp** ↵.

6. Click on the lower viewport.

7. Pan the view so that two of the typical units are centered in the viewport (See Figure 12.36).

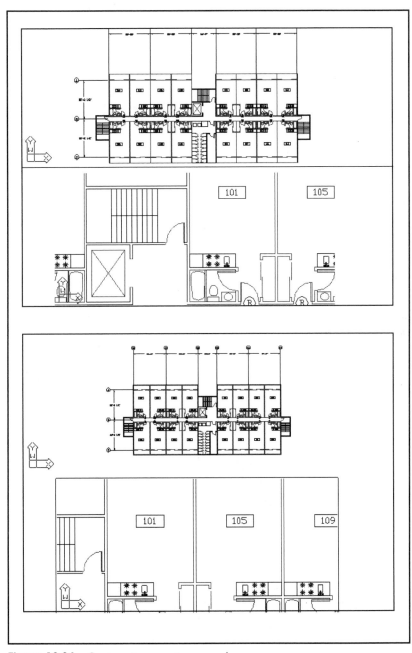

Figure 12.36:   Setting viewport views to scale

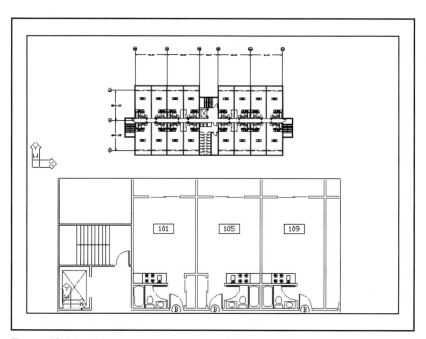

Figure 12.36: Setting viewport views to scale (continued)

8. Enter **Zoom** ↵ again, then enter **1/24xp** ↵ at the **All/Center /Dynamic** prompt. Your view of the unit will be scaled to ½ "=1′ in relation to Paperspace.

You can go back to the Paperspace mode, then use the STRETCH, MOVE or SCALE commands to adjust the width, height, and location of the viewports so that they display only the parts of the unit you want. The view within the viewport itself will remain at the same scale and location, while the viewport changes in size. You can use these commands on a viewport with no effect on the size and location of the objects within the view.

You can also overlap viewports. You can use the Osnap overrides to select geometry within each viewport, even while in Paperspace. This allows you to align one viewport on top of another at exact locations.

You can also add a title block at a 1:1 scale, then plot this drawing while still in Paperspace at a scale of 1 to 1. Your plot will appear just as it does in Paperspace.

SETTING LAYERS IN INDIVIDUAL VIEWPORTS

Another unique feature of Paperspace viewports is their ability to freeze layers independently. You could, for example, display the usual plan information in the overall view of a floor but show only the walls in the enlarged view of one unit.

Settings ➤ Layer Control... ➤ Cur VP ➤ Frz

1. Make the lower viewport the active one.

2. Click on Settings ➤ Layer Control.

3. Click on COMMON | FIXTURE in the list of layers to highlight it.

4. Click on the button labeled FRZ next to the Cur VP: label.

5. Click on **OK**. The active viewport will regenerate with the Fixture layer invisible from the current viewport. It remains visible in the other viewport however (see Figure 12.37).

You might have noticed the other two similar buttons next to the label New VP. These two buttons control layer visibility in any new viewports you might create next, rather than controlling existing viewports.
Now save and exit the Xref-1 file.

IF YOU WANT TO EXPERIMENT...

You may want to experiment further with Paperspace in order to become more familiar with it. Try the following exercise. In it you will add two more viewports using the MVIEW and COPY commands.

1. Open the Plan file you used for the Paperspace exercise.

2. At the command prompt, type **Pspace** to go to Paperspace.

3. Turn on the Vport layer and STRETCH the lower viewport so that it occupies the lower-right third of the screen (see panel 1 of Figure 12.38).

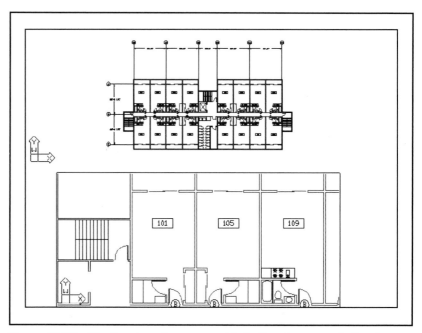

Figure 12.37: The Drawing editor screen with the Door layer turned off in the active viewport

4. To create a new viewport, issue the MVIEW command.

5. At the **OFF/ON/Hideplot** prompt, pick the lower-left corner of the screen.

6. At the **Other corner** prompt, size the viewport so that it is similar to the viewport to the right, as shown in panel 1 of Figure 12.38.

7. Press **Ctrl-C** to stop the drawing regeneration.

8. Use the COPY command to copy the lower-right viewport to the left. This time let the drawing regeneration occur. Note that the view in the copied viewport is identical to that in the original.

9. At the command prompt, type **Mspace** to switch over to Modelspace.

10. Pick the lower-left viewport.

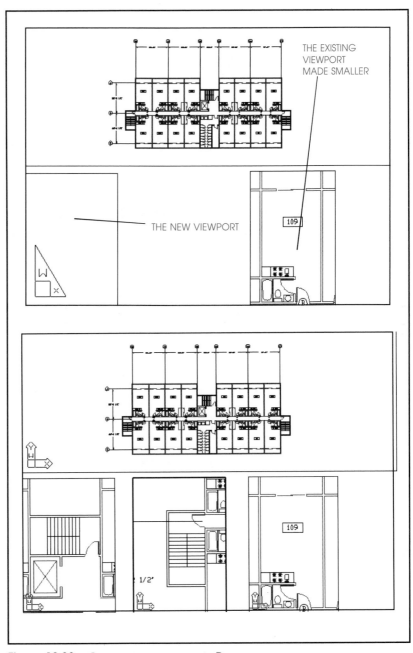

Figure 12.38: Creating new viewports in Paperspace

11. Type **Regen**. Notice that only the current viewport regenerates.

12. Issue the ZOOM command and use the Dynamic option to move your view to the elevator area. Notice that you get a miniature version of the ZOOM Dynamic view.

13. Arrange the views in the other viewport to look like panel 2 of Figure 12.38.

SUMMARY

This chapter concludes the apartment building tutorial. Although you haven't drawn the complete building, you've already learned all the commands and techniques you need to do so. Figure 12.39 shows you a completed plan of the first floor. You can add the symbols shown in this figure to the Plan file to complete your floor plans and practice using AutoCAD. Since buildings like this often have the same plans for different floors, the plan for the second floor can also represent the third floor. Combined with the first floor, this will give you a three-level apartment building. This project would also have a ground-level garage, which would be a separate file. The Gridline file you created earlier can be used in the garage file as a reference for dimensions. The other symbols can be blocks stored as files that can be retrieved in other files.

Most of your work will involve drawing lines, arcs, and circles, but not everything can be drawn with these objects. In the next chapter, you will learn how to draw more complex shapes such as complex curves and solid, filled areas.

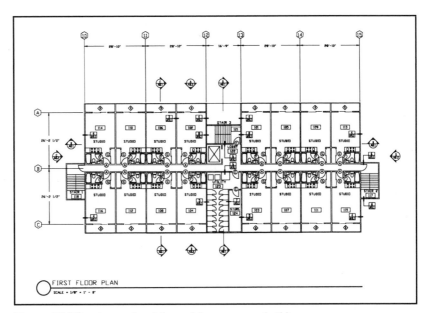

Figure 12.39:   A completed floor of the apartment building.

Using MVSetup to Set Up Paperspace

If you prefer, you can use a feature that automates the Paperspace setup. This feature is an AutoLISP utility called MVSetup. It automatically sets up viewports in Paperspace and offers a set of title blocks. The following describes MVsetup and how to use it.

1. Click on View ➤ Layout ➤ MV Setup. If Tilemode is set to 1, you will see the following message:

   Paperspace/Modelspace is disabled. The pre-R11 setup will be invoked unless it is enabled. Enable Paper/Modelspace? <Y>:

2. If you enter **N**, you will get a series of prompts asking you for the unit style, sheet size, and scale of your drawing. Options to the prompts will appear in the side menu.

3. Once you have responded to the prompts, a border will be drawn representing the Modelspace work area for the scale and sheet size you specify, and you will exit MVSetup.

4. If you respond to step 1 by pressing ↵ to accept the default **Y**, you get the following message.

MVSetup, Version 1.15, (c) 1990-1992 by Autodesk, Inc.
Align/Create/Scale viewports/Options/Title block/Undo:

This is the same prompt you get if you issue MVSetup with Tilemode set to 0. The following describes each of these options.

Align lets you align features of one viewport to those of another, or rotate a viewport view.

Create lets you create a set of viewports by choosing from a set of predefined viewport layouts.

Scale viewports lets you set the scale of each viewport individually or globally.

Options lets you adjust several preferences for the MVSetup utility, such as default limits, default layers for title blocks, units, and whether title blocks are inserted or cross referenced.

Title Block inserts a title block from a set of predefined title blocks. You can add your own custom title blocks to this set.

Undo will undo the last MVSetup option you used.

13

▼ ▼ ▼ ▼ ▼

DRAWING
CURVES AND
SOLID FILLS

FAST TRACK

514 ▶ To sketch with AutoCAD

Click on Draw ➤ Line ➤ Sketch, then click on a point to start the temporary sketch line. Click on a point to stop the sketch line, then press **R** to make the temporary sketch line permanent. Enter **Q** ↵ to exit the sketch mode.

520 ▶ To draw a polyline arc

Click on Draw ➤ Polyline ➤ 2D, pick a start point, then enter **A** ↵. You can then specify a center point, direction, second point, or endpoint for the arc in a way similar to the Arc command.

520 ▶ To smooth out a polyline

Click on Modify ➤ Polyedit, click on the polyline to smooth, then enter **F** ↵. Press ↵ to exit the Pedit command.

526 ▶ To join a polyline with another object

First make sure that the polyline and the object to join meet exactly end to end. Click on Modify ➤ PolyEdit, then click on the polyline. Enter **J** ↵, then select the object you want to join. Press ↵ to confirm your selection, then press ↵ again to exit the Pedit command.

527 ▶ To change the width of a polyline

Click on Modify ➤ PolyEdit, then click on the polyline you wish to widen. Enter **W** ↵, then enter the new width. Enter ↵ to exit the Pedit command.

529 ▶ To convert a line or arc into a polyline

Click on Modify ➤ PolyEdit, then click on the line or arc you wish to convert. Hit ↵ at the next prompt, then enter ↵ to exit the Pedit command.

537 ▶ To vary the width of a polyline

Click on Modify ➤ PolyEdit, then click on the polyline you wish to widen. Enter **E** ↵, then press ↵ until the X marker is on the vertex of the polyline where you want to start to vary the width. Enter the width you want at the current point, then enter the width you want at the next vertex. Enter **R** ↵ to see the resulting new widths. Press ↵ to go to the next vertex or **X** ↵ to exit the Pedit command.

538 ▶ To turn a polyline into a spline curve

Click on Modify ➤ PolyEdit, then click on the polyline you wish to turn into a curve. Enter **S** ↵, then enter ↵ to exit the Pedit command.

543 ▶ To mark an object off into equal divisions

Click on Construct ➤ Divide, click on the object you want to mark, then enter the number of divisions you want.

546 ▶ To make equally spaced copies of an object along a curved path

First turn the object you want to copy into a block. Next, click on Construct ➤ Divide. Click on the object defining the curved path, enter **B** ↵, then enter the name of the block you just created. Finally, enter the number of divisions along the path.

547 ▶ To solid fill a circular area

Click on Draw ➤ Donut. Enter the center hole diameter, enter the overall diameter, then pick points placing the solid filled circle.

In *Chapter 11*, you traced a drawing by using the normal lines and arcs. In this chapter, you will use polylines to trace curves. Polylines offer many options for creating forms, including solid fills. We will look at these options and a few other object types that allow you to include solid fills in your drawings.

DRAWING SMOOTH CURVES

▼ NOTE

You don't have to trace a drawing to use the Sketch command. You may want to use Sketch just to draw freehand images in AutoCAD.

From time to time you will have to trace curved, rather than rectilinear, objects. The Sketch command allows you to draw curves in a freehand style with a series of short line segments that give the appearance of a continuous, smooth line using a polyline. A polyline is composed of several lines linked together that act like a single object. If you draw a square with polylines, instead of a set of four connected lines, the entire box acts like one object. You can use polylines to design fonts, draw concentric boxes, or draw thick lines such as traces on a circuit board. You can even vary the thickness of a polyline, making it taper and expand as you like.

You draw a polyline by using the PLINE command on the Draw menu or the SKPOLY option on the Sketch menu. The only difference between the two is that SKPOLY uses the SKETCH command to generate the polyline, while PLINE allows you to draw it as you would a normal line.

DIGITIZING CURVES WITH THE SKETCH COMMAND

Figure 13.1 shows a simple contour map. The contour lines (similar to those on geological or relief maps) represent elevation, and the numbers on them represent their height in feet. Tracing or drawing this contour map will give you a good feel for the Sketch and polyline commands.

This first exercise requires the use of a digitizing tablet. If you don't have a tablet, skip to the next section on drawing curves with the PLINE command.

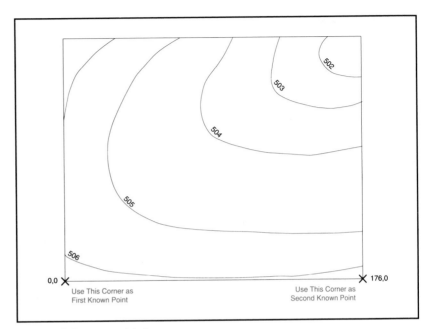

Figure 13.1: A simplified contour map

Draw ➤ ▨ Line ➤ Sketch

1. Open a new file called **Site** and set up the drawing for $\frac{1}{16}"=1'-0"$ on an $8\frac{1}{2} \times 11"$ sheet.

2. Photocopy Figure 13.1 and calibrate the tablet as you did in *Chapter 11*. For a reference line, use the bottom two corners of the rectangle enclosing the site contours. Use 0,0 for the lower-left corner and 176,0 for the lower-right corner.

3. While still in the tablet mode, enter **Sketch** ↵ at the command prompt.

4. At the **Record Increment** prompt, enter ′**Skpoly** ↵; then, at the **New Value for Skpoly** prompt, enter **1** ↵.

> ▼ NOTE
>
> Setting Skpoly to 1 causes the Sketch command to draw with polylines rather than with standard lines (see *Appendix D* for a list of system variables).

▼▼▼▼▼

▼ TIP

To find the appropriate record increment, use Assist ➤ Inquiry ➤ Distance and measure approximately 22° of arc along the smallest curve you will be tracing.

5. At the **Record increment '-0 1/8":** prompt, enter **5'** ↵ to specify your SKETCH line segment length (see Figure 13.2).

6. Now you are in the sketch mode. The **Record increment** prompt appears, asking you to enter a value for the line segment length.

As I said above, the Sketch command draws a series of short lines to simulate a continuous sketched line. The smaller the record increment, the shorter the line segments and the smoother the appearance of the sketch line. If the number you enter here is too small for your drawing scale, however, the Sketch line will use up too much memory and slow down drawing.

AutoCAD offers a default value of ⅛", which is fine for drawings at full scale on the default work area of 9"×12". Since you are drawing at a different scale, you must adjust this value. Generally, it is best to pick a value that allows at least four line segments for the smallest half circle you will draw (see Figure 13.3). We estimate that length to be 5' for this exercise, so we entered **5'** at step 5 above.

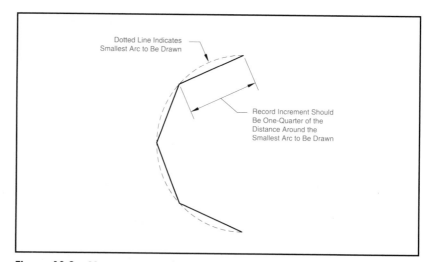

Figure 13.2: How to estimate the SKETCH record increment

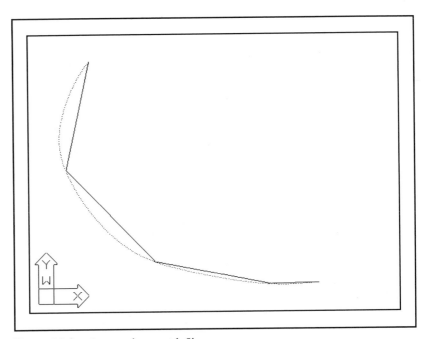

Figure 13.3: A curve drawn with 5′ segments

▼ NOTE

The pick button or *P* key acts as a toggle to raise and lower the stylus. It tells the AutoCAD cursor when to draw but doesn't physically move the stylus.

▼ NOTE

The **Please raise pen!** message appears when your drawing file becomes very complex or if your computer has limited memory. AutoCAD will begin to use disk space as temporary storage, but before it does, it asks you to raise the pen while it prepares to write to disk.

1. At the **Sketch. Pen eXit Quit Record Erase Connect.** prompt, verify that the tablet mode is on and ortho mode is off.

2. Start to trace the contour lines on the site plan, by placing your stylus or puck at the beginning of a contour line, then pressing the pick button or the **P** key.

3. If you get the **Please raise pen!** prompt accompanied by a beep, type **P** (you may have to press the key twice).

4. When the **Thank you. Lower the pen and continue.** prompt appears, continue to trace the contour line.

5. You will notice a rubber-banding line appear at 5′ intervals. As the line reaches a 5′ length, it becomes fixed, then another rubber-banding line continues. When you reach the end of the contour line, press the pick button again. Your line is temporarily drawn.

6. To permanently save it as a line, pick Record from the Sketch menu or type **R**. A line drawn with Sketch is temporary until you use Record to save it.

7. Trace the rest of the contour lines.

8. Choose **Exit** or press ↵ to exit the Sketch command. Your drawing will look like Figure 13.4.

▼ NOTE

If you need help, refer to the section on configuring your digitizing tablet menu in *Appendix B.*

9. Now reconfigure your tablet to its previous condition, using the Reconfig option on the Tablet menu, so you can use the digitizing tablet menu if you wish. Once you have done this, exit the Site file.

You can use the TEXT command to enter the elevations shown on the original site plan. When you are prompted for a text angle, use the cursor to visually set an angle tangent to the contour line.

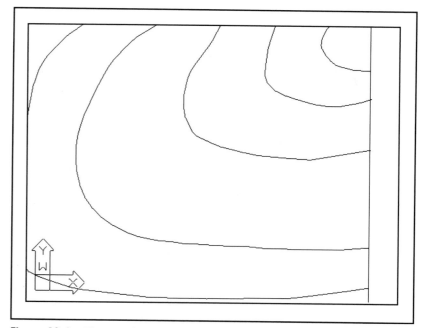

Figure 13.4:   The traced contour lines

Other Sketch Options

Before we continue with smoothing the contours, let's take a quick look at some of the other options you didn't get to try in the last exercise.

The **Connect** option allows you to continue a line from the end of the last temporary line drawn. You pick Connect or type **C**, then move the cursor to the endpoint of the temporary line. AutoCAD automatically starts the line and you just continue to draw. This option works only in the pen-up mode.

The **period** option, which is not available on the menu, allows you to draw by moving the cursor to the desired position, then pressing the period key to draw a line segment. First you start a SKETCH line, then you set the pen up. Then move the cursor to the position for the next endpoint and press the period key. A line segment will be drawn from the endpoint of the last line segment to the current cursor position. This is quite similar to the way you normally draw lines, only without the rubber-banding line. The period option is useful when you are sketching along, then suddenly find you must draw a long, straight line segment.

The **Record, Erase, Quit,** and **Exit** options control recording lines and exiting SKETCH. As we said above, the Record option is used to save a temporary sketched line. Once a line has been recorded, you must edit it as you would any other line. *Erase* allows you to erase temporary lines *before* you record them. *Quit* ends the SKETCH command without saving unrecorded lines. On the other hand, the *Exit* option on the Sketch menu automatically saves *all* lines you have drawn, then exits the SKETCH command.

▼ TIP

Instead of using SKETCH to trace the contours with your tablet, you can use PLINE to trace short line segments over the photocopy of the map. Use longer line segments for broad curves and shorter segments where curves are tight.

You have completed the first stage in creating smooth curves. But polylines are made up of short, straight lines, not arcs. Next you will have to use the PEDIT command to smooth the line segments into arcs. Before you do this, take a look at an alternate way of drawing the polyline contours without a digitizer in the side bar *Scaling Curves with the Pline Command.*

Scaling Curves with the Pline Command

If you don't have a tablet, use a grid to scale the site plan as described in *Chapter 11*, or just draw the site plan freehand using Draw ➤ Line ➤ Sketch ➤ Skpoly. Here are instructions on how to use a grid to scale the site plan.

1. Start a new file called **Contgrid** and draw a grid that is 176'×136' with 8' intervals.

2. Plot the grid out on tracing paper at a scale of 1=364. This is the scale of the drawing in Figure 13.1.

3. Overlay the plot onto the figure and mark some reference points on your grid that correspond to points on the contour line.

4. Return to your grid drawing in AutoCAD and connect the reference points by using Draw ➤ Polyline ➤ 2D.

5. At the **From point** prompt, pick a point at the beginning of one of the contours on your grid.

6. At the **Arc/Close/Halfwidth/Length/Undo/Width/ <Endpoint of line>:** prompt, continue to pick reference points on your grid.

7. Once you finish one contour, press ↵ to exit Polyline.

8. Repeat the process to draw the other contours.

As you pick points, line segments appear, just as with the LINE command. Take care to space the line segments closer together when you come to tighter curves.

SMOOTHING POLYLINES

Next you will convert the contour line segments into smooth curves.

Modify ➤ ⤵ Polyline Edit

1. Click on Modify ➤ Polyline Edit. This menu option starts the Pedit command.

2. At the **PEDIT Select objects:** prompt, pick a contour line.

3. At the **Close/Join/Width/Edit vertex/Fit/Spline/Decurve /Ltype gen/Undo/eXit:** prompt, press **F** ↵ to select the *Fit curve* option. This causes the polyline to smooth out into a curve.

4. At the **Close/Join/Width/Edit vertex/Fit/Spline/Decurve /Ltype gen/Undo/eXit:** prompt, press ↵ to end the Pedit command.

5. Then press ↵ to start the Pedit command again and repeat the process for the next contour line. Keep doing this until all the lines are smoothed.

> **▼ TIP**
>
> You can also enter **Pline** ↵ at the command prompt to start a polyline.

Your contours are complete. The Fit curve option under the Pedit command causes AutoCAD to convert the straight line segments of the polyline into arcs. The endpoints of the arcs pass through the endpoints of the line segments and the curve of each arc is dependent on the direction of the adjacent arc. This gives the effect of a smooth curve.

LOOKING AT POLYLINES' ADVANTAGES

In the next exercise, you will begin a drawing of the top view of the joint in Figure 13.5 to see some other ways that polylines can be used.

Draw ➤ ⤵ Polyline ➤ 2D

1. Save the contour map, then open a new file called **Joint2d**. Don't bother to use the Setup option as you will do this drawing with the default settings.

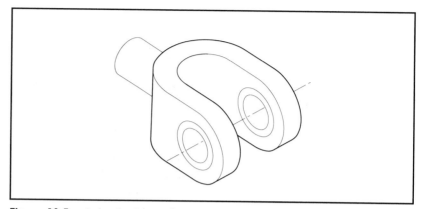

Figure 13.5: A sketch of a metal joint

2. Click on Draw ➤ Polyline ➤ 2D.

3. At the **From point** prompt, enter a point at coordinate **3,3** to start your polyline.

4. At the **Arc/Close/Halfwidth/Length/Undo/Width /<Endpoint of line>:** prompt, enter **@3<0** ↵ to draw a horizontal line of the joint.

5. At the **Arc/Close/Halfwidth**… prompt, enter **A** ↵ to continue your polyline with an arc.

6. At the **Angle\CEnter\CLose\Direction\Halfwidth \Line\Radius\Second pt\Undo\Width\ <Endpoint of arc>:** prompt, enter **@4<90** ↵ to draw a 180° arc from the last point you entered. Your drawing looks like Figure 13.6.

7. Continue the polyline with another line segment. To do this, enter **L** ↵.

8. At the **Arc\Close\Halfwidth**… prompt, enter **@3<180** ↵. Another line segment continues from the end of the arc.

9. Press ↵ to exit Pline.

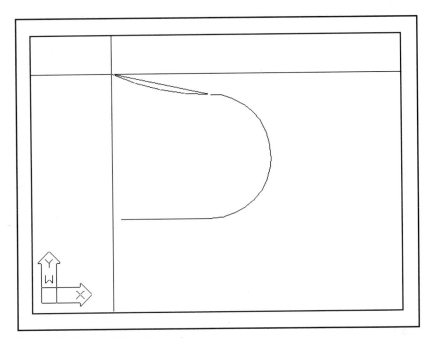

Figure 13.6: A polyline line and arc

You now have a sideways U-shaped polyline that you will use in the next section to complete the top view of your joint. Let's pause from the exercise to look at some of the options you didn't use.

The **Close** option draws a line segment from the last endpoint of a sequence of lines to the first point picked in that sequence. This works exactly like the Close subcommand on the Line menu.

The **Length** option enables you to specify the length of a line that will be drawn at the same angle as the last line entered.

The **Halfwidth** option allows you to create a tapered line segment or arc by specifying half its beginning and ending widths (see Figure 13.7).

The **Width** option allows you to create a tapered line segment or arc by specifying the full width of the segment's beginning and ending points.

The **Undo** option deletes the last line segment drawn.

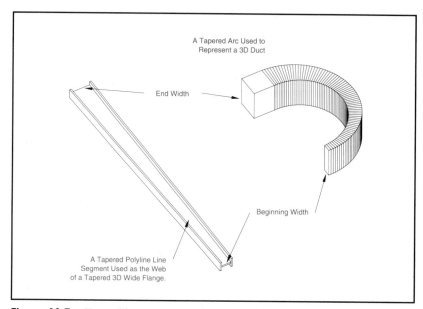

Figure 13.7: Tapered line segment and arc created with Halfwidth

▼ NOTE

The FILLET command can be used to fillet all the vertices of a polyline composed of straight line segments. To do this, first set your fillet radius, then select the polyline option under the FILLET command and pick the polyline you want to fillet.

The FILL ON and FILL OFF options on the Pline side menu allow you to turn off the filling of solid polylines. These options are explained in detail later in this chapter, in the section on solid fills.

EDITING POLYLINES

You can edit polylines with many of the standard editing commands. You can change the properties of a polyline using CHANGE, while STRETCH can be used to displace vertices of a polyline. TRIM, EX-TEND, and BREAK also work with polylines.

In addition, there are many editing capabilities offered only for polylines. You've already seen how you can smooth out a polyline using the Fit Curve option under the Pedit command. Let's take a closer look at some of the other Pedit options by continuing with our top view of the joint. Next, you will use the OFFSET command to quickly add the inside portion of the joint.

Construct ➤ 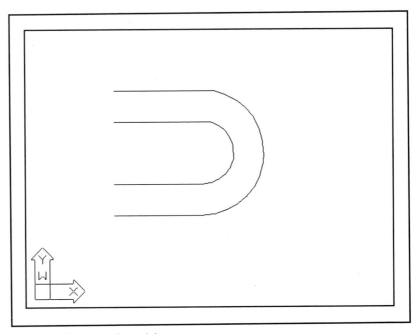 Offset

▼ TIP

A very complex polyline containing hundreds of vertices may not offset properly. If you have problems offsetting complex polylines, break the polyline up into smaller segments, then try the OFFSET command on these segments.

1. Click on Construct ➤ Offset.
2. At the **Offset distance** prompt, enter **1**.
3. At the **Select object…** prompt, pick the U-shaped polyline you just drew.
4. At the **Side to offset** prompt, pick a point toward the inside of the U. A copy of the polyline appears in a concentric fashion (see Figure 13.8).

As you can see, OFFSET makes a concentric copy of a polyline. This can be very useful where you need to draw complex parallel curves like the ones in Figure 13.9.

Figure 13.8: The offset polyline

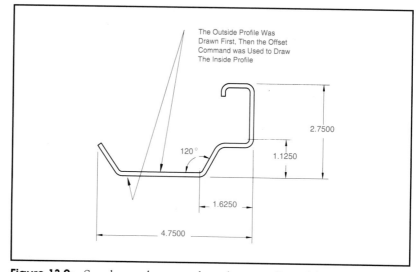

Figure 13.9: Sample complex curves drawn by using offset polylines

Modify ➤ ↵ Polyline Edit / Join

1. Complete the top view of the joint by connecting the ends of the polylines with two short line segments (see Figure 13.10).

2. Click on Modify ➤ Polyedit.

3. At the **Select polyline** prompt, pick the outermost polyline.

4. At the **Close/Join/Width** prompt, enter **J** ↵ for the Join option.

5. At the **Select objects** prompt, pick all the objects you have drawn so far. Then press ↵.

6. Press ↵ when you are done. Now all the objects are joined into one polyline.

By using the Width option under the Pedit command, you can change the thickness of a polyline. Let's change the width of the polyline to give the outline of the joint some thickness.

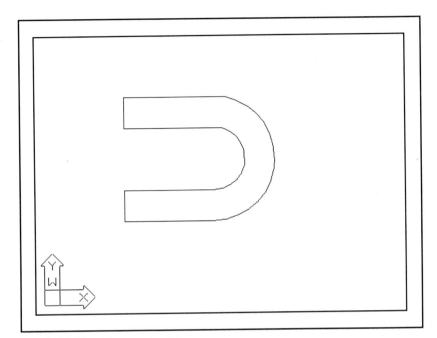

Figure 13.10:   The joined polyline

Modify ➤ Polyline Edit / Width

1. Click on Modify ➤ Polyedit again and pick the polyline. Then press ↵.

2. At the **Close/Join/Width** prompt, enter **W** for the Width option.

3. At the **Enter new width for all segments:** prompt, enter .03 for the new width of the polyline. The line changes to the new width (see Figure 13.11). You now have a top view of your joint.

4. Press ↵ to exit the Pedit command.

5. Save this file.

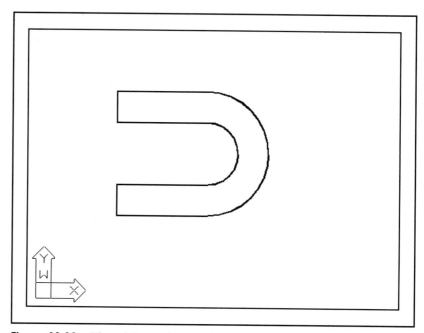

Figure 13.11: The polyline with a new thickness

▼ TIP

You can change the thickness of regular lines and arcs by using Pedit to change them into polylines and then using the Pedit ➤ Width option to change their width. **Ltype gen** controls how noncontinuous line types pass through the vertices of a polyline. If you have a fitted or spline curve with a noncontinuous line type, you will want to turn this option on.

Let's briefly look at a few of the Pedit options you didn't try firsthand.

Close connects the two endpoints of a polyline with a line segment. If the polyline you selected to be edited is already closed, this option changes to Open.

Open removes the last segment added to a closed polyline.

Spline smooths a polyline into a Bézier curve. I will discuss this option in more detail later in this chapter.

Edit Vertex lets you edit each vertex of a polyline individually. We will take a detailed look at this option in the next section.

▼ ■ ■ ■ ■

Turning Objects into Polylines

There may be times when you will want to convert regular lines, arcs, or even circles into polylines. You may want to change the width of lines, or join lines together to form a single object like a boundary. The following describes the steps to take to convert lines, arcs, and circles into polylines.

1. At the **Select polyline** prompt, pick the object you wish to convert. If you want to convert a circle to a polyline, you must first break the circle so that it becomes an arc of 359°.

2. At the **Entity selected is not a polyline. Do you want to turn it into one? <Y>** prompt, press ↵. The object is converted into a polyline.

EDITING VERTICES

One of the Pedit options we haven't discussed, Edit Vertex, is almost like a command within a command. Edit Vertex allows you to fine-tune your polyline by giving you control over its individual vertices. Since there are numerous suboptions under the Edit Vertex option, we'll discuss it in depth in this section. Try these on the Site drawing you did at the beginning of the chapter.

When using Edit Vertex, you must be careful about selecting the vertex to be edited. There are ten options under Edit Vertex, and you often have to exit it and use Fit Curv to see the effect of these options on a curved polyline. When you select Edit Vertex you get the prompt

Next/Previous/Break/Insert/Move/Regen/Straighten/Tangent/
Width/eXit:

and the Edit Vertex side menu appears.

The Next and Previous options enable you to select a vertex for editing. When you start the Edit Vertex option, an X appears on the selected polyline showing you its beginning. As you select Next or Previous, the X moves from vertex to vertex to show which one is being edited.

▼ **TIP**

You can determine the direction of a polyline by noting the direction the X moves in when you use the Next option. It is important to know the direction of a polyline for some of the other Edit Vertex options.

To select Next:

1. Press ↵ to enter the default, Next. The X moves to the next vertex.

To select Previous:

1. Enter **P** for Previous. The X moves in the opposite direction and the default becomes *P*.

The Break option breaks the polyline between two vertices. To use this option, follow these steps.

1. Position the X on one end of the segment you want to break.

2. Pick Break from the Edit Vertex menu or enter **B**.

3. At the **Next/Previous/Go/eXit <N>:** prompt, use Next or Previous to move the X to the other end of the segment to be broken.

4. When the X is in the right position, pick Go from the Edit Vertex menu or enter **G**, and the polyline will be broken (see Figure 13.12).

The Insert option inserts a new vertex.

1. Position the X before the new vertex.

2. Pick Insert from the Edit Vertex menu or enter **I** ↵.

3. When the prompt **Enter location of new vertex:** appears and a rubber-banding line appears originating from the current X position (see Figure 13.13), pick a point indicating the new vertex location. The polyline is redrawn with the new vertex.

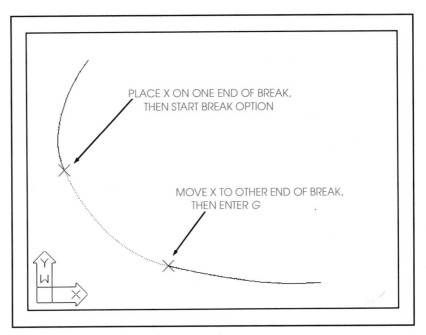

Figure 13.12:   How the Break option works

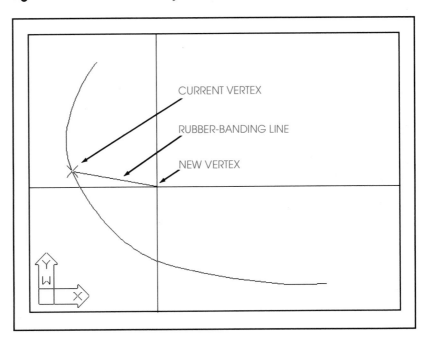

Figure 13.13:   The new vertex location

The inserted vertex appears between the currently marked vertex and the *next* vertex, so this option is sensitive to the direction of the polyline. If the polyline is curved, the new vertex will not immediately be shown as curved (see panel 1 of Figure 13.14). You must smooth it out by exiting the Edit Vertex option and then using the Fit Curv option as you did to edit the site plan (see panel 2 of Figure 13.14). You can also use the STRETCH command to move a polyline vertex.

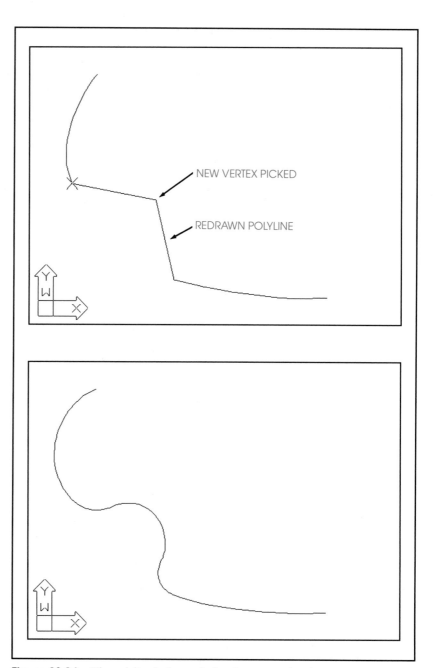

NEW VERTEX PICKED

REDRAWN POLYLINE

Figure 13.14: The polyline before and after the curve is fitted

The Move option allows you to move a vertex.

▼ **TIP**

You can also move a polyline vertex using its grip.

1. Use the Next or Previous option to place the X on the vertex you wish to move.

2. Pick Move from the Edit Vertex menu or enter **M** ↵.

3. When the **Enter new location:** prompt appears and a rubber-banding line appears originating from the X (see panel 1 of Figure 13.15), pick the new vertex position. The polyline is redrawn (see panel 2 of Figure 13.15). Again, if the line is curved, the new vertex appears as a sharp angle until you use the Fit Curv option (see panel 3 of 13.15).

▼ **NOTE**

The Straighten option offers a quick way to delete vertices from a polyline.

The Straighten option straightens all the vertices between two selected vertices.

1. Select the starting vertex for the straight line.

2. Pick Straighten from the menu or enter **S**.

3. At the **Next/Previous/Go/eXit:** prompt, move the X to the other end of the straight line.

4. Once the X is in the proper position, pick Go from the Edit Vertex menu or enter **G** ↵. The polyline straightens between the two selected vertices (see Figure 13.16).

The Tangent option alters the direction of a curve on a curve-fitted polyline.

1. Position the X on the vertex you wish to alter.

2. Pick Tangent from the Edit Vertex menu or enter **T** ↵. A rubber-banding line appears (see panel 1 of Figure 13.17).

3. Point the rubber-banding line in the direction for the new tangent, then press the pick button. An arrow appears indicating the new tangent direction (see panel 2 of Figure 13.17).

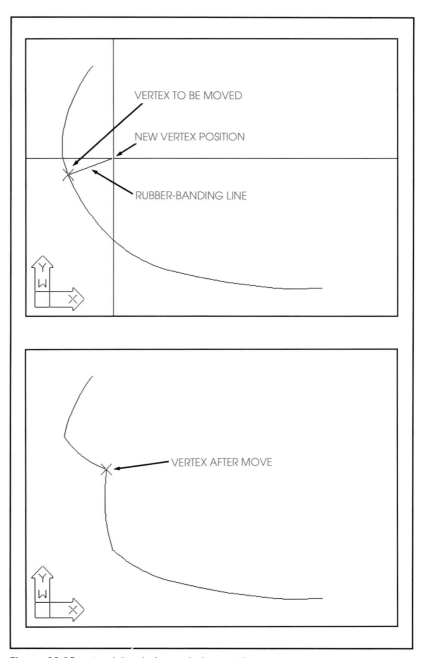

Figure 13.15: A polyline before and after straightening

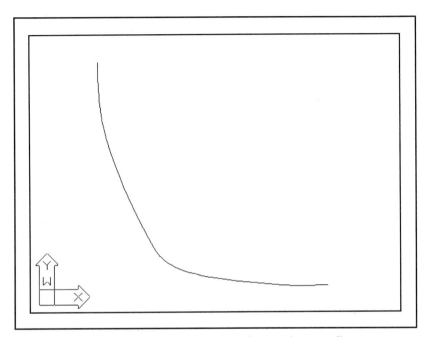

Figure 13.15:   A polyline before and after straightening (continued)

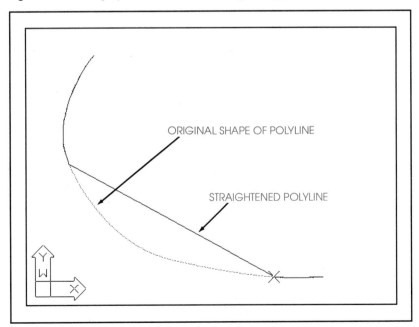

Figure 13.16:   Picking a new location for a vertex, with the polyline before and after the curve is fitted

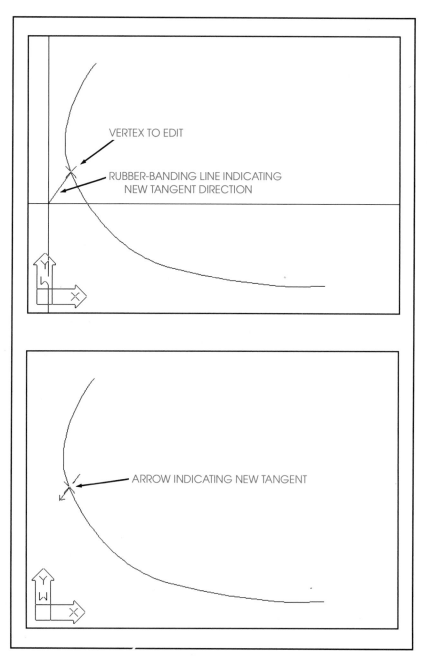

Figure 13.17: Picking a new tangent direction, using the polyline after the Fit Curv option.

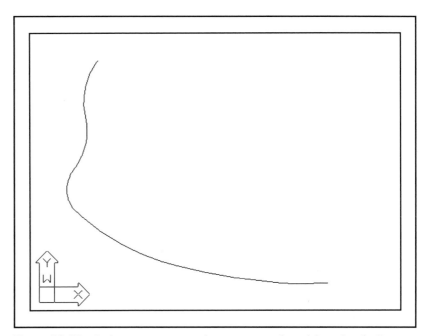

Figure 13.17:   Picking a new tangent direction, using the polyline after the Fit Curv option (continued)

Don't worry if the polyline shape does not change. You must use Fit Curv to see the effect of Tangent (see panel 3 of Figure 13.17).

Finally, there is the Width option. Unlike the first Width option under the Pedit command, this option enables you to alter the width of the polyline at any vertex. By doing this you can taper or otherwise vary polyline thickness.

1. Place the X at the beginning vertex of a polyline segment.

2. Pick Width from the Edit Vertex menu or enter **W** ↵.

3. At the **Enter starting width** prompt, enter a value indicating the polyline width desired at this vertex.

4. At the **Enter ending width** prompt, enter the width for the next vertex.

Again, don't be alarmed if nothing happens after you enter this value. To see the result of the Width option, you must exit the Edit Vertex option (see Figure 13.18), then use the Regen option.

The Undo option undoes the last Edit Vertex option used. You can use the Regen option any time.

Pick eXit from the Edit Vertex menu or enter **X**. This brings you back to the Pedit **Close/Join/Width** prompt.

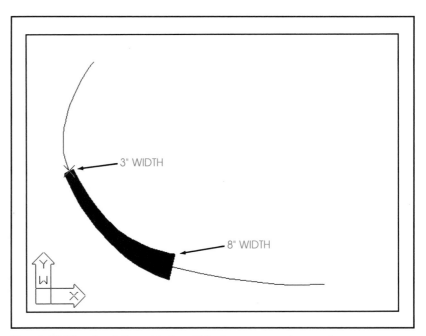

Figure 13.18: A polyline with the width of one segment increased

USING SPLINE CURVES

The Spline option under the Pedit command (named after the spline manual drafting tool) offers a way to draw smoother and more controllable curves than those produced by the Fit Curv option. A spline does not pass through the vertex points like a fitted curve. Instead, the vertex points act like weights pulling the curve in their direction. The spline polyline only touches its beginning and end vertices. Figure 13.19 illustrates this point.

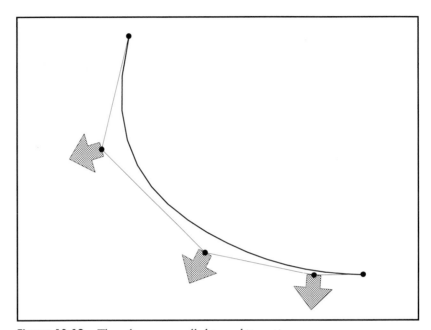

Figure 13.19:   The spline curve pulled toward its vertices

Suppose you received more detailed information about your contour map and you wanted to edit the contour in the upper-right corner of your contour map. Let's see how using a spline curve might influence the way you edit a curve.

1. Open the file containing the contour map.

2. ZOOM in on the upper-right corner contour.

3. To change the contour into a spline curve, start the Pedit command and pick the polyline to be curved.

4. At the **Close\Join\Width** prompt, pick Spline from the Pedit menu or enter **S** ↵. Your curve will change to look like Figure 13.20.

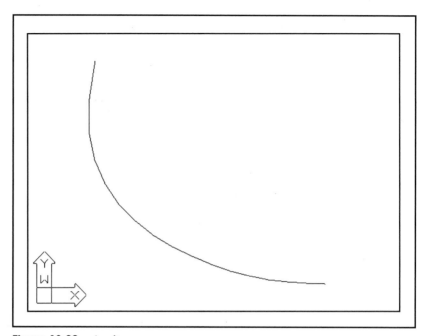

Figure 13.20: A spline curve

The curve takes on a smoother, more graceful appearance. It no longer passes through the points you used to define it. To see where the points went and to find out how spline curves act, do the following.

1. Press ↵ to exit the Pedit command and make sure the Noun/Verb mode and the Grip mode are turned on.

2. Click on the curve. You'll see the original vertices appear as grips.

3. Click on the grip that is second from the top of the curve, then move it around. Notice how the curve follows.

4. Pick a point as shown in Figure 13.21. The curve is fixed in its new position.

As you move the grip in step 3, you get immediate feedback on how the curve will look.

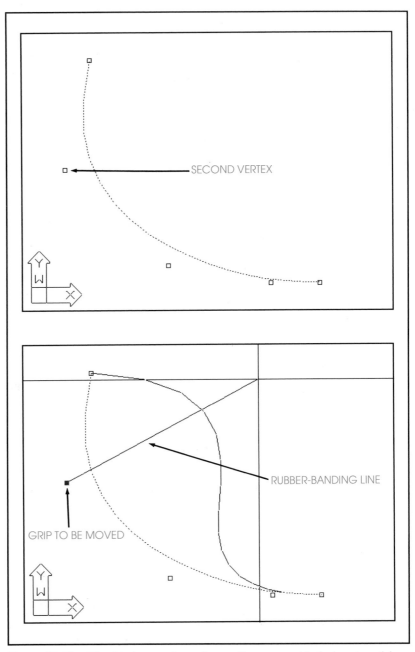

Figure 13.21: The fitted curve changed to a spline curve, with the location of the second vertex and the new curve

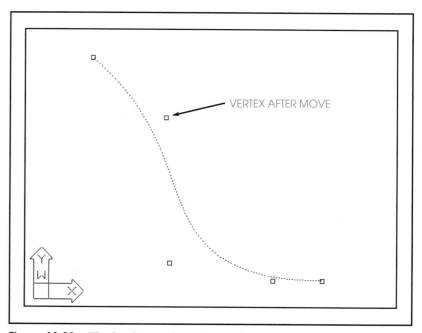

Figure 13.21: The fitted curve changed to a spline curve, with the location of the second vertex and the new curve (continued)

ADJUSTING THE PULL ON SPLINE CURVES

You can adjust the amount of pull the vertex points exert on a spline curve by changing the Splinetype system variable. The Splinetype default value is 6 and will generate what is called a *cubic B-spline* curve. With Splinetype set to 5, the curve becomes what is called a *quadratic B-spline* curve.

You can also adjust the smoothness of a spline curve by using the Splinesegs system variable. The Splinesegs default value is 8. A greater value yields a smoother curve but also creates more segments and therefore causes your drawing file to be larger.

▼ NOTE

Though I discuss the use of Divide and Measure in conjunction with polylines, you can use these commands on any object except blocks and text.

MARKING DIVISIONS ON A CURVE

Polylines used in conjunction with the Divide and Measure commands offer a unique way to mark regular intervals along a curved path. DIVIDE can be used to divide an object into a specific number of equal segments. For example, suppose you needed to mark off the contour into nine equal segments. You could first find the length of the contour by using the LIST command, then sit down with a pencil and paper to figure out exactly what the distances have to be between the marks. But there is another way.

Divide will place a set of point objects on a line, arc, circle or polyline marking off exact divisions. Here's how it works.

Construct ➤ ◣ Divide

▼ TIP

You can also enter **Divide** ↵ at the command prompt to start this command.

1. Click on Construct ➤ Divide.

2. At the **Select objects to divide:** prompt, pick the contour line.

3. At the **<Number of segments>/Block:** prompt, enter **9** ↵. (You are being asked for the number of divisions you want on the selected object.)

The command prompt returns and it appears that nothing has happened. But AutoCAD has placed several points on the contour indicating the locations of the nine divisions. To see these points more clearly, do the following.

Settings ➤ Point Style...

▼ TIP

You can also change the point style by using the Pdmode system variable. The point appears as an X when Pdmode is set to 3. See **Appendix D** for more on Pdmode.

1. Click on Settings ➤ Point Style.... The Point Style dialog box appears (see Figure 13.22).

2. Click on the X point style in the upper-right side of the dialog box, click on the Set Size Relative to Screen radio button, then click on **OK**.

3. Enter **Regen** ↵. A set of Xs appears showing the nine divisions (see Figure 13.23).

▼ TIP

To snap to point objects, you can use the NODES Osnap override.

The DIVIDE command uses POINT objects to indicate the division points. POINT objects are created by using the POINT command; they

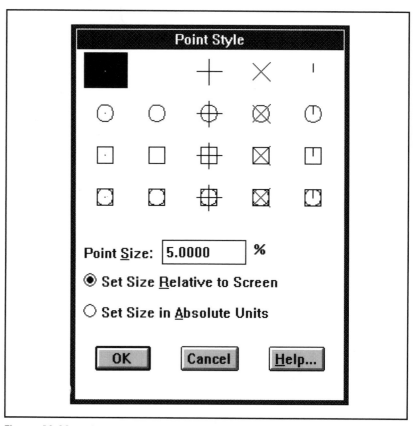

Figure 13.22:   The Point Style dialog box

MEASURE is AutoCAD's equivalent of the divider tool in manual drafting. A divider is a V-shaped instrument used to mark off regular intervals along a curve or line. It is similar to a compass.

usually appear as dots. Unfortunately, such points are nearly invisible when placed on top of other objects. But, as you have seen, you can alter their shape using the Point Style dialog box. You can use these X points to place objects or references to break the object being divided. DIVIDE itself does not actually cut the object into smaller divisions.

The MEASURE command acts just like DIVIDE, but instead of dividing an object into equal-length segments, MEASURE will mark intervals of a specified distance along an object. For example, suppose you need to mark off some segments along the contour that are exactly 5' apart. Try the following exercise to see how MEASURE is used to accomplish this task.

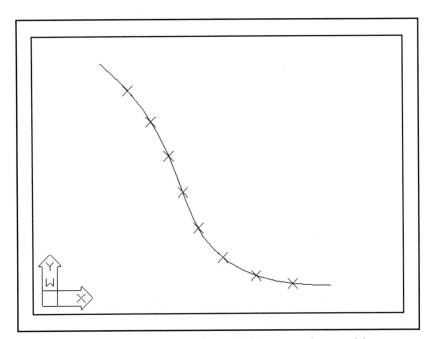

Figure 13.23: Using the DIVIDE and MEASURE commands on a polyline

---

Construct ➤ 📐 Measure

1. Click on Construct ➤ Measure.

2. At the **Select object to measure:** prompt, pick the contour at a point closest to its lower endpoint. We'll explain why this is important later.

3. At the **<Segment length>/Block:** prompt, enter 5′ ↵. The X points will appear at the specified distance.

4. Now exit this file.

In the last exercise, we asked you to pick the contour near its bottom endpoint. The point you pick on the object to be measured will determine where MEASURE will begin measuring. If you had picked the top of the contour, you would have gotten different results, since the measurement would have started at the top and not the bottom.

<table>
<tr><td>▼</td></tr>
<tr><td>■</td></tr>
<tr><td>■</td></tr>
<tr><td>■</td></tr>
<tr><td>■</td></tr>
</table>

Marking Off Intervals Using Blocks instead of Points

You can also use the Block option under the DIVIDE and MEASURE commands to place blocks at regular intervals along a line, polyline, or arc. To use blocks as markers, take the following steps.

1. First be sure the block you want to use is part of the current drawing file.

2. Start the Divide or Measure command.

3. At the **<Segment length> Block:** prompt, enter B.

4. At the **Block name to insert:** prompt, enter the name of a block.

5. At the **Align block with object? <Y>** prompt, press ⏎, if you wish the blocks to follow the alignment of the selected object. (Entering an **N** ⏎ causes each block to be inserted at a 0 angle.)

6. At the **Number of segments:** prompt, enter the number of segments. The blocks appear at regular intervals on the selected object.

One example where you might use DIVIDE's or MEASURE's Block option is to place a row of sinks equally spaced along a wall. Or you could use it to make multiple copies of an object along an irregular path defined by a polyline.

FILLING IN SOLID AREAS

You saw above how you can create a solid area by increasing the width of a polyline segment. But suppose you want instead to create a simple solid shape or a very thick line. AutoCAD provides the SOLID, TRACE, and DONUT commands to help you draw simple filled areas.

DRAWING LARGE SOLID AREAS

I've seen people use hatch patterns to fill in solid areas. Using a hatch pattern is a great way to fill irregular shapes; however, hatches tend to dramatically increase file size, thereby increasing loading and regeneration time. To keep file size down, use solids and polylines to do solid fills whenever possible.

Solids are four-sided polygons that are filled solid. They also plot as solid fills. To draw them, take the following steps.

Solid

▼ **NOTE**

The SOLID command draws a four-sided solid area, so the first point you pick will be one area's corners.

▼ **NOTE**

Selecting the third point (step 4) is where things get a little tricky. If you are drawing a square, your third point represents the corner *diagonal* to the last corner you picked (see Figure 13.24).

1. Enter **Solid** ↵ at the command prompt.

2. At the **First point:** prompt, pick a point indicating the first corner of the solid filled area.

3. At the **Second point:** prompt, pick the next corner of your solid area.

4. At the **Third point:** prompt, pick a point that is diagonal to the rectangular area you are trying to fill—as in a Z pattern.

5. At the **Fourth point:** prompt, pick the final corner of your fill. A solid area appears between the four points you selected.

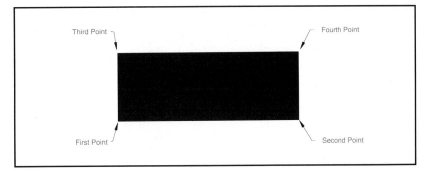

Figure 13.24:   Points for a solid square

6. The **Third point:** prompt appears again, allowing you to continue your fill pattern. You select a sequence of points in a Z pattern again. If you were to pick points in a circular pattern, you would end up with a filled area shaped like a bow tie (see Figure 13.25).

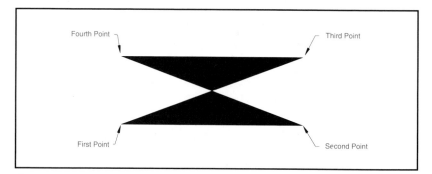

Figure 13.25:   An area filled by picking points in a clockwise pattern

You can create solid filled areas with more than four sides by entering more points in a Z pattern (see Figure 13.26). There is no limit to the number of points you can select. To end the SOLID command, press ↵ without picking a point.

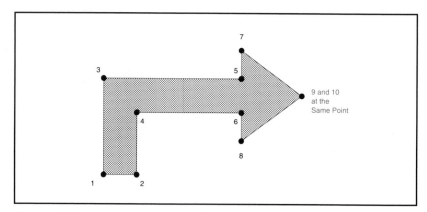

Figure 13.26:   How to use SOLID to fill in an odd shape

DRAWING FILLED CIRCLES

If you need to draw a thick circle like an inner tube or a solid filled circle, do the following.

1. Enter **Donut** ↵ at the command prompt.

2. At the **Inside diameter:** prompt, enter the desired "hole" diameter. This value determines the opening at the center of your circle.

3. At the **Outside diameter:** prompt, enter the overall diameter of the circle.

4. At the **Center of doughnut:** prompt, click on the desired location for the filled circle. You can continue to select points to place multiple donuts (see Figure 13.27).

5. Press ↵ to exit this process.

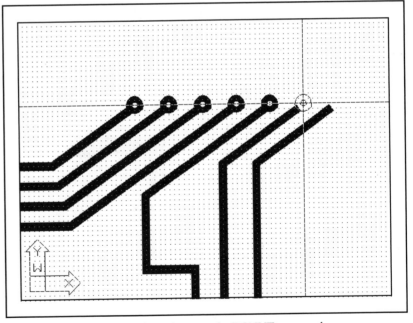

Figure 13.27:   Drawing wide circles using the DONUT command

If you need to fill only a part of a circle, like a pie slice, you can use the Donut command to draw a full circle, then use the Trim or Break command to cut out the portion of the donut you don't need.

TOGGLING SOLID FILLS ON AND OFF

▼ NOTE

You can shorten regeneration and plotting time if solids are not filled in.

Once you have drawn a solid area with the PLINE, SOLID, or DONUT command, you can control whether the solid area actually appears as filled in. When FILL is turned off, thick polylines, solids, traces, and doughnuts appear as outlines of the solid areas (see Figure 13.28).

To turn the solid filled areas on and off, do the following.

1. Enter **Fill** ↵ at the command prompt.

2. At the **ON/OFF <ON>:** prompt, enter **on** or **off** depending on whether you want areas to be filled in.

▼ WARNING

You will have to issue the REGEN command to display the effects of the FILL command.

You can also control solid-fill visibility by using the Solid Fill check box in the Drawing Aids dialog box. You can get to this dialog box by clicking on Settings ➤ Drawing Aids....

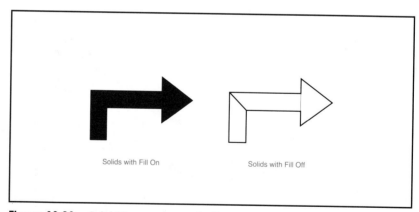

Solids with Fill On   Solids with Fill Off

Figure 13.28: Solid fills turned on and off

OVERLAPPING
SOLID LINES AND SHADED FILLS

If you use a raster plotter or laser printer that is capable of converting solid areas into screened or gray shaded areas, you may encounter the problem of shading areas overlapping lines and hiding them. This problem may not be apparent until you actually plot the drawing; it frequently occurs when a gray area is bounded by lines (see Figure 13.29).

Most other graphics programs have specific tools to handle this problem. These tools are most commonly called *Move To Front* or *Move To Back*, indicating that you move an object in front of or behind another object.

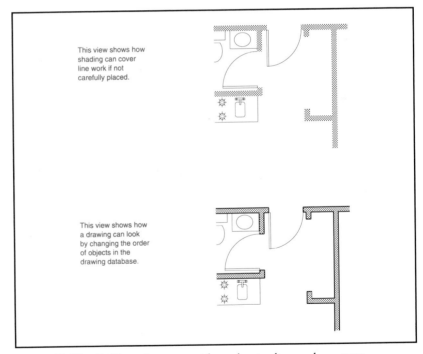

This view shows how shading can cover line work if not carefully placed.

This view shows how a drawing can look by changing the order of objects in the drawing database.

Figure 13.29: Problems that occur with overlapping lines and gray areas

While there isn't a specific command in AutoCAD to perform a move to front, there is hope. Here is how to bring one object in front of another.

1. Select the objects you want to be in the front of the gray surfaces.

2. Click on Construct ➤ Copy.

3. At the **Base point:** prompt, enter **@**.

4. At the **Second point:** prompt, enter **@** again.

5. Click on Modify ➤ Erase ➤ Select.

6. Enter **P** ↵ to select the previously selected objects.

7. Before you plot, click on Settings ➤ Selection Settings ➤ Entity Sort Method.

8. Make sure the Plotting check box is checked.

If you are sending your plots to a PostScript device, make sure the PostScript Output check box is checked in step 8.

IF YOU WANT TO EXPERIMENT...

There are many valuable uses for polylines beyond those covered in this chapter. We encourage you to become familiar with this unique object so you can take full advantage of AutoCAD.

To further explore the use of polylines, try the exercise shown in Figure 13.30. It will give you an opportunity to try out some of the options we discussed in this chapter that weren't included in exercises.

SUMMARY

Polylines are not the easiest objects to use, but, as you have seen, they are helpful where regular lines and arcs won't work. They can be used where you need to control the thickness of lines in your drawing or where curves must be carefully drawn.

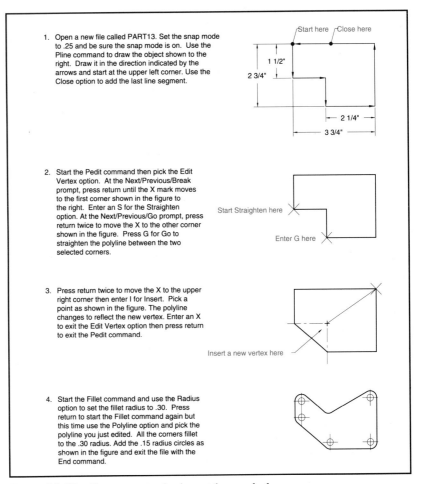

1. Open a new file called PART13. Set the snap mode to .25 and be sure the snap mode is on. Use the Pline command to draw the object shown to the right. Draw it in the direction indicated by the arrows and start at the upper left corner. Use the Close option to add the last line segment.

2. Start the Pedit command then pick the Edit Vertex option. At the Next/Previous/Break prompt, press return until the X mark moves to the first corner shown in the figure to the right. Enter an S for the Straighten option. At the Next/Previous/Go prompt, press return twice to move the X to the other corner shown in the figure. Press G for Go to straighten the polyline between the two selected corners.

3. Press return twice to move the X to the upper right corner then enter I for Insert. Pick a point as shown in the figure. The polyline changes to reflect the new vertex. Enter an X to exit the Edit Vertex option then press return to exit the Pedit command.

4. Start the Fillet command and use the Radius option to set the fillet radius to .30. Press return to start the Fillet command again but this time use the Polyline option and pick the polyline you just edited. All the corners fillet to the .30 radius. Add the .15 radius circles as shown in the figure and exit the file with the End command.

Figure 13.30: Drawing a simple plate with curved edges

You have already learned how to use the DIST command to find exact distances. You may want to be able to find areas or other properties of your drawing, or to find out how much disk space you have left or where a file is located. In the next chapter, we will look at ways to get information about your drawing.

14

GETTING
AND
EXCHANGING
DATA FROM
DRAWINGS

FAST TRACK

558 ▶ **To find the area of a simple shape**

Select Assist ➤ Inquiry ➤ Area, then click on points defining the outline of the area. When you are done, press ↵.

562 ▶ **To retrieve the last area calculation value**

Enter **Setvar** ↵ **Area** ↵ at the command prompt.

562 ▶ **To find the area of a complex shape**

Enter **Bpoly** ↵ at the command prompt. At the Polyline creation dialog box, click inside the areas that impact the area calculation. Press ↵ when you are done. Select Assist ➤ Inquiry ➤ Area, then enter **A** ↵ **E** ↵. Click on the polylines defining the gross areas, then press ↵. Enter **S** ↵ **E** ↵, then click on the areas to be subtracted from the gross areas. Press ↵ when you are done.

570 ▶ **To get an overall view of a drawing's status**

Click on Assist ➤ Inquiry ➤ Status. A listing of the drawing's status will appear.

572 ▶ **To see the amount of time spent on a drawing**

Select INQUIRY ➤ TIME from the root menu or enter **Time** ↵ at the command prompt.

575 ▶ To unlock a file that you know is currently not being used

Select File ➤ Utility ➤ Unlock file. Locate and double-click on the name of the file you wish to unlock.

583 ▶ To export a DXF file

Select File ➤ Import/Export ➤ DXF Out. At the dialog box, enter the name for your DXF file. At the **Enter decimal place…** prompt, press ↵.

584 ▶ To import a DXF file

Select File ➤ Import/Export ➤ DXF In. At the dialog box, double-click on the file name to import.

584 ▶ To import or export an IGES file

Select File ➤ Import/Export ➤ IGES In or IGES Out. At the file dialog box, enter the name you want for your export file, or, if you are importing a file, locate and click on the file name you want to import.

586 ▶ To export a PostScript EPS file

Select File ➤ Import/Export ➤ PostScript Out. Enter a name for your EPS file in the dialog box, then answer the prompts that follow.

AutoCAD drawings contain a wealth of data. You can find graphic information such as distances and angles between objects, as well as precise areas and the properties of objects. But as you become more involved with AutoCAD, you will find that you need data of a different nature. The various settings in a drawing become important as you begin to work in groups. The amount of time you spend on a drawing becomes important when you are billing computer time. As your projects become more complex, file maintenance requires a greater degree of attention. To take full advantage of AutoCAD, you will want to exchange much of this data with other people and other programs.

In this chapter, you will explore the ways in which all types of data can be extracted from AutoCAD and made available to you, your coworkers, and other programs. First, you will discover how to get specific data on your drawings. Then you will look at ways to exchange data with other programs such as word processors, desktop-publishing software, and even other CAD programs.

GETTING INFORMATION ABOUT A DRAWING

AutoCAD can instantly give you precise information about your drawing, such as the area, perimeter, and location of an object; the base point, current mode settings, and space used in a drawing; and the time at which a drawing was created and last edited. In this section you will practice getting this type of information from your drawing.

FINDING THE AREA OR LOCATION OF AN OBJECT

If you are an architect, engineer, or facilities planner, you might want to know the square-foot area of a room or a section of a building. A structural engineer might want to find the cross-sectional area of a beam. In this section you will practice finding the areas of both regular and irregular objects.

First you will get the square-foot area of the living room and entry of your studio unit plan.

▼ TIP

To find absolute coordinates in a drawing, you can use the ID command. Enter **id**, or pick ID from the Inquiry menu. You will get the prompt **ID Point**. You can then use the Osnap overrides to pick a point. Its *x*, *y*, and *z* coordinates will be displayed on the prompt line.

Assist ➤ Inquiry ➤ Area

1. Start AutoCAD and open the Unit file.

2. ZOOM into the living room and entry area.

3. Click on Assist ➤ Inquiry ➤ Area or enter **Area** ↵.

4. At the **<First point>/Entity/Add/Subtract:** prompt, pick the lower-left corner of the living room near coordinate 15'-0", 6'-10" (see Figure 14.1).

5. At the **Next point:** prompt, pick the upper-left corner of the kitchenette near coordinate 15'-0", 25'-5".

6. Continue to pick the corners (as shown in Figure 14.1) outlining the living room and entry area until you have come full circle to the first point. You don't need to pick the first point a second time.

7. When you complete the circuit, press ↵.

You will get the message **Area = 39570.00 sq in (274.7917 sq ft), Perimeter = 76'-0"**.

There is no limit to the number of points you can pick to define an area. This means you can obtain the areas of very complex shapes.

Using the Entity option, you can also select circles and polylines for area calculations. Using this option in conjunction with another AutoCAD utility called Bpoly, you can quickly get the area of a bounded space. You may recall from the discussion on Hatch patterns in *Chapter* 6 that a polyline is drawn when you use the Boundary Hatch function. Bpoly is a subset of Boundary Hatch. You'll remember that Boundary Hatch generates a polyline that conforms to the outline of a boundary. Bpoly generates the polyline without adding the hatch. Here's how to use it.

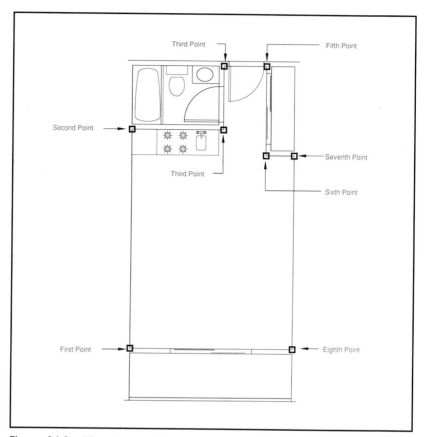

Figure 14.1: The points to select to find the living room and entry area

Bpoly ⏎

1. Set the layers so the doors and fixtures are turned off and the door headers are on.

2. Enter **Bpoly** ⏎. You get the Polyline creation dialog box (see Figure 14.2).

3. Click on the Pick Points button. The dialog box closes.

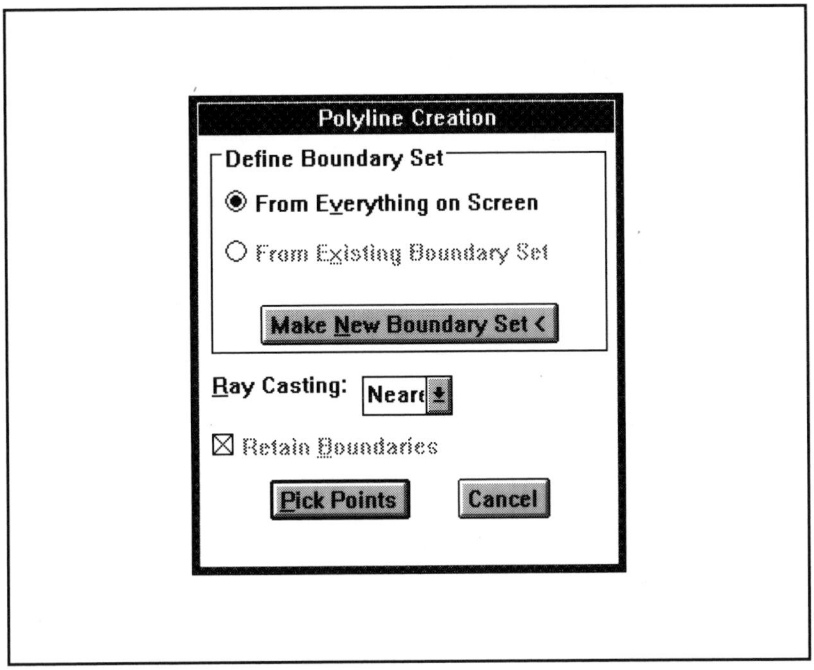

Figure 14.2:   The Polyline Creation dialog box of the Bpoly command

4. At the **Select internal point** prompt, click on the interior of the unit plan. You see the outline of the interior highlight (see Figure 14.3).

5. Press ↵. Nothing seems to have happened, but Bpoly has drawn an outline of the floor area using a polyline.

6. Click on any line that bounds the interior area. The boundary highlights, showing you where the new polyline occurs.

7. Click on Assist ➤ Inquiry ➤ Area or enter **Area** ↵, then enter **E** ↵ for the Entity option.

8. Click on the boundary. You get the same area message you got in the previous exercise.

> ▼ NOTE
>
> The polyline boundary is drawn on the current layer so it is visible when drawn over an object of a different color from the current layer.

The Bpoly command creates a polyline that conforms to the boundary of an area. This feature, combined with the ability of the Area command

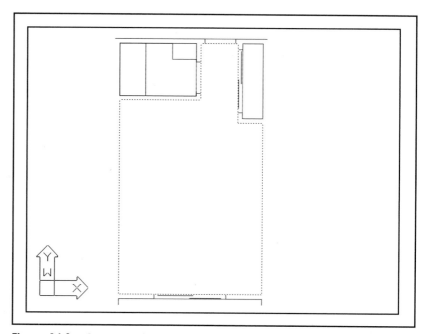

Figure 14.3: Once you select a point on the interior of the plan using Bpoly, an outline of the area is highlighted.

to find the area of a polyline, makes short work of area calculations. However, there is one caveat to using Bpoly: you must be sure the area you are trying to define has a continuous border. If there are any gaps at all, no matter how small, Bpoly will give you an error message.

FINDING THE AREA OF COMPLEX SHAPES

The Bpoly command works well if the area you want to find is not of a complex shape. But some shapes are so complex that you must also enlist the aid of the other Area command options. The following exercise guides you through the use of the Add, Subtract, and Entity options of the Area command. Using the Add and Subtract options, you can maintain a running total of several separate areas being calculated. This gives you flexibility in finding areas of complex shapes.

Next, you'll look at how you can keep a running tally of areas. In preparation for the next exercise, follow these steps.

1. Exit the Unit file, then open a new file named **Flange**. Don't bother to save changes in the Unit File.

2. Draw the object shown in Figure 14.4 (use the dimensions for reference only).

3. Use the Pedit command (as described in *Chapter 13*) to turn the arcs into polyline arcs before you start the AREA command.

Now study the shape to see what rectangular areas can be selected first. Figure 14.5 shows the areas that can be determined by selecting points. Then you must determine the areas to be subtracted from the area calculation. When AutoCAD calculates a polyline area, it automatically connects the endpoints. The entire area of the large arc in the flange will be calculated, including the area covered by the smaller

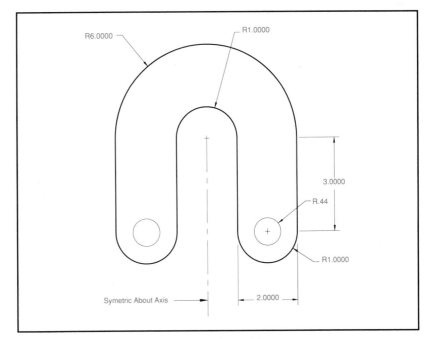

Figure 14.4: A flange to a fictitious mechanical device

concentric arc defining the inside of the flange (see Figure 14.6). This means that the area of the smaller arc will have to be subtracted from the overall area calculation.

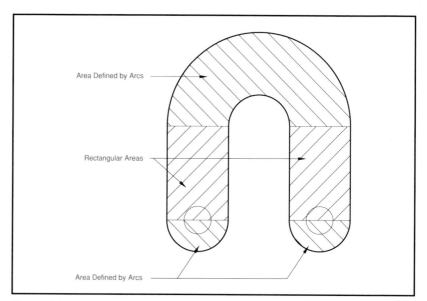

Figure 14.5: The flange broken down into types of areas

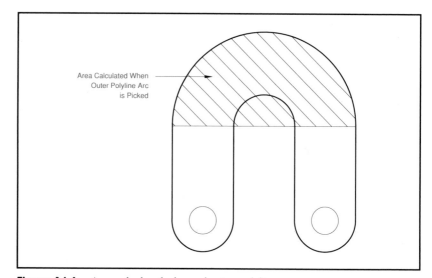

Figure 14.6: Area calculated when selecting polyline arcs

Finding the Gross Area

Once you have made these determinations, you can proceed to use the AREA command to find the gross area. First, take the areas of the rect-angular shapes.

Assist ➤ Inquiry ➤ Area

Add

Subtract

Entity

1. Click on Assist ➤ Inquiry ➤ Area to start the Area command again.

2. Enter **A** ↵ for the Add option.

3. Pick the four corners of one rectangle, then press ↵. This causes AutoCAD to calculate the area of that rectangle:

   ```
   Area = 6.0000, Perimeter = 10.0000
   Total area = 6.0000
   <First point> /Entity/Add/Subtract:
   ```

4. Pick the corners of the other rectangle and press ↵ again.

Once you have picked the second set of corners, the area value in the prompt changes:

```
Area = 6.0000, Perimeter = 10.0000
Total area = 12.0000
<First point> /Entity/Add/Subtract:
```

The new area is twice the first area calculated because AutoCAD adds the previously calculated area to the current area and both rectangular areas measured are the same (see Figure 14.7).

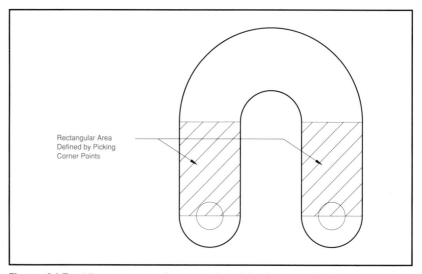

Figure 14.7: The two rectangular areas selected for the area calculation

You may have noticed that as you select points in step 3, the prompt reads **(ADD mode) Next point:**. This prompt helps remind you that you are in Add mode. Also, if you were to press ↵ without selecting a point, you would remain in the AREA command. AutoCAD assumes you want to continue to add to or subtract from your area count whenever you are in Add or Subtract mode. Whenever you enter either of these modes, AutoCAD maintains a running count of the areas you are selecting and leaves you in the AREA command so you can continue to add areas to or subtract them from your running total.

You are still in the Area command. Continue by adding the area defined by the polyline arcs.

1. Enter **E** ↵ to select the Entity option.

2. At the **<ADD mode> Select circle or polyline:** prompt, pick the outer polyline arcs (see Figure 14.8). As you pick the arcs, the running total area is displayed above the prompt, along with the area and perimeter of the object selected.

3. When you are done selecting the arcs, press ↵. This brings you back into the point-selection mode.

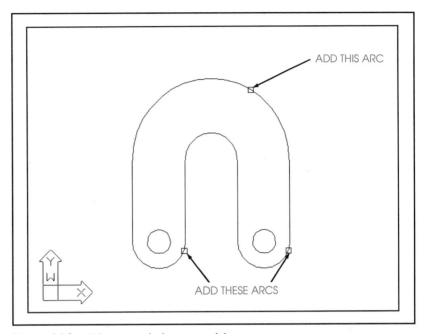

Figure 14.8:   Where to pick the outer polyline arcs

Subtracting Unwanted Areas from the Area Calculation

Now that you've got the gross area, you must subtract those areas from the current running total area that you don't want to include as part of the area count.

1. At the **First point/Entity/Add/Subtract:** prompt, enter **S** ↵ or pick Subtract from the Area menu.

2. At the **<First point>/Entity/Add:** prompt, pick the Entity option again, since you are going to subtract the area defined by one polyline arc and the circles.

3. At the **<SUBTRACT mode> Select circle or polyline:** prompt, pick the two circles and the arc defining the inside of the flange, as shown in Figure 14.9.

4. Once you are done, you see the final total area above the prompt line:

```
Total area = 26.4940
<SUBTRACT mode> Select circle or polyline:
```

5. To exit the AREA command, press ↵ twice.

You must remember that whenever you press ↵ during an area calculation, AutoCAD automatically connects the first and last points and returns the area calculated. You can then continue to select points or objects defining areas, but the additional areas will be calculated from the next point you pick.

This last exercise was intended to give you practice in using some of the other area command options. Looking back, you could have used the Bpoly command to first outline the main area of the part, then used the Area command's Add, Subtract, and Entity options to quickly get an area count. You could then have saved the Bpoly polyline for future reference or erased it.

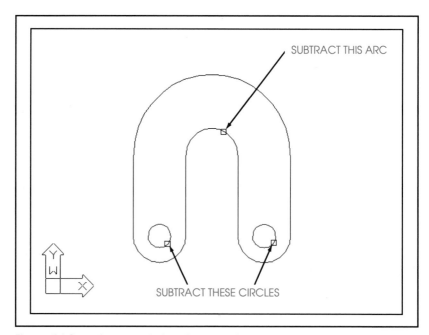

Figure 14.9: Where to pick the subtractive objects

In this example, you obtained the area of a mechanical object. However, the same process works for any type of area you want to calculate. It can be the area of a piece of property on a topographical map, or the area of a floor plan.

You can use the Entity option to find an irregular area like the one shown in Figure 14.10, as long as it is a polyline. Remember that if the polyline is not closed, the AREA command assumes the first and last points picked are connected and calculates the area accordingly.

Once you find the area of an object, you often want to record it somewhere. You could write it down in a project log book, but this is easy to overlook. Another way to store area information is to use *attributes*. For example, in a building project, you can create a block that contains attributes for room number, room area, and date since the room area was last taken. You might make the area and date attributes invisible so only the room number appears. This block would be inserted into every room. Once you find the area, you can easily add it to your block attribute with the DDATTE command. In fact, such a block could be used with any drawing in which you wished to store area data.

▼ TIP

Appendix A lists an AutoLISP program that lets you easily record area data in a drawing file.

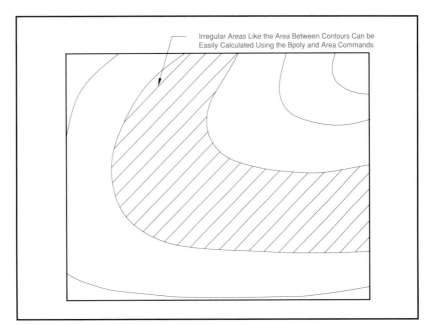

Figure 14.10: The site plan with an area to be calculated

FINDING OUT ABOUT THE DRAWING STATUS

When you begin to work on large projects with others, it becomes increasingly important to keep track of a drawing's setup. The STATUS
command enables you to obtain some general information about the
drawing you are working on, such as the base point, current mode settings, and workspace or computer memory use. STATUS can be especially helpful when you edit a drawing someone else has worked on,
because you may want to identify and change settings for your own style
of working. When you pick Status from the Assist ➤ Inquiry menu, you
get a list like the one shown in Figure 14.11.

Here is a brief description of what each item means.

154 entities in C:\ACAD\Drawing: First, the number of entities or objects is listed.

Modelspace limits are X: Tells you the coordinates of the
Modelspace limits. (See *Chapter 3* for more details on limits.)

Modelspace uses: Indicates the area the drawing occupies. This
would be equivalent to the extents of the drawing.

**Over: If shown, means that part of it is outside the limit
boundary.

Display shows: Indicates the area covered by the current view.

Insertion base, Snap resolution, and Grid spacing lines: Tell
you what the current default values are for those mode settings.

Current space: Indicates whether you are in Modelspace or
Paperspace.

Current layer: Indicates the current default layer.

Current color: Indicates the color new objects are assigned.

Current linetype: Indicates the linetype new objects are
assigned.

Current elevation/thickness: Indicates the current default Z
coordinate for new objects, plus the default thickness of objects.
These are both 3D-related settings (see *Chapter 15* for details).

```
543 entities in E:\ACAD\UNIT
Model space limits are X:     0'-0"    Y:     0'-0"   (Off)
                        X:    44'-0"    Y:    34'-0"
Model space uses        X:    14'-7"    Y:     2'-5"
                        X:    29'-5"    Y:    31'-3"
Display shows           X:     0'-0"    Y:     0'-0"
                        X: 46'-11 1/8"  Y:    34'-0"
Insertion base is       X:    15'-0"    Y:     2'-5"    Z:     0'-0"
Snap resolution is      X:     0'-1"    Y:     0'-1"
Grid spacing is         X:     1'-0"    Y:     1'-0"

Current space:        Model space
Current layer:        WALL
Current color:        250
Current linetype:     BYLAYER -- CONTINUOUS
Current elevation:       0'-0"   thickness:     0'-0"
Fill on  Grid off  Ortho off  Qtext off  Snap on  Tablet off
Object snap modes:    None
Free disk: 5865472 bytes
```

Figure 14.11:   The status screen

Fill, Grid, Ortho, Qtext, Snap, and Tablet: Indicate the status of these options.

Object snap modes: Indicates the current default object snap setting.

Free disk: Tells you how much space you have left on your hard disk for AutoCAD's temporary files.

For more information on memory use, see *Appendix A*.

KEEPING TRACK OF TIME

The TIME command allows you to keep track of the time spent on a drawing for billing purposes or to analyze time spent on a project. You can also use TIME to check the current time and find out when the drawing was created and most recently edited. Because the AutoCAD timer uses the time set on your computer, you must be sure the time is set correctly in DOS.

To access the TIME command, enter **Time** ↵ at the command prompt, or select INQUIRY ➤ TIME from the root menu; you get a message like the one in Figure 14.12.

The first three lines tell you the current date and time, the date and time the drawing was created, and the last time the drawing was saved or ended. The fourth line shows the total time spent on a drawing from its creation. The elapsed timer allows you to time an activity, such as changing the width of all the walls in a floor plan or redesigning a piece of machinery. You can turn the elapsed timer on or off, or reset it, by entering **on, off,** or **reset** at the prompt shown as the last line of the message. The timer will not show any time spent on a drawing between the last time it is saved and the time a QUIT command is issued. The last line tells you when the next automatic save will be.

```
Command: time

Current time:              20 Jul 1993 at 14:15:45.390
Times for this drawing:
  Created:                 16 Jul 1993 at 08:51:41.930
  Last updated:            19 Jul 1993 at 14:33:00.130
  Total editing time:      0 days 02:24:29.390
  Elapsed timer (on):      0 days 02:24:29.390
  Next automatic save in:  0 days 01:58:00.700

Display/ON/OFF/Reset:
```

Figure 14.12: The Time screen

GETTING INFORMATION
DURING ANOTHER COMMAND

If you've been working through the tutorial, you'll have noticed that once in a while I'll mention a system variable in conjunction with a command. You can check the status or change the setting of a system variable while you are in the middle of another command. To do this, you simply enter the system variable preceded by an apostrophe.

For example, if you have started to draw a line, and you suddenly decide you need to rotate your cursor 45°, you can do the following.

1. At the **To point** prompt, enter 'snapang.

2. At the **New value for SNAPANG** prompt, you can enter a new cursor angle. Once you have entered an angle value, you are returned to the LINE command with the cursor in its new orientation.

You can also recall information like the last area or distance calculated by AutoCAD. Since the Area system variable duplicates the name of the Area command, you must enter 'Setvar ↵ Area ↵ to read the last area calculation. Setvar is a command that lets you list all the system variables and their status, as well as access each system variable individually.

The system variables give you direct access to detailed information about your drawing. They also let you fine-tune your drawing and editing activities. You may want to review *Appendix D* to familiarize yourself with all the system variables available. You certainly don't have to memorize them all at once; just be aware that they are available.

MANAGING FILES IN AUTOCAD

As your projects become more complex and your library of drawings and symbols expands, you will find yourself devoting a good deal of effort to organizing your files. Backing up, deleting, renaming, or even just searching for files begins to take more of your time. Fortunately, AutoCAD offers a variety of ways to let you perform your file housekeeping with the minimum of hassle.

USING THE FILE UTILITIES

You can perform a series of simple file operations directly from Auto-CAD by clicking on File ➤ Utilities. You see the dialog box shown in Figure 14.13.

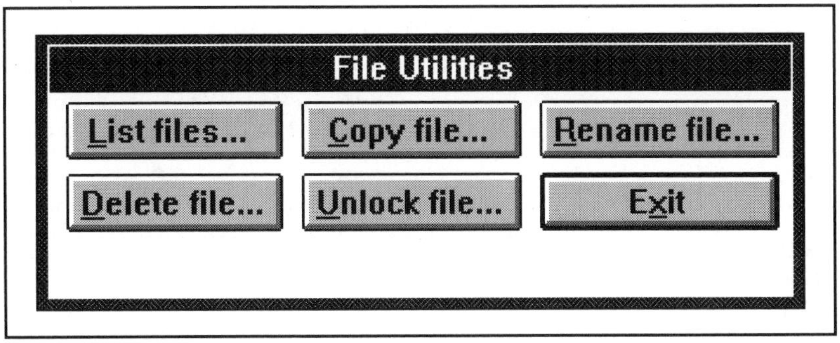

Figure 14.13: The File Utilities dialog box

The function of each of the buttons in the File Utilities dialog box is pretty self-explanatory. When you click on one of these buttons, you get the standard File dialog box.

List files simply lists the files in any directory. You can also filter the list using the Pattern input box.

Copy file copies a file by selecting its new location using the directory list, then entering a new name in the input box.

Rename file renames a file by first letting you locate the source file using the two list boxes, then entering a new file name in the file name input box.

Delete file deletes a file. A warning message appears asking if you are sure you want to delete the file.

Unlock file unlocks locked drawing or password files (see next section).

▼ NOTE

Drawing files are not the only files that are locked. Nearly all types of AutoCAD files, from menu files to font files, are locked while they are being read from disk. They are unlocked, however, once file access has been completed and the file in question has been loaded.

UNLOCKING FILES ON A NETWORK

In a network, there is a potential for more than one person to access a file at the same time. If more than one person tried to edit the same file at the same time, it could be disastrous. For this reason, AutoCAD provides file locking. Whenever anyone opens a file to edit, AutoCAD creates a small lock file that exists only during the time the drawing file is being edited; once the file is closed, the lock file is erased. If you try to edit this drawing at the same time someone else is editing it, AutoCAD will detect the lock file and return this message:

```
Waiting for file: Plan1.DWG
Locked by John Doe at 11:55 am on 12/25/92
Press Ctrl-C to cancel
```

AutoCAD continuously attempts to access the file every five seconds until either the drawing file is closed by the other person or you cancel the operation by pressing **Ctrl-C**. If you cancel, you get the message:

```
Access denied: Plan1.DWG
Press RETURN to continue:
```

You must then wait your turn to access this file.

Sometimes, however, a lock file may exist even though its associated drawing file has been closed. This can occur when someone abnormally aborts an editing session by using the **Ctrl-Alt-Del** key combination. When an orphaned lock file exists, you must manually unlock a file by using File ➤ Utility ➤ Unlock file. You can also use DOS to delete the lock file. You can recognize a lock file by its extension. Table 14.1 shows a list of lock file extensions and their AutoCAD file counterparts.

If you are using AutoCAD on a network, be certain that the file you are trying to load is not currently being edited before you try to unlock it.

LINKING ATTRIBUTES TO SPREADSHEETS WITH DDE

If you use AutoCAD with Excel or Lotus 1-2-3 for Windows, you can export and link attribute data quickly using a feature of Windows called Dynamic Data Exchange (DDE). In simple terms, DDE lets programs communicate with each other and share data. In theory, you can use DDE to link AutoCAD with virtually any other Windows program. In practice, you need a C programmer to write the appropriate AutoCAD

Table 14.1: AutoCAD File Extensions and Their Lock File Counterparts

FILE DESCRIPTION	STANDARD EXTENSION	LOCK FILE EXTENSION
Drawing backup	.BAK	.BKK
AutoCAD configuration	.CFG	.CFK
Drawing	.DWG	.DWK
Binary data exchange	.DXB	.DBK
DXF drawing interchange	.DXF	.DFK
Attribute data in DXF format	.DXX	.DXK
AutoShade filmroll	.FLM	.FLK
Iges drawing interchange	.IGS	.IGK
Line type definition	.LIN	.LIK
Compiled menu	.MNX	MNK
Converted old drawing	.OLD	.OLK
Plot configuration parameters	.PCP	.PCK
Plot file	.PLT	.PLK
Login file	.PWD	.PWK
Shape and font	.SHX	.SXK

Table 14.1:   AutoCAD File Extensions and Their Lock File Counterparts (continued)

FILE DESCRIPTION	STANDARD EXTENSION	LOCK FILE EXTENSION
Slides	.SLD	.SDK
Attribute template	.TXT	.TXK
Xref log	.XLG	.XLK

ADS application to facilitate DDE links. Fortunately, Autodesk supplies AutoCAD with a sample ADS application that allows you to link AutoCAD drawings with Excel and Lotus 1-2-3. The following exercise shows you how you can use DDE to create an Excel spreadsheet from your attribute data. You'll use the attribute data you created in Chapter 10.

▼ NOTE

The Work File Input box should contain the name of an existing spreadsheet.

1. While in AutoCAD, open the Plan file.

2. Switch to the Program Manager and start Excel, then arrange the Excel and AutoCAD windows so you can view both programs at the same time.

3. Go to the AutoCAD window and click on Edit ➤ DDE ➤ Dialog. You will see the DDE Initiate Conversation dialog box (see Figure 14.14). The DDE Application input box should show *Excel* for Microsoft Excel, or *123w* for Lotus 1-2-3 for Windows. The Work File input box should show the name of an existing spreadsheet file or default file name. You can use the name Sheet1 for Excel. Finally, be sure the Automatic update box is checked.

4. Optionally, you can enter the drive, directory, and path name and program file name for Excel in the Command Line input box at the bottom of the dialog box. This will ensure that

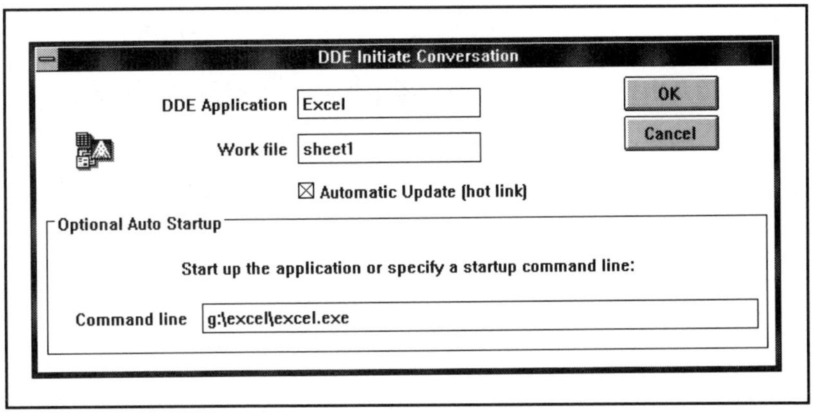

Figure 14.14: The DDE Initiate Conversation dialog box

Excel will be opened whenever you export data from AutoCAD.

5. Click on OK to close the dialog box.

6. Click on File ➤ DDE ➤ Attr Filter 1. This tells AutoCAD to export only the Attribute data and tag name from your drawing.

7. Click on File ➤ DDE ➤ Export Drawing. The Attribute data will appear in the Excel spreadsheet.

The spreadsheet contains all the attribute data from your drawing and some additional columns of data. Each row contains the attribute data for one block. The attribute values are in columns adjacent to the attribute tag names.

You will notice two additional columns for each attribute value. These columns are the entity handles for these attributes. Entity handles allow AutoCAD to identify the exact attribute in the drawing that corresponds to the information in the spreadsheet. For this reason, you will want to leave these two columns alone.

This exercise demonstrates how you can quickly export attribute data to a spreadsheet without intermediate steps. In addition to quick export of data, DDE allows you to update data across the two programs. In the following exercise, you will make changes to the attribute values in your AutoCAD drawing by changing spreadsheet cells.

1. Find the row that shows room number 116. Room numbers should appear in column H.

2. Locate the Material designation in this row and change Wood to Metal. You may have to scroll to the right to find this column.

3. Go to AutoCAD, then click on Modify ➤ Text ➤ Attribute, then click on the entry door to unit 116. Notice that the value for the door material now shows Metal.

4. Return to Excel, click on File ➤ Exit. At the Save file dialog box, click on No. You'll see a message warning you that a DDE link exists. Click OK.

If you make changes to the spreadsheet file independent from the AutoCAD session, you can later update the AutoCAD file to reflect those changes by re-establishing the link from AutoCAD, then using File ➤ DDE ➤ Update Drawing. To update the spreadsheet from the drawing, perform the same steps in the exercise above, using the Export Drawing options again.

OTHER DDE OPTIONS

You've seen how you can quickly export attribute data using the DDE feature of Windows and AutoCAD. Table 14.2 describes the other options available on the Files ➤ DDE menu.

Here, you were able to make a link to a program using tools available within AutoCAD. If you are willing to do a little more work, you can accomplish much more with DDE. Chapter 21 describes how you can further enhance your use of AutoCAD through DDE.

Table 14.2: Other DDE Options on the File ➤ DDE menu

OPTION	FUNCTION
Export SSet	Exports a selected set of objects to the spreadsheet.
Export Blocks	Exports block information.
Export Drawing	Exports the entire drawing.
Import Changes	Imports changes made in the spreadsheet. Use this when the Automatic Update option in the DDE dialog box is left unchecked.
Dialog	Brings up the DDE Initiate Conversation dialog box. This dialog box lets you set the spreadsheet program, Excel or 123W, the file name, and the location of the program file.
No Filters	Exports all data to the spreadsheet in DXF format.
Attr Filter 1	Exports only Attribute data including tag names.
Attr Filter 2	Exports only attribute data excluding tag names.
Unload DDE	Unloads the DDE ADS application.

LINKING AND EMBEDDING AUTOCAD DRAWINGS IN OTHER PROGRAM DOCUMENTS

Windows offers a feature called Object Linking and Embedding, or OLE. OLE lets you include documents from one application in a document of another application. For example, you could include an AutoCAD file within a word processing document. The AutoCAD file would appear as a drawing in the word processor. When you click on that icon, AutoCAD will start up and open the file.

▼ TIP

When you use Object Embed, the pasted drawing is not dependent on an external AutoCAD drawing file. You can give the document with the embedded drawing to anyone who has AutoCAD release 12 for Windows and they can edit the pasted drawing themselves. When Object Link is used, an associated drawing file must be present to edit the pasted drawing. You can, however, paste different views from a linked drawing.

By *linking* or *embedding* AutoCAD files in a word processor document, you can include descriptive text with a drawing, and ensure that the drawing is up to date. The person reading the file can then read the instructions, then double click on the drawing to open and edit the file. Such a tool can be a great aid in managing projects and communicating ideas to others.

To see how you can link an AutoCAD file to another document, take the following steps.

1. Open an AutoCAD file.

2. Click on Edit ➤ Copy Link, then select the portion of the drawing you wish to include in the other document.

3. Open the Windows Write application.

4. Click on Edit ➤ Paste Special.

5. At the dialog box, click on AutoCAD from the list, then click on the Paste button. The drawing appears in the Write document.

You now have a link between your Write document and the AutoCAD file. With Copy Link, any changes made to the drawing will be detected by the word processor and you will be given the option to update the pasted version of the drawing. If you use Edit ➤ Copy Embed to export your drawing, you will be able to open the AutoCAD file by double clicking on the pasted drawing from within the word processor document. Of course, you can also add text either above or below the drawing to describe its contents or whatever.

If you prefer, you can also use the Object Packager application that comes with Windows (see Figure 14.15) to embed drawings into other documents. See your Windows manual for more on this.

OLE offers many other functions and operates in a variety of ways. Not every Windows program supports OLE (and each program varies the way it implements OLE). As you have seen, the Windows Write application supports OLE as well as Word for Windows and Microsoft Excel.

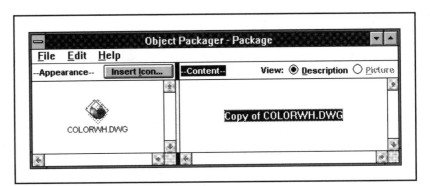

Figure 14.15: The Object Packager application

EXCHANGING CAD FILES

Eventually, you will have to exchange your AutoCAD drawings with someone who has a different CAD program. You have two main vehicles for doing this, the .DXF and .IGS file formats. This section discusses how you go about reading and writing files in these formats.

USING THE .DXF FILE FORMAT

A .DXF file is a file containing all the information needed to reconstruct a drawing. It is often used to exchange drawings created with different programs. Many micro-CAD programs, including some 3D perspective programs, can generate or read files in .DXF format. You may want to use a 3D program to view your drawing in a perspective view, or you may just have a consultant who uses a different CAD program that accepts .DXF files. There are many 3D rendering programs that read .DXF files on both the IBM PC and compatibles and on Apple Macintosh computers. Most 2D drafting programs also read and write .DXF files.

To export your current drawing as a .DXF file, do the following.

1. Click on File ➤ Import/Export ➤ DXF Out or enter **Dxfont** ↵. A file dialog box appears.

2. Enter the name you wish to give your .DXF file in the File name input box.

3. Click on **OK**.

4. At the **Enter decimal places of accuracy (0 to 16)/Entities/Binary <6>:** prompt, press ⏎ to accept the default or enter a value to increase or decrease the decimal accuracy of your .DXF file.

You have two other options at step 4. You can specify that your .DXF file be written in a Binary format by entering **B** ⏎ in step 4. This helps make the file smaller, but some other CAD programs are unable to read the binary version of .DXF files.

You also have the option to select specific objects for export by entering **E** ⏎ at the prompt in step 4. You are then prompted to select objects. Once you are done, you see the **Enter decimal places of accuracy** prompt again.

To import .DXF files, follow these steps.

1. Click on Import/Export ➤ DXF In or enter **Dxfin** ⏎. A file dialog box appears.

2. Using the dialog box, locate and select the .DXF file you wish to import.

3. Double-click on the file name. The .DXF file will begin importing.

If the import drawing is large, AutoCAD may take several minutes.

USING THE IGES FORMAT

▼ **TIP**

If you need to convert a release 12 drawing to a release 9 or 10 format, you can use Igesout to export your drawing, then use Igesin in release 9 or 10. Unfortunately, you will lose layer names and fonts with this method.

IGES, which stands for Initial Graphics Exchange Specifications, is perhaps the most prevalent format for CAD data exchange (it is even described in the U.S. National Bureau of Standards document NBSIR 88-3813).

There are several versions of the IGES format. AutoCAD release 12 supports IGES 4.0 and can read files that conform to IGES versions as early as 2.0. In the event that you need to exchange data with a CAD system that uses IGES, you can select File ➤ Import/Export ➤ IGES In or IGES Out. These options are simple and straightforward to use, so I won't go into a lengthy description of them here. Just be aware that AutoCAD supports the IGES format in case you need to create such a file.

USING AUTOCAD IN DESKTOP PUBLISHING

As you probably know, AutoCAD is a natural for creating line art, and because of its popularity, most desktop-publishing programs are designed to import AutoCAD drawings in one form or another. Those who employ desktop-publishing software to generate user manuals or other technical documents will probably want to be able to use AutoCAD drawings in their work. In this section, we will discuss ways to output AutoCAD drawings for use by the two most popular desktop-publishing programs available for the IBM PC: PageMaker and Ventura.

▼ TIP

If you are a circuit board designer or drafter, you will want to use the PostScript Out option to output your layout to linotronic typesetting devices. This will save time and file size since this option converts AutoCAD entities into true PostScript descriptions.

EXPORTING DRAWINGS TO PAGEMAKER AND VENTURA

There are two methods for transferring AutoCAD drawings to Page-Maker and Ventura. Since they each accept both HPGL and PostScript files, you can either have AutoCAD plot to a file using an HPGL plotter configuration, or you can use the PostScript Out option found under the File menu. Since these two formats are quite popular, most other desktop-publishing packages will support one or other of these formats. First, let's look at how you export an HPGL file:

HPGL Output

1. Configure your plotter setting for a Hewlett-Packard plotter (HPGL). Just about any of the Hewlett-Packard plotter options will work.

2. Click on File ➤ Plot, then use the Device and Default Selection dialog box to set the default plotter to Hewlett-Packard.

3. PLOT your drawing to a file.

Another method for file transfer is to use the Encapsulated PostScript (EPS) format. If you use PostScript fonts in your drawing, then the PostScript output file will contain the proper code to utilize the true PostScript fonts in your output device.

PostScript Output

1. Click on File ➤ Import/Export ➤ PostScript Out. A file dialog box appears, allowing you to enter the name of the PostScript output file.

2. Once you enter a name, you are asked what to plot. Enter the option you desire.

3. At the **Include a screen preview image in the file? (None/EPSI/TIFF) <None>:** prompt, press ↵.

4. At the **Size units (Inches or Millimeters) <Inches>:** prompt, press ↵.

5. At the **Plotted Inches=Drawing Units or Fit or ? <Fit>:** prompt, press ↵. You then see the following list:

STANDARD VALUES FOR OUTPUT SIZE

Size	Width	Height
A	8.0000	10.5000
B	10.0000	16.0000
C	16.0000	21.0000
D	21.0000	33.0000
E	33.0000	43.0000
F	28.0000	40.0000
G	11.0000	90.0000
H	28.0000	143.0000
J	34.0000	176.0000

**STANDARD VALUES FOR
OUTPUT SIZE**

Size	Width	Height
K	40.0000	143.0000
A4	7.8000	11.2000
A3	10.7000	15.6000
A2	15.6000	22.4000
A1	22.4000	32.2000
A0	32.2000	45.9000

6. At the **Enter the Size or Width,Height (in Inches) <A>:** prompt, enter the appropriate sheet size. Chances are, if you are importing AutoCAD documents into PageMaker or Ventura, you'll want the A size, or you can enter a custom width and height at this prompt.

7. AutoCAD displays the message

   Effective plotting area: *X.XX* wide by *Y.YY* high

   where *X.XX* and *Y.YY* are the width and height of the output image. AutoCAD will take a moment to generate the file, then return to the command prompt.

8. If you choose to enter EPSI or TIFF at step 2 above, where you are asked if you want a preview image, you will get the following prompt:

   Screen preview image size (128x128 is standard)?
   (128/256/512) <128>:

You can enter a value for the image size in pixels. The preview image is somewhat crude, but it is only provided to allow easy identification of the art when it is pasted into a document. For this reason, you may not want to increase the size from the default unless the image cannot be identified easily using the default value.

IMPORTING HPGL AND POSTSCRIPT FILES INTO PAGEMAKER AND VENTURA

HPGL or PostScript plot files can be easily imported into PageMaker 4.0 or Ventura 4.0. PageMaker users must first ensure that the HPGL and PostScript import drivers have been installed. You can then use the File ➤ Place option to place either of these two format drawings into your documents.

Ventura users must use the File ➤ Load Text/Picture... option, then, at the dialog box, click on the Line Art radio button. You can then choose either HPGL or PostScript from the list box. Once you've chosen a file format, you see a File dialog box. You can then locate and load the plot file. If you select HPGL, you will see an additional dialog box asking you for the Hewlett-Packard plotter model number, Pen widths, and drawing size.

HPGL plot files will appear accurately in the document of either program. PostScript files, however will appear as a gray box in PageMaker and a box with an X through it in Ventura. If you use the TIFF preview image option while plotting the PostScript file, a crude preview image will appear in place of the box, but the actual output from your printer will be of high quality. In fact, if you use PostScript fonts in your drawing, your output will contain the same high-quality fonts you specified.

EXPORTING TIFF, GIF, PCX, AND FAX FILES

In *Chapter 11*, I described ways to import TIFF, GIF, PCX, and Post-Script files into AutoCAD. And you've just seen how you can export PostScript files. You can also export to these formats as well as to a wide variety of other raster format files, including FAX group III.

There are numerous reasons for wanting output in one of these raster formats. You may want to use a raster format for your desktop-publishing program, instead of the two options just described. Or you may want to use one of your drawings in a paint or rendering program, perhaps to add a texture map to 3D Studio for example. If you're putting together a presentation, you may want to have slides made of some of your CAD drawings. If you are producing a multimedia presentation, you will most

▼
■
■
■
■

Transferring AutoCAD Drawings with the Clipboard

If you're in a hurry, you can use the Windows Clipboard to transfer AutoCAD graphics into other Windows programs. You have the option to transfer graphics in either bitmap or vector format. The Bitmap format is faster but only offers mediocre quality. The vector format is slower but produces results similar to the HPGL file transfer method described earlier.

To transfer AutoCAD graphics to the Clipboard in the bitmap format, click on Edit ➤ Copy Image. The cursor will change to a smaller cross. Use this plus-shaped cursor to window the area you want to place in the Clipboard.

To transfer AutoCAD graphics to the Clipboard in a vector format, click on Edit ➤ Copy Vector. The AutoCAD prompt will display the familiar **Select objects** prompt. You can then select the objects you want to copy to the Clipboard.

Once you've transferred the AutoCAD graphics to the Clipboard, you can then use the Edit ➤ Paste option in any other Windows program to add the graphics to your desktop-published or word-processed document.

likely prefer to use raster images. With AutoCAD's raster output capabilities, you won't have to resort to an intermediate translator to obtain raster files. The following describes how to access this feature:

1. Click on File ➤ Configure.

2. As the prompt at the bottom of the screen suggests, press ↵ to get through the opening screen.

3. At the configuration list menu, enter **5** ↵ to select the Configure Plotter option.

4. At the Plotter configuration menu, enter **1** ↵ to add a plotter to your configuration.

5. Press ↵ twice. You will get a list of plotter options. Enter the number that corresponds with the item labeled

   Raster file export ADI 4.2 - by Autodesk

   You will see the following list

   Supported models:
   1. 320 × 200 (CGA/MCGA Colour)
   2. 640 × 200 (CGA Monochrome)
   3. 640 × 350 (EGA)
   4. 640 × 400
   5. 640 × 480 (VGA)
   6. 720 × 540
   7. 800 × 600
   8. 1024 × 768
   9. 1152 × 900 (Sun standard)
   10. 1600 × 1280 (Sun hi-res)
   11. User-defined
   Enter selection, 1 to 11 <1>:

6. Enter the number corresponding to the resolution you want. Next, you'll see the following list:

   1. GIF (CompuServe Graphics Interchange Format)
   2. X Window dump (xwd compatible)
   3. Jef Poskanzer's Portable Bitmap Toolkit Formats
   4. Microsoft Windows Device-independent Bitmap (.BMP)
   5. TrueVision TGA Format
   6. Z-Soft PCX Format
   7. Sun Rasterfile
   8. Flexible Image Transfer System (FITS)
   9. PostScript image
   10. TIFF (Tag Image File Format)
   11. FAX Image (Group 3 Encoding)
   12. Amiga IFF / ILBM Format

7. Enter the number that corresponds to the type of file you want to be able to export. A series of prompts will then ask you questions pertaining to the option you choose.

8. When you are done answering the prompts, you will return to AutoCAD's drawing editor. You can now select the raster format at the Plot Configuration dialog box.

The range of raster output options is quite comprehensive. Chances are, if you need raster output from AutoCAD, at least one of the options from the previous list should fill your needs. The FAX Image format is perhaps the most interesting option, offering the ability to plot to a remote location via a fax machine.

IF YOU WANT TO EXPERIMENT...

If you use a desktop-publishing program in your work, you may want to experiment with different ways of exporting AutoCAD files to it. Add a Hewlett-Packard plotter to your plotter configuration, then try the following exercises.

1. Open the Unit plan.

2. Start the PLOT command.

3. Click on Device and Default Selection, then click on the Hewlett-Packard plotter listed.

4. Check the Plot to file check box.

5. Use the Size button in the Paper Size and Orientation group to set the size to **11×17**.

6. Enter **1/2"** in the Plotted Inches input box and **1'** in the Drawing Units box.

7. Accept the default settings for the rest of the plotter prompts.

8. When the plotting is done, EXIT AutoCAD.

9. Next, open your desktop-publishing program. Start a new file called **Unitdtp**.

If you are using PageMaker:

1. Pick Place from the Files menu.

2. At the Place File dialog box, enter the appropriate path and file name to access the Unit plot file.

3. You may get another dialog box asking for a file format type. If this happens, pick HPGL from the list of formats.

4. When your cursor changes to an icon reflecting the type of drawing file you are importing, pick the upper-right corner of your page, and your drawing will appear. You may have to resize it to fit on the page.

If you are using Ventura:

1. Pick Load Text/Pictures from the Files menu.

2. When the Load Text/Pictures dialog box appears, pick the Line-Art radio button. The dialog box changes to show several new options.

3. Pick the HPGL button then pick **OK**.

4. At the Open Files dialog box, go to the directory where the Unit plot file is stored, then pick the file name from the list.

5. When the Ventura main screen returns, you will see the plot file listed in the Files List box. Double-click the name, and the drawing appears in your current frame.

Now try adding a few notes to your drawing, and then print out the file.

SUMMARY

In this chapter, you have seen how AutoCAD allows you to access information ranging from the areas of objects to information from other programs. You may never use some of these features, but knowing they are there may help you when you are trying to solve a production problem.

You've just completed Part III of our tutorial. If you've followed the tutorial from the beginning, this is where I start handing out diplomas. You have reached expert status in 2D drawing and should be competent enough to tackle any drawing project thrown at you. You need only to log in some time on some real projects to round out your experience. From now on, you really won't need to follow the book in order. If you're interested in 3D, you can continue to Part IV, where you'll get thorough instructions on 3D drawing and imaging with AutoCAD. Otherwise, you can skip to Part V to become a full-fledged AutoCAD power user.

Also, the appendices are packed with information you can refer to if you have specific questions or problems. Of course, you can use the whole book as a ready reference to answer questions as they arise or to refresh your memory about specific commands.

Good luck!

PART FOUR

MODELING
■
AND
■
IMAGING IN 3D

While 2D drafting is the workhorse application, AutoCAD's 3D capabilities give you a chance to expand your ideas and look at them in a new light. After using 3D to help develop your designs, you may find it difficult to imagine what you would do without it. Part Four gives you control of AutoCAD's powerful 3D capabilities by taking you through them step by step. You will discover how 3D can help you and your co-workers visualize your ideas and turn them into successful presentations for your clients.

15

INTRODUCING 3D

FAST TRACK

605 ▶ To extrude 2D lines to form vertical surfaces

Click on Modify ➤ Change ➤ Properties then select the objects you want to extrude. At the dialog box, enter the height you want in the Thickness input box, then click on **OK**.

609 ▶ To view your drawing in 3D

Click on View ➤ Set View ➤ Viewpoint ➤ Set Vpoint, then enter −1,−1,1. This will place your viewpoint below and to the left of your drawing, looking downward at your drawing at a 35° angle. You can then use View ➤ Set View ➤ Viewpoint ➤ Set Vpoint to make adjustments to your view.

623 ▶ To turn your wire frame view into a hidden line view

Set up the 3D view you want, then click on Render ➤ Hide.

624 ▶ To shade your view to show volume

Set up the 3D view you want, then click on Render ➤ Shade. If you want to shade the surfaces so they have more depth, enter **Shadedge** ↵ 1 ↵ before you shade your view.

630 ▶ To select points in 3D space relative to existing geometry

When prompted to pick a point, enter **.xy** ↵, then select an Osnap mode. Click on the geometry you want to locate the point in the XY axes. You are then free to specify a Z coordinate either by using the Osnap modes again or by entering a Z value. You can also use this method to align points to other geometry in 2D.

631 ▶ To move or copy objects in the Z axis

Issue the Move or Copy command, select the objects you want to edit, then press ↵. At the **Base point** prompt, pick any point. At the **Second point** prompt, enter a relative Cartesian coordinate and include the Z coordinate (@0,0,8′, for example). You can also use grips to copy and move objects in the Z axis, or, if 3D geometry already exists in the drawing, you can use Osnap overrides to grab 3D geometry to indicate displacements.

637 ▶ To draw basic 3D shapes such as spheres, wedges, and cones

Click on Draw ➤ 3D Surfaces ➤ 3D Objects. Click on the desired object from the icon menu then click on **OK**; then answer the set of prompts that follow. The prompts help describe the shape and size of the object.

637 ▶ To convert a 3D view into a 2D drawing

Use the File ➤ Configure option to add a PostScript plotter configuration. Set up your 3D view, then plot it to a file using the new PostScript plotter configuration. Open a new file, then use File ➤ Import/Export ➤ PostScript In to import the Plot file.

641 ▶ To save a hidden line or shaded view for later retrieval

Enter **Mslide** ↵ at the command prompt after you have created the hidden line removal or shaded view. At the file dialog box, enter the name for your saved view. Your view becomes a slide file you can retrieve at any time while in AutoCAD. (You cannot, however, edit a slide.)

Viewing an object in three dimensions helps you get a sense of its true shape and form. It also helps you conceptualize the design, which in turn allows you to make better design decisions. Finally, it helps you communicate your ideas to those who may not be familiar with the plans, sections, and side views of your design.

A further advantage to drawing in three dimensions is that you can derive 2D drawings from your 3D model that might otherwise take considerably more time with standard 2D drawing methods. For example, you could model a mechanical part in 3D then quickly derive its top, front, and right side views using the techniques discussed in this chapter.

AutoCAD allows you to turn any drawing you create into a 3D model by changing the properties of the objects that make it up. AutoCAD does this through a combination of two types of objects: *extruded 2D objects* and *3dfaces*.

In this chapter, you will use AutoCAD's 3D capabilities to see what your studio apartment looks like from various angles.

> **▼ NOTE**
>
> A *3dface* is an object created by AutoCAD that acts like a three-dimensional surface.

CREATING A 3D DRAWING

One way AutoCAD creates three-dimensional forms is by *extruding* two-dimensional objects. This means that to draw a cube, you first draw a square using lines or polylines, then extrude the square by giving them a *thickness* (see Figure 15.1). This thickness is a value given as a z coordinate. Imagine that the screen's drawing area is the drawing surface. A 0 z coordinate is on that surface. A z coordinate greater than 0 is a position closer to you and above that surface. Figure 15.2 illustrates this point.

When you draw an object with thickness, you don't see the thickness until you view the drawing from a different angle. This is because normally your view is perpendicular to the imagined drawing surface. At that angle, you cannot see the thickness of an object because it projects toward you, just as a sheet of paper looks like a line when viewed from one end. To view an object's thickness, you must change the angle at which you view your drawing.

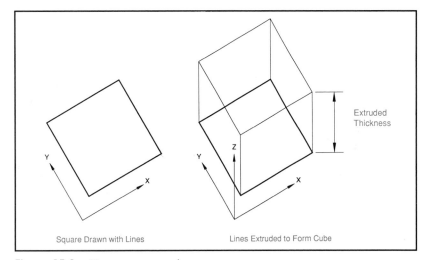

Figure 15.1:   How to create a cube

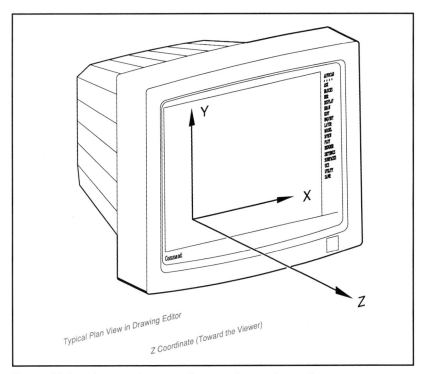

Figure 15.2:   The z coordinate in relation to the x and y coordinates

You can also set AutoCAD so that everything you draw has an *elevation*. Normally, you draw on the imagined surface, but you can set the z coordinate for your drawing elevation so that whatever you draw is above that surface. An object with an elevation value other than 0 rests not on the imagined drawing surface but above it—or below, if the z coordinate is a negative value (see Figure 15.3).

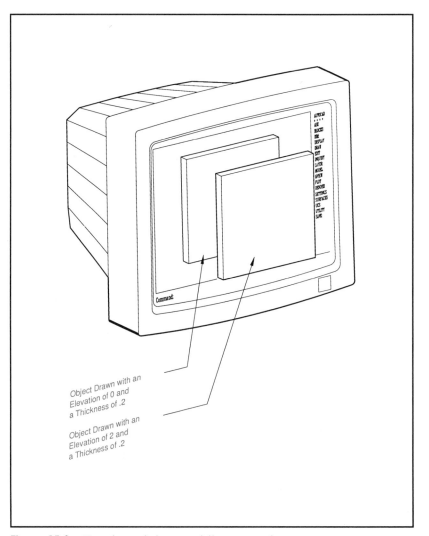

Object Drawn with an Elevation of 0 and a Thickness of .2

Object Drawn with an Elevation of 2 and a Thickness of .2

Figure 15.3: Two identical objects at different z coordinates

CHANGING A 2D PLAN INTO A 3D MODEL

In this exercise, you will turn the 2D studio unit drawing into a 3D drawing by changing the properties of the wall lines. You will also learn how to view the 3D image.

View ➤ Set View ➤ Viewpoint ➤ Set Vpoint

▼ TIP

You can also issue the Vpoint command by entering **Vpoint** ↵ at the command prompt.

1. Start AutoCAD and open the Unit file.

2. Set the current layer to Wall and turn off all the other layers except Jamb.

3. Turn on the grid if it isn't on already. Your screen should look like Figure 15.4.

4. Click on View ➤ Set View ➤ Viewpoint ➤ Set Vpoint. This starts the Vpoint command that allows you to view the studio unit in 3D.

5. At the **Rotate/<viewpoint><0'-0",0'-0",0'-1">:** prompt, enter **-1,-1,1** ↵. The default value is a list of the x, y, and z coordinates of your last viewing location relative to your object. Your view looks as if you are standing below and to the left of your drawing rather than directly above it (see Figure 15.5). The grid shows you the angle of the drawing surface.

6. Use the VIEW command and save this view as 3D.

7. Click on Modify ➤ Change ➤ Properties.

8. At the object-selection prompt, use a window to pick the entire drawing and press ↵.

9. At the Change Properties dialog box, double-click on the Thickness input box and enter **8'**, then click on **OK**.

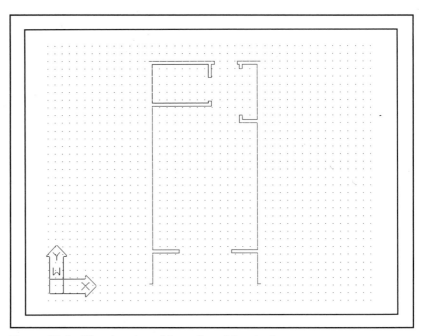

Figure 15.4: The plan view of the walls and door jambs

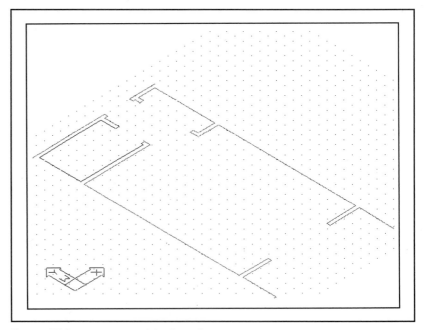

Figure 15.5: A 3D view of the floor plan

The walls and jambs now appear to be 8′ high. You are able to see through the walls because this is a wire frame view. A wire frame view shows the volume of a 3D object by showing the lines representing the intersections of surfaces. Later we will discuss how to view an object as if the surfaces were opaque. Figure 15.6 shows the extruded wall lines.

Next you will change the elevation of the door headers by moving them in the Z axis using grips.

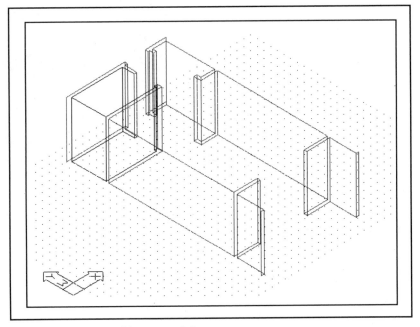

Figure 15.6:   The wall lines extruded

Grips ➤ Stretch

Modify ➤ 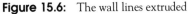 Change ➤ Properties

1. Enter Z↵ .8x ↵ to get a better view, then turn on the Ceiling layer. The door headers appear as lines on the floor where the door openings are located.

2. Click on the two magenta lines representing the header over the balcony door.

3. Shift-click on the midpoint grips of these lines.

4. Click again on one of the hot grips.

5. At the ***STRETCH*** prompt, enter @0,0,7′ ↵. The lines move to a new position 7′ above the floor (see Figure 15.7).

6. Click on Modify ➤ Change ➤ Properties and change the thickness of the header to 1′ using the Thickness input box.

7. Click on **OK**.

8. Click on the four lines representing the door header for the closet and entry.

9. Repeat steps 3 through 7. Your drawing will look like Figure 15.8.

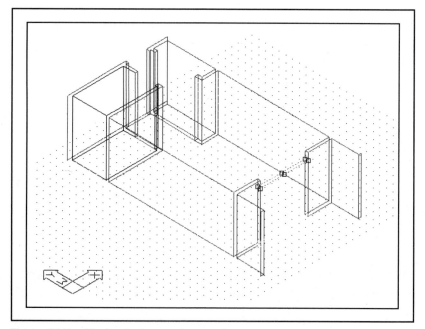

Figure 15.7: The header lines at the new elevation

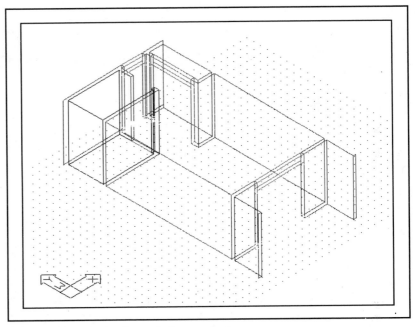

Figure 15.8:   The headers with the new thickness

You could have used the Move command to move the lines to their new elevation. You would enter the same **@0,0,7′** at the **Second point** prompt for Move. Since you must preselect objects to edit them using grips, you save a step by not having to preselect the lines a second time for the Modify ➤ Change ➤ Properties option.

CREATING A 3D OBJECT

Though you may visualize a design in 3D, you will often start sketching it in 2D and later generate 3D views. If you know from the start what the thickness and height of an object are to be, you can set these values so that you don't have to extrude the object later. If you use the same thickness and elevation often, you can even create a template file with these settings so they are readily available when you start your drawing. The command for setting thickness and elevation is ELEV.

Settings ➤ Entity Modes

▼ NOTE

You can also use the Elevation and Thickness system variables to set the default elevation and thickness of new objects.

1. Click on Settings ➤ Entity Modes. The Entity Creation Modes dialog box appears (see Figure 15.9).
2. Enter 3" in the Elevations input box.
3. Enter 12" in the Thickness input box.
4. Click on **OK**.
5. The grid changes to the new elevation. Now as you draw objects, they appear 12" thick at an elevation of 3". Draw a circle representing a planter at one side of the balcony (see Figure 15.10). Make it 18" in diameter. The planter appears as a 3D object with the current thickness and elevation settings.

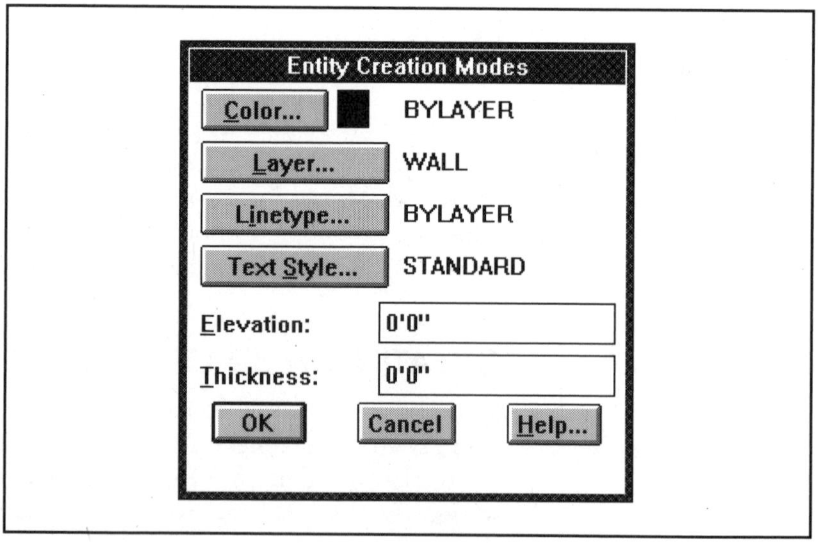

Figure 15.9: The Entity Creation Modes dialog box

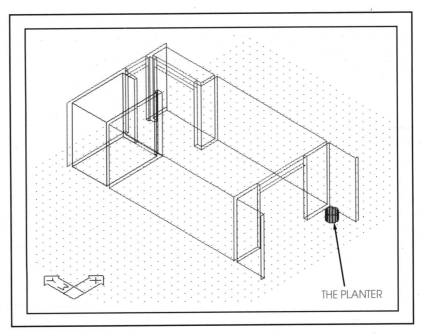

THE PLANTER

Figure 15.10:   The planter

Extruding forms is a very simple process, as you have seen. You just have to keep track of thicknesses and elevations. With these two properties, you can create nearly any three-dimensional form you need. Next you will discover how to control your view of your drawing.

VIEWING A 3D DRAWING

Your first 3D view of a drawing is a wire frame view. It appears as an open model made of wire; none of the sides appear solid. This section describes how to manipulate this wire frame view so you can see your drawing from any angle. We will also describe how, once you have selected your view, you can view your 3D drawing as a solid object with the hidden lines removed.

View ➤ Set View ➤ Viewpoint ➤ Axes

1. Click on View ➤ Set View ➤ Viewpoint ➤ Axes. You get a screen that helps you visually select your 3D view (see Figure 15.11). The three lines converging at one point compose the coordinate tripod.

2. Move your mouse around. The tripod rotates to show your orientation in relation to the X, Y, and Z axes of your drawing. Each line is labeled to indicate which axis it represents. Above and to the right of the tripod is a target with a small cursor. As you move your mouse, the cursor follows, staying near or within the target.

3. Move the cursor around the center of the target. Note how the tripod appears to rotate, indicating your changing view (see Figure 15.12). This target shows you your viewpoint in relation to the drawing.

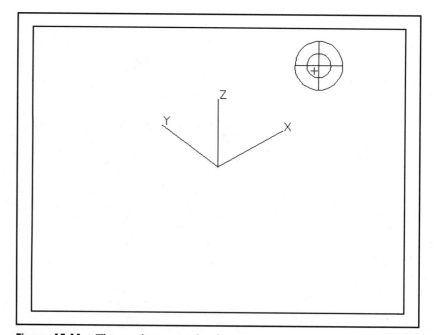

Figure 15.11: The coordinate tripod and target

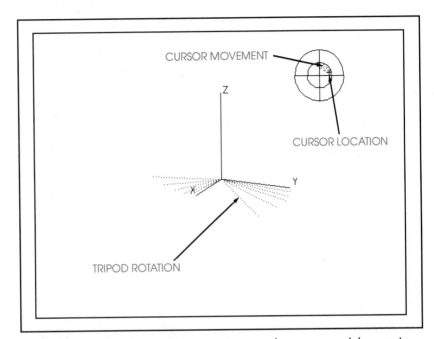

CURSOR MOVEMENT

CURSOR LOCATION

TRIPOD ROTATION

Figure 15.12: How the tripod rotates as you move the cursor around the target's center

4. Toggle on the dynamic coordinate readout if it isn't on already. As you move the cursor, the readout tells you your x,y coordinates in relation to the target's center.

5. Move the cursor closer to the center. The coordinate readout approaches 0,0, and the Z axis of the tripod begins to foreshorten until it is no longer visible (see Figure 15.13). This shows that you are almost directly above the drawing, as you would be in a 2D view.

6. Position the cursor as shown in Figure 15.13 and pick this point. Your drawing will look something like Figure 15.14. Now you can see that your view does indeed look like a plan view. The closer to the target's center you move the cursor, the higher in elevation your view will be.

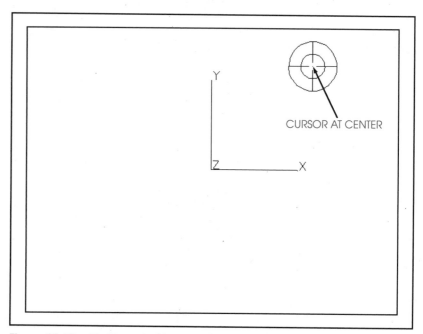

Figure 15.13: The Z axis foreshortened

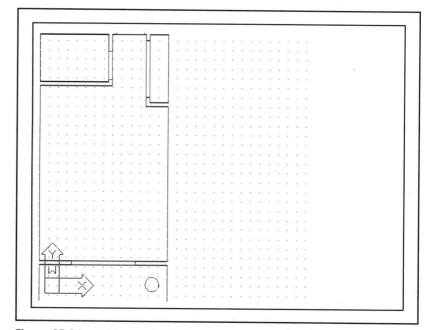

Figure 15.14: A 3D view that looks like a 2D view

UNDERSTANDING COORDINATE VALUES AND THE VIEWPOINT PROMPT

Let's take a moment to look at the relationship between coordinate values you enter at the **Enter view point** prompt and the coordinate tripod. In an earlier exercise, when you entered a coordinate value at the **Viewpoint** prompt, you were specifying the x, y, and z values for your position in relation to the origin of the coordinate tripod. The coordinate tripod graphically shows your orientation to the drawing. The coordinate values are not meaningful in themselves, only in relation to each other. The origin of the coordinate tripod, in this case, is your entire drawing and not the actual drawing origin (see Figure 15.15). The negative x value places your viewing position to the left of your drawing. The negative y places your position 270° in relation to your drawing. The positive 1 value for the Z axis lifts your view above the surface. As you go through the following exercise, you will see more clearly the relationship between your view and these coordinates.

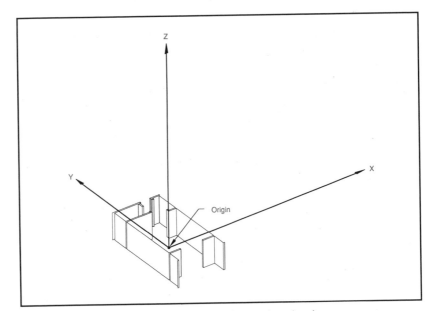

Figure 15.15: The coordinate tripod superimposed on the plan

UNDERSTANDING THE VIEWPOINT AXES TARGET

The cursor's position in relation to the target's center is your viewpoint in relation to your drawing. You might think of the target as a schematic plan view of your drawing, with the cursor being your position in relation to the plan (see Figure 15.16). For example, if you place the cursor just below and to the left of the center, your view will be from the lower-left corner of your overall drawing, like your view of the floor plan in the first exercise. If you place the cursor above and to the right of the center, you will view your drawing from the upper-right corner.

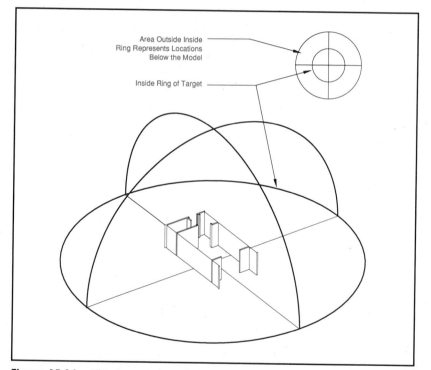

Figure 15.16:   This diagram shows how the viewpoint axes target relates to your drawing.

View ➤ Set View ➤ Viewpoint ➤ Axes

VPOINT defaults: the x and y values are very low, while the z value is relatively high. This tells you that you are very close to the origin in the X and Y axes but far from it in the Z axis.

It is a little difficult to tell what is going on because you can see right through the walls. Don't worry; as you work with 3D, you will become more accustomed to this type of view.

1. Click on View ➤ Set View ➤ Viewpoint ➤ Axes. The tripod and target appear.

2. Look at the target. As you move the cursor closer to its inner ring, the x and y lines begin to flatten until, as you touch the circle, they are parallel (see Figure 15.17). This first ring represents a directly horizontal position on your drawing surface.

3. Position the cursor as shown in Figure 15.17 and click on this position. Your drawing will look as if you are viewing the drawing surface edge on and the walls from the side (see Figure 15.18).

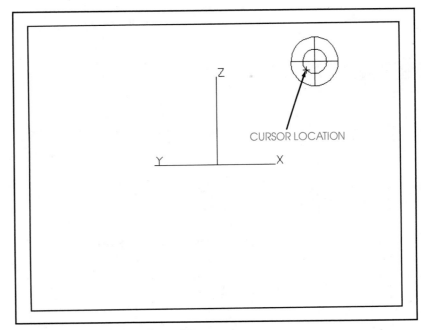

Figure 15.17:   The parallel X and Y axes

Figure 15.18: View of walls from side

▼ NOTE

VPOINT defaults: this time the x and y values are high, while the z value is 0 or close to it. This tells you that the previous view was from an elevation of 0.

▼ NOTE

If you want to get back to a plan view of your drawing, click on View ➤ Set View ➤ Viewpoint ➤ Set Vpoint and enter 0,0 or pick plan from the Vpoint menu. When you do this, you will notice that your 2D view looks just the way it did before you extruded the walls. As I explained earlier, this is because you are viewing the wall lines edge on.

4. Click on the View ➤ Set View ➤ Viewpoint ➤ Axes command again.

5. Move the cursor to the outermost ring of the target. The Z axis line foreshortens again. This ring represents a view located underneath your drawing, as if you were looking at the back of the screen.

6. Pick a point just inside this outer ring, as shown in Figure 15.19. You will get a view something like Figure 15.20.

At first you might think that this is just another view from above the drawing. However, if you look carefully at the position of the bathroom in relation to the rest of the unit, you will notice that it appears to be mirrored, just like any drawing viewed from the back of the drawing sheet.

Now return to the view you used to edit the Unit drawing.

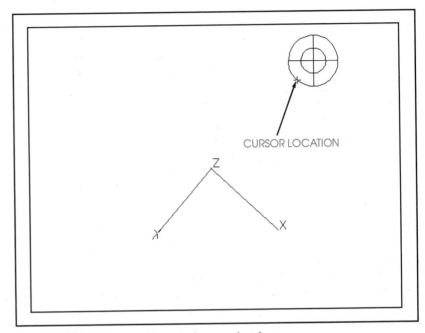

Figure 15.19: The cursor location for an underside view

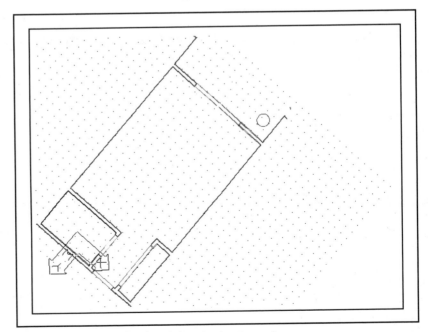

Figure 15.20: The plan from below the drawing surface

View ➤ Set View ➤ Viewpoint ➤ Set Vpoint

1. Click on View ➤ Set View ➤ Viewpoint ➤ Set Vpoint or enter **Vpoint** ↵.

2. Enter **–1,–1,1** ↵. You will see the drawing from a viewpoint similar to the one you started with.

3. Using View ➤ Set View ➤ Named view, save this view and give it the name **3D**.

4. Finally, turn on all the layers except Notes. You will see the rest of the drawing still in a 2D form.

Notice that when you extruded the walls, the interior bathroom walls did not change with the others. This is because those walls are part of a block. You can change the elevation of a block, but you cannot change its thickness. You must redefine the block to change the thickness of the objects it contains.

USING THE VPOINT ROTATE OPTION

A more direct way of obtaining a view from a 3D drawing is by using the rotate option under the VPOINT command.

View ➤ Set View ➤ Viewpoint ➤ Set Vpoint Rotate

1. First turn off all the layers except Wall and Ceiling.

2. Click on View ➤ Set View ➤ Viewpoint ➤ Set Vpoint, then pick rotate from the side menu or enter **R** ↵.

3. At the **Enter angle in X-Y plane in X axis <225>:** prompt, enter **45** ↵ to get a view at the opposite side of the apartment.

4. At the **Enter angle from X-Y plane <35>:** prompt, press ↵ to accept the default value. You get a new view of the apartment from the opposite side of your current view (see Figure 15.21). Figure 15.22 illustrates what these values represent.

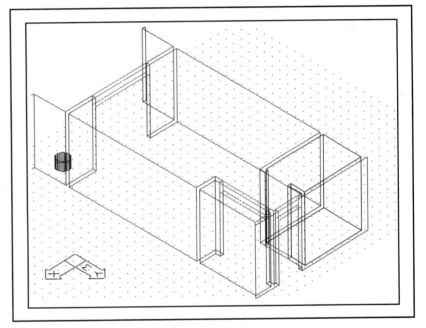

Figure 15.21:   The new view of the apartment

If you like, you can visually choose the rotational angle of your view. To do this, follow these steps.

1. Click on Assist ➤ Inquiry ➤ ID Point or enter **ID** ↵ and pick a point at the center of the apartment.

2. Start the VPOINT command and select the rotate command as before. A rubber-banding line will appear with one end at the point you selected and the other end on the cursor (see Figure 15.23).

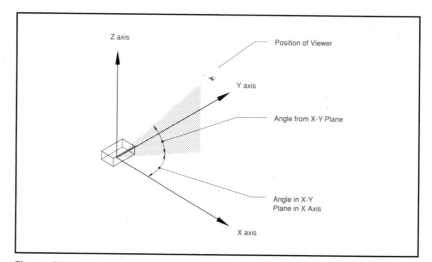

Figure 15.22: The view angles and what they represent

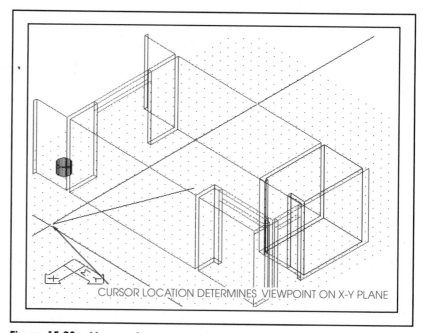

Figure 15.23: How to select a view angle using the cursor

▼ NOTE

The position of the cursor will determine your view position. With the Osnap modes you can even use part of your apartment model as a reference.

▼ WARNING

You cannot use the rubber-banding line to select the view height; you must enter a value.

3. At the **Enter angle from XY plane from X Axis** prompt, pick a point indicating the position you wish to view the model from.

4. At the **Enter angle from the x,y plane** prompt, enter a value as before.

Your view will change to reflect your new view angle.

USING A DIALOG BOX TO SELECT 3D VIEWS

A third way to select 3D views is by indicating an angle in plan and elevation using a dialog box graphic.

1. Click on View ➤ Set View ➤ Viewpoint ➤ Presets or enter Ddvpoint ↵. The Viewpoint Presets dialog box appears (see Figure 15.24). The square dial to the left lets you select a viewpoint location in plan, similar to the target you used earlier. The semicircle to the right lets you select an elevation for your viewpoint.

2. Click on the number *135* in the upper left of the square dial, then click on the box labeled *60* in the right-hand semicircle.

3. Click on **OK**. Your view changes to the new settings you just made.

Other settings in this dialog box let you determine whether the selected view angles are relative to the World Coordinate System or the current User Coordinate System (I'll discuss the User Coordinate System in *Chapter 16*). You can also go directly to a plan view.

VISUALIZING YOUR MODEL

From time to time, you will want to get an idea of how your model looks with hidden lines removed. This is especially true of complex 3D models. Often object intersections and shapes are not readily apparent until you can see what object lies in front of others.

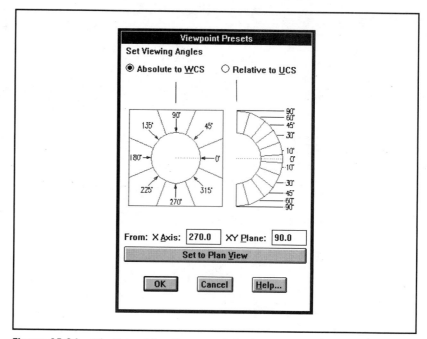

Figure 15.24: The Select View Direction dialog box

AutoCAD provides two viewing commands that can help. First, the Hide command allows you to quickly view your drawing with hidden lines removed. You can then assess where surfaces are and get a better feel for the model. Hide is also an option in the plot command, allowing you to create hard-copy line drawings of a 3D model. You can then render the hard copy using manual techniques if you want.

The second command, Shade, offers the ability to add a sense of solidity to the image by adding color to surfaces. Shade has a variety of settings that let you control how colors are applied. This option is better suited to presentations and as a visualization tool where Hide may be inadequate. Unfortunately, you cannot plot a view generated by the Shade command. You can, however, store it as a slide file for independent viewing. I'll discuss Slides in more detail later.

REMOVING HIDDEN LINES

Release 12's hidden line removal has been vastly improved over earlier versions. Here's how it works.

Render ➤ Hide

1. Restore the view you saved earlier as 3D.

2. Click on Render ➤ Hide or enter **Hide** ⏎. AutoCAD will display the message

   ```
   HIDE Regenerating drawing
   Hidden lines:  value%
   ```

   where *value*% changes as it calculates the hidden line removal. On a very fast computer, such as a 486/50, you won't even notice the value change. When AutoCAD is done, the value reads 100% and the hidden line image appears (see Figure 15.25).

The hidden line view will remain until your drawing is regenerated. You cannot use the VIEW command to save a view with hidden lines removed. You can, however, save this view as a slide.

While it did not take much time to perform a hidden line removal on this drawing, the more complex the 3D drawing, the longer it will take to hide. But even the most complex model you create will probably not take more than several minutes. This is a vast improvement over earlier releases of AutoCAD, where it took hours to perform a hidden line removal.

SHADING YOUR 3D MODEL

If you're used to looking at wire-frame 3D images, the Hide command is usually good enough to give you an idea of how your model looks. But

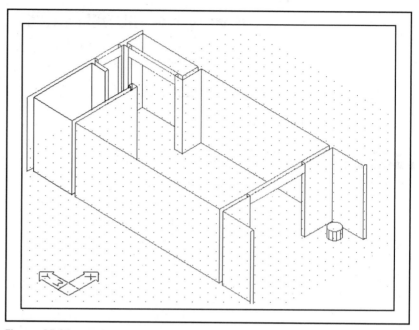

Figure 15.25: Hidden lines removed

you might want to get a feel for the form your model is taking on. The Shade command can help you see volumes better than the Hide command. To see how it works, try the following.

1. Click on View ➤ Set View ➤ Viewpoint ➤ Set Vpoint.

2. At the prompt, enter **–2,– 4,3**. This changes your view so your line of sight is different to each wall surface.

3. Click on Render ➤ Shade or enter **Shade** ↵. Just as with Hide, AutoCAD displays a message telling you that it is regenerating the drawing. In a short time, the shaded view appears.

4. Enter **Shadedge** ↵ at the command prompt.

5. At the **New value for SHADEDGE** prompt, enter **1** ↵.

6. Click on Render ➤ Shade again. Notice that the shaded image looks more realistic and less cartoon-like (see Figure 15.26).

7. Enter Shadedge ↵ again, but this time enter **0** ↵ at the **New value for SHADEDGE** prompt.

8. Render the drawing a third time. Now only the surfaces appear with no edges showing.

In step 2, I asked you to change your view slightly so your line of sight was at a slightly different angle to the different walls. Had you not changed your view, Shade would shade all the walls with the same intensity in steps 6 and 8. This is because Shade renders a view as if a light source emanates from the same direction as the viewer. If all the walls are at the same angle to the view, they all receive and reflect the same amount of light. With the model slightly turned, light then reflects off each surface differently.

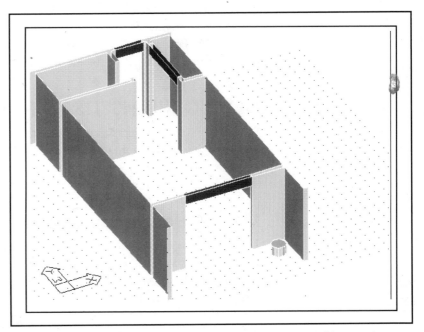

Figure 15.26: The Unit plan shaded with Shadedge system variable set to 1

You used the Shadedge system variable to change the way surfaces were rendered. The following gives a description of each of the four settings.

0 Shades the surfaces with no edge highlighting.

1 Shades the surfaces and highlights the edges.

2 Shades the surfaces with the background color and the edges with the surface color.

3 Shades the surface with the entity color and the edges with the background color.

Another system variable called Shadedif can affect the contrast of colors between different surfaces. A higher number increases contrast, while a lower number decreases contrast. The default setting is 70 with a range between 0 to 100. You may want to experiment with this setting on your own.

There is a third method for visualizing your model that allows you to place different light sources in your drawing. The AutoCAD rendering functions let you adjust light reflectance of surfaces, smooth out faceted surfaces like spheres and cylinders, and place light sources accurately. You'll get a chance to work with AutoCAD rendering functions in *Chapter 16*. For now, let's look at other factors that affect how a 3D model will look when it is shaded or when hidden lines are removed.

GETTING THE RESULTS YOU WANT

Working in 3D is tricky because you can't see exactly what you are drawing. You must alternately draw then hide or shade your drawing from time to time to see exactly what is going on. Here are a few tips on how to keep control of your 3D drawings.

Making Horizontal Surfaces Opaque

To make a horizontal surface appear opaque, you must draw it with a wide polyline, a trace, a solid, or a 3dface. For example, if you were to draw a table, you could represent the tabletop with a rectangle and give it the appropriate thickness, but the top would appear to be transparent when the lines were hidden. Only the sides of the tabletop would become opaque. To make the tabletop opaque, you can use the SOLID command (or a wide trace or polyline) to draw a filled rectangle and give it the appropriate thickness. When the lines are hidden, the table top appears to be opaque (see Figure 15.27). This technique works even with the Fill setting off.

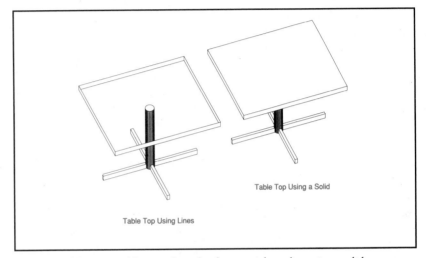

Table Top Using a Solid

Table Top Using Lines

Figure 15.27:   One table using lines for the top and another using a solid

If you use a circle as an extruded form, the top surface appears opaque when you use the Hide command. Where you want to show an opening at the top of a circular volume, as in a circular chimney, you can use two 180° arcs (see Figure 15.28).

If you have complex horizontal surfaces, you can use a combination of wide polylines, solids, and 3dfaces (described later) to create them. For example, a sidewalk on a street corner would use a donut for the rounder corner, then solids or 3dfaces at either side for the straight portion of the sidewalk. It's OK to overlap surfaces to achieve the effect you want.

Setting Layers Carefully

We should mention that the Hide command hides objects that are obscured by other objects on layers that are turned off. For example, if a couch in the corner of the studio unit is on a layer that is off when you

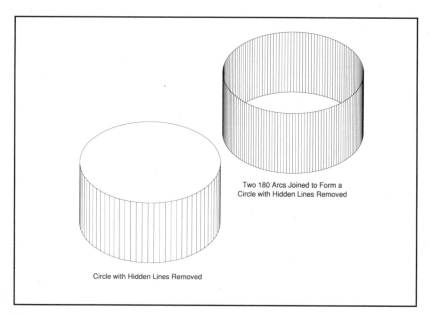

Two 180 Arcs Joined to Form a
Circle with Hidden Lines Removed

Circle with Hidden Lines Removed

Figure 15.28: A circle and two joined arcs

use Hide, the lines behind the couch are hidden even though the couch does not appear in the view (see Figure 15.29). You can, however, freeze any layer containing objects that you do not want to affect the hidden-line removal process. You can also use AutoCAD's regional modeler (described in *Chapter 18*) to draw complex 3D surfaces with holes.

DRAWING 3D SURFACES

So far you have just extruded existing forms or have set AutoCAD to draw extruded objects. Extruded forms have their limitations. Using just extruded forms, it's hard to draw diagonal surfaces in the Z axis. AutoCAD provides 3dface to give you more flexibility in drawing surfaces in three-dimensional space. It produces a 3D surface where each corner can be given an x, y, and z value. By using 3dfaces in conjunction with extruded objects, you can create a 3D model of just about anything. When you view these 3D objects in a 2D plan view, you will see them as 2D objects showing only the x and y positions of their corners or endpoints.

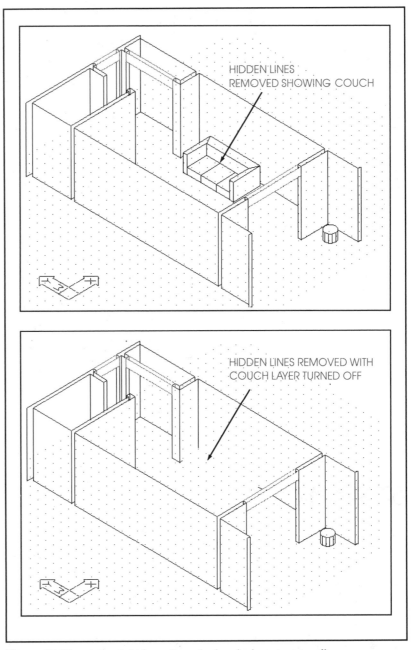

Figure 15.29: A couch hiding a line whether the layer is on or off

USING FILTERS

Before you start using 3D surfaces, you should have a good idea of what the z coordinate values are for your model. The simplest way to construct surfaces in 3D space is to first create some layout lines to help you place the endpoints of 3dfaces.

AutoCAD offers a method for 3D point selection called *filtering* that makes the selection of z coordinates easier. Filtering allows you to enter an x, y, or z value by picking a point on the screen and telling AutoCAD to use only the x, y, or z value of that point or any combination of those values. If you don't specify a z coordinate, the current elevation setting is assumed.

In the following exercises, you will add a stair rail to the studio apartment. In doing this, you will practice using 3dfaces and filters. Start by doing some setup. You will work on a copy of the Unit file, so you can keep the old Unit plan for future reference.

1. Restore the view you saved earlier as 3D using View ➤ Set View ➤ Named View.

2. Save the Unit file and create a new file called **Unitloft** using the Unit file as a prototype.

3. Click on Settings ➤ Entity Modes, and at the Entity Creation Modes dialog box, set the Thickness and Elevation to 0.

4. Click on **OK**.

5. Set the current layer to Wall.

Now you are ready to lay out your stair rail.

1. Click on Draw ➤ Line ➤ Segments.

2. At the **From point** prompt, pick the .xy option side menu, or enter **.xy** ↵. (By doing this you are telling AutoCAD that you are going to first specify the x and y coordinates for this beginning point, then later indicate the z coordinate.)

3. At the **From point: .xy of** prompt, pick a point along the same axis as the bathroom wall 3′- 6″ from the right side wall

of the unit near coordinate 25'- 6",25'-5", to create the first line at the bottom of the stair rail.

4. At the **(need Z):** prompt, enter **9'** ↵ (the z coordinate).

5. At the **to point** prompt, pick .xy again from the side menu or enter **.xy** ↵.

6. Enter **@12′ <270**.

7. At the **(need Z):** prompt, enter **0** ↵.

8. Press ↵ to end the LINE command. Your drawing should look like Figure 15.30.

Now you will copy the line vertically to draw the top of the stair rail.

▼ TIP

Filters can also be used in a 2D drawing to select an x or y component of an object you wish to align a point to.

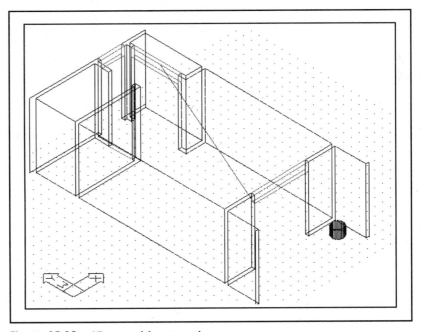

Figure 15.30:   3D view of the stair rail

Construct ➤ 🎲 Copy

1. Click on Construct ➤ Copy.

2. Select the 3D line you just drew, then press ↵.

3. At the **Base point of displacement** prompt, pick any point on the screen.

4. At the **Second point of displacement** prompt, enter **.xy** ↵, then enter **@** ↵ . This tells AutoCAD that your second point will maintain the x,y coordinates of the first.

5. At the **(need Z):** prompt, enter **3′6"** ↵ to place the copy 3′-6" on the Z axis. A copy of the 3D line appears 3′-6" above the original.

In step 3 you were able to specify that the second point used the same x and y coordinates of the base point. You then needed to enter only the z value for the second point. In the earlier exercise, you used a relative coordinate to move door headers to a position 7′ higher than their original location. You could have used the same method here to copy the line vertically. Here, you got a chance to see how the .xy filter works.

USING 3DFACES

Sometimes you will want to draw a solid surface so that when you perform a hidden line removal, objects will appear as surfaces rather than wire frames. If you continue to draw the side of the stair rail using lines, the side of the stair rail will appear transparent. The next step is to fill the side in using 3dfaces. It generally makes life easier to first draw a wire frame of your object using lines, then use their endpoints to fill in the surfaces.

Draw ➤ 🖾 3D Surfaces ➤ 3D Face

▼ NOTE

When the **Third point:**
prompt appears again, you can
draw more 3dfaces if you like.
The additional 3dface uses the
last two points selected as the
first two of its four corners,
hence the prompt for a third
point.

1. ZOOM into the two lines you just created using the zoom window shown in Figure 15.31.

2. Click on Draw ➤ 3D Surfaces ➤ 3DFace.

3. At the **First point:** prompt, use the Osnap overrides to pick the first of the four endpoints of the 3D lines you drew. Be sure the ortho mode is off.

4. As you continue to pick the endpoints, you will get the following series of prompts:

   Second point:
   Third point:
   Fourth point:

5. When the **Third point:** prompt appears again, press ⏎ to end the 3DFace command. A 3dface appears between the two 3D lines.

   It is difficult to tell if they are actually there until you use the Hide command, but you should see vertical lines connecting the endpoints of the 3D lines. These vertical lines are the edges of the 3dface (see Figure 15.32).

Construct ➤ 🝔 Copy
Render ➤ Hide

1. COPY the 3dface you just drew 5" horizontally in the 0 angle direction.

2. Use the 3DFace command to put a surface on the top and front sides of the rail as indicated in panel 1 of Figure 15.33.

3. Use the Intersec Osnap override to snap to the corners of the 3dfaces.

The 3DFace command acts like the Solid command except that with 3DFace, you pick four points in a circular fashion as shown in Figure 15.32. Once you've drawn one 3dface, you can continue to add more by selecting more points.

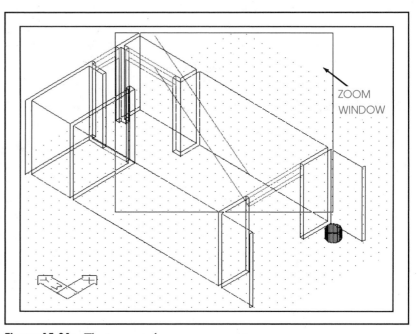

Figure 15.31: The zoom window .

The filter options on the 3DFace menu enable you to enter points as you did for the line command. You can also use the Endpoint and Midpoint Osnap overrides to snap to the endpoints and midpoints of the edges of 3dfaces. In addition, you can snap to the corners of 3dfaces by using the Intersec override.

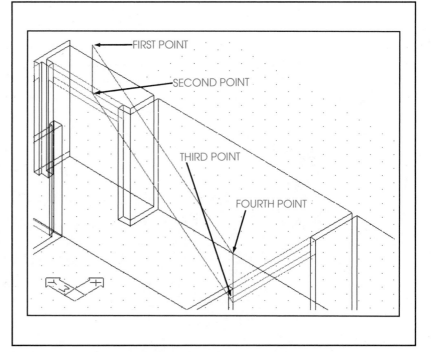

Figure 15.32: The 3dface

4. Use Render ➤ Hide to get a view that looks like panel 2 of Figure 15.33.

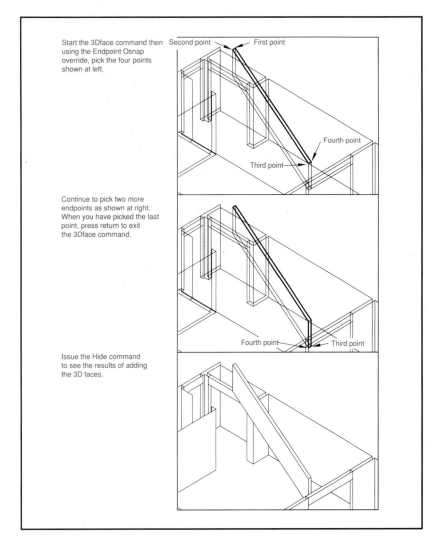

Figure 15.33: The top and front faces of the stair rail, and the stair rail with the hidden lines removed

5. END out of the Unitloft file. You won't be using it in any future exercise, but you can use it to experiment with 3dfaces. You may want to add some stair treads by using the SOLID command to draw the first tread, then arraying it and using CHANGE to alter each stair tread's elevation.

HIDING UNWANTED SURFACE EDGES

When using the 3DFace command, you are limited to drawing surfaces with four sides. You can create more complex shapes by simply joining several 3dfaces. For example, if you want to draw an odd shape, you can draw three joined 3dfaces, as shown in Figure 15.34. Unfortunately, you are left with extra lines that cross the surface. You can hide those lines by using the Invisible option under the 3DFace command in conjunction with the Splframe Setvar variable.

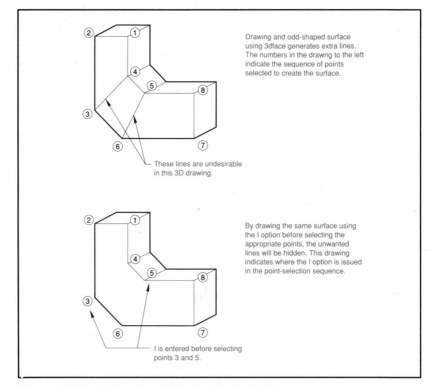

Figure 15.34: Hiding the joined edge of multiple 3dfaces

▼ TIP

When you are drawing two 3dfaces sequentially, only one edge needs to be invisible to hide their joining edge.

▼ TIP

AutoCAD comes with an AutoLISP utility that lets you change a visible 3dface edge to an invisible one (see *Chapter 19*).

To make an edge of a 3dface invisible, start the 3DFace command as usual. While selecting points, enter **I** or select Invisible from the 3DFace side menu just before you pick the first point of the edge to be hidden.

You can make invisible edges visible for editing by setting the Splframe system variable to 1. This is exactly what the ShowEdge option on the 3DFace side menu does. The HideEdge option on the side menu will set Splframe to 0, which causes AutoCAD to hide the invisible edges.

This invisible function can be useful in both 3D and 2D drawings. You can use 3DFace in place of the SOLID command when you want to draw a surface with a complex shape but don't want the surface to be a solid fill.

USING AUTOCAD'S 3D SHAPES

AutoCAD provides several 3D shapes, among them cones, spheres, and torus shapes. All are made up of 3dfaces. To use them, follow these steps.

1. Click on Draw ➤ 3D Surfaces ➤ 3D Objects. The 3D objects icon menu appears (see Figure 15.35).

2. If you select an object, either from the list to the left or from an icon, AutoCAD will prompt you for the points and dimensions that define the 3D object. Then AutoCAD draws the object using an AutoLISP program written to generate it. This provides quick access to shapes that would otherwise be time-consuming to create.

TURNING A 3D VIEW INTO A 2D AUTOCAD DRAWING

I know of one company that uses AutoCAD 3D models to study their designs. Once a particular part of a design is modeled and the design is

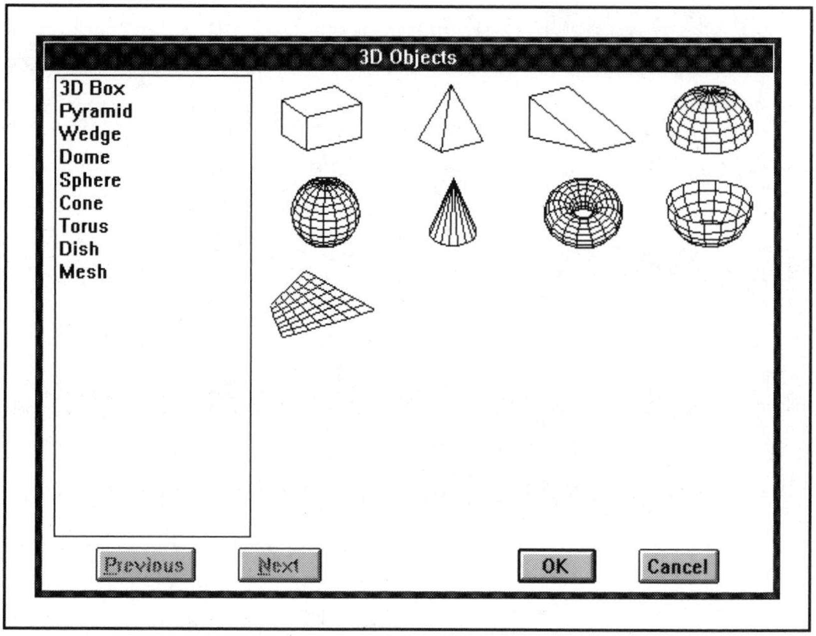

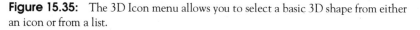

Figure 15.35: The 3D Icon menu allows you to select a basic 3D shape from either an icon or from a list.

approved, they convert the model into 2D elevations, ready to plug into their elevation drawing. Here is how it can be done.

1. Use File ➤ Configure to add a PostScript plotter to the configuration list. You can have more than one Post-Script configuration if you already have one set up.

2. While configuring the PostScript plotter, set the resolution to 1250 dpi.

3. When you are prompted for a configuration name, give it a name that will help you remember it, like *1250 PostScript*.

4. Open the 3D drawing and set up your 3D view, then start the Plot command.

Things to Watch Out for When Editing 3D Objects

You have seen how you can use the Copy command on 3D lines and 3dfaces. You can also use the MOVE and STRETCH commands on 3D lines, 3dfaces, and 3D shapes to modify their z coordinate values, but you have to be careful with these commands in 3D. Here are a few tips to keep in mind while editing in 3D.

■ The Scale command will scale an object's z coordinate value, as well as the standard x and y coordinates. For example, suppose you have an object with an elevation of two units. If you use the Scale command to enlarge that object by a factor of four, the object will have a new elevation of two units times four, or eight units. If, on the other hand, that object has an elevation of zero, its elevation will not change because zero times four is still zero.

■ Array, Mirror, and Rotate can also be used on 3D lines, 3dfaces, and 3D shapes, but these commands won't affect their z coordinate values. Z coordinates can be specified for base and insertion points, so care should be taken when using these commands with 3D models.

■ Using the Move, Copy, or Stretch command with object snaps can produce some unpredictable and unwanted results. As a rule, it is best to use point filters when selecting points with Osnap overrides. For example, to move an object from the endpoint of one object to the endpoint of another on the same z coordinate, invoke the .xy filter at the **Base point** and **Second point** prompts before issuing the endpoint override. Proceed to pick the endpoint of the object you want, then enter the z coordinate or just pick any point to use the current default z coordinate.

■ When you create a block, the block will use the UCS active at the time the block is created to determine its own local coordinate system. When that block is later inserted, it will orient its own coordinate system with the current UCS (UCS is discussed in more detail in *Chapter 16*).

5. At the Plotter Configuration dialog box, be sure you set Device and Default selection to use the 1250 PostScript plotter, and that you are plotting to a file. Also be sure the Hide Lines check box is checked.

6. Use the Optimization dialog box to make sure no lines are overlapping in the plot.

7. After you have plotted the 3D drawing, open a new file to receive the plot.

8. Use the File ➤ Import/Export ➤ PostScript In option to import the plot.

CREATING AND USING SLIDES

3D graphics are often handy for presentations, and 3D AutoCAD images are frequently used for that purpose, as well as for producing drafted 2D drawings. You may want to show off some of your 3D work directly from the computer screen. If your drawings are complicated, however, your audience may get impatient waiting for the hidden lines to be removed. Fortunately, AutoCAD provides a tool to let you save a view from your screen in a form that will display quickly.

The MSLIDE and VSLIDE commands will save a view as a file on disk. Such a view is called a slide. You can display a slide any time you are in the AutoCAD drawing editor. Slides display at redraw speed no matter how complex they may be. This means you can save a slide of a hidden line view of your 3D drawing and recall that view quickly at any time.

Slides can also be used as a reference tool during editing sessions instead of panning, zooming, or viewing. A slide cannot be edited, however, nor will it be updated when you edit the drawing. In the following exercise, you will make a few slides of the Unit file.

▼ NOTE

Slides can be used with Autodesk Animator Pro to become part of animations or other presentation material. From Animator Pro, you can then export your slides to Autodesk 3D Studio for texture maps.

Mslide ↵

1. Open the Unit file and enter **hide** to get a hidden line view of the unit.

2. Enter **Mslide** ↵ or click on AutoCAD ➤ Utility ➤ Slides ➤ Mslides from the side menu.

3. At the File dialog box, Pick **OK** to accept the default file name. The default slide name is the same name as the current drawing with the .SLD extension. AutoCAD will save the current view on disk as a slide with the file name *Unit.SLD*. The actual drawing file is not affected.

4. ZOOM into the bathroom and use the Mslide command to save another view called **Unitbath**, this time without the hidden lines removed.

5. When the File dialog box appears, highlight the File input box.

6. Type **unitbath** and press ↵, then pick **OK**.

VIEWING SLIDES

Now that you've saved two views, let's see how to view them.

Vslide ↵

1. ZOOM back to the previous view and enter **Vslide** ↵ or pick VSLIDE from the side menu. Vslide enables you to view a slide created with the Mslide command.

2. At the File dialog box, enter **unitbath**.

3. Click on **OK**. The slide of the bathroom appears. Although you can move the cursor around the view and start commands in the normal way, you cannot edit or obtain information from this slide.

4. Pick VSLIDE from the Slides menu again.

5. This time click on **OK** at the dialog box to accept the default slide file name, *Unit*. The 3D view of the unit will appear with its hidden lines removed. Since slides display at redraw speed, you don't have to wait to view the unit without its hidden lines.

6. Click on View ➤ Redraw to return to the drawing being edited.

7. Open the Plan file and use the VSLIDE command to view the Unitbath slide again.

8. Now create a slide of the Plan file and call it **Plan1**.

> ▼ NOTE
>
> Any command that performs a redraw will also return you to the current drawing.

> ▼ NOTE
>
> Observe how you are able to call up the slide from any file, not just the one you were in when you created the slide.

Next, you'll get to see how you might automate a slide presentation using the slides you just created.

AUTOMATING A SLIDE PRESENTATION

As I mentioned in *Chapter 7*, SCRIPT can be used like the batch file in DOS to run a sequence of commands automatically. Let's create a Script file to automatically show your slides.

Delay

1. Open a new file called **Show**.

2. Use a text editor to create a file called **Show.SCR**, and enter the following lines into this file.

```
vslide ↵
unit ↵
delay 3000 ↵
vslide ↵
```

```
unitbath ↵
delay 3000 ↵
vslide ↵
Plan1 ↵
```

These lines of text are a sequence of predetermined instructions to AutoCAD that can be played back later. Each line is entered at the AutoCAD command prompt, just as you would enter it through the keyboard. Note that the VSLIDE command appears before the name of each slide. It is followed by the line delay 3000, which tells AutoCAD to pause roughly 3,000 milliseconds after each VSLIDE command is issued (you can substitute another value if you like). If no delay is specified, as soon as the slide is completed, the next slide comes up.

Now try playing the script.

▼ TIP

You can have the slides continually repeat themselves by adding the RSCRIPT command at the very end of the Show file you just created. You may want to do this if your presentation is intended for casual viewing as an exhibit in a display area with people passing through. To stop a repeating script, press the Backspace key.

1. Return to AutoCAD, then enter **Script** ↵ or click on AutoCAD ➤ Utility ➤ Script from the root menu.

2. At the File dialog box, highlight and pick the file you just created (Show) from the file list, then pick the **OK** box.

The slides you saved will appear on the screen in the sequence in which you entered them in the Show.SCR file.

CREATING A SLIDE LIBRARY

You can group slide files together into one file to help keep your slides organized. For example, you could group slides by project or drawing type. Slide libraries also save disk space, as they often use less space than the total used by the individual slide files.

Slide libraries are also used to create icon menus. AutoCAD provides a file called Acad.SLB that contains all the icons for the standard AutoCAD menus. This file includes all the slides used for the font, hatch pattern, and 3D view icon menus. I will discuss how to create icon menus in *Chapter 21*.

To create a slide library, follow these steps in a DOS window.

Slidelib.EXE

▼ **TIP**

To quickly get to DOS from Windows, use the MS-DOS icon in the Accessories program group.

1. Use a word processor and make a list of the slides you want to include in the library. For the slides you created earlier, it should look like the following:

   unit
   unitbath
   plan1

   Do not include the .SLD extension in the name.

2. Save this list as a DOS text or ASCII file in your AutoCAD support directory. You can give this file any name you like. For this example, call it **Slide1.LST**. Be sure it is saved in the same directory as your slide files.

▼ **WARNING**

Do not include the file extension; the Slidelib utility program automatically adds the file extension .SLB. For example, if you enter **Plans** as the library name in the above example, a slide library file called **Plans.SLB** is created.

3. Use the Slidelib.EXE program in your AutoCAD directory (if you set up a Support subdirectory, it may be there). Be sure your Slidelib.EXE file is in the same directory as your slide list file and slide files.

4. At the DOS prompt, enter **slidelib Myslides < slide1.lst** ↵. A file named **Myslides.SLB** will be created. The library name can be any legal DOS file name.

Now let's test your slide library. To view a slide from a slide library, you use the VSLIDE command. This time, however, you will specify the file name differently. Instead of picking a slide name from the dialog box, you must enter the name at the prompt line in a special format. The name must be entered with the library name first, followed by the individual slide name in parentheses.

Vslide ↵

1. Open a new temporary file called **Temp**, and at the AutoCAD command prompt, enter **vslide** ↵.

2. At the File dialog box pick the Type it box. The dialog box disappears.

3. At the **Slide file< current file name>:** prompt, enter **My-slides(plan1)** ↵. The slide will appear in the drawing area.

To use slide libraries from scripts, you use the slide library and slide name following the VSLIDE command, as in the following example:

```
vslide
myslides(unit)
delay 3000
vlside
myslides(unitbath)
delay 3000
vslide
myslides(plan1)
delay 3000
rscript
```

You've seen how you can save and display 3D views quickly and how you can automate a presentation of slides using scripts. With these tools, you can create an impressive, fast-paced presentation.

Another use for slides is in file management. You may reach the point where you can't remember which AutoCAD drawing file goes with which drawing. Making a slide of every drawing you do gives you visual

▼ WARNING

If you placed the slide library file in a directory different from the current one, be sure you enter the directory name before the slide library name.

▼ WARNING

One disadvantage to using slides for file management is that slide files take up disk space. This can be a problem since AutoCAD files tend to use disk space up rapidly. However, slide files can be transported to other computer systems without translation, giving you more flexibility when using dissimilar systems on a network.

references for your drawing files. To hunt for a file, you just open a temporary drawing file, then look through your slide files to find the drawing. This is much faster than opening each drawing file until you find what you're looking for.

IF YOU WANT TO EXPERIMENT...

One thing I haven't mentioned is that 3D modeling can be fun. You get to see your ideas take shape. 3D can help you visualize your ideas more clearly. In some cases, it can show you things that a traditional 3D chipboard model cannot.

The following exercise is really just for fun. It shows you how you can do a limited form of animation using 3D viewpoints, the Mslide command, and scripts.

▼ TIP

Slides can be imported into Autodesk Animator or Animator Pro, allowing you to produce smooth animation sequences.

1. Open the Unit plan.

2. Do a hidden line removal, then use Mslide to create a slide called **V1**.

3. Use Assist ➤ Inquiry ID point and pick a point in the center of the floor plan. This marks the view center for the next step.

4. Enter **Vpoint** ↵ **R** ↵ at the command prompt.

5. At the **Enter angle at XY plane** prompt, enter **235** ↵, then press ↵ at the next prompt.

6. Do another hidden line removal, then use Mslide again to create a slide called **V2**.

7. Repeat steps 4 through 6, but this time increase by ten the angle value you entered at step 5 to enter **245**. At step 6, increase the slide name by one to **V3**.

8. Keep repeating steps 4 through 6, increasing the angle value by ten each time and increasing the slide file name by one. Repeat these steps at least five more times.

9. Create a script file called Animate.SCR containing the following lines (the ↵ is just to show you to press ↵ at the end of each line):

```
Vslide v1 ↵
Vslide v2 ↵
Vslide v3 ↵
Vslide v4 ↵
Vslide v5 ↵
Vslide v6 ↵
Vslide v7 ↵
Vslide v8 ↵
Rscript ↵
```

10. Return to AutoCAD, then enter **Script** ↵. Click on **Animate** at the file dialog box; then click **OK** and watch the show.

11. Press **Ctrl-C** or the Backspace key to end the show.

Try creating an animation that moves you completely around the unit plan.

To practice drawing in 3D, you may want to try turning the kitchenette of your 3D unit drawing into a 3D object. Make the cooking top 30" high and add some cabinet doors.

SUMMARY

Once you have used AutoCAD's 3D capabilities, you see how simple a process using 3D really is. Most important, 3D can help you visualize an object without resorting to complex mathematics to input your image.

If you are not totally satisfied with the 3D views generated by AutoCAD alone, you may want to try using a separate program to further enhance your 3D drawings. In the next chapter, we will cover the advanced 3D features of AutoCAD.

16

▼ ▼ ▼ ▼ ▼

USING
ADVANCED
3D FEATURES

FAST TRACK

657 ▶ **To get a plan view of any UCS**

Click on View ➤ Set View ➤ Plan View, then click on the desired UCS from the last cascading menu. You have the choice of the current UCS, the World Coordinate System, or you can select a saved UCS from a dialog box.

662 ▶ **To change the display of the UCS Icon**

Click on Settings ➤ UCS ➤ Icon, then select the desired setting for the UCS icon. You can turn it on or off, or set it so it shows the location of the current UCS's origin.

663 ▶ **To divide the screen into tiled viewports for easy 3D editing**

Click on View ➤ Layout ➤ Tiled Vports, then at the Tiled Viewports icon menu, click on the desired viewport layout.

682 ▶ **To recall a UCS**

Click on Settings ➤ UCS ➤ Named UCS, then at the dialog box, click on the name of the UCS you wish to recall. Click on the **Current** button, then click on **OK**.

682 ▶ **To save a UCS**

Click on Settings ➤ UCS ➤ Named UCS, then at the dialog box, click on the *No Name* UCS. At the input box toward the bottom of the dialog box, enter the new name, then click on the **Rename To** button to the left. You cannot do this with either *WORLD* or *PRE-VIOUS*, as these are names reserved for the World Coordinate System and the UCS command's Previous option.

685 ▶ To draw a non-linear 3D Surface

First, use lines and 3D polylines to lay out your surface. Use arcs, lines, and polylines to define the edges of your surface. Be sure the objects defining the edges touch end to end. Finally, click on Draw ➤ 3D Surfaces ➤ Edge Defined Patch and select the edge objects one at a time in a circular fashion.

687 ▶ To set the number of facets in a 3D mesh

Enter **Surftab1** or **Surftab2** at the command prompt, then enter the number of facets you want per surface axis.

690 ▶ To draw a surface that is "stretched" over two objects

Draw two objects that define the two sides of the 3D object you want to create. Click on Draw ➤ 3D Surfaces ➤ Ruled Surface, then click on the two objects.

693 ▶ To extrude a shape in a circular fashion like a lathe

First, draw the profile of the object to be extruded in a circular motion (swept), then draw a line representing the center axis of the circular motion. Click on Draw ➤ 3D Surfaces ➤ Surface of Revolution. Click on the profile, then click on the line.

699 ▶ To draw a predefined shape such as a cone or sphere

Click on Draw ➤ 3D Surfaces ➤ 3D Objects. At the 3D Objects icon menu, click on the type of object you desire, then click on **OK**. Answer the prompts that follow. You can then edit the basic shapes to your exact needs.

AutoCAD offers an extended set of tools for creating 3D drawings. You can create 3D models of objects with few limitations on shape and orientation. This chapter focuses on the use of these tools, which allow you to easily generate 3D forms and view them in both the perspective and orthogonal modes.

MASTERING THE USER COORDINATE SYSTEM

The *user coordinate system*, or UCS, allows you to define a coordinate system in 3D space. You can use all the same commands used in 2D drawings and apply them to 3D drawings.

As you work with AutoCAD, you will notice the L-shaped icon in the lower-left corner of the screen. This icon contains the letters W, X, and Y. The W indicates that you are currently in what AutoCAD calls the World Coordinate System, while the X and Y indicate the positive directions of the *x* and *y* axes. Up until now, you have been working in the *World Coordinate System,* or WCS for short (this is defined by AutoCAD and is unchangeable). This is a global system of reference from which you can define other user coordinate systems.

It may help to think of these AutoCAD user coordinate systems as different drawing surfaces, or two-dimensional planes. You can have several user coordinate systems at any given time. By setting up these different UCSs, you are able to draw as you would in the World Coordinate System in 2D, yet draw a 3D image. For example, if you wanted to draw a house in 3D with doors and windows on each of its sides, you could set up a UCS for each of the sides. Then you could move from UCS to UCS to add your doors and windows (see Figure 16.1). Within each of these UCSs, you could draw your doors and windows as you would in a typical 2D drawing. You could even insert elevation views of doors and windows you had created in other drawings.

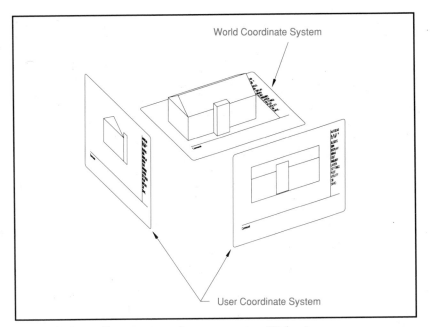

Figure 16.1:   Different user coordinate systems in a 3D drawing

DEFINING A UCS

In the first set of exercises, you will draw a chair that you can later add to your 3D unit drawing. By drawing this chair, you will be exposed to the use of the user coordinate system as well as to the use of some of the other 3D capabilities available in AutoCAD.

View ➤ Layout ➤ MV Setup

1. Start AutoCAD and open a new file called **Barcelon**.

2. Set your drawing up as an architectural drawing with a scale of 1" = 1'-0" on an 8½ × 11" sheet, then click on View ➤ Zoom ➤ All.

3. Click on Draw ➤ Rectangle and draw a rectangle measuring 20" in the x axis and 30" in the y axis. Position the rectangle so the lower-left corner is at the coordinate 2'-0",2'-0". This will be the seat of your chair.

4. Draw another rectangle 17" in the *x* axis and 30" in the *y* axis just to the right of the previous rectangle. This will be the back of your chair (see Figure 16.2).

5. Click on Modify ➤ Change ➤ Properties.

6. At the **Select objects:** prompt, select the two rectangles.

7. At the Change Properties dialog box, enter **3** in the Thickness input box, then click on **OK**. This will give the seat and back a thickness of 3".

8. Click on View ➤ Set View ➤ Viewpoint ➤ Set Vpoint and enter **–1,–1,1** ↵ in response to the prompt. See *Chapter 15* if you need to refresh your memory on this command. This will give you a 3D view from the lower left of the rectangles.

9. Enter **Zoom** ↵ **.7x** ↵ to zoom out a bit and give yourself some room to work.

▼ NOTE

Remember that it helps to think of a UCS as a drawing surface situated on the surface of the object you wish to draw or edit.

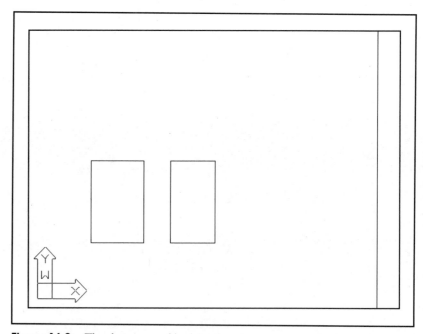

Figure 16.2: The chair seat and back in plan view

Notice that the UCS icon appears in the same plane as the current coordinate system. The icon will help you keep track of which coordinate system you are in. Now you can see the chair components as 3D objects.

Next, you will define a UCS based on one side of the seat.

AutoCAD ➤ UCS 3Point

▼ NOTE

You have several other options, which allow you to define, save, restore, or delete your UCS. We will look at these options later in this chapter.

▼ NOTE

Whichever choice you make will establish the origin point of your UCS.

▼ NOTE

The default value, 2'-1", 2'-0", 0'-0", indicates the positive direction of the *x* axis of the current coordinate system.

▼ NOTE

The prompts shown in steps 4 and 5 are asking you for the direction of the *x* axis (step 4) and of the *y* axis (step 5) in your new UCS.

1. Pick UCS from the Root menu or enter **UCS** ↵ at the command prompt. This is the command you use to define and switch between coordinate systems.

2. Click on next ➤ 3 Point from the side menu or enter **3** ↵ to select the 3Point option. This option allows you to define a UCS based on three points you select.

3. At the **Origin point <0,0,0>:** prompt, use your cursor and the Endpoint Osnap override to pick the bottom of the lower-left corner of the rectangle representing the seat (see label 1 in Figure 16.3).

4. At the **Point on positive portion of the X axis <'-1",2'-0", 0'- 0">:** prompt, use your cursor and the Endpoint Osnap override to pick the bottom of the lower-right corner of the rectangle (see label 2 in Figure 16.3).

5. At the **Point on positive - Y portion of the UCS X-Y plane <0'- 0",2'-0",2'-1">:** prompt, pick the top of the left-hand corner of the rectangle, just above the corner you picked for the origin of the UCS (see label 3 in Figure 16.3). The UCS icon changes to indicate your new UCS. The cursor also changes to reflect your new coordinate system.

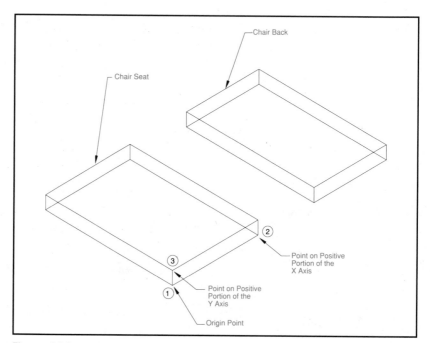

Figure 16.3: Selection points to define a new UCS

Now that you have defined a UCS, you may want to save it so that you can return to it in a later editing session.

UCS ↵
Save

1. Issue the UCS command again.

2. At the **UCS** prompt, use the Save option by entering **S** ↵.

3. At the **?/Desired UCS name:** prompt, enter the name **Side**.

Now you can issue the UCS command and use the Restore option whenever you want to return to this UCS.

VIEWING A UCS IN PLAN

Next, you will want to arrange the seat and back and draw the legs of the chair. It will be easier to accomplish this by viewing the chair from the side. To do this, you need to view your newly created UCS as if it were a 2D view. First, you will save the current 3D view so you can return to it easily later on.

View ➤ Set View ➤ Plan View ➤ Current UCS

1. Use View ➤ Set View ➤ Named View ➤ to open the View Control dialog box (see Figure 16.4), then click on the **New** button to save this view.

2. Give this view the name **3DLL**, then click on the **Save View** button.

3. Click on **OK** to return to the drawing.

4. Click on View ➤ Set View ➤ Plan View ➤ Current UCS. The view changes to show the two objects from their sides (see Figure 16.5).

5. Enter **Zoom** ↵ **.7x** ↵ to view more of the drawing and to give yourself some room to work.

WORKING IN A UCS

You could have given these rectangles a different elevation to lift them off the World Coordinate System plane. Instead, you will change their elevation by using the standard MOVE command while viewing them on edge. In this exercise you will see how you can use standard editing commands to draw in 3D.

1. Issue the MOVE command and use a crossing window to select both the chair seat and back.

2. MOVE them vertically in the current UCS y axis 8.5", just as you would if you were moving any object in 2D. You should have a screen that looks like Figure 16.6.

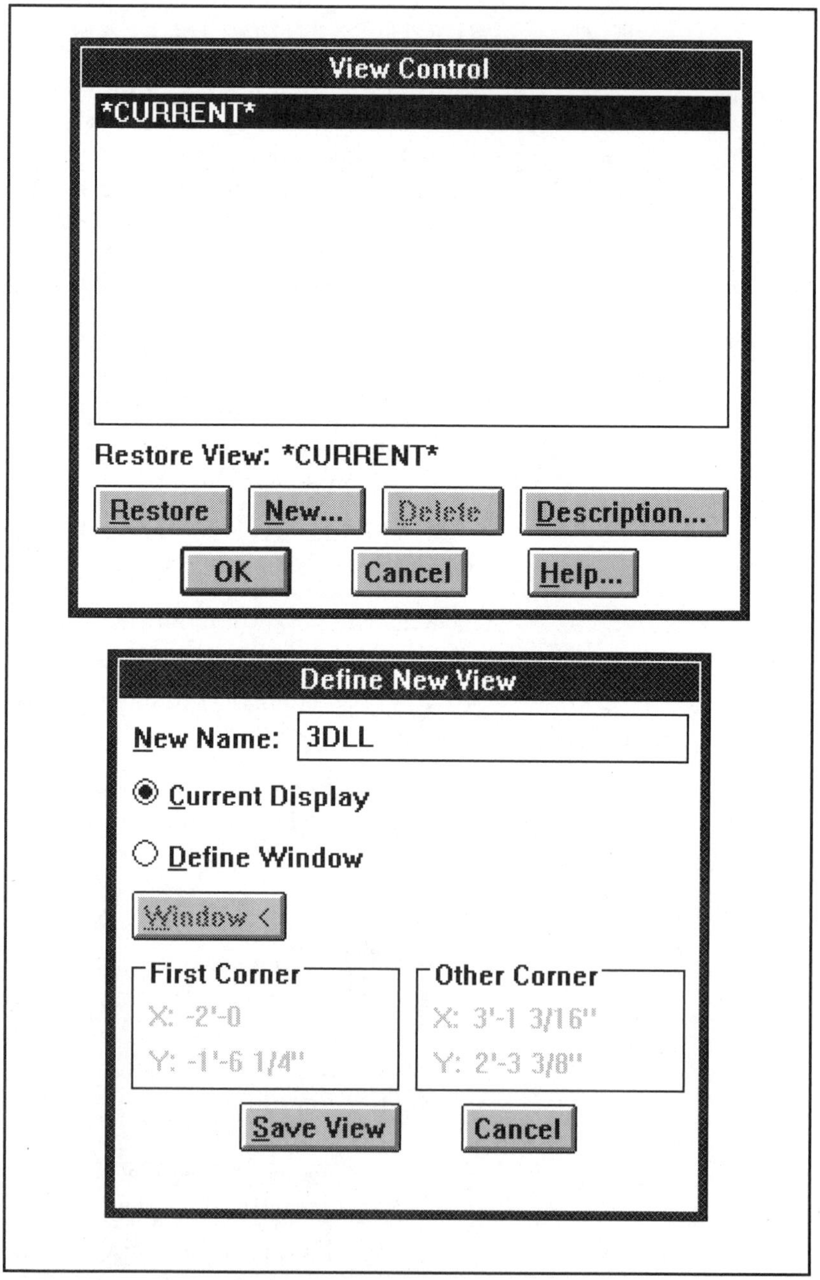

View Control

CURRENT

Restore View: *CURRENT*

Restore   New...   Delete   Description...

OK   Cancel   Help...

Define New View

New Name: 3DLL

◉ Current Display

○ Define Window

Window <

First Corner
X: -2'-0
Y: -1'-6 1/4"

Other Corner
X: 3'-1 3/16"
Y: 2'-3 3/8"

Save View   Cancel

Figure 16.4: The View Control dialog box

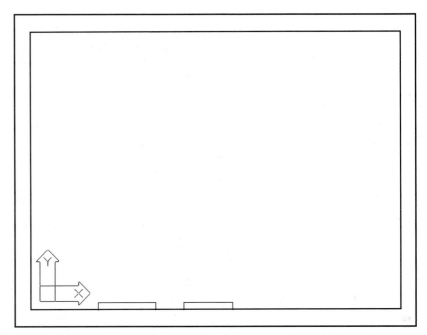

Figure 16.5: The newly defined UCS in plan view

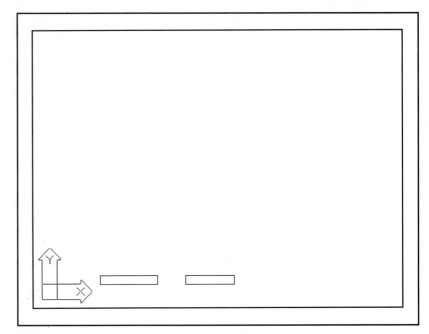

Figure 16.6: Elevating the chair seat and back

Next, you will move the chair seat and back to their proper locations. The grips feature will make quick work of this operation.

Grips ***ROTATE***

1. Be sure the Grips feature and Noun/Verb selection are turned on. Window the rectangle representing the seat back.

2. Click on the upper-left grip, then press ↵ twice to get to the ***ROTATE*** mode.

3. At the **Rotation angle** prompt, enter **80** ↵ for a rotation angle of 80°. You can also visually select a rotation angle using your cursor.

4. Click on the bottom-right grip, and this time press ↵ once to get to the ***MOVE*** mode.

5. Using the Endpoint Osnap override, click on the upper-right corner of the other rectangle to the left, as shown in Figure 16.7.

6. Window both rectangles, then click on the same grip point you did previously at the intersection of the two rectangles.

7. Press ↵ twice to get to the ***ROTATE*** mode, then enter **−10** to rotate both rectangles −10°. Use Figure 16.7 as a guide.

▼ NOTE

If you need some help with the 3DFace command, see the section in *Chapter 15* entitled *Using 3dfaces*.

You can get a 3D view of the chair to see your progress.

1. Use View ➤ Set View ➤ Named View to restore the view you saved earlier as *3DLL*. Your screen should look like Figure 16.8.

2. Use the 3DFace command to draw a surface over the top sides of the chair seat and back. Start the 3dface in the leftmost corner of the seat and work in a counterclockwise fashion.

3. ZOOM in on the chair so you can pick points more easily.

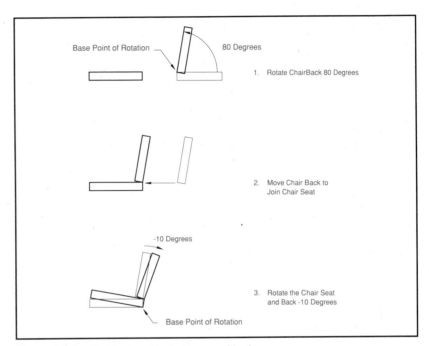

Figure 16.7:   Positioning the chair seat and back

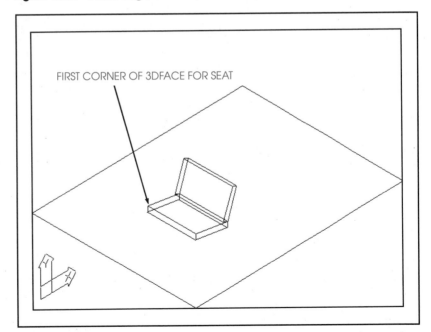

Figure 16.8:   The 3D view of your drawing so far, showing where to pick points for the 3dface

Normally, when picking points for 3dfaces, it doesn't matter where you start selecting points, but for the purpose of this tutorial, select points for the seat's 3dface starting at the leftmost corner and work in a counterclockwise fashion. The way you create the chair seat will affect how some UCS command options work later in this chapter.

CONTROLLING THE UCS ICON

So far, you have used only the UCS 3Point option to create other coordinate systems. There are several other options available to allow easy creation of and access to the UCS function. In the following section, you will want to set the UCS icon to show the current UCS origin location as well as its orientation. The following exercise shows how to control the UCS icon.

Settings ➤ UCS ➤ Icon ➤ Origin

Click on Settings ➤ UCS ➤ Icon ➤ Origin. The UCS icon will move to a location below the chair.

Now, whenever a new UCS is defined, the UCS icon will shift its location to show you not only the orientation of the UCS but also its origin. This will be useful in later exercises. When you click on Settings ➤ UCS ➤ Icon ➤ Origin, you are actually issuing the UCSICON command. Let's take a moment to look at the options offered by the UCSICON command.

Origin, the option you used in the exercise, will force the UCS icon to appear at the location of the current UCS's 0,0,0 origin point. If the UCS's origin is off the screen, the UCS icon appears in the screen's lower-left corner.

The **On** and **Off** options allow you to control whether the UCS icon is displayed or not.

NoOrigin turns off the Origin option.

All causes any changes made to appear in all visible viewports.

USING VIEWPORTS TO AID IN 3D DRAWING

In *Chapters* 6 and *12*, you were introduced to viewports. In this next section, you will use viewports to view your 3D model from several sides at the same time. This can be helpful in creating and editing your 3D drawing, since it allows you to refer to different portions of your drawing without having to change views. In *Chapter 12*, you created viewports from Paperspace. This time, you'll create viewports directly in Modelspace.

View ➤ Layout ➤ Tiled Vports

1. Click on View ➤ Layout ➤ Tiled Vports. An icon menu appears showing you the different viewport options (see Figure 16.9).

2. Highlight the icon that shows three viewports, two on the left side of the screen and one on the right (see Figure 16.9), then click on **OK**.

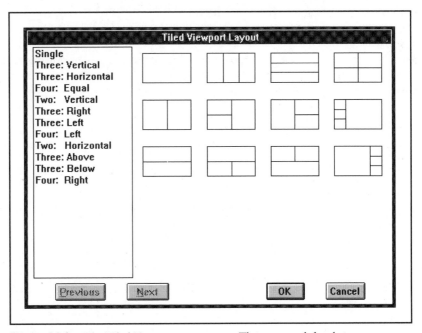

Figure 16.9:   The Tiled Viewports icon menu. These are predefined viewport settings that let you quickly access the Modelspace viewport feature.

▼ NOTE

You may notice that the UCS icon in the upper-left viewport has changed. It now looks like a broken pencil. This icon tells you that you are viewing the current UCS edge-on in that viewport.

Now you see three of the same images in each viewport. Each viewport can display a different view of your drawing.

1. Click on the upper-left viewport to activate it, then issue the PLAN command.

2. Enter **W** for WCS at the plan prompt. The view will change to a plan view of your chair.

3. Enter **Z** ↵ **.7x** ↵ to allow some room in the view.

4. Pick the lower-left viewport to be active.

5. Issue PLAN again, but this time press ↵ at the plan prompt to accept the default, *Current UCS*. The side view of your chair will appear in this viewport.

6. Enter **Z** ↵ **.7x** ↵ again to allow some room in this view.

7. PAN this view up so you can draw the legs of the chair more easily.

8. Switch to the 3D view on the right and enlarge this view to get a better look at the chair in 3D. You should have a screen similar to Figure 16.10.

▼ NOTE

Be sure that the Splinetype system variable is set to 6, the default value. Enter **'splinetype**, then **6**. (Release 10 and earlier must use **'SETVAR**.) By making the curves splines, you can easily adjust them using the Edit vertex option.

Now let's finish off the chair by adding legs.

Draw ➤ ⤵ Polyline ➤ 2D

1. Go to the side view of the chair and draw two spline curved polylines as shown in Figure 16.11. You may have to adjust your view so you can draw the legs more easily.

2. Use the grips of the polyline to adjust its curve if necessary.

3. Using Modify ➤ Polyedit, give the polylines a width of 0.5".

4. Use Modify ➤ Change ➤ Properties to give the polylines a thickness of −2". Notice that as you draw and edit the polyline, it appears in both the plan and 3D views.

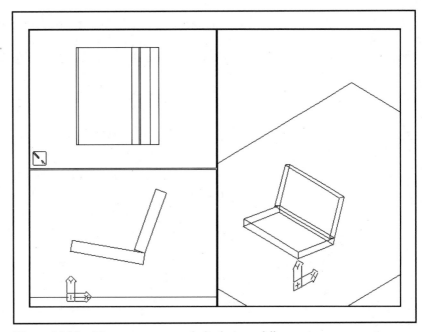

Figure 16.10: Three viewports, each displaying a different view

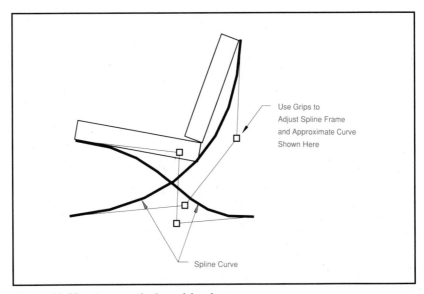

Use Grips to
Adjust Spline Frame
and Approximate Curve
Shown Here

Spline Curve

Figure 16.11: Drawing the legs of the chair

Polylines are the best entities to use for 3D, because you can generate complex shapes easily by giving polylines thickness and width. Once you are done drawing the legs, go to the plan view.

1. Click on the upper-left viewport, then click on Settings ➤ UCS ➤ Named UCS.

2. At the UCS Control dialog box, click on *WORLD*, then click on the **Current** button and finally, click on **OK**.

3. Toggle the ortho mode on and COPY the polylines representing the chair legs to the opposite side of the chair in roughly the same location. Your screen should look similar to Figure 16.12.

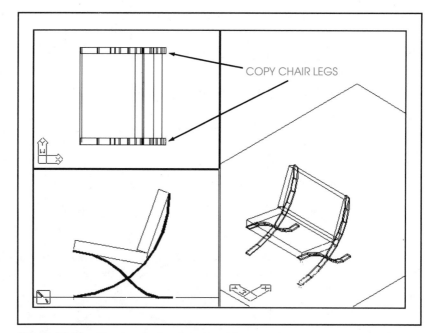

Figure 16.12: Copying the legs from one side to another

▼ **NOTE**

Notice that the broken-pencil UCS icon has shifted to the viewport in the lower-left corner. This tells you that your current UCS is perpendicular to the plane of that view.

▼ **NOTE**

You could also have used the MIRROR command to copy the chair legs. A mirrored object in 3D maintains its z coordinate values while mirroring its x and y coordinates.

Your chair is now complete.

1. Click on the viewport to the right.

2. Issue a Hide command to see what the chair actually looks like when it is viewed as a solid (see Figure 16.13).

3. Click on View ➤ Layout ➤ Tiled Vports, then click on the word *Single* in the list to the left.

4. Click on **OK**. The 3D view fills the screen in preparation for the next set of exercises.

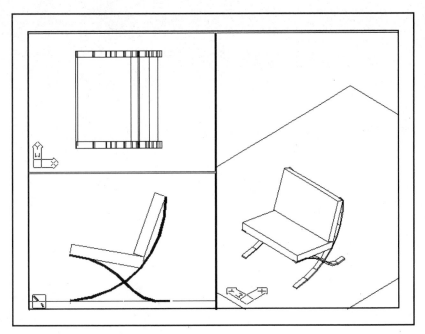

Figure 16.13:   The chair in 3D

CONTROLLING THE UCS

There are a number of other ways to define a UCS. You can, for example, use the 3dface of your chair as the definition for a UCS. In the following set of exercises, you will get some practice moving your UCS around. Learning how to move effortlessly between UCSs is crucial to your ability to create 3D models, so try to pay special attention to the command options shown in these exercises.

This first exercise shows how you can define a UCS in the current view plane.

UCS ↵
View

Enter **UCS** ↵, then enter **V** ↵, or click on UCS ➤ next ➤ View from the root menu. The UCS icon will change to reflect the orientation of the newly created UCS.

AutoCAD uses the current UCS origin point for the origin of the new UCS. By defining a view as a UCS, you can enter text to label your drawing, as in a technical illustration. Text entered in a plane created in this way will appear normal (see Figure 16.14).

▼ TIP

You can also use Paperspace to add notes to 3D views.

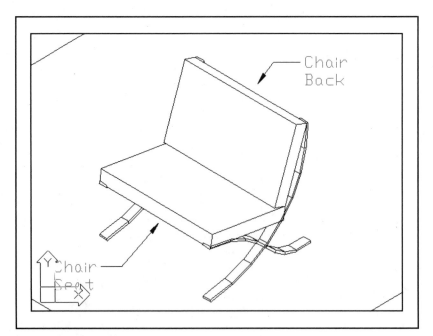

Figure 16.14: Using the View option of the UCS command

Another UCS option allows you to define a UCS based on the orientation of an object. This can be helpful when you want to work on a predefined object to fill in detail on its surface plane.

UCS ↵
Entity

1. Enter **UCS** ↵, then enter **E** ↵, or click on UCS ➤ next ➤ Entity from the Root menu.

2. At the **Select object to align UCS:** prompt, pick the 3dface used to define the top surface of the chair seat. The UCS icon will shift to reflect the new coordinate system's orientation (see Figure 16.15).

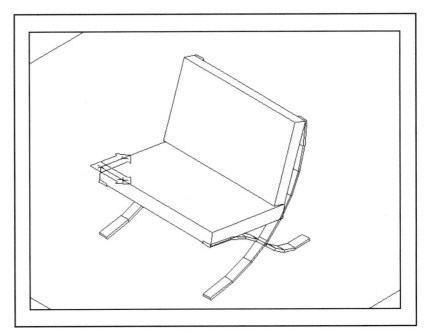

Figure 16.15:   Using the Entity option of the UCS command

You may recall that earlier you were asked to draw the 3dface for the seat in a specific way. The location of the UCS origin and its orientation are dependent on how the 3dface was created. Table 16.1 describes how an object will determine the orientation of a UCS.

Table 16.1: Effects of Objects on the Orientation of a UCS

OBJECT TYPE	UCS ORIENTATION
Arc	The center of the arc establishes the UCS origin. The x axis of the UCS passes through the pick point on the arc.
Circle	The center of the circle establishes the UCS origin. The x axis of the UCS passes through the pick point on the circle.
Dimension	The midpoint of the dimension text establishes the origin of the UCS origin. The x axis of the UCS is parallel to the x axis that was active when the dimension was drawn.
Line	The endpoint nearest the pick point establishes the origin of the UCS and the x,z plane of the UCS contains the line.
Point	The point location establishes the UCS origin. The UCS orientation is arbitrary.
2D Polyline	The starting point of the polyline establishes the UCS origin. The x axis is determined by the direction from the first point to the next vertex.
Solid	The first point of the solid establishes the origin of the UCS. The second point of the solid establishes the x axis.
Trace	The direction of the trace establishes the x axis of the UCS with the beginning point setting the origin.

Table 16.1:   Effects of Objects on the Orientation of a UCS

OBJECT TYPE	UCS ORIENTATION
3dface	The first point of the 3dface establishes the origin. The first and second points establish the x axis. The plane defined by the face determines the orientation of the UCS.
Shapes, Text, Blocks, Attributes, and Attribute Definitions	The insertion point establishes the origin of the UCS. The object's rotation angle establishes the x axis.

There may be times when you want to work in a UCS that has the same orientation as the current UCS but is offset. For example, you may be making a drawing of a building that has several parallel walls offset in a sawtooth fashion (see Figure 16.16). You can easily hop from one UCS to another, parallel one by using the Origin option.

UCS ↲
Origin

▼ TIP

You can also start this option by clicking on Settings ➤ UCS ➤ Origin.

1. Enter **UCS** ↲, then enter **O** ↲, or pick UCS ➤ next ➤ Origin from the Root menu.

2. At the **Origin point <0,0,0>:** prompt, pick the bottom end of the chair leg, just below the current UCS origin. The UCS icon will shift to the end of the leg with its origin at the point you picked (see Figure 16.17). At this prompt, you can either enter the new origin coordinate or pick a point on your drawing.

Now suppose you want to change the orientation of the x, y, or z axes of the current UCS. You can accomplish this by using the X, Y, or Z option of the UCS command. Let's try rotating the UCS about the z axis to see how this works.

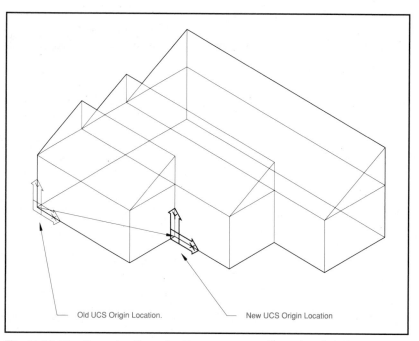

Old UCS Origin Location.   New UCS Origin Location

Figure 16.16: Example of how the Origin option can be used to shift the UCS

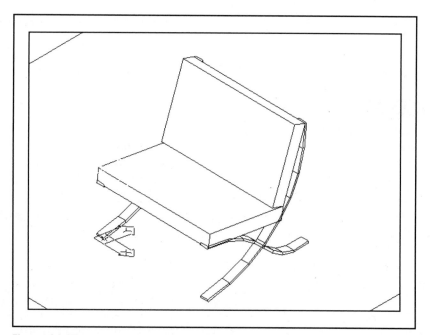

Figure 16.17: Moving the origin of the UCS

UCS ↵

X,Y,Z

▼ TIP

You can also start this option by clicking on Settings ➤ UCS ➤ Axis ➤ X, Y, or Z.

▼ WARNING

Because your cursor location is in the plane of the current UCS, it is best to either pick a point on an object using the Osnap overrides or use the coordinate filters.

1. Issue the UCS command again and enter **Z** ↵, or pick UCS ➤ next ➤ Z from the Root menu. This will allow you to rotate the current UCS about the *z* axis.

2. At the **Rotation angle about Z axis <0>:** prompt, enter **90** for 90°. The UCS icon rotates to reflect the new orientation of the current UCS (see Figure 16.18).

Similarly, the *X* and *Y* options allow you to rotate the UCS about the current *x* and *y* axes respectively, just as you rotated the UCS about the *z* axis.

Finally, you can skew the UCS by using the ZAxis option. This can be useful if you need to define a UCS based on a *z* axis determined by two objects.

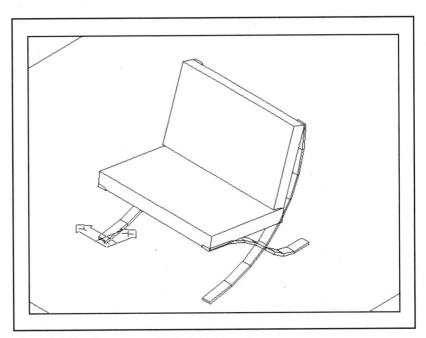

Figure 16.18: Rotating the UCS about the *z* axis

UCS ↵

ZAxis

1. Issue the UCS command again, then enter **ZA** ↵, or pick UCS ➤ next ➤ ZAxis from the root menu.

2. At the **Origin point <0,0,0>:** prompt, press ↵ to accept the default, which is the current UCS origin. You can shift the origin point at this prompt if you like.

3. At the **Point on positive portion of Z-axis <0'-0",0'-0", 0'-1">:** prompt, use the Endpoint Osnap override and pick the other chair leg end, as shown in Figure 16.19. The UCS will twist to reflect the new z axis of the UCS.

Now we've finished our tour of the UCS command. Set the UCS back to the World Coordinate System and END out of this file.

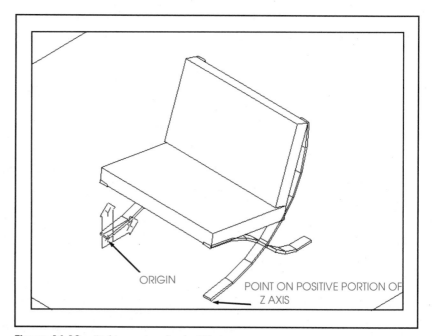

Figure 16.19:   Picking points for the ZAxis option

If you prefer using the UCS command from the keyboard, Table 16.2 describes its options.

With all these options, you can define just about any UCS you will need in the course of your drawing activities.

USING 3D MESHES

In the previous example, you drew a chair composed of objects that were mostly straight lines or extruded curves. All the forms in that chair could be defined in planes perpendicular to each other. At times, you will want to draw objects that do not fit so easily into perpendicular or parallel planes. The following exercise shows you how you can create more complex forms using some of AutoCAD's other 3D commands.

Table 16.2:   UCS Command Options and Corresponding Dialog Box Buttons

UCS OPTION NAME	DEFINE NEW USER COORDINATE SYSTEM DIALOG BOX OPTION
Origin	New origin
ZAxis	New origin, z axis
3point	Origin, x axis, Plane
Entity	Align with entity
View	Align with view
X	Rotate about x axis
Y	Rotate about y axis
Z	Rotate about z axis
Prev	
Restore	
Save	
Del	
?	List Existing UCSs

LAYING OUT A 3D FORM

In this next group of exercises, you will draw a butterfly chair. This chair has no perpendicular or parallel planes to work with. For this reason, you will start by setting up some points that you will use for reference only. This is similar in concept to laying out a 2D drawing. These points will define the major UCSs needed to construct the drawing. As you progress through the drawing construction, notice how the reference points are established to help create the chair.

Vpoint ↵

1. Open a new file called **Btrfly** and set up an architectural drawing at 1" = 1'-0" scale on an 8½ × 11" sheet.

2. Click on Draw ➤ Rectangle and draw a rectangle 20" square with its first corner at coordinate 36,36.

3. Use the OFFSET command to offset the square 4" out so you have two concentric squares, the outer square measuring 28".

4. MOVE the 28" square to the left 2". Your screen should look similar to Figure 16.20.

5. Enter **Vpoint** ↵ to start the Vpoint command.

6. At the **Rotate/<viewpoint>** prompt, enter **–1,–.75,.5**. This will give you a view from the lower-left side of the rectangles.

7. Move the outer rectangle in the Z axis so that its elevation is 30". To do this, first click on the outer rectangle, then click on one of its grips.

8. Press ↵ to enter the ***MOVE*** mode, then enter **@0,0,30** ↵. By entering @0,0,30, you are telling AutoCAD to move the rectangle a 0 distance in both the x and y axes and 30" in the z axis.

9. Use the LINE command and draw lines from the corners of the outer square to the corners of the inner square, as in Figure 16.21. This is the layout for your chair.

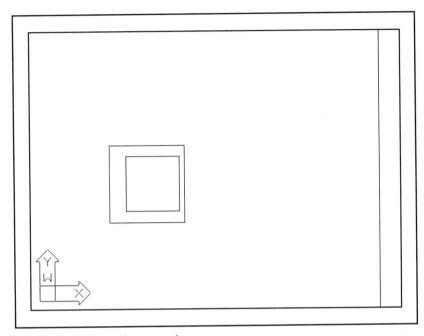

Figure 16.20:   Your drawing so far

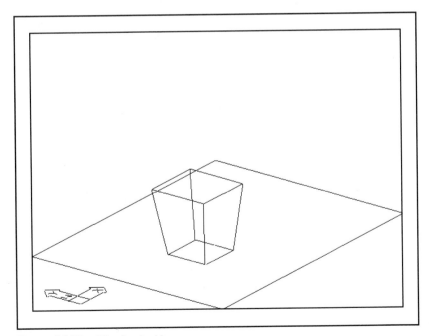

Figure 16.21:   The finished layout

▼ WARNING

All objects, with the exception of lines, 3dfaces, 3dmeshes, and 3D polylines, are restricted to the plane of your current UCS. The PLINE command can only be used to draw polylines in one plane, while the 3DPOLY command allows you to create a polyline in three dimensions. Three-dimensional polylines cannot, however, be given thickness or width.

In this exercise, you used relative Cartesian coordinates to locate the second point for the MOVE command. For commands that accept 3D input, you can also specify displacements by using the *spherical* and *cylindrical coordinate formats*. The spherical coordinate format lets you specify a distance in 3D space while specifying the angle in terms of degrees from the x axis of the current UCS and degrees from the x–y plane of the current UCS (see panel 1 of Figure 16.22). For example, to specify a distance of 4.5" at a 30° angle from the x axis and 45° from the x–y plane, enter **@4.5<30<45**. What this means is that you enter the direct distance followed by a less-than sign; then the angle from the x axis of the current UCS; then another less-than sign; then the angle from the x–y plane of the current UCS. Using the spherical format to move the rectangle in the exercise, you would enter **@30<0<90** at the **Second point** prompt.

The cylindrical coordinate format, on the other hand, lets you specify a location in terms of a distance in the plane of the current UCS and a distance in the z axis. You also specify an angle from the x axis of the current UCS (see panel 2 of Figure 16.22).

For example, to locate a point that is a distance of 4.5" in the plane of the current UCS, at an angle of 30° from the x axis, and a distance of 3.3" in the z axis, you enter **@4.5<30,3.3**. What this means is that you enter the distance of the displacement as it relates to the plane of the current UCS; then the less-than sign; then the angle from the x axis; then a comma; then the distance in the z axis. Using the cylindrical format to move the rectangle, you would enter **@0<0,30** at the **Second point** prompt.

USING A 3D POLYLINE

Next, you will draw the legs for your chair. For this you will use a 3D polyline. This is a polyline that can be drawn in 3D space.

Draw ➤ ⟲ Polyline ➤ 3D

1. Zoom into the frame so you can select the points on the frame more easily.

2. Click on Draw ➤ Polyline ➤ 3D or enter **3dpoly** at the command prompt.

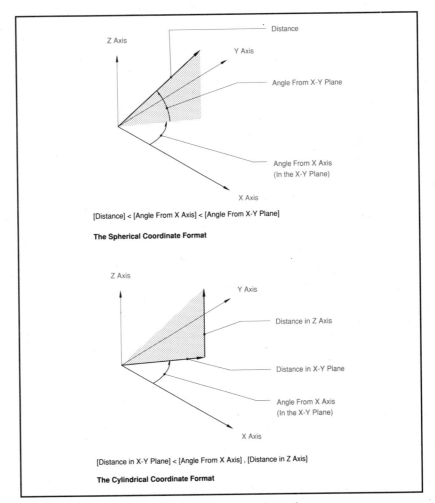

Figure 16.22:   The spherical and cylindrical coordinate formats

3. At the **First point:** prompt, pick a series of points as shown in Figure 16.23 by using the Endpoint and Midpoint Osnap overrides.

4. Draw another 3D polyline in the mirror image of the first (see Figure 16.23).

5. ERASE the rectangles and lines that make up the frame. You have just drawn the legs of the chair.

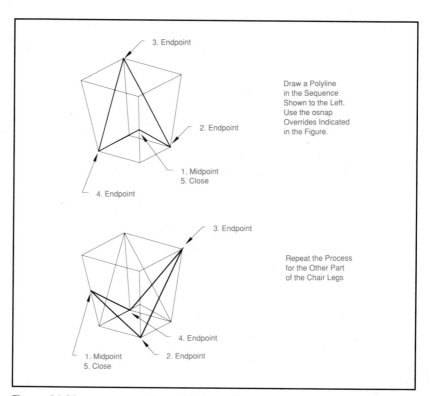

Figure 16.23: Drawing the legs of the butterfly chair

CREATING A 3D SURFACE

Next, you will draw the seat of the chair. The seat of a butterfly chair is usually made of canvas and drapes from the four corners of the chair legs. To draw the seat, you will first define the perimeter of the seat using arcs, then you will use the EDGESURF command to form the shape of the draped canvas. EDGESURF will create a surface based on four objects defining the edges of that surface. In this example, you will use arcs to define the edges of the seat.

To draw the arcs defining the seat edge, you must first establish the UCSs in the planes of those edges. Remember that in the last example you created a UCS for the side of the chair before you could draw the legs. In the same way, you must create a UCS defining the planes that contain the edges of the seat.

UCS
Save
Restore

1. Issue the UCS command and use the 3Point option to create a UCS using the three points shown in the top view of Figure 16.24.

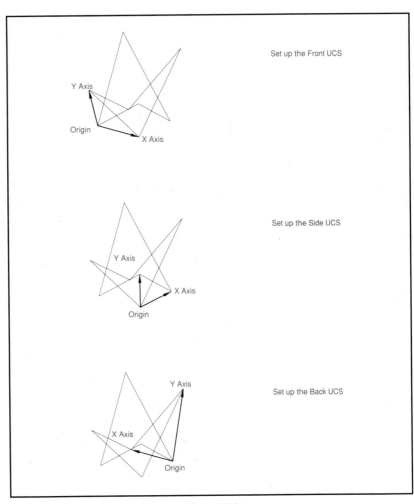

Figure 16.24: Defining and saving three UCSs

2. Click on Settings ➤ UCS ➤ Named UCS. The UCS Control dialog box appears (see Figure 16.25).

3. Highlight the *NO NAME* item in the list box, then, in the input box, change the name to **Front**.

4. Click on the **Rename To** button next to the input box, then click on **OK**. You have just renamed the new current UCS *Front*.

5. Define a UCS for the side of the chair, then use the UCS Control dialog box to rename this UCS **Side**, just as you did with the previous UCS.

6. Define the UCS for the back of the chair and name it **Back** using the UCS Control dialog box. Use Figure 16.24 for reference.

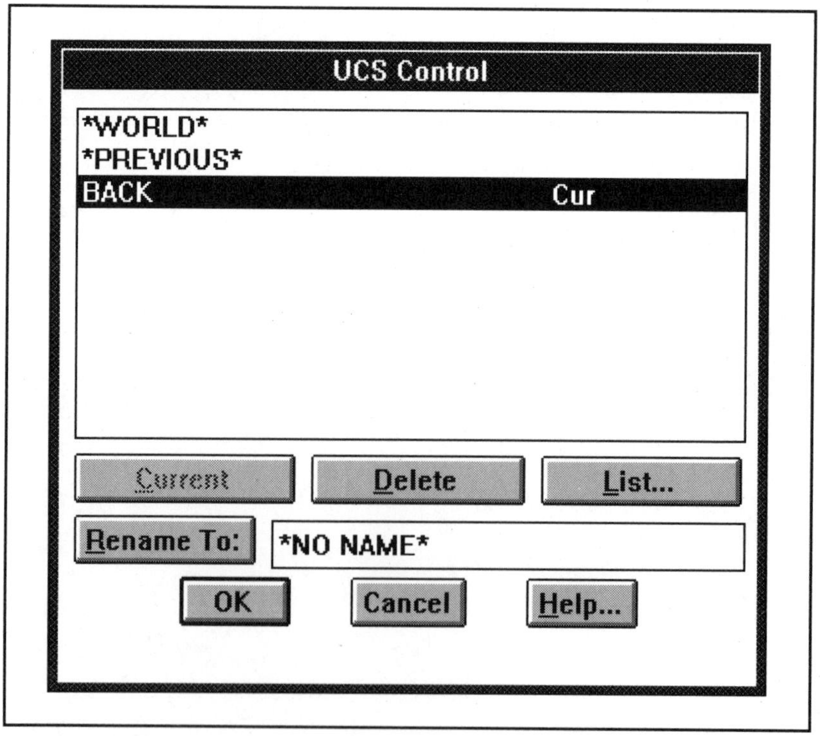

Figure 16.25: The UCS Control Dialog box

▼ NOTE

If you need help with the ARC command, refer to *Chapter 3*.

▼ NOTE

As you pick the endpoints, you may get the message **Entities not parallel with the UCS were ignored.** This message tells you that AutoCAD only draws arcs in the current UCS. Only lines, 3D polylines, and other 3D entities can be drawn in three-dimensional space. All other objects can be drawn only in the current UCS.

7. Open the UCS Control dialog box again and highlight FRONT.

8. Click on the **Current** button below the list, then click on **OK**. This makes the Front UCS current.

9. Click on Draw ➤ Arc ➤ Start, End, Direction, then draw the arc defining the front edge of the chair (see Figure 16.26). Use the Endpoint Osnap override to pick the top endpoints of the chair legs as the endpoints of the arc.

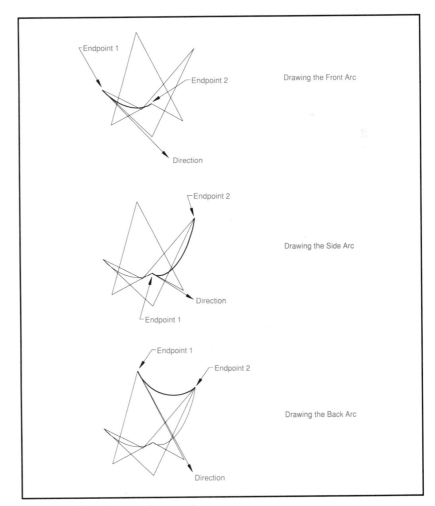

Figure 16.26: Drawing the seat edge using arcs

10. Repeat steps 7 through 9 for the UCS you saved as **Side**, and then again for the UCS named **Back**—each time using the top endpoints of the legs for the endpoints of the arc.

Next, you will mirror the side edge arc to the opposite side. This will save you from having to define a UCS for that side.

UCS
Mirror

1. Use the UCS Control dialog box to make the World Coordinate System (*WORLD*) current. The reason for doing this is that you want to mirror the arc along an axis that is parallel to the plane of the WCS. Remember that you must go to the coordinate system that defines the plane you wish to work in.

2. Click on the arc you drew for the side of the chair. This is the one drawn on the Side UCS.

3. Click on the midpoint grip of the arc, then press ↵ or the right mouse button four times to get to the **MIRROR** mode.

4. Enter **C** ↵ to select the Copy option.

5. Enter **B** ↵ to select a new base point for the mirror axis.

6. At the **Base point** prompt, use the Intersec Osnap override to pick the intersection of the two legs in the Front plane.

7. Next, use INTERSEC to pick the intersection of the two legs in the Back plane. Refer to Figure 16.27 for help. The arc should mirror to the opposite side and your chair should look like Figure 16.28.

8. Press **Ctrl-C** to clear the grips.

▼ WARNING

The arcs, or any set of objects used to define the boundary of a mesh with the Edgesurf command, must be connected exactly end to end in order for that command to work properly.

Let's finish off this chair by adding the mesh representing the chair seat.

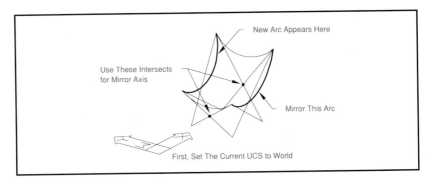

Figure 16.27:   Mirroring the arc defining the side of the chair seat

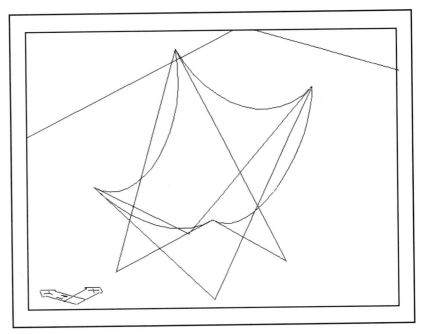

Figure 16.28:   Your drawing so far

Draw ➤ 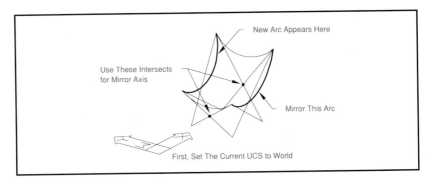 3D Surfaces ➤ Edge Defined Patch

1. Click on Draw ➤ 3D Surfaces ➤ Edge Defined Patch or
   enter **Edgesurf** ↵ at the command prompt.

2. At the **Select edge 1:** prompt, pick the arc on the Front UCS.

3. At the **Select edge 2:** prompt, pick the next arc on the Side UCS.

4. Continue to pick the other two arcs in succession. The arcs must be picked in a circular fashion and not crosswise. A mesh will appear filling the space between the four arcs. Your chair is complete and you've come to the end of the 3D surfaces exercises.

5. Issue the Hide command to get a better view of your chair. You should have a view similar to Figure 16.29.

6. Save this file.

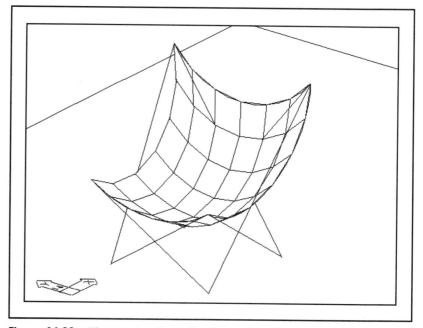

Figure 16.29: The completed butterfly chair

ADJUSTING THE
SETTINGS THAT CONTROL MESHES

As you can see, the seat is made up of rectangular segments. If you want to increase the number of segments in the mesh, you can change the Surftab1 and Surftab2 system variables. Surftab1 controls the number of segments along edge 1, the first edge you pick in the sequence, and Surftab2 controls the number of segments along edge 2. AutoCAD refers to the direction of the first edge as m and the other direction as n. These two directions can be loosely described as the x and y axes of the mesh, with m being the x axis and n being the y axis.

Figure 16.30 shows the chair with settings of 24 for Surftab1 and 12 for Surftab2. The default value for these settings is 6. If you would like to try different Surftab settings on the chair mesh, you must erase the existing mesh, change the Surftab settings, then use the Edgesurf command again to define the mesh. See *Chapters 13* and *14* and *Appendix D* for more on system variables.

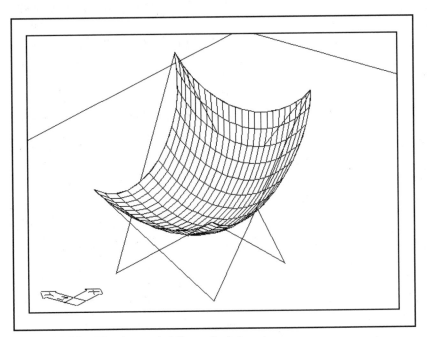

Figure 16.30:   The chair with different Surftab settings

EDITING A MESH

You can edit meshes in a way similar to editing polylines by using the PEDIT command. This command is the same as Modify ➤ Polyedit. When you issue PEDIT and pick a mesh, you get the prompt

Edit vertex/Smooth surface/Desmooth/Mclose
/Nclose/Undo/eXit <X>:

The following describes what each of the options does:

Edit vertex allows you to relocate individual vertices in the mesh. A detailed discussion of this option follows this list.

Mclose and **Nclose** allow you to close the mesh in either the *m* or *n* direction of the mesh. When either of these options is used, the prompt line will replace the corresponding Mclose or Nclose with Mopen or Nopen, allowing you to open a closed mesh.

Smooth surface acts in a similar way to the Spline option when you edit polylines. Rather than having the mesh's shape determined by the vertex points, *Smooth surface* will adjust the mesh so that mesh vertices act as control points that pull the mesh, much as a spline frame pulls a spline curve.

You can adjust the amount of pull the vertex points exert on a mesh by using *Smooth surface* in conjunction with the Surftype system variable. If you'd like to know more about these settings, see *Appendix D*.

Desmooth reverses the effects of *Smooth Surface*.

EDITING VERTICES IN A MESH

If you want to move a specific vertex in the mesh, you can use the Edit vertex option of the Pedit command. To use this option, do the following:

1. Click on Modify ➤ PolyEdit or enter **Pedit** ↵.

2. Click on the Mesh you want to edit.

3. Enter **E** ↵.

You then see the prompt

Vertex (0,0): Next/Previous/Left/Right/Up/Down/Move
/REgen/eXit <N>:

and an X appears on the vertex to be edited. The following describes
each of these options:

Next and **Previous** allow you to move the X quickly along the *n* axis of the mesh to another vertex.

Left and **Right** move the X one vertex at a time along the *n* axis.

Up and **Down** move the X along the *m* axis one vertex at a time.

Move lets you relocate a vertex once you have placed the X on the vertex you want to edit.

REgen regenerates the mesh to show the effects of any changes you make to a smooth mesh.

The m and n axes mentioned above are like the mesh's own local coordinate. Their direction depends on how the mesh is created.

Now that you've seen meshes, let's move on and try out some of the other 3D surface drawing commands.

OTHER SURFACE DRAWING COMMANDS

In the last example, you used the Edgesurf command to create a 3D surface. There are several other 3D surface commands available that allow you to generate surface shapes easily. In the next section, you will explore some of the possible uses of these commands.

CREATING A 3DMESH BY GIVING COORDINATES

If you need to draw a mesh like the one in the previous example, but you want to give exact coordinates for each vertex in the mesh grid, you can use the 3Dmesh command. For example, if you have data from a

▼ **TIP**

All the objects described in the following section, along with the meshes described earlier, are actually composites of 3dfaces. This means that these 3D objects can be exploded into their component 3dfaces, which in turn can be edited individually.

survey of a piece of land, you can use 3Dmesh to convert your data into a graphic representation of its topography. Another use of 3Dmesh is to plot mathematical data to get a graphic representation of a formula.

Since you must enter the coordinate for each vertex in the mesh, 3Dmesh is better suited in scripts or AutoLISP programs where a list of coordinates can be applied automatically to the 3Dmesh command in a sequential order.

USING TWO OBJECTS TO DEFINE A SURFACE

Rulesurf draws a surface between two 2D objects like a line and an arc or a polyline and an arc. It is useful for creating extruded forms that transform from one shape to another along a straight path. Let's see firsthand how this command works. First you'll draw two objects that you will use with Rulesurf.

1. Open a new file called **Table**.

2. Set up this drawing in the same way as the other two drawings.

3. While in the WCS, draw an arc forming a semicircle with a radius of 12".

4. Draw a line connecting the two endpoints of the arc (see Figure 16.31).

5. Next, change your viewpoint to view the drawing in 3D.

6. Move the line 10" in the z axis.

Now you are ready to connect the two objects with a 3D surface using Rulesurf.

Draw ➤ 🔳 3D Surfaces ➤ Ruled Surface

1. Click on Draw ➤ 3D Surfaces ➤ Ruled Surface or enter Rulesurf⏎.

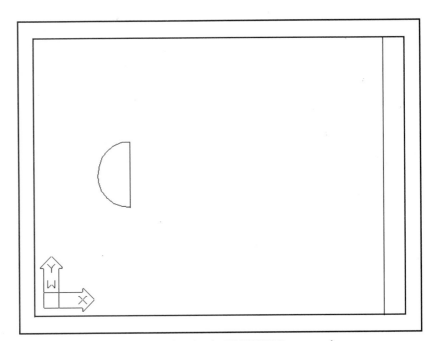

Figure 16.31:   Drawing two edges for the RULESURF command

The position you use to pick the second object will determine how the surface is generated.

You may have noticed that the surface you drew in each instance was made up of six segments. Just as with the Edgesurf command, you can control the number of segments that appear by adjusting the Surftab1 system variable.

2. At the **Select first defining curve** prompt, locate the cursor toward the lower end of the arc and click on it.

3. At the **Select second defining curve** prompt, locate the cursor toward the upper end of the line and click on it. The surface will appear (see Figure 16.32).

The segments defining the surface cross each other. The crossing effect is caused by picking the defining objects near opposite endpoints. The arc was picked near its lower end, while the line was picked toward the top end.

1. ERASE the surface you just drew.

2. Click on Draw ➤ 3D Surfaces ➤ Ruled Surface again, but this time pick the defining objects at or near the same end. You should get a surface similar to the one in Figure 16.33.

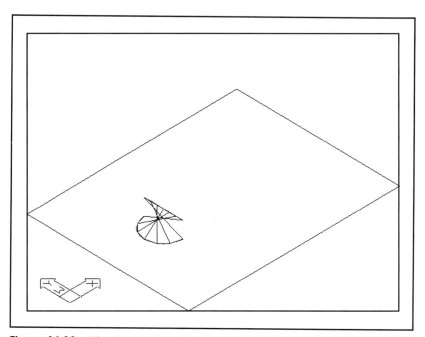

Figure 16.32: The RULESURF surface

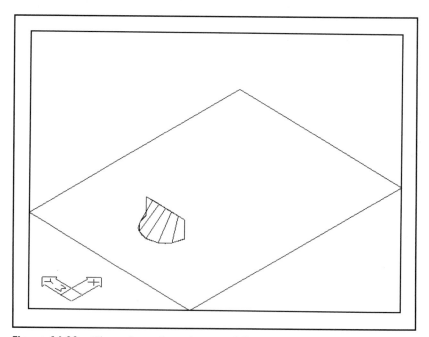

Figure 16.33: The surface redrawn by using different points to select the objects

Now finish the table by following the instructions in Figure 16.34, then save the file.

DRAWING EXTRUDED AND ROTATED 3D FORMS

In *Chapter 15*, you learned how you can extrude objects in the *z* axis by using the CHANGE command and changing an object's thickness. Other commands allow you to extrude an object in a linear or circular fashion in any direction in space. In the following example, you will draw a simple lever-type door handle to see how these other extrusions can be accomplished.

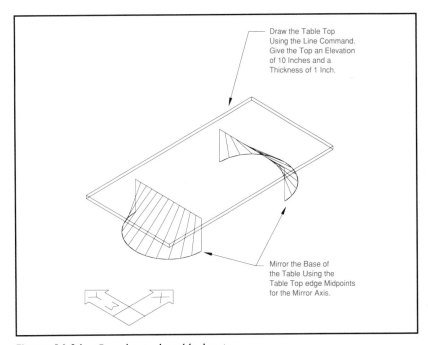

Draw the Table Top Using the Line Command. Give the Top an Elevation of 10 Inches and a Thickness of 1 Inch.

Mirror the Base of the Table Using the Table Top edge Midpoints for the Mirror Axis.

Figure 16.34: Completing the table drawing

Draw ➤ 🖿 3D Surfaces ➤ Surface of Revolution
(Revsurf)

1. Open a new file called **Handle** and set it up as an architectural drawing at full scale on an $8\frac{1}{2} \times 11$" sheet.

2. Draw a circle to the left of the center of the screen with a 0.4" radius.

3. Draw a vertical line 0.5" to the right of the circle. This line will be the axis about which you will extrude the circle to form the curved portion of the handle.

4. Enter **Vpoint** ↵ and enter **−1,−1,1** to get a 3D view of your circle from the lower left of the WCS.

5. Draw ➤ 3D Surfaces ➤ Surface of Revolution or enter **revsurf** ↵ at the command prompt. Revsurf allows you to extrude an object in an arc or circle.

6. At the **Select path curve** prompt, pick the circle. The path curve is an object that defines the shape to be extruded. In this case it is a circle.

7. At the **Select axis of revolution** prompt, pick the line to the right of the circle below its midpoint. The axis of revolution is the axis about which the path curve will be rotated to form the extrusion.

8. At the **Start angle** prompt, press ↵. This prompt allows you to enter the beginning angle of the circular extrusion. This angle is in relation to the object you selected for extrusion. The default, 0, will start the extrusion at the position of the object, while a greater or lesser value will offset the beginning of the extrusion.

▼ NOTE

The included angle prompt allows you to control the distance of the extrusion. If you press ↵ without entering anything, the object will be extruded a full 360°.

▼ TIP

To determine the direction of extrusion, you can apply the *right-hand rule*. Imagine placing your right hand along the axis of rotation with your thumb pointing away from the end closest to the pick point. The direction in which your fingers curl is the direction of the positive extrusion.

9. At the **Included angle (+=ccw, −=cw) <Full circle>:** prompt, enter **90** ↵ for a 90° extrusion. The circle will extrude in a 90° arc toward the screen (see Figure 16.35).

At the **Included angle** prompt, you can enter a value in degrees—180, for example—if you want the extrusion to be only a partial circle. You can control the direction of the extrusion by entering either a plus or a minus sign before the degree value. You can also control the direction by selecting one or the other end of the line defining the axis of revolution. I directed you to select a point below the middle of the line so the extrusion would be in a direction toward you. Had you picked a point above the midpoint, the extrusion would have taken a path in the opposite direction, or away from you.

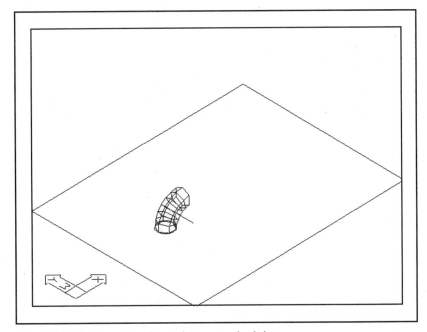

Figure 16.35: Extruding the circle in a circular fashion

You can use circles, arcs, lines, and polylines for your extruded shape and lines or polylines for your axes. You can control the number of segments in the extrusion by setting Surftab1 to a higher or lower value. Surftab2 will control the number of segments in the object. For example, if you set Surftab1 to 24, you will have 24 segments in the extrusion arc, giving the arc a smoother appearance. If you set Surftab2 to 24, the circle making up the extruded shape will be composed of 24 segments. This has the effect of giving your handle a rounded appearance rather than a hexagonal one (see Figure 16.36). The more segments you use, though, the larger your drawing file becomes, so keep the Surftab settings as low as possible without sacrificing appearance.

Let's continue by drawing the straight part of the handle. First, you will have to set up a new UCS in preparation for the next 3D object command. Create a UCS perpendicular to the WCS with its x axis aligned with the x axis of the WCS. Do this in the following way.

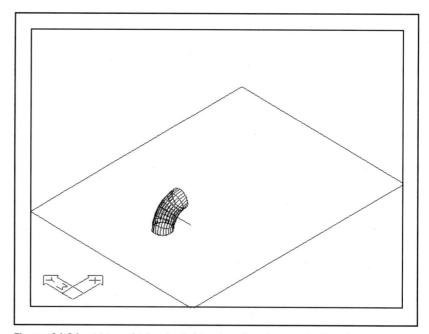

Figure 16.36: Using a higher Surftab2 value when drawing the handle

Settings ➤ UCS ➤ Axis ➤ X

1. Click on Settings ➤ UCS ➤ Axis ➤ X.

2. At the **Rotation angle about the X axis** prompt, enter **90** ↵. This rotates the UCS 90° in the positive direction. The right-hand rule applies here also.

Your UCS icon will change to reflect the orientation of your new UCS. Now you are ready to draw the straight part of the handle using the Tabsurf commmand. To prepare Tabsurf, you will have to rotate the circle used for the Refsurf extrusion –90° in the current UCS.

Grips **ROTATE**

1. ZOOM into the circle.

2. Click on the circle, then click on its center grip.

3. Press ↵ twice to get to the **ROTATE** mode.

4. Enter **B** ↵ to select a different base point for the rotation axis, then use the Endpoint Osnap override to pick the end of the line you used earlier during the Revsurf command.

5. Enter **–90** ↵ to rotate the circle –90°.

6. Draw a line 5" long in the x,y plane of the WCS (see Figure 16.37). This line will be used by the next command, Tabsurf, to define the direction and distance you want the rotated circle to be extruded.

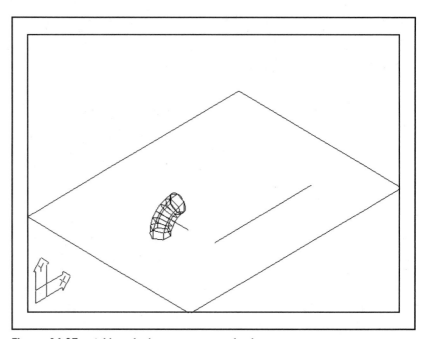

Figure 16.37: Adding the line representing the direction vector

Draw ➤ 🖅 3D Surfaces ➤ Tabulated Surface

7. Click on Draw ➤ 3D Surfaces ➤ Tabulated Surface or enter **Tabsurf** ↵ at the command prompt. Tabsurf extrudes objects in a straight line.

8. At the **Select path curve:** prompt, pick the circle. Here, you are being asked to select the object you want to extrude. If you need to, zoom in close to the circle so you will be able to pick it more easily.

9. At the **Select direction vector:** prompt, pick the line you drew to define the path of the extrusion. The point you pick on the line will determine the direction of the extrusion. The endpoint closest to your pick point on the direction vector will be the base point of the extrusion. The opposite end of the direction vector will indicate the direction of the

Surftab1 controls the number of segments that are used for the path curve. The higher the Surftab setting, the smoother the circle will be. You can use either a line or polyline as the direction vector, and you can use circles, arcs, lines, or polylines as objects to extrude.

extrusion. So, if you pick a point on the line closest to the circle, the extrusion will occur toward the line in the positive x direction. If you pick a point on the line farthest from the circle, the extrusion will occur away from the line (see Figure 16.38). At this point, you should know enough to add the escutcheon plate for the door handle (see Figure 16.39).

10. Finish the drawing and END out of the file.

This completes our look at 3D objects. You have had a chance to practice using nearly every type of object available in AutoCAD. You might want to experiment with the predefined 3D shapes offered in the Draw ➤ 3D Surfaces ➤ 3D objects icon menu.

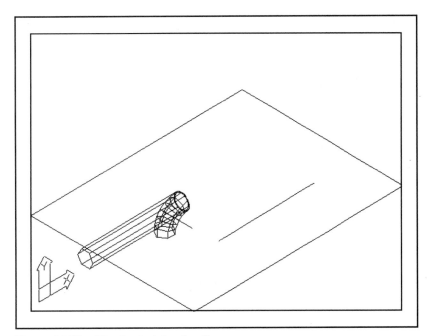

Figure 16.38:   The finished door handle

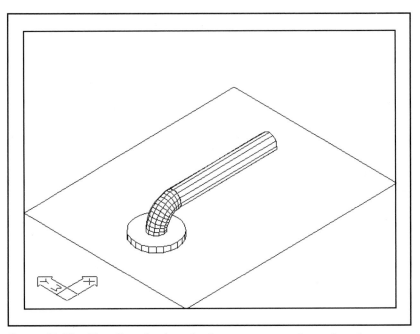

Figure 16.39:   The effect of picking the direction vector end away from the extruded object

IF YOU WANT TO EXPERIMENT...

You've covered a lot of information in this chapter, so it may be a good idea to play with these commands to help you remember what you've learned. Try the exercise shown in Figure 16.40.

SUMMARY

Mastering AutoCAD's 3D capabilities may seem difficult at first, but once you become familiar with the few commands I have shown you in this chapter, you will be creating 3D drawings quickly and easily. The UCS is the key element in developing 3D drawings. If you intend to use AutoCAD's 3D capabilities, try to become as familiar as possible with this very useful function. Of course, being familiar with all the other AutoCAD commands covered so far will also help.

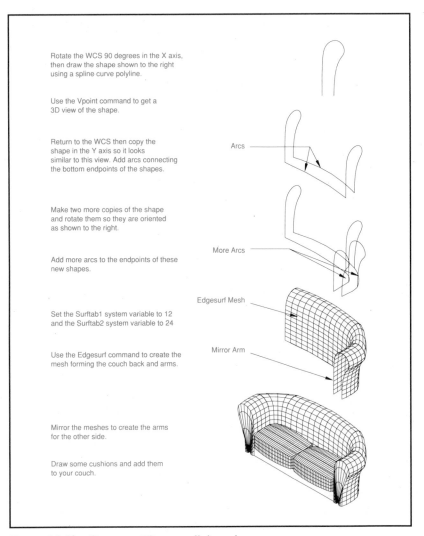

Rotate the WCS 90 degrees in the X axis, then draw the shape shown to the right using a spline curve polyline.

Use the Vpoint command to get a 3D view of the shape.

Return to the WCS then copy the shape in the Y axis so it looks similar to this view. Add arcs connecting the bottom endpoints of the shapes.

Make two more copies of the shape and rotate them so they are oriented as shown to the right.

Add more arcs to the endpoints of these new shapes.

Set the Surftab1 system variable to 12 and the Surftab2 system variable to 24.

Use the Edgesurf command to create the mesh forming the couch back and arms.

Mirror the meshes to create the arms for the other side.

Draw some cushions and add them to your couch.

Arcs

More Arcs

Edgesurf Mesh

Mirror Arm

Figure 16.40: Drawing a 3D overstuffed couch

In the next chapter, you will take a look at ways to view your drawing. You've already seen how you can shade and perform a hidden line removal. With AutoCAD's rendering feature, you can smooth out facets on rounded surfaces, control lighting, and change the way surfaces reflect light. With the Dview command, you can view your model in perspective and adjust the focal length of your view.

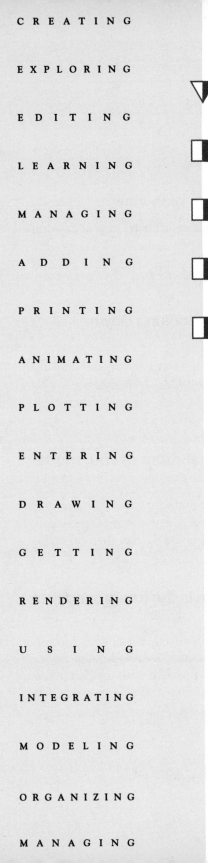

CREATING

EXPLORING

EDITING

LEARNING

MANAGING

ADDING

PRINTING

ANIMATING

PLOTTING

ENTERING

DRAWING

GETTING

RENDERING

USING

INTEGRATING

MODELING

ORGANIZING

MANAGING

17

RENDERING
AND
ANIMATING
3D DRAWINGS

FAST TRACK

706 ▶ To get a perspective view from a plan view

Click on View ➤ Set View ➤ Dview, then select parts of your drawing that will help you get your bearings. Enter **PO** ⏎, then pick a target and camera location. Finally, enter **D** ⏎ and use the slide bar to select a distance.

706 ▶ To change your view so you are looking down at your model

Click on View ➤ Set View ➤ Dview then select parts of your drawing that will help you get your bearings. Enter **CA** ⏎, then enter **T** ⏎⏎. Move your cursor until you get the camera angle you want, then click the left mouse button. Finally, press ⏎ to exit Dview.

706 ▶ To change the focal length to get more of your model in the view

Click on View ➤ Set View ➤ Dview, then select parts of your drawing that will help you get your bearings. Enter **Z** ⏎. Enter a new focal length value or move the cursor until you get a view you like, then press the pick button. Enter ⏎ to exit Dview.

706 ▶ To cut out portions of your model in the foreground that obscure your view

Click on View ➤ Set View ➤ Dview, then select parts of your drawing that will help you get your bearings. Enter **CL** ⏎. Move the slide bar to the far left, then gradually move it toward the right until the part of the foreground you want removed disappears. Press the pick button when you are done, then press ⏎ to exit Dview.

726 ▶ To add lights to your model

While in a plan view, click on Render ➤ Lights. Click on **New**, then select the type of light you want to add. Enter a light name, then click on **Modify** to select the location of the light. Click on **OK**, then click on **OK** again in the Lights dialog box.

735 ▶ To ensure all surfaces are rendered

Click on Render ➤ Preferences, then click on **Other Options**. Make sure the Discard Back Faces option is not checked, then click on **OK**. Click on **OK** again at the Rendering Preferences dialog box.

740 ▶ To add gradient and smooth shading

Click on Rendering ➤ Preferences, then click on **Smooth Shading** in the dialog box. Click on **OK** to exit the dialog box.

744 ▶ To add a finish to a surface

Click on Render ➤ Finishes, then click on **Import**. Click on the finish you want, then click on **OK**. At the **Enter new finish location** prompt, press ↵. Click on **Entities**, then click on the objects you want to attach the finish to. Press ↵ when you are done with your selection, then click on **OK**.

749 ▶ To store an image of a rendered view

Click on Render ➤ Files ➤ Save Image, then click on the image format you want. Enter a name for the image if it is to be different from the default. Click on **OK**.

So far, your views of 3D drawings have been in *parallel projection*. This means that parallel lines appear parallel on your screen. Though this type of view is helpful while constructing your drawing, you will want to view your drawing in true perspective from time to time to get a better feel for what your 3D model actually looks like. In the first part of this chapter, you will explore the use of the Dview command, which allows you to see your drawing in *true perspective*.

Once you've gotten familiar with Dview, you will be introduced to AutoCAD's rendering capabilities in the second half of the chapter. This is perhaps the only chapter where you will need a system capable of displaying 256 colors. Most computers set up for AutoCAD use an SVGA display capable of at least 800×600 display resolution and 256 colors, so this shouldn't be a problem. But if your renderings don't look similar to the ones in the figures, it is possible that your system does not support 256 colors. Check your display card manual if you have problems.

GETTING PERSPECTIVE VIEWS

Dview is a complex command, so I've broken the exercises into small, manageable parts that describe the use of each Dview option. With this in mind, you may want to begin these exercises when you know you have an hour or so to complete them all at one sitting.

Now let's begin!

View ➤ Set View ➤ Dview

1. Open the Barcelon file you created in the first part of *Chapter 16*. Be sure you are in the world coordinate system; issue the PLAN command so you have a plan view of the chair.

2. Issue the ZOOM All command to get an overall view of the drawing.

3. Click on View ➤ Set View ➤ Dview or enter **Dview** ↵ at the command prompt.

4. At the **object selection** prompt, pick the chair seat and back. You will use these objects as references while using the Dview command.

5. At the **CAmera/TArget/Distance/POints/PAn/Zoom/ TWist/CLip/Hide/Off/Undo/<eXit>:** prompt, select the appropriate option. These options are covered in the remaining exercises in this chapter.

The screen will change to show only the objects you selected.

Dview uses *dynamic dragging*, which allows you to preview your perspective view. For this reason, you are asked to select objects that will allow you to get a good idea of your view without slowing the dynamic-dragging process. If you selected the whole chair, the view-selection process would be much slower because the whole chair would have to be dragged during it.

SETTING UP YOUR VIEW

AutoCAD uses the analogy of a camera to help determine your perspective view. As with a camera, your perspective view will be determined by the distance from the object, camera position, view target, and camera lens type.

View ➤ Set View ➤ Dview ➤ Points

To determine the camera and target positions:

In the next set of exercises, be sure you press the pick button as I indicate in the text when selecting views. If you press the ↵ key or corresponding mouse return button, your view will return to the default orientation, which is usually the last view selected.

1. Enter **PO** ↵ at the Dview prompt or click on Options ➤ Points from the side.

2. At the **Enter target point** <*current point*>: prompt, pick the center of the chair. This will allow you to adjust the camera target point, which is the point at which the camera is aimed.

3. At the **Enter camera point** <*current point*>: prompt, pick the lower-left corner of the screen. This places the camera location, the position from which you are looking, below and to the left of the chair on the plane of the WCS (see Figure 17.1).

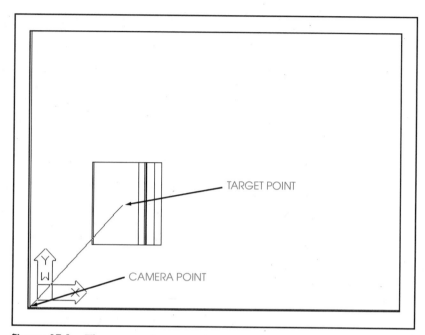

Figure 17.1:   The target and camera points

Your view will change to reflect your target and camera locations (see Figure 17.2). The Dview prompt returns, allowing you to further adjust your view.

If you like, you can press ↵ at the object-selection prompt without picking any object, and you will get the default image, a house, to help you set up your view (see Figure 17.3). You can also define a block and name it **Dviewblock**. AutoCAD will search the current drawing database. If it finds Dviewblock, it will use it as a sample image to help you determine your perspective view. Dviewblock should be defined in a one-unit cubed space.

ADJUSTING DISTANCES

Next, you will adjust the distance between the camera and target.

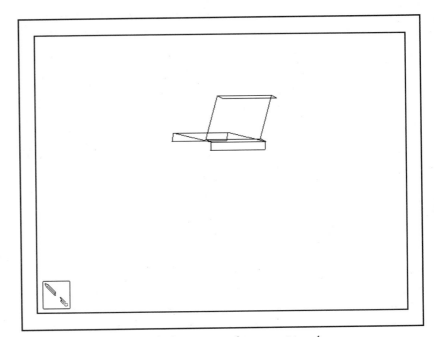

Figure 17.2:   The view with the camera and target positioned

View ➤ Set View ➤ Dview Distance

1. Enter **D** ⏎ or click on Distance from the side menu. A slide bar will appear at the top of the screen.

2. At the **New camera/target distance** <*current distance*>: prompt, move your cursor from left to right. The chair appears to enlarge or reduce. You also see that the position of the diamond in the slide bar moves. The slide bar gives you an idea of the distance between the camera and the target point in relation to the current distance.

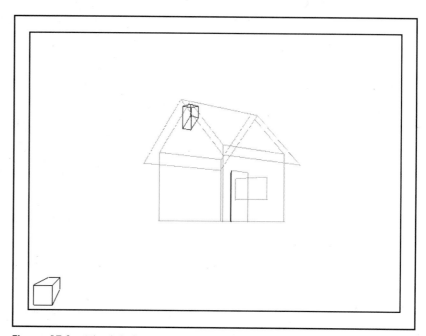

Figure 17.3:   The default sample image used with Dview

3. As you move the diamond, you see lines from the diamond to the 1× value, 1× being the current view distance. As you move the cursor toward the 4× mark on the slide bar, the chair appears to move away from you. Move the cursor toward 0× and the chair appears to move closer.

4. Move the cursor further to the left. The chair appears to fly off the screen when you move the cursor to the extreme left. This is because your camera location is moved so close to the chair that the chair disappears beyond the view of the camera. It is as if you were sliding the camera along the floor toward the target point. The closer to the chair you are, the larger and farther above you the chair appears to be (see Figure 17.4).

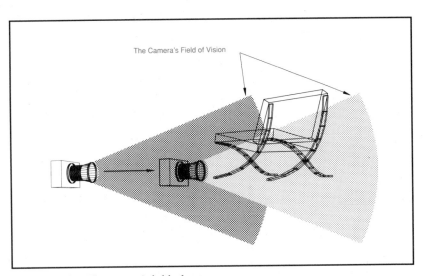

Figure 17.4: The camera's field of vision

The Distance option actually serves two functions: aside from allowing you to adjust your camera to target distance, it also turns on the perspective view mode. The Off option changes the view back to a parallel projection.

5. Adjust your view so it looks similar to Figure 17.5. To do this, move the diamond in the slide bar between the 1× and 4× marks.

6. Press the pick button on your mouse when you have the view you want. The slide bar disappears and your view is fixed in place. You may also notice that you are now viewing the chair in perspective.

ADJUSTING THE CAMERA AND TARGET POSITIONS

Next, you will want to adjust your view so you can see the whole chair. You are still in the Dview command.

View ➤ Set View ➤ Dview Target

1. Enter **TA** ↵ or pick TArget from the side menu.

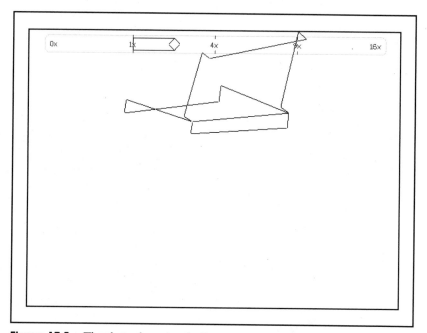

Figure 17.5: The chair after using the Distance option

2. At the [T]oggle angle in/Enter angle from X-Y plane <.00>: prompt, move your cursor slowly in a side-to-side motion. The chair moves in the direction of the cursor in an exaggerated manner. The sideways motion of the cursor simulates panning a camera from side to side across a scene (see Figure 17.6).

3. Center the chair in your view, then move the cursor slowly up and down. The chair moves in the opposite direction to the cursor. The up-and-down motion of the cursor simulates panning a camera up and down.

4. Watch the coordinate readout as you move the cursor up and down. It displays the camera's vertical angle as you move the cursor. Moving the cursor down causes the readout to list increasing negative numbers; moving the cursor up causes the

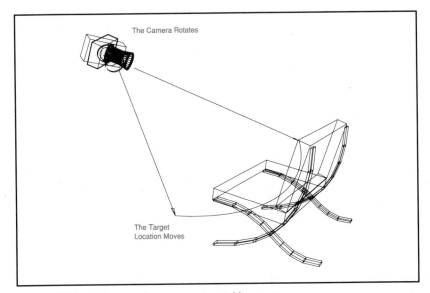

Figure 17.6:   Adjusting the target option is like panning your camera across a scene.

readout to list increasing positive numbers. This coincides with the prompt that asks for an angle from the X-Y plane. If you knew the exact camera angle you wanted from the X-Y plane, you could enter it now.

5.   Enter **T** ↵ to select the Toggle angle option. The prompt changes to read **[T]oggle angle from/Enter angle in X-Y plane from X axis** <*current angle*>:. Now as you move your cursor from left to right, the coordinate readout displays the angle of the camera relative to the X axis of the horizontal (X-Y) plane. If you knew the exact camera angle you wanted from the X axis of the X-Y plane, you could enter it now.

6.   Position the view of the chair so it look similar to Figure 17.7, then press the pick button. You've now fixed the target position.

▼ TIP

If you lose your view of the chair but remember your camera angle, you can enter it at the **Enter angle in X-Y plane** prompt to help relocate your view.

In steps 4 and 5, I said you could enter an angle value indicating either the vertical or horizontal angle to the target. Once you enter a value or just press ↵, the angle becomes fixed in either the vertical or horizontal

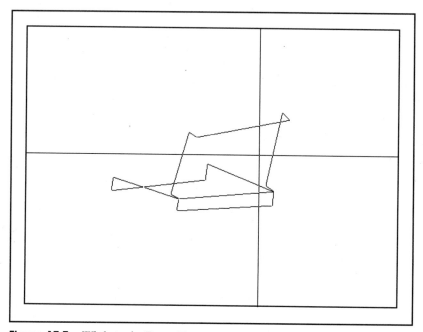

Figure 17.7: While in the Dview Target option, set up your view so it looks similar to this figure.

direction. Then, as you move your cursor, the view's motion will be restricted to the remaining non-fixed direction.

CHANGING YOUR POINT OF VIEW

Next, you will want to adjust the camera location to one that is higher in elevation.

View ➤ Set View ➤ Dview Camera

1. Enter **CA** ↵ to select the Camera option.

2. At the **[T]oggle angle in/Enter angle from XY plane <11>:** prompt, move your cursor slowly up and down. As you move the cursor up, your view changes as if you were rising

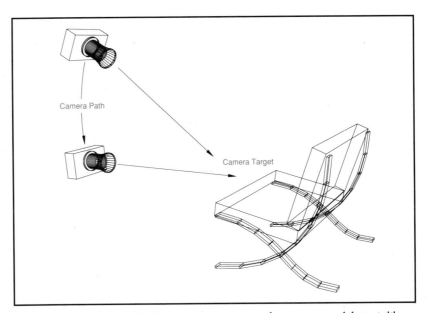

Figure 17.8: While in the Camera option, moving the cursor up and down is like moving your camera location up and down in an arc.

above the chair (see Figure 17.8). The coordinate readout displays the camera's angle from the horizontal X-Y plane as you move the cursor. If you know the angle you want, you could enter it now.

3. Move the cursor down so you have a view that is roughly level with the chair, then move the cursor from side to side. Your view changes as if you were walking around the chair, viewing it from different sides (see Figure 17.9).

4. Enter **T** ↵ to toggle the angle in X-Y plane option. The prompt changes to read **[T]oggle angle from/Enter angle in XY plane from** *x* axis **<−144>:**. Now as you move the cursor from side to side, the coordinate readout lists the camera's angle to the target point relative to the X axis. If you know the horizontal angle you want, you can enter it now.

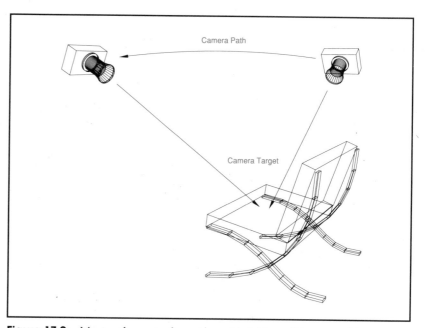

Figure 17.9: Moving the cursor from side to side is like walking around the target position.

5. Position your view of the chair so it is similar to the one in Figure 17.10, then press the pick button.

In steps 2 and 4, I said you could enter an angle value indicating either the vertical or horizontal angle to the camera. Once you indicate a value, either by entering a new one or just by pressing ↵, the angle becomes fixed in either the vertical or horizontal direction. Then, as you move your cursor, the view's motion will be restricted to the remaining non-fixed direction.

USING ZOOM AS A TELEPHOTO LENS

The Zoom option allows you to adjust the cone of vision of your view, much like a telephoto lens in a camera. It allows you to expand your view to include more of your drawing or narrow the field of vision to focus on a particular object.

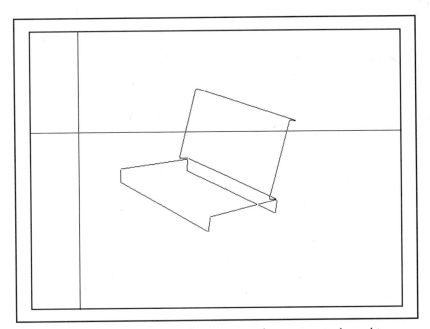

Figure 17.10:   Set up your camera location so you have a view similar to this one.

View ➤ Set View ➤ Dview
Zoom

If you don't have a perspective view (obtained by using the Distance option) and you use the Zoom option, you will get the prompt **Adjust zoom scale factor <1>:** instead of the **Adjust lenslength** prompt. The Adjust zoom prompt acts just like the standard Zoom command.

1. Enter **Z** ↵ at the Dview prompt. As you move your cursor from side to side, the chair appears to shrink or expand. You also see a slide bar at the top of the screen. This slide bar lets you see your view in relation to the last zoom setting, indicated by a diamond. You can either enter a value for a different focal length or visually select a view using the slide bar.

2. At the **Adjust lenslength <50.000mm>:** prompt, press ↵ to accept the *50.000mm* default value.

TWISTING THE CAMERA

The Twist option lets you adjust the angle of your view in the view frame. It is like twisting the camera to make your picture fit diagonally across the frame.

View ➤ Set View ➤ Dview
Twist

1. Enter **TW** ↵ for the Twist option.

2. At the **New view twist <0>:** prompt, press ↵ to keep the current 0° twist angle.

3. Press ↵ again to exit the Dview command, and the drawing will regenerate showing the entire chair in perspective (see Figure 17.11).

In the next section, you will look at one special Dview option that lets you control what is included in your 3D views.

USING CLIPPING
PLANES TO HIDE PARTS OF YOUR VIEW

At times, you may want a view that would normally be obscured by objects in the foreground. For example, if you try to view the interior of your unit drawing, the walls closest to the camera obscure your view. The Clip option under the Dview command allows you to eliminate objects in either the foreground or background so you can control your views more easily. In the case of the apartment unit, you can set the Front Clip option to delete any walls in the foreground that might obscure your view of its interior (see Figure 17.12).

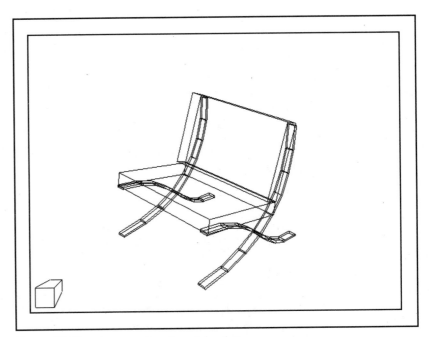

Figure 17.11:   A perspective view of the chair

View ➤ Set View ➤ Dview
Clip

1. Open the 3D Unit file you saved in *Chapter 15* and set up a perspective view using Figure 17.13 as a guide.

2. Click on View ➤ Set View ➤ Dview or enter **Dview** ⏎ for the Front Clip option.

3. When the **object-selection** prompt appears, select the entire drawing.

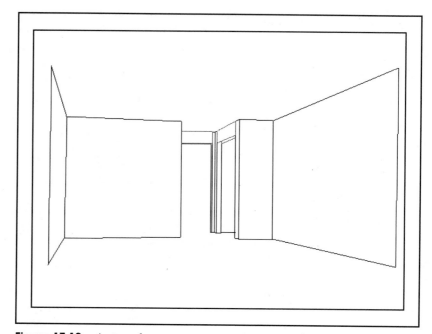

Figure 17.12: A view of an apartment unit interior using the front clipping plane

4. Using the **Points** option, approximate the target and camera locations shown in Figure 17.13. You can use the dynamic coordinate readout to help you locate the camera in relation to the target point.

5. Use the Distance option and enter **30′** to set the target-to-camera distance accurately.

6. Use the Camera option and enter **4.75** to place the camera angle at 4.75° from the floor.

7. When the Camera option's [**T**]**oggle angle from** prompt appears, press ↵ to accept the default.

8. Use the Target option to center the room on the screen. First, center it vertically, then horizontally, so it looks roughly like Figure 17.12.

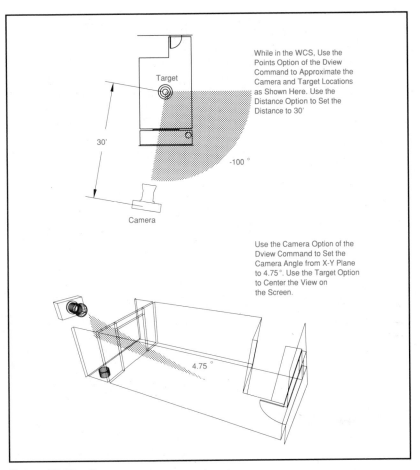

While in the WCS, Use the Points Option of the Dview Command to Approximate the Camera and Target Locations as Shown Here. Use the Distance Option to Set the Distance to 30'

Target

30'

-100 °

Camera

Use the Camera Option of the Dview Command to Set the Camera Angle from X-Y Plane to 4.75°. Use the Target Option to Center the View on the Screen.

4.75 °

Figure 17.13:   Setting up your perspective view

With this view the walls between the interior of the unit and the balcony obscure the interior. Next you will learn how to make the wall invisible using Dview's Clip option.

1. While still in the Dview command, enter **CL** ↵ for the Clip option.

2. At the **Back/front<off>:** prompt, enter **F** ↵. A slide bar appears at the top of the screen.

3. As you move the diamond on the slide bar from left to right, the walls in the foreground will begin to disappear, starting at the point closest to you. Moving the diamond from right to left brings the walls back into view. You can select a view either by using the slide box or by entering a distance from the target to the clipping plane.

4. At the **Eye/<distance from target>< current distance>:** prompt, move the slide bar diamond until your view looks similar to Figure 17.13, then press the pick button to fix the view.

5. To make sure the clipping plane is in the correct location, preview your perspective view with hidden lines removed. Enter **H** ↵ at the Dview prompt. The drawing will regenerate with hidden lines removed.

There are several other Dview Clip options that let you control the location of the Clip plane. The following describes the other options.

Back operates in the same way as the Front option, but instead of clipping your view in front of the view target, it clips the view behind the view target (see Figure 17.14).

Off turns off any clipping planes you may have set up.

▼ **TIP**

The quickest and easiest way to establish a perspective view is to first use VPOINT to set up your 3D view orientation, then start Dview and use the Distance option right off the bat to set your camera to target distance. Once this is done, you can easily use the other Dview options as you like, or exit Dview to see your perspective view.

You've now completed the Dview command exercises. I hope these exercises gave you a better understanding of how Dview can be used to get exactly the image you want.

If you like, you can use View ➤ Set View ➤ Named View to save your perspective views. This can be helpful if you want to construct several views of a drawing to play back later as part of a presentation. You can also use the Hide and Shade options on the Render pull-down menu to help you visualize your model. In the next section, I will discuss the rendering functions built into AutoCAD. These functions take the Shade command one step further to let you control lights and surface reflectance.

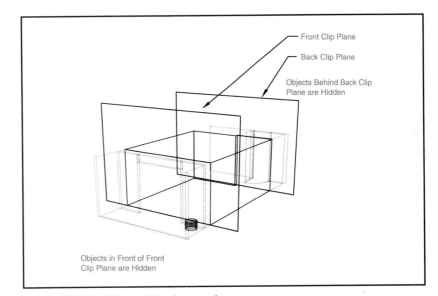

Figure 17.14: Effects of the clipping planes

RENDERING A 3D MODEL

The render function uses the analogy of a movie set to let you set up different rendered views. Each set contains lights and camera locations. The lights can be point sources like light bulbs or directed sources, which act like spot lights. Camera locations are determined through the Dview and View commands.

CONFIGURING THE RENDERER

If you haven't used the render feature before, the first time you attempt to use it, you will get the following prompt:

```
AVE_RENDER
Copyright (C) 1991-1992 Autodesk, Inc.  All Rights Reserved.
Release 2.0.6b  October 13, 1992
AVE_RENDER is not yet configured.
```

> Select rendering display device:
> 1. AutoCAD's configured P386 ADI combined display/rendering driver
> 2. Windows MDI rendering driver
> 3. None (Null rendering device)
> Rendering selection <1>:

Enter 1 if you are using the standard AutoCAD Windows display driver. You will then get a listing as follows:

> Select rendering hard copy device:
>
> 1. None (Null rendering device)
> 2. Windows MDI Rendering driver
> 3. Rendering file (256 color map)
> 4. Rendering file (continuous color)
>
> Rendering hard copy selection <1>:

These are optional hard copy rendering formats. Press 2 ↵ to select the Windows MDI rendering driver. I'll explain this choice later in this chapter.

When you are done, you are returned to AutoCAD. Your system may use a different display driver, which will cause the configuration prompts to be slightly different from those shown here. If you need to reconfigure the renderer, you can do so by clicking on Render ➤ Preferences to open the Rendering Preferences dialog box. From there, click on the **Reconfigure** button. You will get a similar set of prompts to those shown here. For more on the general configuration of AutoCAD, see *Appendix B*.

SETTING UP THE RENDERER

Before you begin to set up your lights, you will want to make some minor adjustments to the renderer's preference settings.

1. Click on Render ➤ Preferences or enter **Rpref** ↵. The Rendering Preferences dialog box appears (see Figure 17.15).

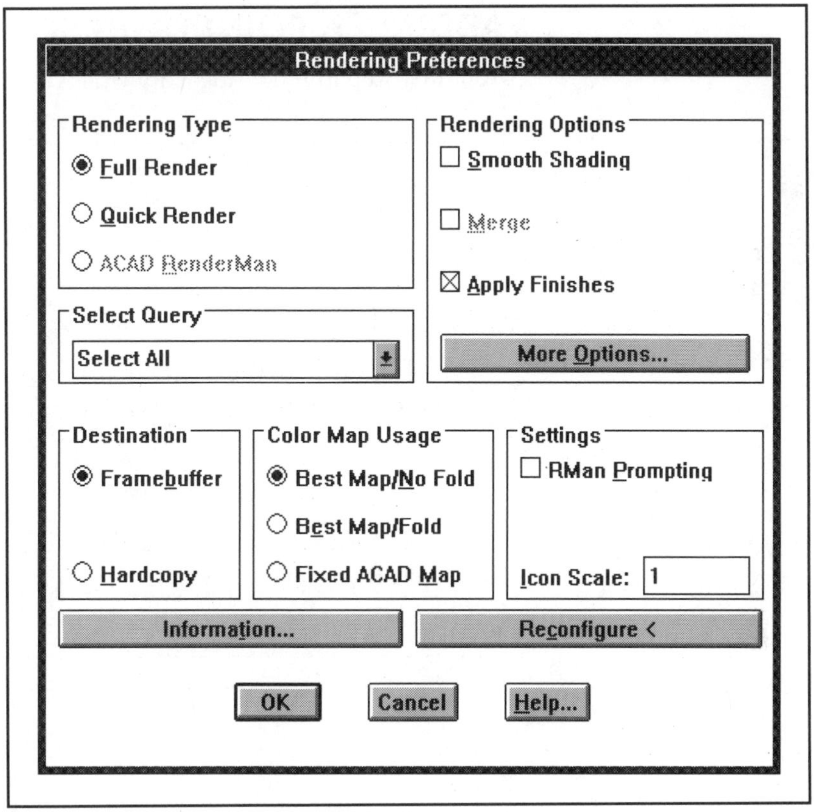

Figure 17.15: The Rendering Preferences dialog box.

2. Click on the input box labeled Icon Scale in the Settings button group, then enter **24**. As you start to insert lights into your model, you will see icons that indicate the location of your light sources. This setting tells AutoCAD how big to make those icons so they will be visible in the model.

3. Click on **OK** to close the dialog box.

You will return to this dialog box a bit later. Now you are ready to add some lights.

ADDING A POINT LIGHT SOURCE

Your first step in rendering a drawing is to set up some lighting.

Render ➤ Views
Render ➤ Lights
Point

1. First, use View Control dialog box to save the current perspective view as **pers1**. The View Control dialog box can be accessed throught Render ➤ Views.

2. Change your view to a plan view so it looks like Figure 17.16.

3. Use the View Control dialog box again to save the plan view as **Plan** so you can easily return to it as you work.

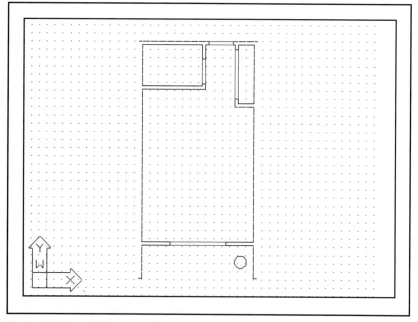

Figure 17.16: A Plan view of unit

4. Click on Render ➤ Lights or enter **Light** ↵. The Lights dialog box appears (see Figure 17.17).

5. Click on the **New** button. Another dialog box appears with a set of radio buttons (see Figure 17.18). These buttons offer three types of light sources.

6. Click on the button labeled Point Light, then click on **OK**. The New Point Light dialog box appears (see Figure 17.18).

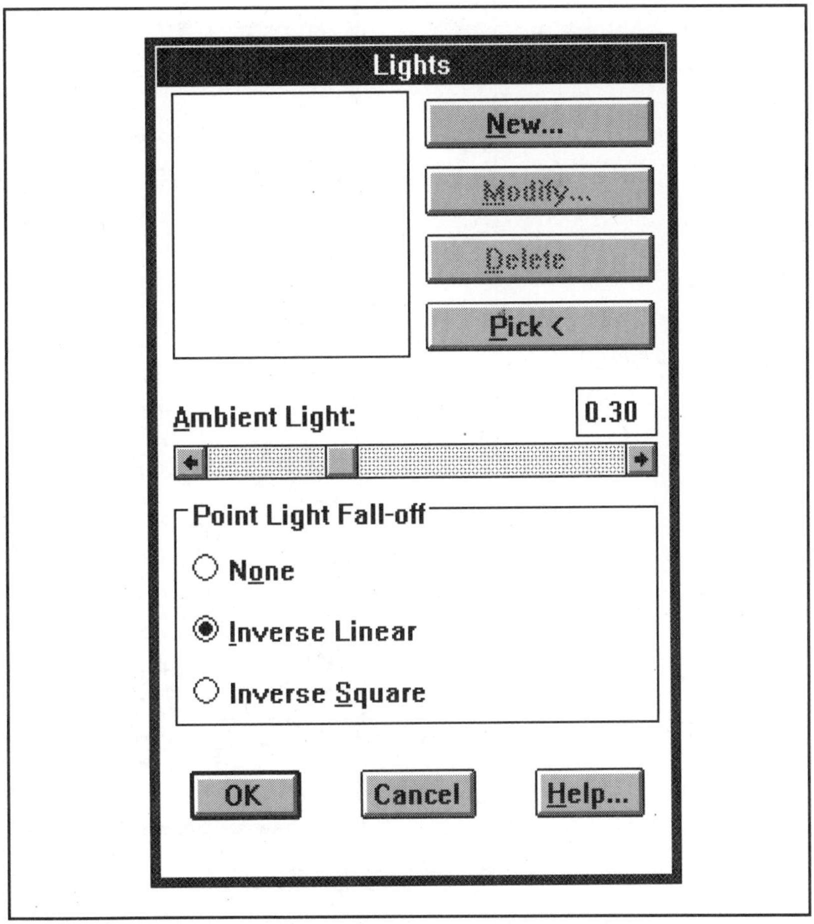

Figure 17.17: The Lights dialog box

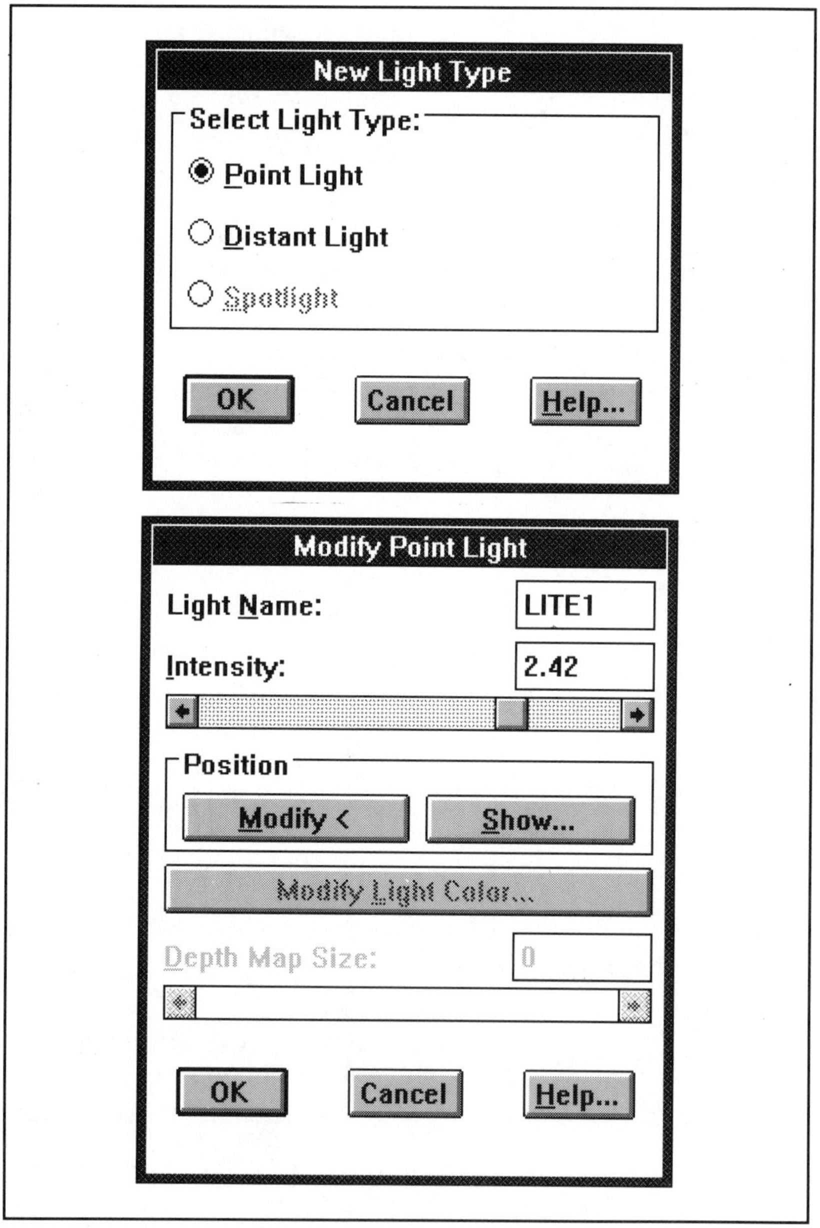

Figure 17.18:   The New Point Light dialog box

7. In the Light Name input box toward the upper right of the dialog box, enter **lite1** for the light name. The renderer allows you to use several light sources for a scene, and many scenes can use the same light source. Give each light source a name so you can distinguish among them. We arbitrarily named the light **lite1** for this exercise, but you can give it any name you like.

8. Next, click on the **Modify** button. The dialog box temporarily closes to reveal the plan with a graphic representing the point light source (see Figure 17.19).

9. At the **Enter light location** prompt, enter **.xy** ⏎ and pick a point in the center of the unit (see Figure 17.19).

10. At the **(need Z)** prompt, enter **8′**. Using the .xy filter allows you to place the light at a specific location in the plan and specify the light's height as well. Once you enter the Z value, the dialog box returns.

11. Click on **OK**. You return to the Lights dialog box. You now see *Lite1* in the list box. You've just created your first point source light. Click on **OK** to exit the dialog box.

In step 8, you might have noticed the words lite 1 inside the point light graphic. This is the name you gave this light source earlier in this command. This graphic is actually a block containing attributes needed to generate your shaded view. The attributes hold such information as the coordinates of the light source and its name. This information will be used by the renderer to determine how to shade your model.

ADDING A DIRECTED LIGHT SOURCE

You can also add a directed light source. In fact you can add as many point or directed light sources as you want, depending on the kind of lighting you require for your shaded model.

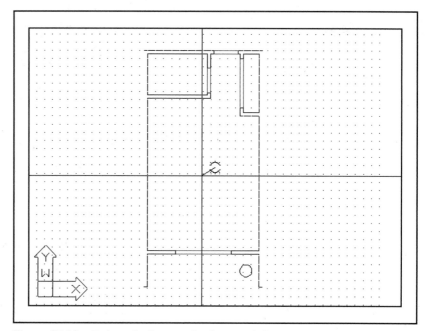

Figure 17.19:   Picking the location for the point light source

Understanding the Light Sources Types

In step 5 of the *Adding a Point Light Source* exercise, you saw a dialog box that let you choose from three different light source types. Here is a brief description of the available light sources and what they are used for.

Ambient Light is general lighting in the model. It has no specific source or direction. You can think of it as the kind of light you get on an overcast day. Such lighting casts no shadows and the light is evenly distributed.

Directed Light is similar to ambient light in that it is used as general lighting. But unlike ambient light, directed light emits light in a specific direction. Its most common use might be to simulate sunlight. You would use it to differentiate the effect of light on planar surfaces that lie in different directions.

▼

■

■

■

■

> **Point Light** is similar to a light bulb. It is a well defined light source whose light is emitted radially in all directions away from its center. The intensity of point light diminishes or "falls off" as you move further away from the source.
>
> **Spotlights** are only available if you are using Autodesk Renderman in conjunction with AutoCAD. This type of light will cast shadows and can produce a light "spot" on lighted surfaces. The spot can have a soft edge, much like a real spotlight might produce.

Render ➤ Light
Distant

1. Click on Render ➤ Light once again, then click on **New** in the Lights dialog box.

2. Click on the Distant Light radio button, then click on **OK**.

3. In the New Distant Light dialog box, enter **1D** for the light name.

4. Click on **Modify** to place the light. The dialog box temporarily closes.

5. At the **Enter light target** prompt, enter **.xy** ↵ and pick a point in the middle of the wall at the left of the unit (see Figure 17.20).

6. At the **(need Z)** prompt, enter **4′** for the height of the target point.

7. At the **Enter light location** prompt, use the .xy filter to pick a point in the upper right of the drawing area (see Figure 17.21). Enter **20′** ↵ for the z value or height of the directed source.

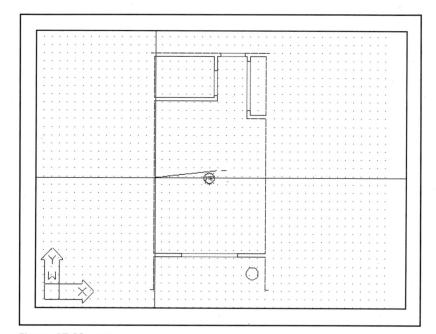

Figure 17.20: The target point for the directed light source

8. In the New Distant Lights dialog box, click on **OK**, then
   again in the Lights dialog box. You're now ready to set up
   your view. Another graphic appears. This time the graphic
   looks like a spotlight (see Figure 17.22). Notice the *1D* inside
   the graphic. This graphic, like the point source graphic, is a
   block on the Ashade layer.

SETTING UP AND ADJUSTING A VIEW

For the final step, set up a view that will let you see the overall effect of
your lighting.

1. Click on View ➤ Set View ➤ Dview and then select the
   entire unit plan.

2. Enter **PO** ↵ to select the target and view point.

3. At the **Enter target point** prompt, pick a point at the center
   of the unit.

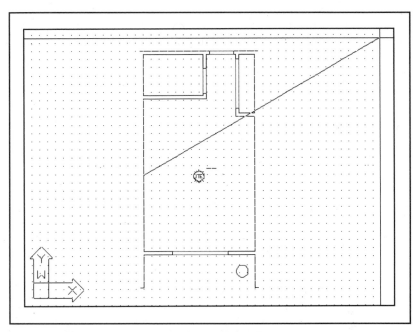

Figure 17.21: The location of the directed light source

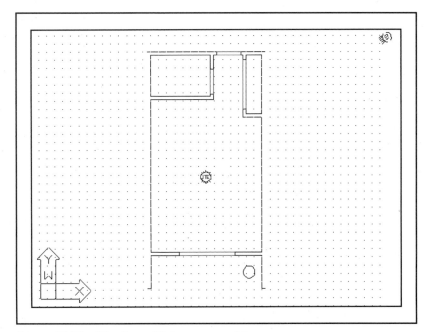

Figure 17.22: The directed light source graphic

4. At the **Enter camera point** prompt, enter **.xy** and pick a point in the extreme lower-right corner of the screen.

5. At the **(need Z)** prompt, enter **30′** ↵.

6. Using the Distance and Target options, adjust your view of the unit so it is centered in the screen and looks roughly like Figure 17.23.

7. Press ↵ to exit the Dview command.

8. Click on Render ➤ Render. You will get a view similar to Figure 17.24.

If you're rendering appears to be missing some surfaces, as in Figure 17.24, one of the renderer's settings may be set to render only one side

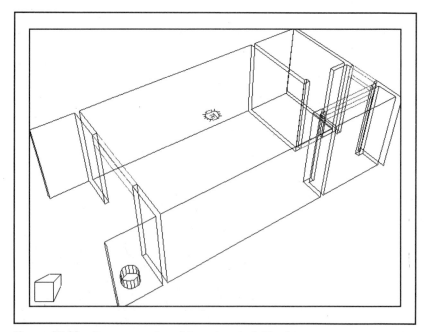

Figure 17.23: Set up your view of the unit to look like this

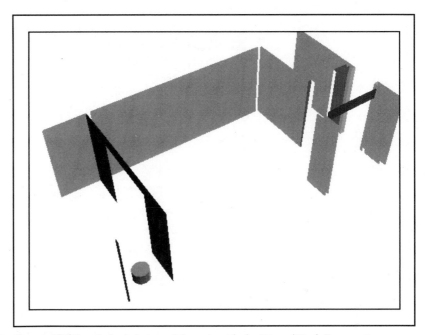

Figure 17.24:   A shaded view of the unit with the Discard Back Faces option turned on.

of a surface. This option is provided to save time in rendering. You can, however, set up rendering preferences to automatically render both sides of a surface.

1. Click on Render ➤ Preferences or enter **Rpref** ↵.

2. In the Rendering Preferences dialog box, click on **More Options**. The Full Render Options dialog box appears (see Figure 17.25).

3. Click on the Discard Back Faces check box so it is not checked, then click on **OK**.

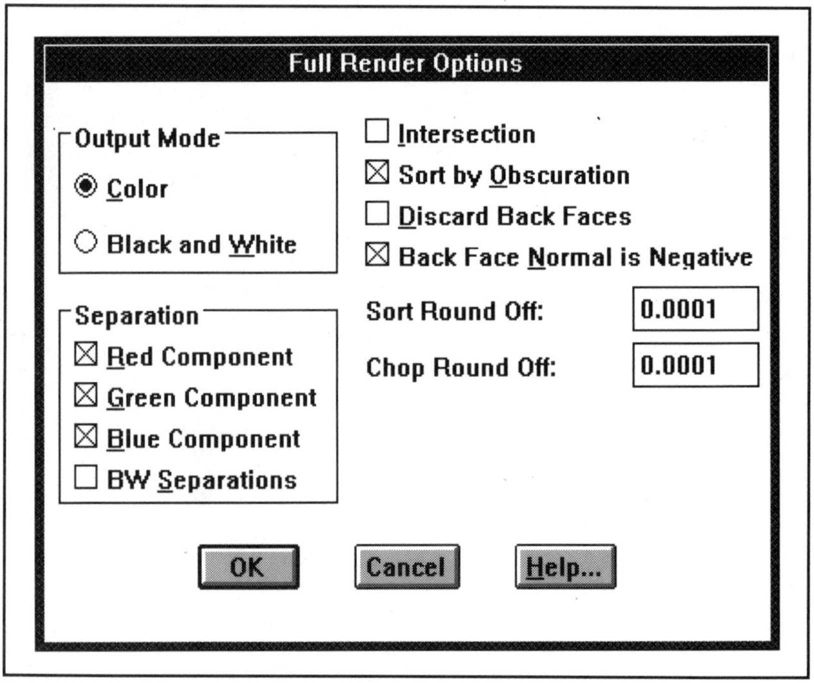

Figure 17.25:   The Full Render Options dialog box

4. Click on **OK** in the Rendering Preferences dialog box, then render the drawing again. This time all the walls appear (see Figure 17.26).

SAVING YOUR LIGHT AND VIEW COMBINATIONS

Once you have found the perfect combination of lights and views, you can save these settings together as scenes. You can then recall them later for further rendering or editing.

1. Click on Render ➤ Scenes or enter **Scene** ↵. The Scene dialog box appears (see Figure 17.27). The list box lists any existing saved scenes in the file. Right now, there are none. You can create a new scene, modify an existing one, or delete a scene from the list box.

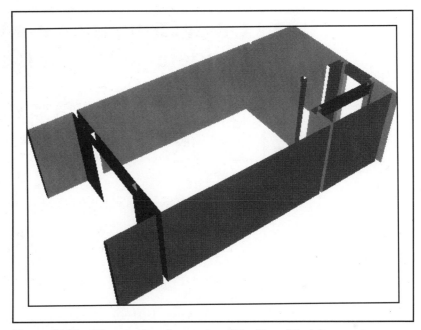

Figure 17.26:   The unit plan after turning off the Discard Back Faces option

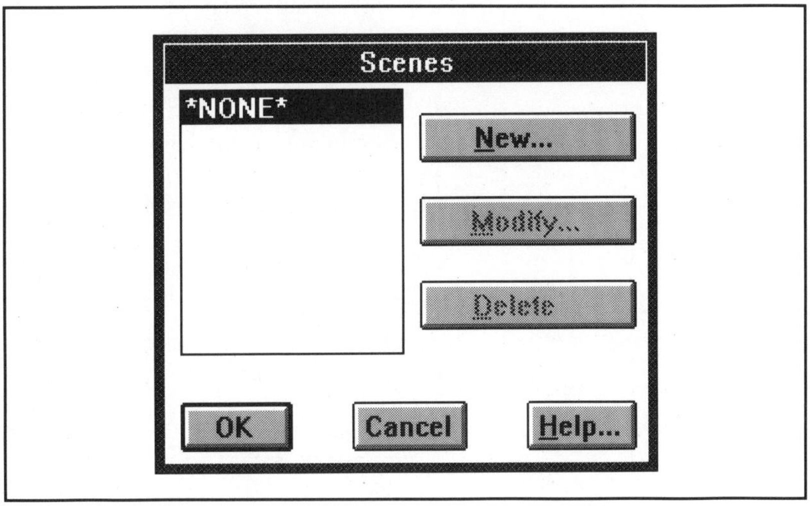

Figure 17.27:   The Scene dialog box

Other Options on the Full Rendering Options Dialog Box

You've just seen how you can set up the renderer to include all sides of surfaces to be rendered. There are numerous other settings in the Full Rendering Options dialog box that you won't get to use in this tutorial. You will probably want to experiment with these other settings, so here is a list describing them so you won't be completely in the dark:

Output Mode: This button group offers two radio buttons, labeled Color, and Black and White. These two radio buttons let you control whether your image is rendered in color or black and white. If you plan to include the rendering in a piece of black-and-white printed matter, you may want to select Black and White to get a better idea of how your rendering will look when it is printed.

Separations: This button group offers the option to make AutoCAD render only the Red, Green, and Blue components of a rendering for four color separations used to make transparencies. Normally all three colors are checked, so all the colors are rendered on the screen. The Black and White option causes AutoCAD to render each color separation in a greyscale. These greyscale separations will give a more accurate representation of your image when used to create color filters for projection.

Intersection: This check box forces AutoCAD to find the intersection of objects when it does its rendering. In the real world, two objects cannot occupy the same space at the same time. In AutoCAD, however, they can. This can cause some odd things to occur at rendering time. Checking this box reduces intersection problems but it can also increase rendering time.

Sort by Obscuration: This check box forces AutoCAD to check for overlapping surfaces. It can increase rendering time but will improve rendering accuracy.

Discard Back Faces: This check box forces AutoCAD to render only one side of a surface and ignore the other side. If you construct all your faces in the same direction, you can turn this setting on to save rendering time. In practice, you probably won't have time while constructing your model to worry whether surfaces are constructed properly for this option.

Back Face Normal Is Negative: This option works in conjunction with the Discard Back Faces option. With this option, you can determine which side of a face is rendered. If you render a scene and nothing appears, try changing this setting.

Sort Round Off: This input box lets you control the degree of accuracy AutoCAD applies to the Sort by Obscuration option.

Chop Round Off: This input box lets you control the degree of accuracy AutoCAD applies to the Intersection option.

2. Click on **New**. The New Scene dialog box appears. You can highlight the combination of lights and saved views from the list, then enter a name for your scene in the input box in the upper-right corner of the dialog box.

3. You won't save a scene here, so press the Escape key, then click on **Cancel** in the Scene dialog box.

ADJUSTING LIGHTING CONDITIONS

Many of the surfaces seem to have the same light intensity, giving the view a flat appearance. You can adjust the lighting that affects your shaded model by using the Lights dialog box.

Render ➤ Lights ➤ Modify
Intensity

1. Click on Render ➤ Lights, then at the Lights dialog box, highlight lite1 in the list.

2. Click on the **Modify** button. The Modify Point Light dialog box appears. This is identical to the New Point Light dialog box you saw when you first created this light.

3. Click and drag the slide bar toward the left until the intensity input box shows a value of about 170.

4. Click on **OK**, then click on **OK** in the Lights dialog box.

5. Render the view again. Now the surfaces have a bit more variation.

Here you turned down the intensity of the point source light located in the middle of the unit. This allows the walls to show more subtle reflectance properties.

The walls in the foreground seem a bit dark. To increase the general lighting of a rendering, you can increase the ambient lighting.

Render ➤ Lights ➤ Ambient

1. Open the Lights Dialog box and click and drag the slide bar labeled Ambient up to the middle of the bar.

2. Render the scene again.

Now the darker walls aren't so dark and you can begin to see more of its form (see Figure 17.28).

ADDING GRADIENT AND SMOOTH SHADING

To add a final touch of realism, you can set Render to shade flat surfaces in a gradient rather than just a single intensity.

1. Click on Render ➤ Preferences.

2. Click on the button labeled Smooth Shading in the Rendering Options button group.

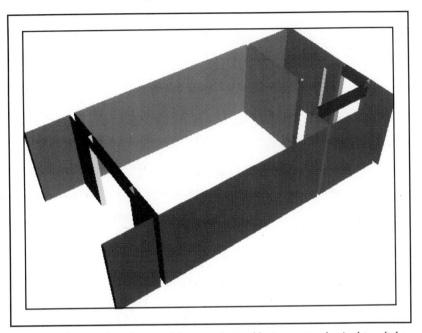

Figure 17.28:   A shaded view of the unit obtained by increasing the Ambient light setting

3. Click on **OK**, then render the model again. Notice how the interior walls now appear to get brighter as they get closer to the light source.

This time the rendering took longer to perform. You may want to reserve the Smooth Shading option for those renderings that really need it. The Unit plan doesn't really show off the Smooth Shading feature as it applies to meshes. Let's take a look at another 3D model to see how smooth shading can improve the look of faceted surfaces.

UNDERSTANDING THE PREFERENCES DIALOG BOX

You've used the Preferences dialog box a few times now, so you know what some of the options do. You won't get to use all the options in this tutorial, so here is a review of all the Preferences options for your future reference:

Rendering Type lets you choose from a Full Render, the one you've been using, a Quick Render that allows you to get an idea of how a rendering will look in a complex 3D model, and the ACAD RenderMan rendering option for photo-realistic rendering. Full Render takes the most time but generates the best image. The ACAD RenderMan option is available only if you purchase Autodesk RenderMan. You will get a chance to use the Quick Render option later.

Rendering Options lets you control whether smooth shading is applied and whether finishes are applied or ignored (see the next section for more on finishes). Smooth shading will smooth out facets in meshes and give gradient shading on flat surfaces. The Merge option is for compositing images in a frame buffer and can only be used if you have selected a frame buffer in your Renderer configuration. The **More Options** button offers advanced rendering options (see the *Other Options on the Full Rendering Options Dialog Box* side bar).

Destination lets you select the destination of your rendering. The Framebuffer option sends the output to the screen, while the Hardcopy option lets you print your rendering. Hardcopy is available only if you have configured the Renderer for a hardcopy device.

Color Map Usage lets you select the method AutoCAD uses to select colors for the rendering. AutoCAD will try to use all 265 colors, though the first 16 are reserved for the different parts of the screen. Best Map/No Fold causes AutoCAD to use the top 240 colors only. Best Map/Fold causes AutoCAD to make a best fit at using all available 256 colors. Fixed ACAD Map forces AutoCAD to use all the 256 colors in a fixed way.

Settings lets you determine whether to allow for prompting where options affect RenderMan output. It also lets you determine the scale factor for light and finish icons.

Information displays information on the current configuration of the renderer.

Reconfigure lets you reconfigure the renderer to use different display and output devices.

ADJUSTING SURFACE REFLECTANCE

One of the main features of the Rendering function is its ability to assign surface reflectance to objects individually. Surface reflectance might be likened to shininess. A surface with high reflectance, like chrome, will deflect light with little distortion. A surface with low reflectance, like a wall painted with a matte color, will scatter light in all directions.

The AutoCAD Renderer lets you set the surface reflectance of objects in your drawing. The settings have an infinite range of permutation, so I'll show you how the basic functions work, and you can experiment with them on your own.

1. Open the Sextant file in the AutoCAD sample directory.

2. Click on Render ➤ Preferences, and in the Rendering Preferences dialog box, click on **Quick Render**. This file is considerably larger than the Unit plan and will take much longer to render, so you will use the Quick Render feature to get a quick look at the rendering later on.

3. Click on **More Options**, and in the Quick Render Options dialog box, click on the Discard Back Faces check box (if it is checked) to deactivate this option, then click on **OK**.

4. Click on **OK** to close the Rendering Preferences dialog box.

5. Click on Render ➤ Lights, then click on **New**.

6. Click on the Point Lights radio button in the next dialog box, then click on OK.

7. Enter **lite1** for the Light Name, then click on the **Modify** button.

8. At the **Enter light location** prompt, enter **315,42,240** ↵. I've already located the light for you, though you can place your own later if you like.

9. Finally, click on **OK**, then in the Light dialog box, set the ambient light slide bar so the ambient input box reads 66.

10. Render the model.

You will see a series of messages and the rendered sextant will appear in a few minutes. This image shows you what the sextant looks like without any special reflectance applied. Next, you set up part of the sextant to reflect light like a metallic object.

1. Click on Render ➤ Finishes. The Finishes dialog box appears (see Figure 17.29).

2. Click on **Import**. The Import Preset Finishes dialog box appears (see Figure 17.30). These are a set of finishes that come with AutoCAD. You can also create your own and store them for retrieval.

3. Double click on Specular from the list. The dialog box temporarily closes.

4. At the **Enter new finish location** prompt, enter **0,0** ↵. This places a finish icon at the origin of the drawing. It isn't really important where this icon goes, so long as you know where you put it and what it's for. The Finishes dialog box returns. Notice that Specular is now listed in the list box to the left and is highlighted.

5. Click on the **Modify** button. The Modify Finishes dialog box appears. This dialog box lets you control the reflectance characteristic of a finish setting. Notice that most of the settings are set to 0 except for the specular component, which is set all the way up to 1.

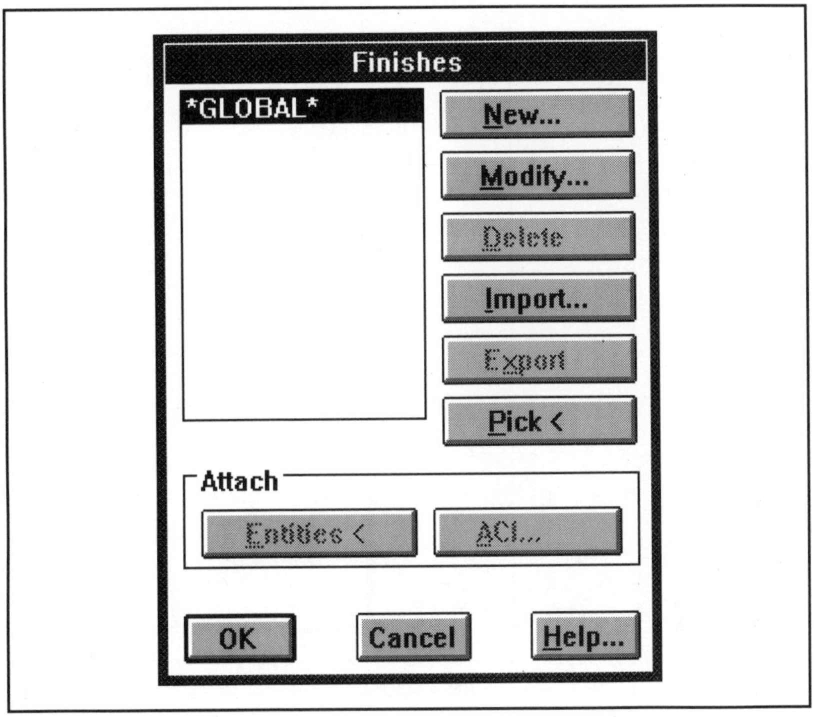

Figure 17.29:   The Finish dialog box

6. Click on the button labeled **Preview finish**. A sphere appears, giving you a preview of how a surface will be rendered with this finish (see Figure 17.31).

7. Click on **OK**, then in the Finishes dialog box, click on **Entities**. The dialog box closes temporarily.

8. At the **Select object to attach SPECULAR to:** prompt, click on all the yellow components of the sextant, then press ↵ to finish your selection.

9. Click on **OK**.

10. Now render the sextant again.

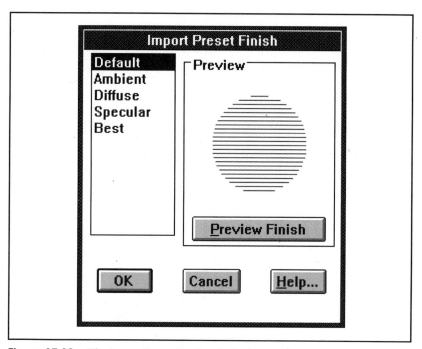

Figure 17.30:   The Import Preset Finishes dialog box

This time, the yellow components of the sextant appear shiny. Take a moment to look at the Modify Finish dialog box again. You've seen what the preview button does. You can play with the settings, then click on the preview button to see the effect.

UNDERSTANDING THE MODIFY FINISH DIALOG BOX

Here is a brief listing of what each component of the Modify Finish dialog box does.

> **Ambient** controls the amount of ambient light the finish reflects. If Ambient is set high, the finish gains in overall brightness.

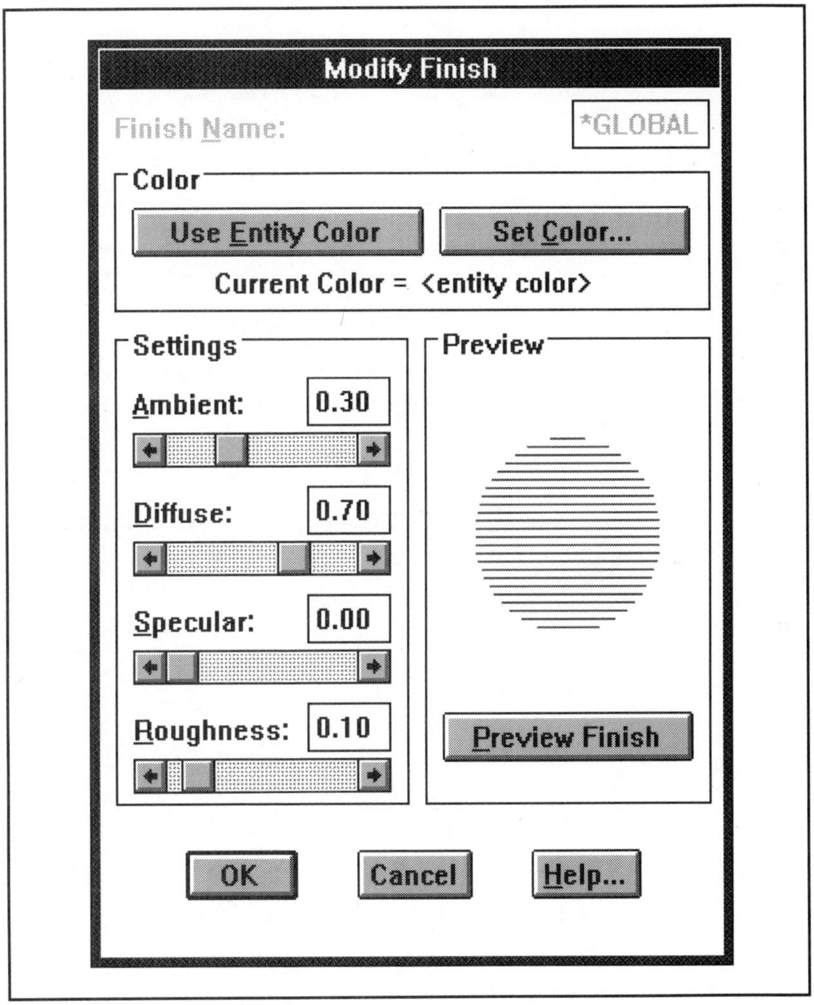

Figure 17.31: The Modify Finish Dialog box with the preview sphere rendered

Diffuse controls the dullness of the finish. You could think of this as the opposite of Specular. If Diffuse is set high, the finish scatters light uniformly in all directions. A high setting also shows matte planar surfaces better.

Specular controls the shininess of a finish. A high specular value causes light to reflect off a surface with little or no scattering of light.

Roughness controls the "spread" of a specular reflection. A high roughness value causes the specular reflection to disperse over a greater area, like a satin finish on metal. If Specular is set to 0, then Roughness has no effect.

Use Entity Color causes the render to use the color of the object in the finish during the final rendering.

Set Color lets you set a different color from the object the finish is applied to. A dialog box appears showing you a color wheel from which you can choose a color.

Understanding the Finish Dialog Box

You've just seen how a finish can be applied to a surface. You can import, modify, and save any number of finishes to get your model looking just the way you want. The vehicle for retrieving finishes is the Finishes dialog box. You got a chance to use it briefly in the previous exercise. Here is a listing of the other components you didn't get to try out.

New opens a dialog box identical to the Modify Finishes dialog box just described. You can then create a finish with the exact settings you want.

Modify, as you have seen, lets you modify the finish that is highlighted in the list box to the left.

Delete removes a finish from the Finishes list box and from your drawing. If you use this, be sure you have saved your finish under the Export option.

Import, as you have seen, will import a predefined finish.

Export saves a finish you may have created or modified. If you have modified a finish, rename it before you export to preserve the original finish.

Pick lets you select a finish from your model.

Entities, as you have seen, lets you attach a finish to a set of objects. The dialog box temporarily closes and you are asked to select objects to attach the finish to.

ACI lets you attach a finish to objects in your model based on their AutoCAD Color Index (ACI). Another dialog box appears showing you a list of the AutoCAD colors listed by their number index.

SAVING AND VIEWING RENDERED VIEWS

When you've got the image you want to keep, you will want to store it as a file. To do this, you use Render ➤ File… ➤ Save Image. This brings up the Save Image dialog box (see Figure 17.32).

The dialog box is fairly clear in its function. The button group to the left lets you select the file format for your rendering. TGA, TIFF, and GIF are fairly common formats. RND is AutoCAD's own format for AutoShade. The **Options** button offers file compression options for those file formats that offer them.

Once you save a view, you can recall it at any time by clicking on Render ➤ File ➤ Replay Image. You get the typical file dialog box. The Pattern input box shows *.tga* by default, though you can also view .TIF and .GIF files. Locate the rendered image file you want and double click on it. It appears in the drawing screen.

RENDERING TO A SEPARATE WINDOW

If you prefer, you can have AutoCAD render to a separate window. This separate render window offers some additional options not found when rendering to the AutoCAD window.

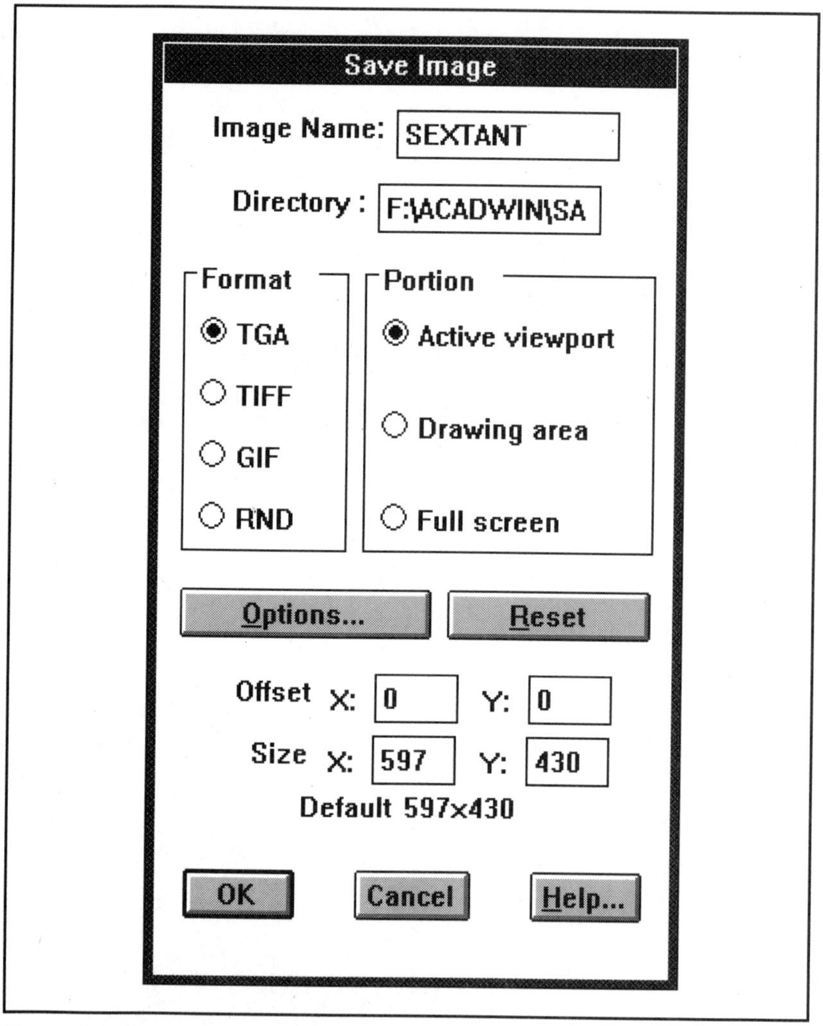

Save Image

Image Name: SEXTANT

Directory : F:\ACADWIN\SA

Format
- ⦿ TGA
- ○ TIFF
- ○ GIF
- ○ RND

Portion
- ⦿ Active viewport
- ○ Drawing area
- ○ Full screen

[Options...]   [Reset]

Offset X: 0   Y: 0

Size X: 597   Y: 430

Default 597x430

[OK]   [Cancel]   [Help...]

Figure 17.32: The Save Image dialog box

▼ NOTE

If your renderer is not configured to render to a window,
you can re-configure the
renderer by clicking on
Render ➤ Preferences, then
on the Reconfigure... button.
Press ⏎, then AutoCAD will
request changes. Reconfigure
the hardcopy option for the
Windows MDI rendering
driver.

You may recall that in the beginning of this chapter, I asked you to configure the rendering hard copy selection for the Windows MDI rendering driver. MDI stands for Multiple Document Interface. By choosing this driver, you can render your model to a window, then make further settings to the image before you save it.

Before you can render to a window, you must first click on Render ➤ Preferences and change the Destination option to Hardcopy. AutoCAD will open a separate window to display the rendering (see Figure 17.33). From this window, you can control the properties of your rendered view. To set the image properties, click on Files ➤ Options …. You get the dialog box shown in Figure 17.34.

The following describes the purpose of the button groups in this dialog box. Be aware that radio button options take effect the next time you render, while check box options take effect immediately.

Size in Pixels options let you set the size of the image based on pixels.

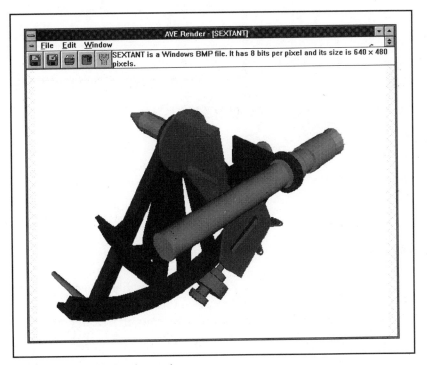

Figure 17.33: The render window

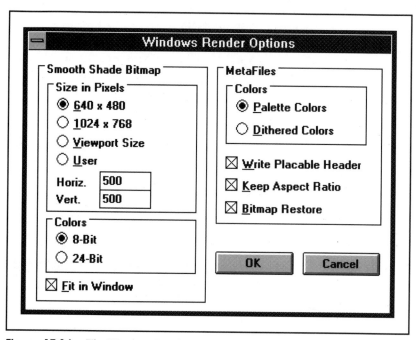

Figure 17.34: The Windows Render Options dialog box

MetaFiles options let you control the way colors are displayed, the aspect ratio of the image, and how the file is stored. *Palette Colors* displays the image using the current Windows Palette. *Dithered Colors* simulates 24-bit color through a process called dithering. *Write Placeable Header* adds the Aldus Placeable Header code to the file. *Keep Aspect Ratio* forces the image to maintain its original aspect ratio regardless of the window shape. *Bitmap Restore* allows faster display of metafile images. None of these options takes effect unless the image is rendered with the full render option on and with smooth shading off.

Color Depth lets you control whether the file is to be saved as an 8-bit (256 colors) or 24-bit (16 million colors) file. Even if your display is only 8 bit, you can still save the rendering as a 24-bit color image. Note that 24-bit color increases the file size.

> **Fit in Window** disables all the options under *Size in Pixels* and sizes the image to fit in the window.

In addition to the image controls, the render window offers several other options from the pull-down menu:

> **File ➤ Open** lets you view saved .WMF and .BMP files.
>
> **File ➤ Save** saves the image as either a Windows .BMP or .WMF file depending on how the image is rendered. (See MetaFiles in the Windows Render Options listed earlier.)
>
> **File ➤ Print** lets you print your rendering to the Windows system printer. You can control the number of copies, image lightness, and, if you want to enlarge your printout, tiling of copies. This tiling option lets you print a large image on several sheets of paper. You can then paste the pages together to form the complete image.
>
> **Edit ➤ Copy** copies the image to the Clipboard.

Finally, you will notice the buttons in the toolbar of the render window. These buttons duplicate the Open, Save, Print, Copy, and Options functions found in the pull-down menus. You may want to click on these buttons to familiarize yourself with their functions.

ADVANCED RENDERING WITH OTHER PROGRAMS

While AutoCAD offers excellent surface shading functionality, there are third-party alternatives to AutoCAD's renderer that offer unique capabilities. Two of the more notable products are RenderStar from Modern Medium and 3D Studio from Autodesk.

SHADING WITH RENDERSTAR

RenderStar is a third-party product that gives AutoCAD 3D models lifelike realism. Perhaps the most significant feature of RenderStar is its speed of rendering. A typical rendering can take a matter of seconds where AutoCAD would take several minutes.

Another unique feature of RenderStar is that image resolution is independent of the display device installed in your computer. You can render an image using up to 9000-pixel×9000-pixel resolution. This is significant if you intend to produce high-resolution hard copy in large formats or if you want to transfer your images to slides using high-resolution film recorders. At lower VGA resolutions, RenderStar is perhaps the fastest rendering program available for AutoCAD, which makes it ideal for developing 3D animations.

Surface maps, bump maps, opacity maps, and glass simulation are all part of RenderStar. If you have a scanner, you can even incorporate photographic images in your rendering.

▼ NOTE

In the USA, write: Render-Star, Modern Medium Inc., 6601 N.E., 78th Court A-8, Portland, OR 97218, or call (503) 252-3668; in Europe, write: Modern Medium BV, Prinsenhofsteeg 10, 1012 EE, Amsterdam, The Netherlands, or call 31/20-224480.

RENDERING AND ANIMATING WITH 3D STUDIO 2.0

If you want the ultimate in 3D rendering and animation, you will want to use 3D Studio 2.0. 3D Studio imports AutoCAD.DXF and .FLM files directly. You can then add a virtually infinite range of surface features to your model. Texture, opacity, and bump maps are supported, as well as a reflectance map that does a decent job of simulating glass reflections, even in animations.

Once you've fine-tuned your rendering in 3D Studio, you can animate it with what is perhaps the easiest and most comprehensive set of animation tools available on a personal computer. Architectural walk-throughs are extremely simple. Kinetic animation, where objects move independently in a scene, can also be achieved with a minimum of training and effort.

For the advanced animator, 3D Studio offers rotoscoping and external procedures for animated surfaces. Rotoscoping lets you map an animation to a surface of an object. An example of this might be an animated walk-through of a room with a television on showing the 6 o'clock news. With the external procedures feature, you can create programs that animate surfaces. 3D Studio comes with several you can try out, such as a ripple generator or a tornado.

You can render in 256 colors and save your animations in GIF or Autodesk Animator Pro formats (see Figure 17.35). Or, for a more professional-looking rendering or animation, you can use the .TGA file format to store your images in 24- or 32-bit color. Support is also offered for professional-level frame accurate video recording equipment. Many video production houses use 3D Studio to do flying logos and other commercial video works.

Finally, if you have a CD-ROM drive, you can take advantage of the 3D Studio world creation toolkit. This is a CD that contains hundreds of 3D objects and clip art, Targa and .GIF files for wood and marble, sample animations, and full models you can use in your own animations.

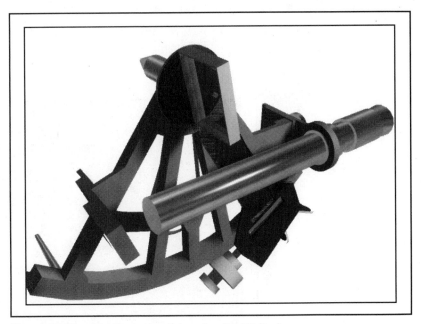

Figure 17.35:   The Sextant model rendered in 3D Studio

IF YOU WANT TO EXPERIMENT...

You've covered a lot of information in this chapter, so it might be a good idea to play with these commands to help you remember what you've learned. Try the following exercise to test what you've learned about Dview.

1. Make a copy of the unit plan and insert the chairs and other objects you created earlier in this chapter. Use Figure 17.36 as a guide.

2. Once you have inserted the furnishings, use the Dview command to create an interior view. You can go through the Dview Clip exercise again to get a view similar to the one in Figure 17.36.

3. Once you have the view on screen, save it, then use the rendering features to set up some lights and finishes.

4. Render the scene, then save the rendered scene as a .TGA file.

Figure 17.36: Inserting the furniture into the Unit plan

SUMMARY

In this brief tutorial, you were exposed to some of AutoCAD's rendering functions. It is a deceptively simple program that contains many more adjustment options than we can cover in one chapter. I hope that, despite its brevity, this tutorial has given you a sense of AutoCAD's potential as a rendering tool. Designers can use AutoCAD to help develop and document their designs. With AutoCAD's file-export capabilities, product manuals can easily use desktop-publishing systems to incorporate 2D and 3D design drawings. Illustrators can also take advantage of AutoCAD's PostScript capabilities to add shaded images to desktop-publishing and other typesetting systems that are capable of importing Encapsulated PostScript files.

In the next chapter, you will look at 3D solid modeling with AutoCAD's Mechanical Drafting Extension. This add-on product for AutoCAD lets you easily produce 3D forms using the concept of positive and negative solid shapes to determine volumes.

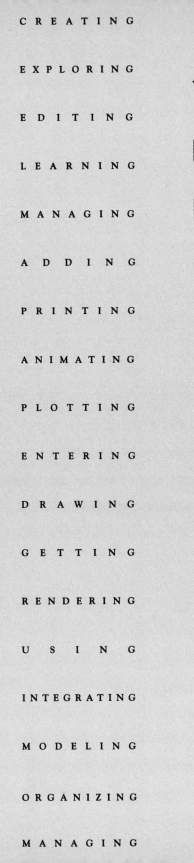

18

MASTERING 3D SOLIDS WITH THE ADVANCED MODELING EXTENSION

FAST TRACK

▽

766 ▶ To draw a 3D primitive

Click on Model ➤ Primitives, then click on the desired primitive from the dialog box. Answer the prompts regarding the size and shape of the primitive.

769 ▶ To convert an extruded 2D polyline into a 3D solid

Click on Model ➤ Solidify, then click on the extruded polyline.

774 ▶ To join two solids to form one shape

Click on Model ➤ Union, then click on the two solids you want to join.

778 ▶ To do a hidden line removal on a solid

Click on Model ➤ Display ➤ Mesh, then click on the solid you want to view using hidden line removal. Next, click on Render ➤ Hide.

780 ▶ To change the shape of a primitive in a composite solid

Click on Model ➤ Modify ➤ Change Prim. Click on the solid containing the primitive you want to change. Click on the primitive to change, then enter the best option.

790 ▶ To convert a 2D polyline into a solid

Click on Model ➤ Extrude, then click on the polyline. Answer the prompts regarding the height of the extrusion and the taper angle.

792 ▶ To convert a 2D polyline into a rotated solid

Click on Model ➤ Revolve, then click on the polyline profile. Answer the prompt regarding the axis of revolution, including the angle.

798 ▶ To fillet the corner of a solid

Click on Model ➤ Modify ➤ Fillet Solids. Click on the edges you want filleted, then enter the fillet radius.

802 ▶ To turn a solid model into paperspace top, front and right side view

Click on View ➤ Layout ➤ MV Setup, then press ↵ at the prompt. Next, enter **C** ↵↵ to create the viewport layout in Paperspace. Enter **2** at the text screen. Select two points defining the area for the four viewports, then enter the spacing between viewports.

809 ▶ To generate a cross-section profile of a solid

While in Modelspace, Click on Model ➤ Display ➤ Section Solid. Indicate the orientation of the cross-section plane, then indicate the origin of the cross section.

810 ▶ To use boolean subtraction on 2D objects

First create a closed 2D polyline outline of the object. Also draw 2D polyline representations of areas you want to subtract from the outline (circles and polygons will also work). Click on Model ➤ Solidify, then click on the polylines. Click on Model ➤ Subtract, then select the main outline. Next, select the objects you want to subtract from the main outline. Other boolean operations are also possible.

815 ▶ To find the physical properties of a solid model

Click on Model ➤ Inquiry ➤ Mass Properties, then click on the solid you want information on.

So far, you have been creating 3D models according to a method called *surface modeling*: as you drew, you used 3dfaces to give your models form and the appearance of solidity. Surface modeling is tricky to use; however, most microcomputers can handle it without much difficulty. But there is another method that CAD systems use to create 3D computer models. This method is called *solid modeling*.

Solid modeling is a way of defining 3D objects as solid forms instead of wire frames with surfaces attached. When you create a 3D model using solid modeling, you start with the basic forms of your model—cubes, cones, and cylinders, for instance. These basic solids are called *primitives*. Then you begin to add or subtract from your forms using more of these primitives, much as if you were carving a block of clay into geometric shapes. For example, to create a model of a tube, you first create two solid cylinders, one smaller in diameter than the other. Then you align the two cylinders so that they are concentric and you tell AutoCAD that the smaller of the two cylinders is a negative object. The larger of the two cylinders then becomes a tube whose inside diameter is that of the smaller cylinder, as shown in Figure 18.1.

There are many advantages to solid modeling, especially if you are involved in mechanical design and engineering. It is easier to create models by using solid modeling. With surface models, just drawing a cube requires several steps. But with solids, you can create a cube with one command. Having created a model, you can assign materials to it and have the computer find physical properties of the model such as center of mass and weight.

Solid modeling was once thought to require more computational power than most personal computers could offer. But with the rapid advancement of microcomputer hardware, it is becoming well within the reach of most PC users. AutoCAD now offers solid modeling functions in the form of the Advanced Modeling Extension, or AME. This is a software module that you can purchase separately from AutoCAD, though it requires AutoCAD to work.

▼ **NOTE**

AutoCAD includes a 2D version of the AME called the Regional Model. The Regional Model lets you apply boolean operations to 2D objects. This can help you generate complex 2D shapes with a minimum of effort. A brief tutorial of this feature is offered in the section called *Using 3D Solid Operations* on 2D Drawings later in this chapter.

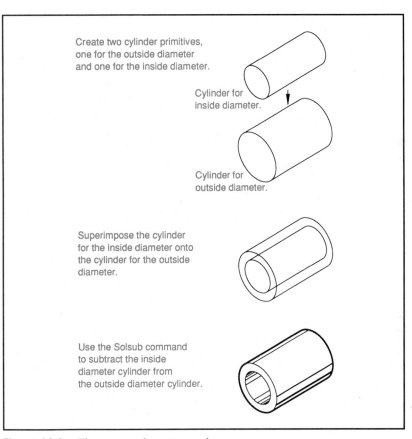

Figure 18.1:   The process of creating a tube

UNDERSTANDING SOLID MODELING

I have already compared solid modeling to creating a model from clay and using simple shapes to add detail. In the AME, several primitives are available (see Figure 18.2).

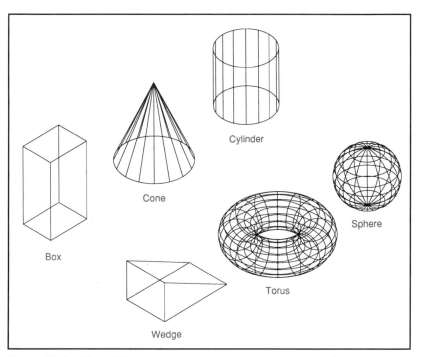

Figure 18.2: The AME primitives

These shapes—cube, wedge, cone, cylinder, sphere, and donut or *torus*—can be joined in one of three ways to produce secondary shapes.

- **Unions** join two primitives so that they act as one object.
- **Subtractions** use one object to cut out a shape in another.
- **Intersections** use only the intersecting region of two objects to define a solid shape.

These three ways of joining solids are called *boolean operations*. The word *boolean* comes from the name of a nineteenth-century mathematician, George Boole. Figure 18.3 shows these three ways of joining objects with a cube and a cylinder as examples. Joined primitives are

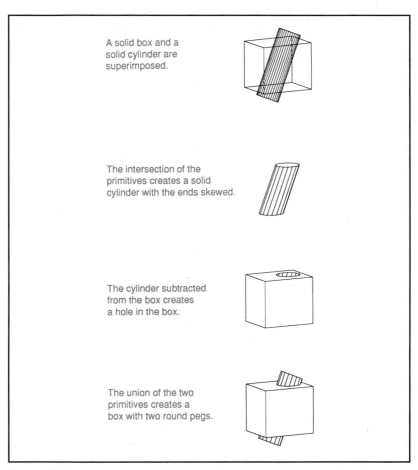

A solid box and a
solid cylinder are
superimposed.

The intersection of the
primitives creates a solid
cylinder with the ends skewed.

The cylinder subtracted
from the box creates
a hole in the box.

The union of the two
primitives creates a
box with two round pegs.

Figure 18.3:   The Union, Subtraction, and Intersection of a cube and a cylinder

called *composite solids*. You can join primitives to primitives, composite
solids to primitives, and composite solids to other composite solids.

Now let's take a look at how these concepts let us create models in
AutoCAD.

CREATING SOLID FORMS

In this section, you will begin to draw the object shown in Figure 18.4. In the process, you will explore how solid models are made by creating primitives and then setting up special relationships between them.

CREATING PRIMITIVES

Primitives are the basic building blocks of solid modeling. At first, it may seem limiting to have only six primitives to work with, but consider the varied forms you can create with just a few two-dimensional objects. Let's begin by creating the basic mass of our fictitious part.

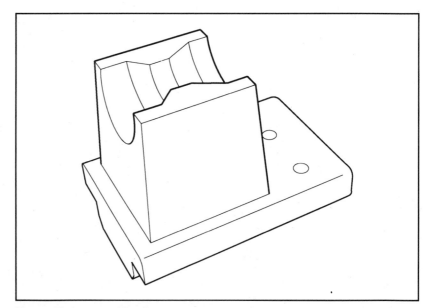

Figure 18.4: A steel bracket

(Load Ame)

Solbox

1. Open a new file called **Bracket**.

2. Set the Snap spacing to 0.5 and turn on the grid and snap modes.

3. Turn on the dynamic coordinate readout by pressing **F6**. I'll use the readout to help guide you in selecting points in the exercises that follow.

4. Click on Model ➤ Primitives. The AME Primitives dialog box appears (see Figure 18.5).

5. Click on the box in the upper-left corner of the dialog box, then click on **OK**.

6. At the **Baseplane/Center/<Corner of box><0,0,0>** prompt, pick a point at coordinate 3,2.5.

7. At the **Cube/Length/<Other corner>:** prompt, enter **@7,4** ↵ to create a box with a length of 7 and a width of 4.

8. At the **Height:** prompt, enter **1** ↵. (This prompt is asking for the height of the box in the Z axis.)

▼ NOTE

These messages appear frequently when you are creating or modifying solids. Since AutoCAD AME often takes a minute or two to perform calculations, the messages are a way of telling you that AutoCAD is working and that your computer hasn't frozen due to some malfunction.

You see the following messages appear at the prompt:

Phase I - Boundary evaluation begins.
Phase II - Tessellation computation begins.
Updating the Advanced Modeling Extension database.

and a rectangle appears in the drawing.

You've now drawn your first primitive, a box that is 7" long by 4" wide by 1" deep. Let's change our view so we can see the box more clearly.

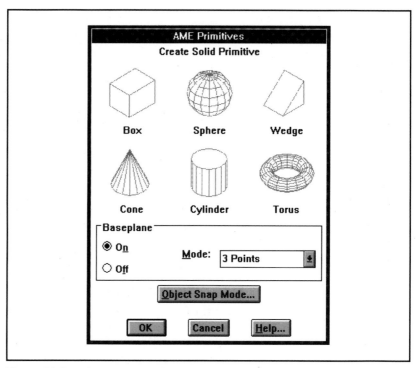

Figure 18.5: The AME Primitives dialog box

View ➤ Set View ➤ Viewpoint ➤ Set Vpoint
Z ↵

Use the VPOINT command to shift your view so that you are looking at the WCS from the lower left.

1. Click on View ➤ Set View ➤ Viewpoint ➤ Set Vpoint.

2. At the **Rotate/<viewpoint>:** prompt, enter **–1,– 1,.5**.

3. Enter **Z** ↵. At the **All/Center/Dynamic** prompt, enter **.6x**. Your screen will look like Figure 18.6.

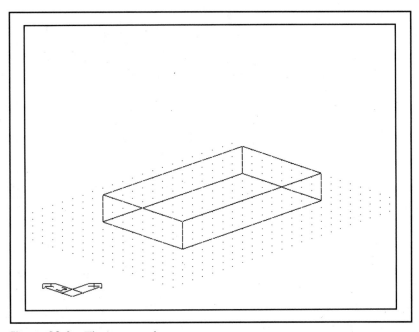

Figure 18.6:   The screen so far

TURNING AN EXTRUDED
2D POLYLINE INTO A 3D SOLID

Now let's add another box to form the lower lip of the bracket. This time, you'll create a box primitive from a polyline.

Draw ➤ ⤶ Polyline

1. Click on Draw ➤ Polyline ➤ 2D.

2. At the **From point** prompt, start the polyline from the coordinate **.5,2.5**.

3. Continue the polyline around to create a rectangle that is 1"
   in the X axis and 3" in the Y. Do this by entering the following set of polar coordinates:

   @1<0 ↵ @3<90 ↵ @1<180 ↵ C ↵

The last C that you entered closes the polyline. Your drawing will look
like Figure 18.7.

Use the CHANGE command to change the thickness of the polyline
you just drew to 1".

Model ➤ Solidify

1. Click on Modify ➤ Change ➤ Properties.

2. At the **Select objects** prompt, pick the polyline, and press ↵.

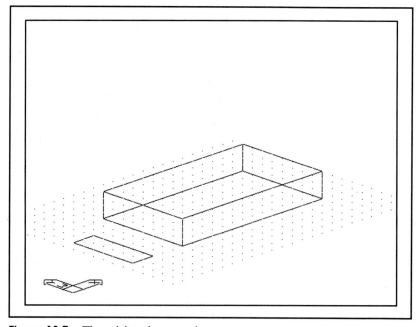

Figure 18.7:   The polyline drawn in place

3. At the Change Properties dialog box enter **1** in the Thickness input box, then click on **OK**.

4. Click on Model ➤ Solidify or enter **solidify** ↵ at the command prompt.

5. At the **Select objects** prompt, click on the polyline you just drew, then press ↵. The polyline will blink as the command prompt returns.

6. Enter **R** ↵ to redraw the screen. Though it may be difficult to tell by looking at it, the polyline has been converted into a solid, as shown in Figure 18.8.

You've now drawn two box primitives using the SOLBOX and the SOLIDIFY commands. Just for variety's sake, you created the smaller box by converting a polyline into a solid, though you could just as easily have used SOLBOX. SOLIDIFY will convert polylines, circles, and

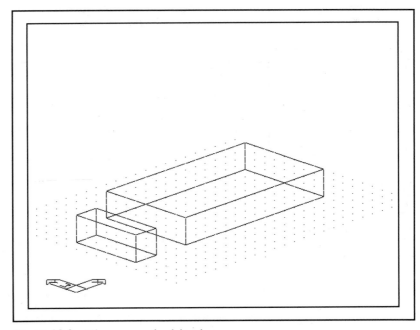

Figure 18.8:   The converted polyline box

traces as long as they have a thickness greater than 0. Regular lines, 3D lines, 3dfaces, and 3D polylines cannot be solidified.

Before you continue, I'd like to introduce the commands for AME primitives you haven't had a chance to use yet. The following describes these other primitives and how they are constructed (see Figures 18.9–18.12).

SOLCONE draws a solid circular cone or a cone with an elliptical base. Drawing a circular cone is much like drawing a circle with an added prompt asking for a height. The Ellipse option acts like the ELLIPSE command, again with the added prompt for height. This command appears as Cone on the pull-down menu.

SOLSPHERE creates a spherical solid. This command acts like the circle command, but instead of drawing a circle it draws a sphere. This command appears as Sphere on the pull-down menu.

SOLTORUS creates a doughnut-shaped solid. You are prompted for two diameters or radii, one for the diameter or radius of the torus and another for the diameter or radius of the tube portion of the torus. This command appears as Torus on the pull-down menu.

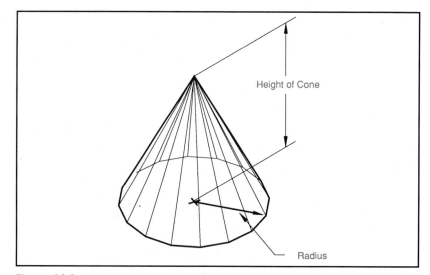

Figure 18.9: Drawing a solid cone

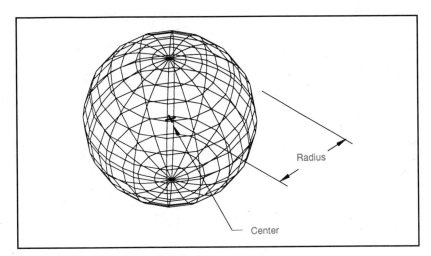

Figure 18.10:   Drawing a solid sphere

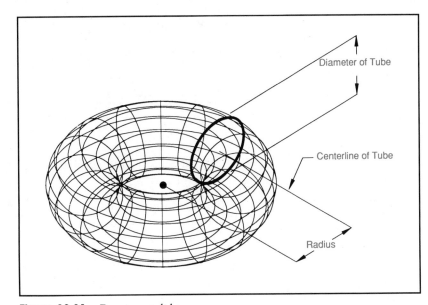

Figure 18.11:   Drawing a solid torus

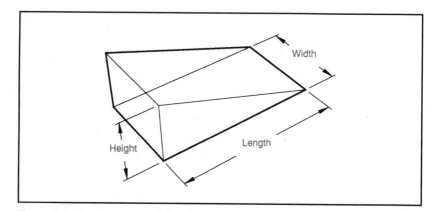

Figure 18.12: Drawing a solid wedge

SOLWEDGE creates a wedge-shaped solid. This command acts much like the SOLBOX command you used to draw the bracket. The point you pick at the **Corner of wedge** prompt determines the tall side of the wedge. This command appears as Wedge on the pull-down menu.

JOINING PRIMITIVES

Now let's see how these two objects are joined. First you'll move the new box into place, then join the two boxes to form a single solid.

Model ➤ Union

1. Start the Move command, pick the smaller of the two boxes, then press ↵.

2. At the **Base point** prompt, use the Endpoint override and pick the upper-left corner of the box as shown in panel 1 of Figure 18.13.

3. At the **Second point** prompt, pick the lower-left corner of the larger box, as shown in panel 2 of Figure 18.13.

4. Click on Model ➤ Union.

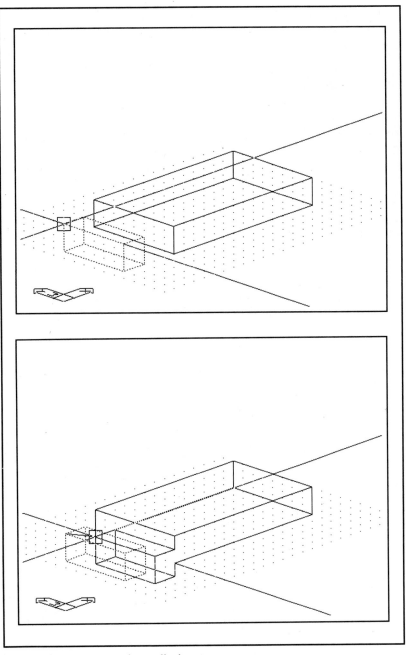

Figure 18.13: Moving the smaller box

5. At the **Select objects** prompt, pick both boxes, then press ↲. You get the same prompts as when you created the boxes. When the Solunion command is done, your drawing will look like Figure 18.14.

As you can see from the figure, the form has joined to appear as one object. It also acts like one object when you select it. You now have a composite solid made up of two box primitives.

Now let's place some holes in the bracket. In the next exercise, you will discover how to create negative forms to cut out portions of a solid.

Model ➤ Primitives

1. Click on Model ➤ Primitives.

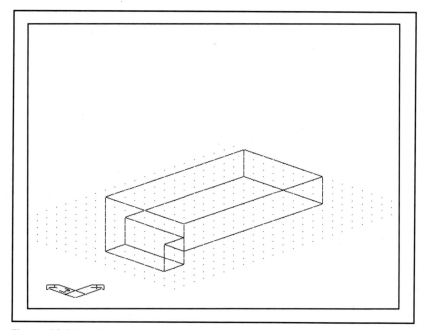

Figure 18.14: The two boxes joined

2. At the AME Primitives dialog box, click on the Cylinder, then click on **OK**. Alternately, you can enter **solcyl** at the command prompt.

3. At the **Baseplane/Ellipse/<center point>:** prompt, pick a point at the coordinate 9,5.5.

4. At the **Diameter/<radius>:** prompt, enter **.25** ↵.

5. At the **Center of other end/<Height>** prompt, enter **1.5** ↵. The solid's prompts appear and the cylinder is drawn, as shown in Figure 18.15.

You have the cylinder primitive, but you still need to define its relationship to the composite solid you created from the two boxes.

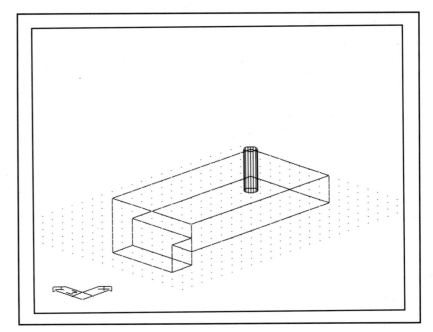

Figure 18.15: The cylinder added to the drawing

Model ➤ Subtract

1. Click on Model ➤ Subtract or enter **Solsub** ↵.

2. At the **Source object… Select objects:** prompt, pick the composite solid of the two boxes, then press ↵.

3. At the **Objects to subtract from them… Select objects:** prompt, pick the cylinder, then press ↵. AutoCAD will display several prompts as it goes to work, then the objects will blink. The cylinder has now been subtracted from the bracket.

Notice that the hole now conforms to the depth of the bracket. Remember that I asked you to draw the cylinder at a height of 1.5", not 1", which is the thickness of the bracket. Having drawn the cylinder taller than needed, you can see that AutoCAD, when it performed the subtraction, ignored the portion of the cylinder that doesn't affect the bracket. AutoCAD will always discard the portion of a primitive that isn't used in a SOLSUB operation.

VIEWING A SOLID

As you've learned in the earlier chapters in *Part IV*, wire-frame views such as the one you have of the bracket are a bit difficult to decipher. You cannot tell for sure that the subtracted cylinder is in fact a hole. You might think that you can perform a hidden-line removal now to view the bracket in its true form. But before you do that, you must tell the AME to create a surface model of the solid. This next exercise shows you how to do this.

Model ➤ Display ➤ Mesh
Render ➤ Hide

1. Click on Model ➤ Display ➤ Mesh or enter **Solmesh** ↵.

2. At the **Select solids to be meshed... Select objects:** prompt, pick the bracket, then press ⏎. You see several messages telling you that the AME is working. When SOLMESH is done, the drawing blinks and the message *Done* appears on the command prompt.

3. Click on Render ➤ Hide. Now you see the bracket as a solid and you can also see that the cylinder is a hole (see Figure 18.16).

As you build your solid model, the AME keeps track of the model's properties. The model is maintained as a solid in a database that the AME controls. But AutoCAD is still a 3D surface drawing program, so in order to represent the solid properly in AutoCAD, you must create a 3D surface facsimile. Solmesh is a tool of the AME's that lets you easily create that facsimile. Solmesh must be used whenever you intend to use the Hide command after you have edited a solid.

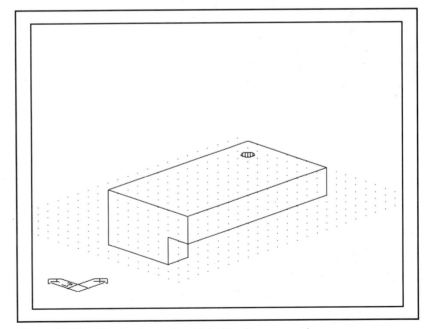

Figure 18.16:   The bracket so far with hidden lines removed

EDITING A SOLID

So far, you've created a composite solid of both unioned and subtracted forms. You were able to use the MOVE command to move a solid into place before you joined it to another solid. As long as you haven't used a boolean operation to join solids, you can use standard AutoCAD commands to move, copy, or scale them. But editing primitives that are a part of an existing composite solid requires the use of some new tools.

MODIFYING A COMPOSITE SOLID

In the next set of exercises, you'll use several new tools to make some changes and additions to your bracket. You'll start by adding another hole to the bracket.

Model ➤ Modify ➤ Change Prim

Next

Instance

Move

Model ➤ Subtract

1. Issue the REGEN command to return to a wire-frame view of your drawing.

2. Click on Model ➤ Modify ➤ Change Prim or enter **solchp** ↵ at the command prompt.

3. At the **Select Solid:** prompt, pick the bracket. AutoCAD will take a moment to find all the primitives that make up the composite.

4. At the **Select Primitive:** prompt, pick the cylinder representing the hole. Once you pick it, the cylinder in its entire height is highlighted.

5. At the **Color/Delete/Evaluate/Instance/Move/Next/Pick/ Replace/Size/eXit <N>:** prompt, press ↵ to accept the

> **▼ NOTE**
>
> You can think of the Solchp command as a Chprop command for solids. It lets you change the properties of a solid without having to take the solid apart and recreate it.

default Next option. Notice that one of the other primitives highlights. Press ↵ again. Now the next primitive highlights. Press ↵ a third time to highlight the cylinder again. This shows that the Next option simply selects the next primitive in the composite.

6. Enter **I** for the Instance option. Instance makes a copy of the primitive you select. AutoCAD will work for a moment, then return to the prompt.

7. At the **Color/Delete/Evaluate** prompt, enter **M** to move the cylinder.

8. At the **Base point of displacement:** prompt, use your cursor to pick the coordinate 9,5.5, which is the center of the cylinder at its base.

9. At the **Second point of displacement:** prompt, enter **@2<-90**. The original cylinder moves to the new location (see Figure 18.17).

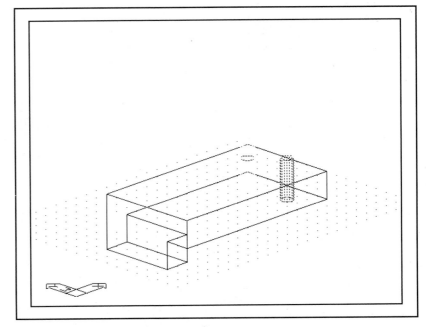

Figure 18.17: The cylinder in a new location

10. Enter **X** to exit the Solchp command. AutoCAD takes a moment to update the model, then it appears with the cylinder in its new position. But remember that you made a copy of the cylinder before you moved it.

11. Issue the REGEN command and that copy appears, as shown in Figure 18.18.

The new cylinder is not a part of the composite.

1. Click on Model ➤ Subtract or enter **Solsub** ↵.

2. At the **Source objects** prompt, pick the composite, then press ↵.

3. At the **Object to subtract** prompt, pick the new cylinder, then press ↵. The bracket appears with the second hole in place (see Figure 18.19).

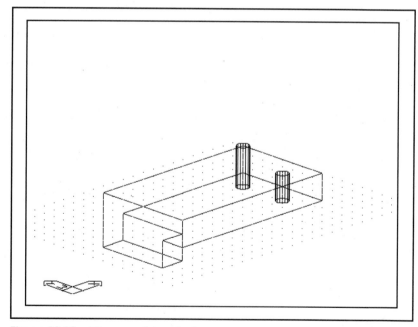

Figure 18.18: The copy of the cylinder

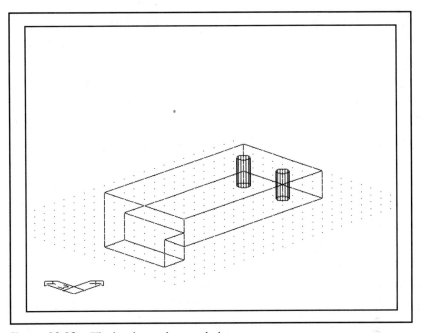

Figure 18.19:   The bracket with a new hole

You were able to add a hole by copying and moving an existing cylinder. You could have drawn a cylinder and placed it where you needed the second hole, then performed a solid subtraction. Doing it the first way, however, gave you a chance to use the Instance and Move options under the Solchp command.

But there are many other options available with the Solchp command. Let's see how you can change the dimensions of a primitive within a composite by using the Size option.

Model ➤ Modify ➤ Change Prim
Size

1. Click on Model ➤ Modify ➤ Change Prim again or enter **solchp** ↵.

▼ **NOTE**

The **Specify x** prompt asks you to specify the dimension of the box in the MCS's X axis (see note next to Figure 18.20 for more on MCS). The default value, 7, is the current X dimension of the primitive.

2. At the **Select Solid:** prompt, pick the composite solid.

3. Then at the **Select Primitive:** prompt, pick the large box primitive.

4. At the **Color/Delete/Evaluate** prompt, enter **S** to select the Size option.

5. At the **Specify x <7>:** prompt, enter **7.5** ↵. Simultaneously with this prompt, an icon appears on the box, as shown in Figure 18.20.

6. At the **Specify y <4>:** prompt, enter **5** ↵. This prompt is asking for the dimension in the MCS's Y axis.

7. At the **Specify z <1>:** prompt, press ↵ to accept the default dimension for the Z axis. As in steps 5 and 6, the default value is the box's current dimension—this time in the MCS's Z axis. The box primitive changes to the new dimensions as shown in Figure 18.21.

▼ **NOTE**

This icon shows you a temporary coordinate system called the Motion Coordinate System or MCS. It is used to help you identify the axis to which the prompt is referring. If you look carefully at the icon, you will notice that each point has a different number of arrow tips. The number of tips identifies the axis: the axis with one tip is the X axis; two tips denote the Y axis; and three the Z axis.

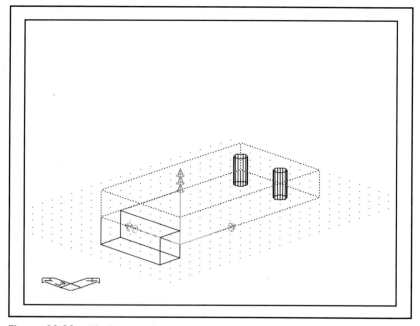

Figure 18.20: The Motion Coordinate System icon

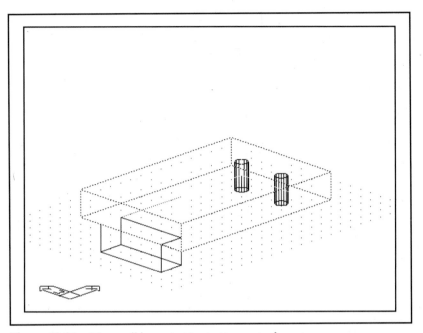

Figure 18.21:   The small box primitive in its new configuration.

▼ WARNING

You will get a different set of prompts from the Size option depending on the type of primitive you select. This exercise shows what happens for solid boxes. For solidified polylines, you will be asked for new **Z** axis dimension and a taper angle (see the section *Extruding a Polyline* later in this chapter). For other primitives, you are asked for the same dimensions you entered when you first created the primitive.

8. Enter **X** to exit the SOLCHP command. AutoCAD recalculates the new solid form and displays the changes, as shown in Figure 18.22.

DEFINING A UCS FROM A SOLID

In previous chapters, you saw how the user coordinate system can help you draw in 3D. Since the next part of the bracket starts on the top of your current composite solid, it will help if you can create a UCS on the top of the bracket. The next exercise shows how this is done using the solid modeler's own form of the UCS command.

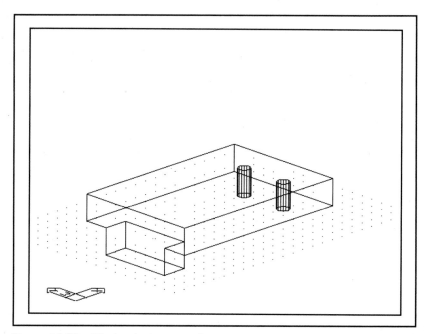

Figure 18.22: The bracket's new configuration

Model ➤ Utility ➤ SolUCS
Settings ➤ UCS ➤ Icon ➤ Origin

▼ NOTE

When using this command, you have to think in terms of surface modeling. Since the line you picked represents the edge of two 3dfaces (the one on top of the bracket and the one at the back of the bracket), you may not get the face you want at your first pick. The **<OK>/Next** prompt lets you highlight the other 3dface that is associated with the edge line you pick.

1. Click on Model ➤ Utility ➤ SolUCS or enter **solucs** ↵.

2. At the **Edge/<Face>:** prompt, press ↵ to accept the default. This prompt asks you if you want to use an edge of your solid model to define a UCS or if you want to use a surface of the solid.

3. At the **Select a face…** prompt, pick the line representing the back top corner of the bracket, as shown in Figure 18.23. The top edge of the bracket highlights.

4. At the **Next/<OK>:** prompt, Enter **N** ↵ to move to the other 3dface. The back face of the bracket highlights, as shown in Figure 18.24.

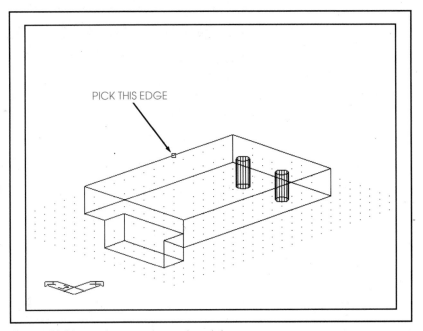

Figure 18.23: Picking an edge on the solid

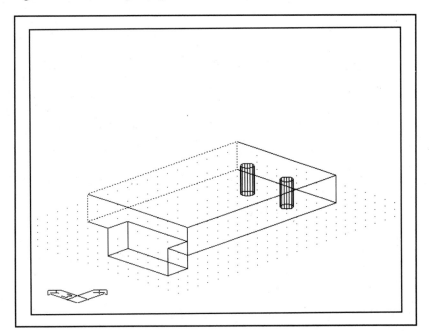

Figure 18.24: Selecting a surface for the SolUCS command

▼   # Other Solchp Options

You still haven't tried some of the other options under the Solchp command. In the space of this tutorial, I can't walk you through an exercise that involves all these options, so here is a brief description of what each of them can do. With this information, you should know enough to experiment on your own.

Color	Changes the color of a primitive.
Delete	Deletes a primitive. If the primitive is part of a composite, it will separate the primitive then give you the option of keeping it or deleting it completely from the drawing.
Evaluate	Forces the AME to update the solid's database. This is useful if you have made several changes in a complex composite. The command has no apparent effect on your screen.
Pick	Lets you select another primitive to edit by picking it instead of using the Next option to go to the next primitive.
Replace	Lets you replace one primitive within a composite with another. The replacing primitive must not be a part of the current composite solid. If you want to replace one primitive with another that *is* a part of the composite, you can first use the Instance option to make a free-standing copy of the replacement primitive. Instance will do this even though the primitive is a part of a composite solid.

5. Enter **N** ↵ again to return to the top face, then press ↵. Notice the orientation of the UCS icon: it has rotated 180° from the WCS.

6. Click on Settings ➤ UCS ➤ Icon ➤ Origin. The UCS icon shifts to the upper-back corner, showing you that it is now aligned with the top face of the bracket.

Solucs performs the same function as the Entity option under the UCS command. It creates a UCS aligned with an object. You cannot use the UCS command's Entity option on solids, so SolUCS was created as a substitute.

Now you're ready to add the top part of the bracket. Just keep in mind that the current UCS is 180° from the WCS, so the coordinates are turned upside down.

CONVERTING 2D OBJECTS TO SOLIDS

Early in this chapter, you created a solid from a polyline. For the most part, however, you have been creating solids by using the AME primitives and editing tools. The AME also provides a few tools that let you create some complex primitive shapes besides the standard ones you saw earlier. These tools use 2D polylines as their basis for creating solids. In this section, you'll add the top portion of the bracket with these tools.

EXTRUDING A POLYLINE

As you learned earlier, you can convert a polyline into a solid by using the Solidify command. But Solidify needs a polyline with thickness before it can do its work. Solext also converts a polyline, but unlike Solidify it doesn't require your polyline to have a thickness.

Draw ➤ 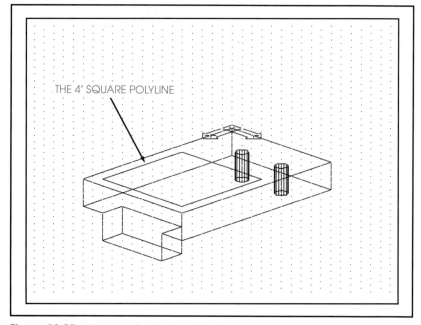 Polyline ➤ 2D
Model ➤ Extrude

1. Draw a 4"×4" closed polyline. Do this by starting at the back left corner of the bracket at coordinate 7,0.5, then drawing the 4×4 square to fit in the top of the composite solid as shown in Figure 18.25.

2. Click on Model ➤ Extrude or enter **solext** ↵ at the command prompt.

3. At the **Select regions, polylines and circles for extrusions… Select objects:** prompt, pick the polyline you just drew, then press ↵. (As the prompt indicates, you can pick polylines or circles.)

4. At the **Height of extrusion:** prompt, enter **4** ↵.

THE 4" SQUARE POLYLINE

Figure 18.25: Drawing the 4"×4" polyline box

▼ NOTE

In step 5, you can indicate a taper for the extrusion. You specify a taper in terms of degrees from the Z axis. You can enter a negative value to taper the extrusion outward or press ↵ to accept the default, 0°, to extrude the polyline without a taper.

5. At the **Extrusion taper angle from Z <0>:** prompt, enter **4** for 4° of taper. The extruded polyline appears, as shown in Figure 18.26.

REVOLVING A POLYLINE

While Solext works fine for rectangular forms, you may want to draw an object that is circular. The Solrev command is designed to let you create a solid that is revolved or swept in a circular path. You might think of Solrev as acting like a lathe that lets you carve a shape from a spinning shaft. In this case, the spinning shaft is a polyline, and instead of carving it, you define the profile, then revolve the profile about an axis.

In the following exercise, you will draw a solid that will form a slot in the tapered box.

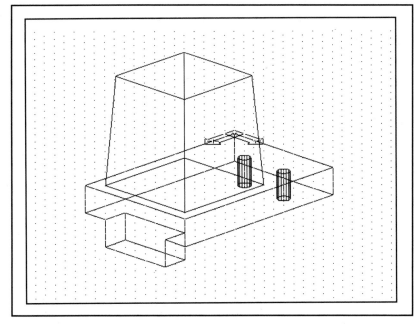

Figure 18.26: The extruded polyline

UCS
Pline
Solrev

1. ZOOM into the top of the tapered box so that you have a view similar to Figure 18.27.

2. Turn the snap mode off.

3. Click on Settings ➤ UCS ➤ Origin.

4. At the **Origin** prompt, use the Endpoint Osnap override and pick the top corner of the box, as shown in Figure 18.27.

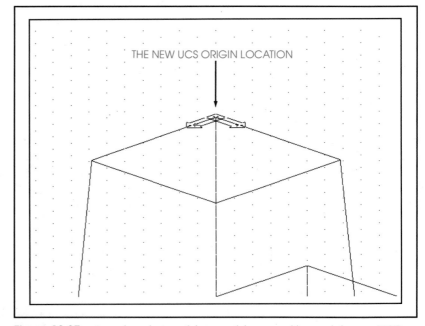

THE NEW UCS ORIGIN LOCATION

Figure 18.27: An enlarged view of the top of the tapered box and the new UCS location

5. Set the Snap distance to 0.125 and, with the coordinate readout turned on, draw a polyline using the following coordinates:

   –0.375, 1.625
   @1.25<270
   @.875<0
   @1<30
   @0.625<0
   @1<330
   @1.25<0
   @1.25<90

6. Press ↵ when you are done. Your drawing should look like Figure 18.28.

7. Click on Model ➤ Revolve or enter **solrev** at the command prompt.

8. At the **Select region polyline or circle for revolution...**
   Select objects: prompt, pick the polyline you just drew, then press ↵.

9. At the **Axis of revolution - Entity/X/Y/<Start point of axis>:** prompt, use the Endpoint Osnap override and pick the beginning endpoint of the polyline you just drew.

10. Turn on the ortho mode (press the **F8** function key) and turn off the snap mode (press the **F9** function key). Then pick a point to the far left of the screen so that the rubber-banding line is parallel with the X axis of the current UCS.

11. At the **Include angle <full circle>:** prompt, press ↵ to sweep the polyline 360°. AutoCAD will take a few moments to calculate the revolution, then the revolved form will appear, as shown in Figure 18.29.

You have just created a solid that will be subtracted from the tapered box to form a slot in the bracket.

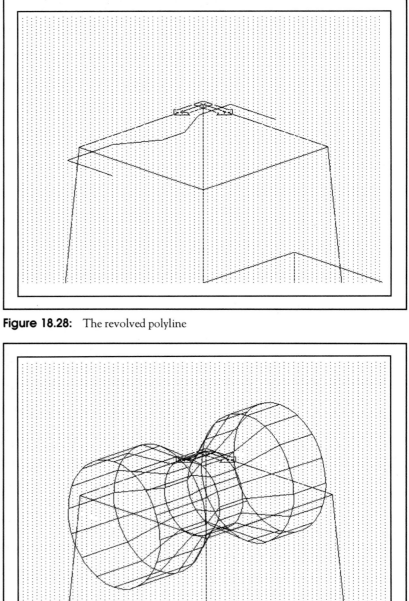

Figure 18.28:   The revolved polyline

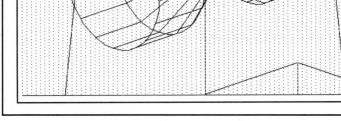

Figure 18.29:   Drawing the polyline

FINE-TUNING A SOLID'S SHAPE

The AME offers tools to simplify some of the more common editing tasks. You can add chamfers and fillets to composite solids and primitives. Another command aids you in positioning both composites and primitives. In this section, you will finish off your bracket with the help of these tools.

MOVING AND ROTATING A SOLID

Before you subtract the revolved shape from the tapered box, you can change its position. Its current location places it off the box's center. You can use the standard AutoCAD commands such as MOVE and ROTATE, but the AME offers Solmove, a command that combines both of them. Solmove is easy to use, though at first it may seem a bit arcane.

Model ➤ Modify ➤ Move Object
Solsub

1. Choose Model ➤ Modify ➤ Move Object or enter **solmove** ↵.

2. At the **Select object**s prompt, pick the revolved solid, then press ↵. The MCS appears.

3. At the **<Motion description>/?:** prompt, enter **ty.0935** ↵—the reason for this is discussed below. The solid moves 0.0935" in the Y axis of the MCS. Since this is such a small distance, you won't see much change in your drawing.

4. When the **<Motion description>/:** prompt returns, this time enter **ry5** ↵. The solid rotates 5° about the Y axis of the MCS.

5. When the **<Motion description>/:** prompt returns again, press ↵ to exit the Solmove command.

6. Use the SOLSUB command to subtract the revolved solid from the tapered box. Your drawing should look like Figure 18.30.

Now let's look at what you entered to move the revolved solid. In the first instance, you entered **ty.0935** to move the solid 0.0935 inches in the Y axis. The *t* told Solmove that you wanted to perform a *translation*, otherwise known as a move. The *y* told Solmove you wanted the move to occur along the Y axis. Finally, the *0.0935* told Solmove the distance for the move. The motion description is not too complicated once you see firsthand what it does!

In the next operation, you entered **ry5**. The *r* stands for rotate, the *y* stands for the Y axis, and the *5* represents 5° of rotation. You could have entered **–5** to rotate the solid in the opposite direction. Here, the right-hand rule applies. If you imagine placing your right hand on the Y axis with your thumb pointing in the positive direction, your fingers will point in the positive direction of rotation.

Once you get used to motion descriptions, you will find that they are real timesavers when it comes to positioning solids.

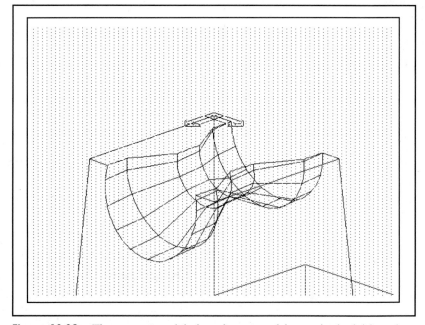

Figure 18.30: The composite solid after subtraction of the revolved solid from the tapered solid

If you enter a question mark at the **<Motion description>** prompt, you get the following listing:

```
a(efuw) - align with selected coordinate system
r(xyz)degrees - rotate about selected axis
t(xyz)distance - translate along selected axis
e - sets axis to edge coordinate system
f - sets axis to face coordinate system
u - sets axis to user coordinate system
w - sets axis to world coordinate system
o - restore motion to original position
For more information, type HELP SOLMOVE.
```

The second and third lines of this listing will help you remember how to enter a motion description. For example, the second line indicates that the syntax of a motion description is r followed by an x, y, or z, which is then followed by a degree value.

The first line shows the syntax of a motion description you didn't try. The a[efuw] motion description lets you align a solid with an axis defined by a solid's edge, solid's face, and a UCS or the WCS. The following list gives a more detailed description of these Solmove options.

Ae: Lets you align an object along the edge of a solid. When you use this motion description, you are prompted to select an edge to define the destination coordinate system. Once you pick an edge, the solid moves into a position aligned with that edge. You can then use the translate or rotate motion descriptors to precisely locate the solid.

Af: Lets you align an object along a face of an object. When you use this motion description, you are prompted to select a face. You can then pick the edge of the face you want. A face will highlight and you will get the **<OK>/Next** prompt. If the highlighted face is not the one you want, you can enter **N** for next; otherwise you can press ↵, and the solid will align with the selected face.

Au: Aligns the solid with the current user coordinate system.

Aw: Aligns the solid with the world coordinate system.

O: Returns the solid to the position it was in when you started the Solmove command.

ROUNDING AND CHAMFERING CORNERS

Your bracket has a few sharp corners on it. You may want to round these corners to give it a more realistic appearance. For this purpose, the AME gives you a solid-model version of the CHAMFER and FILLET commands.

Model ➤ Modify ➤ Fillet Solids

1. ZOOM back to your previous view of the overall drawing.

2. Click on Model ➤ Modify ➤ Fillet Solids or enter **solfill** ↵.

3. At the **Select edges to be filleted (Press ENTER when done):** prompt, pick the edges indicated in panel 1 of Figure 18.31. As you pick them, they are highlighted. When you are done, press ↵.

4. At the **Diameter/<radius> of fillet <0.00>:** prompt, enter **.25**. AutoCAD will take a minute or two to recreate the solid with the filleted corners. Your drawing will then look like panel 2 of Figure 18.31.

Solfill doesn't do a perfect job on the corners where three fillets meet. But you can derive a 2D projection of a 3D view and then clean up any rough spots using standard 2D editing commands. You'll learn how to do that a bit later. Now let's try chamfering a corner.

Solcham

1. Click on Model ➤ Modify ➤ Chamfer Solids or enter **solcham**.

2. At the **Select base surface:** prompt, pick the lowermost edge of the small box primitive as shown in panel 1 of Figure 18.32.

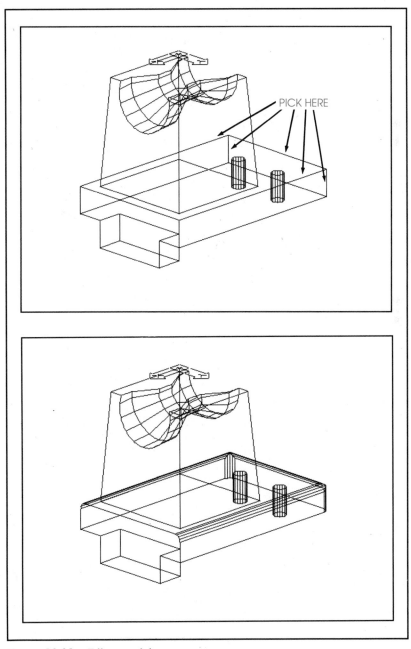

Figure 18.31: Filleting solids

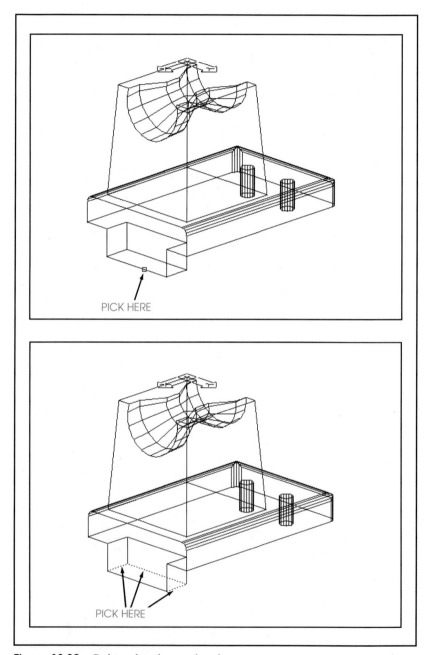

Figure 18.32: Picking the edges to chamfer

3. At the **<OK>/Next** prompt, if the outline of the bottom face of the primitive is not highlighted, enter **N** ↵; otherwise press ↵ to accept the current highlighted face. As with previous occurrences of this prompt, you can either select another face, if the highlighted face is not the one you want, or press ↵ to accept the current face.

4. At the **Pick edges to be chamfered (Press ENTER when done):** prompt, pick the three edges shown in panel 2 of Figure 18.32.

5. At the **Enter distance along first surface <0.00>:** prompt, enter **.25** ↵.

6. At the **Enter distance along second surface <0.25>:** prompt, enter **.4** ↵. (Notice that the default is the same as the value you entered for the previous prompt.) AutoCAD takes a minute to reconstruct the solid with the chamfers. When it is done, your drawing looks like Figure 18.33.

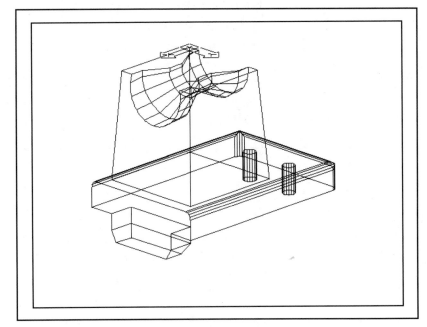

Figure 18.33: The chamfered edges

To finish off the part, join the extruded part with the base.

1. Click on Model ➤ Union.

2. At the **select object** prompt, click on the two solids, then press ↵. AutoCAD will display the usual messages and join the two parts.

ENHANCING THE 2D DRAWING PROCESS

Using AME to model a part such as the one in the previous tutorial may seem a bit on the exotic side, but there are definite advantages to modeling in 3D, even if you only want to draw the part in 2D as a page in a set of manufacturing specs. The following exercise show you how you can quickly generate a working drawing from your 3D model.

DRAWING A STANDARD TOP, FRONT, AND RIGHT SIDE VIEW

One of the more common types of mechanical drawings is the orthogonal projection. This is a style of drawing that shows the top, front and right side view of an object. Optionally, a 3D image is also added for clarity. You can derive such a drawing within a few minutes, once you have created your 3D solid model. The first step is to select a sheet.

Settings ➤ Layer Control
View ➤ Layout ➤ Setup
Title Block

1. Set the UCS back to World, then create a layer called **title**, then make this new layer the current one. This will be the layer for your title block.

2. Click on View ➤ Layout ➤ MV Setup.

3. At the **Enable Paperspace/Modelspace** prompt, press ↵ to enable Paperspace.

4. At the **Align/Create/Scale** viewport prompt, enter **T** ↵ to select the Title block option.

5. At the **Delete objects/Origin/Undo/<Insert Title Block>** prompt, press ↵. The screen flips to text mode and you see a numbered list of sheet sizes.

6. At the **Add/Delete/Redisplay/<Number of entry to load>** prompt, enter **9** for a C size sheet. AutoCAD will flip to graphics mode and draw a title block.

7. At the **Create a drawing called ansi-c.dwg** prompt, enter **N** ↵, then press ↵ again to exit MVSetup.

Setting Up a Set of Standard Views

As you can see, MVSetup offers a range of predefined engineering sheets for you to use. The next step is to get your viewport set up.

Settings ➤ Layer Control
View ➤ Layout ➤ Setup
Create Viewports

1. Create a new layer called **Views** and make this new layer the current one. This will be the layer for the new viewports MVSetup will create.

2. Click on View ➤ Layout ➤ MVSetup again.

3. At the **Align/Create/Scale viewports** prompt, enter **C** ↵ to use the Create option.

4. At the **Delete objects/Undo/<Create viewports>** prompt, press ↵ to accept the default. A numbered list of four options appears on the screen.

5. At the **Redisplay/< Number of entry to load>** prompt, enter **2** ↵ to select the Std. Engineering option. This option generates four viewports with special characteristics, as you will see in a moment.

6. At the **Bounding area for viewports First point** prompt, pick a point toward the lower-left corner of the title block (see Figure 18.34).

7. At the **Other corner** prompt, pick a point as shown in Figure 18.34.

8. At the **Distance between viewports in X** prompt, enter **.5** ↵. Here you are telling MVSetup how much space to put between each viewport horizontally.

9. At the **Distance between viewports in Y** prompt, press ↵. Notice that the default is the same as the X distance you just entered. This tells MVSetup how much space to leave between the viewports vertically. AutoCAD will work for a moment to set up the top, front, and right-side view of the 3D part you drew.

10. Press ↵ to exit MVSetup.

Scaling Viewports Uniformly

Now you have a title block and your view's layout. The next step is to scale your drawing to the appropriate size for this sheet. Once again, you'll use MVSetup.

View ➤ Layout ➤ Setup
Scale Viewports

1. Click on View ➤ Layout ➤ MVSetup.

2. At the **Align/Create/Scale viewports** prompt, enter **S** ↵ for Scale viewports.

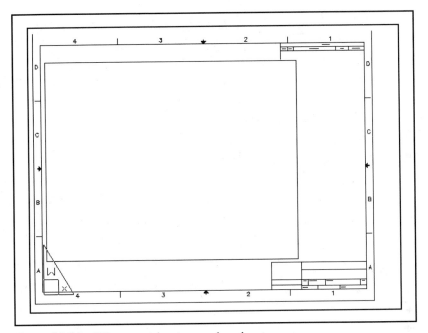

Figure 18.34: Where to pick points to place the viewports

3. At the **Select objects** prompt, click on the four viewports, then press ⏎. Remember that to select a viewport, you click on its border.

4. At the **Set zoom scale factor for viewports Interactively/ <Uniform>** prompt, press ⏎ to accept the Uniform default. This causes all viewports to be scaled to the same scale factor.

5. At the **number of Paperspace units** prompt, enter ~**.5** ⏎.

6. At the **number of Modelspace units prompt**, press ⏎ to accept the default value of 1. This and the previous prompt combine to give your drawing a scale of $\frac{1}{2}'' = 1''$.

7. Press ⏎ to exit the MVSetup option.

Creating Hidden Line Views Automatically

You've got just about everything complete. The views are in place and in scale, but mechanical drawings usually represent hidden geometry by dashed lines. In the next exercise, you will see how AME can quickly generate the hidden line views for you.

Model ➤ Display ➤ Profile Solids

1. Enter **MS** ↵ to go to Modelspace.

2. Click on the viewport in the upper left of the title block showing the top view.

3. Click on Model ➤ Display ➤ Profile Solids.

4. At the **Select objects** prompt, click on the model in the upper left, then press ↵.

5. At the **Display hidden profile lines on separate layer** prompt, press ↵ to accept the default Y.

6. At the **Project profile lines onto a plane** prompt, press ↵ again.

7. At the **Delete tangential edges** prompt, press ↵ again.

8. Repeat steps 2 through 6 for each of the other three viewports. Remember to click on the viewport before using the AME Profile Solids option.

The drawing doesn't look like it has changed, but a good deal of information has been added to your drawing. The next and final step will show you the results of your efforts.

Linetype ↵
Load
Settings ➤ Layer Control
Ltscale ↵

1. Load the Hidden2 linetype using the Linetype command.

2. Click on Settings ➤ Layer Control. Notice all the new layers in the list box of the dialog box. These were created by AME.

3. Highlight all the layers that begin with *PH-*. These are the layers that contain the hidden line information.

4. Click on the Set Ltype button, and in the Select Linetype dialog box, double-click on the Hidden2 linetype. This sets the hidden line layers to the appropriate line type.

5. Click on the **Clear All** button, then click on the layers 0 and Views to highlight them.

6. Click on the **OFF** button to turn these layers off, then click on **OK**. You don't want to see the original solid model you created on layer 0 or the viewport borders, so you turn their layers off.

7. If you get a warning message that the current layer is off, click on **OK**.

8. Finally, enter **Ltscale** ↵, then enter **2** ↵ to set the line type scale to 2. Your drawing will look like Figure 18.35.

You had to get through a lot of steps to get the final drawing, but compared to actually having to draw these views by hand, you may have saved yourself a great deal of time. In addition, as you will see later in this chapter, you have more than just a 2D drafted image. To finish this drawing off, you only need to add some dimensions and labels.

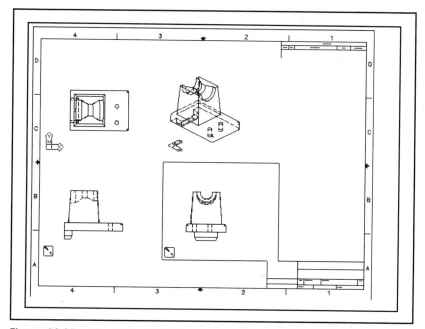

Figure 18.35: The finished 2D layout of your 3D solid model

DRAWING A SECTION

One element of your drawing that is missing is a cross section. The AME will draw a cross section through any part of the solid model you want. In the following exercise, you will draw a cross section, and at the same time, you will see what AME has done to create the views in the previous exercise.

1. First, save your drawing. You may not want to save the results of the following steps.

2. Click on Views ➤ Tilemode ➤ On. Return to your model and you will see a few extra elements in the drawing (see Figure 18.36). When the AME created the four profile views, it actually created these 2D images you see strewn across the screen.

3. Turn layer 0 on. You will see your model superimposed on the 2D profiles.

Model ➤ Display ➤ Section Solid

4. Now set the current layer to 0 and turn off all the layers except 0. You will want to keep the profile images, but they will get in your way while you create your section drawing.

5. Click on Model ➤ Display ➤ Section Solid.

6. At the **Select object** prompt, click on the solid and press ↵.

7. At the **Sectioning plane by Entity/Last/Zaxis/View/XY/YZ /ZX/<3points>** prompt, enter **ZX** ↵. This tells AME you want to cut the solid in the plane defined by the X and Z axis.

8. At the **Point on ZX plane** prompt, pick the midpoint of the back-top surface (see Figure 18.37). AME will work for a minute, then the section cut appears.

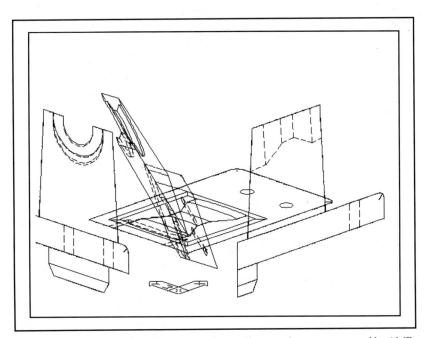

Figure 18.36: The solid model showing the profile views that were generated by AME

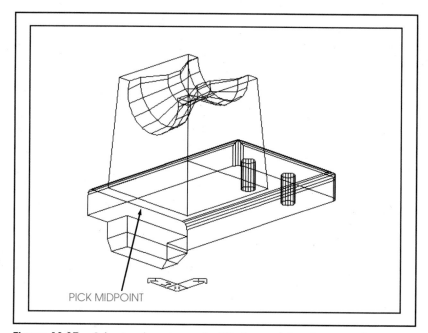

PICK MIDPOINT

Figure 18.37: Selecting the point on the ZX plane to define the section location and the final section cut

The section cross hatching and outline are two separate objects placed on the current layer. You can move them away from the solid model, then create another viewport in the Paperspace layout you did earlier.

USING 3D SOLID OPERATIONS ON 2D DRAWINGS WITHOUT AME

If you don't have AME, you can still take advantage of some of the features I've described in this chapter. AutoCAD comes with a 2D version of the AME called the Regional Model. The Regional Model lets you apply boolean operations to 2D forms. As an optional exercise, try the following:

1. If you have been working through the 3D solids tutorial, save the bracket drawing now.

2. Open the Regdemo file in the Sample directory. You will see two versions of a wrench, a completed one at the bottom and one showing the components of the wrench toward the top (see Figure 18.38).

3. Click on Model ➤ Subtract.

4. At the **Select objects** prompt, click on the green outline of the top version of the wrench, then press ↵.

5. At the **Objects to subtract from them** prompt, click on all the hexagonal shapes, including the pair of concentric hexagons to the left.

6. Press ↵ when you are done selecting objects. The hexagons are subtracted from the wrench outline.

7. Rotate the wrench you just created 90°, then move it on top of the lower wrench so the two form a cross.

8. Click on Model ➤ Union.

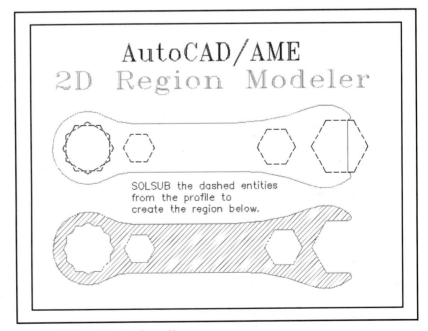

Figure 18.38:   The Regdemo file

9. At the **Select Objects** prompt, click on both wrenches, then press ↵ to confirm your selection. The two wrenches become one very odd-looking wrench.

10. Now return to the Bracket drawing to complete the rest of the chapter.

Here you used two boolean operations, Subtract and Union, to create a new object. You can use the Intersect function as well.

To create a 2D object for boolean operations, you must first draw the outlines of the objects using a closed polyline, then apply the Regional Model's Solidify command to the objects. Do this by clicking on Model ➤ Solidify, then click on the polylines you want to solidify. Once polylines are solidified, you can then use the Subtract, Union, or Intersect options on the Model menu to create new objects.

If you don't have the AME, you can use the Regional Model to generate complex 3D surfaces that might include holes or unusual bends (see Figure 18.39).

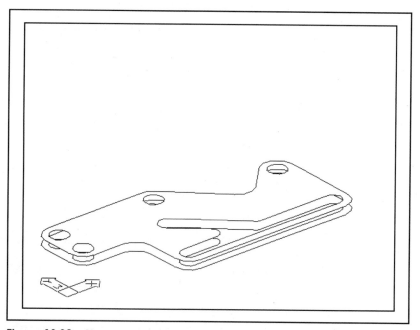

Figure 18.39: You can use the Regional Model to create complex 2D surfaces for use in 3D surface modeling.

To accomplish this, you create the outlines of the surfaces using closed polylines, solidify them using the Regional Model, make any subtractions necessary, then use the Model ➤ Display ➤ Mesh option on the objects. The Mesh option then creates a 2D surface that is opaque to the Hide and Shade commands.

If you need to modify a 2D region, use the Model ➤ Modify ➤ Change Prim or the Solchp command to make changes. See *Editing a Solid* earlier in this chapter.

ACCESSING THE AME SYSTEM VARIABLES

The AME has its own set of system variables that affect such things as the hatch pattern on cross sections and the color of the motion description axis icon. To simplify the use of the AME system variables, AutoCAD has provided yet another dialog box. To access this dialog box, you click on Model ➤ Setup ➤ Variables. The AME System Variables dialog box appears (see Figure 18.40).

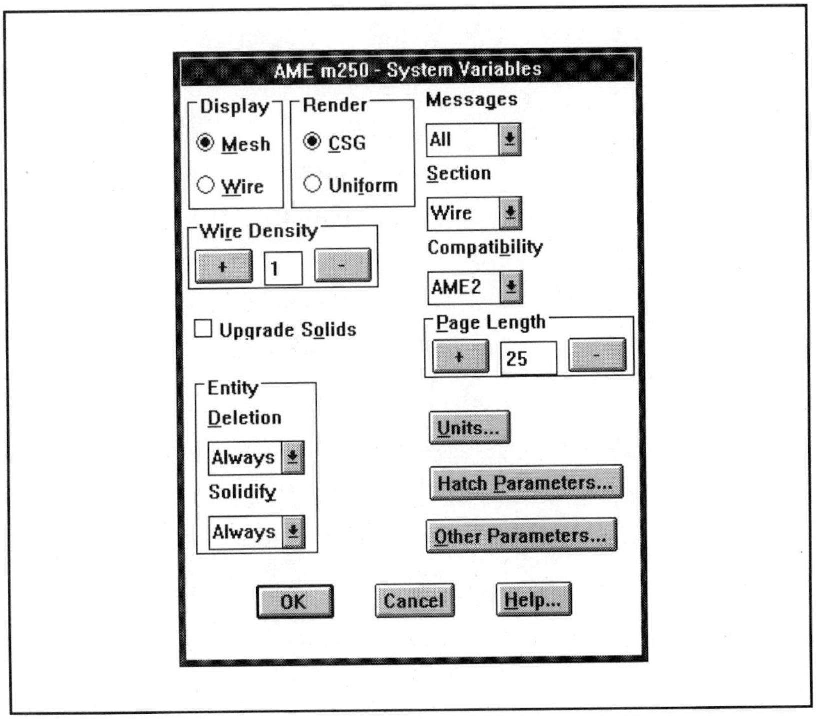

Figure 18.40:   The AME system variables dialog box

The following list describes what each item in the dialog box does.

Display [soldisplay] controls whether the model is displayed as a mesh or wireframe.

Render [solrender] controls whether composite solids are displayed in one uniform color or in multiple colors (CSG).

Wire Density [solwdens] controls the wire density of new objects.

Upgrade Solids [solupgrade] upgrades existing single-precision solids from earlier versions of AME to double-precision floating point.

Entity contains two pop-up lists. Deletion [soldelent] controls whether AME deletes old or unused solids, or extruded or revolved objects. Solidify [solsolidify] controls whether objects are automatically solidified or not.

Messages [solservmsg] controls the level of message reporting provided by AME.

Section [solsectype] controls the type of object created by the Solsect command.

Compatability [solamecomp] controls compatability between AME1 and AME2 command and scripts.

Page Length [solpagelen] controls the length of text screen messages.

Units [solareau] controls the area units used to calculate area.

Hatch Parameters brings up a dialog box that lets you specify the type and scale of hatch patterns used for section cuts. These settings can also be controlled by Solhangle (hatch pattern angle), Solhpat (hatch pattern), and Solhsize (size or scale of hatch pattern).

Other Parameters controls mass properties settings [soldecomp, solsubdiv] and the color of the Motion Coordinate System (MSC) Icon [solaxcol].

FINDING THE PROPERTIES OF A SOLID

All of this effort to create a solid model isn't just to create a pretty picture. Once your model is built and drawn up, you can obtain information about its physical properties. In this section, you will look at a few of the commands that let you gather such information.

FINDING A MODEL'S MASS PROPERTIES

You can find the mass, volume, moment of inertia, and other physical properties of your bracket by using the SOLMASSP command. These properties can also be recorded as a file on disk so you can modify your model and still keep a record of its properties before it was modified.

Model ➤ Inquiry ➤ Mass Properties

▼ TIP

You may have noticed that the list showed mass properties in metric units. If you need information in another unit system, you can select British units (feet, pounds), CGS units (centimeters, grams), or SI units (meters, kilograms) from the Sol-Inquiry menu.

1. Click on Model ➤ Inquiry ➤ Mass Properties or enter **solmassp** ↵.

2. At the **Select objects** prompt, pick the composite solid. AutoCAD will work for a moment, then a dialog box will display a list of the object's properties, as shown in Figure 18.41.

At the bottom of the dialog box is a button labeled **File**. You can save this information to a file on disk by clicking on this button.

DEFINING THE MATERIAL OF A MODEL

Before the AME can determine the mass properties of a solid, it must know about the material the solid is made of. AME uses material definitions stored with the drawing to determine the properties of an object. You can create a new definition by using the SOLMAT command. You can also edit an existing definition (that is, a material definition built into the AME), or assign a definition to a solid by using SOLMAT.

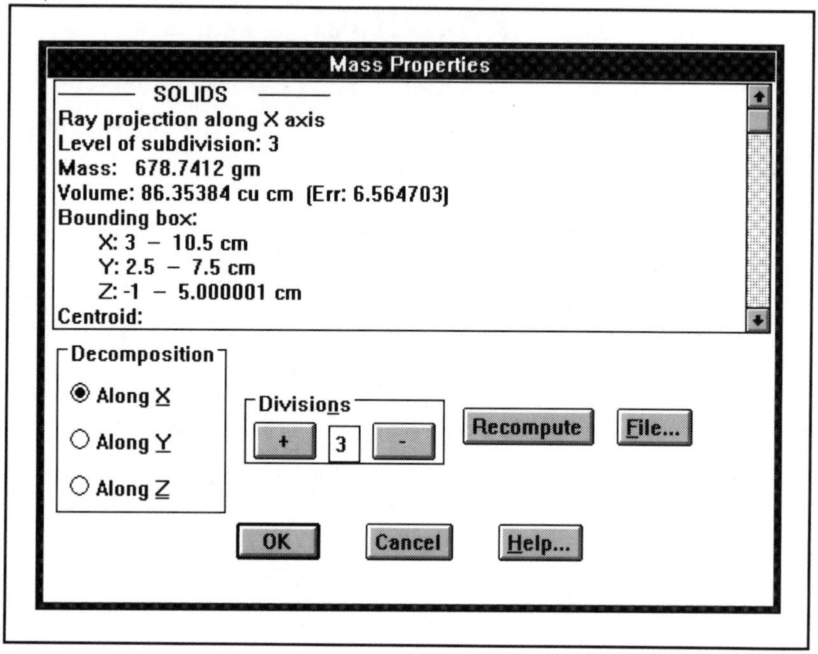

Figure 18.41: A list of the bracket's properties

AME comes with definitions for aluminum, bronze, and mild steel, to name a few. The default material is mild steel. Here is a list of the properties that go into a definition.

- Density
- Young's Modulus
- Poisson's ratio
- Yield strength
- Ultimate strength
- Thermal conductivity
- Linear expansion coefficient
- Specific heat

If you are a mechanical or structural engineer, these properties should be familiar to you. To describe their meaning would be beyond the scope of this tutorial. But if you understand material properties, you can simulate a material, then assign that material to your solid model. Once this is done, you can use the SOLMASSP command to find the specific properties of the model.

Let's see what a material definition looks like. Before you can list one, you must first load it.

Model ➤ Utility ➤ Material

1. Click on Model ➤ Utility ➤ Material or enter **solmat**. The Material Browser dialog box appears (see Figure 18.42).

2. Highlight the Bronze material in the list to the left, then click on Load. Bronze is added to the list of materials in the Drawing list to the right.

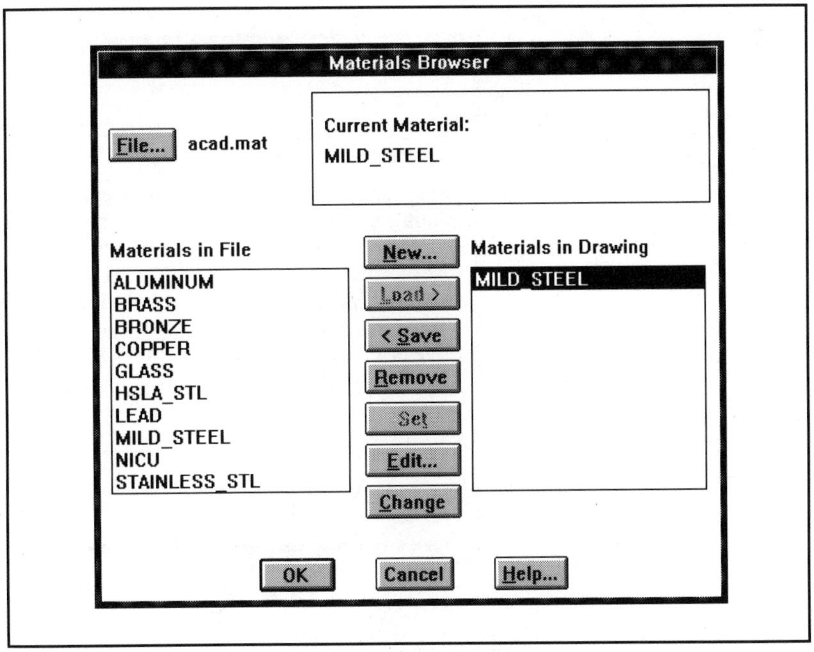

Figure 18.42: The Material Browser lets you load a predefined material from a list of materials. These materials are stored in a file called Acad.MAT.

3. Highlight Bronze in the right list, then click on Edit. The Material Properties dialog box appears (see Figure 18.43). You can make changes to a material's property by highlighting the property in the list and editing its value in the value input box. You could then save your modified property as a new material and store it in the Acad.MAT file.

Now let's assign Bronze to the bracket.

1. Click on **Cancel** to exit the Material Properties dialog box, then at the Material Browser dialog box, highlight Bronze in the right-hand list. Be sure to also deselect Mild_steel.

2. Click on the **Change** button. The dialog box closes momentarily.

3. At the **Select objects** prompt, click on the solid model, then press ↵. The dialog box returns.

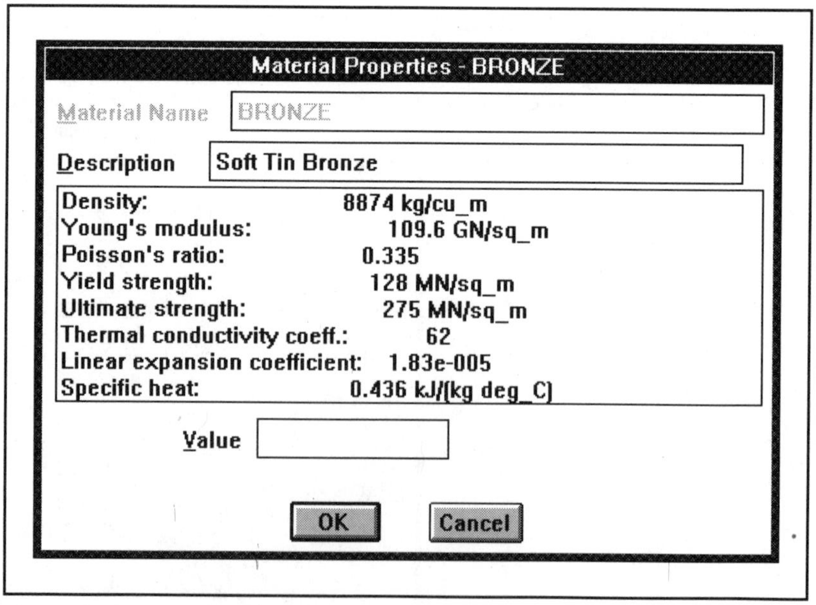

Material Properties - BRONZE

Material Name: BRONZE

Description: Soft Tin Bronze

Density:	8874 kg/cu_m
Young's modulus:	109.6 GN/sq_m
Poisson's ratio:	0.335
Yield strength:	128 MN/sq_m
Ultimate strength:	275 MN/sq_m
Thermal conductivity coeff.:	62
Linear expansion coefficient:	1.83e-005
Specific heat:	0.436 kJ/(kg deg_C)

Value:

OK   Cancel

Figure 18.43: The Material Properties dialog box lets you edit the properties of the selected material.

4. Click on **OK**. Now if you use the Solmassp command on the bracket, you will get a listing reflecting the bronze material.

Finally, two other commands, Sollist and Sollarea, give you basic information about your model. Sollist lets you find the coordinates of an edge or face of the general construction of the model. Sollarea calculates the total surface area of a solid model. Each of these commands simply asks you to select an object, after which it returns the information to you on a text screen. Sollist can be accessed using Model ➤ Inquiry ➤ List Object and Sollarea can be accessed using Model ➤ Inquiry ➤ Area Calc.

IF YOU WANT TO EXPERIMENT...

While this chapter has focused on a mechanical project, you can still use solids to help simplify the construction of 3D architectural forms. If your interest lies in architecture, try drawing the window in Figure 18.44.

The file you create with the WBLOCK command can be inserted into other drawings that need windows. Imagine trying to create this window without the AME!

SUMMARY

You've gotten a glimpse of the AME through this tutorial. You should be comfortable enough with AutoCAD by now to explore this AutoCAD enhancement at your own pace.

This concludes *Part IV, Modeling and Imaging in 3D*. In *Part Five*, you will learn how flexible AutoCAD can be through its many customizable features. You'll also learn about some of the little-known tools that AutoCAD has to offer.

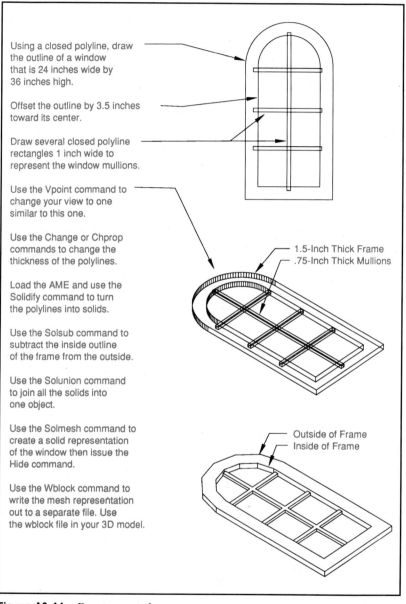

Using a closed polyline, draw
the outline of a window
that is 24 inches wide by
36 inches high.

Offset the outline by 3.5 inches
toward its center.

Draw several closed polyline
rectangles 1 inch wide to
represent the window mullions.

Use the Vpoint command to
change your view to one
similar to this one.

Use the Change or Chprop
commands to change the
thickness of the polylines.

Load the AME and use the
Solidify command to turn
the polylines into solids.

Use the Solsub command to
subtract the inside outline
of the frame from the outside.

Use the Solunion command
to join all the solids into
one object.

Use the Solmesh command to
create a solid representation
of the window then issue the
Hide command.

Use the Wblock command to
write the mesh representation
out to a separate file. Use
the wblock file in your 3D model.

1.5-Inch Thick Frame
.75-Inch Thick Mullions

Outside of Frame
Inside of Frame

Figure 18.44: Drawing a window

Bonus Utilities: Drawing Solid Gears and Maximizing Part Layouts

I'd like to draw your attention to a set of utilities that offer many timesaving functions. These utilities are AutoLISP and ADS applications that can be found in the API and Sample subdirectories of your AutoCAD directory. The following list shows you the file names and what they do. Space is limited in this book, so I can only give brief descriptions. Try experimenting with these utilities on your own. You may find one or two of them indispensable in your work.

Tip: The Wblksol.Lsp utility in the Samples subdirectory lets you WBLOCK a solid without losing its solid properties. See *Chapter 19* for more information.

ASM.EXP lets you assemble solids by selecting and comparing geometry. Once loaded, two commands are available:

> *Solcontact* places two flat surfaces together
> *Solalign* aligns two solids based on their axis features

DESIGN.EXP generates six standard machine parts. Once loaded, six commands are available:

> *Solshaft* creates a cylindrical shaft incuding a keyway
> *Solwheel* creates a solid wheel with a keyway
> *Solgear* creates a solid gear
> *Solbear* creates a solid bearing bracket
> *Solbolt* creates a bolt
> *Solnut* creates a nut

DRILL.EXP generates a hole in a solid. Once loaded, enter **Soldrill** to place the hole.

LAYOUT.EXP calculates the maximum number or 2D regions that will fit inside another region.

Gear creates a 2D region in the shape of a gear
Sheet creates a 2D region in the shape of a rectangle
Layout finds the maximum number of regions that will fit onto another region, then shows you the placement of the first region on the second

OFFSOL.EXP offsets a region. Its main purpose is to show shrinkage.

Soloff offsets a closed polyline made up of lines only
Solmac creates a tool path taking into consideration tool diameter

SOLVIEW.EXP Creates orthographic projected views in Paperspace.

Solview create a viewport in Paperspace of an orthogonal projection of a 3D solid. One orthogonal viewport must already exist
Soldraw creates a profile image of the view prepared by Solview

To load any of these files, Click on File ➤ Applications. At the Load ADS and AutoLISP dialog box, click on **File**, then locate the desired utility in the \ACADWIN\API\SAMPLE\ dirrectory. When you return to the Load ADS dialog box, highlight the desired utility from the list, then click on **Load**.

PART FIVE

CUSTOMIZATION—
■
TAKING AUTOCAD
■
TO THE LIMIT

I have often heard people call AutoCAD an operating system for graphics. They are referring to the fact that you can use AutoCAD to build other graphics applications, just as MS-DOS has been used to build database, spreadsheet, and word processing programs. With Part Five, we begin a series of chapters on how you can take AutoCAD to the limit by using features that are often overlooked or neglected. You will learn how you can build your own special applications, and will see how easy it is to customize AutoCAD to perform just the tasks you want. In the process, you will become a true AutoCAD power user.

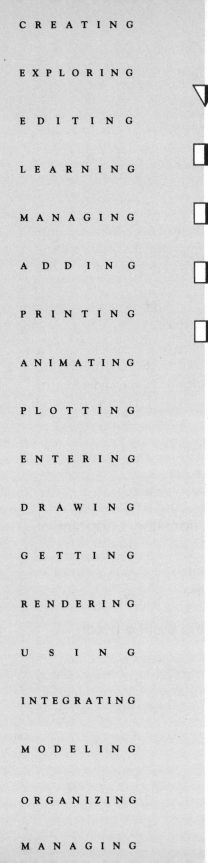

19

▼ ▼ ▼ ▼ ▼

AUTOCAD'S HIDDEN TREASURES

FAST TRACK

829 ▶ To load an AutoLISP program

Click on File ➤ Applications, then click on the **Files…** button. Locate the AutoLISP program you want to load from the Files dialog box and double-click on it. Highlight the program name from the list box then click on **OK**.

832 ▶ To filter a selection by layer

At the **Select objects** prompt, click on Assist ➤ Object Filters…. At the dialog box, click open the pop-up list in the Select Filter button group and click on **Layer**. Click on the **Select…** button and select the layer name. Click on **Add to list**, then click on **Apply**. Select the set of objects you want filtered then press ↵.

838 ▶ To find the centroid of a triangle

Click on Assist ➤ Calculator. Enter **(end + end + end) / 3** ↵. Using the square cursor, pick the three endpoints of the triangle.

839 ▶ To start a line 5" in the Y axis from the endpoint of another line

Start the line command. At the **From point** prompt, click on Assist ➤ Calculator, then enter **end + [0,5]** ↵.

840 ▶ To add two distances together and input a polar coordinate simultaneously

At any **To point** or **Second point** prompt, click on Assist ➤ Calculator, then enter **[@ *distance1* + *distance2* < *angle*]** ↵ where *distance1* and *distance2* are the two distances to be added and *angle* is the desired angle of the polar coordinate.

846 ▶ To explode a mirrored block

Using File ➤ Applications, load Xplode.LSP from the AutoCAD Samples subdirectory. Enter **Xplode** ↵ at the command prompt then pick the mirrored block.

847 ▶ To export a solid and retain its solid modeling data

Using File ➤ Applications, load Wblksol.LSP from the AutoCAD Samples subdirectory. Enter **Wblksol** ↵ at the command prompt. Click on the solid you want to export.

849 ▶ To have AutoCAD load your favorite AutoLISP programs automatically at startup

With your favorite text editor, open a new DOS text file and call it **Acad.LSP**. Enter the line **(load "*lisp-filename*")** where *lisp-filename* is the name of the AutoLISP file you want to load. Include drive and path information with the name if the file is not in the current DOS path. In place of the usual back slash (\ ) for DOS directory listings, use a forward slash (/). Do this for each utility you want loaded automatically.

850 ▶ To create a keyboard macro

Flip to text mode. Enter **(defun c:***progname* **()** ↵ where *progname* is the name you want to give your macro. Next, enter **(command "***com-name***" "***key1***" "***key2***" "***key3***"…)** ↵ where *com-name* is the name of the command you want to use and *key1*, *key2*, etc. are the exact keystrokes you need to execute your macro. Finally, enter **)** ↵ to finish your macro. To use your macro, enter *com-name* ↵.

AutoCAD offers a wealth of features that can enhance your productivity. Unfortunately, many of them lie buried in its documentation and are therefore often overlooked. In this chapter, I'll help you uncover the hidden features that most users miss or have problems understanding. As an introduction to customization, you'll load and run several handy AutoLISP utilities that come with every AutoCAD package. You'll also get a chance to see how you can use AutoLISP to create keyboard shortcuts for your favorite commands.

▼ NOTE

This chapter assumes some familiarity with Windows. If you need help, consult *Appendix C, A Windows Primer*.

Since customization often involves third-party add-ons, I'll also discuss some third-party products that can help you make AutoCAD fit your particular work environment.

PUTTING AUTOLISP TO WORK

Most high-end CAD packages offer a macro or programming language to help users customize their systems. AutoCAD has AutoLISP, which is a pared-down version of Common LISP, a popular artificial intelligence language. There is also the Autodesk Development System (ADS) that allows C programmers to develop utilities and full applications that work with AutoCAD. Chances are you won't get too involved with ADS, except as an end user. AutoLISP, however, offers the intermediate and advanced AutoCAD user many advantages.

Don't let AutoLISP scare you. In many ways, it is just a set of AutoCAD commands that help you build your own features. The only difference between AutoCAD commands and AutoLISP is that when using AutoLISP you have to follow a different set of rules. But this isn't so unusual. After all, you had to learn some basic rules about using AutoCAD commands—how to start commands, for instance, and how to use command options.

While the thought of using AutoLISP may seem a little intimidating, it doesn't really require a lot of computer knowledge to use it. In this section, you will see how you can get AutoLISP to aid you in your everyday editing tasks without actually doing any programming.

LOADING AND RUNNING AN AUTOLISP PROGRAM

As I mentioned, AutoCAD comes with several AutoLISP programs ready to use. These programs are in the form of ASCII text files with the extension .LSP. Before you can use them, you must load them while in the drawing editor. Here's how you load an AutoLISP program.

1. Start AutoCAD, then open the Unit File.

2. Click on File ➤ Applications. The Load ADS and AutoLISP Files dialog box appears (see Figure 19.1).

3. Click on the **File** button. The File dialog box appears. Notice that it shows files with the .EXP extension. Many of these files are ADS applications, which are similar to AutoLISP programs.

4. In the Directories list, double-click on Sample, then from the file list, double-click on Chroma.LSP. The Files dialog box closes and you'll see the Chroma.LSP file in the list box of the Load ADS and AutoLISP Files dialog box.

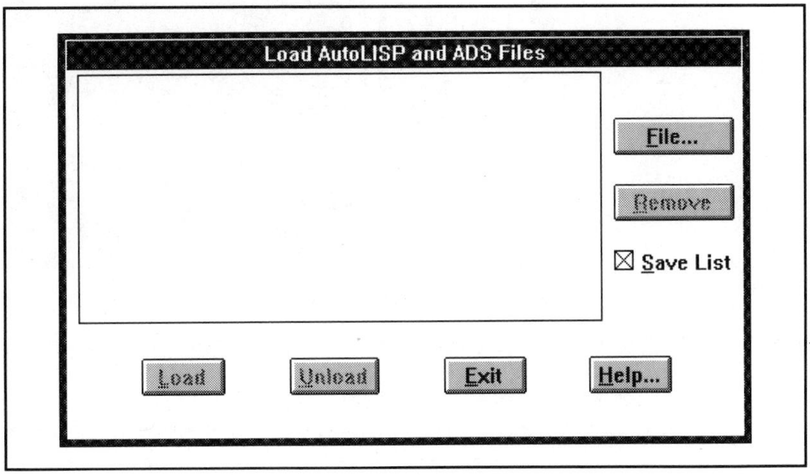

Figure 19.1: The Load ADS and AutoLISP Files dialog box

5. Highlight the Chroma.LSP file in the list, then click on the **Load** button. You will see the message **C:COlor loaded. Type CO or Color to select a color.**

6. Now enter **CO** ↵. The Color dialog box appears. This dialog box is similar to the one you see when you pick **Set Color** from the Layer Control dialog box (see Figure 19.2).

7. From here, you can click on a color to make it the default color for any new objects you create. Two other buttons, **Bylayer** and **Byblock**, let you set the color to these options. Click on **Cancel** to exit this dialog box.

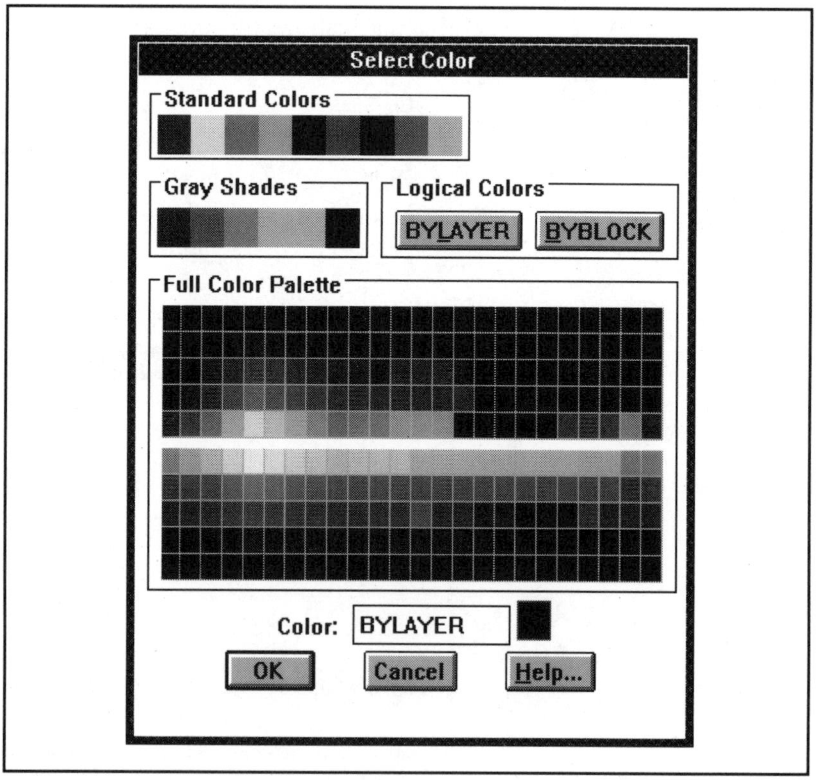

Figure 19.2: The Color dialog box

You have just loaded and used an AutoLISP utility. As you saw from the file dialog box, there are several other utilities you can load and try out. I'll introduce you to a few more of these utilities later on, but for now, let's look at the Load AutoLISP and ADS Files dialog box a little more closely.

UNDERSTANDING THE LOAD AUTOLISP AND ADS FILES DIALOG BOX

The Load AutoLISP and ADS Files dialog box, which I'll call simply the LISP dialog box from now on, gives you a great deal of flexibility in managing your favorite AutoLISP or ADS utilities. As you saw from the previous exercise, you can easily find and select utilities using the dialog box. Once you locate a file, it becomes part of the list in the LISP dialog box, saving you from having to hunt down your favorite utility each time you want to use it.

Even when you exit AutoCAD, the LISP dialog box will retain the name of any ADS or AutoLISP files you select. This is because, by default, the Save List check box in the LISP dialog box is checked. If you don't want to retain items in the list, uncheck this box.

You can remove an item from the list by highlighting it then clicking on the **Remove** button. As with any other list box, you can highlight multiple items and load them all at once.

USING THE OBJECT FILTER AND CALCULATOR

While the name of this chapter implies that you will learn about the hidden wonders of AutoCAD, the utilities described in this section are actually built into AutoCAD's menu system. Chances are you've looked at some of the menu options I haven't discussed in the tutorial. Many of the pull-down menu options are self-evident in what they do and how they work. Two options, however, bear some explanation. These are *Object Filters* and *Calculator*.

FILTERING SELECTIONS

The Object Filters option on the Assist pull down menu is actually an AutoLISP utility that lets you select a set of objects based on their properties. To see how it works, try the following exercise.

Suppose you need to isolate just the walls of your drawing in a separate file. You could turn off all the layers except the wall layer. Then you could use the WBLOCK command and select the remaining walls, using a window to write the wall information to a file. Filters can simplify the operation by allowing you to select groups of objects based on their properties.

1. Start the WBLOCK command and, in the Create Drawing File dialog box, enter **unitwall** in the File input box, then pick **OK**.

2. Press ↵ at the **block name** prompt, then enter **0,0** at the **Insertion base** prompt.

3. At the **object-selection** prompt, click on Assist ➤ Object Filters.... The Filters dialog box appears (see Figure 19.3).

4. Click open the pop-up list in the Select Filter button group.

5. Scroll down the list until you see the layer option listed, then highlight Layer.

6. Click on the button next to the pop-up list labeled **Select**.... You will see a list of layers.

7. Double-click on the Wall layer.

8. At the Entity Selection Filters dialog box, click on the **Add to List** button toward the bottom of the Select Filter button group. You see *Layer = Wall* added to the list box.

9. Click on **Apply**. The dialog box closes.

10. Use a window to select the entire unit plan. Only the objects assigned to the wall layer are selected.

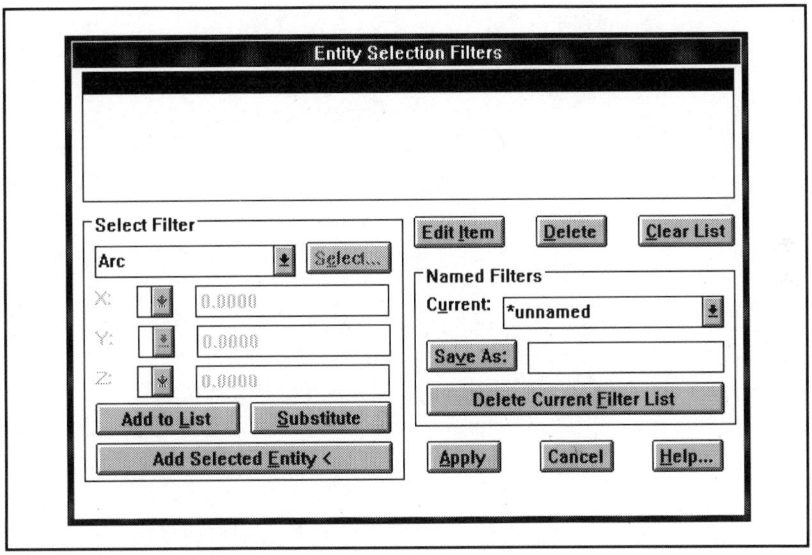

Figure 19.3: The Filters dialog box lets you select objects based on their properties.

11. Press ↵. You see the message *Exiting Filtered selection. 24 found.*

12. Press ↵ again to complete the WBLOCK command. All the walls are written out to a file called **Unitwall**.

In this exercise, you were able to filter out a layer using the Object Filters option. You first started the WBLOCK command. Then, at the Select objects prompt, you opened the Entity Selection Filters dialog box, which enabled you to select the basis for your filter (namely, the Wall layer). Once a filter is selected, you then select the group of objects you want AutoCAD to filter through. AutoCAD finds the objects that match the filter requirements and passes those objects to the current command. As you've seen from the exercise, there are a lot of options to choose from in this utility. The following goes into more depth on the use of object filters.

UNDERSTANDING THE ENTITY SELECTION FILTERS DIALOG BOX

To use the Entity Selection Filters dialog box, you first select the criteria for filtering from the pop-up list. If the criteria you select is a named item, like layers, line types, colors, or blocks, you can then click on the **Select** button to select specific items from a list. If there is only one selection, the **Select** button is grayed out.

Once you've determined what to filter, you must add it to the list by clicking on the **Add to List** button. The filter criteria then appears in the list box at the top of the dialog box. Once you have something in the list box, and it is highlighted, you can then apply it to your current command or apply the list to a command at a later time. Table 19.1 shows you all the criteria available from the pop-up list.

Saving Filter Criteria

If you prefer, you can preselect a filter criteria. Then at any **Select objects** prompt, you can click on Assist ➤ Object Filters, highlight the appropriate filter criteria in the list box, and click on **Apply**. The contents of the Entity Selection Filters list box remain in place for the duration of the current editing session.

You can also save a set of criteria by entering a name in the input box next to the **Save As** button. Once the name is entered, click on the **Save As** button. The criteria list data is saved in a file called **Filter.NFL**. You can then access the criteria list at any time by clicking open the Current pop-up list box and clicking on the name of the saved criteria list.

Filtering Objects by Location

You might notice the X, Y, and Z pop-up lists just below the main Select Filter pop-up list. These pop-up lists become accessible when you select a criteria that describes a geometry or a coordinate, such as an arc's radius or center point, for example. You can use these lists to further filter selections with greater than (>), less than (<), equal to (=), or not equal to (!=) comparisons (called *relational operators*). For example, suppose you want to grab all the circles whose radii are greater than 4.0 units. You select Circle radius from the Select Filters pop-up list; then,

Table 19.1:   Filter Options

Arc	Elevation	Solid Point 3	3Dface Point 3
Arc Center	Layer	Solid Point 4	3Dface Point 4
Arc Radius	Line	Text	Thickness
Attribute	Line Start	Text Position	Viewport
Attribute Position	Line End	Text Value	Viewport Center
Attribute Tag	Line Type	Text Style Name	Xdata ID
Block	Normal Vector	Text Height	** Begin AND
Block Name	Point	Text Rotation	** End AND
Block Position	Point Position	Trace	** Begin OR
Block Rotation	Polyline	Trace Point 1	** End OR
Circle	Shape	Trace Point 2	** Begin XOR
Circle Center	Shape Position	Trace Point 3	** End XOR
Circle Radius	Shape Name	Trace Point 4	** Begin NOT
Color	Solid	3Dface	** End NOT
Dimension	Solid Point 1	3Dface Point 1	
Dimension Style	Solid Point 2	3Dface Point 2	

in the X pop-up list, you select the > sign. Next, you enter **4.0** in the input box to the right of the X pop-up list. Finally, you click on Add to List. You see the item

    Circle Radius > 4.0000

added to the list box at the top of the dialog box. Here you used the greater-than sign to indicate a circle radius greater than 4.0 units.

Creating Complex Selection Sets

There will be times when you will want to create a filter list that is somewhat complex. For example, you may want to filter out all the door blocks on the layer floor2 *and* all arcs with a radius equal to 1. To do this, you use the *grouping operators* found at the bottom of the Select Filters pop-up list to build a list as follows:

```
** Begin OR
** Begin AND
Entity = Block
Layer = Floor2
** End AND
** Begin AND
Entity = Arc
Arc Radius = 1.0000
** End AND
** End OR
```

Notice that the Begin and End operators are balanced, that is, for every *Begin OR* or *Begin AND*, there is an *End OR* or *End AND*. This list may look rather simple, but it can get confusing, mostly because of the way we normally think of the terms *and* and *or*. If a criteria is bounded by the AND grouping operators, then the objects must fulfill both criteria before they are selected. If a criteria is bounded by the OR grouping operators, then the objects fulfilling either criteria will be selected.

To build the list shown previously, do the following:

1. First select **Begin OR from the Select Filter pop-up list, then click on **Add to List**.

2. Do the same for the **Begin And criteria.

3. Click on Block from the pop-up list, then click on **Add to List**.

4. For the Layer, click on Layer from the pop-up list, then click on **Select**... and select the layer name. Then click on **Add to List**.

5. Select **End AND from the pop-up list and click on **Add to List**.

6. Do the same for **Begin AND.

7. Select Arc from the pop-up list, then click on **Add to List**.

8. Select Arc Radius from the pop-up list, then enter **1.0** in the input box next to the X pop-up list. Be sure an equals sign shows in the X pop-up list. Then click on **Add to List**.

9. Select ** End AND from the pop-up list, then click on **Add to List**.

10. Do the same for **End OR.

If you make an error in any step, you can highlight the item, select an item to replace it, then click on the **Substitute** button instead of the **Add to List** button. If you just need to change a value, you can click on **Edit Item** toward the center of the dialog box.

FINDING GEOMETRY WITH THE CALCULATOR

Another not-so-hidden treasure is the *geometry calculator*. This calculator acts like most calculators; it adds, subtracts, divides, and multiplies. If you enter an arithmetic expression like *1 + 2*, the calculator returns *3*. This can be useful for doing math on the fly, but the Geometry Calculator does much more than arithmetic, as you will see in the next examples.

Finding the Midpoint between Two Points

One of the most common questions I've heard from AutoCAD users is "how can I locate a point midway between two objects?" In the past, I've had to explain that you first have to draw a construction line between the two objects, then use the midpoint override to select the midpoint of the construction line. With release 12, this operation has been greatly simplified. The following describes how you would start a line midway between the center of an arc and the endpoint of a line. You may want to draw a line and an arc and try this out.

▼ TIP

You can enter 'Cal ↵ instead of clicking on Assist ➤ Calculator to use the calculator.

1. Start the line command, then at the **From point** prompt, click on Assist ➤ Calculator.

2. At the >> **Expression:** prompt, enter (end + cen)/2 ↵.

3. At the >> **Select entity for END snap:** prompt, click on the endpoint of a line.

4. At the >> **Select entity for CEN snap:** prompt, click on an arc. The line will start midway between the arc's center and the endpoint of the line.

Here you used Osnap modes as part of an arithmetic expression. The calculator treats them as temporary place-holders for point coordinates until you actually pick the points at the prompts shown in steps 3 and 4.

The expression (end + cen)/2 finds the average of two values. In this case, the values are coordinates, so the average is the midpoint between the two coordinates. You can take this one step further and find the centroid of a triangle using the expression (end + end + end)/3.

Note than only the first three letters of the Osnap mode are entered. Table 19.2 shows what to enter in an expression for Osnap modes.

I've included two items in the list that are not really object snap modes, though they work in a similar way to the Osnap modes when they are used in an expression. The first is *Rad*. When you include Rad in an expression, you get the prompt

Select circle, arc or polyline segment for RAD function:

You can then select an arc, polyline arc segment, or circle, and its radius is used in place of Rad in the expression.

The other item, *Cur*, prompts you for a point. It performs a similar function to the Osnap modes, but instead of looking for specific geometry on an object, it just locates a point.

Table 19.2: The Geometry Calculator's Osnap modes

CALCULATOR OSNAP	MEANING
End	Endpoint
Ins	Insert
Int	Intersection
Mid	Midpoint
Cen	Center
Nea	Nearest
Nod	Node
Qua	Quadrant
Per	Perpendicular
Tan	Tangent
Rad	Radius of object
Cur	Cursor Pick

Finding a Point Relative to Another Point

Another common question I hear is "how do I start a line at a relative distance from another line?" The following describes how to start a line from a point that is 2.5" in the X axis and 5.0" in the Y axis from the endpoint of another line, again using the calculator.

1. Start the line command, then at the **From point** prompt, click on Assist ➤ Calculator.

2. At the **>> Expression:** prompt, enter **end + [2.5,5.0]** ↵.

3. At the **>> Select entity for END snap:** prompt, pick the endpoint. The line starts from the desired location.

In this example, you used the Osnap endpoint mode to indicate a point of reference. This is added to Cartesian coordinates in square brackets, describing the distance and direction from the reference point. You could have entered any coordinate value within the square brackets. You could also have entered a polar coordinate in place of the Cartesian coordinate as in the following:

    end + (5.59<63)

You don't have to include the at sign since the calculator assumes you want to add the coordinate to the one indicated by the endpoint Osnap mode. Also, you don't have to include every coordinate in the square brackets. For example, if you want to indicate a displacement in only one axis, you can leave out a value for the other two coordinates as in the following examples:

    (4,5) = (4,5,0)
    (,1) = (0,1,0)
    (,,2) = (0,0,2)
    () = (0,0,0)

Adding Feet and Inch Distances on the Fly

One of the more frustrating situations I've run across is having to stop in the middle of a command to find the sum of two or more distances. For example, you might start the move command, select your objects, pick a base point, then realize you don't know the distance for the move, but you do know that the distance is the sum of two values. Unfortunately, one value is in feet and the other is in inches. Usually in this situation, you would get out pen and paper or, if you've got one, a foot and inch calculator, then figure out the distance, then return to your computer to finish the task. The geometry calculator puts an end to situations like this. The following example shows what to do if you want to move a set of objects a distance that is the sum of 12'-6–5/8" and 115-3/4".

1. Issue the Move command, select objects, then pick a base point.

2. At the **Second point** prompt, Click on Assist ➤ Calculator.

3. At the **>> Expression:** prompt, enter **[@12'6.625 + 115.75" < 45]** ↵. The objects move into place at the proper distance.

In this example, you are mixing, whole inches and feet. Under normal circumstances, this could be a time-consuming calculation. Notice that the format for feet and inches follows the standard AutoCAD syntax of no space between feet and inch values, and a hyphen between inches and fractional inches. The coordinate value in square brackets can have any number of operators and values as in the following:

(@4 * (22 + 15) - (23.3 / 12) + 1 < 13 + 17)

This expression shows that you can also apply operators to angle values.

Understanding the Calculator

You may be noticing that there are some patterns emerging in the way expressions are formatted for the calculator. Here are some guidelines to remember as you use the calculator:

- Coordinates are enclosed in square brackets
- Nested or grouped expressions are enclosed in parentheses
- Operators are placed between values as in simple math equations
- Object snaps can be used in place of coordinate values

I've tried to show you some of the more common uses of the calculator. Table 19.3 lists the operators and functions available in the calculator.

You may want to experiment with these other functions on your own. The geometry calculator is capable of much more than what I've shown you here. Unfortunately, due to limited space, I can't describe its full capabilities. Still, the processes described in this section will be invaluable to you as you use AutoCAD. If you want to know more about the geometry calculator, consult the AutoCAD Extras Manual that comes with release 12 of AutoCAD.

Table 19.3: The Geometry Calculator's Functions

OPERATOR /FUNCTION	WHAT IT DOES	EXAMPLE
+ −	Add Subtract numbers or vectors	2 − 1 = 1 [a,b,c] + [x,y,z] = [a+x, b+y, c+z]
* /	Multiply Divide numbers or vectors	2 * 4.2 = 8.4 a*[x,y,z] = [a*x, a*y, a*z]
^	Exponentiation of a number	3^2 = 9
sin	Sine of angle	sin (45) = 0.707107
cos	Cosine of angle	cos (30) = 0.866025
tang	Tangent of angle	tang (30) = 0.57735
asin	Arcsine of a real number	asin (0.707107) = 45.0
acos	Arccosine of a real number	acos (0.866025) = 30.0
atan	Arctangent of a real number	atan (0.57735) = 30.0
ln	Natural log	ln (2) = 0.693147
log	Base-10 log	log (2) = 0.30103
exp	Natural exponent	exp (2) = 7.38906
exp10	Base-10 exponent	exp10 (2) = 100
sqr	Square of number	sqr (9) = 81.0
abs	Absolute value	abs (−3.4) = 3.4
round	Rounds to nearest integer	round (3.6) = 4
trunc	Drops decimal portion of real number	trunc (3.6) = 3
r2d	Converts radians to degrees	r2d (1.5708) = 90.0002
sqrt	Square root of value	sqrt(4)=2
*	Scalar value of vectors (returns a real)	[a,b,c]*[x,y,z]=ax+by+cz
&	Vector product of vectors (return a vector)	[a,b,c]&[x,y,z]= [(b*z)−(c*y), (c*x)−(a*z),(a*y)−b*x)]

Table 19.3: The Geometry Calculator's Functions (continued)

OPERATOR /FUNCTION	WHAT IT DOES	EXAMPLE
d2r	Converts degrees to radians	d2r (90) = 1.5708
pi	The constant pi	3.14159
vec	Vector between two points	vec ([2,2],[4,4]) = (2.0,2.0,0.0)
vec1	1 unit vector between two points	vec1 ([2,2],[4,4]) = (0.707107,0.707107,0.0)

EDITING IN 3D

AutoCAD provides two utilities for moving objects in 3D space. They offer the ability to perform some of the more common moves associated with 3D editing and can be found on the Modify pull-down menu.

ALIGNING OBJECTS IN 3D SPACE

In mechanical drawing you often create the parts in 3D, then show an assembly of the parts. The Align utility can greatly simplify the assembly process. The following describes how it works. In the description, I use the term *source object* to describe the object you want to move, and *destination object* to describe the object you want the source object to align with.

1. Click on Modify ➤ Align.

2. At the **Select objects** prompt, select the 3D source object you want to align to another part then press ↵.

3. At the **1st source point** prompt, pick a point on the source object that is the first point of an alignment axis, like the center of a hole or the corner of a surface.

4. At the **1st destination point** prompt, pick a point on the destination object where you want the first source point to move to.

5. At the **2nd source point** prompt, pick a point on the source object that is the second point of an alignment axis, like another center point or other corner of a surface.

6. At the **2nd destination point** prompt, pick a point on the destination object indicating how the first and second source points are to align in relation to the destination object.

7. At the **3rd source point** prompt, you can press ⏎ if two points are adequate to describe the alignment. Otherwise, pick a third point on the source object that, along with the first two points, best describes the surface plane you want aligned with the destination object.

8. At the **3rd destination point** prompt, pick a point on the destination object that, along with the previous two destination points, describes the plane you want the source object to be aligned to. The source object will move into alignment with the destination object.

Figure 19.4 gives an example of how the Align utility works.

ROTATING AN OBJECT IN 3D

If you just want to rotate an object in 3D space, the Rotate 3D option in the Modify pull-down menu can simplify the operation. When you click on Modify ➤ Rotate 3D, you are asked to select objects. Once you've selected the objects, you get the following prompt:

Axis by Entity/Last/View/Xaxis/Yaxis/Zaxis/<2points>

This prompt is asking you to describe the axis of rotation. The following describes each of the options presented in the prompt.

Entity allows you to indicate an axis by clicking on an object. If you select this option, you are prompted to pick a line, circle,

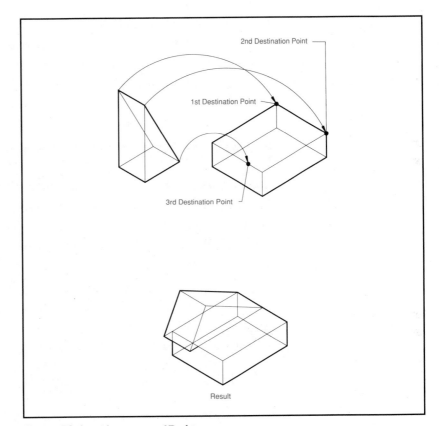

Figure 19.4: Aligning two 3D objects

arc, or 2D polyline segment. If you click on a line or polyline line segment, the line is used as the axis of rotation. If you click on a circle or arc or polyline arc segment, the line passing through the center of the circle or arc and perpendicular to its plane is used.

Last uses the last axis used for a 3D rotation. If no previous axis exists, you are returned to the Axis prompt.

View uses the current view direction as the direction of the rotation axis. You are then prompted to select a point on the view direction axis to specify the exact location of the rotation axis.

Xaxis/Yaxis/Zaxis uses the standard X, Y, or Z axis as the direction for the rotation axis, you are then prompted to select points on the X, Y, or Z axis to locate the rotation axis.

<2points> uses two point you provide as the endpoints of the rotation axis.

EXPLODING MIRRORED BLOCKS, WBLOCKING SOLIDS, AND MORE

As you've already seen, there is much more to AutoCAD than meets the eye. There are many other utilities that add sorely needed functionality to AutoCAD. For example Xplode.LSP lets you explode mirrored blocks. Wblksol.LSP will let you export a solid as an independent file without losing its solid model data.

The lists in the next two sections represent only a few of the sample AutoLISP programs supplied with AutoCAD. I have left out various programs that serve chiefly as demonstrations of AutoLISP features without offering any significant applications to most users. Other programs are used by AutoCAD through its menu system.

A full tutorial on each of these programs would make this chapter prohibitively long, and you should feel comfortable enough with AutoCAD by now to experiment with them on your own. You may find some of them useful in your day-to-day work. Before you can use them, you must first load them individually in the manner described in the first section of this chapter.

SAMPLES FROM THE SAMPLE DIRECTORY

The following list briefly describes the sample AutoLISP programs found in the Sample subdirectory of the AutoCAD directory.

■ **Alias.LSP** provides you with a list of command aliases that are in the Acad.PGP file.

- **Attredef.LSP** will globally redefine attributes contained in a block. Before using this, you must first create the elements of the redefining block. Use this when you need to globally change an attribute definition's location in a block.

- **Bmake.LSP** Creates a block through a dialog box. Bmake.DCL must be in the current directory path.

- **Chface.LSP** will quickly relocate a corner of a single 3dface.

- **Chroma.LSP** lets you select a default color from a dialog box.

- **Cl.LSP** first creates a layer called **Cl** then draws a center line through the arc or circle you select.

- **DDtype.LSP** lets you view the contents of an ASCII file in a dialog box.

- **Dellayer.LSP** deletes the contents of a layer.

- **Edge.LSP** allows you to easily change the visibility of edges on a 3dface.

- **Hole.LSP** creates countersinks and counterbores in 3D solids.

- **Julian.LSP** converts Julian date used by AutoCAD to standard calendar format.

- **Project.LSP** can be used to get a 2D wireframe drawing from a 3D view. Project.LSP actually contains three commands. *Project* lets you select the type of projection. *Project1* projects the 2D image onto the current UCS. *Project2* lets you define the construction plane for the 2D image.

- **Solmaint.LSP** detaches unused wireframe elements from solids, thereby keeping a solid model's file size down. Unused wireframe elements are anonymous blocks, which are purged automatically upon re-entering the drawing.

- **Stlsup.LSP** allows automatic creation of common Stereo Lithography support structures. AME 2.0 supports STL output.

- **Wblksol.lsp** allows you to WBLOCK a solid without losing the solid model data.

- **Xplode.LSP** performs the same function as the EXPLODE command, but instead of exploded objects being placed on the layer 0, exploded blocks are placed on the same layer as the original unexploded object. It also allows you to explode mirrored blocks.

- **Xdata.LSP** attaches extended data types to selected objects.

- **Xrefclip.LSP** automatically attaches an Xref and creates a Paperspace viewport of an area you define using a window.

SAMPLES FROM THE SUPPORT DIRECTORY

The following list briefly describes the sample AutoLISP programs found in the Support subdirectory of the AutoCAD directory.

- **Asctext.LSP** can be used to import ASCII text files into your drawing. See *Chapter 8* for details on its use.

- **Ddrename.LSP** lets you rename named elements like layers, blocks, and line types through a dialog box.

- **3darray.LSP** is a 3D version of the ARRAY command.

- **Ptext.LSP** lets you enter text using word-wrap capabilities normally found in word processing software.

- **Plud.LSP** allows you to toggle between the two modes of line-type generation along a polyline.

▼ TIP

Off Broadway Systems in Oakland, California, offers one of the biggest independent AutoCAD bulletin boards in the United States. There is a small fee for logging on. Their modem number is (510) 547-5264.

As a final note to this section, I'd like to encourage you to use all the resources available for free or shareware AutoLISP utilities. The Autodesk CompuServe forum is a great place to find useful, and often free, AutoLISP programs, as well as information about AutoCAD and other Autodesk products. You can often get the latest information on new products, updates, bug fixes, and more from the Autodesk forum. If you don't have a modem, it may well be worth purchasing one just to obtain the utilities available there. There are also many other bulletin boards across the country devoted to AutoCAD users. They will often have utilities available either for a small fee or completely free.

Other sources for AutoLISP utilities are the two AutoCAD journals, *Cadence* and *Cadalyst*. Both offer sections that list utilities written by readers and editorial staff. If you don't already have a subscription to one of these publications, and you want to know more, their addresses are:

> *Cadence*
> Ariel Communications, Inc.
> 12710 Research Blvd., #250
> Austin, TX 78720
> (512) 250-1700

> *Cadalyst*
> Aster Publishing
> 859 Willamette St.
> P.O. Box 10460
> Eugene, OR 97440-2460
> (503) 343-1200

Finally, there are the disks offered at the back of this book. They include some free- and shareware utilities you that you will find quite useful. If you find the shareware utilities useful, please take the time to register them. This will encourage the authors of the shareware to continue their efforts in providing low-cost software.

LOADING AUTOLISP PROGRAMS AUTOMATICALLY

If you find some of the above AutoLISP programs useful, you can combine them into a single file called Acad.LSP. Place Acad.LSP in your AutoCAD directory, and the programs will be loaded automatically every time you open a drawing file.

You can use a simple word processor such as DOS 5.0's Edit or earlier DOS versions of Edlin to combine the files or you can enter the following at the DOS prompt:

```
Copy Bmake.LSP+Dellayer.LSP+Edge.LSP  acad.lsp
```

The file **Acad.LSP** will be created and the contents of the listed AutoLISP file will be copied into it. Be sure the AutoLISP files you want are in the current directory.

If you already have an Acad.LSP file, you can append AutoLISP programs to it by including Acad.LSP in the list of file names to be copied, as in the following:

```
Copy Acad.LSP+Bmake.LSP+Dellayer.LSP+Edge.LSP
acad.lsp
```

An alternative to combining the actual AutoLISP files into one Acad.LSP file is to simply include the command line entry to load each utility in the Acad.LSP file. For example, to have AutoCAD automatically load the Bmake.LSP, Dellayer.LSP, and Edge.LSP utilities, you would create an Acad.LSP file that contains the following:

```
(load "Bmake")
(load "Dellayer")
(load "Edge")
```

This is how you would load AutoLISP utilities from the command prompt. Notice that the .LSP extension does not have to be included. The advantage of using this abbreviated method is that you can easily manage what files get loaded by using a text editor to edit and view your Acad.LSP file.

CREATING KEYBOARD MACROS WITH AUTOLISP

So far, you have seen how you can load and run existing AutoLISP programs. But you can write some simple programs of your own to create what are called *keyboard macros*. Macros are like script files; they are strings of predefined keyboard entries. Macros often simplify the repeated use of commands and options. For example, you might find that, while editing a particular drawing, you often use the Rotate command to rotate objects 90°. You could quickly create a macro while in AutoCAD, as follows.

(Defun)

1. Open the Unit file and, at the command prompt, enter the following:

   (defun C:R90 () (command "rotate" pause "" "@" "90"))

   Be sure you enter the line exactly as shown here. If you make a mistake while entering this line, use the Backspace key to back up and start over.

2. Next, enter **R90** ↵ at the command prompt. The Rotate command will start and you will be prompted to select an object.

3. Click on the entry door. The door immediately rotates 90° (Figure 19.5). You've just written and run your first AutoLISP program! Let's take a look at what you did in detail.

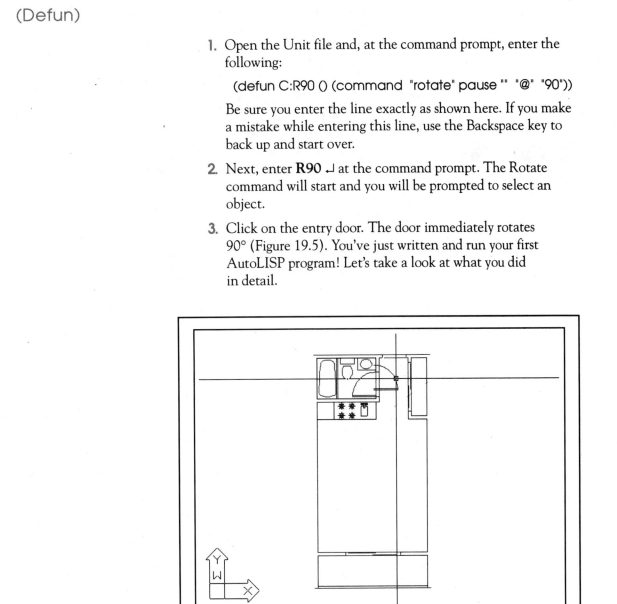

Figure 19.5: The door rotated

The macro you entered is a very simple AutoLISP program (see Figure 19.6). It starts out with a parenthesis, as do all AutoLISP programs, followed by the word *DEFUN*. Defun is an AutoLISP function that lets you create commands; it is followed by the name you want to give the command. The command name is preceded by a C:, telling Defun to make this command accessible from the command prompt. If the C: were left off, you would have to start R90 using parentheses, as in *(R90)*.

After the command name, two parentheses follow. This is called the *argument list*. I won't go into details about it here. Just be aware that these two parentheses must follow the command name.

Finally, a list of words follows, enclosed by a set of parentheses. This list starts with the word *command*. Command is an AutoLISP function that tells AutoLISP that whatever follows should be entered like regular keyboard input. The one odd item in the list is the word *pause*. This is an AutoLISP function that tells AutoLISP to pause for input. In this particular macro, AutoLISP pauses to let you pick an object to rotate.

You might notice that most of the items in the list are enclosed in quotation marks. Literal keyboard input must be enclosed in quotation

▼ NOTE

Notice that the rest of the list is nearly the exact set of keyboard entries needed to rotate a single object 90°.

(DEFUN C:R90 ( ) (command "rotate" pause " " "@" "90"))

AutoLISP function to define a command.

Name of command.

Argument list.

AutoLISP function to issue standard AutoCAD commands.

AutoCAD Rotate command.

AutoLISP function to pause for user input.

Double quotes have the same affect as pressing RETURN.

Keyboard input.

The at sign to respond to the Rotate commands Base point prompt.

A 90 degree value to respond to the Rotate commands Rotate angle prompt.

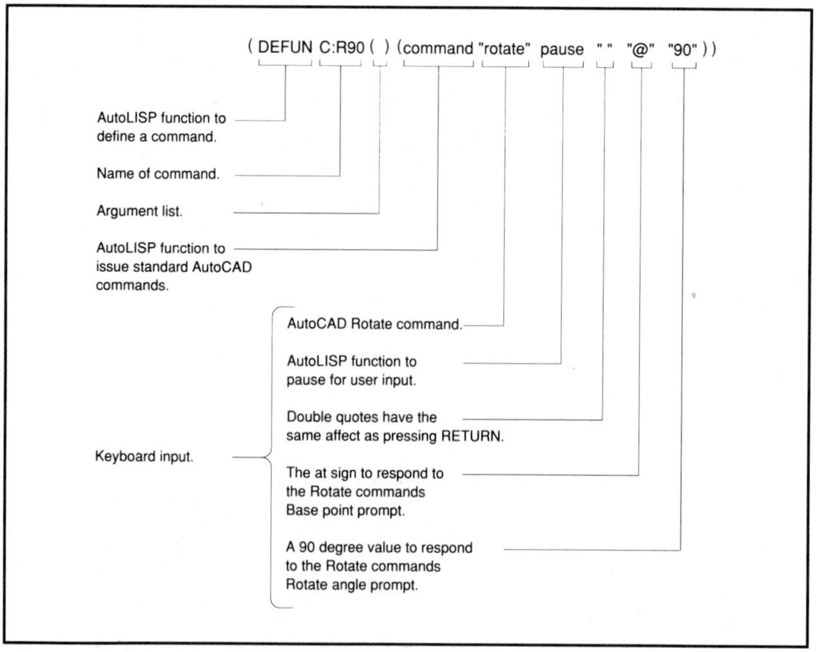

Figure 19.6: Breakdown of the R90 macro

marks in this way. The Pause function, on the other hand, does not require quotation marks, since it is a proper function AutoLISP can recognize.

Finally, the program closes with two right parentheses. All parentheses must be balanced in an AutoLISP program, so these two parentheses close the parenthesis that starts at the Defun function and the Command function.

Once you enter a program such as this, at the command prompt, AutoCAD remembers it until you exit the current file. If you want to use this macro again during a different editing session, you have to re-enter it as you did in the exercise. You can, however, create a permanent record of your macros by copying your AutoLISP macro into an ASCII text file, or including it in a toolbar button. I'll describe how you can customize the toolbar buttons in Chapter 21. The file must have the .LSP extension.

Figure 19.7 shows the contents of just such a file called Keycad.LSP. This file contains the macro you used above along with several others. The other macros are simple command abbreviations that reduce the number of keystrokes needed to start some of the most commonly used commands. Table 19.4 shows the command abbreviations and what

Table 19.4:   Command Abbreviations (Macros) for Keycad.LSP

ABBREVIATION	COMMAND OR ACTION TAKEN
R90	ROTATE object 90°
ZW	ZOOM Window
ZP	ZOOM Previous
ZM	ZOOM Vmax
MO	MOVE @
CO	COPY @
ST	STRETCH
FL	FILLET 0 radius
BR	BREAK F
CH	CHANGE Layer
MI	MIRROR Delete

```
(DEFUN C:R90 () (command "rotate" pause "" "@" "90"))
(DEFUN C:ZW () (command "zoom" "w"))
(DEFUN C:ZP () (command "zoom" "p"))
(DEFUN C:ZM () (command "zoom" "v"))
(DEFUN C:ST () (command "stretch" "c"))
(DEFUN C:FL () (command "fillet" "r" "0" "fillet"))
(DEFUN C:BR () (command "break" pause "F"))
(DEFUN C:MV (/ gp) (setq gp (ssget)) (command "move" gp "" "@"))
(DEFUN C:CO (/ gp) (setq gp (ssget)) (command "copy" gp "" "@"))
(DEFUN C:CH (/ gp) (setq gp (ssget)) (command "change" gp "" "p" "LA"))
(DEFUN C:MI (/ gp) (setq gp (ssget)) (command "mirror" gp "" pause pause "Y"))
```

Figure 19.7: The contents of Keycad.LSP

they do. Use your word processor and copy the listing in Figure 19.7. Give this file the name **Keycad.LSP** and be sure you save it as an ASCII file.

Whenever you want to use these macros, instead of entering each one at the command prompt, you load the file just as you loaded the sample AutoLISP files earlier in this chapter, that is, by entering **(load "keycad")**. Once it is loaded, you can use any of the macros by entering the macro name. For example, entering **CH** will start the CHANGE command.

Now you've got some firsthand experience with AutoLISP, I hope these examples will encourage you to try learning more about this powerful tool. *Chapter 20* continues our look at AutoLISP in more detail, but for now let's explore some of AutoCAD's other hidden features.

NEW NAMES FOR OLD COMMANDS

In some of the early exercises, you used keyboard abbreviations to issue AutoCAD commands. These abbreviations are called command aliases and are defined in a file called Acad.PGP. Acad.PGP already has several aliases built into it: the ZOOM command, for example, has the alias of Z. This means that you can enter **Z** at the command prompt and ZOOM will be issued just as if you had entered the full name. Table 19.5 lists all the aliases currently built into the Acad.PGP file.

You can modify the existing aliases or add some of your own to the Acad.PGP file by following the simple format presented there. First the alias is entered, followed by a comma, then the full command name preceded by an asterisk, as in the following example for the ZOOM alias:

    Z, *ZOOM

If you find you use some commands frequently, you may want to use this feature of AutoCAD to simplify your access to them.

Table 19.5: Standard Command Aliases Built into the Acad.PGP File

STANDARD COMMANDS	
ALIAS	**FULL COMMAND NAME**
A	ARC
C	CIRCLE
CP	COPY
DV	DVIEW
E	ERASE
L	LINE
LA	LAYER
M	MOVE
MS	MSPACE
P	PAN
PS	PSPACE
PL	PLINE
R	REDRAW
Z	ZOOM
3DLINE	LINE
SERIAL	_Pkser

Table 19.5:   Standard Command Aliases Built into the Acad.PGP File (continued)

3D SOLID OBJECTS	
ALIAS	**FULL COMMAND NAME**
BOX	SOLBOX
WED	SOLWEDGE
WEDGE	SOLWEDGE
CON	SOLCONE
CONE	SOLCONE
CYL	SOLCYL
CYLINDER	SOLCYL
SPH	SOLSPHERE
SPHERE	SOLSPHERE
TOR	SOLTORUS
TORUS	SOLTORUS

AME COMPLEX SOLIDS	
ALIAS	**FULL COMMAND NAME**
FIL	SOLFILL
SOLF	SOLFILL
CHAM	SOLCHAM
SOLC	SOLCHAM
EXT	SOLEXT
EXTRUDE	SOLEXT
REV	SOLREV
REVOLVE	SOLREV
SOL	SOLIDIFY

Table 19.5: Standard Command Aliases Built into the Acad.PGP File (continued)

AME SOLIDS AND BOOLEAN OPERATIONS	
ALIAS	**FULL COMMAND NAME**
UNI	SOLUNION
UNION	SOLUNION
INTERF	SOLINT
INTERFERENCE	SOLINT SUB
	SOLSUB
SUBTRACT	SOLSUB
DIF	SOLSUB
DIFF	SOLSUB
DIFFERENCE	SOLSUB
SEP	SOLSEP
SEPARATE	SOLSEP

AME MODIFICATION AND QUERY COMMANDS	
ALIAS	**FULL COMMAND NAME**
SCHP	SOLCHP
CHPRIM	SOLCHP
MAT	SOLMAT
MATERIAL	SOLMAT
MOV	SOLMOVE
SL	SOLLIST
SLIST	SOLLIST

Table 19.5:   Standard Command Aliases Built into the Acad.PGP File (continued)

AME MODIFICATION AND QUERY COMMANDS	
ALIAS	**FULL COMMAND NAME**
MP	SOLMASSP
MASSP	SOLMASSP
SA	SOLAREA
SAREA	SOLAREA
SSV	SOLVAR

AME DOCUMENTATION COMMANDS	
ALIAS	**FULL COMMAND NAME**
FEAT	SOLFEAT
PROF	SOLPROF
PROFILE	SOLPROF
SU	SOLUCS
SUCS	SOLUCS

AME MODEL REPRESENTATION COMMANDS	
ALIAS	**FULL COMMAND NAME**
SW	SOLWIRE
WIRE	SOLWIRE
SM	SOLMESH
MESH	SOLMESH

USING THIRD-PARTY SOFTWARE

One of the biggest reasons for AutoCAD's popularity is its strong third-party software support. AutoCAD is like a chameleon; it can change to suit its environment. Out of the box, AutoCAD may not fulfill the needs of some users. With one of the over three hundred third-party add-ons, however, AutoCAD can be tailored to your specific needs.

In this section, I discuss a few of the third-party add-ons that are popular today. My goal here is to inform you of the possibilities open to you while using AutoCAD. Don't be discouraged if you don't see exactly what you need; I can't possibly cover all the different add-on programs in this section. There are several sources for more detailed information, including listings of all the available programs. Again, you should check with *Cadence* and *Cadalyst* magazines and with your AutoCAD dealer.

AUTOCAD-SPECIFIC FILE VIEWERS

▼ NOTE

Most AutoCAD viewing utilities offer direct plotting of files, multiple windows so you can view several files at once, block viewers that allow you to view blocks within drawings, zooming and panning of viewed files, file conversion, and much more.

Although there are several great general-purpose file managers you can use with AutoCAD, the ones I want to discuss here are aimed directly at AutoCAD users. These programs not only list drawing files but also let you view files without having to start up AutoCAD. The features don't stop there either. The prices for these products range from $100 to $300. One product, AutoManager, is offered not only for MS-DOS, but also for OS/2 and Unix.

But there is an even greater, more compelling reason for using an AutoCAD viewer program. Perhaps one of the greatest sources of resistance to using AutoCAD and CAD in general in an office environment is the fact that people not directly using the program are locked out from using and viewing drawing files. This is especially a source of concern for project managers and design firm principals who, with manual drafting techniques, could normally look over the shoulder of someone doing the drawing. With CAD, these people have less access to drawings, and therefore feel they have less control over the drawing production process.

AutoCAD file viewers remove the barriers between the drawings and the non-AutoCAD users. They are an excellent way to let non-AutoCAD users look at AutoCAD files without having to learn AutoCAD. Since many viewers are easy to learn, casual and non-AutoCAD users are no longer locked out of the AutoCAD world (see Figure 19.8).

A thorough discussion of all the AutoCAD viewers would require a chapter's worth of information, so I won't attempt one here. Many of the AutoCAD-related journals such as *Cadence* and *Cadalyst* have reviewed these products, so contact them for further details if you are interested. Here is a list of some of these viewers and their addresses. Note that not all of these file viewers are for Windows.

Slick!   CAD Systems Unlimited, Inc., 5201 Great America Pkwy, #443, Santa Clara, CA 95054, (408) 562-5762

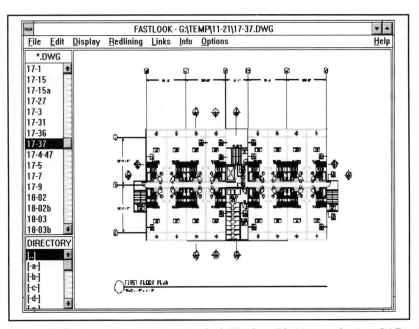

Figure 19.8:   A sample screen from Fastlook Windows File Manager for AutoCAD

Autovue	Les Cimmetry Systems, Inc., 1430 Massachusetts Ave., #306, Cambridge, MA 02138-3810, (514) 735-3219
Automanager (Windows)	Cyco International, 1908 Cliff Valley Way, #2000, Atlanta, GA 30307, (404) 634-3302
Quick-see	The Great Softwestern Co., Inc., 919 S. Carroll Blvd., #203, Denton, TX 76201, (817) 383-4434
Autoview	Premier Design Systems, Inc., 1107 Kenilworth Dr., #100, Towson, MD 21204, (410) 494-8444
Drawing Librarian	SoftSource, 301 W. Holly, Bellingham, WA 98225, (206) 676-0999
Fastlook for Windows	Kamel Software, Inc., 1215 Gallant Fox Wy., Chuluota, FL 32766, (407) 366-1173

ADDING FONTS TO AUTOCAD

▼ NOTE

If you would like more information on these products, contact: CAD Lettering Systems, P.O. Box 850, Oldsmar, FL 34677; or Autograf, 608 Sonora Ave., Glendale, CA 91201.

Perhaps one of the first things AutoCAD users do to customize their systems is to add a set of fonts to replace AutoCAD's standard ones. There are probably more vendors of AutoCAD fonts than of any other type of add-on. Let's take a look at a few of the offerings.

Some third-party vendors offer a wide range of fonts, including Helvetica, Times Roman, and monospaced versions of Roman fonts. Two notable products, CAD Lettering Systems's Letterease and Xfonts from Autograf Utilities, offer accurate renditions of popular fonts in both outline and solid forms. These fonts provide the near-typeset-quality text you need for applications in which the text appearance is important, such as drawing title blocks or special labels.

▼ NOTE

See *Chapter 14* for more information on using PageMaker and Ventura with AutoCAD.

You can also obtain high-quality text by entering it with a desktop-publishing program, such as PageMaker or Ventura. However, drawing size is limited by the output size used by the desktop-publishing program.

As I mentioned in *Chapter* 8, you can also use the hundreds of PostScript fonts available from Adobe and other font foundries. There are even some public domain and shareware PostScript fonts on CompuServe.

ENHANCING THE VGA DISPLAYS

Studies have shown that display speed in CAD programs has a direct effect on a user's productivity. While waiting several seconds may not seem significant, those seconds have a major impact. As great a program as AutoCAD is, it is not exactly a speed demon. Fortunately, there are several add-on software products that boost AutoCAD's display performance at reasonable prices.

These products can add what is called *display list processing* to your AutoCAD system. Such programs, called *display list drivers*, or DLDs, take advantage of AutoCAD's ADI interface to control your display's functions.

DLDs work by storing the display information in a special database list, much like the virtual display AutoCAD uses for dynamic pans and zooms. This list can be stored in RAM memory or on your computer's hard disk. A special program feature allows the software to access this list at a much faster rate than it can by the standard AutoCAD method for accessing the display database.

DLD software in conjunction with your hard disk or expanded or extended memory can dramatically reduce pan and zoom times. In most cases, pans and zooms take one-half to one-fifth the time of a typical redraw. Some even offer what is called a pop-up *bird's eye* window (Figure 19.9). Bird's-eye windows allow you to get an overall view of your drawing so you can quickly determine where to place your next view. This is similar to the Dynamic option under the ZOOM command, only the bird's eye view appears instantaneously.

There are some limitations to DLDs, however. DLDs do not improve regeneration speed, and in fact, some DLDs actually increase regeneration times. DLDs also take up much of your computer's memory, especially if you use AutoCAD's AME extension. If you are using resident programs, you can run into memory conflicts using DLDs.

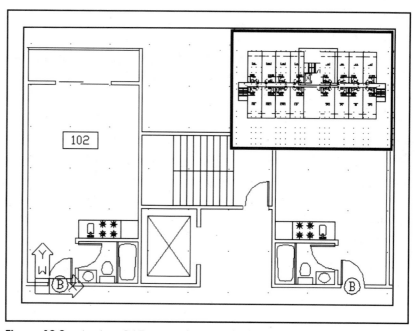

Figure 19.9: An AutoCAD screen showing a bird's-eye view

Still, in most cases, DLDs are worth the several hundred dollars they often cost. Again, you may want to consult the AutoCAD-related journals for detailed reviews of these utilities.

CUSTOM TAILORING AUTOCAD

So far, I have discussed third-party products that are useful to virtually all AutoCAD users. But there are products aimed at specific types of AutoCAD applications. The needs of an architect, for example, are far different from those of a mechanical designer, so third-party developers have created some specialized tools that help users of specific types of AutoCAD applications.

Most of these add-ons come complete with parts or symbols libraries, AutoLISP and ADS programs, and menus all integrated into a single package. These packages offer added functions to AutoCAD that simplify and speed up the AutoCAD user's work. For example, most AEC add-ons (that is, add-ons for architectural or engineering construction) offer utilities for drawing walls, inserting doors and windows, and creating schedules. These functions can be performed with the stock AutoCAD package but usually require more effort without the aid of an add-on product. If you have the time, you can create your own system of symbols, AutoLISP programs, and menus, and often this is the best way of molding AutoCAD to your needs. But often users want to have a ready-made solution, and this is where these add-ons become useful.

Such third-party add-ons are available for AEC, mechanical, civil engineering, piping, mapping, finite element analysis, numeric control, GIS, and many other applications. They can save you a good deal of frustration and time, especially if you find the right one to fill your needs. Like so many things, however, third-party add-ons can't be all things to all people. It is likely that no matter what add-on you purchase, you will find something lacking. In searching for add-ons, make sure that there is some degree of flexibility in the package, so if there is something you don't like, you can change it or add to it later.

If you want to know more about third-party add-ons, you can consult several sources. Autodesk publishes an applications catalog that can be purchased from your AutoCAD dealer. Also, Ariel Communications publishes *Resources*, a directory that lists many AutoCAD-related products (see margin note).

▼ TIP

Write for: *Resources*, Ariel Communications, Inc., P.O. Box 203550, Austin, TX 78720-3550; or call (512) 250- 1700.

IF YOU WANT TO EXPERIMENT...

Just for fun, you may want to try the AutoLISP program in Figure 19.10. This program is an AutoCAD version of a mathematical game used to determine how seemingly random events can create very nonrandom patterns. The game is described in Figure 19.11.

Carefully copy the program from the bonus disk onto your AutoCAD directory. Load Chaos.LSP as you would load any other AutoLISP utility, then enter **chaos**. You will be asked to pick three corners and a start point. Pick any point on the screen and watch the pattern unfold. To exit the program, enter **Ctrl-C** or **Ctrl-Break**.

```
                              CHAOS.LSP



;Chaos.LSP    This is a game that demonstrates the creation of patterns
;             from seemingly random events.
;_____


;function to find the midpoint between two points
(defun mid (a b)
 (list (/ (+ (car a)(car b)) 2)
       (/ (+ (cadr a)(cadr b)) 2)
 )
)

;function to generate random number
(defun rand (pt / rns rleng lastrn)
 (setq rns (rtos (* (car pt)(cadr pt)(getvar "tdusrtimer"))))
 (setq rnleng (strlen rns))
 (setq lastrn (substr rns rnleng 1))
 (setq rn (* 0.6 (atof lastrn)))
 (fix rn)
)

;The Chaos game
(defun C:CHAOS (/ pta ptb ptc rn count lastpt randn key)
 (princ "\nPick 3 points at random: ")
 (setq pta (getpoint))                         ;define point a
 (setq ptb (getpoint))                         ;define point b
 (setq ptc (getpoint))                         ;define point c
 (setq lastpt (getpoint "Pick a start point:")) ;pick a point to start
 (while (/= key 3)                             ;while pick button not pushed

  (setq randn (rand lastpt))                   ;get random number
  (cond                                        ;find midpoint to a b or c
   ( (= randn 0)(setq lastpt (mid lastpt pta)) ) ;use corner a if 0
   ( (= randn 1)(setq lastpt (mid lastpt pta)) ) ;use corner a if 1
   ( (= randn 2)(setq lastpt (mid lastpt ptb)) ) ;use corner b if 2
   ( (= randn 3)(setq lastpt (mid lastpt ptb)) ) ;use corner b if 3
   ( (= randn 4)(setq lastpt (mid lastpt ptc)) ) ;use corner c if 4
   ( (= randn 5)(setq lastpt (mid lastpt ptc)) ) ;use corner c if 5
  );end cond
  (grdraw lastpt lastpt 5)                      ;draw midpoint
  (setq key (car (grread T)))                   ;test for pick
 );end while
);end Chaos
.
```

Figure 19.10: The Chaos.LSP program listing

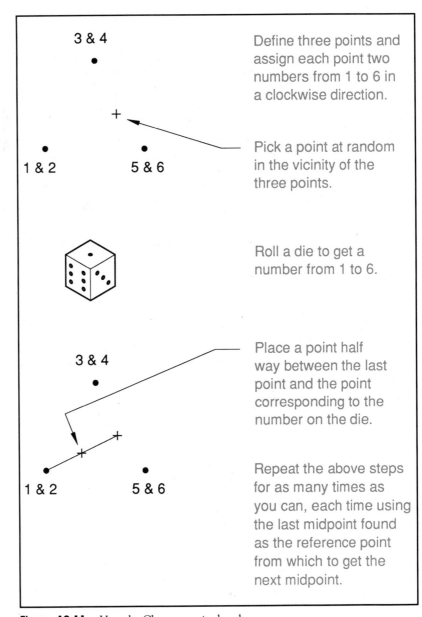

3 & 4 Define three points and assign each point two numbers from 1 to 6 in a clockwise direction.

1 & 2 **5 & 6** Pick a point at random in the vicinity of the three points.

Roll a die to get a number from 1 to 6.

3 & 4 Place a point half way between the last point and the point corresponding to the number on the die.

1 & 2 **5 & 6** Repeat the above steps for as many times as you can, each time using the last midpoint found as the reference point from which to get the next midpoint.

Figure 19.11: How the Chaos game is played

SUMMARY

While AutoCAD is a great CAD program out of the box, you can easily enhance its capabilities through the use of thousands of utilities available from many different resources. I've shown you just a few that are available immediately. For others, you'll have to do a little research. But if you've ever wondered why AutoCAD doesn't have this function or that command, chances are it does. You simply have to find the right utility that performs the function you're looking for and add it to AutoCAD.

Even if you can't find the right utility or third-party add-on, you can often create new functions yourself using either menus or AutoLISP programming. In the next chapter, you'll get a more detailed look at how you can customize AutoCAD's menus and how AutoLISP can work to save you time.

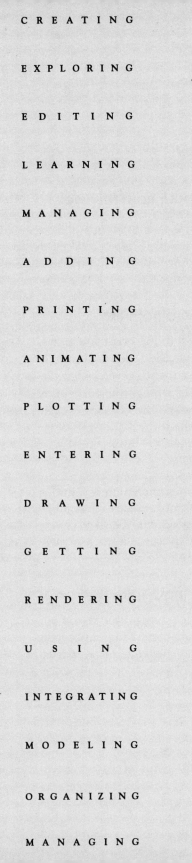

20

EXPLORING
AUTOLISP

FAST TRACK

878 ▶ To set up a program to get point input from the user

Include the Getpoint function. For example, to prompt the user to select a point and store that point in a variable, use the following **(setq** *myvariable* (getpoint "Select a point: ")). The item in double quotes becomes the prompt. The point the user selects is assigned to *myvariable*.

884 ▶ To extract a coordinate from a coordinate list

Use the Nth function. For example, to extract the Y coordinate from a variable that contains a coordinate list, use the following: **(nth 1** *mycoordinate*), where *mycoordinate* is a varible that has been assigned a coordinate value. If *mycoordinate* equals *(1.0 2.0 3.0)*, you will get the number *2.0* as the result of the sample expression. The *1* in the example indicates the second element of the coordinate list.

885 ▶ To combine elements into a list

Use the List function. For example, to combine three numbers into a coordinate list, use the following: **(list 1.0 2.0 3.0)**, where each number following the List function is an X, Y, or Z coordinate. This will create the list *(1.0 2.0 3.0)*. Text can also be combined into a list, but each text string must be enclosed by double quotes.

886 ▶ To set up a program to obtain text input from the user

Include the Getstring function. For example to prompt the user to enter his or her name, use the following: **(setq** *username* (getstring "Enter your name: ")), where *username* is the variable used to hold the person's name.

889 ▶ To set up a program to obtain a selection set from the user

Use the Ssget function. For example, to assign a set of objects to a variable, use the following: **(setq** *selections* (ssget)). When AutoCAD executes this expression, the user is prompted to select objects. The user can then use all the standard selection options to select objects. Then, whenever the *selections* variable is called, the selected items will be used.

893 ▶ To have your program execute one expression or another based on a condition

Use the If function. For example if you want to have AutoCAD start a line at a point only if a particular coordinate variable exists, use the following: **(if** *point1* (command "line" *point1*)), where *point1* is the variable to be tested for.

896 ▶ To have your program repeat an expression or several expressions while a condition exists

Use the While function. For example, if you want AutoCAD to continually obtain points from the user until the user presses ↵, use the following: **(while** *point1* (setq *point1* (getpoint "Pick a point: "))). When the user presses ↵, the variable *point1* is assigned a nil value and While stops evaluating its arguments. You can include more than one expression within a While expression.

In the last chapter, you were introduced to AutoLISP, AutoCAD's macro and programming language. You learned that you can take advantage of this powerful tool without really having to know anything about its internal workings. This chapter is designed to show you how you can take control of AutoLISP to do the things you want to do. You will learn how to store information such as text and point coordinates, how to create smart macros, and how to optimize AutoLISP's operation on your computer system.

Just be prepared to spend lots of time with your computer—not because programming in AutoLISP is all that difficult, but because it is so addicting! You've already seen how easy it is to use AutoLISP programs. I won't pretend that learning to program in AutoLISP is just as easy, but it really isn't as hard as you may think. And once you've created your own first program, you'll be hooked.

UNDERSTANDING THE INTERPRETER

▼ NOTE

Formulas such as this are called *expressions* in AutoLISP.

You access AutoLISP through the AutoLISP *interpreter*, which is a bit like a hand-held calculator. When you enter information at the command prompt, the interpreter *evaluates* it, then returns an answer. By *evaluate*, we mean it performs the instructions described by the information you provide. You could say that evaluation means "find the value of."

The information you give the interpreter is like a formula. Let's examine the interpreter's workings in more detail.

(Evaluation)

1. Start AutoCAD and open a new file called **Temp20a**. You'll use this file just to play around with AutoLISP so don't worry about saving it.

2. At the command prompt, enter **(+ 2 2)** ↵. The answer, 4, appears on the prompt line. AutoLISP evaluates the formula (+ 2 2) and returns the answer, 4.

▼ NOTE

A *function* is an instruction telling the AutoLISP interpreter what to do. In many ways it is like an AutoCAD command. A very simple example of a function is the math function Add, represented by the plus sign. AutoLISP has many built-in functions; in addition, you can create your own.

By entering information this way, you can perform calculations or even write short programs on the fly.

Another calculator-like capability of the interpreter is its ability to remember values. You probably have a calculator that has some memory. This capability allows you to store the value of an equation for future use. In a similar way, with the AutoLISP interpreter you can store values using *variables*.

DEFINING VARIABLES WITH SETQ

A variable is like a container that holds a value. That value can change many times in the course of a program's operation. Variables are assigned values through the use of the Setq function. For example, let's assign the numeric value **1.618** to a variable named Golden. This value, often referred to as the *golden section*, is a ratio of a rectangular area's height to its width. Aside from having some interesting mathematical properties, the golden section is said to represent a ratio that occurs frequently in nature.

Setq !

1. Enter **(setq Golden 1.618)** ↵ at the command prompt. The value 1.618 appears just below the line you enter. The value of Golden is now set to 1.618. Let's check it to make sure.

2. Enter **!Golden** ↵ at the command prompt.

The value **1.618** appears at the prompt. The exclamation point acts as special character that extracts the value of an AutoLISP variable at the prompt. From now until you quit AutoCAD, you can access this value at any time by preceding the variable name with an exclamation point.

The AutoLISP interpreter enables you to use math formulas as responses to prompts. You can also use values stored as variables in the same way. Let's see how we can use the variable Golden as the radius for a circle.

Draw ➤ Circle !

1. Click on Draw ➤ Circle ➤ Center, Radius.

2. At the **center point** prompt, pick a point in the center of your screen.

3. At the **radius** prompt, enter **!Golden** ↵. A circle appears with the radius of 1.618. Check this using Assist ➤ Inquiry ➤ List (see Figure 20.1).

Numbers aren't the only things that can be stored by using Setq; you can also store a variety of other types of data.

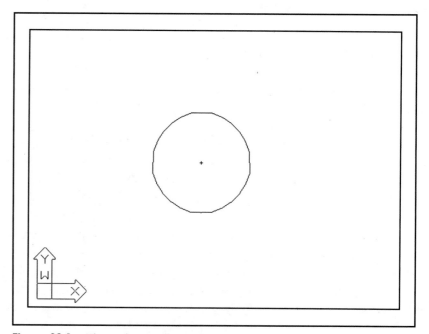

Figure 20.1:   The circle using Golden as the radius

UNDERSTANDING DATA TYPES

Variables are divided into several categories called *data types*. Categorizing data into types lets AutoLISP determine precisely how to evaluate the data and keep programs running quickly. A computer stores different types of data differently, so the use of data types helps AutoLISP communicate with the computer more efficiently. Also, data types aid your programming efforts by forcing you to think of data as having certain characteristics. The following descriptions will give you an idea of what some of these data types are.

Integers are whole numbers. When a mathematical expression contains only integers, only an integer is returned. For example, the expression (/ 2 3)—two divided by three—will return the value 0, because the answer is less than one. Integers are best suited for counting and numbering. The numbers 1, –12, and 144 are all integers.

Real numbers, often referred to as **reals** or **floats**, are numbers that include decimals. When a mathematical expression contains a real number, a real number is returned. For example, the expression (/ 2.0 3) will return the value 0.66667. Real numbers are best suited for situations where accuracy is important. Examples of real numbers are 0.1, 3.14159, and –2.2.

Strings are text values. They are always enclosed in double quotes. Here are some examples of strings: "1", "George", and "Enter a value".

Lists are groups of values enclosed in parentheses. Lists offer a convenient way to store whole sets of values in one variable. There are actually two classes of lists: those meant to be evaluated, and those intended as repositories for data. In the strictest sense, since they are enclosed in parentheses, AutoLISP programs are lists. Here are some examples of lists: (6.0 1.0 0.0), (A B C D), and (setq golden 1.618).

Finally, there are two basic elements in AutoLISP: *atoms* and *lists*. We have already described lists. An atom is an element that cannot be taken apart. Atoms are further grouped into two categories, *numbers* and *symbols*. A number can be a real number or an integer. A symbol, on the other hand, is often a name given to a variable, like *point1* or *dx2*. As you can see, a symbol can use a number as part of its name, however, its name must always start with a letter. You could think of a symbol as a name given to a variable or function as a means of identifying it.

USING ARGUMENTS AND EXPRESSIONS

In the previous exercise, you used the Setq function to store variables. The way you used Setq is typical of all functions.

Functions act on *arguments* to accomplish a task. An argument can be a symbol, a number, or a list. A simple example of a function acting on numbers is the addition of 0.618 and 2. In AutoLISP, this would be entered as

(+ 0.618 2)

This function returns the value **2.618**. This formula, the function followed by the arguments, is called an *expression*. It starts with the left parenthesis first, then the function, then the arguments, and finally the closing right parenthesis.

Arguments can also be expressions, which means you can *nest* expressions. For example, you can assign the value returned by 0.618 + 2 to the variable Golden:

(setq Golden (+ 0.618 2))

This is called a *nested expression*. Whenever expressions are nested, the deepest nest is evaluated first, then the next deepest, and so on. In this example, the expression adding 0.618 to 2 is evaluated first.

Arguments to functions can also be variables. For example, you might have used Setq to assign the value 25.4 to a variable called *Mill*. You could then find the result of dividing Mill by Golden.

1. Enter **(setq Mill 25.4)** ↵ to create a new variable called Mill.

2. Next enter **(/ Mill Golden)** ↵. The slash sign is the symbol for the division function. This returns the value 15.6983. You can assign this value to yet another variable.

3. Enter **(setq B (/ Mill Golden))** ↵ to create a new variable B. Now you have three variables—Golden, Mill, and B—which are all assigned values that you can later retrieve, either within an AutoCAD command (by entering an exclamation point followed by the variable), or as arguments within an expression.

Watching
Parentheses and Quotes

You must remember to close all parentheses when using nested expressions. If you get the prompt

n>

you know you have an incomplete AutoLISP expression. This is the *AutoLISP prompt*. The *n* is the number of missing parentheses or quotes in your expression. If you see this prompt, you must enter the number of closing parentheses indicated by n in order to return to the command prompt. AutoCAD will not evaluate an AutoLISP program that has the wrong number of parentheses. Double quotes enclosing strings must also be carefully closed.

USING TEXT VARIABLES WITH AUTOLISP

Our examples have shown only numbers being manipulated, but text can also be manipulated in a similar way. Variables can be assigned text strings that can later be used to enter values in commands that require text input. You must remember to enclose text in quotation marks as in the following example:

```
(setq text1 "This is how text looks in AutoLISP")
```

This example shows a sentence being assigned to a variable *text1*. Strings can also be *concatenated*, or joined together, to form new strings. Here is an example of how two pieces of text can be added together:

```
(setq text2 (strcat "This is the first part and" "this is the
second part"))
```

Here, the AutoLISP function *strcat* is used to join two strings together. The result is

```
"This is the first part and this is the second part"
```

Strings and numeric values cannot be evaluated together, however. This may seem like a simple statement, but if not carefully considered it can lead to confusion. For example, it is possible to assign the number 1 to a variable as a text string by entering

```
(setq foo "1" )
```

Later, you may accidentally try to add this string variable to an integer or real number and AutoCAD will return an error message.

In our examples, we used Setq and the addition and division functions. These are three functions out of many available to you. All the usual math functions are available, plus many other functions used to test and manipulate variables. Table 20.1 shows some commonly used math functions.

STORING POINTS AS VARIABLES

Point coordinates can also be stored and retrieved in a way similar to numeric values. But since coordinates are actually sets of two or three numeric values, they have to be handled differently. AutoLISP provides

Table 20.1: Math Functions Available in AutoLISP

MATH FUNCTIONS THAT ACCEPT MULTIPLE ARGUMENTS	
FUNCTION	**OPERATION**
(+ *number number*…)	Add
(− *number number*…)	Subtract
(* *number number*…)	Multiply
(/ *number number*…)	Divide
(Max *number number*…)	Find largest number in list
(Min *number number*…)	Find smallest number in list
(Rem *number number*…)	Find the remainder of numbers

MATH FUNCTIONS THAT ACCEPT SINGLE ARGUMENTS	
FUNCTION	**OPERATION**
(1+ *number*)	Add 1 to number
(1− *number*)	Subtract 1 from number
(Abs *number*)	Find the absolute value of number
(Atan *angle in radians*)	Arc tangent of angle
(Cos *angle in radians*)	Cosine of angle
(Exp *nth*)	*e* raised to the nth power
(Expt *number nth*)	*Number* raised to the nth power
(Gcd *integer integer*)	Find greatest common denominator
(Log *number*)	Find natural log of number
(Sin *angle in radians*)	Sine of angle
(Sqrt *number*)	Find the square root of number

the Getpoint function to handle the acquisition of points. Try the following to see how it works.

1. At the command prompt, enter **(getpoint)** ↵. The command prompt will go blank momentarily.

2. Pick a point near the middle of the screen. You see the coordinates of the point you picked appear in the prompt area.

Here, *getpoint* pauses AutoCAD and waits for you to pick a point. Once you do, it returns the coordinate of the point you pick in the form of a list. The list shows the X, Y, and Z axes enclosed by parentheses. You can store the coordinate obtained from Getpoint using the Setq function. Try the following to see how this works.

1. Enter **(setq point1 (getpoint))** ↵.

2. Pick a point on the screen.

3. Enter **!point1** ↵.

Here you stored a coordinate list in a variable called *point1*. You then recalled the contents of Point1 using the exclamation point. You can see that the value of the coordinate is in the form of a list with the X, Y, and Z values appearing as real numbers separated by spaces, instead of the commas you've been used to.

CREATING A SIMPLE PROGRAM

So far, you have seen how you can use AutoLISP to do some math and to store values as variables. AutoLISP has enormous value with these capabilities alone, but you can do a good deal more. In this section, you'll look at how you can combine these three capabilities—math calculations, variables, and lists—to write a simple program for drawing a rectangle.

Defun
Setq
Getpoint
Nth
List
COMMAND

1. First, use the **F2** key to flip to a text display.

2. At the command prompt, enter **(defun c:rectang () ↵**. You will get a new prompt that looks like this:

   ```
   1>
   ```

3. Now, very carefully enter the following several lines. If you make a mistake while typing a line, back up using the ← key, then retype the line. Once you press ↵, you cannot go back to fix a line.

   ```
   (setq Pt1 (getpoint "Pick first corner point:" )) ↵
   (setq Pt3 (getpoint "Pick opposite corner:" )) ↵
   (setq Pt2 (list (nth 0 Pt3) (nth 1 Pt1))) ↵
   (setq Pt4 (list (nth 0 Pt1) (nth 1 Pt3))) ↵
   (command "Pline" Pt1 Pt2 Pt3 Pt4 "C") ↵
   ) ↵
   ```

   Each time you enter a line, you will see the AutoLISP prompt appear. Once you enter the last parenthesis, you return to the standard AutoCAD command prompt.

4. Check what you have entered against this listing to be sure you entered everything correctly. If you find you made a mistake, start over from the beginning and re-enter the program.

▼ **TIP**

You can use AutoLISP programs transparently, as long as the program doesn't contain an embedded AutoCAD command.

When you are done, you get the message **C:RECTANG**. This confirms that you have the rectangle drawing program stored in memory. Let's see it in action.

1. Erase the circle you drew earlier, then enter **rectang** ↵ at the command prompt.

2. At the **Pick first corner point** prompt, pick a point at coordinate 1,1.

3. At the **Pick opposite corner** prompt, pick a point at 6,4. A box appears between the two points you picked (see Figure 20.2).

This program incorporates all the things you've learned so far. Let's see exactly how it works.

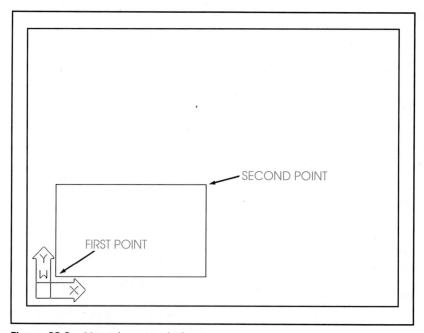

Figure 20.2: Using the rectangle drawing program

DISSECTING THE RECTANGLE PROGRAM

The rectangle program finds the two corner coordinates of a rectangle, which it gets from you as input, then extracts parts of those coordinates to derive the coordinates for the other two corners of the rectangle. Once it knows all four coordinates, it can draw the lines connecting them. Figure 20.3 illustrates what the Rectangle program does. Now let's look at the program in more detail to see how it works.

GETTING INPUT FROM THE USER

In the exercise, you started out with the line (*defun c:rectang* ()). You may recall from *Chapter 19* that Defun is a function that lets you create commands. The name that follows the Defun function is the name of the

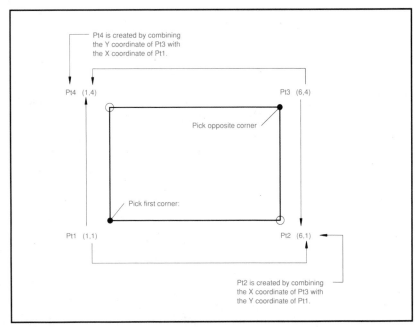

Figure 20.3: The Rectangle program draws a rectangle by getting two corner points of the rectangle then recombining coordinates from those two points to find the other two points of the rectangle.

command as you enter it through the keyboard. The *c:* tells AutoLISP to make this program act like a command. If the *c:* is left off, you must enter (**rectang**) to view the program. The empty parenthesis is an argument list which I'll discuss later.

In the next line the variable *Pt1* is assigned a value for a point you enter using your cursor. *Getpoint* is the AutoLISP function that pauses the AutoLISP program and allows you to pick a point using your cursor, or to enter a coordinate. Once a point is entered, Getpoint returns the coordinate of that point as a list. Immediately following Getpoint is a line that reads: "*Pick first corner point:*". Getpoint allows you to add a prompt in the form of text. You may recall when you first used Getpoint, it caused the prompt to go blank. Instead of a blank, you can use text as an argument to the Getpoint function to display a prompt describing what action to take.

The third line is similar to the second. It uses Getpoint to get the location of another point, then assigns that point to the variable Pt3: (setq Pt3 (getpoint "Pick opposite corner:")). Once AutoLISP has the two corners, it has all the information it needs to find the other two corners of two-dimensional rectangle.

TAKING APART LISTS

The next thing AutoLISP must do is take Pt1 and Pt3 apart to extract their X and Y coordinates, then re-assemble those coordinates to get the other corner coordinates. AutoLISP must take the X coordinate from Pt3, and the Y coordinate from Pt1 to get the coordinate for the lower-right corner of the rectangle (see Figure 20.3). To do this, you use two new functions called *Nth* and *List*.

Nth extracts a single element from a list. Since coordinates are lists, Nth can be used to extract an X, Y, or Z component from a coordinate list. In the fourth line of the program, you see

```
(nth 0 Pt3)
```

Here the zero immediately following the Nth function tells Nth to take element number 0 from the coordinate stored as Pt3. Nth starts counting from 0 instead of 1 so the first element of Pt3 is considered item number 0. This is the X component of the coordinate stored as Pt3.

Try the following to see how Nth works first hand.

1. Enter **!point1** ↵. You see the coordinate list you created earlier using Getpoint.

2. Enter **(nth 0 point1)** ↵. You get the first element of the coordinate represented by *point1*.

Immediately following the first Nth expression is another Nth expression similar to the previous one.

```
(nth 1 Pt1)
```

Here, Nth extracts element number 1, the second element, from the coordinate stored as Pt1. This is the Y component of the coordinate stored as Pt1. If you like, try the previous exercise again, but this time, enter **(nth 1 point1)** and see what value you get.

COMBINING ELEMENTS INTO A LIST

AutoLISP has extracted the X component from Pt3 and the Y component of Pt1. They must now be joined together into a new list. This is where the List function comes in. The list expression looks like this.

```
(list (nth 0 pt3) (nth 1 pt1))
```

You know that the first Nth expression extracts an X component and the second extracts a Y component. Conceptually, the expression says the following:

```
(list X Y)
```

where X is the the value derived from the first Nth expression and Y is the value derived from the second Nth expression. The List function simply recombines its arguments into another list, in this case another coordinate list. Finally, the outermost function of the expression uses Setq to create a new variable called *Pt2* which is the new coordinate list derived from the List function. The following is a schematic version of the fourth line of the Rectangle program, so you can see what is going on more clearly.

```
(setq pt2 (list X Y))
```

You can see that Pt2 is a coordinate list derived from combining the X component from Pt3 and the Y component from Pt1. Try the following exercise to see how List works.

1. Enter **(list 5 6)** ↵. You see the list (5 6) appear in the prompt.

2. Enter **(list (nth 0 point1) (nth 1 point1))** ↵. You see the X and Y coordinates of point1 in a list, excluding the Z coordinate.

The fifth line is similar to the fourth. It creates a new coordinate list using the X value from pt1 and the Y value from pt2:

```
(setq Pt4 (list (nth 0 Pt1) (nth 1 Pt3))).
```

The last line tells AutoCAD to draw a polyline through the four points to create a box:

```
(command Pline Pt1 Pt2 Pt3 Pt4 c).
```

The Command function issues the PLINE command then inputs the variables Pt1 through Pt4. Finally, it enters a c to close the polyline.

GETTING OTHER INPUT FROM THE USER

In your program, you were able to prompt the user to pick some points by using the Getpoint function. There are several other functions that also allow you to pause for input and instruct the user what to do. Nearly all of these functions begin with the *Get* prefix. Table 20.2 shows a list of these *Get* functions. They accept single values or; in the case of points, a list of two values. In the case of Getstring, string values are case-sensitive. This means that if you enter a lowercase letter in response to

Table 20.2: Functions that Pause to Allow Input

FUNCTION	DESCRIPTION
Getint	Allows entry of integer values
Getreal	Allows entry of real values
Getstring	Allows entry of string or text values
Getkword	Allows filtering of string entries through a list of keywords
Getangle	Allows key or mouse entry of angles based on the standard AutoCAD compass points (returns values in radians)
Getorient	Allows key or mouse entry of angles based on UNITS command setting for angles (returns values in radians)
Getdist	Allows keyboard or mouse entry of distances (always returns values as real numbers, regardless of unit format used)
Getpoint	Allows keyboard or mouse entry of point values (returns values as coordinate lists)
Getcorner	Allows selection of a point by using a window*
Initget	Allows you to define a set of keywords for the Getkword function—keywords are strings, as in **(initget " Yes No ")**

*This function requires a base-point value as a first argument. This base point defines the first corner of the window. A window appears, allowing you to select the opposite corner.

Getstring, it will be saved as a lowercase letter, while uppercase letters will be saved as uppercase letters. You can enter numbers in response to the Getstring function, but they will be saved as strings and cannot be used in mathematical operations. Also, AutoLISP will automatically add quotes to string values it returns, so you don't have to enter any.

Just as with Getpoint, all these *Get* functions allow you to create a prompt by following the function with the prompt enclosed by quotation marks, as in the expression

(getpoint "Pick the next point:")

This expression will cause the prompt **Pick the next point** to appear while AutoCAD waits for your input.

The functions Getangle, Getorient, Getdist, Getcorner, and Getpoint allow you to specify a point from which the angle, distance, or point is to be measured, as in the expression

(getangle Pt1 "Pick the next point:")

where *Pt1* is a previously defined point variable. A rubber-banding line will appear from the coordinate defined by Pt1 (see Figure 20.4).

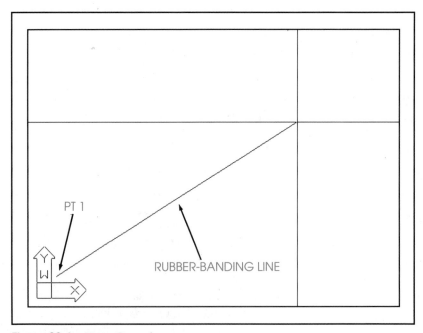

Figure 20.4:   Using Getangle

Once you pick a point, the angle defined by Pt1 and the point you pick are returned in radians. You can also enter a relative coordinate through the keyboard in the unit system currently being used in your drawing. Getangle and Getdist prompt you for two points if a point variable is not provided. Getcorner always requires a point argument and will generate a window instead of a rubber-banding line (see Figure 20.5).

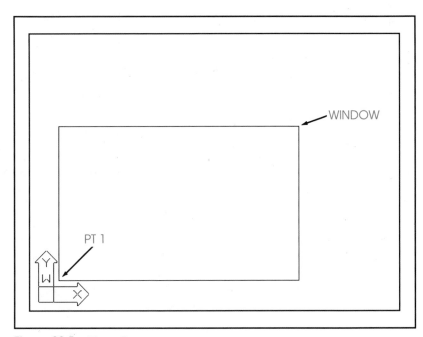

Figure 20.5:   Using Getcorner

SELECTING
OBJECTS WITH AUTOLISP

In *Chapter 19*, I showed you a simple macro created using AutoLISP. That macro lets you rotate a single object 90°. While it did the job, it was limited in that you could only select a single object to rotate. What if you wanted to have that macro rotate a set of objects instead of just one? At this point, you know enough to create a program to do just that.

The only part missing is how to get AutoLISP to select several objects instead of just one. For this you need Ssget.

UNDERSTANDING SSGET

So far, you know you can assign numbers, text, and coordinates to variables. Ssget is a function that assigns a set of objects to a variable. The following shows you first hand how Ssget works.

1. Draw a few random lines on the screen.

2. Enter **(setq ss1 (ssget))** ↵.

3. At the **Select objects** prompt, select the lines using any standard selection method. Notice that you can select objects just as you would at any **Select objects** prompt.

4. When you are done selecting objects, press ↵. You get the messge **<Selection set:** *n***>** where *n* is an integer value.

5. Start the move command, and at the **Select objects** prompt, enter **!ss1** ↵. The lines you selected previously will highlight.

6. Press ↵ then pick two points to finish the Move command.

In this exercise, you stored a selection set as the variable *Ss1*. You can recall the selection set from the command prompt using the exclamation point as you did with other variables earlier.

USING SSGET IN AN EXPRESSION

You can also use the Ss1 variable in an AutoLISP expression. For example, the R90 macro you created in *Chapter 19* could be modified to accommodate the selection of several objects. In the following exercise, it is rewritten to include the Ssget function.

1. Enter **(defun c:r90 (/ ss1)** ↵. You see the AutoLISP prompt appear.

2. Enter **(setq ss1 (ssget))(command "rotate" ss1 "" pause "90"))** ↵ to complete the macro.

3. Enter **r90** ↵ to start the macro.

4. At the **Select objects** prompt, select a few of the random lines you drew earlier.

5. Press ↵ to confirm your selection, then pick a point near the center of the screen. The lines you selected rotate 90°.

This macro starts out in the same way as the one in *Chapter 19*. The defun function tells AutoLISP this is to be a command called *r90*. A list called an *argument list* follows the name of the macro. I'll discuss the argument list a bit later.

Following the argument list is the *(setq ss1 (ssget))* expression you used in the previous exercise. This is where the new macro stops and asks you to select a set of objects to later be applied to the rotate command.

The next expression uses the Command function described in *Chapter 19*. You may recall this Command lets you include standard command line input within an AutoLISP program. In this case, the input starts by issuing the Rotate command. Then it applies the selection set stored by Ss1 to the Rotate command's **Select objects** prompt. Next, the two *""* marks indicate a ↵. The pause lets the user select a base point for the rotation. Finally, the value of 90 is applied to the Rotate command's angle prompt. The whole expression might look like the following when entered at the command prompt.

```
Command: Rotate ↵
Select objects: !Ss1
Select objects: ↵
Base point: pause for input
< Rotation angle >/Reference: 90 ↵
```

In this macro, the Ssget function adds flexibility because it allows the user to select as many objects as he or she chooses. You could use the Pause function, but with pause, you cannot anticipate whether the user will use a window, pick points, or select a previous selection set.

Memory Limitations of Selection Sets

While you can have virtually an unlimited number of variables in a program, you are limited to 128 selection set variables. If the number exceeds 128, AutoCAD will not allow further selection of objects. If this situation arises, you must set some of the selection set variables to nil then use the GC (garbage collection) function to clear the unused variables from memory. The following shows a sample line of AutoLISP code that will free selection sets from memory.

```
(setq ss1 nil ss2 nil ss3 nil ss4 nil...) (GC) ⏎
```

This example shows three things. First, you can assign values to more than one variable using the Setq function. In this example, several selection set variables are set to nil. This is done by alternating the variables and values in the Setq expression. You might also note that you can assign a variable the nil value. Finally, you will notice that the GC function has no arguments at all. Its sole purpose is to free your system of unused memory segments called *nodes*. A full discussion of nodes is beyond the scope of this book. Just be aware that GC, used in conjunction with setting selection-set variables to nil, will free up memory.

CONTROLLING MEMORY USE WITH LOCAL VARIABLES

Selection sets are memory hogs in AutoLISP. You don't want to create too many of them or you will end up crowding AutoLISP's memory reserves. To limit the memory used by selection sets, you can turn them into what are called *local variables*. Local variables are variables that only exist while the program is executing its instructions. Once the program is finished, local variables are discarded. The vehicle for making variables local is the *argument list*. You may recall the empty parentheses that immediately follow the program name in the Rectangle program:

```
(defun c:rectang ()...)
```

If you include a list of variables between those parentheses, then those variables become local. In the new R90 macro you just looked at, the Ss1 selection set variable is included in the argument list to turn it into a local variable.

```
(defun c:r90 (/ ss1)...)
```

▼ WARNING

The space after the / in the argument list is very important. Your macro will not work properly without it.

Note that the argument list starts with a forward slash, then a space followed by the list of variables. Once the R90 program is done with its work, any memory assigned to Ss1 can be recovered.

There are times when you will want a variable to be accessible at all times by all AutoLISP programs. Such variables are known as *global variables*. You can use global variables to store information in the current editing session. You could even store a few selection sets as global variables. To keep memory use down, however, use global variables sparingly. Remember that all variables are global unless you include them in an argument list.

CONTROLLING THE FLOW OF AN AUTOLISP PROGRAM

At some point, you will want to design a program to perform one function or another depending on some existing condition. This type of operation is often referred to as an *if-then-else conditional statement:* If a condition is met, then perform computation A, else perform computation B. AutoLISP offers the If function to facilitate this type of operation.

USING THE IF FUNCTION

The If function requires two arguments. The first argument must be a value that returns a true or a false, or in the case of AutoLISP, *T* for true or *nil* for false. It is like saying "If *true* then do A." You can optionally

▼ **NOTE**

A common use for the if-then-else statement is to direct the flow of a program in response to a user's *yes* or *no* reply to a prompt. If the user responds with a yes to the prompt **Do you want to continue?**, for example, that response can be used in the if-then-else statement to direct the program to continue to perform some function like erasing objects or drawing a box.

supply a third argument, which is the action to take if the value returned is nil. This would be like saying "If true then do A, *else do B.*" Here is how an If expression might look:

```
(if Exst (+ a b) (* a b))
```

In this example, the value of the Exst variable determines which of the two following expressions is evaluated. If Exst has a value, then it returns *T* for true; that is, when AutoLISP evaluates Exst, the value returned is *T*. The expression then will evaluate the second argument, (+ a b). If Exst does not have a value or is nil, then the third expression, (* a b), is evaluated.

There are several special functions that can test variables for specific conditions. For example, you can test a number to see if it is equal to, less than, or greater than another number, as in the following:

```
(if (= A B) (+ A B) (* A B))
```

In this expression, if A is equal to B then the second argument is evaluated.

```
(if (> A B) (+ A B) (* A B))
```

In this expression, if A is greater than B then the second argument is evaluated. The functions that test for T or nil are called *predicates* and *logical operators*. Table 20.3 shows a list of these functions.

Let's see how conditional statements, predicates, and logical operators work together. Suppose you want to write a program that either finds the multiplication of two numbers or simply adds the numbers together. You want the program to ask the user which action to take depending on which of the two values is greater.

▼ **NOTE**

Be sure you include a space after a math or logic function in an expression.

1. Enter the following program at the command prompt, just as you did for the Rectangle program.

```
(defun c:mul-add ( )
(setq A (getreal "Enter first number:" ))
(setq B (getreal "Enter second number:" ))
(if (< A B) (+ a b) (* a b))
)
```

Table 20.3: A List of Predicates and Logical Operators

FUNCTION	RETURNS T (TRUE) IF...
<	one numeric value is less than another
>	one numeric value is greater than another
<=	one numeric value is less than or equal to another
>=	one numeric value is greater than or equal to another
=	two numeric or string values are equal
/=	two numeric or string values are not equal
eq	two values are exactly the same
equal	two values are the same (approximate)
atom	a symbol represents an atom (as opposed to a list)
listp	a symbol represents a list
minusp	a numeric value is negative
numberp	a symbol is a number, real or integer
zerop	a symbol evaluates to zero
and	all of several expressions or atoms return non-nil
not	a symbol is nil
nul	a list is nil
or	one of several expressions or atoms returns non-nil

2. Now run the program by entering **Mul-add** ↵.

3. At the **Enter first number** prompt, enter **3** ↵.

4. At the **Enter second number** prompt, enter **4** ↵. The value 7.0 is returned.

5. Try running it again, but this time enter **4** at the first prompt and **3** at the second prompt. The value *12.0* appears.

In this program, the first two Setq expressions get two numbers from you. The conditional statement that follows, (< A B), tests to see if the first number you entered is less than the second. If this predicate function returns T for true, then (+ a b) is evaluated. If it returns *nil* for false, then (* a b) is evaluated.

You will often find that you need to perform several steps depending on some condition. So far, I've shown you some fairly simple If expressions, but you can have an If expression that evaluates several expressions at once as in the following:

```
(if (= A B) (progn (* A B)(+ A B)(- A B) ))
```

Here, the function *Progn* tells the If function that several expressions are to be evaluated if (= A B) returns *T*.

REPEATING AN EXPRESSION

Sometimes you will want your program to repeatedly evaluate a set of expressions until a particular condition is met. If you are familiar with BASIC or Fortran, you will recognize such a function as a *loop*.

You can repeat steps in a program by using the While function in conjunction with predicates and logical operators. Like the If function, While's first argument must be one that returns a *T* or *nil*.

You can have as many other arguments to the While function as you like, just as long as the first argument is a predicate function.

```
(while test (expression 1) (expression 2) (expression 3)...)
```

The While function isn't the only one that will repeat a set of instructions. The *Repeat* function will also cause a set of instructions to be executed several times, but unlike While, Repeat requires an integer value for its second value as in the following:

```
(Repeat 14 (expression 1)(expression 2)(expression 3)...)
```

In this example, Repeat will evaluate each expression 14 times.

A third function called *Foreach* will evaluate an expression for each element of a list. The arguments to Foreach are first a variable, then a list whose elements are to be evaluated, then the expression used to evaluate each element of the list.

> (foreach *var1* (*list1*) (*expression var1*))

Foreach is a bit more difficult to understand at first, since it involves a variable, a list, and an expression, all working together.

USING OTHER BUILT-IN FUNCTIONS

With just a handful of AutoLISP functions, you were able to create many useful programs. I can't do a tutorial showing you how to use every single AutoLISP function. However, in this final section, I'll describe a few of the other available functions along with brief examples. Though this is far from a complete list, it should be enough to get you well on your way to using AutoLISP. You can then experiment with the functions at your leisure. But remember, using AutoLISP can be addicting!

GEOMETRIC OPERATIONS

These functions are useful for manipulating geometric data. You may also want to look at the Get functions mentioned earlier.

Angle

The Angle function finds the angle between two points. The value returned is in radians.

> (angle '(6.0 4.0 0.0) '(6.0 5.0 0.0))

returns *1.5708*. In this example I show two coordinate lists for arguments, but point variables can also be used.

▼ NOTE

In many of the examples below, I show numeric values or lists as arguments. As with all AutoLISP functions, you can also use variables as arguments, as long as the value of the variable is of the proper data type. You may also notice that in some examples an apostrophe precedes a list. This apostrophe tells AutoLISP not to evaluate the list, but to treat it as a repository of data.

Distance

The Distance function finds the distance between two points. The value returned is in base units. Just like Angle, Distance requires two coordinates as arguments:

(distance '(6.0 4.0 0.0) '(6.0 5.0 0.0))

returns *1.0.*

Polar

The Polar function returns a point in the form of a coordinate list based on the location of a point, an angle, and a distance:

(polar '(1.0 1.0 0.0) 1.5708 1.0)

returns *(0.999996 2.0 0.0)*. The first argument is a coordinate list, the second is an angle in radians, and the third is a distance given in base units. The point must be a coordinate list.

Inters

The Inters function returns the intersection point of two vectors, with each vector described by two points. The points must be in this order: the first two points define the first vector and the second two points define the second vector:

(inters
'(1.0 4.0 0.0)'(8.0 4.0 0.0)'(5.0 2.0 0.0)'(5.0 9.0 0.0)
)

returns *(5.0 4.0 0.0)*. If the intersection point does not lie between either of the two vectors, you can still obtain a point provided you include nil fifth as a argument.

STRING OPERATIONS

These functions allow you to manipulate strings. You can use the command function with string variables to enter text, as in the following:

```
(Setq note "This is a test.")
(command "text" point "2.0" "0" note )
```

In this example, note is first assigned a string value. Then the command function is used to issue the text command and place the text in the drawing.

Substr

The Substr function returns a portion of a string, called a *substring*, beginning at a specified location. A string is returned:

```
(substr "string" 3 4)
```

returns *ring*. The first argument is the string containing the substring to be extracted. The second argument, 3, tells Substr where to begin the new string. This value must be an integer. The third argument, 4, is optional and tells Substr how long the new string should be. Length must also be an integer.

Strcat

The Strcat function combines several strings. The result is a string:

```
(strcat string1  string2  etc....)
```

returns *string1 string2 etc....* In this example, the etc....'s indicate you can have as many string values as you want.

DATA-TYPE CONVERSIONS

While using AutoLISP, you will often have to convert values from one data type to another. For example, since most angles in AutoLISP must be represented in radians, you must convert them to degrees before you can use them in commands. This can be accomplished by using the Angtos function. Angtos will convert a real number representing an angle in radians into a string in the degree format you desire. The following example converts an angle of 1.57 radians into surveyor's units with a precision of four decimal places:

```
(angtos 1.57 4 4)
```

returns *N 0d2'44" E*. The first argument is the angle in radians; the second argument is a code that tells AutoLISP which format to convert the angle to; and the third argument tells AutoLISP the degree of precision desired. This third argument is optional. The conversion codes for Angtos are: 0=degrees; 1=degrees/minutes/seconds; 2=grads; 3=radians; 4=surveyor's units.

Now that you've seen an example of what the Angtos data-type conversion can do, let's briefly look at other similar functions.

Atof and Atoi

Atof converts a string to a real number:

```
(atof "33.334")
```

returns *33.334*. Atoi converts a string to an integer:

```
(atoi "33.334")
```

returns *33*.

Itoa and Rtos

Itoa converts an integer into a string. The argument must be an integer:

```
(itoa "24")
```

returns *"24"*.

Rtos converts a real number to a string. As with Angtos, a format code and precision value is specified:

```
(rtos 32.3 4 2)
```

returns *"2'-8 ¼"*. The first argument is the value to be converted; the second argument is the conversion code; and the third argument is the precision value. The codes are: 1=scientific; 2=decimal; 3=engineering; 4=architectural; 5=fractional.

Fix and Float

Fix converts a real number into an integer by truncating the decimal value:

        (fix 3.3334)

returns *3*.

Float converts an integer into a real number:

        (float 3)

returns *3.0*.

STORING YOUR PROGRAMS AS FILES

▼ WARNING

If you haven't saved it as file, you will have to enter the Box program from the keyboard as you did in the earlier exercise.

When you exit AutoCAD, the rectangle program will vanish. But just as you were able to save the keyboard shortcuts in *Chapter 19*, you can create an ASCII file on a disk containing the program or add it to your Acad.LSP file. That way you will have ready access to it at all times.

To save your programs, open a text editor and enter them just as you entered the rectangle program through the keyboard, including the first line that contains the defun function. Be sure you save the file with the .LSP file name extension. Then you can recall your program using File ➤ Applications.

If you prefer, you can use the manual method for loading AutoLISP programs. This involves the Load AutoLISP function. Just as with all other functions, it is enclosed by parentheses. In *Chapter 19*, you loaded the Chroma.LSP file using the application loader. To use the Load function to load Chroma.LSP, you would enter the following:

```
(Load "Chroma")
```

Load is perhaps one of the simpler AutoLISP functions since it requires only one argument; the name of the AutoLISP file you want to load. Notice that you do not have to include the .LSP extension.

If the AutoLISP file resides in a directory that isn't in the current path, you would include the path in the file name as in the following:

```
(Load "c:/lisp/chroma")
```

Notice that the / is used instead of the usual DOS \ to indicate directories. The / is used because \ has special meaning to AutoLISP in a string value. It tells AutoLISP that a special character follows. You would get an error message if you attempted to use \ in the above example.

As you might guess, the Load function can be a part of an AutoLISP program. It can also be included as part of a menu to load specific programs whenever you select a menu item. You'll learn more about customizing the menu in the next chapter.

SUMMARY

I hope that you will be enticed into trying some programming on your own and learning more about AutoLISP. For a more detailed look at AutoLISP, you may want to try *The ABC's of AutoLISP* by George Omura, from SYBEX. Although AutoLISP is somewhat different from other forms of LISP, you may want to consider studying LISP as background for using AutoLISP. Versions of LISP are available for the PC, and there are a few good introductory books on LISP as well. *LISP: A Gentle Introduction to Symbolic Computation*, by David S. Touretzky (Harper & Row, 1984), and *Common LISPcraft*, by Robert Wilensky (W. W. Norton & Company), are good beginning books that cover the theory behind LISP.

In the next and final chapter of this book, you will learn how to make AutoCAD fit in with your current work environment. You will learn how you can set up menus for your specific applications as well as how to add new hatch patterns and line types. I also discuss the issues you will face when working in groups and networks.

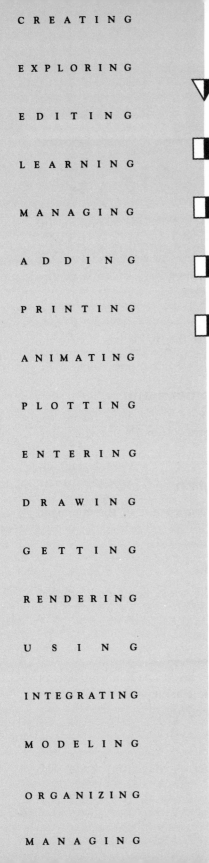

21

INTEGRATING AUTOCAD INTO YOUR PROJECTS AND ORGANIZATION

FAST TRACK

909 ▶ To edit the AutoCAD menu

First make a backup copy of the Acad.MNU file, found in the AutoCAD Support directory. Next, open the Acad.MNU file with a text editor. Make your changes, then save the file as an ASCII or DOS text file.

910 ▶ To load a menu

Enter **Menu** at the command prompt. At the dialog box, locate the menu you wish to load and double-click on it.

916 ▶ To have a menu option call another menu

Include **$S=**_menu_group_name_ or **$P=**_menu_group_name_ before you enter the command keystrokes of the menu option. Be sure you follow the _menu_group_name_ with a space.

919 ▶ To pause for input in a menu option

Include the backslash (\) where you want a pause in the command keystroke sequence of your menu item.

920 ▶ To include long lines in the menu

Use a plus sign at the end of a command keystroke line to indicate that the line continues to the next line.

924 ▶ To create a cascading menu

Start the bracketed label with –>, as in [–>line]. The following lines of the menu group will be part of the cascading menu until AutoCAD encounters <– in a menu label, as in [<– Sketch].

925 ▶ To add an icon menu item

In the icon menu group (***ICON), create a submenu group by adding a title with two asterisks, as in **MYICON**. Start your submenu group with a bracketed label. The next several lines should start with the slide name in brackets, as in [*myslide*], or [*slidlib(myslide)*] if the slide is part of a slide library, followed by the command keystrokes of the menu item.

932 ▶ To add AutoLISP code in a menu

Start by adding a menu label in square brackets, as you normally would for a menu option. Then add your AutoLISP program code. If the program takes several lines, be sure to end each line except the last with a plus sign.

942 ▶ To create a custom line type

Enter **Linetype** at the command prompt. Enter **C** ↵, then enter the name for your new line type. Select the Acad.LIN file at the dialog box, or enter a name for a new line type file, then enter a description for your new line type. Finally, enter the length of each line segment of your new line type, including blank lengths, separated by commas. For example, if you enter **1.5,–1.5** for the line type pattern, you will have a line type that draws a line for 1.5 units then skips 1.5 units before it draws another line segment.

946 ▶ To create a hatch pattern

While in DOS, open the Acad.PAT file, then add your hatch pattern description to the end of the file. The description starts with the name of your pattern preceded with an asterisk, as in ***mypattern**. The following lines describe the line pattern groups. Each group starts with the angle of the line pattern, followed by the origin coordinates, the offset coordinates, and finally the line pattern. The line pattern is described in the same way as a line type pattern.

The reason why microcomputers are so popular may well be their adaptability. Some microcomputer programs, such as AutoCAD, offer a high degree of flexibility and customization, allowing you to tailor the software's look and feel to your requirements. In this final chapter, you will examine how AutoCAD can be made to fit into your work-group and office environment.

The first part of the chapter shows how you can adapt AutoCAD to fit your particular needs. You will learn how to customize AutoCAD by modifying your menus and how to create custom macros for commands that your work group will use frequently. You will also explore how to use other programs to control AutoCAD.

The second part deals with general issues of using AutoCAD in an office. I discuss the problems you may encounter when using AutoCAD in a work group and how to deal with them. I also discuss the management of AutoCAD projects.

LOOKING AT THE MENU STRUCTURE

In *Chapter 19*, we introduced you to the keyboard macro as a way of aiding command selection. A screen menu is like a macro, in that it allows you to create predetermined strings of commands and responses. For example, you could create a screen menu item that automatically sets a new angle for the cursor. This might be useful if you find that you frequently need to work at an angle other than one of 0 or 90°. Or you might create a macro that "remembers" specific coordinates for you. You can also use the screen menu to provide predetermined responses to command prompts. For example, if you have a list of layer names you use all the time, you could turn that list into a screen menu from which you can pick names rather than enter them from the keyboard.

▼ **NOTE**

You can use the Windows Write word processor to edit the AutoCAD menu file. Be sure you open and save the file as a text file, not as a Write file.

Modifying the AutoCAD menu or creating your own is the easiest way to customize AutoCAD. It is also a way to give others in your work group easy access to specialized functions you might create for your office. Before you try this, however, you should be familiar with the way AutoCAD commands work. To write custom menu files, you must also understand the menu structure. In this section we will explore this structure and show you how to create your own menu.

We will concentrate on creating pull-down and side menus, although the digitizing-tablet menu and the puck and mouse-button definitions can be created and modified by the methods described here.

KNOWING WHICH MENU FILE TO EDIT

When AutoCAD first opens a drawing file, it looks on the hard disk for a file called Acad.MNX. This file contains the menu you see displayed on the screen. It also contains the information AutoCAD needs to operate the digitizing-tablet menu and the commands on the buttons of your puck or mouse.

This Acad.MNX file originates as an ASCII file that contains the menu options in an easily editable form. The ASCII file has the name *Acad.MNU*. The Acad.MNX file is the *compiled* version of the Acad.MNU file, which means that it is in a form that AutoCAD can load and read quickly. You can make modifications to the Acad.MNU file, but not to the Acad.MNX file. If you want to customize your menu, you must work on Acad.MNU. If you modify Acad.MNU in any way, AutoCAD will detect this modification and automatically compile Acad.MNU into a new Acad.MNX file when you open a new drawing file. Once the file is compiled, AutoCAD uses only the compiled version.

You can also create other menu files with different names. They must always have the .MNU extension, however. You load an alternate menu by using Utility ➤ Menu. When you load a menu with a name other than *Acad*, it is compiled and the compiled version is given the file extension .MNX. The next time this new menu is loaded, AutoCAD uses the compiled version.

CREATING YOUR FIRST MENU

Before I get into the whys and wherefores of menus, try the following exercise to create a simple menu.

Mymenu.MNU

1. Using the Windows Notepad application, create an ASCII file called **Mymenu.MNU** containing the following:

   ```
   ***Screen
   **first
   (My Menu)
   (Line)^c^cline

   (page 2)$s=second
   **second 2
   (Arc-SED)^c^carc \e \d
   (Rotate90)^c^c(if  (not c:r90)+
   (defun c:r90 (/ ss1)(setq ss1 (ssget))+
   (command "rotate" ss1 "" pause "90") ) );r90
   (page 1)$s=first
   ```

2. Enter ↵ at the end of the last line.

3. Be sure you place this file in your AutoCAD directory.

Once you've stored the file, you've got your first menu. You may have noticed some familiar items among the lines you entered. The menu contains the Line and Arc commands. It also contains the R90 macro you worked on in the previous chapters. This time, the macro is broken into shorter lines.

Now let's see how the menu works in AutoCAD.

LOADING A MENU

In the following exercise, you will load the menu you created previously, then test it out. The procedure for loading menus described here is the same for all menus, regardless of their source.

1. Open an AutoCAD file and enter **menu** ↵ or click on Utility ➤ Menu from the root menu.

2. At the Select Menu File dialog box, locate Mymenu.MNU and double-click on it. Your screen should look similar to Figure 21.1.

3. Click on Line from the side menu. Notice that the Line command starts.

4. Draw a line across the middle of the screen.

5. Pick page 2 from the side menu. The menu changes to the one shown in Figure 21.2.

6. Now pick Arc-SED from the menu. The Arc command starts.

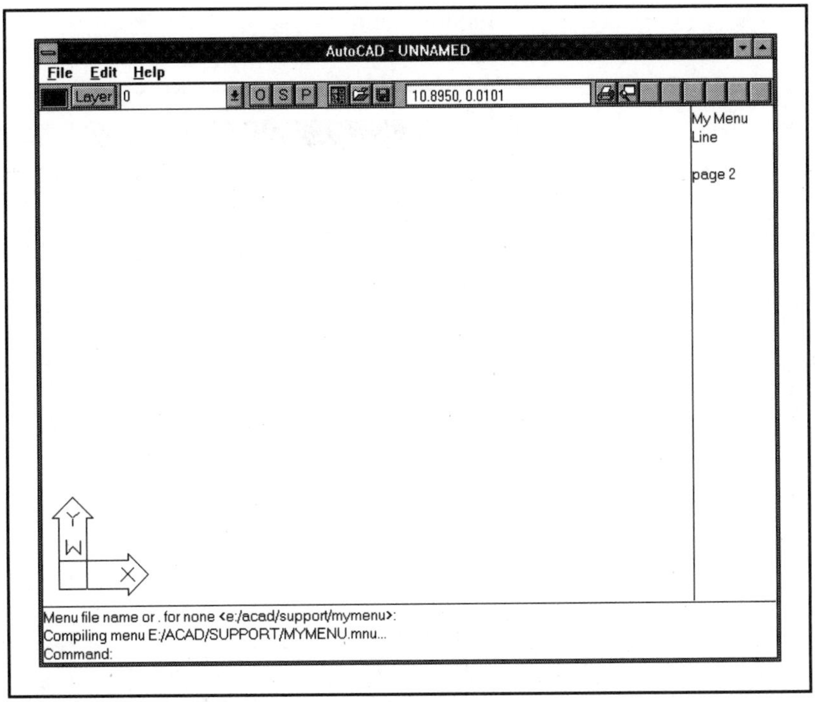

Figure 21.1: The Mymenu menu

7. At the **arc Center/<Start point>:** prompt, pick the beginning of the arc.
8. At the **End point:** prompt, pick the end of the arc.
9. At the **Direction from start point:** prompt, pick a direction for the arc. The arc appears.
10. Try the Rotate90 option and rotate some of the objects on the screen.
11. Pick page 1 from the menu and you will return to the first menu.

▼ NOTE

You might notice that the second button on your mouse does not respond. This is because your menu does not include a ***AUX menu group. The standard AutoCAD menu contains an auxiliary group that defines the second mouse button as ↵.

In just eleven lines of text, you created a menu that contains virtually every tool used to build menus. Now let's take a detailed look at how menus work.

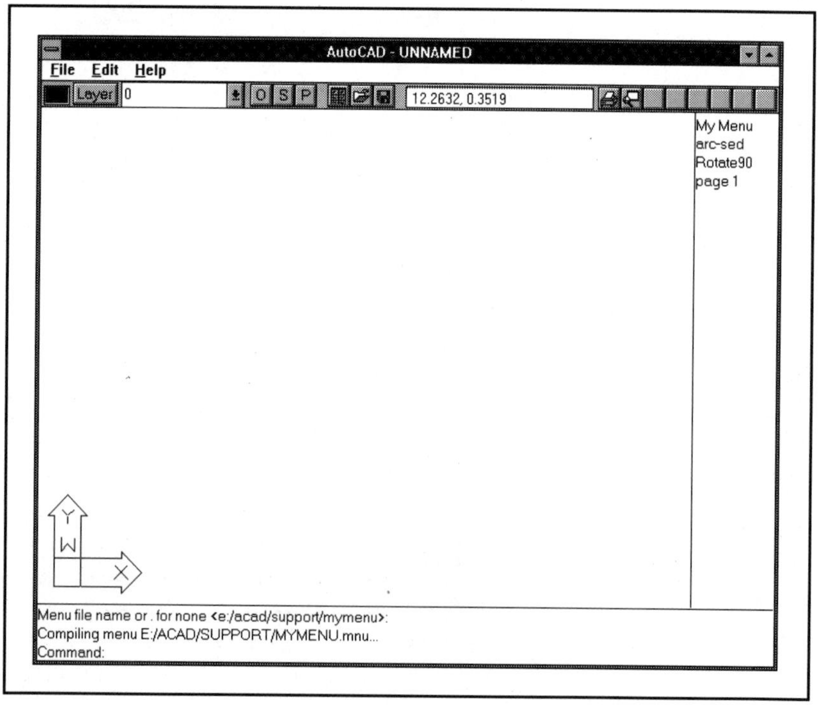

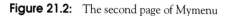

Figure 21.2: The second page of Mymenu

UNDERSTANDING THE ACAD.MNU FILE

The Acad.MNU file is a list of menu items containing the commands related to the items. There are six major menu groups:

- *Side* or *screen* group. Controls the side screen menu. (You created a side menu in your exercise.)

- *Pull-down* or *pop-up* group. Controls pull-down menus.

- *Icon* group. Controls the display of icon menus.

- *Tablet* group. Controls the tablet menu.

- *Button* group. Controls the buttons on your mouse or puck.

- *Auxiliary* group. Controls optional equipment, such as special keyboards, that we will not cover in this book.

Figure 21.3 shows schematically how the file is structured.

Most of the menu items in each menu group act like keyboard input; that is, they contain the keystrokes you would normally enter to start a command or select an option. Additionally, some items call up other menus.

File organization is linear: each menu group follows the next and starts with the group name preceded by three asterisks. Figure 21.4 shows the beginning of the button, auxiliary, and pull-down menu groups in the Acad.MNU file.

The other menu groups are set up in similar ways. Side, icon, and pull-down menu options usually start with the name of the menu option in brackets. This is done when you want to distinguish the actual word that appears on the screen menu from the rest of the menu instructions. As you browse the Acad.MNU file, you might notice that some side menu items are not bracketed. If the menu instructions and the words that appear on the menu are the same in the side menu, the text within the brackets is not needed.

Icon menus start with the name of the slide library and slide name in brackets to identify which slide to display for a particular icon menu option. We will discuss these points in detail next.

▼ NOTE

Pop0 is the first of as many as 16 pull-down menu groups—one group for each pull-down menu. The pull-down, icon, and side menu groups can have submenus.

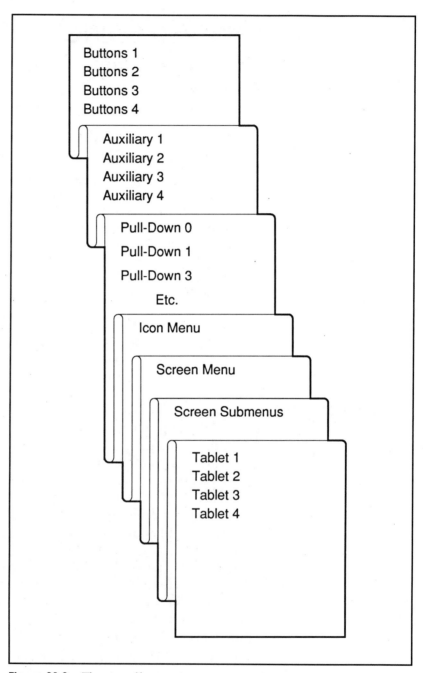

Figure 21.3:   The menu file structure

```
***BUTTONS1
;
$p0=*
^C^C
^B
^O
^G
^D
^E
^T

***BUTTONS2
$p0=*

***AUX1
;
$p0=*
^C^C
^B
^O
^G
^D
^E
^T

***AUX2
$p0=*

***POP0
[Osnap]
[Center]_center
[Endpoint]_endp
[Insert]_ins
[Intersection]_int
[Midpoint]_mid
[Nearest]_nea
[Node]_nod
[Perpendicular]_per
[Quadrant]_qua
[Tangent]_tan
[None]_non
```

Figure 21.4:   The beginning of the Acad.MNU file

UNDERSTANDING THE SIDE MENU

This section shows you how a typical submenu from the screen menu group is put together. In the Acad.MNU file, the Draw submenu looks like Figure 21.5.

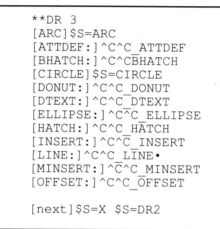

```
**DR 3
[ARC]$S=ARC
[ATTDEF:]^C^C_ATTDEF
[BHATCH:]^C^CBHATCH
[CIRCLE]$S=CIRCLE
[DONUT:]^C^C_DONUT
[DTEXT:]^C^C_DTEXT
[ELLIPSE:]^C^C_ELLIPSE
[HATCH:]^C^C_HATCH
[INSERT:]^C^C_INSERT
[LINE:]^C^C_LINE•
[MINSERT:]^C^C_MINSERT
[OFFSET:]^C^C_OFFSET

[next]$S=X $S=DR2
```

Figure 21.5: The Draw submenu

Each item on the list starts with a word enclosed in brackets. Each word within the brackets is an option on the Draw menu. If you were to remove everything else, you would have the Draw menu as it appears on the screen with the exception of the Last, Draw, and Edit options at the bottom (see Figure 21.6).

The text that follows the item in brackets conveys instructions to AutoCAD in the form of a special code. The code **$S=** tells AutoCAD to display another submenu. The word that follows this code is the name of the submenu to be displayed.

Calling Submenus

If you look at the line containing the Draw option in the beginning of the **screen section, two menus are called for, one named X and another named DR.

(DRAW)$S=X $S=DR

▼ NOTE

In the Mymenu exercise, you created two submenus called **first** and **second**. Within these submenus, you also had the item [page2]$s=second. This line instructs AutoCAD to go to the **second submenu.

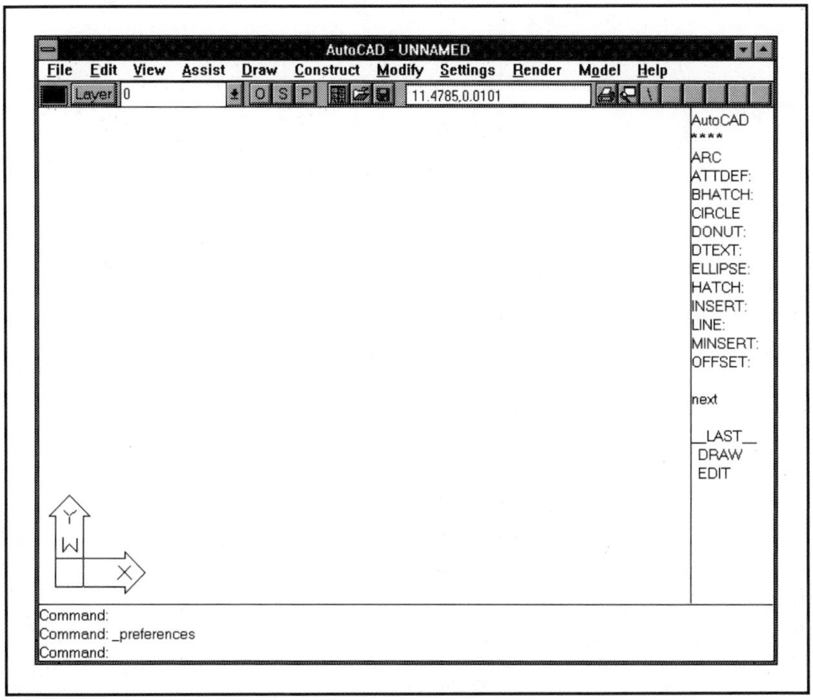

Figure 21.6: The Draw menu

The X submenu displays the Last, Draw, and Edit options (see Figure 21.7). The DR menu displays the rest of the Draw options. Two things are accomplished by calling these two menus together. First, by calling the **X submenu, all items from the previous menu are cleared from the screen. Most of **X is blank except for the bottom few lines. These blanks overwrite the previous menu items. If menus are not overwritten in this way, they will remain on the screen when a shorter menu, like **DR, is called.

Second, the bottom several lines of **X offer menu options that let you navigate through the menu system. As long as the next menu called does not overwrite these bottom options, they remain accessible from the screen menu.

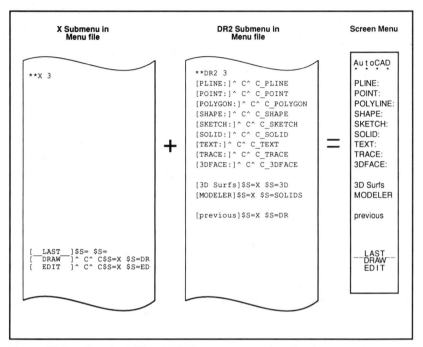

Figure 21.7: How the **X and **DR menus are combined to form one menu on the screen

Submenu names are located at the top of each submenu; they begin with two asterisks. If you look at the top of the DR submenu, you will see two asterisks followed by the letters DR. A 3 follows the letters DR. This number tells AutoCAD to begin displaying the Draw menu on the third line of the menu area. This way, it won't overwrite the two top menu options that help you get back to the opening menu and access the Osnap overrides (see Figure 21.7).

Calling Commands

▼ NOTE

Ctrl-C is typed into the Acad.MNU file as a caret symbol (^) followed by a **C**, not as an actual Ctrl-C key sequence.

Where menu options call commands, you might notice the ^c^c at the beginning of the menu instructions. For example, the Offset menu line ends with ^C^COFFSET. The two Ctrl-C's at the beginning of this text cancel any command that is currently operative. The Offset command follows. This last sequence is written just as it would be entered through the keyboard. Two cancels are issued in case you are in a command that has two levels, such as the DIM command.

You may also notice that there is no space between the second Ctrl-C and the word *OFFSET*. A space on the menu would be the same as a ↵. If there were a space between the two, a ↵ would be entered between the last Ctrl-C and the Offset command, causing the command sequence to misstep.

Another way to indicate a ↵ is by using the semicolon, as in the line

```
(continue)^C^CLINE;;
```

This is how the Continue option appears in the Line submenu. The two semicolons following the word *LINE* tell AutoCAD to start the LINE command, then press ↵ twice to begin a line from the endpoint of the last line entered. AutoCAD automatically issues a single ↵ at the end of a menu line. However, in this case, you want ↵ twice, so they must be represented as semicolons.

Also, a space must be used after a menu call, as in

```
(DIM:)$S=X $S=DIM ^C^CDIM
```

where the calls to the X menu and the Dim menu are each followed by a space. This is the only case where the space and the semicolon have different meanings; otherwise they are interchangeable.

Pausing for User Input

Another symbol used in the menu file is the backslash. This is used when a pause is required for user input. For example, the Arc-SED option you used in your exercise starts the Arc command then pauses for your input.

```
(Arc-SED)^c^carc \e \d
```

The space between **^c^carc** and the backslash (\) has the effect of pressing the **spacebar**. The backslash indicates a pause to allow you to select the starting endpoint for the arc. Once you have picked a point, the **e** is entered to select the Endpoint option under the Arc command. The backslash is again applied to allow you to select a point. Finally, the

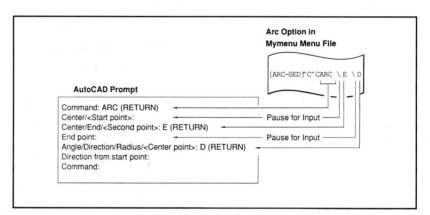

Figure 21.8: How the Arc menu item relates to the Arc command

d is entered to select the Direction option under the Arc command. (The spaces help enter the selection in AutoCAD.) Figure 21.8 illustrates this.

Using the Plus Sign for Long Lines

As you browse through the Acad.MNU file, you may notice that many of the lines have a plus sign (**+**) at the end. The length of each line in the menu file is limited to about 80 characters. You can break a line into two or more lines by adding a plus sign at the end of the line that continues, as in

```
(Rotate90)^c^c(if (not c:r90)+
(defun c:r90 (/ ss1)(setq ss1 (ssget))+
(command "rotate" ss1 "" pause "90") ) );r90
```

This example shows how you would include the R90 AutoLISP macro in a menu. Everything is entered just as it would be with the keyboard. The plus is used for the continuation of the menu line to the next line, and the semicolon is used in place of ↵.

UNDERSTANDING THE PULL-DOWN MENUS

The pull-down menu group is quite similar to the screen menu group, with some minor differences. Try the following exercise to create a small pull-down menu.

1. Make a copy of Mymenu.MNU and call the copy **Mymenu2.MNU**. Next open the file and make changes to it so it looks as follows:

   ```
   ***POP1
   (/MMy Menu)
   (/LLine)^c^cline
   (--)
   (->/oMore)
   (/AArc-SED)^c^carc \e \d
   (<-/RRotate90)^c^c(if  (not c:r90)+
   (defun c:r90 (/ ss1)(setq ss1 (ssget))+
   (command "rotate" ss1 "" pause "90") ) );r90
   (/GMake Group)(setq *ssglobe (ssget))
   (/SSelect Group)!*ssglobe
   ```

2. Add a blank line at the very top of the file. If the space is not present, AutoCAD will display the menu on the side menu area.

3. Open AutoCAD and load Mymenu2.MNU the same way you loaded Mymenu.MNU. Issue the MENU command, then locate and select mymenu2. After it has been loaded, highlight the menu bar and pull down the Mymenu2 menu. The pull-down menu will look like Figure 21.9. Notice that the two new options Make Group and Select Group appear at the bottom.

4. Click on More, and the Arc-SED and Rotate90 options appear as a cascading menu.

5. Experiment with these options to see how they work. Make Group will group objects together. Select Group will allow you to select the group you made with Make Group at any **select object** prompt.

▼ WARNING

I've shown the use of Ssget in the menu example to create groups of entities in AutoCAD. Limit your use of groups to a reasonable number. See **Chapter 20** regarding memory limits and the use of selection sets.

Pull-down menus act like side menus, with a few key differences. Let's see what makes the pull-down menus tick.

To begin with, the first item in the menu group becomes the menu title in the menu bar. You can use up to 14 characters in the title bar's title. Other options in the menu can contain up to eighty characters instead of the restrictive eight characters for the side menu.

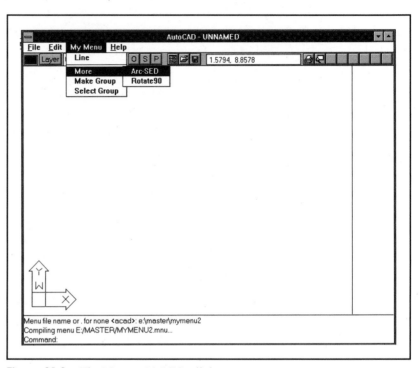

Figure 21.9: The Mymenu2.MNU pull-down menu

Like the side menus, pull-down menus can also contain submenus in the form of cascading menus. There are 10 pull-down menu groups currently in the Acad.MNU file (11 if you include the Osnap pop-up menu), but there can be as many as 16. The Help pull-down menu is built into AutoCAD and cannot be edited. Also, the first 8 items in the Edit menu are hard-coded into AutoCAD. If you look in your Acad.MNU file, the pull-down menu sections appear as shown in Figure 21.10.

Notice the three asterisks preceding the menu group names. Each pull-down menu group corresponds to one of the items on the menu bar. The ***POP0 group is a special group that pops up near the cursor when you hold down the **Shift** key and press the second button on your pointing device. ***POP1 is the pull-down farthest to the left, ***POP2 is the one next to it, and so on. POP1 and POP2 are appended to a set of standard menu options like File ➤ Open and Edit ➤ Copy Objects. These standard options always appear in a menu regardless of what is in the .MNU file.

Adding Accelerator Keys

You will notice that the option names in brackets start with a forward hash mark and an extra letter. These tell AutoCAD which character in the bracketed name is to be used as an accelerator key. In most cases, they are the first character of the word, as in /NNew.... This turns the N into the accelerator key for the New option. But it isn't unusual to see a different character at the beginning, as in /vRecover. Here, it's the lowercase *v* in the word *Recover* that becomes the accelerator key.

```
                  Write - ACAD.MNU
 File   Edit   Find   Character   Paragraph   Document   Help
 ***POP2
 [/EEdit]
 [--]
 [->/DDDE]
   [/SExport Selection Set]^C^C^P(if (null ddesset) (xload "ddeads"))(ddesset);^P
   [/BExport Blocks ]^C^C^P(if (null ddesset) (xload "ddeads"))(ddeblocks);^P
   [/EExport Drawing]^C^C^P(if (null ddedrawing) (xload "ddeads"))(ddedrawing);^P
   [--]
   [/IImport Changes]^C^C^P(if (null ddeupdate) (xload "ddeads"))(ddeupdate);^P
   [/DDialog...      ]^C^C^P(if (null ddedialog) (xload "ddeads"))(ddedialog);^P
   [--]
   [/NNo Filters    ]^C^C^P(if (null ddeformat) (xload "ddeads"))(ddeformat 1);^P
   [/1Attribute Filter 1 ]^C^C^P(if (null ddeformat) (xload "ddeads"))(ddeformat 2);^P
   [/2Attribute Filter 2 ]^C^C^P(if (null ddeformat) (xload "ddeads"))(ddeformat 3);^P
   [--]
   [<-/UUnload DDE    ]^C^C^P(xunload "ddeads");^P
 [--]
 [->/SSelect]
   [/PPoint]$M=$(if,$(getvar,cmdactive),,_select;)\
   [/WWindow]$M=$(if,$(getvar,cmdactive),,_select;)_window
   [/LLast]$M=$(if,$(getvar,cmdactive),,_select;)_last
   [/CCrossing]$M=$(if,$(getvar,cmdactive),,_select;)_crossing
   [/AAll]$M=$(if,$(getvar,cmdactive),,_select;)_all
   [/FFence]$M=$(if,$(getvar,cmdactive),,_select;)_fence
   [/oWPolygon]$M=$(if,$(getvar,cmdactive),,_select;)_wpolygon
   [/yCPolygon]$M=$(if,$(getvar,cmdactive),,_select;)_cpolygon
   [/dAdd]$M=$(if,$(getvar,cmdactive),,_select;)_add
   [/RRemove]$M=$(if,$(getvar,cmdactive),,_select;)_remove
   [/MMultiple]$M=$(if,$(getvar,cmdactive),,_select;)_multiple
   [<-/ePrevious]$M=$(if,$(getvar,cmdactive),,_select;)_previous
 Page 1
```

Figure 21.10: The beginning of the pull-down menu group and the equivalent pop-up menu on the screen

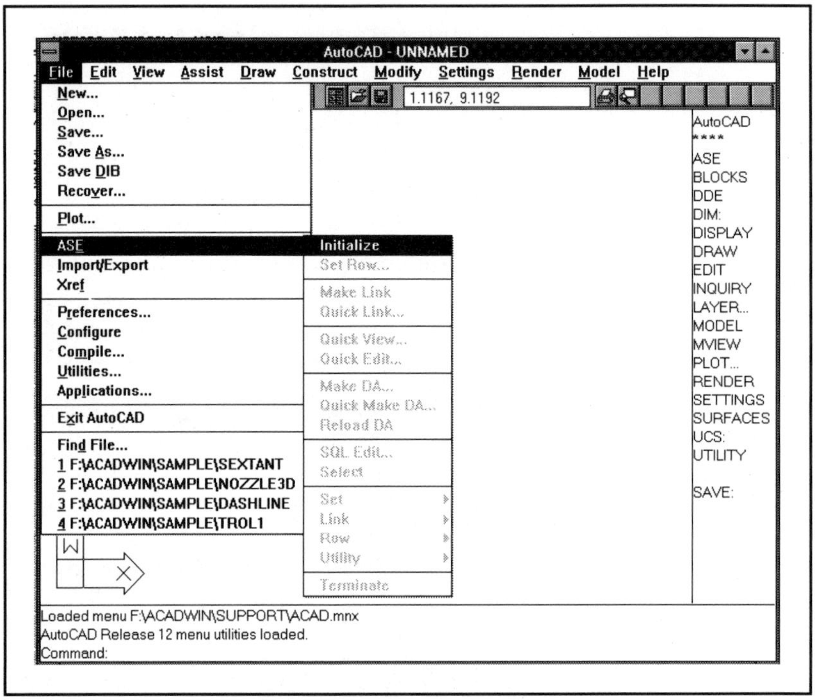

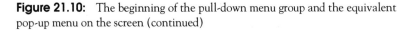

Figure 21.10: The beginning of the pull-down menu group and the equivalent pop-up menu on the screen (continued)

Accelerator keys are not required, but if you like using them, they can be quite helpful in speeding up command access.

Creating a Cascading Menu

Look at the DDE option in the ***POP2 group. It starts with a hyphen and a greater-than sign (**>**). This is the way you indicate a menu item that opens a cascading menu. Everything that follows the [–>/DDDE] menu item will appear in the cascading menu (see Figure 21.10). To indicate the end of the cascading menu, you include a less-than sign (**<**) and a hyphen, as in the [<–?UUnload DDE] menu item further down. Anything beyond this item appears in the main part of the menu. If the last item in a cascading menu is also the last item in the menu group, you must use two less-than–hyphen combos in a row, as in [<–<–/U-Unload DDE].

If you look at the modifications you made to the Mymenu2.MNU file, you will see that the More item included –> and that Rotate90 included <–. This turned the two items Arc-SED and Rotate90 into cascading menu options.

Placing Blanks in Pull-Down Menus

When you converted the Mymenu2.MNU file into a pull-down menu, you had to remove blanks in the menu and replace them with double hyphens. Unlike side menus, pull-down menus do not allow blank menu items.

Two additional options not present in other menus are available in pull-down menus. One is the *double-hyphen* symbol, which is used to divide groups of items in a menu and will expand to fill the entire width of the pull-down menu with hyphens. The other option is the *tilde* symbol (~). If the tilde precedes a bracketed option name, that option will be dimmed when displayed; when picked, it will have no effect. If you have used other programs that offer pull-down menus, you are probably familiar with this effect. When you see a dimmed menu item, it usually means that the option is not valid under the current command.

Placing Bitmap Icons in Pull-Down Menus

The Windows version of AutoCAD allows you to place bitmap icons in the pull-down menus. These icons are hard-coded into the AutoCAD program, so you can only use those icons that are available as a resource to AutoCAD. To make matters more confusing, those icons don't have easily recognizable names. Instead, they use an alphanumeric code. For example, the code for the Arc icon is X3. To include this icon as a pull-down menu option, you would use [^x3^]. For clarity, you can include the name of the icon as in [^X3^Arc]. The word *Arc* is ignored and only the icon is displayed in the menu. Table 21.1 shows the icon codes and the commands they are associated with.

You can add more icons to AutoCAD by editing the ACAD.DLL file with a Windows Resource editor like Borland's Resource Workshop. Be sure you include the name of any new icons in the Stringtable section of the resource file.

Table 21.1:   Icon Codes for Pull-Down Menus

CODE = COMMAND			
X1 = Line	X11 = Hatch	X21 = Array	X31 = Block
X2 = Circle	X12 = Faces 3D	X22 = Offset	X32 = Fillet
X3 = Arc	X13 = Erase	X23 = Divide	X33 = Measure
X4 = UCS	X14 = Move	X24 = Polyline Edit	X34 = Entity Mod
X5 = Polyline	X15 = Rotate	X25 = Mirror	X35 = Break
X6 = Donut	X16 = Scale	X26 = Insert	X36 = Extend
X7 = Ellipse	X17 = Stretch	X27 = Point	X37 = Align
X8 = Polygon	X18 = Trim	X28 = Rectangle	X38 = Change
X9 = 3D Surfaces	X19 = Chamfer	X29 = Text	X39 = Explode
X10 = AME	X20 = Copy	X30 = Dimensions	X40 = Edit Dimensions

ACCESSING THE POP-UP MENU AND OTHER BUTTON OPTIONS

▼ NOTE

The Auxiliary menu groups serve the same functions as the Button menus, but are intended for computers that have built-in mouse support, like the Apple Macintosh and Sun SPARCstations.

You may wonder why AutoCAD provides several Button groups when you are probably going to use only one pointing device. The reason is that if you have a multi-button mouse or digitizer puck, you can have up to four sets of button definitions. One set of definitions might let you set the snap, grid, and ortho modes, while another set may issue your favorite commands. These other sets of button definitions can be accessed using the **Shift, Ctrl**, and combined **Ctrl-Shift** keys in conjunction with a button. You've already used the **Shift** key in conjunction with the second mouse button to open the pop-up menu. This works because the second button menu group in the Acad.MNU file looks like this:

```
***BUTTONS2
$p0=*
```

You may recall that in the screen menu, you call a submenu using the $s= code. This button option uses a similar code to call the POP0 menu group. The *p* in the $*p*0 indicates a pull-down menu. The 0 indicates which of the pull-down menus to access. The asterisk is a code used to open a pull-down menu. The asterisk code is not needed or used in the side menu, because side menus are always in view. If you replace the 0 with 1, the File menu will pop down when you press **Shift**-*second button*.

If you want to add more functionality to your mouse or digitizer puck, create two more button groups, each with a definition for each button on your device. For a mouse, you may have only one or two options for each group. Still, this can add up. The following shows some examples of what you might add to your menu to provide more functions to your mouse buttons, if you have a three-button mouse.

```
***BUTTONS1
(plain old RETURN);

***BUTTONS2
(shift 2)$p0=*
(shift 3)^c^cline

***BUTTONS3
(ctrl 2)^c^c
(crtl 3)u

***BUTTONS4
(ctrl-shift 2)^o
(ctrl-shift 3)^b
```

In this example, the first button group just contains a semicolon for ↵. The second group includes the Osnap pop-up menu and the line command for the third button. Both of these functions are accessed with the **Shift**-*button* combination. The third group supplies the cancel and undo options with a **Ctrl**-*button* combination. The fourth group toggles the ortho (**Ctrl-O**) and snap (**Ctrl-B**) modes with a **Ctrl-Shift**-*button* combination. If you have a two-button mouse, only the first item of each button group will be available. Still, four options is not bad for just two buttons.

UNDERSTANDING ICON MENUS

When I discuss Icon menus, I don't mean the icons that appear in the toolbar or in the pull-down menus. Icon menus are actually dialog boxes that display options in an array of icons, e.g., the hatch options. Icon menus operate in a slightly different way from other menus. Each icon menu is actually a submenu of the icon menu group. In this regard, the icon menu group is similar to the screen menu group. Each icon menu subgroup has a name that is preceded by two asterisks. The subgroup name is followed by a label in brackets. This label appears as the title of the icon menu.

The subsequent menu items are labeled in a slightly different way from most other menu groups. Instead of starting with the name of the option as it might appear on the screen, icon menu options begin with the slide library file name and slide name in brackets. The two icon submenus are shown in Figure 21.11, including portions of their screen counterparts.

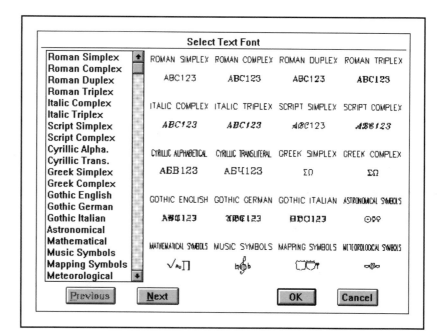

Figure 21.11: The 3D objects and fonts icon submenus, as seen from the Acad.MNU file and on the screen

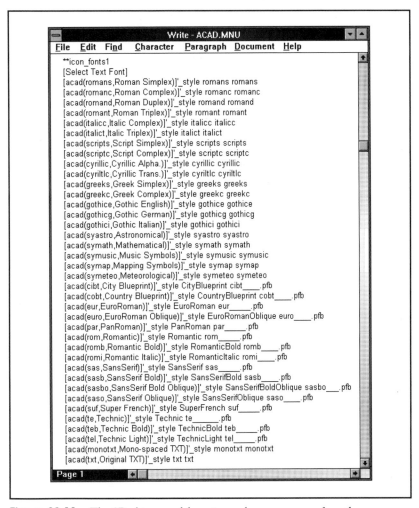

Figure 21.11: The 3D objects and fonts icon submenus, as seen from the Acad.MNU file and on the screen (continued)

Notice that in the 3D objects icon menu, the name of the slide associated with an icon is entered as it would be with the VSLIDE command: the slide library name is followed by the slide name in parentheses.

An icon menu can be called from any other menu by using the code $I=. This code serves the same purpose as $S= in the side menus and $Pn= in the pull-down menus. For example, the Select Text Font icon menu in the sample above is called from the Draw ➤ Text ➤ Set Style... pull-down menu with the following line:

(/SSet Style...)$I=icon_fonts1 $I=*

Notice that the name between the square brackets in the Icon fonts menu adds an extra name to each slide. If you want to show an alternate name in the list box of the icon menu, you include the alternate with the slide name. There are several ways you can use the bracketed portion of the Icon menu.

[*slide name*] displays *slide name* in the list box and displays the slide in the icon menu.

[*slide name,label*] displays *label* in the list box and the slide in the icon menu.

[*slide library(slide name)*] displays *slide name* in the list box and the slide from *slide library* in the icon menu.

[*slide library (slide name,label)*] displays *label* in the list box and the slide from *slide library* in the icon menu.

[*blank*] displays a blank in the list box and a blank in the icon menu. This can be used as a separator.

[*label*] displays *label* in the list box and a blank in the icon menu. This can be used for options that do not require an icon, such as Exit, Previous, or Next.

Also notice that the first item in the submenu is not followed by any instructions or commands. The first item is always the text that appears as the icon menu title (see Figure 21.11).

UNDERSTANDING THE TABLET MENU

A tablet menu is written the same way as a screen menu. The only real difference between the two is in the way the file is presented to you. The tablet menu is set up as rows and columns of boxes, with each box containing a menu item, while the on-screen menu is a long list. It is fairly easy to see how the list structure relates to the screen menu. To understand how the list is converted to the rows and columns of the tablet menu, think of the tablet menu as a list starting from the upper left and moving to the right. When the top row of the tablet menu is full, the next row continues the list, and so on, until each item on the list has a box. A tablet menu containing 200 menu items might appear on the tablet as 25 columns and 8 rows. In fact, this is exactly how the customizable area of your tablet menu template is set up. Figure 21.12 is provided to help you find the corresponding position in the menu file.

You can have up to four tablet menu areas. Your Acad.MNU file uses three of them, reserving the first tablet area for your custom menu items. If you open your Acad.MNU file and go to the heading ***Tablet1, you will see the list shown in Figure 21.13.

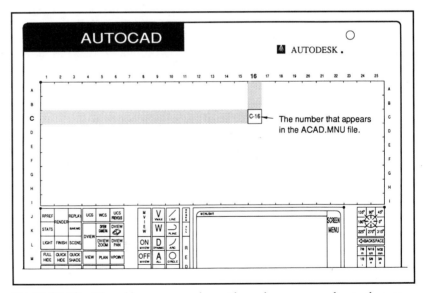

Figure 21.12: The tablet menu template with numbers corresponding to those in Acad.MNU

```
***TABLET1
[A-1]
[A-2]
[A-3]
[A-4]
[A-5]
[A-6]
[A-7]
[A-8]
[A-9]
[A-10]
[A-11]
[A-12]
[A-13]
[A-14]
[A-15]
[A-16]
[A-17]
[A-18]
[A-19]
[A-20]
[A-21]
[A-22]
[A-23]
[A-24]
[A-25]
```

Figure 21.13: The beginning of the tablet menu group

This list continues to T1-25. There are 225 spaces total, which are reserved for your custom menu items in the area at the top of your digitizing tablet.

Each number on the menu template corresponds to a number in brackets, less the *T1* prefix. If you want to add an item to the custom menu area, find the square you want to assign it to, then add the appropriate text to the corresponding line in the tablet menu.

USING AUTOLISP WITH MENUS

As you browse the Acad.MNU file, you will notice that AutoLISP is used frequently as part of menu options. You even included some AutoLISP when you wrote the Mymenu.MNU file at the beginning of this chapter. Remember that, for the most part, menu options act like macros that are read verbatim by AutoCAD, as if they were entered from the keyboard. So it is perfectly legal to include AutoLISP in your menu. In fact, I know some users who embed their treasured AutoLISP programs in the menu as a way to encrypt them. (Since AutoCAD compiles menus into a binary form, .MNX files cannot be viewed or deciphered.)

Another way to use AutoLISP with menus is to create a file containing menu-specific AutoLISP programs in a file with the .MNL extension. Such a file will be automatically loaded with its menu counterpart. For example, you could have a file called Mymenu.MNL containing the R90 AutoLISP macro. Whenever you load the Mymenu.MNU or .MNX file, Mymenu.MNL will automatically load with it, giving you access to the R90 Macro. This method can help you manage and organize any AutoLISP program code you want to include with a menu.

You should also be aware that there is an AutoLISP function that can call a menu. The *Menucmd* function calls an AutoCAD menu group using a code similar to the *$S=* code. For example, if you want to open the File pull-down menu using AutoLISP, you would include the following expression in your AutoLISP program.

```
(menucmd "p3=*")
```

Notice that the dollar sign is left out (remember that the asterisk opens a menu). To get to a screen menu, the Offset menu for example, you would include the following:

```
(menucmd "s=offset")
```

In summary, the codes to remember when writing a menu file are the dollar sign, which tells AutoCAD the menu group you want; the equals sign, which calls other screen menus; the backslash, which pauses for data entry; the semicolon, which signifies a ↵; and the plus sign, for long menu items. Also remember that submenu names start with double asterisks and that the optional number that follows determines the line on which the submenu begins. Menu group names start with three asterisks. Everything else, including the **spacebar**, works as a standard command entry through the keyboard.

▼
■
■
■
■

Auto-Repeat
and Single Selections

In some graphical interfaces, when you select a command or option from a menu, that option remains active until you select another one. You can simulate this mode of operation in AutoCAD by forcing AutoCAD to continually repeat a command selected from a menu. This is done by preceding the menu instructions with an asterisk, as in the following example:

(Erase)*^c^cerase

Whenever you click on this option, the Erase command will be active continually until you select another command from the menu or you press **Ctrl-C**.

Another option common to other graphical interfaces is to allow only a single selection when you click on an object. In AutoCAD, this can be accomplished with the Single selection option. Added to the previous example, the Erase menu option would look like this:

(Erase)*^c^cerase si

If you've ever used Release 9 or 10 of AutoCAD, you know the effects of these two options, since they are integrated into the standard AutoCAD menu of those two versions. In fact, a third option that is used in releases 9 and 10 is called *Auto*. Auto causes AutoCAD to use a window or crossing window selection mode if no object is clicked on. The Auto option is replaced by the Pickauto function in Release 12.

CUSTOMIZING THE TOOLBAR

As you work with AutoCAD, you may find that you use some commands frequently, but you become annoyed by the number of layers of menus you must go through to start those commands. You could restructure the menu using the methods described earlier, but that takes time. Fortunately, AutoCAD lets you quickly define toolbar buttons to your frequently used commands. You can add a command or even a macro to a toolbar button on the fly without having to stop your editing session.

The toolbar already has five buttons pre-defined. They are the Toolbox, Open, Save, Plot, and Zoom. You can redefine these buttons or add definitions to those empty buttons to the right of the Zoom button. The following exercise shows you how to redefine the Open button to the Copy command.

1. With AutoCAD open, move the arrow cursor to the toolbar button that shows an opening file folder and right-click on it. The AutoCAD Toolbar Button 2 dialog box opens (see Figure 21.14).

2. Double-click on the input box, then enter **\3\3copy**.

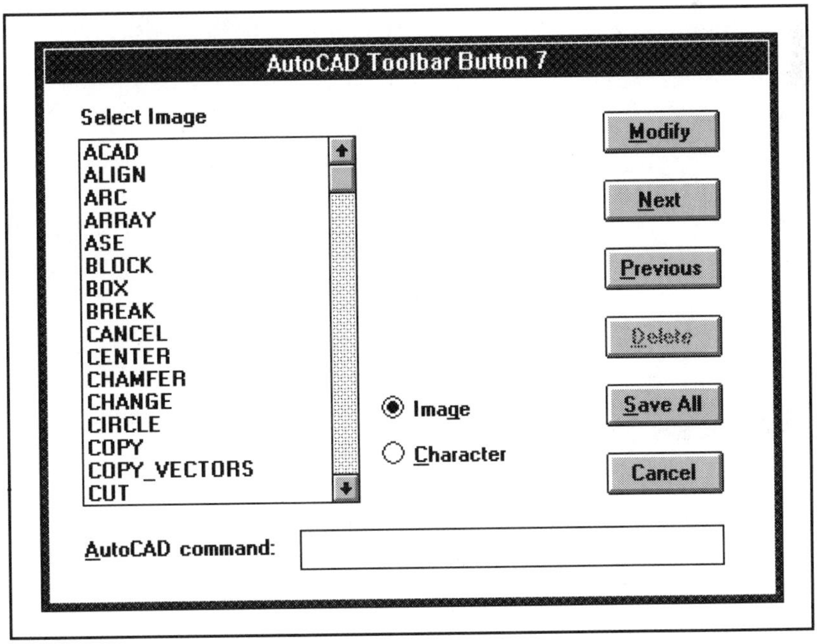

Figure 21.14: The AutoCAD Toolbar Button dialog box.

3. Click on the downward-pointing arrow next to the box labeled *Enter Resource ID*.

4. Scroll up the list until you find Copy, then click on it.

5. Click on OK.

The button now shows the Copy bitmap icon. When you click on it, the copy command is issued.

In step 2, you entered **\3\3copy**. The two **\3**'s are codes used to represent the **Ctrl-C** keystroke sequence. Two Ctrl-C's are used to cancel any command that might be active at the time of the button press. The word *copy* immediately follows. This starts the copy command. You can enter any set of keystrokes in the input box you like. Those keystrokes will in turn be entered whenever you click on the button.

In steps 3 and 4, you located the name for the copy icon. It's called a *resource ID*, because the icon is a special type of data in Windows called a resource. Resources are an integral part of the AutoCAD program. You can access these resources and even edit them with the help of some special programs. In this exercise, you simply selected one of several AutoCAD resources to be used for toolbar button number 2.

You can also use an alphabetical character instead of an icon in the toolbar button. To do this, you click on the Character ID radio button in the AutoCAD Toolbar Button dialog box. Once this is done, the options under the popup list change to uppercase characters.

CUSTOMIZING THE TOOLBOX

▼ NOTE

You can have as many as 128 buttons.

The toolbox can also be customized in a way similar to the toolbar buttons. You can right-click on the toolbox button you want to customize and the Toolbox Customization dialog box appears (see Figure 21.15). You can then enter the AutoCAD command you want to assign to the button in the input box at the bottom of the dialog box. The list box to the left lets you select from a list of bitmap icons. When you click on an icon name, the icon appears in the square toward the center of the dialog box. The Insert and Delete buttons let you add or delete buttons from the toolbox.

Unlike the toolbar, you can also control the shape of the toolbox by changing the value in the box labeled *Icons Per Row*. The default value

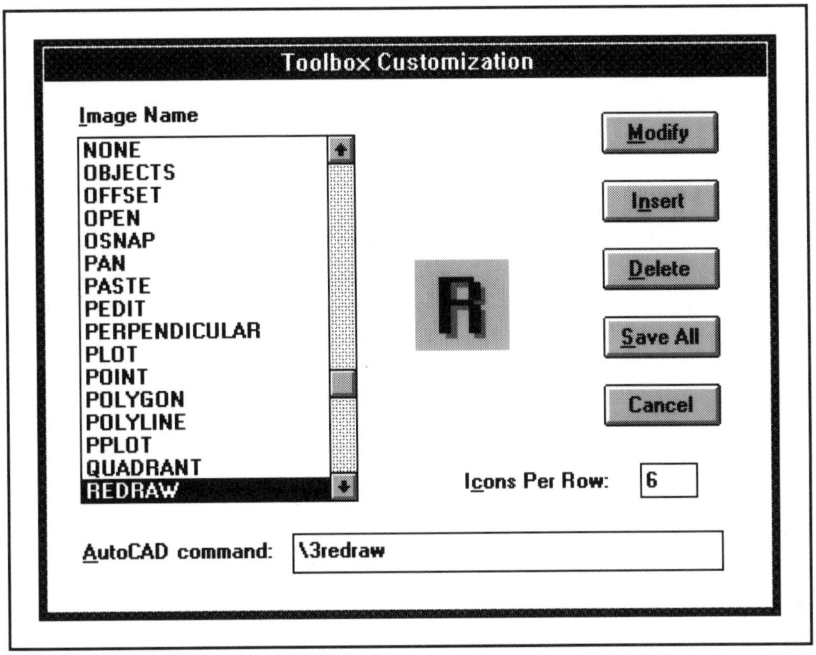

Figure 21.15:   The Toolbox Customization dialog box

is 4, which causes the toolbox to show four columns and ten rows. Changing the value to 2 changes it to a tall, skinny, two-column toolbox.

Since you can add more buttons to the toolbox, you might consider using the toolbox for your custom symbols library. You can, for example, add buttons that issue the insert command and supply the file name for a symbol as in the following:

```
\3\3insert C:\\acadwin\\symbol\\door
```

In this example, the insert command is issued, then a drawing file called *door* in a subdirectory called *symbol* is specified for the insert. The scale factor and rotation angle can then be specified manually.

You can use a product such as Borland's Resource Workshop to add custom bitmap icons to the toolbox to represent your symbols. Borland's Resource Workshop program lets you open the TBAR16.DLL or

▼ ▼ ▼ ▼ ▼

TBAR24.DLL files and add bitmap icons using a paint-like program. Once you add a bitmap icon to these files, and add their names to the Stringtable section of the resource file, they can be selected just as any other built-in icon.

CREATING INTERACTIVE TOOLBAR AND TOOLBOX MACROS

The toolbar and toolbox are great for simplifying your search for frequently used commands. But you can do much more with a little help from AutoLISP. If you read through *Chapter 19*, you saw how you can use AutoLISP to create macros. The toolbar and toolbox let you create and store AutoLISP macros quickly. They also let you quickly test your macros without having to write an AutoLISP file and load it.

To illustrate the use of the toolbar to create interactive macros, let's take the macro created in Chapter 19 and add further functionality to it. Suppose you want to draw a round table with chairs. You can easily draw one chair, but to place more chairs around the table, you must copy the original chair, then rotate it for each new chair. The R90 macro already does part of what we need our macro to do. You will use a variation of it for the new macro.

1. Start AutoCAD, then draw a circle with a rectangle to the right of it as shown in Figure 21.16. The circle represents a table and the rectangle represents a simplified chair.

2. Right-click on a blank toolbar button.

3. Enter the following as a single line in the command-string input box of the Toolbar Button dialog box:

   ```
   \3\3(setq ss1 (ssget))(command "copy" ss1 "" "@" "@"
   "rotate" ss1 "")
   ```

4. Click on the Character ID radio button, then enter **C** in the Character ID popup list.

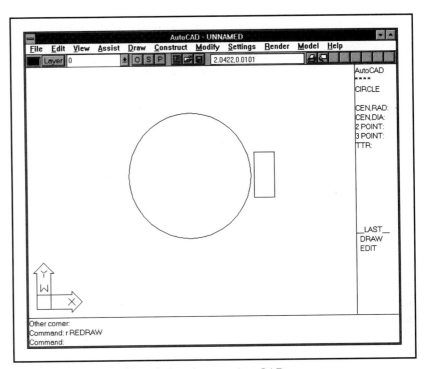

Figure 21.16: The table and chair drawn in AutoCAD

5. Click on OK, then click on the toolbar button you just defined.

6. At the **Select object:** prompt, click on the rectangle then press ↵.

7. At the **Base point:** prompt, select the center of the circle. The rectangle now rotates with the cursor about the base point you selected.

8. Click on a point directly vertical from the base point, then redraw the screen. You should have a copy of the rectangle representing the chair at the top of the circle.

The macro you entered starts out with \3\3, which is the same as entering two **Ctrl-C** commands. This cancels any command that may be currently active. Next, it uses the Setq and Ssget functions

```
(setq ss1 (ssget))
```

discussed in *Chapter 20*. These functions let you select a set of objects to be processed by the rest of your macro. The main part of the macro—

```
(command "copy" ss1 """@" "@" "rotate" ss1 "")
```

—does the work. You will notice that the string of instructions following the word *command* are the same instructions you would give AutoCAD if you were to manually perform the copy and rotate operations. First the word **copy** is entered to start the copy command. Next **ss1** is included to tell the copy command what to copy. A pair of double quotes follow, which act as a ⏎ to close the **Select object:** prompt and move to the next prompt. The two @ symbols are inputs to the **Base point:** and **To point:** prompts. The net effect is that the selected objects are copied in place with no displacement. Finally, the Rotate command is issued and the same set of objects is selected again as indicated by the ss1. The last pair of double quotes again acts as a ⏎ to close the select object prompt and move to the next **Rotate** prompt. From there, you select a base point and rotation angle.

Notice that immediately after the Copy and Rotate commands are invoked, where a **Select object:** prompt would appear, **ss1** is inserted. This ss1 is a variable that represents the set of objects you select at the beginning of the macro in the *(setq ss1 (ssget))* part. Notice too that words that are normally entered from the keyboard are enclosed in double quotes as in the commands **"copy"** and **"rotate"** and **"@"**.

If you need to pause the macro for input, you can use the word *pause*, just as in the R90 macro example in *Chapter 19*.

```
(command "rotate" pause "" "@" "90")
```

The pause in this macro allows the user to select an object for the Rotate command.

Finally, here are two other handy macros you can try. The first one lets you group a set of objects together. The second one selects the group you create with the first.

```
(setq ss1 (ssget))
!ss1
```

If you read Chapter 20, these two macros should be familiar. In fact, the first macro is the first part of the macro discussed earlier in this section. You can use it all by itself to create a selection set that can be retrieved at any time by entering **!ss1** at any **Select object:** prompt. By making !ss1 a macro button, you can click on a button instead of having to enter !ss1 to retrieve the group.

CREATING CUSTOM LINE TYPES AND HATCH PATTERNS

As your needs expand, you may find that the standard line types and hatch patterns are not adequate for your application. Fortunately, you can create your own. In this section, I will explain how you go about creating custom line types and patterns.

VIEWING AVAILABLE LINE TYPES

Although AutoCAD provides the line types most commonly used in drafting (see Figure 21.17), the dashes and dots may not be spaced the way you would like, or you may want an entirely new line type.

Linetype ↵

To create a custom line type, you use the Linetype command. Let's see how this handy command works by first listing the available line types.

1. Open a new AutoCAD file and, at the command prompt, enter **linetype** ↵ or click on SETTINGS ➤ LINETYP: from the root menu.

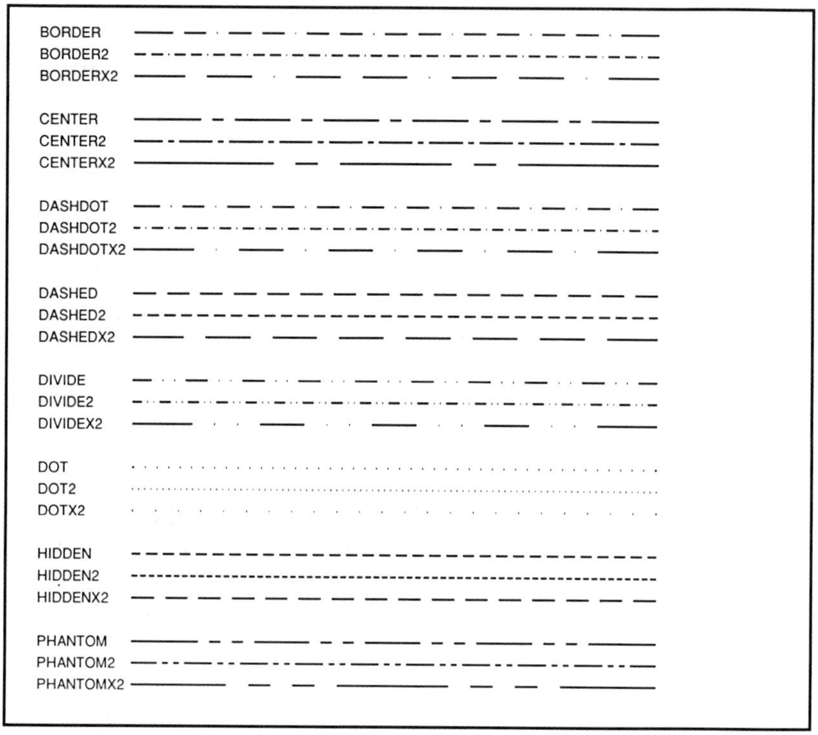

Figure 21.17:   The standard AutoCAD line types

AutoCAD stores the line types in a file called Acad.LIN, which is in the ASCII format. When you create a new line type, you are actually adding information to this file or creating a new file containing your own definitions. If you create a separate line type file, it will also have the extension .LIN. You can edit line types as described here or you can edit them directly in these files.

2. At the **?/Create/Load/Set:** prompt, enter **?** ↵. The File dialog box appears, listing the available line type files.

3. Double-click on ACAD. You get the listing shown in Figure 21.18, which shows the line types available in the Acad.LIN file, along with a simple description of each line.

CREATING A NEW LINE TYPE

Next, let's try creating a new line type.

1. Enter **C** ↵ or pick Create from the side menu.

2. At the **Name of linetype to create:** prompt, enter **Custom** ↵. This will be the name of your new line type. Once you've entered the name, the File dialog box appears. Note that the

```
*BORDER,__ __ . __ .
A,.5,-.25,.5,-.25,0,-.25
*BORDER2,__.__.__.__.
A,.25,-.125,.25,-.125,0,-.125
*BORDERX2,____ .
A,1.0,-.5,1.0,-.5,0,-.5

*CENTER,___ ___ __
A,1.25,-.25,.25,-.25
*CENTER2,__ __ __
A,.75,-.125,.125,-.125
*CENTERX2,____ __
A,2.5,-.5,.5,-.5

*DASHDOT,__ . __ .
A,.5,-.25,0,-.25
*DASHDOT2,_._._._._.
A,.25,-.125,0,-.125
*DASHDOTX2,____ .
A,1.0,-.5,0,-.5

*DASHED,__ __ __
A,.5,-.25
*DASHED2,__ __ __
A,.25,-.125
*DASHEDX2,____
A,1.0,-.5

*DIVIDE,____ . . ___
A,.5,-.25,0,-.25,0,-.25
*DIVIDE2,_..__..__..
A,.25,-.125,0,-.125,0,-.125
*DIVIDEX2,_____ . .
A,1.0,-.5,0,-.5,0,-.5

*DOT,. . . . .
A,0,-.25
*DOT2,..........
A,0,-.125
*DOTX2,. . . .
A,0,-.5

*HIDDEN,__ __ __
A,.25,-.125
*HIDDEN2,_ _ _ _
A,.125,-.0625
*HIDDENX2,____ ___
A,.5,-.25

*PHANTOM,_____ __ __
A,1.25,-.25,.25,-.25,.25,-.25
*PHANTOM2,____ _ _ _
A,.625,-.125,.125,-.125,.125,-.125
*PHANTOMX2,_____ ____
A,2.5,-.5,.5,-.5,.5,-.5
*HIDDEN4,hidden2 with shorter dashes
A,0.1,-0.1
```

Figure 21.18: A listing of standard line types. The lines in the figure were generated with the underline key and the period, and are only rough representations of the actual lines.

title of the dialog box is Create or Append Linetype File. This tells you that you are to enter the name of the line type file you want to create or add to. Let's assume you want to start a new line type file called **Newline**.

3. Enter **Newline** ↵. You will see the **Creating new file...Descriptive text:** prompt. (If you had accepted the default choice (ACAD) in step 2, you would have gotten the prompt **Wait, checking if linetype already defined....** This is done so that you don't inadvertently overwrite an existing line type you may want to keep.)

4. Enter a text description of your line type. Although your actual line type can be composed only of a series of lines, points, and blank spaces, you can use any keyboard character as part of your description. For this exercise, enter the following, using the underline key to simulate the appearance of your line:

   Custom - My own center line _____ _ _____ ↵.

5. At the **Enter pattern (on next line):** prompt, enter

   1.0,- .125,.25,-.125 ↵

6. At the **New definition written to file. ?/Create/Load/Set:** prompt, press ↵ to exit the Linetype command. Once you've created a line type, you must load it to use it, as described in *Chapter 4.*

In this exercise you entered a series of numbers separated by commas. The commas separate the different lengths of the components that make up the line type. The *1.0* following the A is the length of the first part of the line. The A that begins the line type definition is a code that is applied to all line types.

The *-.125* is the blank or broken part of the line. The minus sign tells AutoCAD that the line is *not* to be drawn for the specified length, which is 0.125 units in this example. Next comes the positive value of 0.25. This tells AutoCAD to draw a line segment 0.25 units long after the blank part of the line. A zero value here would draw a dot. Finally, the last negative value, −.125, again tells AutoCAD to skip drawing the line for the distance of 0.125 units. This series of numbers represents one segment that is repeated to form the line (see Figure 21.19). You could create a very complex line type that looks like a random broken line, as in Figure 21.20.

You may be wondering what purpose the A serves at the beginning of the line type code. A line type is composed of a series of line segments and points. The A, which is supplied by AutoCAD automatically, is a code that forces the line type to start and end on a line segment rather than on a blank space in the series of lines. At times AutoCAD stretches the last line segment to force this condition, as shown in Figure 21.21.

You can also create line types outside AutoCAD by using a word processor to edit the Acad.LIN file. The standard Acad.LIN file looks like Figure 21.19.

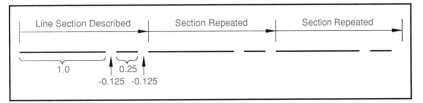

Figure 21.19: Line type description with plotted line

Figure 21.20: "Random" broken line

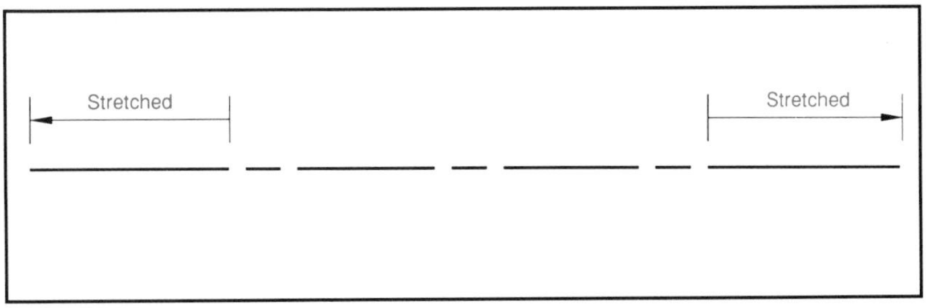

Figure 21.21: Stretched beginning and end of line

This is the same file you saw earlier, with the addition of the code used by AutoCAD to determine the line segment lengths.

Normally, to use a line type you have created, you have to enter its name through the keyboard when you are prompted for a line type during the CHANGE, LAYER, or LINETYPE commands. If you use one of your own line types frequently, you may want to add it to the Acad.LIN file so it will be available on the Linetype setting submenu.

CREATING HATCH PATTERNS

AutoCAD provides 53 predefined hatch patterns you can choose from (see Figure 21.22). If the hatch pattern you want is not available, you have the option of creating your own. In this section I will show you the basic elements of pattern definition.

Unlike the line types, hatch patterns cannot be created while you are in an AutoCAD file. The pattern definitions are contained in an external file named Acad.PAT. This file can be opened and edited with a text editor that can handle ASCII files or with EDLIN. Here is one hatch pattern definition from that file:

```
*square,Small aligned squares
0, 0,0, 0,.125, .125,–.125
90, 0,0, 0,.125, .125,–.125
```

You can see some similarities between the pattern description and the line description. They both start with a descriptive text line, then give numeric values defining the pattern. The numbers have a different meaning, however. This example shows two lines of information. Each line represents a line in the pattern, much like a line in the line type definition. The first line determines the horizontal line component of the pattern, and the second line represents the vertical component. Figure 21.23 shows the hatch pattern defined in the example.

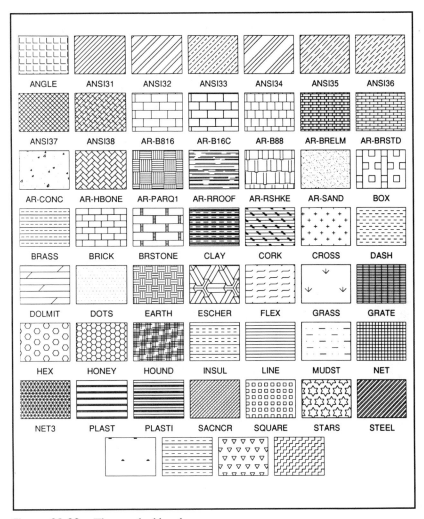

Figure 21.22: The standard hatch patterns

A pattern is made up of *line groups*. A line group is like a line type that is arrayed a specified distance to fill the area to be hatched. A group is defined by a line of code, much as a line type is defined. In the square pattern, two lines are used, one horizontal and one vertical. Each of these lines is duplicated in a fashion that makes the lines appear as boxes when they are combined. Figure 21.24 illustrates this point.

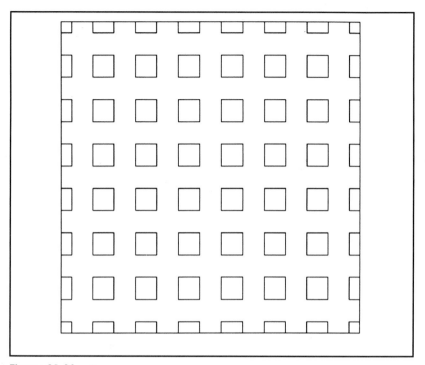

Figure 21.23:   Square pattern

Look at the first line in the definition:

0, 0,0, 0,.125, .125,–.125

This example shows a series of numbers separated by commas. This line
of codes representing one line group actually contains four sets of information. Blank spaces separate these different components. The first
component is the 0 at the beginning. This value indicates the angle of
the line group, as determined by the line's orientation. In this case it is
0 for a horizontal line that runs from left to right. If you have forgotten
what the numeric values for the different directions are, refer back to
Figure 2.6, which shows AutoCAD's system for specifying angles.

The next component is the origin of the line group, 0,0. This does not
mean that the line actually begins at the drawing origin (see Figure 21.25). It gives you a reference point to determine the location of
other line groups involved in generating the pattern.

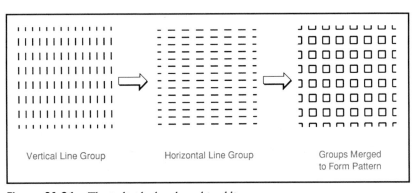

Figure 21.24: The individual and combined line groups

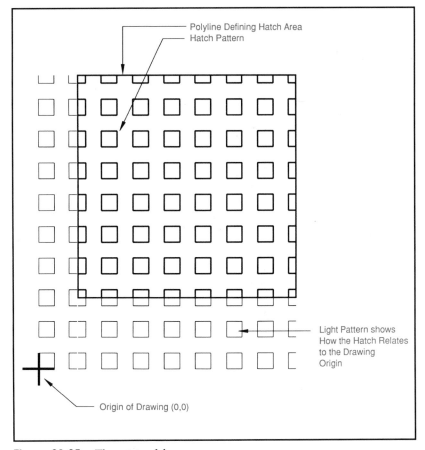

Figure 21.25: The origin of the patterns

The next component is *0,.125*. This determines the distance the line is to be arrayed and in what direction. Figure 21.26 shows what this means in terms of the pattern. This value is like a relative coordinate indicating *x* and *y* distances for a rectangular array. It is not based on the drawing coordinates, but on a coordinate system relative to the orientation of the line. If the line is oriented at a 0° angle, then the code *0,.125* indicates a precisely vertical direction. If the line were oriented at a 45° angle, then the code *0,.125* would represent a 135° direction. In this example, the duplication occurs 90° in relation to the line group, since the *x* value is 0. Figure 21.27 illustrates this point.

Finally, the actual description of the line pattern is given. This value is equivalent to the value given when you create a line type. Positive values are line segments, and negative values are blank segments. This part of the line group definition works exactly like the line type definitions you looked at in the previous section.

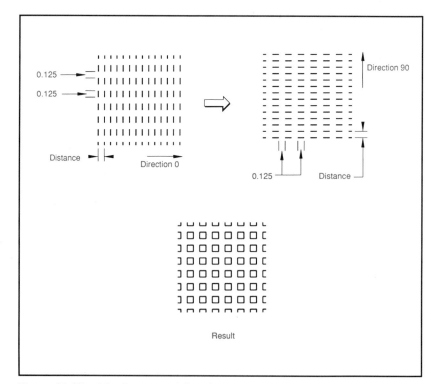

Figure 21.26:   The distance and direction of duplication

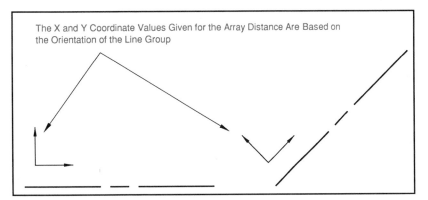

Figure 21.27:   How the direction of the line group copy is determined

▼ Customizable Dialog Boxes

One topic I haven't touched on is AutoCAD's customizable dialog box feature. Beginning with Release 11 for Windows and with Release 12 for other platforms, you can create your own custom dialog boxes. Any dialog box you create is transportable to other platforms and will conform with the standard appearance of those other platforms.

Unfortunately, in order to take advantage of this feature you must have more than a little familiarity with AutoLISP programming, a topic that requires more depth than I can go into in this book. For more information on dialog box customization, I refer you to the AutoCAD Customization Manual that is supplied with AutoCAD Release 12.

This system may seem somewhat limiting, but you can actually do a lot with it. Autodesk managed to come up with 53 patterns—and that was really only scratching the surface.

USING DDE TO CUSTOMIZE AUTOCAD

One of the chief advantages of using Windows is its ability to integrate programs so they work together—almost as if you had one very large program instead of several independent ones. For the most part, you will use Windows ability to multitask and the Windows Clipboard to make your programs work together. With a little more work and a few other programs, you can add functionality to AutoCAD. In this section, you will look at ways you can use Windows' DDE facility to connect programs more intimately with AutoCAD.

CREATING SYMBOLS LIBRARIES WITH VISUAL BASIC

I mentioned earlier that you could use the toolbox as an aid to access your custom symbols library. However, since it is so easy to edit the toolbox, you may prefer to leave it for macros and use another method for adding a symbols library. Another way to customize AutoCAD is to use a program like Microsoft's Visual Basic 2.0 to access your custom symbols library. Visual Basic is a programming environment that lets you create stand-alone custom programs that can send instructions to AutoCAD by way of a Windows DDE link. Don't let Visual Basic scare you. You don't have to be an expert programmer to get useful results from Visual Basic. The following exercise describes how you can create a simple Visual Basic program that inserts symbols from a symbols library. If you have Visual Basic 2.0 you should be able to follow along.

First, you will start by creating the part of the program that makes the link to AutoCAD.

1. Start up Visual Basic. You will see several windows that make up the Visual Basic programming system (see Figure 21.28). The window at the center of the screen is the Form1 window. This is where you construct the interface to your program in a way similar to a dialog box. To the left are the tool buttons and to the right is a Properties List window.

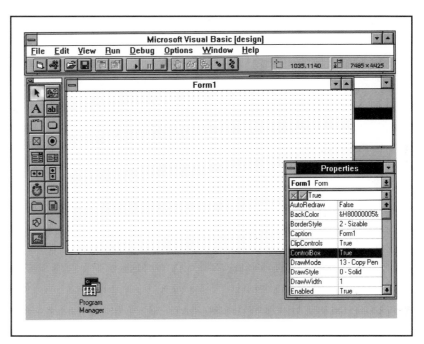

Figure 21.28: The Visual Basic screen

2. Click on View ➤ Code. A window will open. This is where you enter the program instructions or program code as it is referred to.

3. In the Object: popup list, click on General, then enter the following exactly as it's shown:

```
Sub LinkApp (Link As Control, Appname As String, Topic
As String) ↵
CONST NONE = 0 ↵
CONST COLD = 2 ↵
Link.LinkMode = NONE ↵
Link.LinkTopic = Appname + " | " + Topic ↵
Link.LinkMode = COLD ↵
End Sub ↵
```

This is a subroutine that defines some general parameters of the program.

4. Close the window, then click on the **ab** icon in the tool buttons to the left.

5. Click and drag to create a rectangle in the form1 window. You don't have to worry about the size of the rectangle. This step defines a text object which will be used by the program to channel data from the program to AutoCAD through a DDL link.

6. In the Properties window to the right, double-click on the item called *Text*, then enter **AcadText** ↵. As you type, the word appears in the text box in the form1 window. AcadText is now the name of this object.

7. In the Properties window, click on Visible to highlight it, then double-click on it to change its value to False. This causes the text object to be invisible when the program runs.

8. Double-click on a blank area in the Form1 window. You will get the Form1.frm window.

9. Enter the following line in the Form1.frm window.

```
Sub Form_Load ()
LinkApp AcadText, "AutoCAD.DDE", "System"
End Sub
```

The first and last lines should already appear in the window. You only need to enter the line that starts with LinkApp AcadText…. This subroutine makes the DDL link to AutoCAD when the program is run.

10. Close the Form1.FRM window.

Now you have the basis for a program that will link with AutoCAD. Next you will add buttons to the program that will send instructions to AutoCAD.

1. Click on the button icon in the tool button group. This is the rectangle with rounded corners and a drop shadow.

2. Click and drag a rectangle in the Form1 window. A button appears with the word *Command1*.

3. Double-click on the button to open the Form1.frm window again. Notice that the Object popup list shows Command1 and that the Proc: popup list shows Click. You may begin to see that the name in the Object popup list tells you which object you are editing. The Proc popup list tells you the action or process that activates this object.

4. Enter the following in the window:

```
Sub Command1_Click ()
AcadText.LinkExecute "(\3\3Insert door )"
End Sub
```

Just as with the text object, the first and last lines are provided for you. Notice that the text between the square brackets is the keyboard equivalent to starting the Insert command and entering the name of the door block. Also notice the AcadText.LinkExecute statement. This directs the text in the brackets to the AcadText object you created earlier.

5. In the Properties window, find the item called *Caption* and double-click on it. You can now change the label on the Command1 button.

6. Type **DOOR** to change the label of the button to DOOR.

7. Repeat Steps 1 through 6, but this time in Step 4 change the text in the square brackets to read **[\3\3insert toilet]**, then in Step 6 enter the name **TOILET** for the button label.

8. Reduce the size of the Form1 window so it is just large enough to contain the new buttons. You can click and drag the buttons to move them around if you need to. You can also change the size of the buttons by moving their grips.

You've just completed enough of your program to test. You can add more Command buttons as you did in these last seven steps, but first let's see if these two buttons work. In order to use your Visual Basic program, you must first have AutoCAD running.

1. Without closing Visual Basic, start AutoCAD.

2. Return to Visual Basic, then click on Run ➤ Start.

3. Arrange the windows so you can see the AutoCAD window and the Form1 window clearly, then click on the DOOR button. Notice what happens in the AutoCAD window.

4. Click on the AutoCAD window and complete the Insert command.

5. Now return to the Visual Basic program and click on Run ➤ End.

You can add more buttons to your program to include other symbols. Of course, you can have the buttons do other things besides insert symbols. The point is, without much work, you can create a custom application for AutoCAD quickly using Visual Basic.

Once you are happy with your Visual Basic program, you should save it as a project under a new name then use the File ➤ Make .EXE option to create a stand-alone program that you run alongside AutoCAD. Once you create the .EXE file, you can use the File Manager to click and drag it into your AutoCAD program group so you can easily start it while in AutoCAD. You can further enhance your program by using icons in place of the text buttons used in the exercise. Visual Basic comes with a set of icons, or you can use one of the many icon creation tools available as freeware and shareware.

I've shown you how you can use Microsoft Visual Basic 2.0 as an aid to customizing AutoCAD, but you can also use Borland's Object Vision to accomplish the same thing. Both programs are relatively inexpensive. Object Vision is much easier to understand for the non-programmer and it can easily form links to dBASE and Paradox files. But it doesn't offer the ability to create stand-alone programs.

SENDING INSTRUCTIONS TO AUTOCAD FROM EXCEL

In *Chapter 10* you saw how you can have AutoCAD exchange Attribute data between Excel and Lotus 1-2-3 for Windows. You can also set up Excel to return data to your drawing and even have Excel generate drawings based on spreadsheet information. You could, for example, have Excel draw a door and window schedule automatically based on the spreadsheet data generated in Chapter 10. Again, the Windows DDE facility is used for this. The following exercise shows how to establish a DDE link to AutoCAD from Excel using Excel's macro facility. The macro will draw a rectangle whose dimensions are based on spreadsheet data.

1. Start Excel, then in the default spreadsheet named *Sheet1*, enter the value **1,1** in cell A1. This is the starting corner for the rectangle.

2. Enter the value **4** in cell A2 and **6** in cell A3. These are the width and height of the rectangle.

3. Click on File ➤ New, then at the dialog box, click on Macro Worksheet.

4. Enter the following lines into the macro worksheet. Start at cell A1 and add each new line to the next cell down. You should have 18 cells occupied.

```
AutoCAD Link
=INITIATE("AutoCAD.DDE","System")
=EXECUTE(C2,"(\3)")
=EXECUTE(C2,"(LINE )")
=EXECUTE(C2,Sheet1!$A$1)
=EXECUTE(C2,"( )")
=EXECUTE(C2,"(@)")
=EXECUTE(C2,Sheet1!$A$2)
=EXECUTE(C2,"(<0 )")
=EXECUTE(C2,"(@)")
=EXECUTE(C2,Sheet1!$A$3)
=EXECUTE(C2,"(<90 )")
=EXECUTE(C2,"(@)")
=EXECUTE(C2,Sheet1!$A$2)
```

```
=EXECUTE(C2,"(<180 )")
=EXECUTE(C2,"(C )")
=TERMINATE(C2)
=HALT()
```

5. If AutoCAD is not yet running, start it, then set up the Excel and AutoCAD windows so they are both visible.

6. Return to Excel and highlight cell A1 in the macro worksheet, then click on Macro ➤ Run. Watch AutoCAD draw a 4-by-6 rectangle.

7. Back in Excel, change the values in the Sheet1 spreadsheet cells A2 and A3, then run the macros again to see what happens. You will see another rectangle with different proportions in AutoCAD.

This macro works by reading the data from the Sheet1 spreadsheet, then includes that data in the instructions to AutoCAD. When the cells of the macro worksheet are strung together, you get a line that looks something like this:

```
LINE (sheet1-A1) @(sheet1-A2)<0 @(sheet1-A3)<90
@(sheet1-A2)<180 C
```

I've simplified the references to spreadsheet data and enclosed them in parentheses for clarity. When the macro is laid out like this, it is easier to see that the data are in the typical AutoCAD polar coordinate format. The spaces in the macro translate as spaces or hard returns in AutoCAD.

You might notice that the format for the macro text is similar to those in the Visual Basic example shown earlier. The keystrokes to be sent to AutoCAD are enclosed within square brackets which are in turn enclosed in double quotes. The exception to this is where the macro calls values from the spreadsheet—in lines 5, 8, 11, and 14. Here we see the format

```
Sheet1!$A$1
```

in which the spreadsheet name is supplied first, then an exclamation point, then the cell address. The cell address includes dollar signs, so cell A1 is shown as $A$1. In all cases, the macro text is preceded by a C2. This is the cell address of the macro statement describing where to send the macro.

```
=INITIATE("AutoCAD","System")
```

Finally, the macro is closed with the =TERMINATE(C2) and =HALT() statements.

If you prefer, you can have the macro start up AutoCAD if it isn't already running. To do this, add the following two lines below the first cell A1 in the Macro Worksheet.

```
=DIRECTORY("C:\acadwin")
=EXEC("C:\acadwin\acad.exe",1)
```

If you add these lines, be sure you change the A2 in all of the EXECUTE statements to **A4**.

While this is a simple macro, it can be easily modified and expanded to generate a schedule of parts in AutoCAD. Or you could create a macro that draws a part based on data that a non-AutoCAD user would supply through the spreadsheet. For example, you could set up a spreadsheet that lists the different properties of a part with adjacent cells used for user input. You could then write a macro that uses the input cell data to construct a drawing of the part in AutoCAD.

ESTABLISHING OFFICE STANDARDS

You've seen how you can mold AutoCAD to fit into your office's style of work by editing its menus and linking AutoCAD to other Windows programs. But the successful use of AutoCAD is dependent on more than just its interface. Your efforts as a CAD user should include standard methods of operation. You can start by including graphic standards you may already have set up for your office. As you start to use AutoCAD in more of your work, you may want to consider devising methods for communicating drawing file structures and file organization.

Communication is especially important when you are one of many people working on the same project on separate computers. A well-developed set of standards and procedures helps to minimize problems that might be caused by miscommunication. In this section, I give some suggestions on how to set up these standards.

MAKING AUTOCAD EASIER FOR YOUR CO-WORKERS

Not everyone needs to be an AutoCAD expert, but almost everyone involved in design or production should be able to use AutoCAD in order for your firm to obtain maximum productivity from it. Designers especially should be involved, as AutoCAD can show significant time savings in the design phase of a project.

You may want to consider an add-on software package to aid those in your office who need to use AutoCAD, but who are not likely to spend a lot of time learning it. These add-ons automate some of the more frequently used functions of a particular application. They can also provide ready-made office standards for symbols and layers. Add-ons are available for architects, circuit board designers, electrical engineers, civil engineers, and mechanical designers, to name a few.

Add-ons shouldn't be viewed as the only means of using AutoCAD within your office, but rather as aids to casual users and partners to your own custom applications. No two offices work alike and no two projects are exactly the same, so add-ons cannot be all things to all people. Remember, AutoCAD is really a graphics tool whose commands and interface can be manipulated to suit any project or office. And that is the way it should be.

▼ **TIP**

If you are serious about being as productive as possible with AutoCAD, you will want to develop custom applications. See *Chapters 19* and *20* to find out more about customization and third-party software.

ESTABLISHING LAYERING CONVENTIONS

You have seen how layers can be a useful tool. But they can easily get out of hand when you have free rein over their creation and naming. This can be especially troublesome when more than one person is working on the same set of drawings.

With a naming convention, you can minimize confusion between members of a work group. However, a too-rigid naming convention can cause as many problems as no convention at all, so it is best to give

▼ TIP

If you are an architect, engineer, or someone in the construction business, you may want to check out some of the CAD layering standards set forth by the American Institute of Architects (AIA) and the Construction Standards Institute (CSI).

▼ TIP

There are several DOS utilities available that allow you to attach comments to file names. Such a utility helps you overcome the eight-character limit on DOS file names. One such utility, called *Dirnotes*.**COM**, can be found on the PCmagNet forum on CompuServe.

general guidelines rather than force everyone to stay within narrow limits. As I mentioned in *Chapter* 6, you can create layer names in a way that allows you to group them using wildcards. AutoCAD allows up to 31 characters in a layer name, so you can use descriptive names.

Line weights should be standardized in conjunction with layers. If you intend to use a service bureau for your plotting, you may want to check with the staff first because they may ask you to conform to their color and line-weight standards.

ESTABLISHING DRAWING NAME CONVENTIONS

Just as you will want to keep track of layers, so you will need a system to keep track of your drawing files and blocks. This is a little more difficult than keeping track of layers, because DOS limits file names to eight characters. Although blocks can have 31-character names, you may want to limit block names to eight characters, because you will want to turn blocks into external files.

You can design a file-naming system that allows you to identify your drawing files by job number, drawing type, and revision number. The job number may be three digits, the drawing type may be an alphabetic code, and the revision may be an alphanumeric code. For example, a coded file name could be *304B061A.DWG*.

In this example, the first three numbers could be an abbreviation of job number 9304. The next three characters could be a symbol for drawing type B on sheet number 06. Finally, the last two characters could mean revision number 1 and series designation A. You may even want to include a code number to designate symbols.

Unfortunately, this type of code is difficult to learn. Most people prefer easily recognizable names, such as *ELMA02.DWG* for Elm Street project sheet number A02. This recognizable type of name can't convey as much information as a coded name. Still, because most designers and drafters have enough to think about without remembering special codes, it is usually better to base your file-naming system on recognizable names. You may be able to devise a combination of the two systems that offers a word or phrase in conjunction with a code.

LABELING HARD COPIES

A problem you will run into once you start to generate lots of files is keeping track of which AutoCAD file goes with which hard-copy drawing. It is a good idea to place an identifying tag on the drawing in some inconspicuous place that will plot with the drawing. As well as the file name, you should include such information as the date and time the drawing was last edited, who edited it, and what submission the plot was done for. All these bits of information can prove helpful in the progress of a design or production project (see Figure 21.29).

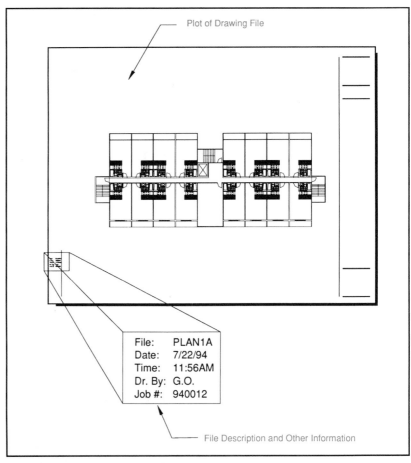

Figure 21.29: Using a small note identifying the file used to generate a drawing can be helpful in drawing management.

USING NETWORKS WITH AUTOCAD

▼ NOTE

In simplified terms, a *dedicated file server* is a storage device, often a computer with a large-capacity hard disk, that acts as a repository of data. A server will often have a tape-backup device to facilitate regular system backup.

In an effort to simplify your file maintenance, you may want to consider installing a network to connect your computers electronically. Networks offer a way to share files and peripherals among computers in different locations. They come in a variety of styles, from very simple software and cable connectors to systems that use what are called *dedicated file servers*, whose special hardware and fiber optics communicate with the computers on the network.

There are two basic types of networks that can be used with AutoCAD: *server-client systems* and *peer-to-peer systems*. The file server offers you a way to maintain files on a single computer. The computers connected to the server are referred to as *clients*, or *nodes*. You can store all of your common symbols, AutoLISP programs, custom menus, and working files on the server, thus reducing the risk of having duplicate files. The client computers are simpler and less powerful. They use the server as their main storage device, accessing programs and data stored on the server through the network. Networks with servers also have all the peripheral output devices connected to the server. This centralized type of system offers the user an easier way of managing files.

A peer-to-peer network does not use a server. Instead, each computer has equal status and can access files and peripherals on other computers on the network. Microsoft's Windows for Workgroups supports this type of network. Generally, peer-to-peer networks are less expensive, since you don't need to dedicate a computer to the single task of server. Peripherals such as plotters and printers are shared between computers. Even hard disks are shared, though access to directories can be controlled at each computer.

A third type of network, a *multitasking-multiuser system*, might also be used. This system is similar to a server-client type of system, with the client computers being nothing more than a monitor and keyboard connected to the "server." Since AutoCAD is so power-hungry, it would be difficult to run more than a few AutoCAD stations on such a system.

▼ NOTE

Release 12 of AutoCAD offers many new features for the network user. Features like file locking and reference files, which are discussed in earlier chapters, let you maintain better file version control over networks. The network version of AutoCAD can operate with systems such as Lantastic, Novell, NFS, and 3Com (3Com users, however must pay special attention to AutoCAD's installation and performance guide).

Networks can be useful tools in managing your work, but they can also introduce new problems. Speed of file access can also be a problem. No matter what form of network you install, you will need a system manager whose duties include backing up files in a server and making sure the output devices connected to the network are operating as they should. Used properly, a network can save time by easing the flow of information between computer users; it must, however, be managed carefully. For more information, consult *Appendix A* for helpful tips on setting up AutoCAD on a network.

KEEPING RECORDS

Computers were supposed to create the paperless office. As you work more and more with them, you may find that quite the opposite is true. Although you may store more information on magnetic media, you will spend a good deal of time reviewing that information on hard copy because it is very difficult to spot errors on a computer monitor. Another level of documentation must also occur when you use AutoCAD on large projects. You will have to have a way of keeping track of the many elements that go into the creation of drawings.

Because jobs vary in their requirements, you may want to provide a layer log to help keep track of layers and their intended uses for specific jobs. Also, to keep track of blocks within files, you may want to keep a log of block names and their insertion values. Finally, you may want to keep a log of symbols. You will probably have a library of symbols that everyone uses. This library will grow as your projects become more varied, so you may want to document these symbols to keep track of them. *Chapter 4* describes a method that lets you keep track of information about AutoCAD through a log file. The AutoCAD log file can be invaluable for coordinating your work with others.

Plotting is an activity that you may also want to keep records for, especially if you bill your clients separately for computer time or for analyzing job costs. A plot log might contain such information as the time spent on plotting, the type of plot that was done, the purpose of the plot, and even plotting problems that arise with each drawing.

Although records may be the last thing on your mind when you are working to meet a deadline, in the long run they can save time and aggravation for you and the people you work with.

UNDERSTANDING WHAT AUTOCAD CAN DO FOR YOU

Many of us have only a vague idea of what AutoCAD can do for our work. We think it will make our drafting go faster but we're not sure exactly how, or we believe it will make us produce better-quality drawings. Some people believe it can make them better designers or allow them to produce professional-quality drawings without having much drawing talent. All these things are true to an extent, and AutoCAD can help you in additional ways that are less tangible than speed and quality.

SEEING THE HIDDEN ADVANTAGES

We have discussed how AutoCAD can help you in both drafting and design work by allowing you to visualize your ideas more clearly, and by reducing the time it takes to do repetitive tasks. AutoCAD also forces you to organize your drawing process more efficiently. It changes your perception of problems and, though it may introduce new ones, the additional accuracy and information it provides minimize errors.

AutoCAD also provides drawing consistency. A set of drawings done on AutoCAD is more legible and consistent, reducing the possibility of errors caused by illegible handwriting or poor drafting. In our litigious culture, this can be a significant feature.

Finally, since AutoCAD is becoming so pervasive, it is easier to find people who can use it proficiently. As this number of people grows, training will become less of a burden to your company.

WHEN TO SET AUTOCAD ASIDE

As helpful as AutoCAD can be, there are times when it is simply not worth making revisions on AutoCAD. Last-minute changes that are minor but pervasive throughout a set of drawings are best made by hand on the most up-to-date hard copy. That way, you don't spend a long time plotting drawings and wasting drawing media.

▼ TIP

Once the project is done, however, you should go back and enter the final changes in AutoCAD just to keep your files up to date.

Only your experience can help you determine the best time to stop using AutoCAD and start making changes by hand. Many factors may affect this decision, such as the size and complexity of the project, the people available, and the nature of the revisions, to name a few.

It is a good idea to have a label on every hard copy of a file so that users know which file to edit when the time comes to make changes.

AFTERWORD

As you have seen, AutoCAD is a powerful software tool, and like any powerful program, it is difficult to master. I hope this last chapter has given you the incentive to take advantage of AutoCAD's full potential. Remember that even after you've learned how to use AutoCAD, there are still many other issues that must be confronted while using AutoCAD in an office environment.

Unlike words, drawings have few restrictions. The process of writing requires adherence to the structures of our language. The process of drawing, on the other hand, has no fixed structure. There are a million ways to draw a face or a building, for example. For this reason, AutoCAD is much less restricted in the way you use it. It has the potential for uses that are yet to be discovered. I encourage you to experiment with AutoCAD and explore the infinite possibilities it offers for solving your problems and communicating your ideas.

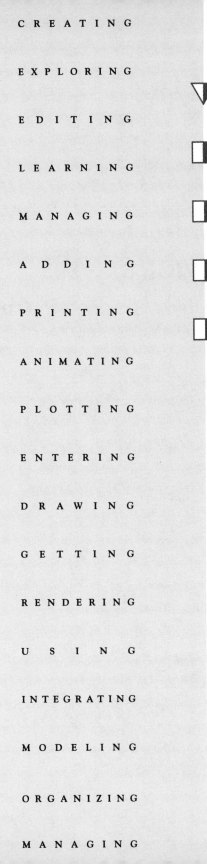

CREATING

EXPLORING

EDITING

LEARNING

MANAGING

ADDING

PRINTING

ANIMATING

PLOTTING

ENTERING

DRAWING

GETTING

RENDERING

USING

INTEGRATING

MODELING

ORGANIZING

MANAGING

HARDWARE
AND
SOFTWARE TIPS

AutoCAD is a resource-hungry program; it requires a fairly sophisticated hardware system to run efficiently. Since many of the components that make up an AutoCAD system are not found on the typical desktop computer, this appendix is provided to help you understand some of the less common ones. I also discuss ways you can improve AutoCAD's performance through software and hardware.

UNDERSTANDING DEVICE DRIVERS

Sometimes a program calls for input and output devices that are not normally connected to a microcomputer and that the operating system does not know how to manage. AutoCAD for Windows provides its own instructions in the form of applications called *drivers* for managing the devices. These drivers are in the form of computer files and can be recognized by their .DLL extension. They also have specific prefixes depending on whether they are display (ds), rendering (rc), plotter (pl) or digitizer (dg) drivers. For example, the standard AutoCAD display driver is DSACAD.DLL. The HPGL2 driver is PLPHPGL2.DLL.

When you configure AutoCAD during the installation process, AutoCAD asks you to select the types of devices you intend to use. This configuration process tells AutoCAD which of the available drivers to use with your particular system.

However, there are many products available that are not listed in the AutoCAD configuration menu. Fortunately, most products imitate some of the more popular input and output devices as a way of maintaining compatibility with AutoCAD. For example, you may have a plotter that emulates the Hewlett Packard line of plotters through the Hewlett Packard Graphics Language (HPGL). If you have a plotter that uses HPGL, you can use it by configuring AutoCAD for a Hewlett Packard plotter, regardless of whether yours is listed in the configuration menu. You can also use the Windows system printer option, which tells AutoCAD to use the printer used by Windows. The Windows system printer can be selected through the Control Panel application.

In addition to the standard, built-in drivers, AutoCAD allows third-party drivers that use what is called the *Autodesk Device Interface* (ADI). Autodesk offers the ADI Toolkit for manufacturers who wish to write drivers for their own hardware. This frees Autodesk from having to write drivers for every device on the market. Virtually every CAD related product on the market today supports AutoCAD through standard interfaces such as HPGL2 or ADI. For the Windows version of AutoCAD, the ADI drivers are also .DLL files.

THE GRAPHICS DISPLAY

A high-resolution display card is a device that allows your computer to display graphic images in greater detail, or *resolution*, than a standard graphics display. Many of the so-called SVGA display cards are inexpensive and offer high-quality output. High-resolution display cards often require a monitor capable of displaying their output. Because of this, the card and monitor combination is often considered a unit.

To improve AutoCAD's performance, Autodesk and other third-party products offer *display list* software. I discuss display-list drivers in *Chapter 19* and in *Appendix B*. The display list gives you nearly instantaneous pans and zooms at the cost of consuming more of your memory. If you are shopping for a display system, consider one that utilizes a graphics processor, such as the Texas Instruments, Tseng Lab ET4000, or Weitek chip used for Microsoft Windows acceleration in conjunction with a display-list software driver. If you are in the market for a complete computer system, you might consider one that uses the VESA local bus. A computer equipped with such a bus, and a local bus display card, can greatly improve overall Windows performance.

POINTING DEVICES

Our most basic means of communicating with computers is the keyboard. It allows us to talk to our computers and, with text-oriented programs, it is a fairly natural link. With Windows, a pointing device is also standard equipment. Most likely, you will use a mouse, but if you are still in the market for a pointing device, choose an input device that generates smooth cursor movement. Some of the lesser-quality input devices cause erratic movement. When looking for an input device other than a mouse, choose one that provides positive feedback, such as a definitive button click when you pick an object on the screen. Many low-cost digitizers have a very poor button feel that can cause errors when you are selecting points or menu options. Display adapters can affect tablet operation as well; some of the more exotic displays will not work at all in conjunction with some tablets.

In general, use a high-resolution mouse if you do not plan to do any tracing. You may also consider a trackball if you are tight on desk space. If you must have the use of a tablet menu, or if you know you are going to trace drawings, then get a digitizer, but be sure it is of good quality.

THE DIGITIZING TABLET

If you need to trace drawings, you should consider a digitizing tablet. It is usually a rectangular object with a penlike *stylus*, or a device called a *puck*, which resembles a mouse. It has a smooth surface on which to draw. The most popular size is 11"×11", but digitizing tablets are available in sizes up to 60"×70". The tablet gives a natural feel to drawing with the computer because the movement of the stylus or puck is directly translated into cursor movement.

A digitizing tablet's puck often has *function buttons*. These buttons can be programmed through the AutoCAD menu file system to start your most frequently used commands, which is much faster than searching through an on-screen menu. You can also select commands from the tablet's surface if you install the *menu template* supplied with AutoCAD. A menu template is a flat sheet of plastic with the AutoCAD commands printed on it. You can select commands simply by pointing at them on the template. If you have a digitizing tablet, refer to *Appendix B*, which tells you how to install a template.

Most digitizers can be used as pointing devices for Windows. Unfortunately, this precludes their use as a tracing device for AutoCAD. For this reason, you may want to have both a digitizer and a mouse connected to your computer. AutoCAD allows you to switch easily from digitizer to mouse using the Mouse/Digitizer Arbitration option under the File ➤ Preferences dialog box.

OUTPUT DEVICES

Output options vary greatly in quality and price. Quality and paper size are the major considerations for both printers and plotters. Nearly all printers give accurate drawings, but some produce better line quality than others. Some plotters give merely acceptable results, while others are quite impressive in their speed and accuracy. Color is optional on both printers and plotters. Some printers produce color printouts, while all pen plotters allow color.

AutoCAD for Windows can use the Windows system printer, so any device that Windows supports is also supported by AutoCAD. AutoCAD also gives you the option of plotting directly to an output device. By plotting directly to the output device, instead of going through Windows, AutoCAD can offer more control over the final output.

PRINTERS

The dot-matrix printer is the least expensive choice for producing a quick-check plot, as long as your drawing isn't larger than 13"×16". It will do a reasonable job of printing your drawing, though it won't produce the best-quality line work, and drawing size is limited to the carriage width of the printer (anywhere from $8^1/_2$" to 13"). The printer's chief advantage is speed. A dot-matrix printer can print any drawing in under ten minutes, regardless of complexity. In contrast, a plotter can take an hour or more, particularly if your drawing contains a lot of text. Some dot-matrix printers also offer color printing.

Most laser printers, with the exception of PostScript printers, fall into the category of dot-matrix printers as far as AutoCAD is concerned. Laser printers have the same limitations as dot-matrix printers, but they are capable of better line quality and higher speeds. They are usually limited to $8^1/_2$ ×11" paper, though you can get 11"×17" laser printers at a premium.

A third alternative is the ink-jet printer. These printers offer speed and quality output with the added advantage of low noise. Some ink-jet printers even accept 17"×22" paper and offer PostScript emulation at 360 dots per inch. Since ink-jet printers are competitively priced, they can offer the best solution for low-cost check plots. And the 17"×22" paper size is quite acceptable for half-size plots, a format that more architects and engineers are using.

PLOTTERS

A plotter is a mechanical drafting device used to draw a computer image on sheets of paper, vellum, or polyester film. Most plotters use pens, though some offer ink-jet, laser, thermal, or electrostatic technology to get the image on paper.

If your drawing is fairly simple, your plotter can give you results in minutes. However, many applications require fairly complex drawings, which in turn take much longer to plot. A typical architectural drawing, for example, takes 45 minutes on a good-quality, large-format plotter using wet-ink pens on polyester film. By using pens capable of faster speeds, you can reduce the time it takes to plot a drawing by 40% and still get an accurate reproduction. When you want large plots, sharp clear lines, or reproduction quality, the pen plotter is the way to go.

Plotters come in one of two configurations: *flatbed* and *drum*. Flatbed plotters are usually large, rectangular machines that carry a pen on an arm much like a large-format drafting arm. They are usually slower than drum plotters and many are less expensive. Some flatbed plotters offer a higher degree of accuracy than the drum plotters. It is also easier to reposition your drawing on the plotter bed for revisions to existing drawings.

Drum plotters are generally faster than their flatbed counterparts. They also take up less space (though some flatbed plotters can be mounted on a wall). They are more commonly used, so availability, service, and parts are more readily available.

Raster plotters are becoming increasingly popular. These plotters can produce large-format drawings in less than half the time taken by pen plotters. However, their line work is often inferior to that of pen plotters, and the laser, thermal, and electrostatic plotters tend to be much more expensive. A few ink-jet plotters however, offer laser speed at pen-plotter prices. If speed and large-format drawings are top priority, nothing can match these devices.

If you need large plots but feel you can't afford a large plotter, many blueprint companies offer plotting as a service. This can be a very good alternative to purchasing your own plotter. Check with your local blueprinter.

POSTSCRIPT PRINTER OUTPUT

If you want to use a PostScript device to output your drawings, the best method is to use the Psout command (File ➤ Import/Export ➤ Post-Script Out). This converts your drawing into a true PostScript file. You can then send your file to a PostScript printer or typesetting machine. This can be especially useful for PCB layout where you require photo negatives for output. If you are an architect who needs presentation-quality drawings, you too may want to consider using the PostScript Out option. Often blueprinters who offer a raster plotter service can produce E-size PostScript output from a PostScript file. The uses of this option are really quite open-ended.

FINE-TUNING OUTPUT FROM THE PSOUT COMMAND

AutoCAD provides the PostScript user with a great deal of control over the formatting of the PostScript file output from Psout; from font-substitution mapping to custom PostScript Prologue data. Most of this control is offered through a file named *Acad.PSF*. This is the master support file for the Psin and Psout commands. You can customize the PostScript file created by Psout by making changes in the Acad.PSF file. Acad.PSF is divided into sections that affect various parts of the PostScript output. Each section begins with a title preceded by an asterisk. The following briefly describes these sections.

*fonts lets you control font substitution. You can assign a PostScript font to an AutoCAD font file or PostScript .PFB file used in the drawing.

*figureprologue defines the procedures used for embedding figures included with Psin PostScript images.

*isofontprologue defines the procedures used to re-encode fonts to be compatible with the ISO 8859 Latin/1 character set.

*fillprologue defines the code used in the Psout file to describe area fills.

*fill is a section where you can include your own custom fill patterns.

Most of these sections, with the exception of the *fonts section, will be of little use to the average user; but if you are a PostScript programmer, you can take advantage of these sections to customize your PostScript output.

You will also want to know about the *Psprolog* system variable. This system variable instructs Psout to include your custom Prolog statement in its PostScript output. (See *Chapter 14* for details on using Psout.) You add your custom prolog to the Acad.PSF using a text editor. The prolog should begin with a section heading that you devise. The heading can say anything, but it must begin with an asterisk like all the other section headings. Everything following the heading, excluding comments, will be included in the Psout output file, up to the next heading or the end of the file. The following shows a sample prolog that converts color assignments to line widths in a way similar to pen plotters.

```
*widthprolog
/ACADLayer { pop } def
/ACADColor { pop pop pop dup 0.5 mul setlinewidth pop}
def
/ACADLtype { pop
userdict /Linedict known not { /Linedict 100 dict def } if
1 index cvn Linedict exch known not {
mark 1 index { dup 0 eq { pop 1 72.0 div } if abs } forall
counttomark 2 add −1 roll astore exch pop
1 index cvn exch Linedict begin def end }
{ pop } ifelse
Linedict begin cvx exec 0 setdash end } bind def
/bd{bind def}bind def /m{moveto}bd /l{lineto}bd
/s{stroke}bd
/a{arc}bd /an{arcn}bd /gs{gsave}bd /gr{grestore}bd
/cp{closepath}bd /tr{translate}bd /sc{scale}bd
/co{concat}bd
/ff{findfont}bd /sf{setfont}bd /sh{show}bd /np{newpath}bd
/sw{setlinewidth}bd /sj{setlinejoin}bd /sm{setmiterlimit}bd
/cl{clip}bd /fi{fill}bd
%%EndProlog
```

A complete discussion of Psout and Psin's PostScript support is beyond the scope of this book. If you are interested in learning more, consult the PostScript section of the AutoCAD Customization manual. You can also learn a lot by looking at the PostScript files produced by Psout, browsing the Acad.PSF file, and consulting the following publications:

> *Understanding PostScript*, David Holzgang, SYBEX Inc.
>
> *PostScript Language Program Design*, Adobe Systems Incorporated, Addison-Wesley Publishing Company, Inc.
>
> *PostScript Language Reference Manual*, Adobe Systems Incorporated, Addison-Wesley Publishing Company, Inc.
>
> *PostScript Language Tutorial and Cookbook*, Adobe Systems Incorporated, Addison-Wesley Publishing Company, Inc.

You can also add a PostScript Plotter to the Plotter configuration. When you do this, AutoCAD plots the drawing as a series of vectors, just like any other plotter. If you have filled areas in your drawing and you are plotting to a PostScript file, filled areas can greatly increase plot file size and the time it takes to plot your PostScript file.

MEMORY AND AUTOCAD PERFORMANCE

Next to your computer's CPU, memory has the greatest impact on AutoCAD's speed. How much you have, and how you use it can make a big difference in whether you finish that rush job on schedule or work late nights trying. In this section, I hope to clarify some basic points about memory and how AutoCAD uses it.

AutoCAD release 12 for Windows is a virtual memory system. This means that when your RAM memory resources reach their limit, part of the data stored in RAM is temporarily moved to your hard disk to make more room in RAM. This temporary storage of RAM to your hard disk is called memory *paging*. Through memory paging, AutoCAD will continue to run, even though your work might exceed the capacity of your RAM.

AutoCAD uses memory in two ways. First, it stores its program code in RAM. The more programs you have open under Windows, the more RAM will be used. Windows controls the use of memory for program code, so if you start to reach the RAM limit, Windows will take care of memory paging. The second way AutoCAD uses memory is for storing drawing data. AutoCAD always attempts to store as much of your drawing in RAM as possible. Again, when the amount of RAM required for a drawing exceeds the actual RAM available, AutoCAD will page parts of the drawing data to the hard disk. Drawing data paging is controlled strictly by AutoCAD. Since RAM is shared with both program code and drawing data, your drawing size and the number of programs you have open under windows will affect how much RAM you have available. For this reason, if you find your AutoCAD editing session is slowing down, try closing other applications you might have open. This will free up more memory for AutoCAD and the drawing file.

AUTOCAD AND YOUR HARD DISK

You will notice that, as paging occurs, AutoCAD will slow down. If this happens frequently, the best thing you can do is add more RAM. But you can also improve the performance of AutoCAD under these conditions by ensuring that you have adequate hard-disk space and that any free hard-disk space has been *defragmented* or *optimized*. A defragmented disk will offer faster access, thereby improving paging speed.

You can also set up a permanent swap file under Windows to improve performance. A permanent swap file will improve the speed at which Windows is able to page RAM to your hard disk. To install a permanent swap file, take the following steps:

1. Remove any unnecessary files, then defragment your hard disk.

2. Under Windows, open the Control Panel program, then double-click on the 386 Enhanced icon. The 386 Enhanced dialog box will appear.

3. Click on the Virtual Memory ... button. The Virtual Memory dialog box appears.

4. Click on the Change button. The dialog box will expand to reveal more options.

5. Select the drive you intend to use for your permanent swap file from the Drive popup list, then select Permanent in the Type popup list.

6. Enter the size you want for your permanent swap file in the New Size input box.

7. Click on the Use 32-bit Disk·Access check box.

8. Close all the dialog boxes by clicking on OK.

Autodesk recommends a swap file that is four times the size of your RAM capacity. This means that if you have 8 megabytes of RAM, you will want a swap file that is 32 megabytes. This gives you a system with up to 40 megabytes of virtual memory.

The permanent swap file will permanently take up space on your hard disk, so when you select a size for the swap file, be sure you leave some room on your drive for other data. If your hard disk is limited in free space, try removing unnecessary files. Autodesk recommends a minimum of 4 Mb of free disk space. If you have a disk optimizer that lets you control which sectors are made free during defragmentation, use the outer-most sectors of your hard drive for swap-file space.

WHAT TO DO FOR *OUT OF RAM* AND *OUT OF PAGE SPACE* ERRORS

Once in a while, you may get the message that you have run out of page space, and AutoCAD terminates your editing session. This is usually due to a full hard disk. Here are two things you can do to free up your hard disk for more page space.

After you have used AutoCAD for some time, you may find some odd-looking files with the .AC$ extension in the directory where your drawings are stored. These files are the temporary memory page files for drawings mentioned earlier. They often appear if AutoCAD has been terminated abnormally. You can usually erase these files without any adverse effect. If you are in a network environment, however, check the time and date of these files before you remove them. They may belong to another user's current editing session, in which case you should not erase them.

If you've gotten rid of all the old swap files, but your disk is still unusually full, there may be lost file clusters filling up your hard disk. Lost clusters are pieces of files that are not actually assigned to a specific file. Often they occur when a program has terminated abnormally. To eliminate lost clusters and free up disk space, run the DOS Chkdsk.EXE (Check Disk) utility, with the /F parameter. Do not run Chkdsk from a DOS window under Windows. Exit Windows first to run Chkdsk. See your DOS manual for more on Chkdsk.EXE.

AUTOCAD MEMORY AND NETWORKS

If you are using a network version of AutoCAD, each computer on the network that uses AutoCAD must have its own configuration file. This means you must set the /C command switch (described in *Appendix B*) to a local drive and directory. Once this is done, you must run the AutoCAD configuration for each client computer. This will ensure that each node will have its own network node name and default log-in name.

Another point to consider is the location of swap files. When drawing files get large, AutoCAD makes heavy use of your hard disk. Swap files are constantly being written and updated. If you are working with AutoCAD on a network, it is especially important to pay attention to where swap files are being written. If you are using a server-client network system, and the network client or node has its own hard disk, you can improve AutoCAD's performance by forcing the program to place drawing swap files on the local drive, instead of on the server. This reduces network traffic, thereby improving AutoCAD's and the network's performance. The following steps show how this is done.

1. Start AutoCAD from the node, then click on File ➤ Configure.

2. At the Configuration menu, enter 7 ↵ to select *Operating Parameters*.

3. At the Operating Parameters menu, enter **5** ↵ to select *Placement of temporary files*. You will see the message

   Enter directory name for temporary files, or DRAWING
   to place them in the same directory as the drawing
   being edited.
   <DRAWING>:

4. Enter a local drive and directory name where temporary files can be stored.

5. Exit the configuration and make sure you save the configuration at the last prompt.

WHEN THINGS GO WRONG

AutoCAD is a complex program, and at times things don't go exactly right. If you run into problems, chances are the problem is not insurmountable. Here are a few tips on what to do when things don't work.

DIFFICULTY STARTING UP OR OPENING A FILE

If you've recently installed AutoCAD but you cannot get it started, you may have a configuration problem. Before you panic, try reconfiguring your system from scratch. To do this, erase the Acad.PWD and Acad.CFG files found in your AutoCAD directory, and start AutoCAD. You will be prompted to configure AutoCAD.

The Acad.PWD file contains authorization data needed to run AutoCAD. This file and the Acad.CFG file are both created when you first configure AutoCAD after installation.

Another common problem is having files locked and unavailable. This can happen to drawing files as well as support files—such as line type, hatch pattern, menu, and shape files. If a file is reported as being locked by AutoCAD, and you know no one else is using the system, locate the file in question, then remove its lock file. See *Chapter 14* for a complete listing of files and their lock file equivalents.

If you are on a single-user system, you may want to turn off the file-locking feature altogether. This can save you the frustration of having to unlock files that are accidentally locked due to system crashes.

RESTORING CORRUPTED FILES

Perhaps one of the most dreaded sights a computer user can see is the message *Error reading drive* C:. Computer hardware is often taken for granted until something goes wrong with it. Unfortunately, the most vulnerable part of your computer system is the hard disk, with the files it contains. You may even know someone who has lost AutoCAD files to an errant disk drive. One day, while you are trying to open a file, your screen responds *FATAL ERROR* or *INTERNAL ERROR*; then panic sets in.

Fortunately, there is hope for lost files. In most cases, AutoCAD will run through a file-recovery routine automatically when it attempts to load a corrupted file. If you have a file you know is corrupted, you can start the file-recovery utility by clicking on File ➤ Recover. You will get the File dialog box, allowing you to select the file you want to recover. Once you enter the name, AutoCAD goes to work. You get a series of messages, most of which have little meaning to the average user. Then the recovered file is opened. You may lose some data, but a partial file is better than no file at all, especially when the file represents several thousand hours of work. Also, there may be situations when a file is so badly corrupted it cannot be restored. You can only hope and pray this doesn't happen to you. By backing up frequently, the inconvenience of such an occurrence can be minimized. You may also want to invest in a hard disk maintenance program such as SpinRite or Norton Utilities. These programs can spot problem areas on your hard disk before they cause trouble.

CHECKING THE CONNECTION WITH YOUR PLOTTER OR DIGITIZER

The most common problem when connecting devices to your computer's serial port is improper cabling and switch settings. Usually proper cabling is supplied with the device, but sometimes it is not. The wires connecting the various pins on your cable must be arranged a certain way. If your plotter or other serial device does not work, check the cabling on your plotter and be sure it conforms to the cabling diagram shown in your AutoCAD installation guide. Also be sure the switches are properly set on your plotter or other serial device to receive and send data to AutoCAD. Again, these settings can be found in the installation guide.

Some devices require special setting up even after AutoCAD has been configured. These usually come with setup instructions. Check the manual that came with the device to be sure you haven't missed its setup options. When all else fails, call your vendor or manufacturer.

Sometimes when you temporarily switch to another program, you may find that upon returning to AutoCAD your digitizer or plotter won't respond. If this occurs, use the Reinit command. This command re-establishes connections to your peripheral devices. See *Chapter 7* for more details on Reinit.

CREATING

EXPLORING

EDITING

LEARNING

MANAGING

ADDING

PRINTING

ANIMATING

PLOTTING

ENTERING

DRAWING

GETTING

RENDERING

USING

INTEGRATING

MODELING

ORGANIZING

MANAGING

INSTALLING AND SETTING UP AUTOCAD

This appendix contains instructions on installing AutoCAD. To follow them, you need Windows 3.1 or greater installed. The instructions also assume some knowledge of Windows. If you need more help with Windows than is provided here, refer to *Appendix C* or your Windows manual. For more information on the AutoCAD package, refer to *Chapter 1*.

BACKING UP THE ORIGINAL DISKS

The program disks you received with your system are the most important part of your AutoCAD package. Without them, you have no AutoCAD program. It is therefore important that you make backup copies of them and use the *copies* to install your program. If you make any fatal errors during the installation, such as accidentally erasing files, you will still have the original disks to work with.

To back up your original disks, you can use the DOS DISKCOPY command, or if you prefer, you can use the File Manager's Disk ➤ Copy Disk option. If you need help with DISKCOPY, consult your DOS manual. If you are using Windows, you can consult the Help option under the File Manager.

Be sure to label your copies the same way the originals are labeled, including the serial number from disk 1. Put your originals in a safe place away from any magnetic sources. If you have a tablet, do not put disks on top of it because the tablet uses a small electrical field to operate. This field can destroy data on a disk.

INSTALLING AUTOCAD

Before you begin the installation process, be sure you have a drive with at least 37 MB of free disk space for the complete installation, including sample files, the help system, and the AME. In addition, you should know the following:

- Your dealer's name and phone number
- Whether you have the Advanced Modeling Extension (AME)

You will also want to have at least an additional 4 Mb of free disk space for AutoCAD *temporary files*, plus another 5 Mb of additional space for the tutorial files you will create. Temporary files are files AutoCAD creates as it works.

To begin your installation, first start up Windows. Next, get the backup disk labeled *Executables-1* and be sure it is not write-protected. Place the disk in drive A or B. From the Program Manager, click on File ➤ Run, then enter **A:setup** or **B:setup** depending on which drive you are installing from. You will get the opening screen. It will stay on for a moment, then the next screen will appear informing you that you must first personalize your copy of AutoCAD. Press ↵ to continue.

When you personalize AutoCAD, you are asked for your name, company, dealer's name, and the dealer's telephone number. This information will be displayed on the opening AutoCAD screen, so don't enter anything you'll regret later.

Once you enter this information, you are asked where to place your AutoCAD files. The tutorial assumes you have AutoCAD on drive C and in a directory called ACADWIN. These are the defaults during the installation so, unless you are an experienced DOS user, press ↵ to accept them when you see these prompts.

The next set of questions asks which set of files you want to install. The tutorials in this book assume that you have installed the entire program. However, you can install just the files you feel you need right now. If you later find you need to install other AutoCAD files, you can run the AutoCAD Setup utility again.

Once you answer all these questions, the actual installation begins and you are prompted for each disk as it is needed. The AutoCAD Setup will install an AutoCAD program group in the Program Manager. The program group will contain a variety of Notepad files which you can view on your own. These files contain last minute information that didn't make it into the final version of the documentation.

THE PROGRAM FILES

If you look at the AutoCAD directory, you will see a number of sub-directories. The following list briefly describes the contents of each sub-directory:

ADS stands for *AutoCAD Development System*. The files contained in this directory are programs and sample codes for ADS. If you are a C programmer who wants to customize AutoCAD, then this directory will be of importance to you. I do not discuss ADS in this tutorial, however.

API stands for *Application Programming Interface*. The files in this directory are for programmers interested in linking applications to the Advanced Modeling Extension. Most users will probably never have to deal with these files.

ASE stands for *AutoCAD SQL Extensions*. The files in this directory are for database programmers interested in linking AutoCAD drawings to SQL servers.

Fonts contains the standard AutoCAD font-definition files, as well as some sample PostScript .PFB files.

Igesfont contains files that help AutoCAD translate to and from the Initial Graphics Exchange Specifications (IGES) CAD format. These files are of concern to you only if you use the IGES translation facility in AutoCAD.

R11supp contains a compressed archive file called R11supp.EXE. When you enter **R11supp.EXE** at the DOS prompt the archive decompresses and you see numerous files ending with the .LSP extension. These are AutoLISP and menu files from AutoCAD release 11. They are offered to those users who intend to exchange release 11 and 12 files frequently, and to those users who want to use the release 11 extension for Windows. Since the Windows release needs the support files from the DOS version, these files can be used with the Windows version of AutoCAD to maintain compatibility.

Sample contains sample drawings and AutoLISP programs; many of the latter are quite useful (see *Chapter 19* for more on these programs).

Source contains the ASCII source files for many of the support files. Included here is the AutoCAD Menu file, which you will learn to use in *Chapter 21*.

Support contains the files that define a variety of AutoCAD's functions, such as fonts, line types, and patterns. You will take a closer look at all these files in *Chapters 19–21*.

Tutorial contains sample files used in conjunction with the tutorials that appear in the various AutoCAD manuals.

CONFIGURING AUTOCAD

In this section, you will learn how to *configure* AutoCAD. By configure, we mean to set up AutoCAD to work with the particular hardware you have connected to your computer. Programs often rely on their own drivers to operate specialized equipment. By configuring AutoCAD, you tell it exactly what equipment it will be working with. With release 12, you can configure AutoCAD at any time during an AutoCAD session.

DOING THE BASIC CONFIGURATION

To perform a basic configuration, follow these steps.

1. Open the AutoCAD program group by double clicking on its icon, then double click on the AutoCAD icon. You will get a message that AutoCAD is not yet configured.

2. Press ↵ and you will get the screen shown in Figure B.1. This tells you that AutoCAD needs to be configured.

3. At the **Press Return to continue** prompt, press ↵. You will get the screen shown in Figure B.2 showing a list of display systems.

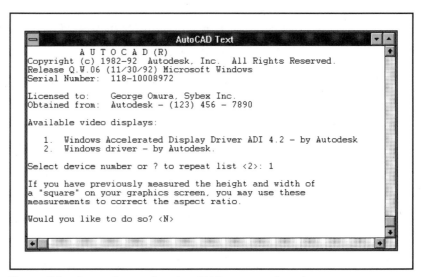

Figure B.1: Screen shown when AutoCAD is not configured

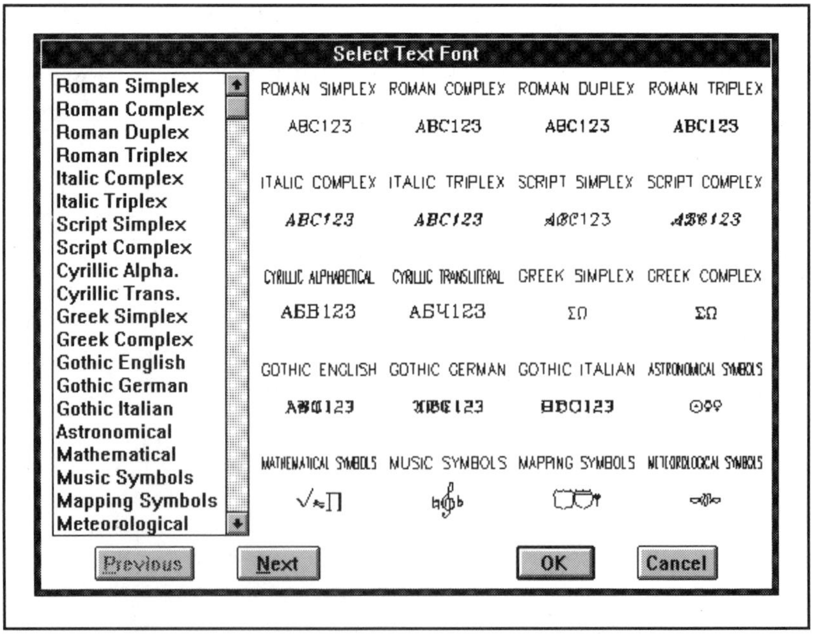

Figure B.2: List of display options

4. At the **Select device number or ? to repeat list <1>:**
prompt, enter the number that corresponds to the display system you are using.

Selecting a Display Option

AutoCAD supplies two display drivers for Windows. The default driver,
DSACAD.DLL, uses the Windows resources to display AutoCAD
drawings. The accelerated display driver, DSDLWIN.DLL, offers enhanced speed under Windows by bypassing Windows to write directly
to the screen. This high-performance driver also offers a display list,
which further increases AutoCAD performance, though at the cost of
greater memory use.

If you choose to use the accelerated display driver, you will have two
additional options to select. The following describes the other options.

> **GDI-bypass** causes AutoCAD to bypass some of the standard
> Windows Graphics Display Interface (GDI) routines that con-
> trol the Windows screen. By enabling this feature, AutoCAD is
> able to draw to the graphics display much faster. This feature is
> only effective, however, when the AutoCAD window is in the
> foreground.

> **Display-list** causes AutoCAD to maintain graphic data in a
> faster display-list format. With this feature enabled, you will see
> a major improvement in pan and zoom speeds. The drawback to
> this feature is that it requires the use of more system memory.

Selecting Input Devices

Once you are done configuring your display, you will get a list of input
device options.

1. Check the list for the number of your device and enter that
number at the prompt at the bottom of the list. If you have
no input device other than the keyboard, choose option 1,
None. Choosing None causes AutoCAD to use the same
pointing device that is used for Windows.

2. Answer any questions regarding your input device. Again, since different input devices offer different options, we cannot provide details on what to select. However, the prompts are usually quite clear, so you shouldn't have any problems.

3. You may also be prompted to select an adapter port for your input device. You will get the prompt

   ```
   Connects to Asynchronous Communications Adapter
   port.
   Standard ports are:
   COM1
   COM2 Enter port name, or address in hexadecimal
   <COM1>:
   ```

   If you have two asynchronous communications ports, or *serial* ports as they are commonly called, you can use this opportunity to tell AutoCAD that you want to connect your input device to a port other than COM1.

4. If you are configuring AutoCAD for a digitizing tablet, you will see a series of prompts referring to Mole Mode. See *Configuring Your Digitizing Tablet*, later in this appendix, for a detailed description of this feature. This section also describes how to set up your tablet to use a tablet template.

Be sure you plug your input device into the proper serial port. If you don't know which port is COM2, you may have to experiment by switching ports and seeing which one works.

Selecting Output Devices

Printer and plotter configuration works the same way as display and input device configuration. You are shown a numbered list, at the bottom of which is a prompt asking you to enter the number of the device you wish to connect to.

1. Enter the number corresponding to your printer or plotter.

2. As with the input device, you are prompted for a serial or parallel port assignment. You are also prompted for the printer or plotter default options that are displayed during AutoCAD's PLOT command. *Chapter 7* describes the different options in detail.

3. For now, take the default settings presented to you for the plotter settings. You can always change them later.

Note: You can configure multiple plotters and printers if you so desire. To do this, while in AutoCAD, pull down the File menu at the far left of the menu bar and click on Configure. At the configuration screen, enter **5**. You are presented with the following list:

```
Plotter Configuration Menu
0. Exit to configuration menu
1. Add a plotter configuration
2. Delete a plotter configuration
3. Change a plotter configuration
4. Rename a plotter configuration
```

You have a variety of options to choose from, including the addition of more printers or plotters to the configuration list. You can even have multiple instances of the same plotter or printer if you want.

Answering General Questions about Your System

Once you've finished configuring your peripherals, AutoCAD asks you some general questions about your system configuration.

1. If you have the network version of AutoCAD, you will get the following prompt:

```
Login Name:
Enter default login name or . for none <Your name and
company.>:
```

The network version of AutoCAD locks files when they are being edited. This prevents two people on the network from attempting to edit the same file simultaneously. The log-in name is used to identify the computer on the network that is currently using a locked file.

You can press ↵ to accept the default name, which is the same as the one used during the installation. If you enter a period (.) at this prompt, AutoCAD will prompt you for a log-in name every time you open a drawing file. You can always come back and change the log-in name, so press ↵ to accept the default for now.

2. Next, you are prompted for a server authorization.

   ```
   Server authorization:
   AutoCAD serial number is 123-45678900
   Enter the maximum number of users for this package
   <1>:
   ```

   Here, you must enter the number of users your package is authorized for.

3. Once you enter the number, you are prompted for the authorization code:

   ```
   Enter server authorization code for this package <0>:
   ```

   Your authorization code can be found on the version label placed on the spine of your AutoCAD slip case.

4. Once you enter the code, you get the next prompt:

   ```
   Do you wish to run the executable from a read-only
   directory? <N>
   ```

This prompt is significant only if your network requires read-only permission on shared executable files, as in 3Com networks. If you answer Y, then you are prompted for a sharable directory for server temporary files. You should then enter a full path name, including disk-drive designation. Press ↵ at this prompt. You then get the prompt:

```
Enter a password to restrict unauthorized changes to the
server authorization or . for none<> :
```

5. Enter a name for a password to protect the server configuration. If you later forget the password, however, you will have to reinstall AutoCAD. You are then prompted to reenter the password:

   Please retype password to verify:

6. Retype the password. You then get the prompt:

   Do you wish to enable file-locking? <Y>:

7. Enter **N** ↵ for no if you are on a single user system. If you are installing AutoCAD on a network, answer **Y**.

Finishing Up

Once you are done with the configuration, you will get a list of the devices you selected (see Figure B.3).

```
Current AutoCAD configuration


  Video display:      SVADI Super VGA ADI 4.2 - by Autodesk

SVADI v1.8d (21jun92).  Universal Super VGA ADI (Display/Render)
DOS Protected Mode ADI 4.2 Driver for AutoCAD.
Config file is E:\ACAD\DRV\SVADI.CFG
Configured for: Tseng ET4000.  Text font: 8x16.
Display - 1024x768 in 256 colors on Black background.
Rendering - 320x200 in 256 colors.


    Version: A.1.18

  Digitizer:          Microsoft Mouse Driver ADI 4.2 - by Autodesk
                      Microsoft Mouse
    Version: A.1.18

  Plotter:            Hewlett-Packard (HP-GL) ADI 4.2 - by Autodesk
                      7585
    Port: Asynchronous Communications Adapter COM1 at address 3F8 (hex)
    Version: A.1.18


Press RETURN to continue:
```

Figure B.3: Screen showing configured hardware options

1. Press ↵ and you will get the Configuration menu and a prompt asking you to enter a selection (see Figure B.4).

2. Press ↵ to accept the default, 0. The following message will appear:

   > If you answer N to the following question, all configuration changes you have just made will be discarded. Keep configuration changes? <Y>

3. If you wish to save your current configuration, press ↵ to accept the default, Y. AutoCAD will start up. Now you can begin drawing.

```
                A U T O C A D  (R)
Copyright (c) 1982-92  Autodesk, Inc.  All Rights Reserved.
Release 12 (6/21/92) 386 DOS Extender
Serial Number:  117-10058471
EVALUATION VERSION -- NOT FOR RESALE
Licensed to:    George Omura, Sybex Inc.
Obtained from:  Autodesk - (123) 456-7890

Configuration menu

   0.  Exit to drawing editor
   1.  Show current configuration
   2.  Allow detailed configuration

   3.  Configure video display
   4.  Configure digitizer
   5.  Configure plotter
   6.  Configure system console
   7.  Configure operating parameters

Enter selection <0>:
```

Figure B.4:   The Configuration menu

SETTING PREFERENCES

Once you've done the basic configuration, you are ready to use AutoCAD. But you can further modify other features of AutoCAD through the Preferences dialog box (see Figure B.5). This dialog box can

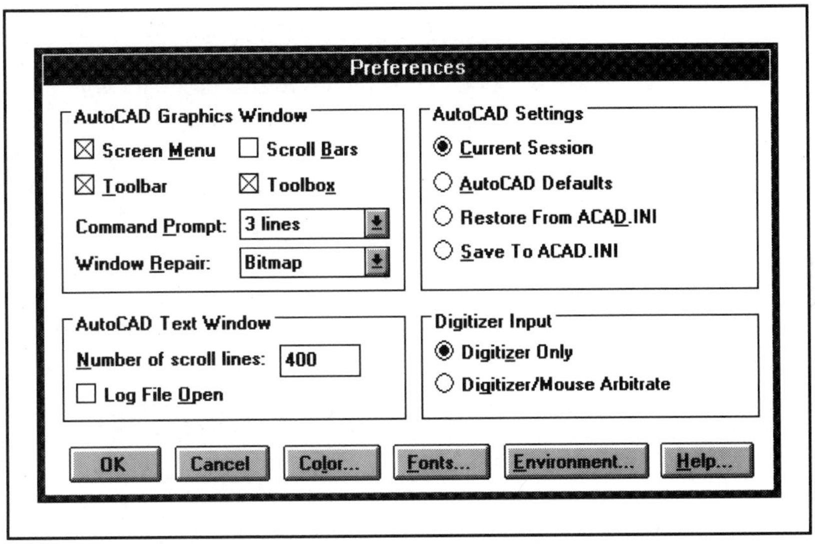

Figure B.5:   The Preferences dialog box lets you control the general appearance of AutoCAD, as well as a variety of other AutoCAD settings.

be accessed by clicking on File ➤ Preferences…. The following describes the settings available in this dialog box according to button groups.

AUTOCAD GRAPHICS WINDOW

The controls in this group let you control the various parts of the AutoCAD window. The two check boxes, Screen Menu and Status Line, turn the screen menu and status line on or off. The *Command Prompt* popup menu list lets you control the number of text lines displayed in the command prompt area. You can set this value to none to hide the command prompt entirely.

The Screen Repair radio buttons let you set how the window image is repaired. Bitmap is best suited for super high resolution displays, 1280×1024 or greater. Fastdraw is best suited for VGA and Super VGA resolutions. You may want to experiment with these settings to see which offers the fastest redraw times for your system.

AUTOCAD SETTINGS

The radio buttons in this group let you store or recall the preference settings. AutoCAD Defaults will restore the standard AutoCAD settings. Restore from ACAD.INI will restore the settings found in the ACAD.INI configuration file. Save To ACAD.INI will save the current settings to the ACAD.INI file. These settings then become the default for later sessions. Current Session tells AutoCAD to use the current preference settings for the current session only. The **OK** button must be pressed before any of these options takes effect.

AUTOCAD TEXT WINDOW

The settings in this group let you control properties of the text window which can be accessed by pressing the F2 function key. The Number of scroll lines input box lets you control how many lines of text AutoCAD maintains in the text window before discarding them. To view earlier lines, you can use the scroll bar in the text window. The Log File Open checkbox lets you store data from the text window in a text file. The text file can then be viewed, edited, and printed with any word processor. When this item is checked, a log file is opened, and from then on, anything that appears in the command prompt will be written to the file. Note that when the log file is opened, you cannot access it with any other application. When the Log File Open box is unchecked, the log file is closed. You are then able to view the log file using any word processor. You can set the location and name of the log file using the Environment... button at the bottom of this dialog box. See *Environment...* described later in this section.

DIGITIZER INPUT

These two radio buttons let you control how AutoCAD works with your Digitizer, if you have one installed. When Digitizer Only is selected, AutoCAD will respond to digitizer movement and input only. With Digitizer/Mouse Arbitration selected, AutoCAD will respond to both the digitizer and Mouse depending on which pointing device is moving.

Note: If you are using the digitizer mole mode described later in this appendix, AutoCAD will respond only to the mouse while the digitizer is in the digitizer mode.

SYSTEM PRINTER SELECTION

These two radio buttons let you determine whether AutoCAD plots to the Windows device (Use Control Panel Configuration) or the device you selected during the AutoCAD configuration (Use AutoCAD Configuration).

COLOR...

This button opens the Color dialog box (see Figure B.6). From this dialog box, you can set the color for the various parts of the AutoCAD graphics and text windows. You can click on the graphic to the left to

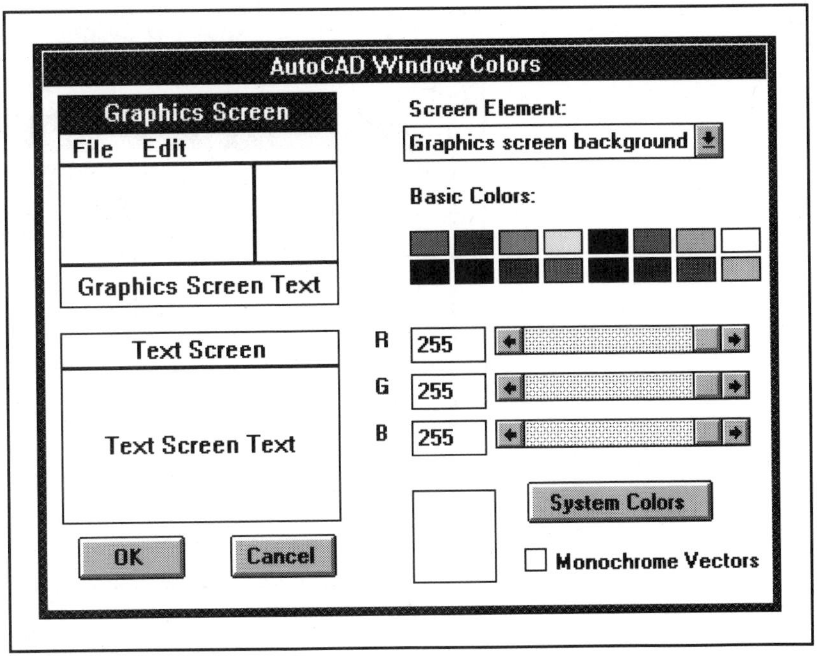

Figure B.6:   The Color dialog box

select the part of the screen you want to set. Then you can use the RGB sliders or the basic color samples to set the color. The System Colors button will set the windows to those settings found in the Windows Control Panel settings.

FONTS...

This button opens the Font dialog box (see Figure B.7). From this dialog box, you can set the font, font style, and size of the text that appears in the command prompt, screen menu, and text window. By reducing the size of the font, for example, you can increase the size of the drawing area.

ENVIRONMENT...

This button opens the Environment dialog box (see Figure B.8). From here, you can determine where AutoCAD is to look for or place various resource files. See *Other AutoCAD Settings* for more information on these settings.

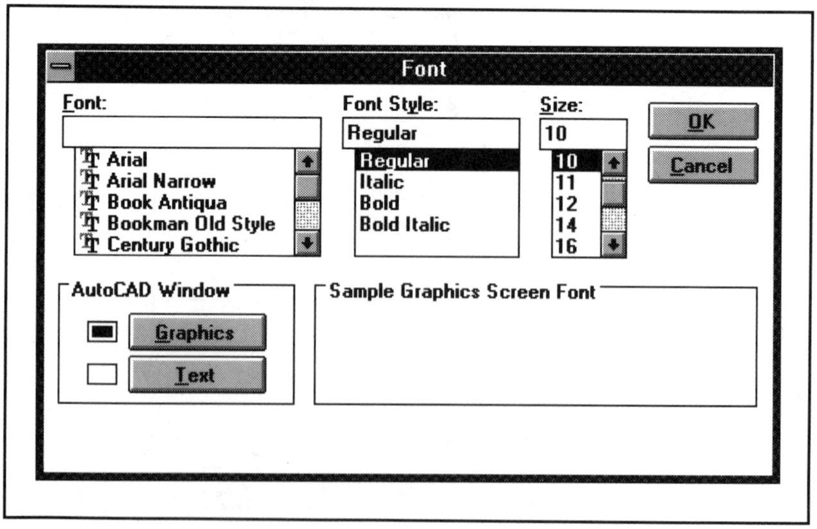

Figure B.7: The Font dialog box

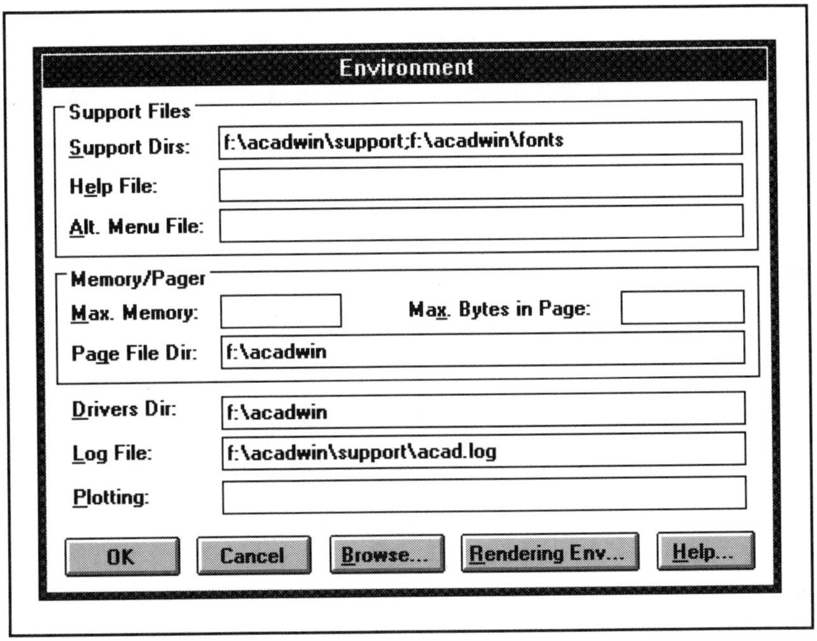

Figure B.8:   The Environment dialog box

CONFIGURING YOUR DIGITIZING TABLET

If you are using a digitizer with AutoCAD for Windows, you will need to select some additional configuration options. These other options allow you to add flexibility to your digitizer or to add a menu template. As an alternative, you may choose to configure your tablet as the Windows pointing device, in which case, the options in this section will not apply.

MAKING YOUR DIGITIZER ACT LIKE A MOUSE

If you are using a digitizer tablet, during the configuration you will be asked the following questions pertaining to the *mole mode* feature. If you do not use the mole mode feature, you can only use your digitizer to select points in the drawing area and pick menu options from the screen menu. You cannot access the toolbar, pull-down menus or any other window outside of AutoCAD. To get to these other areas, you will have to use your standard Windows pointing device. With the mole mode feature activated, you will be able to access the toolbar and pull-down menus with your digitizer, though you will still be restricted to using the digitizer in AutoCAD.

To try out the mole mode, accept the default by pressing return at the following set of prompts during the digitizer configuration:

```
Do you want to configure your digitizer as a mole? <Y>
Do you want an audible mole/context state indicator? <N>
Do you want an visible mole/context state indicator? <Y>
Do you want to assign a CURSOR BUTTON to toggle
modes? <N>
Do you want a PRIMARY MOLE area? <Y>
Enter lower-left hand corner now.
Enter upper-right hand corner now.
Do you want a SECONDARY MOLE area? <N>
Do you want a PRIMARY TOGGLE area? <N>
Do you want a SECONDARY TOGGLE area? <N>
```

After the fifth prompt, you are prompted to select the primary mole area. This can be any part of your digitizer you are not using for anything. For now, you can use the top third of the digitizer. This area is normally reserved for custom digitizer overlays. Once you are done, and are running AutoCAD, you will be able to move your pointer into the mole area to make your digitizer act like a mouse.

If you are using a single primary mole area, you cannot use the mole area for tracing nor can you use the mole area to select commands from a tablet overlay menu. However, If you need to use the entire tablet for an overlay menu, you can use a *toggle area* in conjunction with a *secondary mole* area to make a tablet area serve two functions.

If you choose to use a toggle area, you will be prompted to select two corners defining the toggle area on your tablet. This area can be very small and should be placed near the mole area. The toggle area is used only to switch the mole area on and off. This way you can use an area on your digitizer for both a mole area and to select commands. Another option is to select a button on your digitizer puck to turn the mole area on and off.

Note: If you choose to use a toggle area and a secondary mole area, you may want to use the screen pointing area to double as the mole area. The next section describes the screen pointing area.

The second and third prompts in the mole configuration let you turn on a sound or visual aid to tell you the mole mode status. If you choose the visible mole indicator, the AutoCAD Window title bar will display the word *Mole* or *Digitizer* depending on which mode the digitizer is currently in. The sound option simply beeps each time you toggle from mole to digitizer mode.

If you have both a mouse and a digitizer connected to your computer, you can still use both devices for AutoCAD.

CONFIGURING THE TABLET MENU AREA

If you own a digitizing tablet, and you would like to use it with the AutoCAD tablet menu template, you must configure your tablet menu.

1. The first step is to securely fasten your tablet menu template to the tablet using the plastic registration pins provided with the template. Be sure the area covered by the template is completely within the tablet's active drawing area.

2. Next, start AutoCAD if it isn't already running.

3. Move your pointing device to the menu area to the right of the screen. Highlight the word SETTINGS on the Root menu, then press your pick button.

4. Now pick Next, then TABLET from the side menu. Then pick Config from the side menu (if your tablet has already been configured once, pick Re-cfg). You will get the prompt

   Digitize upper left corner of menu area 1:

   For the next series of prompts, you will be locating the four tablet menu areas, starting with menu area 1 (see Figure B.9).

5. Locate the position indicated in Figure B.9 as the upper-left corner of menu area 1. Place your puck or stylus to pick that point. The prompt will change to

   Digitize lower left corner of menu area 1:

6. Again, locate the position indicated in Figure B.9 as the lower-left corner of menu area 1.

7. Continue this process until you have selected three corners for four menu areas.

8. When you are done selecting the menu areas, you will get the prompt

   Digitize lower left corner of screen pointing area:

   Pick the position indicated in Figure B.9.

9. Finally, you get the prompt

   Digitize upper right corner of screen pointing area:

   Pick the position indicated in Figure B.9. Now you are done.

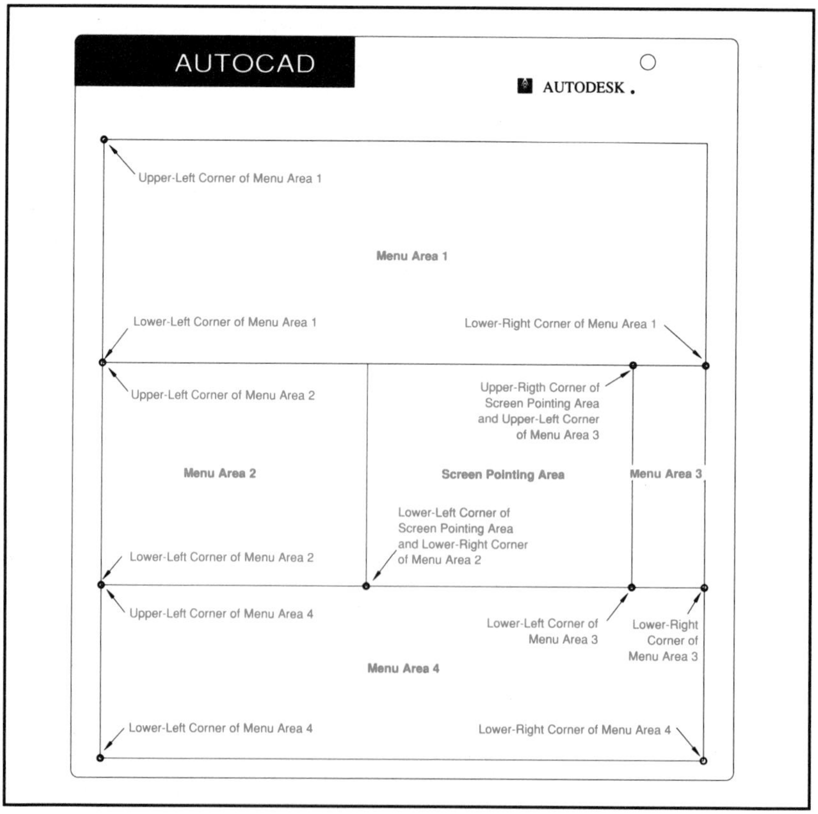

Figure B.9: How to locate the tablet menu areas

AutoCAD will remember this configuration until you change it again. Quit this file by entering **quit** through the keyboard. Or quit by clicking on File ➤ Exit AutoCAD.

KEEPING MULTIPLE CONFIGURATIONS

There may be times when you want to have AutoCAD configured in more than one way. For example, you may want to have one configuration where the drawing editor's status line, prompt area, and menu area are not shown, so a drawing fills the entire screen. (See *Chapter 1* for the location and appearance of these areas on the display.) This configuration is desirable for presentations. At the same time, you will want to use the standard screen configuration when you create and edit drawings.

AutoCAD stores its configuration information in two files. These files are ACAD.CFG and ACAD.INI. When you first install and configure AutoCAD, these two files are created and placed in the Acadwin directory. You can, however, tell AutoCAD to store alternative versions of these files in other directories, then set up an AutoCAD icon to start and run AutoCAD based on these alternate settings. The following steps take you through the process of creating a second version of the AutoCAD icon with a different configuration.

1. First create a subdirectory under the Acadwin directory where you can store your new configuration files. For this example, I'll call it config2.

2. Copy the ACAD.CFG and ACAD.INI files from the \Acadwin directory to the \Acadwin\Config2 directory.

3. With the AutoCAD program group open, highlight the AutoCAD Icon.

4. From the Program Manager menu bar, click on File ➤ Copy. The Copy Program Item dialog box appears.

5. Open the To Group popup list, locate the AutoCAD program group name, and click on it. AutoCAD should now appear in the To Group list box.

6. Click on OK. A copy of the AutoCAD icon appears in the AutoCAD program group.

7. With the new AutoCAD program icon highlighted, click on File ➤ Properties. The Program Item Properties dialog box appears (see Figure B.10).

8. Edit the contents of the Command Line input box so that it shows the following

   ```
   C:\acadwin\acad.exe /C C:\acadwin\config2 /S
   C:\acadwin\support
   ```

The Command line input box tells Windows where to find the AutoCAD program. The /C and /S in the example are called command line switches. The /C lets you specify the location of the configuration files. The /S lets you specify where AutoCAD should look for support files. The switch appears first in the line, followed by the file location. This example assumes that AutoCAD is installed in drive C. Be sure you specify the correct drive for your installation.

9. You can optionally change the icon to a different one by clicking on the Change Icon button. You can also change the title that appears below the icon by editing the Description input box.

10. When you are done, click on OK. Your new configuration is ready to set up.

11. Double-click on the newly created AutoCAD icon, then run the configuration process described earlier in this appendix, this time, using different settings.

12. Use the Preferences option under the File menu to set up your preferences for this version of AutoCAD.

You can create as many different versions of AutoCAD as you like, using these steps. Note that you aren't making copies of the program; you are only making copies of the program items in the Windows program group.

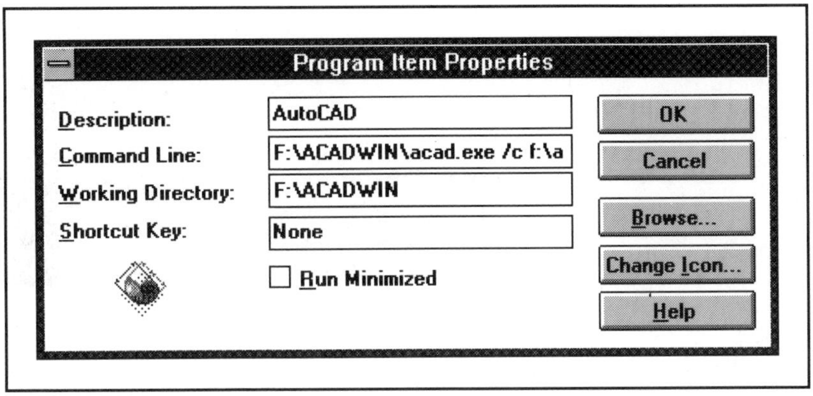

Figure B.10:   The Program Item Properties dialog box

OTHER AUTOCAD SETTINGS

There are a variety of other AutoCAD settings you can control either through command switches or through the *DOS environment*. The DOS environment is a small portion of memory used to store data. When AutoCAD starts up, it looks in that environment for any information that may be specifically set aside for it. You can place data in the environment using the DOS Set command. For example, to direct AutoCAD to look in Acadwin\Support and Acadwin\font directories for support files, you would enter the following at the DOS prompt:

SET ACAD=C:\ACAD\SUPPORT;C:\ACAD\FONTS

You can include this line in a batch file that starts Windows so the environment is set before you run AutoCAD for Windows. Table B.1 gives a listing of these other environment settings and their uses. It also shows the commands switches that can be used to make some of these settings.

These variables are entered at the DOS prompt just as described for the ACAD variable in the previous example. You can also control these settings from within AutoCAD. To do this, click on File ➤ Preferences, then in the Preferences dialog box, click on Environment .... The Environment dialog box appears (see Figure B.8). You can then enter values for these settings in the appropriate input boxes.

Table B.1: The AutoCAD DOS Environment Variables

ENVIRONMENT VARIABLE	COMMAND LINE SWITCH	ENVIRONMENT DIALOG NAME	PURPOSE
ACAD	/S	Support Dirs:	Indicates the directory or directories for support files.
NA	/C	NA	Indicates where configuration files are found
ACADALTMNU	NA	Alt. Menu File:	Indicates where to find alternate tablet menu files
ACADDRV	/D	Drivers Dir:	Indicates where to find the Protected mode ADI drivers
ACADHELP	NA	Help File:	Indicates where to find the AutoCAD help files
ACADLOGFILE	NA	Log File:	Indicates where AutoCAD is to place command prompt log file

Table B.1: The AutoCAD DOS Environment Variables (continued)

ENVIRONMENT VARIABLE	COMMAND LINE SWITCH	ENVIRONMENT DIALOG NAME	PURPOSE
ACADMAXMEM	/M	Max. Memory	Indicates the maximum amount of memory in bytes that AutoCAD requests from the operating system
ACADPAGEDIR	NA	Page File Dir:	Indicates the directory where page files are stored
ACADMAXPAGE	NA	Max. Bytes in Page	Indicates the maximum number of bytes to be sent to the first page file
ACADPLCMD	NA	Plotting:	Indicates the shell command AutoCAD is to use for plot spooling
AVECFG	NA	Rendering Env... ➤ Config. File Dir:	Indicates where to store the renderer's configuration files

Table B.1: The AutoCAD DOS Environment Variables (continued)

ENVIRONMENT VARIABLE	COMMAND LINE SWITCH	ENVIRONMENT DIALOG NAME	PURPOSE
RDPADI	NA	NA	Indicates the location of the protected mode ADI rendering drive for the renderer
RHPADI	NA	NA	Indicates the location of the protected mode ADI hard copy rendering driver for the renderer
AVEFACEDIR	NA	Rendering Env … ➤ Face File Dir:	Indicates the location for storing the renderer's temporary files
AVEPAGEDIR	NA	Rendering Env… ➤ Page File Dir:	Indicates the location for the renderer's RAM page files
AVEDFILE	NA	Rendering Env… ➤ AVERDFILE:	Indicates where .RND rendering files are displayed

USING THE FILE MANAGER TO OPEN AUTOCAD FILES

You might also want to set up Window's File Manager to automatically start AutoCAD and load a file. Using the File Manager can help you locate and manage your AutoCAD files and keep control over your projects. To set up the File Manager to do this, take the following steps:

1. Open the File Manager.
2. Locate and highlight any AutoCAD drawing file.
3. Pull down the File menu and click on Associate.
4. At the Associate dialog box, click on Browse.
5. At the Browse dialog box, locate Acad.EXE in the Acadwin directory and double-click on it.
6. Back at the Associate dialog box, click on **OK**.

Now you can use the File Manager to open AutoCAD files by just clicking on the AutoCAD file drawing name. The directory of the file you double-click on becomes the default working directory.

SETTING UP A WORKING DIRECTORY

The tutorials in this book assume you are working from the directory where the program files are stored. However, if you prefer, you can use another directory to store your files. The following steps describe how you set up a working directory for AutoCAD.

1. Create your working directory either in DOS using the MD command or in the File Manager using File ➤ Create Directory ....
2. Highlight the AutoCAD icon in the AutoCAD program group and click on File ➤ Properties from the Program Manager pull-down menu.

3. In the Program Item Properties dialog box, double-click on the Working Directory input box, then enter the name of your working directory. You can use the Browse button to use a file dialog box to locate your directory.

4. Click on OK.

This new working directory will be the default whenever you open the file dialog box in AutoCAD. You can also use these same steps to set up a working directory for any other Windows program.

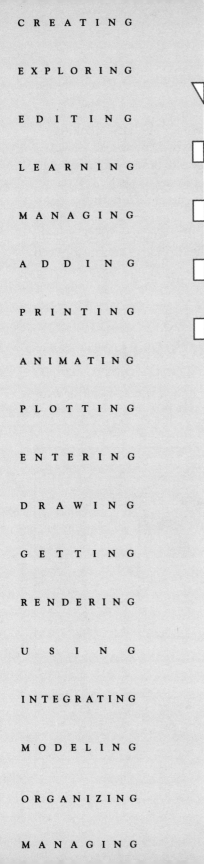

CREATING

EXPLORING

EDITING

LEARNING

MANAGING

ADDING

PRINTING

ANIMATING

PLOTTING

ENTERING

DRAWING

GETTING

RENDERING

USING

INTEGRATING

MODELING

ORGANIZING

MANAGING

A
WINDOWS
PRIMER

In this appendix, I explain some of the more common Windows functions for those readers who are not familiar with Windows. You may also want to consult your Windows manual or any of the publications by SYBEX that describe the use of Windows in detail, such as *Mastering Windows 3.1 Special Edition*, 1993. The first part of this appendix discusses how to get around in Windows. The rest describes two of the essential built-in applications that come with Windows, the Program Manager and the File Manager. I assume that Windows has already been installed on a 386 or 486 computer.

STARTING UP WINDOWS
AND THE OPENING SCREEN

Once Windows is installed, you start it up by entering WIN ↵ or WIN/3 ↵ at the DOS prompt. You first see the opening banner, then the Windows desktop appears (see Figure C.1).

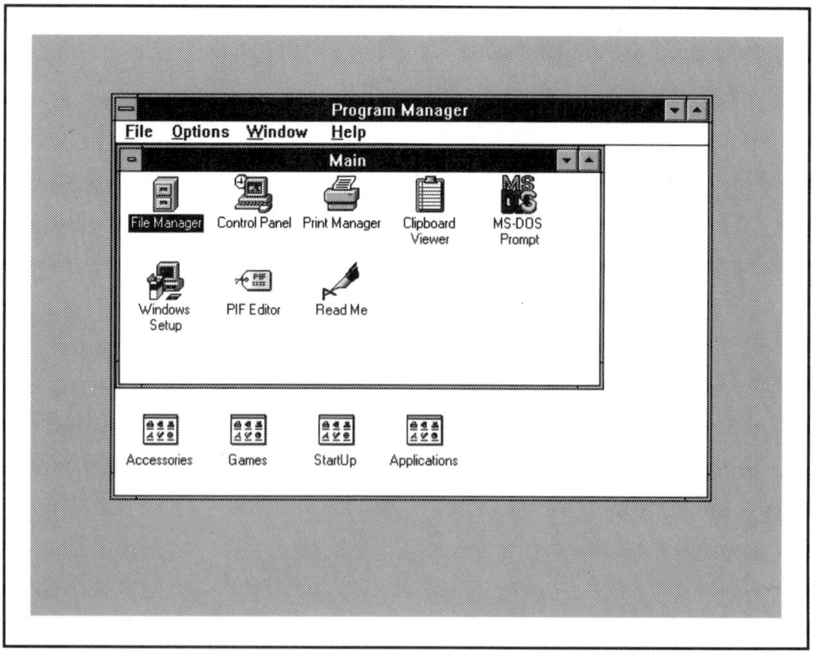

Figure C.1: The opening Windows banner and the Windows desktop

Figure C.1 shows the Windows screen as it appears after Windows is first installed. It shows you the components of the desktop and a typical window. You may want to refer to this figure as you read through this appendix.

The entire screen space on which Windows operates is called the desktop. You can think of the desktop as a workspace on which you arrange your windows. If you are working on someone else's computer, chances are the screen you see will be different from the figure, just as someone else's desk might be arranged differently from your own. Don't be alarmed. I'll explain how to navigate the desktop next.

UNDERSTANDING THE WINDOWS DESKTOP

As its name implies, Windows provides an environment where programs are viewed through rectangles called windows. You can have multiple windows open, and you can change the size and location of these windows to suit your needs. Windows can overlap each other, or they can be arranged side by side in what is called a *tiled* arrangement. You can even shrink the windows so they appear as small icons on the desktop. As you look at Figure C.1, you see two windows already open. Their titles are shown at the top. The main window is called the Program Manager. Within the Program Manager are other windows and icons that are called program groups. Within these program groups are icons of the programs you use, such as word processors, spreadsheets, and AutoCAD. When you first install Windows, you see five program groups entitled Main, Accessories, Applications, Games, and StartUp. Main contains several useful programs, such as the File Manager and the Control Panel. Accessories contains a word processor, the Cardfile, the Calculator, the Calendar, the Paint program, and more. Applications contains any programs Windows finds on your computer during installation. Games contains two sample Windows games. Start Up is a program group reserved for programs you want started automatically when Windows is opened.

You can create your own groups to organize your programs into separate and distinct categories. You may, for example, have a group you call Graphics to hold all of your graphics-related programs, and another group called DTP to hold your word processing and desktop publishing programs. Often, when you install new Windows software, new groups will be created just for that program. Before you get into working with program groups, let's try working with the windows themselves.

MOVING AND RESIZING WINDOWS

Any window can be re-sized and moved to let you arrange your desktop. To change the shape of a window, try the following steps:

1. Move the arrow cursor to the right border of a window until the arrow changes to a double sided arrow, as shown in Figure C.2.

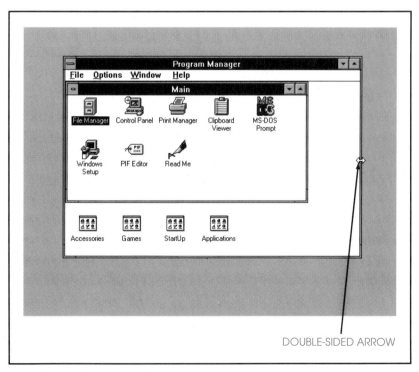

Figure C.2:   A double sided arrow at the window border

2. Press and hold down the left pick button of your mouse and move the mouse from side to side. Notice that the window changes in width as you move your mouse. When you let go of the mouse button, the window stays where you left it and the cursor returns to its normal shape.

3. Move the arrow cursor to the lower-left corner of the window. Notice that the cursor changes to a double arrow pointing in a diagonal direction.

4. With the cursor in the corner diagonal shape, press and hold down the pick button. Now as you move the mouse, the corner moves with it, allowing you to change both the height and width of the window. Once you let go of the mouse button, the window becomes fixed in its last position.

5. Move the cursor to the window title bar at the top of the Program Manager window, then press and hold the mouse button. Now as you move the mouse, the entire window moves with the mouse. Let go of the button and the window is fixed in its last position.

You have just seen how you can reshape and move a window. In these steps, you were asked to press and hold down your mouse button while you moved the mouse. This action is called *click and drag*. You will use this mouse action frequently in Windows and in AutoCAD.

TURNING A WINDOW INTO AN ICON AND BACK AGAIN

Under Windows, you can have several programs open at once. Each program appears in its own window. You may want to temporarily remove a window from the desktop to view other windows. This operation can be accomplished using the arrow button in the upper-right corner of a window.

To temporarily remove a window, you use the downward arrow button.

1. Move your cursor to the button with the downward-pointing arrow in the upper-right corner of the Program Manager window, then press and release the left mouse button. The window closes down to an icon in the lower-left corner of the desktop. The button you just clicked on is called the *Minimize button*. You can now click and drag the icon to move it to another position on the desktop.

2. Move your cursor to the Program Manager icon, then press the left mouse button twice quickly. The icon is restored to an open window.

In step 2, you pressed the mouse button twice to "open" an icon into a window. Pressing the mouse button twice rapidly is called a "double click." You will use this action frequently in both Windows and AutoCAD, so you may want to practice closing windows and double clicking on their icons until you get a feel for how this action works.

When a program is minimized, that doesn't mean that it has been closed or is inactive. You can minimize a program that is performing some activity, like a database sort, and the program will continue to run in its minimized state.

ENLARGING A WINDOW TO FILL THE SCREEN

If you want to work in and view one window exclusively, you can force a window to fill the entire desktop. To do this, try the following steps:

1. Place the arrow cursor on the upward-pointing button in the upper-right corner of the Program Manager window, then click on it. The window expands to fill the screen. The button with the upward-pointing arrow is called the *Maximize button*. Notice that the upward-pointing arrow has changed to one that points both up and down. This new button is called the *Restore button*.

2. Click on the Restore button. The window changes back to its previous size and the Restore button turns back into a Maximize button.

All windows have the Maximize, Minimize, and Restore buttons in their upper-right corner. When a window appears at the desktop level, the Maximize button makes the window fill the desktop. If the window is within another window, like a program group within the Program Manager window, the Maximize button makes the window fill the bounding window. When a window is maximized, you cannot adjust its size.

CONTROLLING YOUR WINDOWS FROM A MENU

All of the functions described so far can also be accessed from the control menu box. This is the square located in the upper-left corner of every window. When you click on this box, the control menu appears. This menu also appears when you click on a minimized or iconized program. From this menu, you can maximize or minimize a window, switch to another program window, or exit a program entirely. The contents of the control menu vary from window to window, but the following describes the control menu's most common options:

Restore opens a minimized or iconized window.

Move lets you move a window using the keyboard's cursor keypad.

Size lets you resize a window using the keyboard's cursor keypad.

Close closes the window entirely. Clicking on this option from a program window will cause the program to terminate. If a file is open, you are given the option to save the file or discard any changes. You can also double-click on the control menu box to close a window.

Switch To … opens the Task dialog box. This dialog box lets you switch to another program by double clicking on its name from a list. It also lets you arrange the windows on the desktop, or close an application in the list. The Task dialog box can also be opened by double clicking on any blank area of the desktop.

As an alternative to the Switch To ... option, you can quickly switch from one window to another by holding down the Ctrl key and pressing the Tab key simultaneously. A small rectangle appears in the middle of the screen showing an icon and a program name. If you let go of the Ctrl key, you are switched to the program indicated by the rectangle. If you continue to hold down the Ctrl key and press Tab again, another program name appears in the rectangle. You can continue to press the Tab key while maintaining your hold on the Ctrl key to cycle through all the available applications.

FINDING WHAT YOU WANT IN A WINDOW

Often a Window will contain more information than can fit into the screen. In a typical DOS program such as a word processor, you would use the PageUp or PageDown cursor key to move through the document. While most Windows word processors maintain the use of the cursor keys, you have an additional tool called the scroll bar to help you move through a document. Scroll bars appear to the right and at the bottom of a window whenever a document becomes too large to fit within a window (see Figure C.3). The scroll bar to the right lets you move up and down in the document, while the bottom scroll bar lets you move from side to side.

At either end of the scroll bar are arrows. You can click and hold your mouse button on these arrows to dynamically scroll the document. This action causes the contents of a window to gradually move across the window. You can also click and drag the square button found between the arrows of the scroll bar. This action lets you move rapidly to a location in your document. Finally, you can click on the space between the square button and the arrows to display the portion of the document that is next to the current view. For example, if you click on the bar just below the square button, the window will shift downward to the portion of the document just below the current visible area. This action is similar to pressing the PageDown key in a word processor.

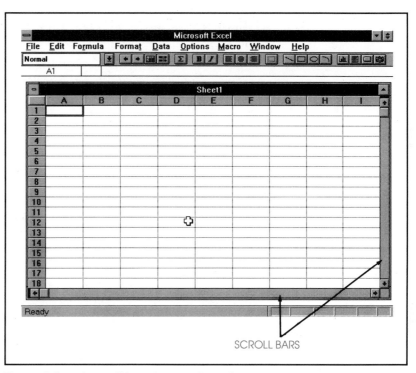

Figure C.3: The scroll bars of Microsoft Excel

USING PROGRAMS UNDER WINDOWS

Now that you understand a little about manipulating windows, you can begin to explore the use of programs within windows. One major difference between programs under DOS and Windows is that Windows lets you have several programs open at once. You can, for example, have AutoCAD open along with your favorite word processor and spreadsheet program. You can then easily switch between the programs. You can even have a window running into DOS, allowing you to run non-Windows programs. Other features of the Windows environment allow you to easily exchange data between programs. For example, you can quickly copy an AutoCAD drawing to your desktop publishing program using a Windows feature called the Clipboard.

UNDERSTANDING THE PROGRAM MANAGER

The Program Manager is perhaps the most important window application you will work with. It gives you access to all of your other programs, as well as other maintenance utilities for Windows, such as the File Manager, which lets you manipulate files on your hard disk; and Control Panel, which lets you adjust your Windows environment. This section describes how to use the Program Manager.

Understanding Program Groups

Program groups are like containers that hold programs and files. They provide the means to organizing your programs in a meaningful way. As you have already seen, the program groups can be minimized to appear as icons or opened to reveal their contents. If a program group has been minimized to an icon, you open it by double clicking on its icon. To start a program, you double click on a program's icon within a program group. You can then use the program's File menu to locate and open an existing file or to create a new file.

Program groups are objects that help you arrange your programs and files into categories that make the most sense for you. When you first install Windows, you are given a set of predefined program groups. You can rearrange these groups, create new groups, or delete groups you find unnecessary. You can even click and drag program icons from one program group to another, or you can have the same program icon in several program groups at once. This doesn't mean you have several copies of the program in your computer. Each copy of the program icon is linked to the same program file in your computer.

If you want to create your own program group, or if you want to change the name of a program group, you can do so by using the options under the File menu to the far left of the Program Manager menu bar. To create a new program group, you click on File ➤ New. You then get the first dialog box in Figure C.4. (If you need to know more about dialog boxes, see "Using Dialog Boxes" later in this appendix.)

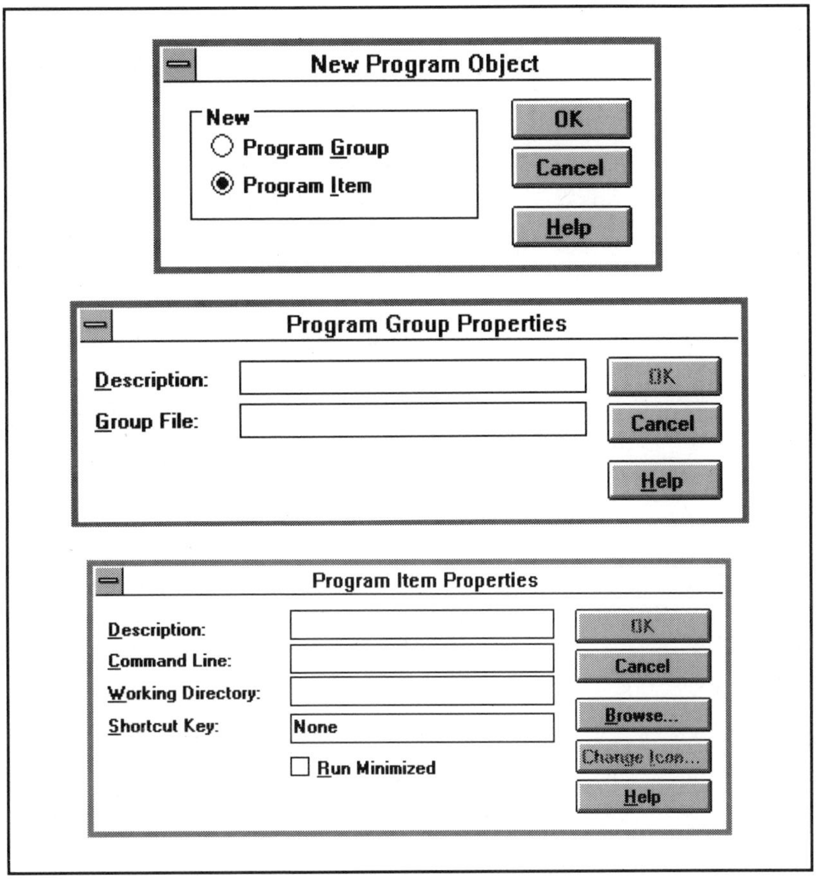

Figure C.4: The New Program Object, Program Group Properties, and Program Item Properties dialog boxes

You are given the choice to create a new Program Group or a Program Item. If you click on the Program Group radio button—the round button next to the label—then click on OK, you will get the second dialog box shown in Figure C.4. You can then enter a description for your new program group by clicking on the rectangular box labeled Description. This rectangular box is called an input box. The description you enter here will appear as the program group's name. You can leave the Group File input box empty. Once you enter a description, you can click on OK to complete the creation of a program group, or Cancel to close the dialog box without creating one.

If instead you click on the Program Item radio button, you get the final dialog box shown in Figure C.4. This dialog box allows you to create an icon that is associated with a program or file on your hard disk. The Description input box lets you give a title to your program item. This title appears as the label under the program icon. The Command Line input box lets you specify a keyboard entry to start a program or batch file, as you would at a DOS prompt. The Working Directory input box lets you specify a default startup directory and the Shortcut Key input box lets you specify a keyboard shortcut to start this program item.

The Change Icon button allows you to select an icon to associate with the program item. When you are done, you can click on OK and a new program icon will appear in the current program group.

If you want to change the title of a program group or icon, you can highlight the icon, then click on File ➤ Properties from the Program Manager menu. The Program Group Properties or Program Item Properties dialog box appears and you can then make your changes by altering the contents of the input boxes.

To delete a program group, you must first minimize it so it appears as an Icon. Make sure it is highlighted, then click on File ➤ Delete. You are asked if you really want to delete the program group.

Arranging the Program Groups

You've seen how you can adjust the size and shape of windows. The Program Manager offers some options that will quickly arrange the program group windows in a preset arrangement. The following describes the three main options under the Window menu of the Program Manager:

Cascade arranges the windows in an overlapping fashion (see Figure C.5). The windows are overlapped to allow you to see the title of each window. You can then click on the title bar of the window you want to work in.

Tile arranges the windows in a side-by-side fashion, much like a set of square or rectangular kitchen tiles would be arranged (see Figure C.5).

Arrange Icons forces the icons of the current active window to be arranged into neat rows and columns.

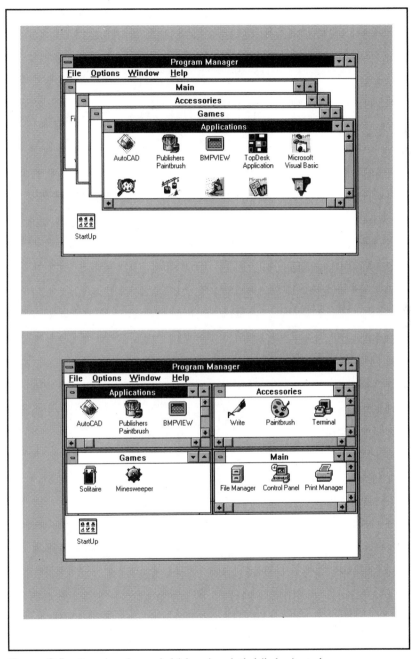

Figure C.5: Samples of cascaded (above) and tiled (below) windows

Just below these three main options is a list of all the program groups within the Program Manager. If you cannot find a program group because it is overlapped by a window, you can use this list to open a program group and make it visible.

USING THE FILE MANAGER

The File Manager is a program that lets you copy, move, and organize the files on your hard disk or floppy drive. It performs a set of standard DOS commands like Copy, Diskcopy, Format, Mkdir, Rmdir, and Ren. In addition, it allows you to view several drives and directories at one time. If properly set up, you can even have the File Manager start a program and open a file automatically, just by double clicking on a file name.

To start the File Manager, double click on the File Manager icon shown in Figure C.6. This can be found in the Main program group if you are using the default program groups. The File Manager window appears (see Figure C.6).

The File Manager window contains another window which in turn is divided in half. The left half of the window shows the directory tree structure of the current drive. The right half of the window shows a list of files in the current directory. You will know the current directory by the open file folder icon in the left half of the window. To view the contents of a different directory, click on the folder representing the directory you want to view.

Notice the row of disk drive icons just below the menu bar. These icons are used to change drives. To view the contents of the D drive, for example, you click on the drive icon labeled *d*. A new directory tree appears along with a new list of files.

You can view the contents of more than one drive by double clicking on a drive icon. This opens another window displaying the drive tree and file list. You also can create a duplicate of the current drive window by clicking on Window ➤ New Window. As with all other windows, the drive windows can be closed by double clicking on the control menu box in the upper-left corner, or minimized by clicking on the Minimize button in the upper-right corner.

Figure C.6: The File Manager icon (above) and window (below)

Selecting Files

Now suppose you want to move a set of files from one directory to another. In the right-hand side of a drive window, you can select a single file by clicking on it. This action highlights the file name. To select a group of files, first click on a file at the top or bottom of the group, then, Shift-click on the file at the other end of the list. All the files between the two files you picked will be highlighted. If you want to select a set of files that appear in random order in the file window, you can hold down the Ctrl key while simultaneously clicking on the files you want to select.

Once files are selected, you can then click and drag them to a directory folder icon in the window to the left. This has the effect of moving the files to a new location. To Copy files to another directory in the same drive, hold down the Ctrl key while you click and drag. As you move the files, a plus sign appears in the moving icon, signifying that you are copying files instead of moving them. You can also click and drag a set of files to a drive icon to copy files across drives. You do not have to hold down the Ctrl key to copy files across drives.

Highlighted files and directories can be erased by pressing the Delete key or by clicking on File ➤ Delete from the File Manager pull-down menu. Entire directories can also be moved by clicking and dragging them.

Associating Files with Programs

Many of the popular DOS file managers allow you to associate a file with a program so that you can highlight a file name and press a key, and the program associated with the file will start up and the file will open. The Windows File Manager also offers this function.

To associate AutoCAD files with the AutoCAD program, first highlight any AutoCAD file with the .DWG file name extension. Next, click on File ➤ Associate. The Associate dialog box appears (see Figure C.7). The file name extension is shown at the top and a list of program files is shown below the extension. You can select the AutoCAD program name from the list or you can click on the Browse menu to locate the ACAD.EXE file using the standard Windows file dialog box.

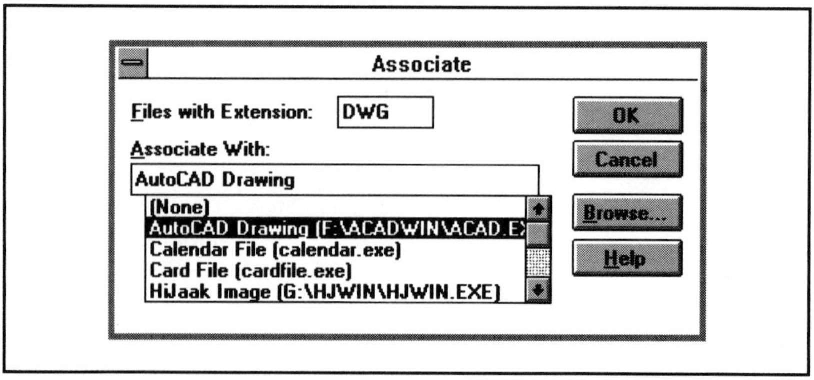

Figure C.7:   The Associate dialog box

Once you've selected a program to associate with the file, click on OK. From then on, you can double click on the AutoCAD file from the File Manager, and AutoCAD will start and the file will open.

Placing Files in a Program Group

Quite often, you will have a handful of files you use frequently. You can provide quick access to such files by placing them in the program group of the associated program. To place a file in a program group, you first open the File Manager, then arrange the Program Manager and File Manager on the desktop so both are visible. You then locate the file in the File Manager and click and drag the file into the desired program group. If the file has been associated with a program as described earlier, the icon of its associated program will appear with the file name below it. Note that this only creates an icon representation of the file and does not actually move the file from one location to another.

Other File Manager Features

The File Manager has a wealth of tools that let you view and manipulate your files. Table C.1 lists the options available and their uses. You will find that most of these other options are easy to use.

USING DIALOG BOXES

Dialog boxes offer an easy way to communicate with AutoCAD and other Windows programs. If you've used Microsoft Windows before, or any other graphical user interface, you should feel right at home with AutoCAD release 12 for Windows. If not, here is a brief primer on dialog boxes.

Table C.1: The File Manager menu options

FILE ➤	
OPTION	**FUNCTION**
Open	Starts the program associated with a highlighted file and opens it.
Move	Moves selected files.
Copy	Copies selected files.
Delete	Deletes selected files.
Rename	Renames selected files.
Properties	Displays the properties of a file such as size, date, time, and attribute.
Run	Starts a program based on typed instructions.
Print	Starts a program associated with a highlighted file, then prints the file.
Associate	Associates a file type with a program.
Create Directory	Creates a directory.
Search	Searches for a file or files in the current directory.
Select Files	Highlights files based on DOS wildcard filters.
Exit	Exits the File Manager.

DISK ➤	
OPTION	**FUNCTION**
Copy Disk	Makes a duplicate of a disk.
Label Disk	Labels a disk. The label appears whenever a directory listing is obtained.
Format Disk	Formats a diskette.

Table C.1:   The File Manager menu options (continued)

DISK ➤	
OPTION	**FUNCTION**
Make System Disk	Makes a bootable diskette.
Select Drive	Lets you select the current drive from a list. The list shows the drive label.

TREE ➤	
OPTION	**FUNCTION**
Expand One Level	Shows the next level of subdirectories of a directory.
Expand Branch	Shows all subdirectories of a directory.
Expand All	Shows all subdirectories of all directories.
Collapse Branch	Hides all subdirectories of the current directory.
Indicate Expandable Branches	Marks directories that contain subdirectories with a plus sign. This also closes all branches.

VIEW ➤	
OPTION	**FUNCTION**
Tree and Directory	Shows both directory tree (left) and file listing (right).
Tree Only	Shows directory tree only.
Directory Only	Show file listing only.
Split	Lets you locate where the directory tree and file listing are divided.

Table C.1: The File Manager menu options (continued)

VIEW ➤	
OPTION	**FUNCTION**
Name	Displays file names only.
All File Details	Displays all file information including size, date, time, and attribute.
Partial Details...	Lets you control what file information is displayed.
Sort by Name	Sorts file list by name.
Sort by Type	Sorts file list by extension.
Sort by Size	Sorts file list by file size.
Sort by Date	Sorts file list by date and time.
By File Type...	Lets you limit the types of files that are displayed.

OPTIONS ➤	
OPTION	**FUNCTION**
Confirmation...	Controls when confirmation dialog appears.
Font...	Controls fonts used to display file names.
Status Bar	Controls the display of the status bar at the bottom of the window.
Minimize on Use	Controls whether the File Manager opens as an Icon or a Full Window.
Save Settings on Exit	Controls whether View and Option settings are saved when the File Manager is closed.

Table C.1:   The File Manager menu options (continued)

WINDOW ➤	
OPTION	**FUNCTION**
New Window	Opens another Tree Directory window to view multiple drives.
Cascade	Arranges Tree Directory windows in an overlapping fashion.
Tile	Arranges Tree Directory windows in a Tiled arrangement.
Arrange Icons	Neatly arranges minimized or iconized tree directory windows.
Refresh	Updates file listing when changes have been made to files outside the File Manager.
Contents	Shows the contents of the File Manager menu.
Search for Help…	Opens a dialog box that lets you search for specific topics in the Help system.
How to Use Help	Offers help on Help.
About File Manager	Displays general information.

THE COMPONENTS

Figure C.8 shows two dialog boxes, each with a set of typical dialog box elements.

There are three major components to dialog boxes. First, at the top of the dialog box is the title. When working with dialog boxes, you'll be able to identify the dialog box you have on your screen by the title at the top. Dialog boxes are broken into groups. These groups are enclosed by a rectangle and are labeled at the top. I will refer to these groups as button groups,

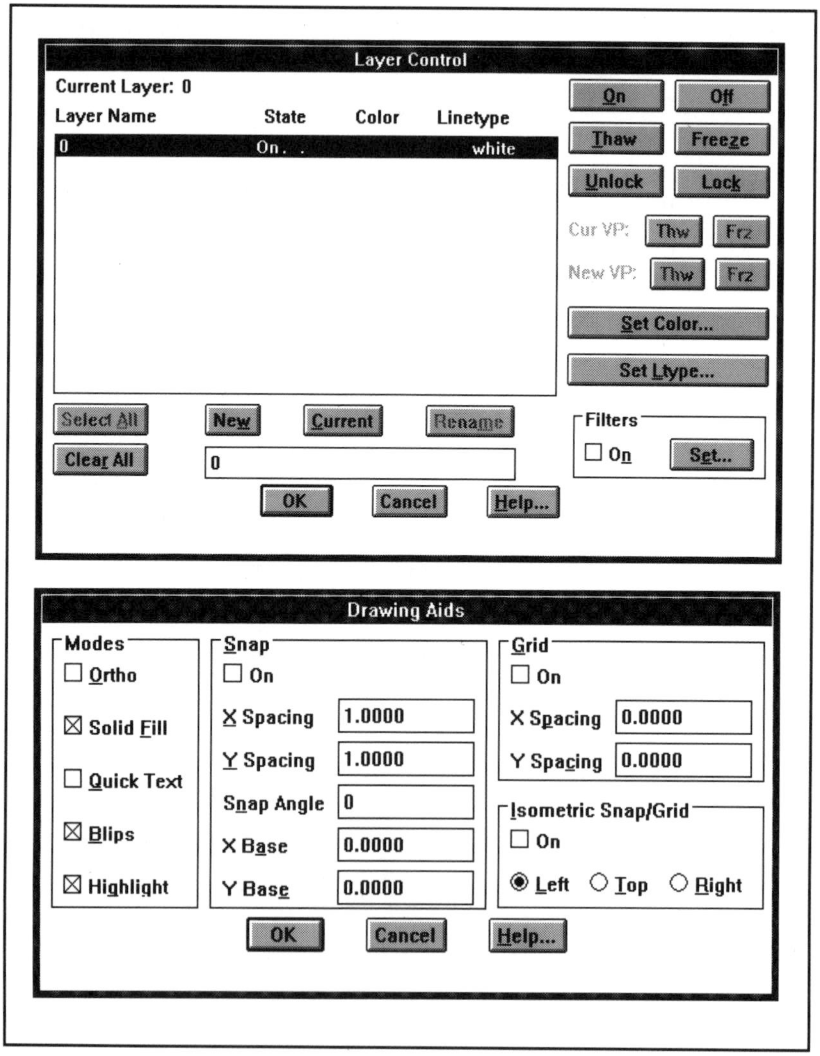

Figure C.8: Typical dialog boxes

even though they don't always contain buttons. Finally, there are the buttons and rectangles that appear scattered over the dialog boxes. The following describes each type of button and how it is used.

Command Buttons

Whenever you see a rectangular button with a *label* on it, you know that when you click on it, an action will immediately take place. Buttons whose names are followed with a series of periods (…) tell you that a dialog box will be opened. Buttons with a < symbol following the label tell you that the screen will clear, allowing you to perform some activity in the graphic screen, such as pick points. When you see a button that is heavily outlined, that means that button is the default and will be activated when you press ↵. Dimmed buttons are unavailable in the current use of the dialog box.

While most buttons serve a specialized purpose, four buttons will appear in nearly every dialog box. Here is a brief description of these buttons.

OK causes the dialog box settings to take effect and closes the dialog box.

Cancel cancels the effect of any changes made to the dialog box and closes the dialog box.

Help opens the Help window of the associated program. Help is frequently context sensitive, so the help window will provide information about the specific dialog box or option being used.

Browse opens another dialog box allowing you to search for an item such as a file or other Windows resource.

The OK, Cancel, and Help buttons are shown in Figure C.9.

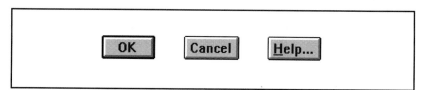

Figure C.9:   A typical set of labeled buttons

Radio Buttons

Whenever there is a set of mutually exclusive options, they are usually presented as *radio buttons*. These are small circular buttons with labels to their right and they are always found in groups (see Figure C.10). When a radio button option is active, it is filled in. You select a radio button option by clicking on the button itself.

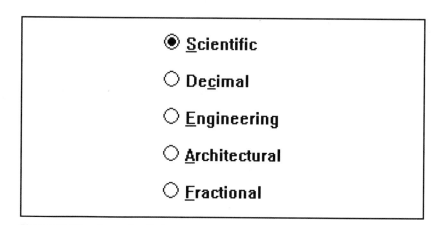

Figure C.10:   A set of radio buttons

Check Boxes

Toggled options are presented as *check boxes*. These are squares that can be blank or have an × through them (see Figure C.11). When the × appears, the option is turned on. A blank square means the option is turned off.

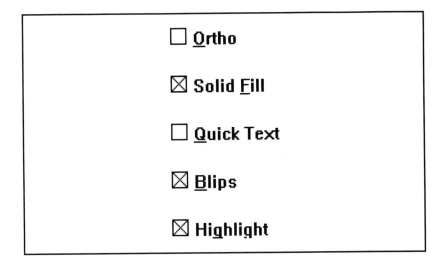

Figure C.11:   A set of check boxes

List Boxes

You will often be presented with a list of items to choose from. These lists appear in *list boxes* (see Figure C.12). You select items from the list by clicking on them. If the function allows multiple selections, you can click on more than one item. When the list becomes too long to show in the list box, a scroll bar appears to the right of the box. You can search for items in a list box by typing the first character of the item you are looking for. Edit boxes are often associated with list boxes.

Layer Name	State	Color	Linetype
0	On . .	. .	white
A-DIM-1	On . .	. .	cyan
A-DIM-5	On . .	. .	9
A-DIMTX-4	On . .	. .	12
A-LIN-5	On . .	. .	9
A-MISC-5	On . .	. .	9
A-SYM-1	On . .	. .	cyan
A-SYM-2	On . .	. .	blue
A-SYM-4	On . .	. .	10
A-SYM-5	On . .	. .	9
A-TX-1	On . .	. .	red
A-TX-4	On . .	. .	12

Figure C.12:   A sample list box

Popup Lists

Sometimes, a *popup list* is used in place of a list box (see Figure C.13). A popup list appears as a rectangle with a downward-pointing arrow on the right side. The default item appears in the rectangle. To open the list, you click on the arrow to the right. You can then click on the desired option. If the list is long, a scroll bar is provided to scroll down the list.

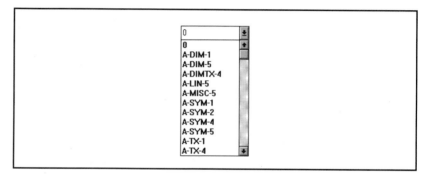

Figure C.13: A sample popup list

Edit Boxes

If an option requires keyboard input from you, an edit box or input box is provided (see Figure C.14). This is a rectangular box that, when you click on it, displays a vertical bar cursor. You can then enter a name or other text or correct any existing text in the box. If text already appears in an edit box, you can double click on the box to highlight the entire text. Then, when you begin to type, your typing will completely replace the original text. A single click on the box will move the vertical bar cursor to the location that you click on. Just as in a word processor, you can also toggle between insert and overtype modes by pressing the **Ins** key. You can also use the left and right arrow cursor keys to move the vertical bar cursor. A click-and-drag will highlight a group of characters in the input box.

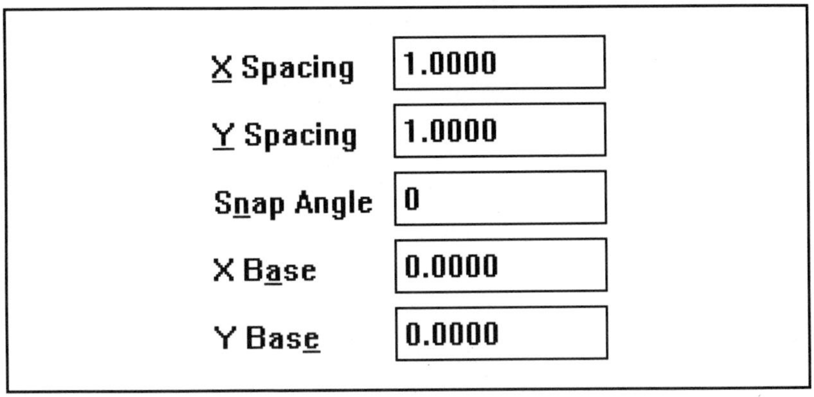

X̲ Spacing	1.0000
Y̲ Spacing	1.0000
Sn̲ap Angle	0
X Ba̲se	0.0000
Y Bas̲e	0.0000

Figure C.14: A typical edit box

KEYBOARD ACCELERATORS

You might notice that the labels for the various menus, buttons, and boxes have underlined characters in them. You can select an option from a dialog box by holding down the **Alt** key and pressing the underlined character in the option name. The option label is then highlighted. Once a label is highlighted, you can move to any other option by just pressing the underlined character in the option label or you can move to the next option by pressing the **Tab** key.

Once a label is highlighted, changing the option depends on the type of button it is. Radio buttons and check boxes are activated using the **spacebar**. Popup lists are opened by pressing the **Alt** key and the ↓ cursor key together. You can then move up and down in the list using the ↑ and ↓ keys. The **Alt-**↑ key closes the list. The **Esc** key closes the dialog box. Labeled buttons are activated by pressing ↵ when they are highlighted.

Pull-down menus work in a similar way. You can pull down a menu by pressing the Alt key in combination with the underlined character of the menu item. For example, to open the File menu, you can press Alt-F. Once the menu is opened, you can select a menu option by pressing the underlined character of the option. For example, to open a file, you can press Alt-F, then O.

You may want to try using the keyboard shortcuts for a while to see if you like them. They are not for everyone, but since you have one hand free while mousing around, you might as well put it to work.

USING WILD CARD CHARACTERS

When specifying files in a file dialog box, you can often filter out groups of files using *wild card characters*. Wild card characters are the asterisk (*) and the question mark (?). They indicate an undefined character. For example, to single out all drawing files whose names begin with A, you would enter the following in a File Name input box:

A*.DWG

With this command, the file list box will only display names that begin with A and have the .DWG file extension. The asterisk tells Windows to accept any character between the A and the period. You could also enter

A*.*

to tell Windows to display all files that start with A no matter what the extension is.

Care must be taken when using the asterisk, because every character that follows is ignored. You cannot designate a file name like

A*TE.DWG

because Windows will ignore the TE between the asterisk and the period.

The question mark performs a similar function to the asterisk, except that it is used to replace individual letters rather than groups of letters. If you want to filter out file names that start and end with specific characters, use the question mark as in

A?????TE.DWG

Here, Windows will display only files with names that start with A, are eight characters long, end with TE, and have the .DWG extension.

CHECKING AND CLEANING UP DISK SPACE

Every AutoCAD user should know about the CHKDSK DOS utility. CHKDSK displays the current status of your disk, including the total space in bytes, the amount of disk space used, and the amount of available RAM. It is also used to help clean your disk of lost files. The name stands for *check disk*. To use CHKDSK, you must have the file CHKDSK.EXE on your hard disk and have the DOS path set to its location. Then, to check drive C, for example, you can enter

    CHKDSK C: /F

at the DOS prompt. The /F in the entry is a command switch that tells the CHKDSK utility to locate and delete any *lost clusters*.

In general terms, files are stored on your hard disk not as a contiguous stream of information, but as bits of information called clusters scattered throughout your disk. Another part of your disk contains the file names and a kind of map called the file allocation table, or FAT, telling DOS the locations of the clusters associated with that file name. Sometimes clusters get lost when a program opens a file but fails to close it properly. This often occurs when you have a power outage while you have a file open, or when a program crashes.

These lost clusters can take up valuable disk space. Fortunately, they can be removed by using CHKDSK with its /F option. If there are any lost clusters, you will see a message like

    18 lost clusters found in 11 chains.
    Convert lost chains to files (Y/N)?

The chains referred to in this statement are lists in the FAT that point to the cluster locations. You could think of chains as a way DOS links clusters to form a file. You can enter N ↵ at this message to delete these lost clusters. If you happen to enter Y, you will find that DOS has created files in the root directory with the name FILE000*n*.CHK where *n* is a sequential number. These are the lost clusters converted to files. You can then view these files using a file viewing utility such as those supplied with Xtree or Norton Utilities to see if they contain data you want to keep.

If you think you need to use CHKDSK.EXE to clean up your hard disk, use it before you start Windows. Do not use it in a DOS window while running Windows.

D

SYSTEM
AND
DIMENSION
VARIABLES

This appendix contains a list of system variables accessible directly from the command prompt, plus a brief description of each variable. These system variables are also accessible through the AutoLISP interpreter by using the Getvar and Setvar functions. I have divided the variables into two sections: *system variables*, and *dimension variables*. The first section covers the general system variables that let you fine-tune AutoCAD. The second section covers those system variables that deal specifically with the dimensioning functions of AutoCAD.

All of these variables can be accessed transparently by entering the variable name preceded by an apostrophe.

SYSTEM VARIABLES

Table D.1 shows the variables that you can set, noting whether they are read-only. Most of them have counterparts in other commands. For example, angdir and angbase can be adjusted using the Units command. Many, like Highlight and Expert, do not have equivalent commands. For easy reference, I have shown the command associated with the variable following the variable name.

Table D.1: System Variables

NAME	ASSOCIATED COMMAND	WHERE SAVED	USE
Acadprefix (read only)	DOS Set	na	The ACAD environment setting
Acadver (read only)	na	na	The AutoCAD version number
Aflags	AttDEF	With drawing	Controls the attribute mode settings: 1 = invisible, 2= constant, 3=verify, 8=preset
Angbase	Units	With drawing	Controls the direction of the 0 angle, relative to the current UCS
Angdir	Units	With drawing	Controls the positive direction of angles: 0= counterclockwise, 1= clockwise

Table D.1: System Variables (continued)

NAME	ASSOCIATED COMMAND	WHERE SAVED	USE
Aperture	Aperture	With configuration	Controls the Osnap cursor target height in pixels
Area (read only)	Area	na	Displays the last area calculation. Use with Setvar or AutoLISP
Attdia	Insert/Attribute	With drawing	Controls the attribute dialog box: 0= no dialog box, 1= dialog box
Attmode	Attdisp	With Drawing	Controls the attribute display mode: 0= off, 1= normal, 2= on
Attreq	Insert	With drawing	Controls the prompt for attributes: 0= no prompt or dialog box for attributes (attributes use default values) 1= normal prompt or dialog box upon attribute insertion
Auditctl	Config	With configuration	Controls whether an audit file is created: 0=disable, 1=enable creation of .ADT file
Aunits	Units	With drawing	Controls angular units: 0=decimal degrees, 1=degrees-minutes-seconds, 2=grads, 3=radians, 4=surveyor's units
Auprec	Units	With drawing	Controls the precision of angular units determined by decimal place
Backz (read only)	Dview	With drawing	Displays the distance from the DVIEW target to the back clipping plane
Blipmode	na	With drawing	Controls the appearance of blips: 0= off, 1=on
Cdate (read only)	Time	na	Displays calendar date/time read from DOS (YYYYMMDD.HHMMSSMSEC)
Cecolor	Color	With drawing	Controls the current default color assigned to new objects
Celtype	Linetype	With drawing	Controls the current default linetype assigned to new objects
Chamfera	Chamfer	With drawing	Controls first chamfer distance

Table D.1:   System Variables (continued)

NAME	ASSOCIATED COMMAND	WHERE SAVED	USE
Chamferb	Chamfer	With drawing	Controls second chamfer distance
Circlerad	Circle	na	Controls the default circle radius: 0=no default
Clayer	Layer	With drawing	Sets the current layer
Cmdactive (read only)	na	na	Displays whether a command, script, or dialog box is active: 1=command active, 2=transparent command active, 4= script active, 8=dialog box active (values are cumulative so 3=command and transparent command are active)
Cmddia	na	With configuration	Controls the use of dialog boxes for some commands: 0=don't use dialog box, 1=use dialog box
Cmdecho	AutoLISP	na	With AutoLISP, controls the display of prompts from embedded AutoCAD commands: 0=no display of prompt, 1=display prompts
Cmdnames (read only)	na	na	Displays the English name of the currently active command
Coords	F6, Ctrl-D	With drawing	Controls coordinate readout: 0= coordinates are displayed only when points are picked, 1=absolute coordinates are dynamically displayed as cursor moves, 2=distance and angle are displayed during commands that accept relative distance input
Cvport	Vports	With drawing	Displays the ID number of the current viewport
Date (read only)	Time	na	Displays the date and time in Julian format
Dbmod (read only)	na	na	Displays the drawing modification status: 1=Entity database modified, 2=Symbol table modified, 4=Database variable modified, 8=Window modified, 16=View modified

Table D.1: System Variables (continued)

NAME	ASSOCIATED COMMAND	WHERE SAVED	USE
Diastat (read only)	Dialog box	na	Displays how the last dialog box was exited: 0=Cancel, 1=OK
Distance (read only)	Dist	na	Displays the last distance calculated by the Dist command
Donutid	Donut	na	Controls the default inside diameter of a donut
Donutod	Donut	na	Controls the default outside diameter of a donut
Dragmode	Dragmode	With drawing	Controls dragging: 0=no dragging, 1= on if requested, 2=automatic drag
Dragp1	na	With configuration	Controls regeneration-drag input sampling rate
Dragp2	na	With configuration	Controls sampling rate of fast-drag input
Dwgcodepage	na	With drawing	Displays the code page of the drawing (see Syscodepage)
Dwgname (read only)	Open	na	Displays the drawing name and drive/directory if specified by user
Dwgprefix (read only)	na	na	Displays the drive and directory of the current file
Dwgtitled (read only)	New	na	Displays whether a drawing has been named: 0=untitled, 1=named by user
Dwgwrite	na	na	Displays the read/write status of the current drawing: 0=read only, 1=read/write
Elevation	Elev	With drawing	Controls current 3D elevation relative to the current UCS
Errno (read only)	na	na	Displays error codes from AutoLISP or ADS applications

Table D.1: System Variables (continued)

NAME	ASSOCIATED COMMAND	WHERE SAVED	USE
Expert	na	na	Controls prompts, depending on level of user's expertise: 0=issues normal prompts, 1=suppresses **About to regen** and **Really want to turn the current layer off** prompts, 2=suppresses **Block already defined** and **A drawing with this name already exists** block command prompt, 3=suppresses **An *item* with this name already exists** prompt for the Linetype command, 4=suppresses **An *item* with this name already exists** for the UCS Save and Vports Save options, 5=suppresses **An *item* with this name already exists** for Dim Save and Dim Override commands.
Extmax (read only)	Zoom	With drawing	Displays upper-right corner coordinate of extents view
Extmin (read only)	Zoom	With drawing	Displays lower-left corner coordinate of extents view
Filedia	dialog box	With configuration	Sets whether a file dialog box is used by default: 0=don't use file dialog box unless requested with a ~, 1=use file dialog box whenever possible
Filletrad	Fillet	With drawing	Controls fillet radius
Fillmode	Fill	With drawing	Controls fill status: 0=off, 1= on
Frontz (read only)	Dview	With drawing	Controls the front clipping plane for the current viewport. Use with Viewmode
Gridmode	Grid	With drawing	Controls grid: 0=off, 1=on
Gridunit	Grid	With drawing	Controls grid spacing
Gripblock	(grips)	With configuration	Controls the display of grips in blocks: 0=show only insertion point grip, 1=show grips of all entities in block

Table D.1:   System Variables (continued)

NAME	ASSOCIATED COMMAND	WHERE SAVED	USE
Gripcolor	(grips)	With configuration	Controls the color of non-selected grips. Choices are integers from 1 to 255: Default=5
Griphot	(grips)	With configuration	Controls the color of hot grips. Choices are integers from 1 to 255: Default=1
Grips	(grips)	With configuration	Controls the use of grips: 0= no grips, 1=enable grips (default)
Gripsize	(grips)	With configuration	Controls the size in pixels of grips. The default is 3
Handles (read only)	Handles	With drawing	Displays the status of entity handles: 0=off, 1=on
Highlight	Select	na	Controls whether objects are highlighted when selected: 0=no highlight, 1=highlighting
Hpang	Hatch	na	Sets the default hatch pattern angle
Hpdouble	Hatch	na	Sets the default hatch doubling for the user defined hatch pattern: 0=no doubling, 1=doubling at 90°
Hpname	Hatch	na	Sets the default hatch pattern name. Use a period (.) to set to no default
Hpscale	Hatch	na	Sets the default hatch pattern scale factor
Hpspace	Hatch	na	Sets the default line spacing for the user defined hatch pattern. Cannot be 0
Insbase	Base	With drawing	Controls insertion base point of current drawing
Insname	Insert	na	Sets the default block or file name for the Insert command. Enter a period (.) to set to no default
Lastpoint	na	na	Sets or displays the coordinate that is normally referenced by the at (@) sign

Table D.1: System Variables (continued)

NAME	ASSOCIATED COMMAND	WHERE SAVED	USE
Lenslength (read only)	Dview	With drawing	Displays the focal length of the lense used for a perspective display
Limcheck	Limits	With drawing	Controls limit checking: 0=no checking, 1=checking
Limmax	Limits	With drawing	Controls the coordinate of drawing's upper-right limit
Limmin	Limits	With drawing	Controls the coordinate of drawing's lower-left limit
Loginname (read only)	Config/startup	With configuration	Displays user's login name
Ltscale	Ltscale	With drawing	Controls the line type scale factor
Lunits	Units	With drawing	Controls unit styles: 1=scientific, 2=decimal, 3=engineering, 4=architectural, 5=fractional
Luprec	Units	With drawing	Controls unit accuracy by decimal place or size of denominator
Macrotrace	DIESEL	na	Controls the debugging tool for DIESEL expressions: 0=disable, 1=enable
Maxactvp	Viewports	na	Controls the maximum number of viewports to regenerate at one time
Maxsort	na	With configuration	Controls the maximum number of items to be sorted when a command displays a list
Menuctl	na	With configuration	Controls whether the side menu changes in response to a command name entered from the keyboard: 0=no menu response, 1=menu response

Table D.1: System Variables (continued)

NAME	ASSOCIATED COMMAND	WHERE SAVED	USE
Menuecho	na	na	Controls messages and command prompt display from commands embedded in menu: 0=display all messages, 1=suppress menu item name, 2=suppress command prompts, 4=Disable ^P toggle of menu echo, 8=debugging aid for DIESEL expressions
Menuname (read only)	Menu	With drawing	Displays the name of the current menu file
Mirrtext	Mirror	With drawing	Controls mirroring of text: 0=no copying of text, 1=copying of text
Modemacro	na	na	Controls the display of user defined text in the status line
Offsetdist	Offset	With drawing	Controls the default offset distance
Orthomode	F8, Ctrl-O, Ortho	With drawing	Controls ortho: 0= off, 1=on
Osmode	Osnap	With drawing	Sets the current default Osnap mode: 0=none, 1=endpoint, 2=midpoint, 4=center, 8=node, 16 = quadrant, 32=intersection, 64=insert, 128=perpendicular, 256=tangent, 512=nearest, 1024=quick. If more than one mode is required, enter the sum of those modes
Pdmode	Point	With drawing	Controls the type of symbol used as a point during the POINT command. Several point styles are available (see Settings ➤ Point style for a display of the different modes)
Pdsize	Point	With drawing	Controls the size of the symbol set by Pdmode
Perimeter (read only)	Area, List	na	Displays the last perimeter value derived from the Area and List command
Pfacevmax (read only)	na	na	Displays the maximum number of vertices per face

Table D.1:   System Variables (continued)

NAME	ASSOCIATED COMMAND	WHERE SAVED	USE
Pickadd	Select/Ddeselect	With configuration	Controls how items are added to a selection set: 0=only the most recently selected item or set of items becomes the selection set (to accumulate objects in a selection set, hold down the Shift key while making your selection), 1=Selected objects accumulate in a selection set as you select them (holding down the Shift key while selecting items removes those items from the selection set)
Pickauto	Select/Ddeselect	With configuration	Controls the automatic window at the **select objects** prompt: 1=automatic window is enabled, 0=automatic window is disabled
Pickbox	Select/Ddeselect	With configuration	Controls the size of the Select object pickbox (in pixels)
Pickdrag	Select/Ddeselect	With configuration	Controls how selection windows are used: 0=click on each corner of the window, 1=Shift click and hold on the first corner then drag and release for the second
Pickfirst	Select/Ddeselect	With configuration	Controls whether you can pick an object or set of objects before you select a command: 0=disabled, 1=enabled
Platform (read only)	na	na	Displays the version of AutoCAD being used
Plinegen	Pline/Pedit	With drawing	Controls how polylines generate linetypes around vertices: 0=linetype pattern begins and ends at vertices, 1=linetype patterns ignore vertices and begin and end at polyline beginning and ending
Plinewid	Pline/Pedit	With drawing	Controls default polyine width
Plotid	Plot	With configuration	Sets the default plotter based on its description

Table D.1: System Variables (continued)

NAME	ASSOCIATED COMMAND	WHERE SAVED	USE
Plotter	Plot	With configuration	Sets the default plotter, based on its integer ID
Polysides	Polygon	na	Controls the default number of sides of a polygon
Popups (read only)	na	na	Displays whether the current system supports pull-down menus: 0=does not support, 1=supports
Psltscale	Pspace	With drawing	Controls Paperspace linetype scaling
Psprolog	Psout	With configuration	Controls what portion of the Acad.PSF file is used for the prologue section of a Psout output file. Give this setting the name of the section you want to use
Psquality	Psin	Configuration	Controls how images are generated in AutoCAD with the Psin command. This is an integer value: 0=only bounding box is drawn, >0=number of pixels per AutoCAD drawing unit, <0=outline with no fills and the absolute value of the setting determines pixels per drawing units
Qtextmode	Qtext	With drawing	Controls the quick text mode: 0= off, 1=on
Regenmode	Regenauto	With drawing	Controls the Regenauto mode: 0=off, 1= on
Re-init	Re-init	na	Reinitializes I/O ports, digitizers, display, plotter, and Acad.PGP: 1=digitizer port, 2=Plotter port, 4=digitizer, 8=display, 16=PGP file reload
Savefile (read only)	Autosave	With configuration	Displays the Autosave file name
Savename (read only)	Save	na	Displays the user file name the file is saved under
Savetime	Autosave	With configuration	Controls the time interval between automatic saves, in minutes: 0=disable automatic save

Table D.1: System Variables (continued)

NAME	ASSOCIATED COMMAND	WHERE SAVED	USE
Screenboxes (read only)	Menu	With configuration	Displays the number of slots or boxes available in the side menu
Screenmode (read only)	na	With configuration	Displays the current display mode: 0=text, 1=graphics, 2=dual screen
Screensize (read only)	na	na	Displays the current viewport size in pixels
Shadedge	Shade	With drawing	Controls how Shade shades a drawing: 0=faces shaded, no edge highlighting, 1=faces shaded, edge highlighting, 2=faces not filled, edges in entity color, 3= faces in entity color, edges in background color
Shadedit	Shade	With drawing	Controls how much ambient versus diffuse light is used to render an image (in percent of ambient light). This can be set from 0 to 100.
Shpname	Shape	na	Controls the default shape name
Sketchinc	Sketch	With drawing	Controls the sketch record increment
Skpoly	Sketch	With drawing	Controls whether the SKETCH command uses regular lines or polylines: 0=line, 1=polyline
Snapang	Snap	With drawing	Controls snap and grid angle
Snapbase	Snap	With drawing	Controls snap, grid, and hatch pattern origin
Snapisopair	Snap	With drawing	Controls isometric plane: 0=left, 1=top, 2=right
Snapmode	F9, Snap	With drawing	Controls snap toggle: 0=off, 1=on
Snapstyl	Snap	With drawing	Controls snap style: 0=standard, 1=isometric
Snapunit	Snap	With drawing	Controls snap spacing given in x and y values
Sortents	Ddselect	With configuration	Controls whether objects are sorted based on their order in the database: 0=disabled, 1=sort for object selection, 2=sort for object snap, 4=sort for redraws, 8=Sort for Mslide, 16=sort for Regen, 32=sort for Plot, 64 = sort for Psout

Table D.1: System Variables (continued)

NAME	ASSOCIATED COMMAND	WHERE SAVED	USE
Splframe	Pline, Pedit, 3Dface	With drawing	Controls the display of spline vertices and the defining mesh of a surface fit mesh. Also controls the display of "invisible" edges of 3dfaces: 0= no display of spline vertices; (only the fit surface of a smoothed 3dmesh is displayed, "invisible" edges are not displayed), 1=display of spline vertices (only the defining mesh of a smoothed 3dmesh is displayed, "invisible" edges are displayed)
Splinesegs	Pline, Pedit	With drawing	Controls the number of line segments used for each spline patch
Splinetype	Pline, Pedit	With drawing	Controls the type of spline curve generated by a Pedit spline: 5=quadratic B-spline, 6=cubic B-spline
Surftab1	Rulesurf, Tabsurf, Revsurf, Edgesurf	With drawing	Controls the number of facets in the M direction of meshes
Surftab2	Revsurf, Edgesurf	With drawing	Controls the number of facets in the N direction of meshes
Surftype	Pedit	With drawing	Controls the type of surface fitting used by the Pedit Smooth option: 5=quadratic B-spline surface, 6=cubic B-spline surface, 8=Bezier surface
Surfu	3Dmeshes	With drawing	Controls surface density in the M direction
Surfv	3Dmeshes	With drawing	Controls surface density in the N direction
Syscodepage (read only)	na	With drawing	Displays the system code page specified in acad.xmf
Tabmode	Tablet	na	Controls the tablet mode: 0=off, 1=on

Table D.1: System Variables (continued)

NAME	ASSOCIATED COMMAND	WHERE SAVED	USE
Target (read only)	Dview	With drawing	Displays the coordinate of a perspective target point
Tdcreate (read only)	Time	With drawing	Displays time and date of file creation in Julian format
Tdindwg (read only)	Time	With drawing	Displays total editing time in Julian format
Tdupdate (read only)	Time	With drawing	Displays the time and date of last update of file in Julian format
Tdusrtimer (read only)	Time	With drawing	Displays user-elapsed time in Julian format
Tempprefix (read only)	Config	With configuration	Displays the location of temporary files
Texteval	na	na	Controls how text input is interpreted: 0=AutoCAD takes all text input literally, 1=AutoCAD interprets "(" and "!" as part of an AutoLISP expression, unless the Text or Dtext command is active
Textsize	Text, Dtext	With drawing	Controls default text height
Textstyle	Text, Dtext	With drawing	Controls the default text style
Thickness	Elev	With drawing	Controls the default 3D thickness of objects being drawn
Tilemode	Mspace/Pspace	With drawing	Controls Paperspace and Viewport access: 0=Paperspace and Viewport entities enabled, 1=strictly Modelspace
Tracewid	Trace	With drawing	Controls trace width

Table D.1: System Variables (continued)

NAME	ASSOCIATED COMMAND	WHERE SAVED	USE
Treedepth	Treestat	With drawing	Controls the depth of the tree structured spatial index affecting AutoCAD database search speed. The first two digits are for the Modelspace nodes and the second two digits affect the Paperspace nodes. Use positive integers for 3D drawings and negative integers for 2D drawings. Using negative values can improve 2D operation speed
Treemax	Regen, Treedepth	With configuration	Limits memory use during regeneration by limiting the maximum number of nodes in the spatial index created with Treedepth
Ucsfollow	UCS	With drawing	Controls whether AutoCAD automatically changes to the plan view of a UCS while in Modelspace: 0=UCS change does not affect view, 1=UCS change causes view to change with the UCS
Ucsicon	Ucsicon	With drawing	Controls the UCS icon: 1=on, 2 = UCS icon appears at origin
Ucsname (read only)	UCS	With drawing	Displays the name of the current UCS
Ucsorg (read only)	UCS	With drawing	Displays the origin coordinate for the current UCS relative to the World Coordinate System
Ucsxdir (read only)	UCS	With drawing	Displays the X direction of the current UCS relative to the World Coordinate System
Ucsydir (read only)	UCS	With drawing	The Y direction of the current UCS relative to the World Coordinate System
Undoctl (read only)	Undo	na	Displays the current state of the Undo feature: 1=Undo is enabled, 2=only one command can be undone, 4=Auto-group mode is enabled, 8=group is currently active

Table D.1: System Variables (continued)

NAME	ASSOCIATED COMMAND	WHERE SAVED	USE
Undomarks (read only)	Undo	na	Displays the number of marks placed by the Undo command
Unitmode	Ddunit/Units	With drawing	Controls how hyphens are used in the coordinate readout when fractional, architectural, and surveyor units are used. 0=hyphen between feet and inches, 1=hyphen between inches and fractions.
Useri1– Useri5	AutoLISP, ADS	With drawing	Five user variables capable of storing integer values
Userr1– Userr5	AutoLISP, ADS	With drawing	Five user variables capable of storing real values
Users1–5	AutoLISP, ADS	na	Five user variables capable of storing string values
Viewctr (read only)	na	With drawing	Displays the center of the current view in coordinates
Viewdir (read only)	Dview	With drawing	Displays the camera viewing direction in coordinates
Viewmode (read only)	Dview	With drawing	Displays view related settings for the current viewport: 1=perspective on, 2=front clipping on, 4=Back clipping on, 8=UCS follow on, 16=Front clip not at eye
Viewsize (read only)	Zoom/View	With drawing	Displays the height of the current view in drawing units
Viewtwist (read only)	Dview	With drawing	Displays the twist angle for the current viewport
Visretain	Layer	With drawing	Controls whether layer setting for Xref's are retained: 0=current layer color, linetype, and visibility settings are retained when drawing is closed, 1=layer settings of Xref drawing are always renewed when file is opened

Table D.1:   System Variables (continued)

NAME	ASSOCIATED COMMAND	WHERE SAVED	USE
Vsmax (read only)	na	na	Displays the coordinates of the upper-right corner of the virtual display
Vsmin	na	na	Displays the coordinates for the lower-left corner of the virtual display
Worlducs (read only)	UCS	na	Displays the status of the WCS: 0= current is not WCS, 1=current is WCS
Worldview	Dview, UCS	With drawing	Controls whether Dview and Viewpoint operate relative to UCS or WCS: 0=current UCS is used, 1=WCS is used
Xrefctl	Xref	With configuration	Controls whether Xref log files are written: 0=no log files, 1=log files written.

USING A DIALOG BOX TO CONTROL DIMENSION SETTINGS

You can control the appearance and format of dimensions by clicking on Settings ➤ Dimension Style from the pull-down menu bar. You the see the Dimension Styles and Variables dialog box (see Figure D.1).

With this dialog box, you can create and recall dimension styles. This can be useful if you are using several formats for your dimensioning. For example, you may want to use an arrow for some dimensions and an architectural style tick for others. By setting up and saving two styles, you can quickly switch between the two arrow styles while you are dimensioning.

CREATING A DIMENSION STYLE

To create a style, enter a style name in the input box at the bottom of the dialog box. This will add a name to the list box on the left. You can then use the buttons to the right to set up your dimension style. You can

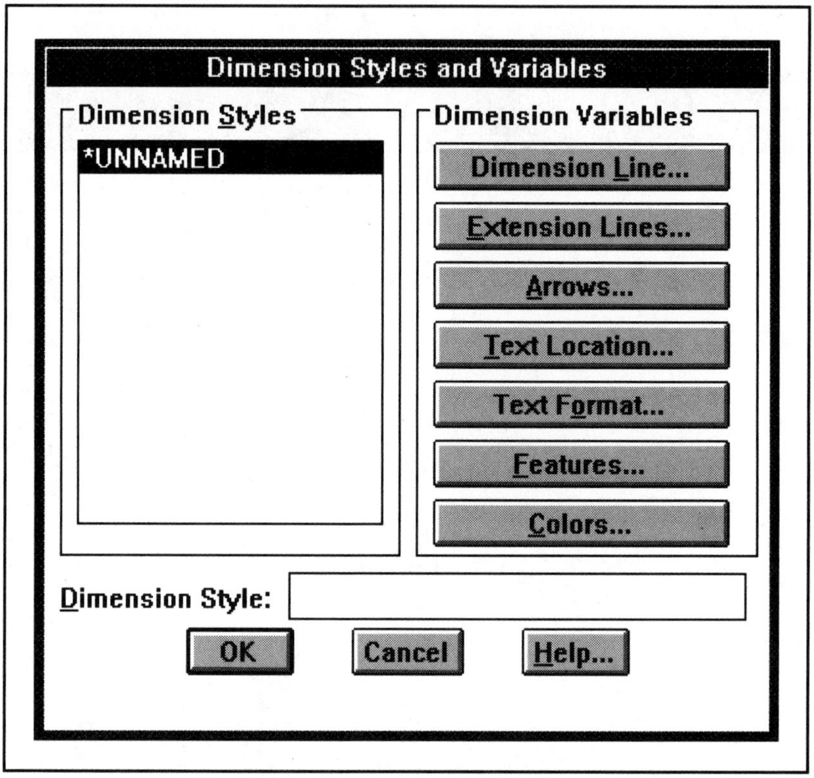

Figure D.1:   Dimension Styles and Variables dialog boxes

then create another dimension style by entering another name in the input box. This creates a copy of the current style and gives it the new name. You can then make setting changes to the new style.

SETTING UP A DIMENSION STYLE

Each button to the right of the dialog box opens another dialog box that controls the variables associated with that particular aspect of AutoCAD's dimensioning system. Toward the top of those sub-dialog boxes, you will see several items that are common to all the sub-dialog boxes (see Figure D.2). Those items perform the following functions:

> **Style name** shows you which dimension style this setting is associated with.

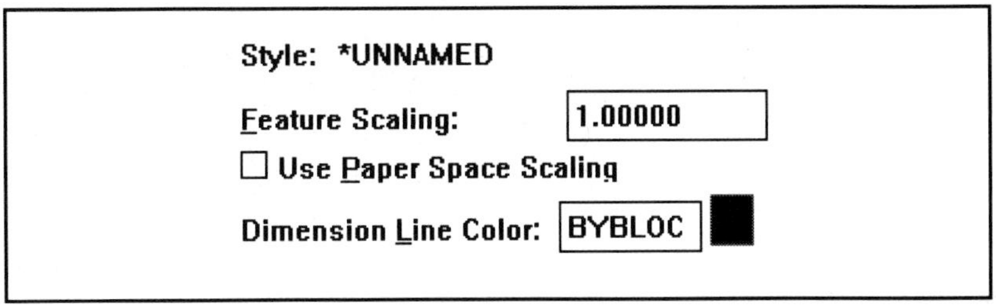

```
Style:  *UNNAMED

Feature Scaling:          1.00000

☐ Use Paper Space Scaling

Dimension Line Color:  BYBLOC ■
```

Figure D.2: Settings found on all Dimension Styles and Variables dialog boxes

> **Feature Scaling** (dimscale) controls the overall scale factor applied to dimensions.

> **User Paper Space Scaling** (dimscale) controls whether AutoCAD computes a dimension scale factor based on the scaling between the current Modelspace viewport and Paperspace. Dimscale is set to 0 if this item is checked.

In the following sections, you will find a description of each of the sub-dialog boxes of the Dimension Styles and Variables dialog box. First a figure of the dialog box is shown followed by a description of its options. Each description shows the related dimension variable in parentheses. The section following this one describes the dimension system variables in detail.

DIMENSION LINES

The Dimension Line subdialog box is shown in Figure D.3.

> **Dimension Line Color** (Dimclrd) controls the color of the dimension line through an input box.

> **Force Interior Line** (Dimtofl) forces a dimension line to be drawn between extension lines even when text is forced out from between the extensions. Interior dimension lines are also forced for radius and circumference dimensions.

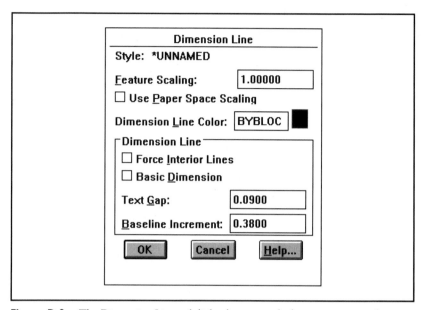

Figure D.3: The Dimension Line subdialog box controls the appearance and placement of the dimension line under various conditions.

Basic Dimension (Dimgap) draws a box around dimension text. This is the same as setting Dimgap to a negative value.

Text Gap (Dimgap) determines the distance between the dimension text and the dimension line whenever the text breaks the dimension line.

Baseline Increment (Dimdli) determines the distance between dimension lines from a common extension line as generated by the Baseline dimension option.

EXTENSION LINES

The Extension Lines sub-dialog box is shown in Figure D.4.

Extension line color (Dimclre) controls the color of the extension line.

Extension above line (Dimexe) controls how far past the dimension line the extension line is to extend.

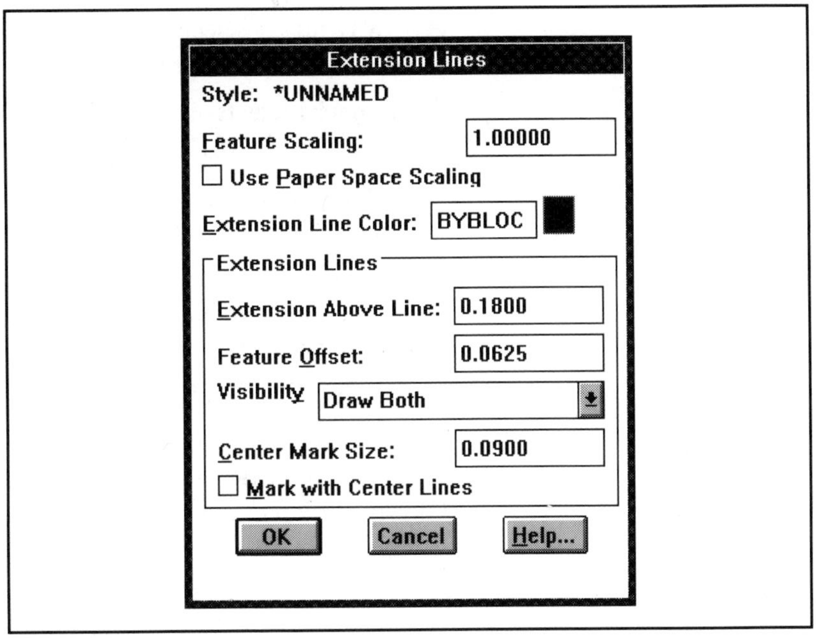

Figure D.4:   The Extension Lines subdialog box controls the appearance of dimension extension lines

Feature Offset (Dimexo) controls how far from the dimensioned feature the extension line is to start.

Visibility (Dimse1, Dimse2) controls whether the first or the second dimension extension is to be drawn. You can suppress the first, second, or both extension lines.

Center Mark Size (Dimcen) controls the center mark size for Center, Diameter, and Radius dimensions.

Mark with Center Lines (Dimcen), when checked, draws a center mark with center lines extending past the dimensioned object. This option makes the Dimcen a negative value.

ARROWS

The Arrows subdialog box is shown in Figure D.5.

Dimension Line color (dimclrd) controls the color of the dimension arrows. This also sets the color of the dimension line.

Arrow (Dimasz) selects the standard AutoCAD arrow for the dimension arrow. This sets Dimtsz to 0.

Tic (Dimtsz) selects a tick mark, usually used in architectural dimensioning, for the dimension arrow. This sets Dimasx to 0.

Dot (dimblk) selects a dot for the dimension arrow. This set Dimblk to a block name called *Dot*.

User (dimblk) lets you use a custom arrow based on a block. You can specify the block name using the User Arrow, First Arrow, and Second Arrow input boxes.

Arrow Size (Dimasz, Dimtsz) controls the size of the arrow.

User Arrow (Dimblk) lets you specify the block name for the custom User Arrow. If you do not specify a block name, an Unknown Block message appears in the lower-left corner of the dialog box.

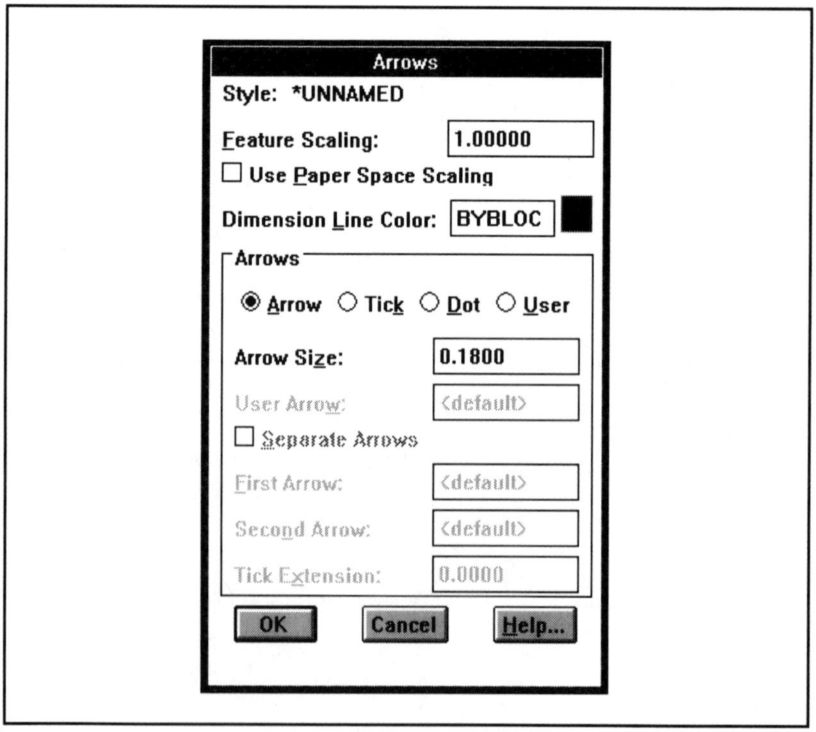

Figure D.5: The arrows sub-dialog box controls the appearance

Separate Arrows (Dimblk1, Dimblk2) lets you specify a different beginning and ending custom arrow when using the User Arrow radio button.

First Arrow (Dimblk1) lets you specify the block name for the first arrow of the separate arrow pair.

Second Arrow (Dimblk2) lets you specify the block name for the second arrow of the separate arrow pair.

Tick Extension (Dimdle) lets you specify how far the dimension line will be drawn past the extension line when using the Tic option.

TEXT LOCATION

The Text Location sub-dialog box is shown in Figure D.6.

Dimension Text Color (Dimclrt) controls the color of the dimension text.

Text Height (Dimtxt) lets you specify a dimension text height when the current text style doesn't have a fixed height value.

Tolerance Height (dimtfac) lets you specify a separate text height for dimension tolerances.

Text Placement/Horizontal (Dimtix, Dimsoxd) lets you specify the general placement of dimension text. Three options are offered: *Default* places text inside extension lines if there is room. For radial dimensions, text is placed outside the radius. This option turns off Dimtix and Dimsoxd. *Force Text Inside* forces text between extension lines and turns Dimtix on and Dimsoxd off. *Text, Arrows Inside* forces both text and arrow inside extension lines. If arrows and dimension lines would normally be drawn outside the extension lines by AutoCAD, they will not be drawn at all with this option. This sets both Dimtix and Dimsoxd on.

Vertical (Dimtad) controls where the text appears relative to the dimension line. It offers three options in a pop-up list. *Centered* places the text in-line with the dimension line, causing the dimension line to be broken. This sets Dimtad off. *Above*

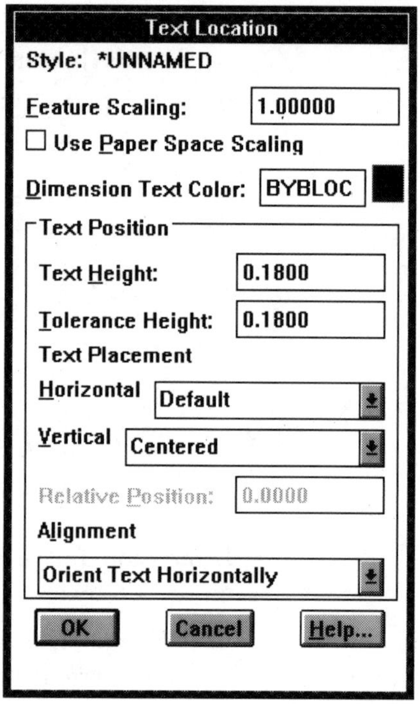

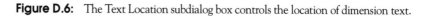

Figure D.6:   The Text Location subdialog box controls the location of dimension text.

places text above the dimension line so the dimension is one continuous line. This sets Dimtad on. *Relative* lets you specify a distance between the dimension text and the dimension line using the Relative Position input box. This sets Dimtad to off.

Relative Position (Dimtvp) lets you specify the distance from the dimension line to the dimension text. To use this option, you must have chosen the Relative option in the Vertical pop-up list. The value you enter is stored with the Dimtvp dimension variable, as the value you enter divided by the text height.

Alignment (Dimtih, Dimtoh) lets you specify whether dimension text is aligned with the dimension line or not. The pop-up list offers four options. *Orient Text Horizontally* forces the text to be horizontal regardless of the dimension line orientation. This sets Dimtih and Dimtoh on. *Align With Dimension Line* causes the text to align with the dimension line. This turns Dimtih off and Dimtoh off. *Aligned When Inside Only* aligns text with dimension lines only when the text appears between extension lines. This sets Dimtih on and Dimtoh off. *Aligned When Outside Only* aligns text with dimension lines only when the text appears outside the extension lines. This turns Dimtih off and Dimtoh on.

TEXT FORMAT

The Text Format subdialog box is shown in Figure D.7.

Length Scaling (Dimlfac) lets you apply a multiplication factor to dimension text. Any dimension found by AutoCAD will be multiplied by the value you enter here.

Scale In Paper Space Only (Dimlfac) controls whether the Length Scaling is applied to Paperspace only. This sets Dimlfac to a negative value. When this is done, dimensions will only use the Length Scaling in Paperspace.

Round Off (Dimrnd) lets you specify a round off value.

Text Prefix (Dimpost) lets you add a prefix to all dimensions. This uses the Dimpost variable and places the value before the <> signs.

Text Suffix (Dimpost) lets you add a suffix to all dimensions. This uses the Dimpost variable and places the value after the <> signs.

Zero Suppression/Feet (Dimzin) suppresses 0′ values in feet and inch dimensions. This is the same as setting Dimzin to 3.

Zero Supression/Inches (Dimzin) suppresses the zero values in feet and inch dimensions. This is the same as setting Dimzin to 2.

Zero Suppression/Leading (Dimzin) suppresses leading zeros in decimal dimensions. This is the same as setting Dimzin to 4.

Zero Suppression/Trailing (Dimzin) suppresses trailing 0's in decimal dimensions. This is the same as setting Dimzin to 8.

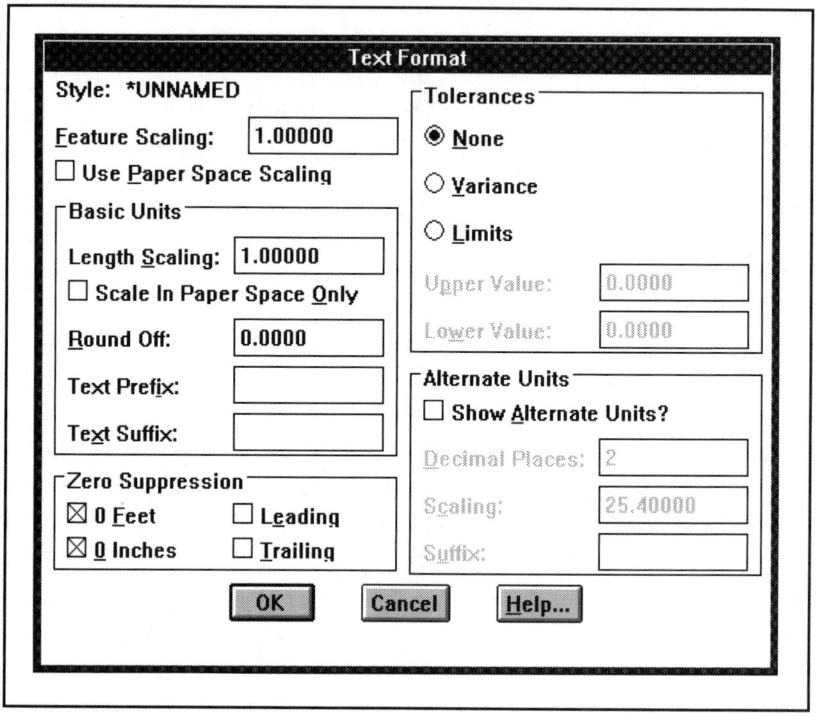

Figure D.7: Options such as additional tolerance dimension, prefixes and suffixes, the appearance of the alternative units, and zero feet and inch values are controlled through this dialog box

Tolerances/None (Dimtol, Dimlim) turns off tolerance dimensions.

Tolerances/Variance (Dimtol, Dimlim) causes the values in the Upper Value and Lower Value input boxes to appear with the dimension text, including a plus/minus sign. This sets Dimtol on and Dimlim off.

Tolerances/Limits (Dimtol, Dimlim) causes AutoCAD to show two stacked dimensions instead of just one. The top dimension is the actual dimension added to the value listed in the Upper Value input box. The lower dimension is the actual dimension minus the value listed in the lower Value input box. This sets Dimtol off and Dimlim on.

Upper Value (Dimtp) sets the value used for the upper limit in the Variance and Limits options.

Lower Value (Dimtm) sets the value used for the lower limit in the Variance and Limits options.

Show Alternate Units? (Dimalt) lets you display a second dimension along with the standard dimension. This second dimension might show the dimension in another format. Dimalt is turned on.

Decimal Places (Dimaltd) lets you set the number of decimal places the alternate dimension carries.

Scaling (Dimaltf) lets you determine the scale factor for the alternate dimension.

Suffix (Dimapost) lets you add a suffix to the alternate dimension as in *mm* for millimeters.

FEATURES

This subdialog box (seen in Figure D.8) provides a quick view to all the previously discussed subdialog boxes. This dialog box may be sufficient for making general changes to the dimension settings.

COLORS

This subdialog box (seen in Figure D.9) provides a quick view of the color, Paperspace, and scaling settings found in all the dimension subdialog boxes that offer these options.

SETTING DIMENSION VARIABLES

This section describes the system variables associated with AutoCAD's dimensioning functions. Through these variables, you can fine-tune the way AutoCAD constructs dimension lines. This is an important feature, since different disciplines have different standards for dimension notation.

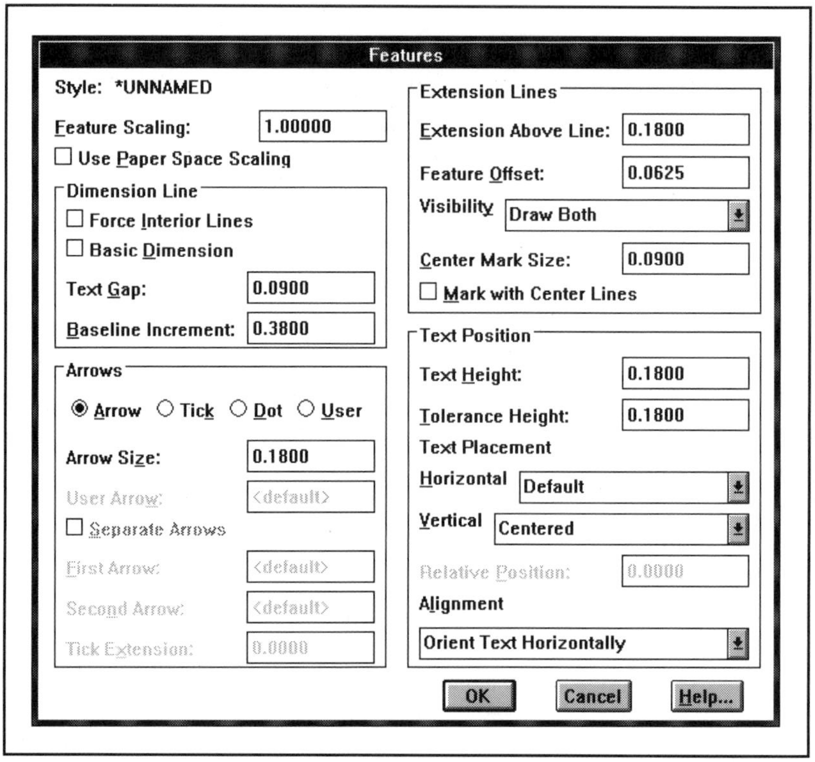

Figure D.8: Options such as additional tolerance dimension, prefixes and suffixes, the appearance of alternate units, and zero feet and inch values are controlled through this dialog box.

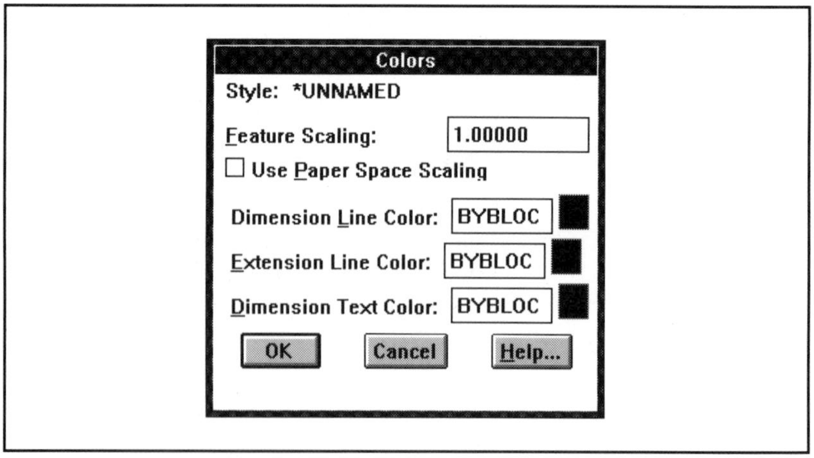

Figure D.9: The Colors subdialog box

Table D.2 shows you a list of the settings that can be modified, their current status, and a brief description of what they do. You can get a similar listing by entering **Dim** ↵ **Status** ↵ at the command prompt. The name of a setting may help you remember its purpose: for example, Dimasz adjusts the arrow size.

If you want to change a setting, you can enter the setting name at the command prompt. You can then change that setting's value.

CONTROLLING ASSOCIATIVE DIMENSIONING

As I said in *Chapter 9*, you can turn off associative dimensioning by using the Dimaso setting. The default for Dimaso is on. The **Dimsho** setting controls whether the dimension value is dynamically updated while a dimension line is being dragged. The default for this setting is on.

SPECIFYING SCALES OF DIMENSION ELEMENTS

In an exercise in *Chapter 9*, you used the Dimscale setting to set the dimension scale. Dimscale controls the overall *scale factor*. The other dimension settings are multiplied by this factor. For example, the default arrow size is $3/16$". With **Dimscale** set to 1, the dimension arrows are drawn at $3/16$". If Dimscale is set to 48, the arrows are drawn at 48 times $3/16$", or 9". The use of an overall scale factor allows quick adjustment of all these settings. Otherwise, you would have to convert every setting individually for every different scale you use.

The **Dimtxt** setting controls text size. Remember that the setting height is multiplied by the Dimscale setting. For example, you could set Dimscale to 48. With a Dimtxt value of $3/16$", that would make your dimension text 9" high. If the current text style has a fixed height, that height overrides this setting. For example, if you had used the Note text style in your dimension example, the text height would have been 6". The **Dimtfac** setting lets you apply a separate scale factor to tolerance factor dimension text. This only affects dimensions created with Dimtol and Dimlim.

Table D.2: The dimension variables

ASSOCIATIVE DIMENSIONING		
SETTING NAME	**DEFAULT SETTING**	**DESCRIPTION**
Dimaso	On	Turns associative dimensions on and off
Dimsho	On	Updates dimensions dynamically while dragging
SCALE		
SETTING NAME	**DEFAULT SETTING**	**DESCRIPTION**
Dimscale	1.0000	Overall scale factor of dimensions
Dimtxt	.18"	Text height
Dimasz	.18"	Arrow size
Dimtsz	0"	Tick size
Dimcen	.09"	Center mark size
Dimlfac	1.0000	Linear unit scale factor
OFFSETS		
SETTING NAME	**DEFAULT SETTING**	**DESCRIPTION**
Dimexo	.0625"	Extension line origin offset
Dimexe	.18"	Amount extension line extends beyond dimension line
Dimdli	.38"	Dimension line offset for continuation or base
Dimdle	0"	Amount dimension line extends beyond extension line

Table D.2: The dimension variables (continued)

	TOLERANCES	
SETTING NAME	**DEFAULT SETTING**	**DESCRIPTION**
Dimtp	0"	Plus tolerance
Dimtm	0"	Minus tolerance
Dimtol	Off	Shows dimension tolerances when on
Dimlim	Off	Shows dimension limits when on

	ROUNDING	
SETTING NAME	**DEFAULT SETTING**	**DESCRIPTION**
Dimrnd	0"	Rounding value
Dimzin	0	Controls display of 0 dimensions. Has four settings: 0, 1, 2, and 3. 0 leaves out zero feet and inches, 1 includes zero feet and inches, 2 includes zero feet, and 3 includes zero inches.

	DIMENSION TEXT ORIENTATION	
SETTING NAME	**DEFAULT SETTING**	**DESCRIPTION**
Dimgap	1/16" or 0.09"	Controls distance between the dimension text and the dimension line.
Dimtfac	1.0"	Controls the scale factor for dimension tolerance text.
Dimtih	On	Text inside extensions is horizontal when on
Dimtoh	On	Text outside extensions is horizontal when on
Dimtad	Off	Places text above the dimension line when on
Dimtix	Off	Forces text between extensions
Dimtvp	0	Controls text position based on numeric value

Table D.2:   The dimension variables (continued)

EXTENSION LINE CONTROL		
SETTING NAME	DEFAULT SETTING	DESCRIPTION
Dimse1	Off	Suppresses the first extension line when on
Dimse2	Off	Suppresses the second extension line when on
Dimtofl	Off	Forces a dimension line between extension lines
Dimsoxd	Off	Suppresses dimension lines outside extension lines

ALTERNATE DIMENSION OPTIONS		
SETTING NAME	DEFAULT SETTING	DESCRIPTION
Dimalt	Off	Alternate units selected are shown when on
Dimaltf	25.4000	Alternate unit scale factor
Dimaltd	2	Alternate unit decimal places
Dimpost	*Suffix/Prefix*	Adds suffix or prefix to dimension text
Dimapost	*Suffix/Prefix*	Adds suffix or prefix to alternate dimension text
Dimblk	*Block name*	Alternate arrow block name
Dimsah	Off	Allows the use of two different arrow heads on a dimension line
Dimblk1	*Block name*	Alternate arrow block name used with Dimsah
Dimblk2	*Block name*	Alternate arrow block name used with Dimsah
Dimstyle	**unnamed*	Name of current dimension style

Table D.2: The dimension variables (continued)

COLORS		
SETTING NAME	**DEFAULT SETTING**	**DESCRIPTION**
Dimclrd	*byblock*	Controls the color of dimension lines and arrows
Dimclre	*byblock*	Controls the color of dimension extension lines
Dimclrt	*byblock*	Controls the color of dimension text

The **Dimasz** setting controls the arrow size. The size indicated is the actual size of the arrows in the plotted drawing, provided the Dimscale option is set to the drawing scale.

The **Dimtsz** setting controls dimension tick-mark size. If this setting is a value greater than 0, the dimensions produce a tick mark. (The arrow still appears when you dimension radii or use leaders for notes.) The value you enter here determines the orthogonal distance from the midpoint of the tick mark to one end (see Figure D.10).

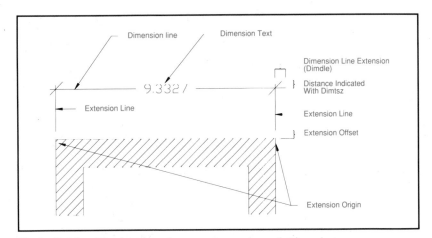

Figure D.10: The dimension line extension setting and tick mark size

Dimcen controls the size of the center mark AutoCAD uses when dimensioning arcs and circles. The center mark is a small cross placed at the center of the circle or arc.

The **Dimlfac** setting affects the numeric value of the dimension. The default setting, *1.0000*, multiplies the distance to be dimensioned by 1 and enters this value as the actual dimension measured. If you want to show the distance converted to millimeters, for example, you make the Dimlfac value 25.4. This multiplies a one-unit distance by 25.4 and displays a dimension of *25.4000*.

Dimlfac is also useful for dimensioning objects in a Paperspace viewport. If Dimlfac is set to a negative value, then the dimension distances in Paperspace will be multiplied by the absolute value of the Dimlfac setting. You might set Dimlfac to **–48**, for example, if a viewport contains a drawing at ¼" scale. Then, any dimension drawn in Paperspace will have its distance value multiplied by 48. Dimensions drawn while in Modelspace will be given a scale factor of 1 so that dimensions reflect true distances.

You can have AutoCAD automatically set Dimlfac to a scale factor appropriate for a particular viewport. If you enter Dimlfac while in Paperspace, you get the prompt:

```
Current value <1.000> New value (viewport):
```

You then respond by entering **V**. You get the prompt:

```
Select viewport to set scale:
```

Finally, you pick a viewport border. Dimlfac will be set to the appropriate value to reflect a true dimension even while dimensioning in Paperspace.

SETTING DIMENSION LINE OFFSETS

Dimexo controls the distance between the point you pick and the beginning of the extension line. Dimexe controls the distance the extension line passes beyond the dimension line (see Figure D.11).

At times it is necessary for AutoCAD to offset dimensions when the Continue or the Baseline option is used. The **Dimdli** setting controls the distance of that offset (see Figure D.12).

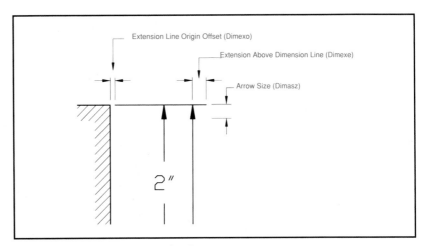

Figure D.11: The extension line offset

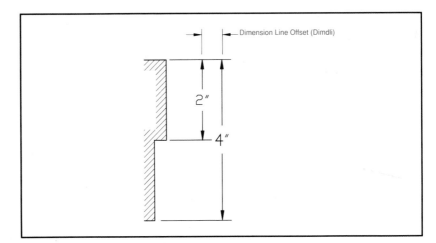

Figure D.12: How Dimdli controls offset distances

The **Dimdle** setting is effective only if you use tick marks. It controls the distance the dimension extends beyond the extension lines (see Figure D.10). This is one setting that is not affected by Dimscale. For example, if you set Dimdle to ⅛", no matter what the Dimscale value is, the dimension line will extend only ⅛" beyond the extension line. The **Dimgap** setting controls the gap between the dimension line and the dimension text when **Dimtad** is turned off. You can also have a box drawn around a dimension as in a reference or basic dimension by setting Dimgap to a negative value. The absolute value of Dimgap will still be taken as the gap between the text and dimension line.

DIMENSIONING WITH TOLERANCES

You may want to indicate a plus tolerance in your dimensions. The **Dimtp** setting determines what that value will be. A 0" setting shows a 0" plus tolerance, for example. The **Dimtm** setting works in the same way as the Dimtp setting, but for minus tolerances. Plus and minus tolerances do not appear unless Dimtol or Dimlim is set *on* (see Figure D.13).

Dimtol controls whether the dimension tolerance values set with Dimtp and Dimtm are added to the dimension text. With Dimtol on, you get a dimension followed by the plus and minus values you specified using Dimtp and Dimtm (see Figure D.14).

Dimlim is similar to Dimtol. However, rather than giving the plus and minus values, it gives two values reflecting the range determined by the dimension and tolerance values (see Figure D.14). Since Dimlim and Dimtol do similar things, if one is turned on the other is automatically turned off.

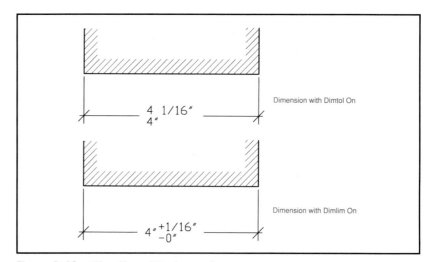

Figure D.13: The effect of Dimlim on dimension text

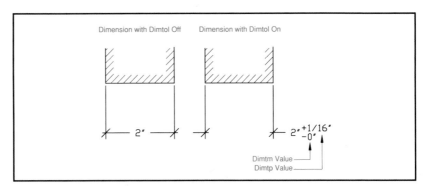

Figure D.14: The effect of Dimtol on dimension text

CONTROLLING DIMENSION ROUNDING

To round the dimension values, use the **Dimrnd** command. A 0.125 value here will round your dimensions to the nearest ⅛ ".

If your measurement system uses feet and inches, the **Dimzin** setting determines how a zero-inch value is displayed. It can be set to one of four integer values: 0, 1, 2, or 3. The setting 0 leaves out zero feet and inches; for example, 1'0" is displayed as 1', and 0'6" is displayed as 6". The setting 1 includes zero feet and inches, 2 includes zero feet only, and 3 includes zero inches only.

POSITIONING DIMENSION TEXT

Dimtih controls whether the dimension text is inserted horizontally or aligned with the dimension line. When Dimtih is on, text is always inserted horizontally. If it is off, the text is aligned with the dimension line except when it does not fit between the extension lines (see Figure D.15).

Dimtoh controls the orientation of dimension text that does not fit between the extension lines. As with Dimtih, when on, it forces the text to be horizontal (see Figure D.16).

When the **Dimtad** setting is on, the dimension text is placed above the dimension line and aligned with it. If you are doing architectural drawings, you will probably want to set Dimtad on (see Figure D.17).

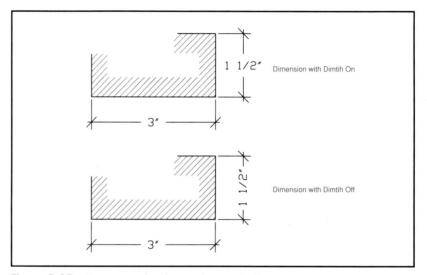

Figure D.15: Text inserted with Dimtih on and off

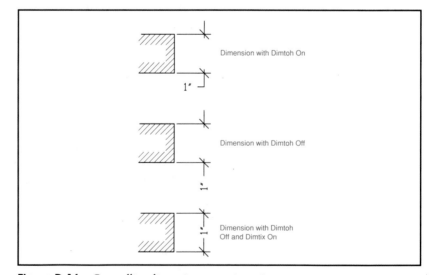

Figure D.16: Controlling dimension text orientation

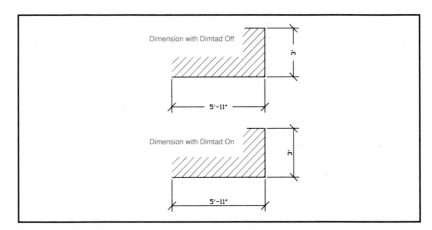

Figure D.17: Dimensions inserted with Dimtad on and off

If you want the dimension text to appear between the extension lines regardless of the length of the text, you can set **Dimtix** on (see Figure D.16). You can control the vertical location of the dimension text by setting **Dimtvp** to a numeric value. If its value is less than .7, the dimension line will split to accommodate the text. Negative values place the text below the dimension line. Dimtad must be off before Dimtvp can take effect.

CONTROLLING DIMENSION LINES

At times, you may not want the first extension line to be drawn, as in Figure D.18. You can control the insertion of extension lines by setting **Dimse1** and **Dimse2** on or off. Setting Dimse1 on suppresses the insertion of the first extension line, while setting Dimse2 on suppresses the second extension line.

Normally, AutoCAD will not draw a dimension line between the extension lines if the dimension text is outside the extensions (see Figure D.16). Setting **Dimtofl** on will force a line to be drawn between extension lines regardless of the text location. For radial and diametric dimensions, Dimtofl set to *on* will force a dimension line to appear inside the circle or arc being dimensioned. If it is used in conjunction with Dimtix, both the dimension text and the dimension line will be forced to appear inside the arc or circle. Dimsoxd will suppress dimension lines that would normally appear outside the extension lines (see Figure D.19).

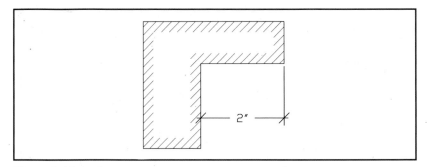

Figure D.18: When you want to suppress an extension line

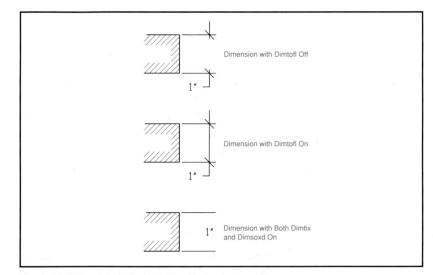

Figure D.19: Controlling dimension line orientation

USING ALTERNATE DIMENSIONS AND ARROWS

Dimalt controls whether the Dimaltf and Dimaltd settings are operative. The **Dimaltf** setting determines a conversion factor for the AutoCAD drawing unit and displays that alternate dimension in brackets. For example, the default setting, *25.4000*, converts the unit measure, inches, to millimeters. If the Dimalt setting is on, a one-inch measurement is displayed along with the alternate millimeter equivalent, 25.4000, in brackets (see Figure D.20). This is useful if you must show dimensions in both English and metric measurements. The **Dimaltd** setting controls the number of decimal places shown when you use Dimaltf.

If you want a dimension suffix or prefix added to your dimensions, you can use the **Dimpost** option. For example, if you want the word *units* always to appear after a dimension value, you can set Dimpost to *units*. A four-unit dimension would read

4 units

instead of just 4. Dimapost has the same effect, except it applies only to alternate dimensions, as in

1" (25.4 *units*)

If you don't want the default arrow or tick mark for your dimension lines, you can create a block of the desired arrow or tick and enter the block name for the **Dimblk** setting. For example, you may want to have a tick mark that is thicker than the dimension lines and extensions. You could create a block of a tick mark on a layer you assign to a thick pen weight, then assign that block to the Dimblk setting.

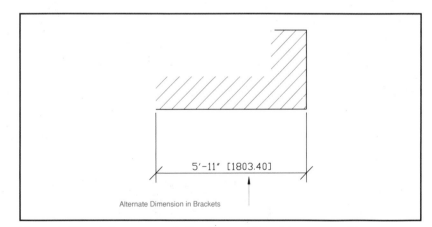

Figure D.20:   A dimension with Dimalt on and Dimaltf set to 25.4000

The original block should be drawn one unit long. The block's insertion point will be the endpoint of the dimension line, so be sure the insertion point is at the point of your arrow. The block will be rotated 180° for the left side of the dimension line. Because the right side's arrow will be inserted with a zero rotation value, orient the arrow so that it is pointing to the right (see Figure D.21).

If you set a block for a different arrow, then decide to use the standard AutoCAD arrow, enter a period as a response to the Dimblk option.

At times, you may want a different type of arrow at each end of the dimension line. To accomplish this, you can use **Dimsah** in conjunction with Dimblk1 and Dimblk2. With Dimsah on, AutoCAD will use arrows defined by **Dimblk1** and **Dimblk2** as arrows for dimension lines. Dimblk1 and Dimblk2 are defined in the same way as Dimblk.

If you know you will use certain dimension settings all the time, you may want to change the default settings in the Acad.DWG file, as we discussed in *Chapter 6*, or set up a template file.

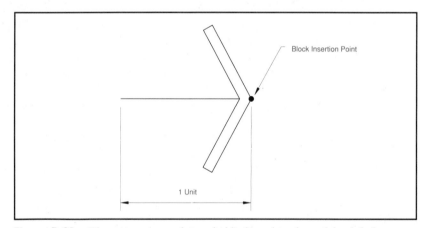

Figure D.21:   The orientation and size of a block used in place of the default arrow

CONTROLLING THE COLOR OF DIMENSION ELEMENTS

Three dimension variables let you control the color of the individual components of a dimension. **Dimclrd** lets you set the dimension line and arrow color. **Dimclre** controls the color of the dimension extension lines. **Dimclrt** controls the color of the dimension text. This can be significant, especially if you use a plotter that allows you to control line weight by the colors in your drawing. For example, if you want the dimension text to be in a heavier line weight than the rest of the dimension lines, you can set Dimclrt to a color that will print or plot in a heavier weight.

When you use any of these dimension variables, you get the prompt **Current value <BYBLOCK> New value**, to which you must respond with a color number. The default BYBLOCK causes the dimension component to take on the color of the layer the dimension is on.

STORING DIMENSION STYLES

After you have changed the dimension variable settings to ones you like, you can save the settings by using the dimension **Save** command. This is not to be confused with the Save command that saves your drawing to disk. The dimension Save command records all of the current dimension variable settings (except Dimaso) with a name you give.

If you enter **Dim1 ↵ save ↵** at the command prompt, you get the prompt:

?/Name for new dimension style:

You can enter a question mark (?) to get a listing of any dimension styles currently saved, or you can enter a name under which the current setting is to be saved.

For example, suppose you change some of your dimension settings as shown in the following list.

Dimtsz	0.044
Dimtad	on
Dimtih	off
Dimtoh	off

These settings are typical for an architectural style of dimensioning. You can save them under the name *Arch*. Then you can go about changing other dimension settings to draw dimensions in another format—surveyor's dimensions on a site plan for example. You could also save them with the dimension Save command. When you want to return to the settings you used for your architectural drawing, you use the dimension Restore command.

RESTORING A DIMENSION STYLE

To restore a dimension style you've saved using the dimension Save command, you use the dimension Restore command. Enter **Dim1** ↵ **Restore** ↵ at the command prompt and you get the prompt:

?/Enter dimension style name or RETURN to select dimension:

Here you have three options. You can enter a question mark (?) to get a listing of saved dimension styles. You can enter the name of a style, such as **Arch**, if you know the name of the style you want. Or you can use the cursor to select a dimension on the screen whose style you want to match.

IMPORTING DIMENSION STYLES FROM OTHER DRAWINGS

Dimension styles are saved within the current drawing file only. You can, however, import a dimension style from another drawing by using the XBIND command, as described in *Chapter 12*. To do this, you first use XREF to attach a cross-reference file. Then you use XBIND to import the dimension style you want. Finally, you use XREF to detach the cross-reference file.

NOTES ON METRIC DIMENSIONING

This book assumes you are using feet and inches as the units of measure. The AutoCAD user community is worldwide, however, and many of you may be using the metric system in your work. As long as you are not mixing English and metric measurements, using the English version of

AutoCAD is fairly easy. Set your measurement system to decimal with the UNITS command, then draw distances in millimeters or centimeters. At plot time, be sure you specify Millimeters at the **Size units** prompt. Also be sure you specify a scale that compensates for differences between millimeters (which are the AutoCAD base unit when you are using the metric system), and centimeters.

If your drawings are to be in both English and metric measurements, you will be concerned with several settings. I've listed those settings here for your convenience:

Dimlfac	Scale factor for dimension values. The dimension value will be the measured distance in AutoCAD units times this scale factor. Set Dimlfac to **25.4** if you have drawn in inches but want to dimension in millimeters. The current default is *1.00*.
Dimalt	Turns the display of alternate dimensions on or off. Alternate dimensions are dimension text added to your drawing in addition to the standard dimension text.
Dimaltf	Scale factor for alternate dimension (i.e., metric). The default is *25.4* which is the millimeter equivalent of 1".
Dimaltd	Number of decimal places displayed in alternate dimension.
Dimapost	Adds suffix or prefix to alternate dimension, as in *4.5mm*.

CREATING

EXPLORING

EDITING

LEARNING

MANAGING

ADDING

PRINTING

ANIMATING

PLOTTING

ENTERING

DRAWING

GETTING

RENDERING

USING

INTEGRATING

MODELING

ORGANIZING

MANAGING

E
▼ ▼ ▼ ▼ ▼

STANDARD
AUTOCAD
COMMAND
LIST

STANDARD
AUTOCAD COMMAND LIST

This appendix provides a comprehensive list of all the standard AutoCAD commands. If it isn't here, chances are it is an AutoLISP or ADS macro. Each command is given a brief description and, if applicable, a listing of options and comments on its operation. Most of these commands are also described quite thoroughly in the tutorial.

COMMAND NAME	DESCRIPTION	OPTIONS/OPERATIONS
About	Displays your serial number and a scrolling list box with the contents of the Acad.MSG file	*na*
Aperture	Controls the size of the Object Snap cursor	Size of aperture is in pixels.
Arc	Draws arcs	**A**=including angle, **C**=center point, **D**=starting point, **E**=endpoint, **L**=length of cord, **R**=radius
Area	Finds the area of selected points, a polyline, or a circle	**A**=add mode, **S**=subtract mode, **E**=select entity to find area
Array	Constructs multiple copies in a matrix or circular pattern	**R**=rectangular, **P**=polar
Attdef	Creates an Attribute definition	**I**=visible/invisible, **C**=constant/variable, **V**=controls verify mode, **P**=controls preset, **Tag**=attribute "ID", **Prompt**=attribute prompt, **default**=attribute default value

COMMAND NAME	DESCRIPTION	OPTIONS/OPERATIONS
'Attdisp	Controls visibility of attributes	**On**=all are made visible; **Off**=all are made invisible; **N**=normal only attributes set to invisible are not shown
Attedit	Edits attributes	You can edit attributes globally or one at time. You can also change attribute text size, orientation, and locations.
Attext	Extracts attribute data	**C**=comma-delimited format, **D**=DXF format, **S**=space-delimited format, **E**=extract from specific entities
Audit	Audits drawing integrity	**Y**=fix errors, **N**=don't fix errors but produce report
'Base	Changes insertion origin	Pick a point
Bhatch	Draws a hatch pattern	Automatic boundary defined by picking a point. Hatch preview offered. *See* Bpoly.
'Blipmode	Controls blips	**On**=show blips, **Off**=don't show blips
Block	Groups objects into a single, named entity	**?**=list existing blocks
Bpoly	Draws a polyline boundary	The boundary must be contiguous or Bpoly will not work properly.
Break	Breaks objects into two parts	Select object, then second point of break, or **F**=pick first and second point.
Chamfer	Joins two lines in a chamfer	**D**=set chamfer distances, **P**=chamfer each vertex of a polyline

COMMAND NAME	DESCRIPTION	OPTIONS/OPERATIONS
Change	Modify an entity's properties	**P**=change common properties, such as: **C**=color, **E**=elevation, **LA**=layer, **LT**=linetype, **T**=thickness. Also changes text height, style, angle, value, line endpoints, and circle radius.
Chprop	Modifies common properties	**C**=color, **LA**=layer, **LT**=linetype, **T**=thickness
Circle	Draws circles	**2P**=based on two diametric points on circle, **3P**=based on three points on circumference, **D**=enter diameter, **R**=enter radius, **TTR**=tangent to two objects and a radius
'Color/'Colour	Sets the default color for new objects	**number**=color number, **name**=color name for standard colors only, **Bylayer**=use layer color, **Byblock**=floating entity color
Compile	Compiles shape or font file	Indicate file name with .SHP extension
Config	Configures AutoCAD	*See* Configuration *in Appendix B.*
Copy	Copies objects	**M**=multiple copies
Dblist	Lists database information for every object in drawing	*na*
Ddattdef	Dialog box to create attribute definition	*See* Attdef.
Ddatte	Dialog box to edit attributes	Displays the attribute prompt and value. Values are editable through input box.
Ddattext	Dialog box to extract attribute data	*See* Attext.

COMMAND NAME	DESCRIPTION	OPTIONS/OPERATIONS
Ddchprop	Dialog box to change properties	*See* Chprop.
Ddedit	Dialog box to edit text	Displays text in an input box, allowing you to edit single lines of text
'Ddemodes	Sets defaults for new objects	Lets you set layer, linetype color, elevation, thickness, and text style
'Ddgrips	Sets the Grips feature	Lets you turn grips on or off and set the grip color and size
Ddim	Controls the dimension settings	Lets you control dimension styles and variables from a series of dialog boxes. *See Appendix D.*
Ddinsert	Dialog box for the Insert function	Lets you insert a block or file and allows you to define insertion point, scale, and rotation angle
Ddlmodes	Dialog box for controlling layers	Lets you set current layer, create new layer, control visibility, color, line type, etc.
'Ddosnap	Dialog box for Osnap settings	Lets you control default Osnap settings and size of Osnap cursor. *See* Osnap.
'Ddrmodes	Dialog box for setting standard modes	Lets you set Grid, Snap, and other drawing modes set by function keys
'Ddrename	Dialog box for renaming items	Lets you rename blocks, line types, layers, text styles, viewports, UCSs, and dimension styles
'Ddselect	Dialog box for setting selection modes	Lets you set Verb/Noun, Shift-pick, click-drag, automatic window, and pickbox size. Also sets entity sort method.

COMMAND NAME	DESCRIPTION	OPTIONS/OPERATIONS
Dducs	Dialog box for setting and recalling UCSs	Lets you save a UCS under a name or list a UCS's coordinates
'Ddunits	Dialog box for unit style settings	Lets you control the unit and angle style as well as the degree of precision for each
'Delay	Used with scripts to delay the execution of the next command	Place just after the command you want to pause in a script. Follow Delay with a value representing milliseconds.
Dim	Starts the dimension mode	While in the dimension mode, you can only enter dimension commands.
Dim1	Allows you to enter a single dimension command	Once entered, you can enter any dimension command once
'Dist	Finds the distance between points	Pick two points
Divide	Marks off an object in equal segments	Select an object, then specify the number of segments you want. Uses point entities as markers by default, but you can use Blocks.
Donut/ Doughnut	Draws a circle with thickness	Specify inside diameter and outside diameter of circle. Specify inside diameter of 0 for solid circle.
'Dragmode	Controls dynamic dragging	**On**=drag when requested with "drag" keyboard entry, **Off**=don't drag at all, **Auto**=drag when applicable

COMMAND NAME	DESCRIPTION	OPTIONS/OPERATIONS
Dtext	Draws text directly in graphic area	Select a start point, style, or justification, then specify height if the style height is set to 0, and rotation angle. You can enter several lines of text. Each ↵ drops the cursor down one line.
Dview	Controls the view of 3D perspectives	**CA**=camera location, **CL**=set clip planes, **D**=camera-to-target distance and turns on perspective mode, **H**=hidden line removal, **Off**=turn perspective off, **PA**=pan view, **PO**=allows selection of target and camera points, **TA**=allows selection of target point by view, **TW**= twist camera view, **U**=undo last option, **X**=exit Dview, **Z**=zoom in/out or set camera focal length, **T**=suboption of CA and TA that toggles between setting angle from xy plane and x axis of xy plane
Dxbin	Inserts .DXB files	*na*
Dxfin	Inserts .DXF files	*na*
Dxfout	Exports .DXF files	**B**=write Binary DXF, **E**=select specific entities to export, **0–16**=floating point precision
Edgsurf	Draws a 3D mesh based on four contiguous objects	Objects must be joined end-to-end exactly, and can be lines, arcs, or polylines.
Elev	Sets the default elevation and thickness for new objects	Can be set from Ddemodes dialog box

COMMAND NAME	DESCRIPTION	OPTIONS/OPERATIONS
Ellipse	Draws an ellipse	**C**=select center point, **R**=specify eccentricity by rotation, **I**=isometric
End	Exits AutoCAD	Drawing is saved and AutoCAD closes.
Erase	Deletes objects	Standard selection options
Explode	Reduces blocks and polylines to basic entities	Nested blocks are not broken down. Spline polylines break down into line segments.
Extend	Extends objects to meet other objects	You can select multiple objects to extend by using a Fence selection option. **U**=undo last extend.
'Files	Dialog box to access file utilities	You can copy, list, delete, unlock, or rename files.
'Fill	Controls visibility of filled objects	**On**=fill solids, traces, and wide polylines, **Off**=show outlines only
Fillet	Joins 2D objects end-to-end or with an arc	**P**=fillet a polyline, **R**=set radius for fillet
Filmroll	Creates a filmroll file (.FLM) for AutoShade or 3D Studio	*na*
'Graphscr	Flips from text to graphics mode	Same as **F1**
'Grid	Sets grid settings	**On**=turn on grid, **Off**=turn off grid, **S**=match Snap spacing, **A**=set grid aspect ratio, *number*=set grid spacing to the number specified, *number*x=set grid spacing to be multiple of Snap setting.

COMMAND NAME	DESCRIPTION	OPTIONS/OPERATIONS
Handles	Assigns permanent value to entities	Handles are accessed through AutoLISP. **On**=turn handles on, **Destroy**=turn handles off and remove all handles from entities.
Hatch	Draws hatch patterns	**name**=predefined pattern, ***name**=predefined pattern exploded, **U**=simple line or cross hatch (allows user to specify spacing and rotation), **?**=list predefined hatch patterns. *See* Bhatch.
'Help/'?	Provides information on commands and operations	If used while in the middle of a command, provides information regarding the current operation
Hide	Performs hidden line removal	*na*
'ID	Displays coordinates of selected point	Asks to select point
IGESIN	Imports IGES files	*na*
IGESOUT	Exports drawing as IGES file	*na*
Insert	Imports file or inserts block	Use **blockname**=*filename* to redefine internal block. **C**=select window to place insert. **?**=list available blocks. *****=insert and explode. Other options are independent X, Y, and Z scale, as well as rotation angle. *See also* Ddinsert.
'Isoplane	Select plane of isometric grid	**L**=left, **R**=right, **T**=top, ↵=toggles between planes (*see also* Ddrmodes)

COMMAND NAME	DESCRIPTION	OPTIONS/OPERATIONS
'Layer	Provides command-line layer control	**C**=set layer color, **F**=freeze a layer, **L**=set layer linetype, **LO**=lock a layer, **M**=create a layer and make it current, **N**=create new layer, **ON**=turn on layer, **OFF**=turn off layer, **S**= set current layer, **T**=thaw layer, **?**=list layers, **U**=unlock layers. For F, N, On, Off, and T options, you can provide multiple layer names by listing them with comma separators. Wildcard characters can also be used.
'Limits	Sets the drawing limits	Select two points to define boundaries of limits. **On**=limits checking on, **Off**=limits checking off. (Limits checking forces objects to be drawn inside limits.)
Line	Draws lines	**C**=Close series of lines, **U**=undo last line segment, ⤶=at start point prompt, starts line from last line or arc
'Linetype	Controls linetype settings	**?**=List linetypes available from linetype file, **C**=create linetype definition, **L**=Load linetype definition, **S**=set current default linetype for new objects
List	Shows properties of objects	Uses standard selection options
Load	Loads shape and text style definitions	Uses standard file dialog box
'Ltscale	Sets the scale for linetypes	Applies to all objects and linetypes

COMMAND NAME	DESCRIPTION	OPTIONS/OPERATIONS
Measure	Marks off specific intervals on objects	**B**=use a block for marking device. The default marking device is a point entity.
Menu	Loads a menu file	Menus settings are stored with drawings. Any AutoLISP programs with the .MNL extension and the same name as the menu are loaded with the menu.
Minsert	Multiple inserts of blocks in an array	Options are similar to those for the Insert command.
Mirror	Creates a reflected copy	You can specify a copy or just mirror an object without copying.
Move	Moves objects	Standard selection options
Mslide	Makes a slide	Specify file name
Mspace	Switch to Modelspace	Can only be used while in Paperspace
Multiple	Repeats the next command	Command is repeated until user enters **Ctrl-C**.
Mview	Controls Paperspace viewports	**On/Off**=turns display of viewport on or off, **Hideplot**=causes hidden line removal of viewport at plot time, **Fit**=fits new viewport in current view, **2/3/4**=creates two, three, or four viewports, **Restore**=restores viewport configurations saved with Vports command
New	Creates new drawing	Dialog box lets you choose a prototype drawing.
Offset	Creates parallel copies	**T**=select a point through which offset passes, *number*=offset distance
Oops	Restores last erasure	*na*

COMMAND NAME	DESCRIPTION	OPTIONS/OPERATIONS
Open	Opens a new file	Dialog box allows you to save or discard current drawing edits.
'Ortho	Forces lines to be vertical or horizontal	Toggle with **F8** key or **Ctrl-O**.
'Osnap	Allows exact selection of object geometry	You can set object snaps to be the default by using Osnap and entering the Osnap mode you want. Use None to turn default Osnaps off.
'Pan	Shifts the current display in a specified direction	*na*
Pedit	Edits polylines, 3D polylines, and meshes	**C**=close a polyline; **D**=decurve a curved polyline; **Edit**=edit polyline vertices; **F**=curve fitted polyline; **Join**=Join polyline to other polylines, arcs, and lines; **L**=controls noncontinuous linetype generation through vertices; **O**=open a closed polyline; **S**=spline curve; **U**=undo last option; **W**=set overall width; **X**=Exit pedit
Pface	Creates a 3D mesh	*na*
Plan	Changes to Plan view of a UCS	**C**=current, **U**=specified UCS, **W**=World Coordinate System

COMMAND NAME	DESCRIPTION	OPTIONS/OPERATIONS
Pline	Draws a 2D Polyline	**H**=set half-width value, **U**=undo last option, **W**=set the beginning and end width of current segment, **A**=switch to drawing arcs, **C**=Close a polyline, **L**=continue previous segment. While in the Arc mode, **A**=arc angle, **CE**=center point, **CL**=close polyline with an arc, **D**=arc direction, **L**=switch to line drawing mode, **S**=second point of a three point arc, **R**=specify an Arc radius.
Plot	Plot a drawing	Uses a dialog box to offer plotter settings. Can be disabled using the Cmddia system variable.
Point	Draws a point entity	Point entities can be changed using the Pdmode and Pdsize system variables.
Polygon	Draws a polygon	**E**=draw a polygon by specifying one edge segment, **C**=circumscribe polygon around a circumference, **I**=inscribe a polygon around a circumference
Psdrag	Controls the Psin drag mode	**0**=show only bounding box in dragged image, **1**=show whole image as it is being dragged
Psfill	Fill polyline with PostScript fill pattern	Pattern appears when plotted to a PostScript device. Not intended for viewing or plotting on pen plotters.
Psin	Import Encapsulated PostScript images	Image quality can be controlled with Psquality.

COMMAND NAME	DESCRIPTION	OPTIONS/OPERATIONS
Psout	Exports drawing to Encapsulated PostScript format	If PostScript fonts are used in the drawing, they will be used with the EPS file.
Pspace	Switch to Paperspace	Only valid in Paperspace when moving from a Modelspace viewport
Purge	Deletes unused named items	Layers, blocks, text styles, linetypes, and dimension styles will be removed if not being used.
Qsave	Saves the drawing	File is saved with no messages or requests from AutoCAD.
Qtext	Displays text as rectangles	**On**=turn on Qtext, **Off**=turn off Qtext. Can also be set using Ddrmodes.
Quit	Exits AutoCAD	Dialog box appears allowing you to save or discard changes to the current drawing.
Recover	Attempts recovery of damaged drawings	AutoCAD automatically attempts a recovery of a damaged file when you try to open it.
Redefine	Restores an Undefined command	*See* Undefine.
Redo	Reverses the last Undo	Can only be used to Redo one Undo
'Redraw	Refreshes the display	Only in current viewport or Modelspace
'Redrawall	Refreshes all viewport displays	*na*
Regen	Regenerates a drawing	Refreshes the display to reflect the latest changes in the drawing database

COMMAND NAME	DESCRIPTION	OPTIONS/OPERATIONS
Regenall	Regenerates all viewports	*na*
'Regenauto	Controls automatic regens	Some commands force a regen. With Regenauto off, you are prompted before a regen is about to occur, allowing you to terminate the current command and avoid the regen.
Reinit	Reinitializes I/O devices	Also reinitializes the Acad.PGP file.
Rename	Renames named items	Layers, blocks, dimension styles, text styles, linetypes, UCSs, Views, and Viewport configurations can be renamed.
'Resume	Resumes a terminated script	*See* 'Script
Revsurf	Creates a surface of revolution	Requires a polyine profile and a line defining the revolution axis
Rotate	Rotate objects	**R**=rotate with respect to an angle
Rscript	Restarts a script from the beginning	*See* 'Script
Rulesurf	Creates a 3D mesh between two curves	Requires the existence of an arc, line, or polyline between which the mesh is drawn
Save	Saves a drawing	A dialog box allows you to determine the name of the file and where it is to be saved.
Saveas	Same as Save	Also renames the current drawing
Scale	Changes the size of objects	**R**=scale relative to another object

COMMAND NAME	DESCRIPTION	OPTIONS/OPERATIONS
'Script	Runs a script file	Script files are files containing the exact keystrokes to perform a series of actions. Virtually no interaction is allowed. Best suited for batch operations.
Select	Selects objects	You can use Select to preselect objects using the standard selection options.
'Setvar	Controls and displays system variables	**?**=show the status of all or selected system variables
Sh	Allows access to DOS commands	*See* Shell.
Shade	Performs Z-buffer shading on 3D models	*See* Shadedge and Shadedif system variables.
Shape	Places a predefined shape in the drawing	**?**=list available shapes in the current drawing. Shapes must be loaded using the Load command.
Shell	Temporarily exits AutoCAD to run DOS software	You can enter a command or program name after entering **Shell** ↵ or you can press ↵ again to issue multiple DOS commands. A full-screen DOS windows is opened. Enter **Exit** ↵ at the DOS prompt to return to AutoCAD.

COMMAND NAME	DESCRIPTION	OPTIONS/OPERATIONS
Sketch	Allows freehand drawing	**C**=connect with last sketch endpoint, **E**=back up over previously drawn temporary lines, **P**=start and stop temporary line drawing, **Q**=discard temporary lines, **R**=save temporary lines, **X**=save temporary lines and exit the sketch command, period (.)=with pen up, draw straight line to current point
'Snap	Controls Snap function	Snap forces the cursor to move in exact increments. *number*=snap increment, **On/Off**=turn snap feature on and off (same as **F9** function key or **Ctrl-B**), **A**=allows differing X and Y snap increments, **R**=rotate snap grid, **S**=allows you to select between standard and isometric snap grids. *See also* Snapang and Snapbase system variables and the Ddrmodes command.
Solid	Draws a four-sided 2D filled polygon	*See* the Fill command.
'Status	Displays general information about the drawing	Offers a quick way to view memory use

COMMAND NAME	DESCRIPTION	OPTIONS/OPERATIONS
Stretch	Stretches vertices	Objects and vertices can be selected separately with careful use of selection options. The last window (i.e. window, Crossing window, Wpolygon, or Cpolygon) determines which vertices are moved. The Wpolygon and Cpolygon selection options offer the most flexibility with this command.
'Style	Creates text styles	You can set text height, width, and obliquing angles, as well as other orientations. This is also where you specify what font file to use.
Tablet	Controls digitizer tablet alignment	**On/Off**=allows you to turn tablet calibration on or off once a tablet is calibrated. **Cal**=calibrates a tablet to match coordinates in the draw space, **Cfg**=configures the tablet for use with a digitizer template.
Tabsurf	Extrudes 2D shapes into 3D surfaces	Requires an object to be extruded and a line used to indicate an extrusion direction. Tabsurf creates a 3D mesh approximating the extrusion, leaving the original 2D object alone.
Text	Creates text	Select a start point, style, or justification, then height if the style height is set to 0, and rotation angle. Text does not appear in the drawing until ↵ is pressed at the end of the text line.

COMMAND NAME	DESCRIPTION	OPTIONS/OPERATIONS
'Textscr	Flips display to text mode	Same as **F1**
'Time	Displays time values	Shows the date the drawing was created, current time in drawing, and offers an elapsed timer
Trace	Draws solid wide lines	Draws lines in one segment behind the current point. You may prefer to use Pline instead of Trace.
Treestat	Displays information on spatial index	AutoCAD uses a binary tree structure to improve its drawing database access. *See* the Treedepth system variable.
Trim	Trims objects back to another object	Several objects can be selected for both trimming and objects to trim to. The Fence selection option offers a quick way to do multiple trims.
U	Undoes one command at a time	*See* Undo
UCS	Controls the User Coordinate System function	**D**=delete UCS, **E**=set extrusion direction, **O**=move origin, **P**=restore previous UCS, **R**=restore a saved UCS, **S**=save the current UCS, **V**=create a UCS aligned with current view, **W**=set current to WCS, **X/Y/Z**=Rotate UCS about the X, Y, or Z axis, **ZA**=define the Z axis using two points, **3**=define a UCS using 3 points, **?**=list existing UCS's. *See also* Dducs.

COMMAND NAME	DESCRIPTION	OPTIONS/OPERATIONS
UCSicon	Controls the UCS icon	**On/Off**=turn the display of the icon on and off, **Or**=when possible, place the icon at the UCS origin, **N**=turn off Or option, **A**=use settings for all viewports.
Undefine	Undefines a built-in AutoCAD command	Undefine is usually used if you want to replace a built-in command with another command you have created using ADS or AutoLISP. You can still issue an undefined command by preceding the command name with a period.
Undo	Undoes one or a series of commands	*number*=number of commands to undo, **A**=turns on or off the treatment of menu macros as single groups; **B**=undo back to placeMark; **C**=controls Undo features by turning on all features (All), limiting Undo to one operation (1), or turning off Undo entirely (None); **E**=marks the end of an undo group; **G**=marks the beginning of an undo group; **M**=placeMark for Back option
'Units	Selects the unit style	*See* Ddunits.
'Views	Saves and restores views	**D**=delete a view, **R**=restore a view, **S**=save a view, **W**=save a windowed view, **?**=list saved views

COMMAND NAME	DESCRIPTION	OPTIONS/OPERATIONS
Vports/ Viewports	Divides the Modelspace display into viewports	**D**=delete a saved viewport configuration, **J**=join two viewports, **R**=restore a viewport configuration, **S**=save the current viewport configuration, **SI**=change to a single viewport, **2/3/4**=divides the current viewport into 2, 3, or 4 viewports, **?**=list current and saved viewport configurations.
Viewres	Controls the display of arcs, circles, and linetypes	When on, Viewres enables virtual display, which in turn offers greater display speed. Viewres values affect how coarse arcs and circles appear in the virtual display.
Vplayer	Controls layer visibility in Paperspace viewports	**?**= list frozen layers in a viewport, **F**=freezes a layer in a viewport, **T**=thaw a layer in a viewport, **R**=reset layer visibility to the default settings, **N**=create a new layer that is frozen in all viewports, **V**=set the default visibility of existing viewports
Vpoint	Selects a viewpoint for 3D views	**R**=sets rotation angle in the XY plane, **X,Y,Z**=specifies a viewpoint coordinate, **↵**=use tripod and compass to determine viewpoint. In all cases, the entire drawing is the target location.
Vslide	Displays slide files	***filename**=pre-load *filename* for next Vslide

COMMAND NAME	DESCRIPTION	OPTIONS/OPERATIONS
Wblock	Saves portions of a file to disk	Generally used to write a block to a file, Wblock can also be used to save portions of a drawing. The following options can be entered at the Block name prompt: **name**=write block name to file, **==**write block to file using the same name as the file, *****=write the entire current file out to a file, **⏎**=write selected objects. You then see the **Select object** prompt. The * option is a quick way to purge a drawing of all its named elements all at once.
Xbind	Imports named elements from an Xref drawing	Block, dimension styles, layers, line types, and text styles can be imported.
Xref	Cross references another drawing with the current one	You can scale, rotate, or mirror cross-referenced files. You can also use object snap modes and set their layers (*see* Visretain system variable). You cannot edit them however. **A**=attach a cross reference, **B**=bind or import a cross reference to become a permanent part of the current drawing, **D**=detach a cross reference, **P**=allows you to view and edit file names that AutoCAD uses for cross references, **R**=reload a cross reference, **?**=displays a list of cross references

COMMAND NAME	DESCRIPTION	OPTIONS/OPERATIONS
'Zoom	Controls the display	*number*=zoom factor relative to drawing limits, *numberX*=zoom factor relative to current view, *numberXP*=zoom factor relative to paperspace, **A**=display limits of drawing, **C**=display a view based on a center point and height, **D**=dynamic pan/zoom feature, **E**=display drawing extents, **L**=display a view based on a lower-left corner and view height, **P**=display a previous view, **V**=display the entire virtual screen, **W**=display an enlargement of a window
3Dface	Draws a four-sided 3D surface	You can make an edge of a 3Dface invisible by entering **I** ↵ before you pick the second point of the side.
3Dmesh	Draws a 3D mesh by specifying each point on the mesh	Points are input column by column in a column-and-row matrix.
3Dpoly	Draws a 3D polyline	3D polylines allow 3D point selection; however, 3Dpolylines cannot have width or thickness.

DIMENSIONING COMMANDS

The following is a list of the dimensioning commands. These commands can only be accessed by entering **Dim** or **Dim1** first. Dim places you permanently in the dimensioning feature and the prompt will change from **Command** to **Dim**. You can exit the Dim feature by entering **Exit** or **Ctrl-C**.

COMMAND NAME	OPTION/OPERATIONS
Aligned	Draws a linear dimension aligned to an angle
Angular	Draws an arc dimension showing degrees
Baseline	Continues a linear dimension from a base extension line
Center	Draws a center mark
Continue	Continues a linear dimension from the last one
Diameter	Dimensions the diameter of an arc or circle
Exit	Returns you to the standard **Command** prompt if you use the Dim command.
Hometext	Restores dimension text to its home position
Horizontal	Draws a horizontal linear dimension
Leader	Draws a pointing leader and a single line of text
Newtext	Lets you change dimension text
Oblique	Changes the angle of extension lines
Ordinate	Draws ordinate dimensions from a UCS origin
Override	Lets you override dimension variables for a selected dimension
Radius	Dimensions the radius of an arc or circle
Redraw	Same as standard Redraw command
Restore	Restores a saved dimension style—used in conjunction with Save
Rotate	Draws a linear dimension at an angle you specify
Save	Saves the current dimension variable settings under a name

COMMAND NAME	**OPTION/OPERATIONS**
Status	Displays the current dimension variable settings
Style	Changes the current text style
Tedit	Lets you move or rotate dimension text
Trotate	Lets you rotate several dimension text objects at once
Undo	Undoes the most recent dimension command
Update	Updates a dimension to the current dimension variable settings
Variables	Displays the dimension variable settings of a specified style
Vertical	Draws linear vertical dimensions

INDEX

This index contains certain typographical conventions to assist you in finding information. **Boldface** page numbers are references to primary topics and explanations that are emphasized in the text. *Italics* indicate page numbers that reference figures. Roman page numbers are standard references. The letter *n* after a page number indicates that the reference is to a margin note on the page.

MASTERING AUTOCAD FOR WINDOWS ON DISK
▼ ▼ ▼ ▼ ▼

As an enhancement to *Mastering AutoCAD Release 12 for Windows*, you can obtain a variety of software utilities that can greatly improve your productivity and help simplify the most common AutoCAD tasks.

The **Mastering AutoCAD Utilities Disk** contains a set of general-purpose AutoLISP utilities plus some applications created using Microsoft's Visual Basic. These utilities are integrated through a menu system for your convenience. The utilities include the following:

Lqpick turns layers off by selecting an object on that layer.

Matchl sets the current layer by selecting an object on that layer.

Lrecord and *Lrestore* record and restore layer settings in Modelspace.

Edsp lets you export text to a file, and later update your drawing to reflect changes in that file.

Blklog and *Laylog* create text files that list the blocks or layers in a drawing.

Thk changes the thickness of lines in a drawing.

Join joins broken lines.

Rxy lets you specify a point as a relative location to an object.

Fence acts like a "cookie cutter" to cut out a portion of a drawing.

Macro is a keyboard macro generator.

Zoom12 adds new features to the Zoom command like zoom in and zoom out.

Dirpad.EXE is a utility to help simplify coordinate input.

On-Screen AEC is a full-featured AutoCAD AEC software add-on that includes features like automatic door insertion, wall cleanup utilities, and a library of architectural symbols including plumbing, electrical, and reference symbols. The utilities and symbols are integrated into an easy-to-use menu system and come with full documentation. This is everything you need to get started and stay ahead with architectural drafting. This package includes the Mastering AutoCAD Utility Disk to further enhance your use of AutoCAD.

AutoPS gives you full control of your PostScript output. While AutoCAD's own Psout command offers PostScript output, you have little control over screening and line weights. AutoPS lets you easily set gray-scale screen density and combine line weights with screening. It also lets you easily control font sizes and styles. In addition to control, AutoPS offers a wide range of utilities that let you set how objects overlap, place text in a curved path, control text line spacing, and more, all integrated through an easy-to-understand menu. A concise 130-page manual is included.

TO ORDER...

To order, just complete this form and send it to the address below, along with a check or money order for the indicated amount per package. California residents add the proper sales tax.

Omura Illustrations, P.O. Box 6357, Albany, CA 94706-6357

- -

Name _____

Address _____

City/State/Zip _____

Country _____

Phone _____

Please send me the following packages:

ITEM	UNIT PRICE	QUANTITY	SUBTOTAL
Mastering AutoCAD Utility Disk	$14.95	_____	_____
On-screen AEC	$50.00	_____	_____
Auto-PS	$150.00	_____	_____
California Sales Tax			_____
Foreign orders other than Canada and Mexico, add US$12.00 for shipping and handling			_____
Domestic UPS 2nd day air, add $9.00			_____
Foreign UPS 2nd day, add US$22.00			_____
Total (make check payable to Omura Illustrations)			_____

Diskette type: $3^1/_2$" ☐ $5^1/_4$" ☐
Type of computer: 386 ☐   486 ☐

Sorry, no credit-card orders. Please allow three weeks for delivery within the United States. UPS orders, one week. **No P.O. Boxes for UPS orders, please.**

SYBEX is not affiliated with Omura Illustrations and assumes no responsibility for any defect in the disks or files.

SYBEX

FREE BROCHURE!

Complete this form today, and we'll send you a full-color brochure of Sybex bestsellers.

Please supply the name of the Sybex book purchased.

_____

How would you rate it?

_____ Excellent   _____ Very Good   _____ Average   _____ Poor

Why did you select this particular book?

_____ Recommended to me by a friend

_____ Recommended to me by store personnel

_____ Saw an advertisement in _____

_____ Author's reputation

_____ Saw in Sybex catalog

_____ Required textbook

_____ Sybex reputation

_____ Read book review in _____

_____ In-store display

_____ Other _____

Where did you buy it?

_____ Bookstore

_____ Computer Store or Software Store

_____ Catalog (name: _____)

_____ Direct from Sybex

_____ Other: _____

Did you buy this book with your personal funds?

_____ Yes   _____ No

About how many computer books do you buy each year?

_____ 1-3   _____ 3-5   _____ 5-7   _____ 7-9   _____ 10+

About how many Sybex books do you own?

_____ 1-3   _____ 3-5   _____ 5-7   _____ 7-9   _____ 10+

Please indicate your level of experience with the software covered in this book:

_____ Beginner   _____ Intermediate   _____ Advanced

Which types of software packages do you use regularly?

_____ Accounting	_____ Databases	_____ Networks
_____ Amiga	_____ Desktop Publishing	_____ Operating Systems
_____ Apple/Mac	_____ File Utilities	_____ Spreadsheets
_____ CAD	_____ Money Management	_____ Word Processing
_____ Communications	_____ Languages	_____ Other _____
		(please specify)

Which of the following best describes your job title?

_____ Administrative/Secretarial   _____ President/CEO

_____ Director   _____ Manager/Supervisor

_____ Engineer/Technician   _____ Other _____
(please specify)

Comments on the weaknesses/strengths of this book: _____

_____

_____

_____

_____

Name _____

Street _____

City/State/Zip _____

Phone _____

PLEASE FOLD, SEAL, AND MAIL TO SYBEX

-- --

SYBEX, INC.
Department M
2021 CHALLENGER DR.
ALAMEDA, CALIFORNIA USA
94501

Object Selection Options
Some of the options available at any Select objects prompt.

Option/Example	Key	Description
Pick	None (default)	Selects single objects. With the Pickadd system variable on, each object picked is added to the selection set. Use a Shift-Click to de-select objects.
Window	W ⏎	Only selects objects that are entirely within the window. With the Pickauto system variable on, a window is used automatically when you click on a blank area and click on a 2nd point to the right.
Crossing	C ⏎	Selects objects that are within and cross through the window. With the Pickauto system variable on, crossing is used automatically when you click on a blank area and click on a 2nd point to the left.
Wpolygon	WP ⏎	Selects objects that are within an irregular polygon. You draw the polygon by picking points defining the polygon's corners. Press ⏎ when you are done drawing the polygon.
Cpolygon	CP ⏎	Selects objects that are within or crossing through an irregular polygon. You draw the polygon by picking points defining the polygon's corners. Press ⏎ when you are done drawing the polygon.
Fence	F ⏎	Selects objects that are crossed over by a line called a *fence*. You draw the fence just as you would draw a line. Press ⏎ when you are done drawing the fence.
Last	L ⏎	Selects the last object that was added to the drawing database.
Previous	P ⏎	Selects the last selection set.
All	All ⏎	Selects everything in the drawing including those on frozen layers and layers that are off. This option can be used in conjunction with the Remove option to select everything except a small group of objects.
Remove	R ⏎	Places you in Remove mode where objects selected are removed from the current selection set. With the Pickadd system variable set to 1, you can also Shift-Click on objects to remove them.
Add	A ⏎	Places you in Add mode where objects selected are added to the current selection set. This is the default mode.